NEUROBIOLOGY OF COMPARATIVE COGNITION

COMPARATIVE COGNITION
AND NEUROSCIENCE

Thomas G. Bever, David S. Olton,
and Herbert L. Roitblat, Senior Editors

NEUROBIOLOGY OF COMPARATIVE COGNITION

Edited by

Raymond P. Kesner
University of Utah
David S. Olton
Johns Hopkins University

LAWRENCE ERLBAUM ASSOCIATES, PUBLISHERS
1990   Hillsdale, New Jersey   Hove and London

Lawrence Erlbaum Associates, Inc., Publishers
365 Broadway
Hillsdale, New Jersey 07642

Library of Congress Cataloging-in-Publication Data

Neurobiology of comparative cognition

(Comparative cognition and neuroscience)
Includes bibliographical references.
1. Comparative neurobiology. 2. Cognitive science.
I. Kesner, Raymond P. II. Olton, David S. III. Series.
QP356.15.N45 1990   156'.34   89-25908
ISBN 0-8058-0133-2
ISBN 0-8058-0639-3 (pbk.)

Printed in the United States of America
10 9 8 7 6 5 4 3 2 1

Contents

PART IV.   NEUROBIOLOGY OF SPATIAL ORGANIZATION

Preface

This book represents a logical and necessary step in the endeavor to relate cognitive and neural functions. Considerable progress has been made in neurocognitive analyses, reflected in many different terms applied to variations of these approaches: cognitive neuroscience, neuropsychology, computational neuroscience, and so forth.

Another important development has been the comparison across species of different kinds of cognitive processes. The field of comparative cognition has grown markedly, and addresses important issues about the nature of cognitive processes, as well as the ways in which these differ across different species of animals. These approaches have implications for our understanding of cognitive processes in individual animals, and for the processes involved in natural selection.

This book, as indicated by its title, represents a first step toward joining together the areas of neurobiology and comparative cognition, a step that can be highly beneficial for each of them. One of the remarkable results from an analysis of the chapters in this book is the clear realization that any given cognitive ability can arise in many different animals and have many different neural bases. In addition, the experimental procedures and theoretical concepts used to analyze any given type of cognitive process, at times, differ markedly depending on the species that is being examined, but at other times reveal a great deal of commonality.

Thus, we hope that this book will make several contributions. First, this book approaches two important complementary scientific strategies that have tended to drift apart. Second, it should help to educate people about the contributions and opportunities that exist in the amalgamation of the comparative basis of neural and cognitive science. An analysis of the many different ways in which science has approached similar issues because of differences in an animal's cognition or nervous system should provide information about the ways in which neural tissue has been designed to solve common adaptive problems. Third, it is hoped that this book will help others to start thinking of the neurobiological basis of cognition within a comparative framework.

The book begins with a discussion of the concepts, issues, and rationale in a truly comparative approach. A simple comparison of the data from two different species of animals is helpful for an empirical analysis, but careful attention to logical deductions from these data is important to address the more important conceptual issues. This initial chapter (by W. Hodos and C. B. G. Campbell) helps to set the framework for a comparative approach.

The remainder of the book is divided into three sections, each one of which presents data on a single cognitive process from several different species. The first topic is "Neurobiology of Communication," and analyses are provided for humans (Chapter 2 by B. Gordon), monkeys (Chapter 3 by U. Jurgens), and birds (Chapter 4 by H. Williams). The second topic is "Neurobiology of Learning and Memory" and analyses are provided for primates (Chapter 5 by E. Murray), turtles (Chapter 6 by A. S. Powers), rodents (Chapter 7 by R. Kesner), fish (Chapter 8 by J. B. Overmier and K. L. Hollis), honeybees (Chapter 9 by R. Menzel), and invertebrates (Chapter 10 by J. H. Byrne). The third topic is "Neurobiology of Spatial Organization" and contributions are provided for humans (Chapter 11 by F. J. Friedrich), primates (Chapter 12 by E. T. Rolls), rodents (Chapter 13 by B. J. Leonard and B. L. McNaughton) and birds (Chapter 14 by V. P. Bingman).

If the investigation of the neurobiology of comparative cognition were completely developed now, we could provide a closing chapter, placing all of these data into a theoretical framework according to the principles outlined by Hodos and Campbell in their introductory chapter. However, the field is still so young that such an endeavor is not yet possible. Nonetheless, each of the contributions is important in its own right, and a comparison of the different enterprises for each of the different species should provide an enlightening insight into neural mechanisms, cognitive processes, experimental techniques, and important conceptual issues. If this book stimulates increased investigations of the neurobiology of comparative cognition, as we hope, the next edition should provide a more systematic comparative analysis.

Raymond P. Kesner
David S. Olton

I Introduction

1 Evolutionary Scales and Comparative Studies of Animal Cognition

William Hodos
University of Maryland

C. B. G. Campbell
Walter Reed Army Institute of Research

Throughout history, humans have had a fascination with animal cognition. Folklore and children's tales of various cultures abound with descriptions of the cognitive abilities of animals: their planning skills, their mastery of spatial relations, their memory feats, their use of concepts and abstractions. These descriptions are put forth as if the animal capabilities were the equivalent of human processes. Likewise, the results of laboratory studies of animal cognition invite comparisons with human cognitive processes. Such comparisons readily lend themselves to speculations about the origins of human cognition in our animal ancestors.

In order for these speculations to be meaningful within the broad context of evolutionary biology, they should be consistent with what is known about the actual evolutionary history of humans and the genealogical lineages from which they were derived (Hodos & Campbell, 1969; Lockard, 1971; Martin, 1974). For example, to compare the performance on some behavioral task of a bony fish (teleost) with those of a bird, a rodent, a carnivore, and a human within an evolutionary framework would be absurd, because none of these animals could be regarded as direct descendents of the ancestral species of the human lineage. No bony fish was ever an ancestor of any bird; no bird was ever an ancestor of any mammal; no carnivore was ever an ancestor of any primate (Carroll, 1987; Colbert, 1980; Romer, 1966).

In this chapter, we discuss several issues that are of importance in any analysis of the evolution of behavior. The first issue concerns the model of species evolution that will be used as the framework for the reconstruction of behavioral evolution. The two models most frequently encountered are the evolutionary or phylogenetic scale and the evolutionary or phylogenetic tree. The choice between

1

these models can have a profound impact on the choice of animals to study and the subsequent interpretation of the results obtained. The second issue concerns the strategies that the experimenter might employ in selecting the animals to be studied in a comparative or evolutionary context. The selection strategy will play an important role in determining the experimenter's ability to interpret his or her results as being related to the mechanisms by which evolution affects behavior, irrespective of specific historical events or as a reconstruction of actual historical trends in behavioral history. The third issue involves the interpretation of the data after the animals have been selected and studied. This issue concerns the purposes for which behavior is categorized and is related to the notion of evolutionary progress.

APPROACHES TO COMPARATIVE PSYCHOLOGY

Hodos and Campbell (1969) discussed two approaches to the study of comparative psychology; (a) a phylogenetic (historical) approach, in which an experimenter attempts to reconstruct evolutionary history by studying animal species that have been derived from common genealogical lineages; and (b) an analysis-of-adaptation approach, in which species to be studied are selected according to some morphological characteristic, mode of life, habitat, behavior pattern, and so forth, irrespective of their phyletic relationships to each other. We stated that both approaches were equally important and equally valid for an understanding of the evolution of behavior and the nervous system. In addition, we rejected the notion that evolutionary scales had any utility for either approach. Yarczower and Hazlett (1977) have argued for a third approach based on anagenesis and evolutionary scales. Several additional papers (Aronson, 1984; Gottlieb, 1984) also have argued that evolutionary scales do have a place in comparative psychology. In this chapter, we reply to these arguments. The debate is of direct relevance to those interested in comparative studies of cognition and the nervous system. Attempts to systematize comparative cognitive data and to draw inferences about the historical origins of the varying cognitive abilities of animals or the origins of human cognitive processes in nonhuman animals must take into account the arguments raised in this debate. Indeed, experimenters may feel obliged to take a position on these issues before beginning systematic, comparative studies or analyses of cognitive data.

SCALES AND TREES

In this section, we compare two organizational approaches for representing the evolutionary history of animals. They are the scale and the tree. A scale may be defined as a graded, ladder-like or staircase-like sequence or a hierarchical classi-

TABLE 1.1
A Comparison of the Phylogenetic
(Evolutionary) Scale Model With the
Phylogenetic Tree Model

Phylogenetic Scale	Phylogenetic Tree
Hierarchical.	Nonhierarchical.
Unilinear.	Multilinear.
Complexity determines the presumed historical sequence.	Presumed historical sequence determined by historical data, independently of complexity.
Complexity increases with time.	Complexity is independent of time.

fication. A tree-like organization has a stem and several or many radiating branches. Table 1.1 lists the main features of the two organizational arrangements.

The seductive similarity between the pre-Darwinian concept of a phylogenetic scale (also referred to as the *scala naturae*) and the phylogenetic trees of the evolutionary biologists has led to many erroneous conclusions about the evolution of the brain and behavior (Campbell, 1976; Hodos, 1970, 1974; Hodos & Campbell, 1969). Consider the organizational scheme illustrated in Fig. 1.1.

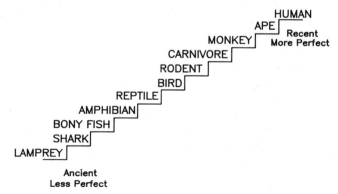

FIG. 1.1.   A phylogenetic or evolutionary scale. This scale is a hierarchical arrangement in which the more ancient, more primitive, and less perfect forms are located at the bottom of the scale and the more recent, more advanced, and more perfect forms are located at the top of the scale. Evolution is represented as a unilinear progression towards humans.

This is a representation of a phylogenetic scale. The figure is, of necessity, made up wholly from our imaginations and intuitions; because the phylogenetic scale has no biological basis, there is no scientific reference source that we could cite to provide a definitive ranking.

Several characteristics of the phylogenetic scale should be noted. First, it is a hierarchy; animals have a higher or lower location on the staircase, depending on their presumed degree of complexity. Second, this hierarchy frequently is offered as a representation of an historical series. Third, if the scale is to be considered as a model of evolution, then the animals represented must have evolved in the indicated sequence. In other words, animals that are presumed to represent lesser degrees of complexity always appear earlier in the sequence. Thus, time also is represented by position on the staircase.

As a model of evolution, the phylogenetic scale has many deficiencies, not the least of which is its unilinear construction. It reinforces the erroneous notion that evolution has proceeded along a single path leading to humans when, in fact, the study of the fossil record leads to quite the opposite conclusion—that vertebrate evolution has proceeded along numerous independent paths. Moreover, each of these has produced a divergence of lineages; hence the biologist's model of an evolutionary or phylogenetic tree, rather than a staircase. One type of tree is shown in Fig. 1.2.

Figure 1.2 differs from Fig. 1.1 in several important respects. First, there is no hierarchy. Birds, for example, are neither higher nor lower than mammals; they are merely on a different branch of the tree. Second, the construction is multi-linear, with the genealogical lines radiating out from a common origin. Different lineages evolve concurrently and independently of one another. Third, the phylogenetic tree is based on actual historical data independent of complexity. Fourth, time is independent of sequence; hence, different stages of evolution in different lineages can appear in the same epoch of time. Moreover, "simpler" animals can evolve later than more "complex" forms.

The two conceptual schemes for comparing animals that are illustrated in Figs. 1.1 and 1.2 lead to very different ways of ordering data for the purpose of comparisons of different animal species or for comparing animals to humans. The *scala naturae* approach of Fig. 1.1 suggests that performance should vary according to position on the staircase. The tree model, though more complex than a unilinear hierarchy, has the advantage that it frees the experimenter from always having to predict that amphibians will always perform more poorly than reptiles, that mammals will always surpass birds, that primates must always excel over other mammals, and so on. The tree model lets the behavioral chips fall where they may. For example, because birds followed a history quite independent from that of mammals, there is every reason to suppose that they may have evolved some capacities, quite on their own, that are superior to those of some mammals. Some bony fishes, as a consequence of the long separation of the ray-finned lineage from the ancestors of amphibians and reptiles, may indeed

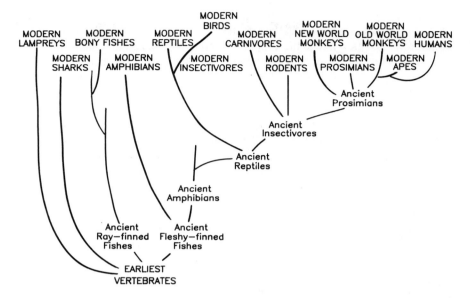

FIG. 1.2.   A phylogenetic tree showing the genealogy of most of the living vertebrate classes. Greater detail is shown among the primates than other orders. Unlike the arrangement in Fig. 1.1, this tree is not a hierarchy, nor are concepts of perfection or advancement represented. Evolution is represented as a multilinear process that has occurred in a number of independent lineages.

have developed behavioral abilities that exceed those of their cousins in the fleshy-finned lineage.

On the other hand, integration of behavioral data from living animals with knowledge of the fossil record of animal evolution does put a number of constraints on the comparisons that can meaningfully be made. First, the living descendents of ancestral lineages generally should not be regarded as "living fossils." When evolutionary biologists use this term, they mean that an extant species has changed very little (in its skeleton and other hard tissues) from its fossilized ancestors. Such living fossils are relatively rare. Some examples of living fossils are the horseshoe crab, the Virginia oppossum, and the tuatara of New Zealand.

In general, descendent species have undergone considerable modifications from the ancestral condition. Indeed, these modifications often are what have permitted the lineage to survive in the face of changing environmental conditions. If their bodies have changed, we must suppose that their behavioral abilities have not remained static either. Therefore, conclusions about the evolution of behavior based on living descendents of ancient lineages must be drawn with extreme conservatism (Simpson, 1958).

Other problems concern uncertainty over genealogical relationships and the lack of appropriate representatives of lineages. As Fig. 1.2 shows, the line of amphibians that gave rise to the amniotes (reptiles, birds, and mammals) became extinct. Moreover, the modern amphibians may have had an independent origin from the fleshy-finned fishes. Although they are amphibians, they are not descended from the same amphibian stock as are the amniotes. Consequently, behavioral observations of modern amphibians may be of little or no value in an attempt to reconstruct amniote behavioral evolution unless they are a part of a phylogenetic reconstruction that contains many species of varying degrees of relatedness. Moreover, data from a single species usually give little useful information in this context. Observations from modern lampreys, sharks, and fishes must be treated with similar caution because each of these, as shown in Fig. 1.2, arrived at the present era via evolutionary paths quite different from those followed by the amniotes.

In a thoughtful and scholarly article, Aronson (1984), a leading advocate of the value of evolutionary scales, described in some detail the history of this approach and argued for the usefulness of the notion of the *scala naturae*, or evolutionary scale, in comparative psychology. He listed the scale as follows: "primitive chordates (such as amphioxus), cyclostomes, bony fishes, amphibia, reptiles, birds, lower mammals, higher mammals, monkeys, apes and humans. Details of the scale and terminology vary considerably depending on individual requirements" (p. 58). Although he stated that this scale is not a genealogy, he added, "we cannot dismiss lightly a characteristic of nature that has been recognized in one way or another from the time of Aristotle to the present day, namely that the animals of the earth, past and present, can be arranged in ascending order based on specific criteria" (p. 59). That one can rank order behavior patterns for a specific purpose has never been an issue of dispute, so long as the ranking is not used in ways that misrepresent well-established bodies of scientific literature. As a hierarchy of complexity or any other criterion, such rankings are useful and meaningful so long as the conclusion is not offered that the higher ranked behaviors evolved from the lower ranked behaviors. One may speculate that such might have been the case; but a firm conclusion requires external corroboration from systematic biology, not the mere existence of the behavioral hierarchy itself. Indeed, a telling point is Aronson's (1984) statement quoted previously that ". . . details of the scale and terminology vary considerably depending on individual requirements." Because the scale is itself arbitrary, judgmental, and not based on an established set of scientific principles, it too easily can be manipulated to fit the hierarchies of behavior. Similarly, the arbitrary and judgmental nature of these hierarchies can lead too easily to the conclusion that those hierarchies that fit the scale must be correct and those that do not must be flawed.

The details of the scale that Aronson (1984) proposed leave much to be desired. For example, he ranked birds far below humans on his scale. We argue that, in many ways, birds have achieved the same grade as primates. Birds are the only other true bipeds besides humans. Like primates, they have a complex social organization, a rich repertoire of vocal communication, they provide intensive and extended parental care, they use tools, they perform extremely well on tests of memory, and they have superb vision and visual perception. How many of the "lower" mammals or "higher," nonprimate mammals can boast the same abilities? Similarly, should not alligators, which provide parental care, establish territories, and defend them by vocalization and threat, be ranked the same as birds with which they have these behaviors in common? Moreover, how do we decide which animals fall into the category of lower mammals and which are the higher mammals? What exactly is the basis of this ranking, and are we not all free to make up any ranking of animals that we like?

Aronson (1984) conceded that the evolutionary scale is not a genealogical series, but he went on to add that:

> Although, as already stated, the steps in the anagenesis of living things do not constitute a common evolutionary lineage, there is, nevertheless, substantial concordance since those lowest on the scale tend to be descendents of the most ancient lines, while those highest on the scale are mostly representatives of the most recent lines. (p. 60))

This statement exposes several weaknesses of the approach that Aronson proposed. First, as Simpson (1967) has cautioned, "To suppose that older groups are ipso factor lower on the scale of evolutionary progress than younger groups, or ancestors than their descendents, or among contemporaries those more like the common ancestor than those less like, is to confuse change with progress" (p. 255). Second, how is one to decide whether a bat or a gazelle or a ferret belong to the higher mammals or the lower mammals? Formal criteria for this assignment are never given. When formal criteria are given, the results sometimes differ considerably from the old rat–cat–monkey–human hierarchy. Consider, for example, Colbert's (1980) assessment of the status of rodents:

> As contrasted with the evolutionary success of man, or the order primates, or of any other mammalian order, the rodents have been supremely successful during most of Cenozoic times. If the range of adaptive radiation, the numbers of species, and the numbers of individuals within a species are criteria of success in evolution, the rodents far outshine all other mammals. . . . All these factors have brought about the long-continued success of the rodents throughout the world. They have persisted where other mammals have failed, and it is quite likely that when human beings decline, at some unforeseeable date in the future, the rodents will still be making their way on earth with unabated vigor. (p. 312)

Finally, the arbitrary and intuitive basis of the evolutionary scale in combination with the arbitrary and axiological assignment of animals to grades seems to invite a form of *ad hoc* theorization that would add little to our understanding of the evolution of behavior or the relationship between behavior and taxonomy.

ADAPTATION

The reconstruction of behavioral history is not the only reason for comparing the performance of different species. An equally important reason, one that is far less constrained by the genealogical problems raised above, is the study of behavior as an adaptive response to pressures of the environment. In this approach to systematizing animal behavior, many constraints are removed. The experimenter is freed from concerns with lineage and the appropriateness of a living animal as a stand-in for its extinct ancestors. Correlations may be made between behavioral performance and habitat or other aspects of the environment. Interdisciplinary approaches may be used to correlate behavioral data with body morphology, brain anatomy, endocrine function, histochemistry, and so on. Theorists may freely construct whatever hierarchies seem to fit the data. In the latter situation, however, extreme caution must be taken not to fall into the trap of the phylogenetic scale and assume that a given hierarchy necessarily represents history. Some hierarchies may in fact represent actual historical sequences; but merely placing the behavioral performance of different species in rank order does not guarantee a representation of history. Only by careful, cautious correlation with the fossil record and other data of systematic biology can reasonable inferences about history be drawn.

The reader should be aware that the concept of "evolutionary adaptation" is presently undergoing a reevaluation by systematic biologists (Northcutt, 1988). The concern is with the interpretation of correlations that have been drawn between structures (or behaviors) and their presumed functions in meeting the challenges of the environment. The problem is that experimenters often do not demonstrate, either by their own research or by appropriate references to the literature, that such structures or behaviors actually have that function in nature. In addition, experimenters should be wary of the possible influences of partial correlations; that is, circumstances in which correlations between two variables exist, not because of any relationship between them, but because each is correlated with a common third variable.

CLADES AND GRADES

When studying morphological features, systematic biologists distinguish between two types of analyses: analysis by clades and analysis by grades. Various authors have defined the term *grade* somewhat differently. Gottlieb (1984), for example, proposed the following: "A grade is a particular level in an ascending series of improvements on any given structure or functional unit of analysis in which the animals may or may not be closely related . . ." (p. 449). Yarczower and Hazlett (1977) have stated that grades are the units of anagenesis, a view that has been adopted by several other behavioral scientists. In contrast, Wiley (1981) presented a definition that would be accepted by most contemporary systematic biologists. His definition, which is based on Simpson (1953, 1961) is: "A grade is a taxon characterized by a general level of organization. . . . grades are composed of individual lineages progressing by parallel (nonhomologous) development through sequences of adaptive zones toward increasingly effective organization levels" (p. 260). In the biologists' sense, the concept of "grade," which antedates the notion of anagenesis, was not devised to indicate levels of evolutionary progress. The behaviorists' use of "grade" thus differs from the meaning of this term as it is commonly understood by systematic biologists.

Wiley (1981) described at length the theoretical controversy within systematic biology over the utility of grades. The controversy is between the phylogenetic taxonomists and the evolutionary taxonomists. The former only make use of genealogical relationships in classifying animals. This approach is known as *cladistics,* and the branching patterns of lineages are known as *clades.* A cladistic analysis is an inference in which the data are arranged according to what is known about the phylogeny of the animals from which the data were collected. The analysis is based on shared characters and the pattern of character distribution.

The evolutionary taxonomists argue that phylogenetics cannot reveal certain aspects of evolution. An important feature of their approach is that they accept paraphyletic groups (i.e., groups either without a common ancestor included or without including all descendent groups) as being "natural" taxa or the equivalent. These paraphyletic groups or "grades" are considered by them to be meaningful evolutionary entities. Among the criteria for the identification of grades are discontinuities or gaps in morphology (or in behavior). The traditional, Darwinian, gradualist approach regards gaps as sampling errors that ultimately will be filled in by new observations. But, when the gaps are filled in by these new data, the basis for the establishment of the grade evaporates. The approach of punctuated equilibrium (Eldredge & Gould, 1972; Gould & Eldredge, 1977) postulates the necessary existence of such gaps, but in so doing it denies that anagenesis plays a major role in shaping evolutionary trends.

Of particular importance in establishing a grade is the development of a unique adaptation. Indeed, those adaptations that permitted the taxon to enter new adaptive zones within the environment often are accorded a higher rank than those that do not. But the extent to which an adaptation is important depends very much on the judgment of the observer. Wiley (1981) observed that: "In practice, grades are not created by evolutionary processes but by taxonomic decisions" (p. 260). He concluded that ". . . grades have no place in taxonomies that purport to be phylogenetically natural" (p. 261).

In contrast to a cladistic analysis, which aids in the reconstruction of the specific history of a particular lineage, an analysis by grades in the Yarczower-Gottlieb sense arranges the data in order of presumed advancement or elaboration. Although an analysis by grades can yield information about how structure or behavior may have changed in response to changes in the environment (Gould, 1976), an important consideration, especially for behaviorists, is to specify in which specific lineage the change has occurred. Failure to do so could have the effect of mixing the proverbial apples and oranges. The resulting "fruit salad" might be tasty in the short run, but ultimately could prove to be quite indigestible.

Capitanio and Leger (1979) described a further problem with grades; namely, a tendency towards circularity in the assignment of ranks to grades when one attempts the marriage of paraphyletic and phylogenetic classifications. Because judgments about relative complexity are required in the assignment of ranks to grades and the phylogeny is known ahead of time, there may be a tendency to be biased in favor of assigning a higher rank to the behavior of the more recently evolved taxon. Thus, the higher ranked behaviors are observed in the more recently evolved taxa.

None of this is intended to deny the usefulness of a grade concept as a means of classifying behavior in a nonphylogenetic context. The concept of grades may serve many useful purposes for ranking, organizing and systematizing behavioral data. For example, in the study of food caching and recovery in birds, one could rank the species according to their ability to recover food. Such a ranking is of interest in its own right. One then could compare the behavior ranking with a ranking of the volumes of certain brain structures, such as the hippocampus (Krebs, Sherry, & Healy, in press). This may constitute a structure–function relationship that offers insights into some aspects of the neural basis of long-term memory. An important consideration, however, is that neither the behavioral nor the morphological ranking will necessarily tell us anything about the evolutionary history of either food caching or the hippocampus. In order to determine those histories, one would require knowledge of the specific genealogical relationships of the individual species of birds. The phylogenetic tree model indicates that different degrees of complexity can occur at the same period of time.

A confusing situation occurs when one attempts to take a classification system that is essentially unnatural (arbitrary), axiological (based on value judgments), and nonphylogenetic (nonhistorical) and impose it upon a natural, phylogenetic system. In other words, grades may be arranged in any ranking scheme that serves to organize the data in a coherent way for a particular purpose; one must not suppose, however, that the particular ranking necessarily represents the historical sequence of events that occurred in a particular lineage or that higher ranked grades necessarily evolved from lower ranked grades.

ANAGENESIS AS A BIOLOGICAL CONCEPT

A biological concept that has received considerable attention in the comparative behavior literature recently is *anagenesis* (Aronson, 1984; Capitanio & Leger,

1979; Gottlieb, 1984; Yarczower & Hazlett, 1977; Yarczower & Yarczower, 1979). Anagenesis has been used to refer to those evolutionary trends that result in "progress" or "improvement" in a given lineage.

In their discussions of anagenesis, Yarczower and Hazlett (1977), Aronson (1984), and Gottlieb (1984) drew heavily on the writings of a number of eminent biologists who have espoused this concept. The reader should be aware, however, that each of these biologists had a different notion of what the term meant and how it should be used, a fact that is not sufficiently emphasized in discussions of anagenesis. The four most frequently cited are Rensch (1959), Huxley (1942, 1957, 1958), Simpson (1949, 1961), and Gould (1976). We add to this list Wiley (1981). In brief, the differences between them are summarized as follows.

Definitions of Anagenesis

Rensch. The first use of the term *anagenesis* generally is attributed to Rensch (1959), although notions of evolutionary progress had earlier been used by a number of biologists. He considered anagenesis to be a progressive advance towards higher levels in particular lineages within the phylogenetic tree and in the tree as a whole. Rensch clearly was influenced by notions of the *scala naturae,* and he frequently referred to levels of the evolutionary scale. Rensch's writings also are indicative of an anthropocentric bias; he continually pointed to the dominant position of humans, their mastery of the planet, the victory of the human brain, and so on. Rensch used anagenesis to refer strictly to advances towards "perfection" of general organization of some major function.

Huxley. In his famous work *Evolution: The Modern Synthesis,* Huxley (1942) discussed the concept of evolutionary progress at some length, although he did not adopt the term *anagenesis* until later, after Rensch had introduced it into the literature. He acknowledged that a major criticism of the notion of progress was that it involved the incorporation of the values of the biologist. Huxley too appears to have difficulty in shaking off the notion that somehow the "scala naturae" has biological validity. Moreover, he offered no guidance on how to determine which animals are higher or lower on the evolutionary scale. He did, however, conclude that the factual basis of evolutionary progress will be discovered if we examine the fossil record to determine what the main types of evolutionary changes have been, whether some of them have led to the development of "higher" forms, and which types of change have been most successful in producing new groups, dominant forms, etcetera. Huxley too had a highly anthropocentric view of evolution and regarded only the line of evolution that led to humans as representing progress; all other lines were blind alleys. An important distinction between Huxley's use of anagenesis and Rensch's is that Rensch regarded only advancement towards perfection as anagenetic. Huxley, in his later writings (1957, 1958), accepted retrogressive trends and the reduction of or loss of parts also to be anagenetic and thereby broadened Rensch's definition to include all types and degrees of biological improvement.

Simpson.   Neither the *scala naturae* nor anthropocentrism appear to be features of Simpson's (1961) approach to anagenesis, which he regarded as the tendency of some major groups to have a fairly consistent and definable evolutionary direction, often characterized by different lineages evolving in parallel. But he still was obliged to deal with the difficult problem of value judgement. He wrote of animals progressing towards increasingly effective organizational levels or grades in clearly definable steps. He cautioned, however, that the concept was meaningless unless the data were taken from animals that were closely related. Thus parallelism (the independent development of similar features in closely related lineages) was a critical feature of anagenesis for Simpson. He specifically ruled out grades formed by convergence (the independent development of similar features in remotely related animals). This restriction seems to make Simpson firmly opposed to the grades formed from the sort of evolutionary scale shown in Fig. 1.1.

Gould.   A conception of anagenesis based on increasingly efficient design principles in an engineering sense was put forth by Gould (1976). He specifically denied an anthropocentric basis for anagenesis. He cautioned that grades that contain more recently evolved animals should not be ranked higher merely on that basis. According to Gould, evaluations of progress must be made after studying the use of a structure throughout the history of the lineage and its relationship to major changes in the environment. These appear to be significant restrictions on the use of the term "anagenesis." Gould warned that processes that are hard to quantify or characterize in an engineering sense are the most difficult in which to recognize advances.

Wiley.   A useful definition of anagenesis was proposed by Wiley (1981). In his definition, anagenesis is ". . . the process by which a genetic or phenotypic character changes within a species whether that change is random or nonrandom, slow or rapid" (p. 8). Note that this definition, which has been stripped of axiology (value judgments), anthropocentrism (the superiority or perfection of humans), and notions of progress, is equivalent to Simpson's (1961) concept of phyletic evolution, which he defined as extensive cumulative change within a single lineage without branching into two or more descendent lineages. Moreover, Simpson himself considered anagenesis to be a subset of phyletic evolution. This is the sense in which the term is used by most modern-day systematic biologists.

Anagenesis and Grades

A common feature of all of these biologists' writings is that none of them advocated the formation of a grade based on a single characteristic of the animal. Many of the grades that have been formed by behaviorists have been on the basis of such single features. Thus, the application of the grades of anagenesis suggested by Yarczower and Hazlett (1977) and Gottlieb (1984), while bearing some resemblance to the preceding notions, are in fact single-character grades. Although such grades would have value for organizing and systematizing data, they would tell us nothing about anagenesis in Simpson's sense or in Gould's sense.

As to the question of whether hierarchies of grades represent historical trends, none of the aforementioned biologists would advocate such conclusions without careful comparison with data from the fossil record and a wide range of extant animals of appropriate lineages. Moreover, none of them advocated the use of anagenesis as a substitute for or alternative to phyletic analysis.

GRADES AND BEHAVIOR

Martin (1974) described four grades of primate social behavior that are well established in the primatology literature:

1. Solitary-living grade
2. Pair-living grade
3. Harem grade (one male, many females)
4. Multiple males and females grade.

As a classification of social arrangements and as a ranking of behavior from simple to complex, these grades are quite satisfactory. But problems arise when one takes the additional steps of assuming that the multiple male–female grade is an "improvement" or "advance" over the harem grade or that the solitary grade represents a "primitive" or ancestral condition and that the higher grades are each derived from the preceding lower grade. By placing the distribution of these grades on a primate phylogenetic tree, Martin showed that the four grades are as widely distributed among the prosimians as among the simians. Moreover, even within the Hominoidea (apes and humans), all four grades of social organization can be found. In other words, at least some of the individual primate lineages appear to have moved back and forth across grades of social organization in the course of their evolution.

Hodos (1970) used a similar approach to the analysis of learning-set performance of various birds and mammals. The performance of these animals could be ranked in order of the rate of acquisition of the task and the final level of performance achieved. One could stop there and state that the data indicated the relative performances of various species irrespective of phylogenetic relatedness. One could make use of certain discontinuities in performance as the basis for forming grades. One could then note, for example, that pigeons and ferrets had achieved the same grade as spider monkeys, that cats and skunks were in a lower grade, in company with marmosets and squirrel monkeys, or that a chimpanzee and a normal-IQ human child were at grades intermediate between a gorilla and a bright human child. Many theorists, however, such as Simpson (1953, 1961) and Rensch (1959), would not accept grades that included species that demonstrated similar performance resulting from convergent evolution. Moreover, a conclusion that this ranking represented historical trends within the various lineages represented should not be drawn until after the data were plotted on a phylogenetic tree and the distribution of performance was observed.

ANAGENESIS AND COMPLEXITY

Evolutionary progress often has been equated with an increase in complexity. But the path from simple to complex is not the only route that evolutionary changes can follow. The paths from more complex adaptations to simpler adaptations, from more elaborate structure to less elaborate structure, and from greater numbers of components to fewer components are all well-trodden routes in the history of morphological evolution. There seems to be little reason to suppose that behavioral evolution always followed the route from simpler to more complex.

A case in point is the evolution of the vertebrate heart. One could construct a sequence of grades based on the number of chambers using the evolutionary scale (1) fishes, (2) amphibians, (3) amniotes. At grade 1 we find a two-chambered heart; at grade 2 we find a three-chambered heart; at grade 3 we find a four-chambered heart. Clearly, we have an increase in complexity and a possible increase in progress. But do we have something that represents a historical sequence? The weight of comparative morphological and embryological data says "no" (Yapp, 1965; Torrey, 1971). The division of the heart into four chambers appears to have occurred in the rhipidistian fishes that were the fleshy finned ancestors of amphibians. The three-chambered heart, rather than representing a precursor of the four-chambered heart, is instead derived from the four-chambered heart as a consequence of the amphibian reliance on the skin as an organ of respiration in addition to the lungs. Because the amphibian skin is an efficient gas exchanger, the venous return to the heart from the body is well oxygenated; therefore, there is no advantage in keeping blood from the body separate from the blood from the lungs.

Capitanio and Leger (1979) pointed out that a rank ordering is an easier task when one is dealing with morphological features than when considering behavior. They offered the example of probability learning by goldfish and rats (Bitterman, 1965), in which the response pattern of "maximizing" (the pattern used by rats) has been regarded as having a higher rank than the "matching" pattern of the goldfish (Yarczower & Hazlett, 1977). Capitanio and Leger (1979) offered arguments that support the opposite interpretation. We are not taking a position on this particular issue; we merely use the controversy to illustrate the judgmental nature of such behavioral grades.

ANAGENESIS AND PROGRESS

A core concept of anagenesis is the notion of "progress." Unfortunately, "progress" often has been confused with "progression." Progress may be defined as a trend in the direction of improvement or a movement towards perfection. Rensch's (1959) original definition of anagenesis was in the context of both progression and biological progress, which was paraphrased by Simpson (1953) as ". . . the tendency of some major groups to have a fairly consistent and definable evolutionary direction, often exhibited by different lineages in parallel" (p. 384). Note that this definition places no value judgment on whether the evolutionary direction is an improvement or an advance towards perfection. Huxley (1957), however, broadened Rensch's definition to include ". . . all types or degrees of biological improvement, from detailed adaptation to general organizational advance" (p. 454). Much of the subsequent criticism of anagenesis has been directed at its association with "progress." As Ayala (1974) has put it, "The notion of progress requires that a value judgement be made of what is better and what is worse, or what is higher and what is lower, according to some axiological standard" (p. 341). Most contemporary systematic biologists have dropped the association of anagenesis with biological progress. Instead, they use anagenesis as a synonym for Simpson's (1961) "phyletic evolution"; that is, evolutionary change within a single taxon without branching.

An important distinction to consider is that between value judgment and scientific judgment. Scientific judgments frequently are made in the course of designing experiments, collecting data, interpreting results. These judgments sometimes involve error, but such errors usually are detected by the self-correcting nature of the scientific method. Value judgments, on the other hand, are highly personal, often arbitrary, and frequently dependent on nonscientific criteria. Thus, they can never be corrected by the usual scientific methods. For example, the phylogenetic trees generated by systematic biologists are based on scientific judgments, and they indeed may be in error in certain features. Certain species may be placed on the wrong limbs of the tree, or what was thought to be one branch may in fact be two or more separate branches. These errors may be detected and corrected by later scientific studies. But value judgments about which lineages represent improvements over others or which species are higher or lower, better or worse, advanced or regressive cannot be tested by subsequent research, because they are not objective; they represent the personal assessments of individuals.

The association of anagenesis with notions of evolutionary progress leads to the assumption that if a specific anagenetic sequence is progressive, then the reverse sequence must be retrogressive. We argue, however, that any adaptive change, if it enables the species to survive, is progressive, irrespective of its direction. It matters not whether the adaptive sequence was from simple to complex or vice versa. An illustration may be seen in the evolution of horses from *Hyracotherium*, an ancestral horse, to *Equus*, the modern horse (Colbert, 1980), which is one of the best documented fossil records.

Hyracotherium was a small animal, about the size of a terrier, with four toes on the foreleg and three on the hind leg. It was adapted to swift running over firm ground. As the animals' environment changed to the hard-packed ground of the prairie, the middle toes evolved into hooves and the lateral toes were suppressed. This might be regarded as progress, because it permitted the animals to succeed in a new adaptive zone. But if the sequence of environmental change had been the reverse, from hard-packed ground to firm ground, then the opposite sequence also would have been called progress. Indeed, if there were no methods for dating the fossils, we would have been totally unable to determine from the bones themselves whether the sequence had been from *Hyracotherium* to *Equus* or from *Equus* to *Hyracotherium*. Either direction would be progressive, depending on the demands of the environment. In other words, it is the fact of change that defines progress rather than the absolute direction. Similar considerations apply to body size. In many lineages, increased body size represents a successful adaptation to the environment; but in some lineages, decreased body size permitted the animals to enter new adaptive zones. For still others, a change in body size led to disaster for the species. Thus, one animal's progress may be another's route to extinction.

Analyses based on "progress" do not take into account the opportunism that is a contributing feature of the success of many adaptations. Being in the right place at the right time with the right adaptation, which indeed may have been evolved for some other purpose entirely, is a common scenario in evolutionary history (Mayr, 1965; Olson, 1976; Simpson, 1958).

ANAGENESIS AND LEVELS OF ORGANIZATION

Aronson (1984) has suggested that the concept of "levels of organization and integration" is an improvement over anagenesis. In our opinion, this concept is virtually identical to anagenesis in the Yarczower-Hazlett and Gottlieb senses and suffers from the same weaknesses. This concept is discussed hereafter. In his article, Aronson forthrightly described the weaknesses of the anagenetic approach:

1. *Evolutionary "progress" cannot be defined objectively.* Aronson quoted numerous distinguished authorities, each of whom offers either a different definition of progress or concludes that it cannot be objectified. After summarizing these opinions, Aronson himself offered no solution.

2. *Objective criteria for distinguishing successive grades do not exist.* Complexity may not be a satisfactory criterion, he stated, because "lower" animals may be complex and higher (and therefore more complex) animals can undergo extinction (Aronson, 1984, p. 72).

He concluded that ". . . for many purposes an intuitive understanding of the meaning of complexity will, at least, temporarily suffice" (p. 72). Although intuition may serve well as the starting point for hypotheses or new directions of exploration, we find it difficult to understand how intuition alone can serve as the foundation for a branch of science.

Aronson (1984) offered the concept of "levels" of integration and organization" as a preferable alternative to anagenesis. It is preferable because it avoids the pitfall of defining progress and instead substitutes "complexity", but:

> . . . not elementary complexity which can easily be described by the number of parts and the number of kinds of parts, but rather an advanced view of complexity that stresses the interrelationships of many different kinds of parts and their integration into new wholes at qualitatively higher levels. (p. 76)

No rules or objective criteria for measuring this advanced view of complexity are given, nor are we told how the qualitatively higher levels may be unambiguously recognized. He merely concluded that:

> There are still serious problems with complexity, especially its measurement, but this is now a subject of considerable attention and there is good basis for expectation that with further study, and especially with the aid of computer technology, solutions to these problems will be available in the near future. p. 76)

We do not share Aronson's optimism that either humans or the *deus ex machina* of the computer will soon solve the problem of finding a measure of complexity (advanced or otherwise) that is free from anthropocentrism, value judgments, preconceptions, and intuitive assessment.

CONCLUSIONS

In our article on the *scala naturae* (Hodos & Campbell, 1969), we suggested that if comparative psychology were to be consistent with the field of biological science, it should have the theory of evolution as its principle underpinning. Because the title of our paper was "Scala naturae: Why there is no theory in comparative psychology," some writers failed to recognize that the paper was an appeal for comparative psychologists to make their theorizing consistent with evolutionary theory and data rather than the phylogenetic (evolutionary) scale. We went on to state that an equally important and equally valid area of study was the "analysis of adaptation." By this we meant the correlation of structure and function. In this approach, investigators are free to study any animals and to group the data in any way that seems reasonable. They can form higher grades and lower grades and as many levels of organization that they see fit, so long as they do not conclude that by making such rankings they are representing history. They may, in fact, have represented history, but they must demonstrate that they have done so by correlation of their grades or levels with independent data of comparative morphology, physiology, and behavior of extant animals as well as data of paleontology.

Anagenesis is not a theory. Anagenesis is a descriptive term for one aspect of the pattern of evolution. Huxley (1957) combined Rensch's global, philosophical, macroevolutionary view of this term with a microevolutionary, nonbranching, ancestor-to-descendent progression concept to ". . . cover all types or degrees of biological improvement, from detailed adaptation to general organizational advance" (p. 454). Modern-day systematic biologists generally use the term in the former sense (detailed adaptation in an unbranched ancestor-to-descendent progression). Gottlieb (1984), and Yarczower and Hazlett (1977), are using the term in the latter sense (general organizational advance). Further, these behavioral scientists are using the term "grade" in a sense that is not in keeping with its current accepted meaning in systematics and evolutionary theory.

Yarczower and Hazlett (1977) and Gottlieb (1984) have made an appeal for an application of anagenesis to animal behavior, in which the notion of evolutionary "progress" is used as the basis for establishing grades. This basically is the Rensch-Huxley approach, which we reject because it is axiological; that is, it depends on value judgments as the basis for determining the rank order of the grades.

In our view, the inherently axiological nature of their view of anagenesis and the lack of objective criteria for determining the ranking of grades whether by "progress" or by "complexity" are weaknesses of such overwhelming magnitude as to invalidate the method. Measurements made with an elastic ruler do not inspire much confidence. Aronson (1984) also has expounded several serious criticisms of this anagenetic approach.

Does anagenesis have any utility in comparative psychology? The answer to this question depends to a great extent on whose definition of anagenesis is being discussed. We reject Rensch's (1959) definition outright because of its highly anthropocentric frame of reference; that is, it has as its measures of progress characteristics usually attributed to humans. For similar reasons, we reject anagenesis as propounded by Huxley (1942, 1957, 1958). The definitions of anagenesis suggested by Simpson (1961), Gould (1976), and Wiley (1981) appear to have some useful applications in the study of animal behavior. The reader should note that the three latter authors did not define anagenesis in precisely the same way. So long as grades based on these definitions are not used to infer sequences of historical events, they can serve useful functions in the systematic study of behavior. Rather than assume that anagenesis is a standard biological concept with an unequivocal meaning, writers should specify the sense in which the term is meant.

One should not lose sight of some important differences among the ways that various writers have used anagenesis. For example, Gould would form grades based on the fact that biological or behavioral changes have occurred and that these changes represent a betterment or an improvement in a mechanical sense. Improvement, for Gould, therefore, would be changes in the direction of greater efficiency, improved adaptation to the environment, invasion of new ecological niches, and so on. The Simpson-Wiley definitions allow no conclusions about the desirability of change or progress. In contrast, the Rensch-Huxley view is based on the scala naturae and therefore assumes that general biological improvement has occurred and that it has been in the direction of human characteristics.

In conclusion, we reject the suggestion that the study of anagenesis constitutes a third approach to the study of animal cognition, in particular, or comparative psychology, in general. In our opinion, the formation of grades of performance is one of the ways of categorizing the adaptation of organisms to their environment. In this application, we have no quarrel with those who would form grades and rank them in some sequence. We do take considerable issue, however, with those who would take these rankings and construct from them "evolutionary scales", representing these rankings as actual historical sequences. If we may be permitted to end on an axiological note, we believe that even though there are considerable differences of opinion and interpretation, the fact that comparative psychologists are now debating the intricacies of evolutionary theory represents an important form of "progress" in this field.

REFERENCES

Aronson, L. R. (1984). Levels of integration and organization: A revaluation of the evolutionary scale. In G. Greenberg & E. Tobach (Eds.), *Evolution and integrative levels* (pp. 57–81). Hillsdale, NJ: Lawrence Erlbaum Associates.

Ayala, F. J. (1974). The concept of biological progress. In F. J. Ayala & T. Dobzhansky (Eds.), *Studies in the philosphy of biology* (pp. 339–355). Berkley: University of California Press.

Bitterman, M. E. (1965). Phyletic differences in learning. *American Psychologist, 20,* 396–410.

Campbell, C. B. G. (1976). What animals should we compare? In R. B. Masterton, W. Hodos, & H. Jerison (Eds.), *Evolution, brain and behavior: Persistent problems* (pp. 107–113). Hillsdale, NJ: Lawrence Erlbaum Associates.

Capitanio, J. P. & Leger, D. W. (1979). Evolutionary scales lack utility: A reply to Yarczower and Hazlett. *Psychological Bulletin, 84,* 876–879.

Carroll, R. L. (1987). *Vertebrate paleontology and evolution.* San Francisco: Freeman.

Colbert, E. H. (1980). *Evolution of the vertebrates.* New York: Wiley.

Eldredge, N. & Gould, S. J. (1972). Punctuated equilibria: An alternative to phyletic gradualism. In T. J. M. Schoff (Ed.), *Models in paleontology* (pp. 82–115). San Francisco: Freeman, Cooper.

Gottlieb, G. (1984). Evolutionary trends and evolutionary origins: Relevance to theory in comparative psychology. *Psychological Review, 91,* 448–456.

Gould, S. J. (1976). Grades and clades revisited. In R. B. Masterton, W. Hodos & H. Jerison (Eds.), *Evolution, brain and behavior: Persistent problems*. Hillsdale, NJ: Lawrence Erlbaum Associates.

Gould, S. J. & Eldredge, N. (1977). Punctuated equilibria: The tempo and mode of evolution reconsidered. *Paleobiology, 3,* 115–151.

Hodos, W. & Campbell, C. B. G. (1969). The scala naturae: Why there is no theory in comparative psychology. *Psychological Review, 76,* 337–350.

Hodos, W. (1970). Evolutionary interpretation of neural and behavioral studies of living vertebrates. In F. O. Schmitt (Ed.), *The neurosciences: Second study program* (pp. 26–39). NY, The Rockefeller University Press.

Hodos, W. (1974). Comparative study of brain–behavior relationships. In I. J. Goodman & M. W. Schein (Eds.), *Birds, brain and behavior* (pp. 15–25). New York: Academic Press.

Huxley, J. S. (1942). *Evolution, the modern synthesis*. London: George Allen and Unwin.

Huxley, J. S. (1957). The three types of evolutionary progress. *Nature, 180,* 454–455.

Huxley, J. S. (1958). Evolutionary processes and taxonomy with special reference to grades. *University of Upsalla Arsskrift,* 21–39.

Krebs, J. R., Sherry, D. F. & Healy, S. D. (in press). Hippocampal specialization of food-storing birds. *Proceedings of the National Academy of Sciences.*

Lockard, R. B. (1971). Reflections on the fall of comparative psychology: Is there a message for us all? *American Psychologist, 26,* 168–179.

Martin, R. D. (1974). The biological basis of human behavior. In W. B. Broughton, (Ed.), *The biology of brains* (pp. 215–250). New York: Wiley.

Mayr, E. (1965). The evolution of living systems. In *The Scientific Endeavor* (pp. 241–250). New York: Rockefeller University Press.

Northcutt, R. G. (1988). Sensory and other neural traits and the adaptionist program: Mackerals of San Marco. In J. Atema, R. R. Fay, A. N. Popper, & W. N. Tavolga (Eds.), Sensory biology of aquatic animals. New York: Springer-Verlag, pp. 869–883.

Olson, E. C. (1976). Rates of evolution of the nervous system and behavior. In R. B. Masterton, W. Hodos & H. Jerison (Eds.), *Evolution, brain and behavior: Persistent problems* (pp. 47–77). Hillsdale, NJ: Lawrence Erlbaum Associates.

Rensch, B. (1959). *Evolution above the species level*. New York: Columbia.

Romer, A. S. (1966). *Vertebrate paleontology*. Chicago: University of Chicago Press.

Simpson, G. G. (1949). *The meaning of evolution*. New York: Yale University Press.

Simpson, G. G. (1953). *The major features of evolution*. New York: Columbia University Press.

Simpson, G. G. (1958). The study of evolution: Methods and present status of theory. In A. Roe & G. G. Simpson (Eds.), *Behavior and evolution* (pp. 7–26). New Haven: Yale University Press.

Simpson, G. G. (1961). *Principles of animal taxonomy*. New York: Columbia University Press.

Simpson, G. G. (1967). *The meaning of evolution*, 2nd Ed. New Haven: Yale University Press.

Torrey, T. W. (1971). *Morphogenesis of the vertebrates*. New York: Wiley.

Wiley, E. O. (1981). *Phylogenetics*. New York: Wiley.

Yapp, W. B. (1965). *Vertebrates: Their structure and life*. New York: Oxford University Press.

Yarczower, M. & Hazlett, L. (1977). Evolutionary scales and anagenesis. *Psychological Bulletin, 84,* 1033–1097.

Yarczower, M. & Yarczower, B. S. (1979). In defense of anagenesis, grades and evolutionary scales. *Psychological Bulletin, 86,* 880–883.

II Neurobiology of Communication

2 Human Language

Barry Gordon
The Johns Hopkins University School of Medicine

Cries and many other forms of vocal utterances in humans clearly have direct functional and neuroanatomical antecedents to those of nonhuman primates (see chap. 3). However, humans also have the natural capacity to communicate information through symbols combined according to rules (*propositional speech*). This chapter presents a selected outline of what is known about the functional basis for this capacity, and about its representation(s) in the brain.

While many sources of data can and have contributed to our current knowledge of language and its cerebral substrate, this chapter draws largely on that obtained from "experiments of nature" in previously normal individuals who have sustained a brain injury affecting their speech or other relevant functions. There are many uncertainties in interpreting such data (Berndt, 1989; Henderson, 1982; Seidenberg, 1988) which we simply gloss over here. However, what has been clearly established over the last century is that language in such patients fractionates in systematic ways, and that some of these regularities reflect the logic of how language is represented in the brain. This logic is presented here.

Figs. 2.1a and 2.1b give the anatomical landmarks of the human left cerebral hemisphere to which we refer.

LANGUAGE AS A SEPARABLE COGNITIVE FUNCTION

Because human language is so intimately associated with most of the activities we regard as uniquely human, and because the interdependence of language and other mental activities has been widely assumed for so long, it is not trivial to report that language functions can not only be dissociated from most other

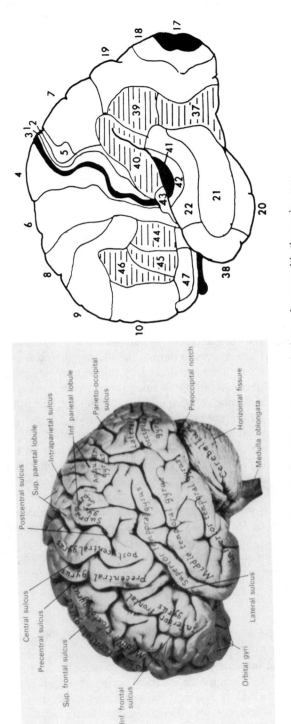

FIG. 2.1a. (left panel). The left cerebral hemisphere of man, with the major neuroanatomic areas of importance in speech processing. The Lateral Sulcus in the photo is also known as the Sylvian fissure.

FIG. 2.1b. (right panel). The left cerebral hemisphere, with areas classified by Brodmann's (1908) cytoarchitectonic scheme. Primary sensory cortices are in black. Regions thought to be unique to humans are striped. (Figure 1a reproduced with permission from M. B. Carpenter (1976). *Human neuroanatomy* (p. 555). Baltimore: Williams & Wilkins. Figure 1b reproduced with permission from C. Trevarthen (1983). Development of the Cerebral Mechanisms for Language. In U. Kirk (Ed.), *Neuropsychology of language, reading, and spelling* (p. 48; Fig. 3.1c). New York: Academic Press.

cognitive activities, but that they seem to be assigned their own separate cerebral territories as well. The two main sources of evidence for these statements are cases in which propositional speech is totally lost—global aphasia—and those in which relatively intact speech functions can be shown to be separated from all or part of other cognitive activities, as in the case of the transcortical aphasias and the sensory-specific anomias.

In *global aphasia*, the capacity for propositional speech is completely abolished, or nearly so. There is little or no residual ability to understand, speak, read, or write propositional speech. However, the affected individual is not without mentation, only without language. Individuals with virtually absent speech abilities can still think, plan, emote, and communicate in other ways; they can see, hear nonverbal sounds, and touch and feel normally. The lesion responsible for global aphasia is usually extensive destruction of the left perisylvian region, which destroys the auditory input routes, the oral output routes, and additional structures responsible for other language functions (Mazzocchi & Vignolo, 1979; Poeck, De Bleser, & Keyserlingk, 1984a) (see Fig. 2.2). These structures serve speech regardless of degree of education (Damasio, Castro-

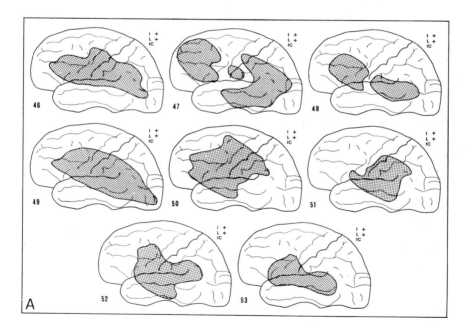

FIG. 2.2. Sample of sites of damage (by CT scan) associated with acute global aphasia. From Mazzocchi & Vignolo, 1979. Reproduced with permission.

Caldas, Grosso, & Ferro, 1976; but see Lecours et al., 1988) or the nature of the native tongue (Chary, 1986). Moreover, what is lost is an ability that transcends the auditory input route or the oral production route of normal individuals, since the prelingually deaf develop language disorders with left perisylvian damage, even though they perceive their language by eye, not ear, and express it with their hands, not their mouths (Chiarello, Knight, & Mandel, 1982; Douglass & Richardson, 1959; Poizner, Klima, & Bellugi, 1987; Underwood & Paulson, 1981). This constancy is even more surprising, given that speech is essentially a sequential transmission medium, whereas American Sign Language has a high degree of parallel information display (Poizner, Klima, & Bellugi, 1987).

The communicative ability that is left after global aphasia typically includes facial expressions, gestures, and a limited vocal repertoire. The latter includes grunts, recurrent consonant-vowel syllables ("dada", "meme") (Poeck, De Bleser, & Keyserlingk, 1984b), stock words and phrases, including expletives ("Yes", "You know how" or "My God!"), and singing (which, while not normal, is usually far better than propositional speech of the same lyrics without the melody [Critchley, 1970; see also Marin, 1982]). Modulation (volume and pitch) of the remaining sounds is typically appropriate for the context. These remaining communicative abilities presumably arise from one of two sources. The emotional, nonverbal expressions in particular are probably the product of anterior temporal lobe and subcortical structures in either hemisphere that are analogous to those in monkeys (chap. 3).

However, the formed utterances of the global aphasic ("My God!") may well be originating from the intact right hemisphere (cf. Knopman et al., 1984; Papanicolaou, Moore, Deutsch, Levin, & Eisenberg, 1988). The question of how much capacity for speech is normally present in the right hemisphere of individuals who are left-dominant for language (which is over 99% of right-handed individuals, and perhaps 60% of left-handers as well; see review by Nass & Gazzaniga, 1987) is a controversial one. The answer is complicated because the right hemisphere clearly has the capacity to gradually develop many language functions if the left hemisphere is damaged, particularly if the damage occurs in childhood, and even more so when it occurs in infancy. Perhaps the most widely accepted position is that the normal right hemisphere of a left-dominant individual has the capacity to understand high frequency, concrete words (words referring to palpable objects), but only limited syntactic ability, and little or no phonologic production capability (Nass & Gazzaniga, 1987). The right hemisphere also normally seems to play a role in comprehension of emotional tone (Ross, 1981) and of humor and metaphor (Wapner, Hamby, & Gardner, 1981).

Therefore, right-handed individuals (and most left handers) normally possess two anatomically independent language systems: the fully functional and dominant one on the left, and a much more limited one on the right. These capabilities raise one of the interpretative problems alluded to earlier: namely, if a function is *lost* from unilateral damage, it can be reasonably thought to have been dependent on that region of the brain. But the functions that *remain* might be coming from either side. Fortunately, the relatively limited capabilities of the right hemisphere usually ensure that we can restrict the scope of this discussion to the left (dominant) hemisphere.

Global aphasia demonstrates how language can be rather selectively eliminated, while other cognitive functions remain intact. What is also observed are conditions wherein some or all other cognitive functions are destroyed, while some language function(s) remain intact. The most extreme example of such disorders is isolation of the speech area (*mixed transcortical aphasia*): This describes patients with an acquired loss of comprehension through every input route (auditory speech, visual signal or reading, etc.) who do not themselves speak spontaneously, but with intact elementary speech input and output processes in that they can repeat what is spoken to them.

An analogous but less global impairment is seen in *transcortical sensory aphasia,* in which comprehension is impaired, even though repetition and speech production are intact (Albert, Goodglass, Helm, Rubens, & Alexander, 1981; Berndt, Basili, & Caramazza, 1987; Luria, 1976). The areas of damage responsible for transcortical sensory aphasia are in the temporo-parietal-occipital junction, just posterior to Wernicke's area (Kertesz, Sheppard, & MacKenzie, 1982; Rubens & Kertesz, 1983). The analogue of transcortical sensory aphasia in the motor domain is *transcortical motor aphasia,* in which comprehension is intact, as is repetition, but spontaneous speech production is markedly reduced (Rubens, 1976; von Stockert, 1974). The responsible lesions (those germane to this discussion) are in the prefrontal area, rostral and dorsal to Broca's area (Freedman, Alexander, & Naeser, 1984).

The focal damage causing isolation of the speech area (mixed transcortical aphasia) is conceptually the combination of transcortical sensory and transcortical motor aphasia: a ring around the perisylvian zone, sparing the zone itself (Fig. 2.3). These conditions therefore demonstrate that the basic mechanisms for speech input/output and for syntax are in the perisylvian region, while the structures involved in access to meaning and to the rest of the brain's functions are outside this area. In isolation of the speech area, the speech regions become functionally and anatomically sequestered from the rest of the brain (Geschwind, Quadfasel, & Segarra, 1968).

The independence of language can also be established by considering cases in which language is spared even though specific cognitive abilities linked to language are impaired, or in which the links themselves are damaged. The clearest examples are modality-specific processing or naming deficits. These have been described for the visual (Ratcliff & Ross, 1981; McCormick & Levine, 1983; McCormick & Levine, 1984), auditory (Denes & Semenza, 1975; Saffran, Marin, & Yeni-Komshian, 1976; Auerbach, Allard, Naeser, Alexander, & Albert,

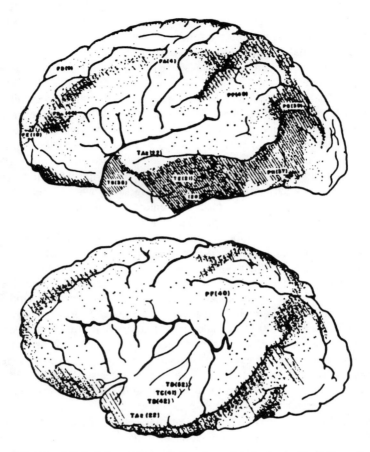

FIG. 2.3.   The left hemisphere lesion in a classic case of isolation of the speech area.The degree of dotting/hatching is roughly proportional to the degree of histologic damage. In the bottom illustration, the Sylvian (lateral) fissure has been spread apart, to show the preservation of the superior part of the temporal lobe and of the insular gyri. (From Geschwind, Quadfasel, & Segarra, 1968, Fig. 7. Reproduced with permission.)

1982; Kohn & Friedman, 1986), and tactile (Geschwind & Kaplan, 1962; Gazzaniga & Sperry, 1967; Yamadori, Osumi, Ikeda, & Kanazawa, 1980) input routes. The responsible lesions have either been within the particular sensory system, or in the pathways connecting the sensory processing system to language.

FRACTIONATION OF PROPOSITIONAL SPEECH

The Classic Aphasic Syndromes

Even though propositional speech as a whole may be an isolatable component of human cognition, there are other pathologic conditions that demonstrate that the abilities underlying propositional speech can be functionally and anatomically subdivided. The classic evidence for this came from the clinical syndromes of *Wernicke's aphasia* and *Broca's aphasia,* which we discuss next. It is important to understand, though, that these classical syndromes are not the optimal introduction to a neurobiology of language, for several reasons. They were defined on the basis of patterns of surface performance, such as "ability to comprehend" or "ability to repeat" (see Table 2.1). We now appreciate that such functions are only the surface product of other processes, and that it is these underlying processes which must be understood to explain speech and its cerebral mechanisms. The other point to be understood is that the classical syndromes are complex conglomerations of deficits. Some are intimately related; some are just accidentally associated because, for example, they are dependent upon the different territories supplied by a single vessel. Therefore, they are a confusing introduction to the fine structure of language representation. However, they are a rich source of evidence as to the nature of the underlying deficits, and they are the

TABLE 2.1
The Clinical Features of Broca's and Wernicke's Aphasias

	Broca's Aphasia	*Wernicke's Aphasia*
Spontaneous speech	Nonfluent, effortful, dropping of small grammatical words, retaining meaningful words, may be poor pronunciation, dysarthria	Fluent, little effort, high output of words, often poor in meaningful words with many circumlocutions, often paraphasias (substitutions of different sounds or words) or neologisms (completely uninterpretable sounds), pronunciation normal, no dysarthria
Comprehension	Usually fairly good, or normal	Poor
Repetition	Poor (consistent with spontaneous speech)	Poor
Naming	Better than spontaneous speech	Poor, often paraphasic

Note: Adapted from Gordon & Moses (1988).

lingua franca of work in this field, the principle route through which patients are identified for research study.

Classically, each of the major syndromes was defined by a major deficit in one area of clinical assessment: Wernicke's aphasia, by inability to comprehend; Broca's aphasia, by inability to produce speech; and *conduction aphasia,* by inability to repeat, despite relatively intact comprehension and production abilities.

Wernicke's Aphasia

Wernicke's aphasia describes a clinical syndrome of acquired aphasia in which speech comprehension is impaired and higher-order aspects of speech production are also affected. The degree of impairment of speech comprehension can vary from mild to nearly complete.

Although Wernicke's aphasia is frequently characterized as an input (receptive) deficit, speech production is typically abnormal too. The following quote is from a Wernicke's aphasic, describing the scene in a standardized picture (of the commotion surrounding a broken window; Fig. 2.4; Marin & Gordon, 1979). The spellings represent an attempt at phonetic transcription:

FIG. 2.4.   The broken window picture (reprinted with permission from Wells & Reusch, 1945).

You go the people goin' . . . an' what's more . . . the . . . eh . . well, you'd have one . . . your beez, your beez. Oh. . . . and then . . . come out in a few minutes . . . How manu, how many beezes. . . . eight many beezes . . . Eera comes a bes an' she an' gone the peesh an' these's the man an' there the young girl, on these she calls an' she's holdin' a koun. Emsin, emshin, I guess. A stickit, stimin . . . (p. 313)

In Wernicke's aphasia, articulation of speech is normal; there is no motor production deficit. Also, it is normally modulated and inflected, and produced fluently and without apparent effort. However, substantive words such as the nouns and major verbs are missing, replaced by generalities ("thing") and by a variety of speech errors (paraphasias). Some of the speech errors can be understood as errors in selecting single phonemes or syllables (phonemic paraphasias, e.g., door → "sloor"). Others are errors in selecting words (verbal paraphasias, e.g., door → "window"), which are usually semantically related to the intended word (semantic paraphasias). Still other speech production errors are completely uninterpretable (neologisms, e.g., "jilsent"). These errors are not shifts to an alternative language, as the Wernicke's aphasic shows no better comprehension of his own speech than anyone else. Similar speech errors occur in other aphasic syndromes, and even in normal speech, but with much lower frequency than in Wernicke's aphasics. Grammatical constructions and grammatical function words and ending are usually preserved, giving the appearance of correct syntactic frames, but on close examination they are often misapplied (paragrammatism) (Butterworth & Howard, 1987).

Repetition of auditory speech is impaired, commensurate with the comprehension and production impairments. Writing is usually well-formed and fluent, but has the same errors as spoken speech. Reading usually (but not always) shows the same comprehension deficits as with spoken speech. The minimal lesion responsible for the clinical picture of acute Wernicke's aphasia is usually in the posterior portion of the superior temporal gyrus (frequently termed "Wernicke's area," but see Bogen & Bogen, 1976) (see Fig. 2.5).

Broca's Aphasia

In partial contrast to Wernicke's aphasia is the clinical syndrome of Broca's aphasia. Clinically, comprehension in Broca's aphasics is normal. Their major clinical problem is in speech production. Broca's aphasics typically have pure motor problems with their speech production, with dysarthric speech, and with errors producing phonemes correctly. Their speech output is labored, and lacks normal rhythms and stress. Instead of complete, flowing sentences, only single words and short phrases can be produced. Usually, these are just the nouns and other substantive words of the intended message. Typically, Broca's aphasics omit grammatical function words such as the prepositions, and grammatical

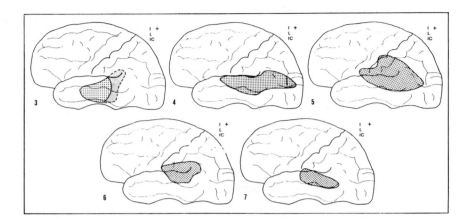

FIG. 2.5. Sample of sites of damage (by CT scan) associated with acute Wernicke's aphasia. From Mazzocchi & Vignolo, 1979. Reproduced with permission.

endings such as number and tense markers. Here is a Broca's aphasic's description of the "Broken Window" scene from Marin & Gordon, 1979 described earlier: "Like the door . . . crash . . . like, pants. . . . shirt . . . shoes . . . the boy . . . the dress . . . Do . . . . you do window?" (p. 312).

The Broca's aphasics' problems with producing grammatical function words and endings cannot be attributed to their motor speech problem. Some Broca's aphasics have the same grammatical difficulty, but little or no motor speech deficit. Also, the deficit depends upon the type of the sound to be produced, not the actual sound itself. "Two" meaning the number can often be said perfectly well, but when the intention is to say "too" or "to," it cannot be spoken. We discuss the grammatical deficit in Broca's aphasics in more detail later in this chapter (under Syntactic Processing Disorders).

The regions in which damage gives rise to persisting Broca's aphasia are not necessarily the same as the ones that have been labeled Broca's area, a constant source of confusion. Broca's area proper is the posterior portions of the second and third divisions of the inferior frontal gyrus (see Fig. 2.1). A lesion of just this area may produce the Broca's aphasia syndrome acutely (see Fig. 2.6), but such a lesion chronically is perhaps more likely to be associated with only motor speech production problems (aphemia: Schiff, Alexander, Naeser, & Galaburda, 1983). To produce a persisting Broca's aphasia, a much larger lesion is necessary, one typically including more posterior regions and deep subcortical structures as well (Mazzocchi & Vignolo, 1979; Mohr et al., 1978).

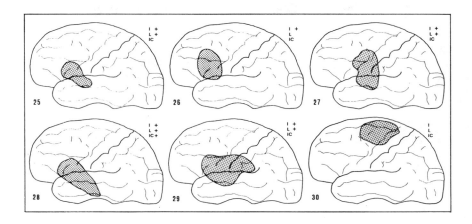

FIG. 2.6.   Sample of sites of damage (by CT scan) associated with acute Broca's aphasia. From Mazzocchi & Vignolo, 1979. Reproduced with permission.

FRACTIONATION OF PROPOSITIONAL SPEECH

Componential Analysis

Although the validity of Broca's aphasia and Wernicke's aphasia as clinical syndromes has been appreciated for over a century, neither syndrome is a suitable starting point for theorizing about the brain. The tasks used to define these conditions—such as speech comprehension and speech repetition—are not primitive brain functions, but are instead the complex products of many different, more basic, functions. The syndromes themselves are more-or-less accidental combinations of impairments, with ill-defined criteria for inclusion or exclusion. Studying the basis of language in the brain with only pathologic performance on such tasks as a guide is like trying to infer the function and structure of the arm in terms of "primitive" functions such as writing and ball throwing ability, by testing these after various kinds of fractures.

Two significant aides for such theorizing—both in the case of the arm, and in the case of language—are to begin with at least an outline of a theory of normal function(s), and to couple this with an appreciation of the requirements of the tasks used to probe for the underlying functions of interest. This strategy appears to be particularly valuable in studying acquired language disorders, since in many instances, cerebral injury seems to impair or delete normal functions, but does not appreciably change the ones already present, nor add new ones. There-

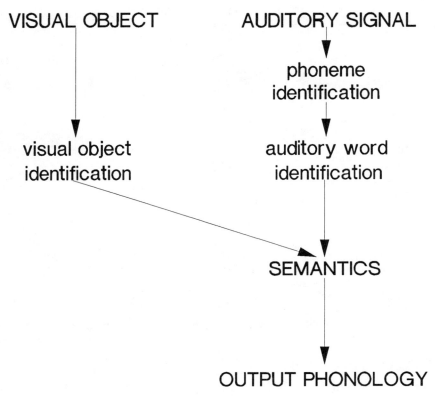

FIG. 2.7. Working model of speech perception, production, and of visual confrontation naming.

fore, a subtractive logic can be used to infer what was once the complete, normal state. This information can then be used to reinterpret, if necessary, the evidence from pathology, and to extend the chain of inference to make a more accurate model of the normal process.

The current processing diagram of language functioning, obtained from such an iterative process, is outlined in Fig. 2.7. More complete outlines can be found in Garrett (1984) and Shallice (1988). As shown in Fig. 2.7, speech production is thought to begin when the meaning of the message is synthesized (*semantics*). From meaning, the sound patterns of individual words are selected (*output phonology*). These, in turn, specify the motor programs for actual articulation of the muscles of the face, jaw, and tongue, and for control of the larynx. Speech comprehension begins with auditory input, from which the signals specific to speech are decoded (*phoneme perception*). These are recognized as words (the *input phonological lexicon*), which then, presumably, access the semantic system so that their meaning can be understood. Syntax is not depicted in the outline, but is discussed later in this chapter. Working from this outline, it is possible to ask more detailed questions about how speech and language functions can be described, and how these functions might be realized by the brain. We discuss several specific components and their possible neuroanatomical corrections from this viewpoint of a componential analysis, and then reconsider the classical clinical syndromes from this perspective.

Phoneme Perception

While the speech sound code is an acoustic signal, it clearly has a number of features and requirements which differentiate it from other sounds. Without presupposing a processing sequence, even at the descriptive level the nearly infinite variations in the acoustic signal must be identified in terms of the much smaller (50-100) set of categories which are used to signify meaning (Lieberman & Blumstein, 1988; Lieberman, Cooper, Shankweiler, & Studdert-Kennedy, 1967). In English, these are the consonants and vowels; many other languages use tone (relative pitch and changes in pitch) as another important dimension of coding. Vowels are relatively simple, sustained (on the order of 200-300 msec) sounds produced by shaping the oscillations produced by the vocal cords with the oropharynx and nasopharynx. Consonants are very brief (on the order of 20 msec) bursts of sounds produced by controlling more explosive air bursts with the tongue, lips, and jaw. Consonants convey most of the linguistic information in the speech signal. The net result of this coding process is that we can appreciate the information in speech at a rate several times faster than the rate at which other forms of acoustic signals can be decoded.

Clearly, we would infer that some specialized processor subserves speech perception. There is, in fact, neurologic evidence from patients with speech comprehension deficits which supports this. Curiously, these are not the patients with Wernicke's aphasia. The comprehension deficit in Wernicke's aphasia seems to be due to impairment in a later stage of processing (Blumstein, 1980). Instead, evidence for the existence and the location of this specialized early speech processor comes from the clinical syndrome of *pure word deafness*. In this very rare condition, hearing is intact, and speech is appreciated as a sound. But speech cannot be understood as language; it sounds as though it is a foreign tongue. Understanding of nonspeech sounds such as music, animal noises, etc., is preserved. Other speech functions, such as production, writing, and reading, are completely intact, or nearly so (Denes & Semenza, 1975; Saffran, Marin, & Yeni-Komshian, 1976).

To a first approximation, then, pure word deafness appears to be a selective loss of the capability for decoding speech sounds. In the few patients who have been tested more extensively, the problem affects perception of consonants rather than vowels (Chocholle, Chedru, Botte, Chain, & Lhermitte, 1975; Denes & Semenza, 1975; Saffran, Marin, & Yeni-Komshian, 1976; see also Auerbach,

Allard, Naeser, Alexander, & Albert, 1982; Yaqub, Gascon, Alsnosha, & Whitaker, 1988), and only some consonants at that (Saffran, Marin, & Yeni-Komshian, 1976). This selective deficit appears to have two causes (Auerbach et al., 1982). One cause is a disorder in perception of rapid transitions, prior to more specific speech (phonemic) identification (Auerbach, et al., 1982). The other is a true disorder of phonemic processing, apart from any central auditory disorder (Chocholle et al., 1975; Denes & Semenza, 1975). The deficit in pre-phonemic, acoustic temporal processing is associated with bilateral superior temporal lobe lesions (Yaqub, Gascon, Alsnosha, & Whitaker, 1988). The minimal lesion responsible for the purely phonemic processing deficit is typically in or around the primary auditory area of the left temporal lobe (Chocholle et al., 1975; Denes & Semenza, 1975). Therefore, it would appear that the specialized encoding of acoustic information to consonantal phonemic categories is accomplished in a relatively small region of the left superior temporal lobe. Vowel perception, which is less temporally demanding and less informationally significant, can be accomplished in either hemisphere (see also Oscar-Berman, Zurif, & Blumstein, 1975; Tallal & Newcombe, 1978).

This specialized processor faces a formidable task in mapping the nearly infinite variety of acoustic signals into the speech codes, but at least there are only a relatively small number of such codes (no more than about 200 distinct sounds across all the world's languages, with each individual language using only a subset of these [Maddieson, 1984]), However, this smaller set of phonologic codes is combined in human language to form a nearly infinite variety of words. It is perhaps reasonable to suppose that this, the recognition of the phonological input lexicon, could be a distinct next stage in auditory speech processing. There is indeed some convergent neurologic evidence to suggest that this is the case. Some of the performance of Wernicke's aphasics can be interpreted as evidence that they can have intact phonemic speech perception (Blumstein, 1980) but a disrupted input phonologic lexicon. Less direct but better established evidence indicates that a stage with the properties of a phonologic lexicon can be disconnected from semantic appreciation of the words (Bramwell, 1897; Kohn & Friedman, 1986). In these cases, during a phase of recovery from more severe aphasias, hearing was intact, and spoken language could be repeated correctly and written to dictation. However, spoken language could not be understood. At the same time, spontaneous speech was largely or almost completely intact, and reading was fairly good to intact. In one case, computed tomography (CT) showed a small lesion of the left posterior superior temporal lobe (possibly involving the primary auditory cortex) that extended up into the supramarginal and angular gyri (Kohn & Friedman, 1986).

Semantic Stage

The model we have presented presupposes that semantic processing of language is separable from its auditory input and production. There are, again, several sources of evidence from cerebral pathology that justify postulating a separable semantic stage. A semantic deficit has been generally conceded to be present in Wernicke's aphasics (Zurif, Caramazza, Myerson, & Galvin, 1974); however, the other deficits in these patients make it difficult to study the semantic impairment alone. The transcortical aphasias discussed earlier imply a separable semantic processing stage, in that they show that speech input processing can be decoupled from semantic appreciation.

More direct evidence comes from patients in whom semantic processing impairments can be identified, unconfounded by other deficits. Three patients whose clinical problem was difficulty in word retrieval (anomia) were found to have a disorder in semantics at the level of single word meaning (Hart & Gordon, in press), as defined by the following tasks: (a) synonym judgments (choosing the synonym of a target word from two candidates); (b) naming to definition (giving a word in response to a definition or description); (c) categorization (deciding if the pair of stimuli belonged to the same category, as in *hammer* and *drill*); and (d) property judgments (given a property such as color, size, or function, determining which response item shared the given property with the target; e.g., given *peas,* determine whether its color was more similar to that of *alligator* or that of *chicken*).

In these patients, and in others who have been characterized as having semantic deficits (De Renzi, Liotti, & Nichell, 1987; Gainotti, Carlomagno, Craca, & Silveri, 1986; Gainotti, Miceli, & Caltagirone, 1979; Sartori & Job, 1988), the common area of damage has been in the left posterior temporal-inferior parietal region. Lesions elsewhere in the cerebral cortex have not been found to produce such deficits (Gainotti, Carlomagno, Craca, & Silveri, 1986). Therefore, it appears that such single-word semantic processing is critically dependent on the left posterior temporal-inferior parietal region.

The left posterior temporo-parieto-occipital junction in man includes the posterior portions of Brodmann's (1909) areas 22 and 21, as well as the phylogenetically recent areas 39 and 37. While the exact functions of these areas are not known, by analogy with studies of nonhuman primates it seems plausible that portions of this region are devoted to higher-level elaboration exclusively within the auditory or visual processing domains, while more posterior and superior regions are concerned with multimodal processing and integration with language (Gross, Schiller, Wells, & Gerstein, 1967; Jones & Peters, 1986; Jones & Powell, 1970; Seltzer & Pandya, 1978). These multimodal regions are also among the areas of the brain which have undergone the greatest expansion in the course of evolution (Sanides, 1975) (see Fig. 2.1b). Therefore, even though it is not yet possible to infer exactly how these regions play a role in single-word semantic appreciation, their neuroanatomic connections and neurophysiologic properties make it plausible that they serve important functions for such abilities.

Subdivisions of Semantic Processing: Category-Specific Deficits. The neuropsychologic evidence also points to a finer-grained differentiation of semantic functions, even though specific neuroanatomic correlations (if any exist) are not yet known.

There is abundant evidence from studies of brain-injured patients that knowledge is represented categorically. This by itself is not a necessarily surprising revelation, since it has long been apparent that human semantic processing makes use of higher-order categories and links between items (e.g., Anderson & Bower, 1973). However, what has been surprising about the neurologic data is that it appears that categorical information is in some way segregated by the brain, so that it can be selectively impaired. The bulk of the relevant evidence comes from patients identified by their impairments in naming pictures of specific categories of items. For example, Hart, Berndt, & Caramazza (1985) described a patient with difficulty naming fruits and vegetables, but not in naming items from other categories. The impairment in this patient proved to be more pervasive than just in naming from pictures. This patient also had difficulty naming when he palpated the object, or tried to name it from its verbal definition. There was no reason to believe this patient's experience with fruits and vegetables had ever been limited in any way. His performance on other items of comparable frequency and saliency was normal. Other patients have been described with similarly specific patterns: for animals (Sartori & Job, 1988), animate objects (Warrington & Shallice, 1984), inanimate objects (Warrington & McCarthy, 1983), body parts (McKenna & Warrington, 1978), and colors (Goodglass, Wingfield, Hyde, & Theurkauf, 1986).

These category-specific deficits seem to obey what might be considered natural categories (such as the difference between animate and inanimate objects), so there might be some basis for believing that evolution has seen fit to dedicate specific neural systems to their representation, which is why they can be selectively dissociated. However, this argument cannot be correct, as at least two patients have been described with category-specific naming deficits that encompass unnatural, man-made categories: indoor objects (Yamadori & Albert, 1973) and household objects (Hart & Gordon, in preparation).

Therefore, it appears that cerebral injury can erase very selective portions of semantic memory. How this data can be explained neurobiologically is as yet unclear. However, the "hidden" or middle levels of many current parallel distributed processing (PDP) learning models frequently code categorical information in a subset of "neuronal" connections (Rumelhart, McClelland, & PDP Research Group, 1986). Such an architecture would permit the selective excision of a category by the right form of chance damage (cf. Wood, 1978), providing a possible account of this data.

Subdivisions of Semantic Processing: Verbal-Visual Dissociations.   A neurobiologic account may be possible at a grosser level for a semantic deficit that has been identified in two other patients, in whom access to visual information via verbal input seems to be selectively damaged. We have extensively studied one of these patients (Hart & Gordon, 1988b). This patient (K.R.) was identified because she had difficulties in naming pictures, but only those of animals. Investigation showed that this naming impairment was not limited to pictures, however, but was also present when trying to name in response to the nonverbal sounds associated with animals (e.g., a dog's bark). These errors could not be attributed to a speech production deficit, as she made errors in writing as well.

Detailed investigation showed that K.R. had marked deficits in verbally accessing the visual perceptual properties of animals. She could not demonstrate much knowledge of the color, size, and even of the number of legs of animals. For example, she could not tell how many legs a snake has ("six"). However, she could easily make these judgments for other perceptual and associative properties of animals, and for any properties of other items. For example, she could report that a stool has 3 or 4 legs. This discrepancy between animals and other items was found regardless of input modality (visual or auditory), stimulus type (words or sounds), the type of the task, or the response mode. Nevertheless, her perceptual knowledge of animals was intact. For example, she could determine whether the color of an animal was correct (e.g., a white sheep) or incorrect (e.g., a green fox). However, even for the pictures that she recognized were colored incorrectly, she should not give the name of the correct color.

Besides K.R., there is another case reported in the literature with such a specific and sharply delimited semantic processing deficit for visual information (Sartori & Job, 1988), although not as clearly defined as in K.R. This additional case supports the interpretation that K.R.'s case is an example of a dissociation caused by the manner in which language and visual information are normally related, rather than by some idiosyncracies on K.R.'s part.

A clue to this relationship between linguistic and visual knowledge can perhaps be found in the neurobiology of primate vision. Visual processing in primates appears to be distinct from that of other modalities up through fairly high levels of representation. In the nonhuman primate, color and form are processed separately from spatial position, and separately from each other, throughout cortical processing stations ranging from the occipital cortex through the inferior temporal lobe (Mishkin, 1982; Ungerleider, 1985; Ungerleider & Mishkin, 1982; Zeki & Shipp, 1988). There are good reasons to believe humans have a similar visual processing organization and neuroanatomic representation (Damasio, Yamada, Damasio, Corbett, & McKee, 1980; Livingstone & Hubel, 1988; Tusa & Ungerleider, 1985).

In contrast to the inferior temporal location of visual information processing, language processing is of course a function of more superior, perisylvian regions. In particular, as we have suggested above, lexical semantic processing appears to be critically dependent on the left posterior temporal-inferior parietal region (Gainotti, Carlomagno, Craca, & Silveri, 1986; Hart & Gordon, 1988a; Hart & Gordon, in press; Warrington & Shallice, 1984).

In keeping with these functional and neuroanatomic distinctions, we suggest that in the normal state, purely verbal knowledge is separate from higher-order visual and other perceptual information, but that all of these systems are highly linked with each other. The linking may be through direct connections, or through higher-level units. The net result is that the verbal system contains tags or connections to, for example, visual representations, but these visual representations do not themselves reside within the verbal representational system.

That K.R.'s deficits were limited to the visual domain can therefore be explained as a consequence of damage to these verbal-to-visual links (in the absence of any direct evidence for damage to the purely verbal or the purely visual systems themselves). K.R. had a lesion of her left temporal lobe, a location broadly consistent with the functional explanation. To account for the category specificity, we must suppose that access between the systems normally requires a conjunction of codes for both visual and animal information, or that K.R.'s illness raised the normal activation threshold so that both sources of information were needed for sufficient activation of information. Chance then determined in her case which combinations of features failed to be sufficient (Gordon, 1982; Wood, 1978; Wood, 1982).

Syntactic Processing Disorders

Syntax was not explicitly labeled part of the normal processing scheme, yet it clearly is a vital feature of language. Syntactic ability has been thought to be central in generating the **creativity** of language. In human language, linguistic symbols can be combined into novel patterns, conveying novel information. This creativity has been thought to be one of the primary characteristics of true symbolic communication, separating man from organisms using simple reflexive messages (Terrace, Petitto, Sanders, & Bever, 1979; Thompson & Church, 1980; but see Savage-Rumbaugh, Rumbaugh, Smith, & Lawson, 1980).

Syntax has also been descriptively singled out as a separable level, akin to the phonemic and semantic levels of speech processing we have discussed. Many elements of language are considered part of syntax. These include the abstract markings of words and other elements in grammatical classes (e.g., the property of being a noun). Through these markings, the elements can be manipulated according to rules without referencing their complete semantic content. The frame of a sentence created by its grammatical function words, affixes, and word order, similarly seems to belong to syntax, existing apart from any particular meaning. Chomsky's famous nonsense sentence "Colorless green ideas sleep furiously" demonstrates how correct syntax can exist even when meaning is completely uninterpretable.

The neurologic evidence does imply that the broad distinction between semantic operations and syntactic operations is respected by the neural substrates of language. As we noted earlier, in isolation of the speech area and in a related problem, termed *transcortical sensory aphasia*, semantic understanding is typically impaired, whereas syntactic operations and knowledge are left intact. In the condition called isolation of the speech area (and also in transcortical sensory aphasia), semantically anomalous sentences (such as, "Elephants are smaller than ants") will be repeated verbatim, without any sign of recognition or surprise, yet grammatically incorrect sentences (such as, "The pen and pencil *is* in my pocket," or "Hand the paper to *she*") will be repeated with grammatical corrections (Berndt, Basili, & Caramazza, 1987; Davis, Foldi, Gardner, & Zurif, 1978; Heilman, Rothi, McFarling, & Rottmann, 1981; Pirozzolo, Christensen, Ogle, Hansch, & Thompson, 1981; Schwartz, Marin, & Saffran, 1979; Whitaker, 1976). This implies that syntactic processing (in production) can remain intact despite profound deficits in semantic comprehension. Perhaps more convincingly, two cases have been reported in which syntactic comprehension (the ability to understand who did something to whom, in sentences of the form "The girl pushed the boy") is preserved despite marked impairment of semantic comprehension on other tasks (Schwartz, Marin, & Saffran, 1979; Gordon et al., 1988). Wernicke's aphasics show some aspects of a similar dissociation, producing sentences with relatively normal syntactic structure even though they have little content (but see Butterworth & Howard, 1987). Other, less easily classified, cases have been reported who also show intact knowledge and execution of syntactic rules despite profound disruptions of semantic knowledge (De Renzi, Liotti, & Nichelli, 1987).

The opposite dissociation, of disrupted syntactic processing despite intact semantic abilities, has also been reported. Broca's aphasics demonstrate relative preservation of substantive words, but impaired syntax in their impoverished, stereotyped word orderings and their omissions of grammatical words and endings (Berndt & Caramazza, 1980).

The descriptive classification of levels of speech processing has clearly had so much congruence with the components revealed by cerebral injury that it has been tempting to imagine that, because syntax has frequently been treated by linguists as a unified entity (e.g., Chomsky, 1965), it would be the product of a single, specialized processing system in the brain. This position was initially thought to be justified by the neurologic evidence. In particular, the syntactic deficit in Broca's aphasia was found to involve comprehension of syntax, as well as its production, just as would be expected if a single system was responsible for both input and output (for reviews, see Berndt & Caramazza, 1980; Kean, 1980; Saffran, Schwartz, & Marin, 1980; Schwartz, Saffran, & Marin, 1980; Zurif, 1980). However, it now appears that the full spectrum of syntactic deficits in aphasia cannot be explained by damage to any single syntactic system. Instead, many different aspects of syntax appear to be fractionated by brain injury. One important dissociation that has been observed is that between syntactic processing in comprehension and in production. The two can be affected independently of each other (Caramazza & Hillis, 1984; Kolk, van Grunsven, & Keyser, 1985; Miceli, Mazzucchi, Menn, & Goodglass, 1983; Nespoulous, et al., 1988). Even in speech production alone, it has become clear that various forms of syntactic expression do not show correlated impairments after damage (Berndt, 1987; Miceli, Silveri, Komani, & Caramazza, in press).

In fact, an increasing volume of detailed case studies has documented even more surprising variations. A patient reported by Howard (1985) was agrammatic in reading but not in auditory comprehension. Agrammatism in writing but not in speech has also been described (Bub & Kertesz, 1982). Furthermore, patients who do not use syntax correctly in their speech may, nonetheless, be able to make correct judgments about their own types of grammatical errors (Isserlin, 1922/1985; Linebarger, Schwartz, & Saffran, 1983).

Clearly, at the present time it does not appear that syntax is a single processing ability. Instead, syntactic abilities are the outcome of a heterogeneous collection of individual processes (cf. Bates, Friederici, & Wulfeck, 1987; Bates, Friederici, Wulfeck, & Juarez, 1988), which are perhaps segregated with specific processing routes (such as phonologic input and output in the case of the transcortical aphasias; see Berndt, Basili, & Caramazza, 1987). Neuroanatomic correlations of these various deficits are just beginning (Tramo, Baynes, & Volpe, 1988).

Individual Variability and Mechanisms of Recovery: Implications

So far, this chapter has presented the functional architecture and the neuroanatomy of language as it exists in the "average" individual. One of the important recent advances in the study of language representation in the brain has been the appreciation of individual differences in language processing, and of individual differences in cerebral organization.

Individual differences in cognitive ability have been apparent for some time (Carroll, 1988). Differences in experience account for some of these, as, for example, in knowledge of birds (Coltheart & Evans, 1981). However, more far reaching are differences between individuals in how even relatively simple psychological tasks are accomplished (Battig, 1975; Cooper, 1976; Hunt, 1978). For example, different subjects apparently use different strategies to decide if two visually presented shapes are the same or different (Cooper, 1976), or to determine whether or not an item has been previously presented (Hunt, 1978). Despite these indications, the nature and range of individual differences in processing within a language are just beginning to be explored (Bates, Bretherton, & Snyder, 1988).

Individual differences in neuroanatomic structures are strikingly apparent in humans (Whitaker & Selnes, 1976). For example, between individuals there is a three-fold difference in the surface area of the primary visual cortex (Stensaas, Eddington, & Dobelle, 1974). There presumably are functional correlates of these differences, but these are not yet known for humans. In animals, however, these differences are also apparent even for relatively basic functions (Livingston & Phillips, 1957; Neafsey et al., 1986). For instance, the cortical stimulation maps of patterns of movement in laboratory rats varies appreciably from animal to animal (Neafsey et al., 1986). We should not expect less variability in the cerebral organization of language in humans, and what direct data there is suggests that this will be the case. When language function is mapped in conscious humans by the technique of applying electric current directly to the cortex, the regions involved in language can be shown to have considerable individual variations (Lesser et al., 1987; Lesser, personal communication; Ojemann, 1978; Ojemann & Whitaker, 1978). While there are some hazards in extrapolating these electrical studies to normal human language, this evidence for variability is consistent with the data from normal individuals who have suffered accidental cerebral damage. The standard correlations presented here (Figs. 2.2 through 2.6) are frequently violated in individual cases. There is much more variability in the location of lesions causing aphasic syndromes than we have discussed and, conversely, in the location of lesions that do not cause the expected problems (Basso, Bracchi, Capitani, Laiacona, & Zanobio, 1987; Basso, Lecours, Moraschini, & Vanier, 1985; Lhermitte, Lecours, Ducane, & Escourolle, 1973; Mazzocchi & Vignolo, 1979; Metter, 1987; Metter, Wasterlain, Kuhl, Hanson, & Phelps, 1981; Poeck, De Bleser, & Keyserlingk, 1984a). In the one systematic survey (to our knowledge) of both positive and negative lesions by computerized tomographic (CT) scanning (Basso et al., 1985), 17% of the patients had unexpected findings. This number may be inflated because of limitations of CT scanning (it shows only structural lesions, and only those of fairly significant size and severity). It may also be inflated because current concepts of the role of different areas of the cortex are probably too narrow (cf. Galaburda & Sanides, 1980). But this data does help support the argument that there is an appreciable variability in the location and extent of the representations of different language functions in different individuals, within and between (Segalowitz & Bryden, 1983) hemispheres.

Possibly closely allied to individual variations in normal representation is the ability for more-or-less complete recovery of function, seen after focal lesions in many regions of the brain, including the language areas. It has been known for some time from animal studies that, for example, a small lesion appropriately placed in the motor cortex can impair motor function. But motor abilities then recover. If a lesion is then made in the surrounding areas, however, function is lost once again, this time with much less complete recovery, if at all. Yet lesions of these adjacent regions would not have produced any appreciable motor impairment had the animal not had the first lesion (Glees & Cole, 1950; Irle, 1987; Marshall, 1984).

These experiments have been interpreted as evidence for a relatively diffuse representation of potential function, which is only expressed in one specific area. A lesion of the specific area is the impetus for a reorganization of the adjacent region to take over the ability (Irle, 1987; Marshall, 1984; Newsome & Wurtz, 1988).

An analogous process seems to occur in humans, and in the speech areas. While the human data is more difficult to interpret than the animal data, since it is less well controlled, small focal lesions can produce speech problems acutely, which fade or change in nature over time (see Pashek & Holland, 1988). In many cases, this is presumably because functions can be taken over by the adjacent brain regions (Levine & Mohr, 1979; Roberts, 1958), instead of (or in addition to) being expressed by the right hemisphere, a possibility mentioned earlier. This may be the reason that, in the case of single-word auditory comprehension, lesions have to involve more than 60 cm^2 of cerebral tissue before they produce persisting deficits (Selnes, Niccum, Knopman, & Rubens, 1984).

This data on variability and on the nature and evolution of deficits after injury is important for several reasons. The first is simply a technical one: It imposes an additional challenge for the study of human language (and other higher cerebral functions), and certainly adds to the uncertainty in trying to make inferences about the cerebral representation of these functions, and in trying to interpret reports of neuroanatomic correlations, when these have been done at different times in the course of the patient's condition.

Secondly, the animal lesion data has also helped to show that the cortical processing map is very highly detailed (Livingstone & Hubel, 1987; Newsome & Wurtz, 1988). Therefore, it suggests that the neuroanatomic associations of language that we have been able to make so far are, in fact, gross underestimations of how finely language is represented in the brain. The evidence from semantic dissociations we have reviewed earlier certainly supports this contention.

Finally, the variability in normal representation, and the potential for recovery, are also important theoretical opportunities. The central nervous system must be constructed in such a way as to permit them to occur. Several recent theoretical explanations of central function have tried to infer fundamental aspects of neural connectivity from these capabilities (Edelman, 1987; Wall, 1988).

SUMMARY AND FUTURE DIRECTIONS

We have seen that propositional speech can be functionally separated from other cognitive operations, and can be shown to depend upon neuroanatomic structures in the left perisylvian region in some essential way, even though the neurobiologic basis for this is unclear. We have also seen that several different functional components of propositional speech can be dissected by brain injury, and that these functions are associated with discrete brain regions, ranging in size from a few cm^2 to many cm^2 (cf. Livingstone & Hubel, 1988; Posner, Petersen, Fox, & Raichle, 1988). The data from brain injured patients also makes it clear that even finer functional distinctions, such as those we have reviewed in semantics and syntax, are implemented in the neural architecture, although their specific neural correlates are not yet understood.

It may be that the structure of functional-brain organization is such that even these smaller cognitive units will be found to have discrete neuroanatomic representations. Even if this is the case, individual variations will make these difficult to discern. However, it is also likely that we are approaching a scale of operations where discrete localization no longer applies. Parallel distributed processing models (Grossberg, 1980; Rumelhart, McClelland, & PDP Research Group, 1986; see also Edelman, 1987) have suggested ways in which cognitive function and neural processing may be related on these smaller scales. Many laboratories are actively pursuing tests of these models with aphasic data.

ACKNOWLEDGMENTS

Preparation of this chapter was supported in part by NINCDS Teacher-Investigator Award 1 KO7 NS00721 and by NINDS Grant No. 1 RO1 NS26553. I thank Patricia Hopkins, Elissa A. Kinch, Tara Spevak, and Pamela Schwerdt for their assistance, and Stephanie Trampbusch for her German translations. The engaging discussions and comments of Drs. Alfonso Caramazza, Ola Selnes, and particularly of Dr. John Hart, Jr., are gratefully acknowledged. The unflagging enthusiasm and omniverous interests of Dr. Oscar S. M. Marin, my teacher and former colleague, have continued to help sustain my own. His contribution to this chapter has therefore been immense.

REFERENCES

Albert, M. L., Goodglass, H., Helm, N. A., Rubens, A. B., & Alexander, M. P. (1981). *Clinical Aspects of dysphasia*. New York: Springer.

Anderson, J., & Bower, G. (1973). *Human associative memory*. Washington, DC: Winston.

Auerbach, S. H., Allard, T., Naeser, M., Alexander, M. P., & Albert, M. L. (1982). Pure word deafness: Analysis of a case with bilateral lesions and a defect at the prephonemic level. *Brain, 105*, 271–300.

Basso, A., Lecours, A. R., Moraschini, S., & Vanier, M. (1985). Anatomoclinical correlations of the aphasias as defined through computerized tomography: Exceptions. *Brain and Language, 26*, 201–229.

Basso, A., Bracchi, M., Capitani, E., Laiacona, M. & Zanobio, M. E. (1987). Age and evolution of language area functions. A study on adult stroke patients. *Cortex, 23*, 475–483.

Bates, E., Bretherton, I., & Snyder, L. (1988). *From first words to grammar: Individual differences and dissociable mechanisms*. New York: Cambridge University Press.

Bates, E., Friederici, A., & Wulfeck, B. (1987). Grammatical morphology in aphasia: Evidence from three languages. *Cortex, 23*, 545–574.

Bates, E. A., Friederici, A. D., Wulfeck, B. B., & Juarez, L. A. (1988). On the preservation of word order in aphasia: Cross-linguistic evidence. *Brain and Language, 33*, 323–364.

Battig, W. F. (1975). Within-individual differences in "cognitive" processes. In R. L. Solso (Ed.), *Information processing and cognition: The Lovola symposium* (pp. 195–228). Hillsdale, NJ: Lawrence Erlbaum Associates, Inc.

Berndt, R. S. (1987). Symptom co-occurence and dissociation in the interpretation of agrammatism. In M. Coltheart, G. Sartori, & R. Job (Eds.), *The cognitive neuropsychology of language* (pp. 221–233). London: Erlbaum.

Berndt, R. S. (1989). Repetition in aphasia: Implications for models of language processing. In F. Boller, & J. Grafman (Eds.), *Handbook of neuropsychology.* (pp. 329–348). New York: Elsevier.

Berndt, R. S., Basili, A., & Caramazza, A. (1987). Dissociation of functions in a case of transcortical sensory aphasia. *Cognitive Neuropsychology, 4,* 79–107.

Berndt, R. S., & Caramazza, A. (1980). A redefinition of the syndrome of Broca's aphasia: Implications for a neuropsychological model of language. *Applied Psycholinguistics, 1,* 225–278.

Blumstein, S. (1980). Neurolinguistic disorders: Language–brain relationships. In S. B. Filskov & T. J. Boll (Eds.), *Handbook of clinical neuropsychology.* New York: Wiley.

Bogen, J. E., & Bogen, G. M. (1976). Wernicke's region—where is it? *Annals New York Academy of Sciences, 280,* 834–843.

Bramwell, B. (1897). Illustrative cases of aphasia. *Lancet, 1,* 1256–1259.

Brodmann, K. (1909). Vergleichende Lokalisationlehre der Grosshirnrinde in ihren Prinzipien dargestellt auf Grund des Zellenbaues. Leipzig: J. A. Barth.

Bub, D., & Kertesz, A. (1982). Deep agraphia. *Brain and Language, 17,* 146–165.

Butterworth, B., & Howard, D. (1987). Paragrammatisms. *Cognition, 26,* 1–37.

Caramazza, A., & Hillis, A. E. (1989). The disruption of sentence production: Some dissociations. *Brain and Language, 36:*625–650.

Carroll, J. B. (1988). Individual differences in cognitive functioning. In R. C. Atkinson, R. J. Herrnstein, G. Lindzey, & R. D. Luce (Eds.), *Stevens' handbook of experimental psychology (2nd ed.).* New York: John Wiley & Sons.

Chary, P. (1986). Aphasia in a multilingual society: A preliminary study. In J. Vaid (Ed.), *Language processing in bilinguals: Psycholinguistic and neuropsychological perspectives* (pp. 183–197). Hillsdale, NJ: Lawrence Erlbaum Associates.

Chiarello, C., Knight, R., & Mandel, M. (1982). Aphasia in a prelingually deaf woman. *Brain, 105,* 29–51.

Chocholle, R., Chedru, F., Botte, M. C., Chain, F., & Lhermitte, F. (1975). Psychoacousic study of a case of 'cortical deafness'. *Neuropsychologia, 13,* 163–172.

Chomsky, N. (1965). Aspects of the Theory of Syntax. Cambridge, MA: M.I.T. Press.

Coltheart, V., & Evans, J. St. B. T. (1981). An investigation of semantic memory in individuals. *Memory & Cognition, 9,* 524–532.

Cooper, L. A. (1976). Individual differences in visual comparison processes. *Perception & Psychophysics, 19,* 433–444.

Critchley, M. (1970). *Aphasiology and Other Aspects of Language.* London: Edward Arnold.

Damasio, A. R., Castro-Caldas, A., Grosso, J. T., & Ferro, J. M. (1976). Brain specialization for language does not depend on literacy. *Archives of Neurology, 33,* 300–301.

Damasio, A., Yamada, T., Damasio, H., Corbett, J., & McKee, J. (1980). Central achromatopsia: Behavioral, anatomic, and physiologic aspects. *Neurology, 30,* 1064–1071.

Davis, L., Foldi, N. S., Gardner, H., & Zurif, E. B. (1978). Repetition in the transcortical aphasias. *Brain and Language, 6,* 226–238.

Denes, G., & Semenza, C. (1975). Auditory modality-specific anomia: Evidence from a case of pure word deafness. *Cortex, 11,* 401–411.

De Renzi, E., Liotti, M., & Nichelli, P. (1987). Semantic amnesia with preservation of autobiographic memory. A case report. *Cortex, 23,* 575–597.

Douglass, E., & Richardson, J. C. (1959). Aphasia in a congenital deaf-mute. *Brain, 83,* 68–80.

Edelman, G. M. (1987). *Neural Darwinism: The theory of neuronal group selection.* New York: Basic Books.

Freedman, M., Alexander, M. P., & Naeser, M. A. (1984). Anatomic basis of transcortical motor aphasia. *Neurology, 34,* 409–417.

Gainotti, G., Carlomagno, S., Craca, A., & Silveri, M. C. (1986). Disorders of classificatory activity in aphasia. *Brain and Language, 28,* 181–195.

Gainotti, G., Miceli, G., & Caltagirone, C. (1979). The relationships between conceptual and semantic-lexical disorders in aphasia. *International Journal of Neuroscience, 10,* 45–50.

Galaburda, A., & Sanides, F. (1980). Cytoarchitectonic organization of the human auditory cortex. *Journal of Comparative Neurology, 190,* 597–610.

Garrett, M. (1984). The organization of processing structure for language production: Applications to aphasic speech. In D. Caplan, A. Lecours, & A. Smith (Eds.), *Biological perspectives on language.* Cambridge, MA: MIT Press.

Gazzaniga, M. S., & Sperry, R. W. (1967). Language after section of the cerebral commissures. *Brain, 90,* 131–148.

Geschwind, N., & Kaplan, E. (1962). A human cerebral disconnection syndrome. *Neurology, 12,* 675–685.

Geschwind, N., Quadfasel, F. A., & Segarra, J. M. (1968). Isolation of the speech area. *Neuropsychologia, 6,* 327–340.

Glees, P., & Cole, J. (1950). Recovery of skilled motor function after small repeated lesions of motor cortex in macaque. *Journal of Neurophysiology, 13,* 137–148.

Goodglass, H., Wingfield, A., Hyde, M., & Theurkauf, J. C. (1986). Category specific dissociations in naming and recognition by aphasic patients. *Cortex, 22,* 87–102.

Gordon, B. (1982). Confrontation naming: Computational model and disconnection simulation. In M. A. Arbib, D. Caplan, & J. C. Marshall (Eds.). *Neural models of language processess.* New York: Academic Press.

Gordon, B., Hart, J., Lesser, R. P., Selnes, O. A., Fisher, R., & Uematsu, S. (1988, October). *Dissociations in mixed transcortical aphasia produced by direct cortical electrical stimulation.* Paper presented to the Academy of Aphasia, Montreal.

Gordon, B. & Moses, H., III. (1988). Aphasia and other disorders of higher cognitive function. In A. M. Harvey, (Eds.), *The principles and practice of medicine* (22nd ed.). New York: Appleton-Century-Crofts.

Gross, C. G., Schiller, P. H., Wells, C., & Gerstein, G. L. (1967). Single-unit activity in temporal association cortex of the monkey. *Journal of Neurophysiology, 30,* 833–843.

Grossberg, S. (1980). How does a brain build a cognitive code? *Psychological Review, 87,* 1–51.

Hart, J., Berndt, R. S., & Caramazza, A. (1985). Category-specific naming deficit following cerebral infarction. *Nature, 316,* 439–440.

Hart, J., & Gordon, B. (1988a). Semantic and phonologic deficits in anomia: CT study. *Neurology, 38 (Supp 1),* 300.

Hart, J., & Gordon, B. (1988b, October). *Implications for semantic organization from a case of category specific anomia.* Paper presented at the Annual Meeting of the Academy of Aphasia, Montreal.

Hart, J., & Gordon, B. (in press). *Delineation of single-word semantic comprehension deficits in aphasia, with anatomic correlation. Annals of Neurology.*

Heilman, K. M., Rothi, L., McFarling, D., & Rottmann, A. L. (1981). Transcortical sensory aphasia with relatively spared spontaneous speech and naming. *Archives of Neurology, 38,* 236–239.

Henderson, L. (1982). *Orthography and word recognition in reading.* New York: Academic Press.

Howard, D. (1985). Introduction to "On Agrammatism" (Ueber Agrammatismus), by Max Isserlin, 1922. *Cognitive Neuropsychology, 2,* 303–307.

Hunt, E. (1978). Mechanics of verbal ability. *Psychological Review, 85,* 109–130.

Irle, E. (1987). Lesion size and recovery of function: Some new perspectives. *Brain Research Reviews, 12,* 307–320.

Isserlin, M. (1922/1985). On agrammatism. *Cognitive Neuropsychology, 2,* 308–345.

Jones, E. G., & Peters, A. (Eds.). (1986). *Cerebral Cortex.* New York: Plenum.

Jones, E. G., & Powell, T. P. S. (1970). An anatomical study of converging sensory pathways within the cerebral cortex of the monkey. *Brain, 93,* 793–820.

Kean, M. L. (1980). Grammatical representation and the description of language processing. In D.

Caplan (Ed.), *Biological studies of mental processes* (pp. 239–268). Cambridge, Mass: MIT Press.

Kertesz, A., Sheppard, A., & MacKenzie, R. (1982). Localization in transcortical sensory aphasia. *Archives of Neurology, 39,* 475–478.

Knopman, D. S., Selnes, O. A., Niccum, N., & Rubens, A. B. (1984). Recovery of naming in aphasia: Relationship to fluency, comprehension and CT findings. *Neurology, 34,* 1461–1470.

Kohn, S. E., & Friedman, R. B. (1986). Word-meaning deafness: A phonological-semantic dissociation. *Cognitive Neuropsychology, 3,* 291–309.

Kolk, H. H. J., van Grunsven, M. J. F., & Keyser, A. (1985). On parallelism between production and comprehension in agrammatism. In M. L. Kean (Ed.), *Agrammatism* (pp. 165–206). Orlando, FL: Academic Press.

Lecours, A. R., et al. (1988). Illiteracy and brain damage 3: A contribution to the study of speech and language disorders in illiterates with unilateral brain damage (initial testing). *Neuropsychologia, 26,* 575–589.

Lesser, R. P., Lueders, H., Klem, G., Dinner, D. S., Morris, H. H., Hahn, J. F., & Wyllie, E. (1987). Extraoperative cortical functional localization in patients with epilepsy. *Journal of Clinical Neurophysiology, 4,* 27–53.

Levine, D. N., & Mohr, J. P. (1979). Language after bilateral cerebral infarctions: Role of the minor hemisphere in speech. *Neurology, 29,* 927–938.

Lhermitte, F., Lecours, A. R., Ducarne, B., & Escourolle, R. (1973). Unexpected anatomical findings in a case of fluent jargon aphasia. *Cortex, 9,* 437–449.

Lieberman, A. M., Cooper, F. S., Shankweiler, D. P., & Studdert-Kennedy, M. (1967). Perception of the speech code. *Psychological Review, 74,* 431–461.

Lieberman, P., & Blumstein, S. E. (1988). *Speech physiology, speech perception, and acoustic phonetics.* Cambridge: Cambridge University Press.

Linebarger, M., Schwartz, M., & Saffran, E. (1983). Sensitivity to grammatical structure in so-called agrammatic aphasics. *Cognition, 13,* 361–392.

Livingston, A., & Phillips, C. G. (1957). Maps and thresholds for the sensorimotor cortex of the cat. *Quarterly Journal of Experimental Psychology, 42,* 190–205.

Livingstone, M. S., & Hubel, D. H. (1987). Connections between layer 4B of Area 17 and the thick cytochrome oxidase stripes of Area 18 in the Squirrel monkey. *The Journal of Neuroscience, 7,* 3371–3377.

Livingstone, M. S., & Hubel, D. H. (1988). Psychophysical evidence for separate channels for the perception of form, color, movement, and depth. *The Journal of Neuroscience, 7,* 3416–3468.

Luria, A. R. (1976). *Basic problems of neurolinguistics.* Paris: Mouton.

Maddieson, I. (1984). *Patterns of sounds.* New York: Cambridge University Press.

Marin, O. S. M. (1982). Neurological aspects of music perception and performance. *The psychology of music* (pp. 453–477). Academic Press, Inc. New York.

Marin, O. S. M., & Gordon, B. (1979). Neuropsychological aspects of aphasia. In H. R. Tyler & D. M. Dawson (Eds.), *Current neurology* (Vol. 2, pp. 305–343). Boston: Houghton Mifflin.

Marshall, J. F. (1984). Brain function: Neural adaptations and recovery from injury. *Annual Review of Psychology, 35,* 277–308.

Mazzocchi, D., & Vignolo, L. A. (1979). Localisation of lesions in aphasia: Clinical-CT scan correlations in stroke patients. *Cortex, 15,* 627–654.

McCormick, G. F., & Levine, D. A. (1983). Visual anomia: A unidirectional disconnection. *Neurology, 33,* 664–666.

McCormick, G. F., & Levine, D. A. (1984). Reply to Margolin [letter]. *Neurology, 34,* 398–399.

McKenna, P., & Warrington, E. K. (1978). Category-specific naming preservation: A single case study. *Journal of Neurology, Neurosurgery, and Psychiatry, 41,* 571–574.

Metter, E. J. (1987). Neuroanatomy and physiology of aphasia: Evidence from positron emission tomography. *Aphasiology, 1,* 3–33.

Metter, E. J., Wasterlain, C. G., Kuhl, D. E., Hanson, W. R., & Phelps, M. E. (1981). FDG positron emission computed tomography in a study of aphasia. *Annals of Neurology, 10,* 173–183.

Miceli, G., Mazzucchi, A., Menn, L., & Goodglass, H. (1983). Contrasting cases of Italian agrammatic aphasia without comprehension disorder. *Brain and Language, 19,* 65–97.

Miceli, G., Silveri, M. C., Romani, C., & Caramazza, A. (in press). Variation in the pattern of omissions and substitutions of grammatical morphemes in the spontaneous speech of so-called agrammatic patients. *Brain and Language,*

Mishkin, M. (1982). A memory system in the monkey. *Philosophical Transactions of the Royal Society of London, 298B,* 85–95.

Mohr, J. P., Pessin, M. S., Finkelstein, S., Funkenstein, H. H., Duncan, G. W., & Davis, K. R. (1978). Broca aphasia: Pathologic and clinical aspects. *Neurology, 28,* 311–324.

Nass, R. D., & Gazzaniga, M. S. (1987). Cerebral lateralization and specialization in human central nervous system. In F. Plum (Ed.), *Handbook of physiology V (The nervous system)* (pp. 701–761). Baltimore: Williams and Wilkins.

Neafsey, E. J., Bold, E. L., Haas, G., Hurley-Gius, K. M., Quirk, G., Sievert, C. F., & Terreberry, R. R. (1986). The organization of the rat motor cortex: A microstimulation mapping study. *Brain Research Reviews, 11,* 77–96.

Nespoulous, J. L. et al. (1988). Agrammatism in sentence production without comprehension deficits: Reduced availability of syntactic structures and/or of grammatical morphemes? A case study. *Brain and Language, 33,* 273–295.

Newsome, W. T., & Wurtz, R. H. (1988). Probing visual cortical function with discrete chemical lesions. *Trends in Neurosciences, 11,* 394–399.

Ojemann, G. A. (1978). Organization of short-term verbal memory in language areas of human cortex: Evidence from electrical stimulation. *Brain and Language, 5,* 331–340.

Ojemann, G., & Whitaker, H. (1978). Language localization and variability. *Brain and Language, 6,* 239–260.

Oscar-Berman, M., Zurif, E. B., & Blumstein, S. (1975). Effects of unilateral brain damage on the processing of speech sounds. *Brain and Language, 2,* 345–355.

Papanicolaou, A. C., Moore, B. D., Deutsch, G., Levin, H. S., & Eisenberg, H. M. (1988). Evidence for right-hemisphere involvement in recovery from aphasia. *Archives of Neurology, 45,* 1025–1029.

Pashek, G. V., & Holland, A. L. (1988). Evolution of aphasia in the first year post-onset. *Cortex, 24,* 411–423.

Pirozzolo, F. J., Christensen, K. J., Ogle, K. M., Hansch, E. C., & Thompson, W. G. (1981). Simple and choice reaction time in dementia: Clinical implications. *Neurobiology of Aging, 2,* 113–117.

Poeck, K., De Bleser, R., & Keyserlingk, D. G. von (1984a). Computed tomographic localization of standard aphasic syndromes. In F. C. Rose (Ed.), *Progress in aphasiology* (pp. 71–89). New York: Raven Press.

Poeck, K., De Bleser, R., & Keyserlingk, D. G. von (1984b). Neurolinguistic status and localization of lesion in aphasic patients with exclusively consonant–vowel recurring utterances. *Brain 107,* 199–217.

Poizner, H., Klima, E. S., & Bellugi, U. (1987). *What the hands reveal about the brain.* Cambridge, MA: MIT Press.

Posner, M. I., Petersen, S. E., Fox, P. T., & Raichle, M. E. (1988). Localization of cognitive operations in the human brain. *Science, 240,* 1627–1631.

Ratcliff, G., & Ross, J. E. (1981). Visual perception and perceptual disorder. *British Medical Bulletin, 37,* 181–186.

Roberts, L. (1958). Functional plasticity in cortical speech areas and integration of speech. *Archives of Neurology and Psychiatry, 79,* 275–250.

Ross, B. H. (1981). The more, the better? Number of decisions as a determinant of memorability. *Memory & Cognition, 9,* 23–33.

Rubens, A. B. (1976). Transcortical motor aphasia. In H. Whitaker, & H. A. Whitaker (Eds.), *Studies in neurolinguistics (Vol. 1,* pp. 293–303). New York: Academic Press.

Rubens, A. B., & Kertesz, A. (1983). The localization of lesions in transcortical aphasias. In A. Kertesz (Ed.), *Localization in neuropsychology* (pp. 245–268). New York: Academic Press.

Rumelhart, D. E., McClelland, J. L., & PDP Research Group (1986). *Parallel distributed processing: Explorations in the microstructure of cognition. Vol. 1.* Cambridge, MA: MIT Press.

Saffran, E. M., Marin, O. S. M., & Yeni-Komshian, G. H. (1976). An analysis of speech perception in word deafness. *Brain and Language, 3,* 209–228.

Saffran, E. M., Schwartz, M. F., & Marin, O. S. M. (1980). The word order problem in agrammatism: II. Production. *Brain and Language, 10,* 263–280.

Sanides, F. (1975). Comparative neurology of the temporal lobe in primates including man with reference to speech. *Brain and Language, 2,* 396–419.

Sartori, G., & Job, R. (1988). The oyster with four legs: A neuropsychological study on the interaction of visual and semantic information. *Cognitive Neuropsychology, 5,* 105–132.

Savage-Rumbaugh, E. S., Rumbaugh, D. M., Smith, S. T., & Lawson, J. (1980). Reference: The linguistic essential. *Science, 210,* 922–925.

Schiff, H. B., Alexander, M. P., Naeser, M. A., Galaburda, A. M. (1983). Aphemia: Clinical–anatomic correlations. *Archives of Neurology, 40,* 720–727.

Schwartz, M. F., Marin, O. S. M., & Saffran, E. M. (1979). Dissociations of language function in dementia: A case study. *Brain and Language, 7,* 277–306.

Schwartz, M., Saffran, E., & Marin, O. (1980). The word order problem in agrammatism: I. Comprehension. *Brain and Language, 10,* 249–262.

Segalowitz, S. J., & Bryden, M. P. (1983). Individual differences in hemispheric representation of language. In S. J. Segalowitz (Ed.), *Language functions and brain organization* (pp. 341–372). Orlando: Academic Press.

Seidenberg, M. (1988). Cognitive neuropsychology and language: The state of the art. *Cognitive Neuropsychology, 5,* 403–426.

Selnes, O. A., Niccum, N., Knopman, D., & Rubens, A. B. (1984). Recovery of single word comprehension: CT-scan correlates. *Brain and Language, 21,* 72–84.

Seltzer, B., & Pandya, D. N. (1978). Afferent cortical connections and architectonics of the superior temporal sulcus and surrounding cortex in the rhesus monkey. *Brain Research, 149,* 1–24.

Shallice, T. (1988). *From neuropsychology to mental structure.* New York: Cambridge University Press.

Stensaas, S. S., Eddington, D. K., & Dobelle, W. H. (1974). The topography and variability of the primary visual cortex in man. *Journal of Neurosurgery, 40,* 747–755.

Tallal, P., & Newcombe, F. (1978). Impairment of auditory perception and language comprehension in dysphasia. *Brain and Language, 5,* 13–24.

Terrace, H. S., Petitto, L. A., Sanders, R. J., & Bever, T. G. (1979). Can an ape create a sentence? *Science, 206,* 891–902.

Thompson, C. R., & Church, R. M. (1980). An explanation of the language of a chimpanzee. *Science, 208,* 313–314.

Tramo, M. J., Baynes, K., & Volpe, B. T. (1988). Impaired syntactic comprehension and production in Broca's aphasia: CT lesion localization and recovery patterns. *Neurology, 38,* 95–98.

Tusa, R. J., & Ungerleider, L. G. (1985). The inferior longitudinal fasciculus: A reexamination in humans and monkeys. *Annals of Neurology, 18,* 583–591.

Underwood, J. K., & Paulson, C. J. (1981). Aphasia and congenital deafness: A case study. *Brain and Language, 12,* 285–291.

Ungerleider, L. G. (1985). The corticocortical pathways for object recognition and spatial perception. In, *Pattern recognition mechanisms.* Vatican City: Pontificiae Academiae Scientiarvm Scripta Varia.

Ungerleider, L. G., & Mishkin, M. (1982). Two Cortical Visual Systems. In D. J. Ingle, M. A. Goodale, & R. J. Mansfield (Eds.), *Analysis of visual behavior* (pp. 549–586). Cambridge, MA: MIT Press.

von Stockert, T. R. (1974). Aphasia sine aphasia. *Brain and Language, 1,* 277–282.

Wall, J. T. (1988). Variable organization in cortical maps of the skin as an indication of the lifelong adaptive capacities of circuits in the mammalian brain. *Trends in Neuroscience, 11,* 549–557.

Wapner, W., Hamby, S., & Gardner, H. (1981). The role of the right hemisphere in the apprehension of complex linguistic materials. *Brain and Language, 14,* 15–33.

Warrington, E. K., & McCarthy, R. (1983). Category specific access dysphasia. *Brain, 106,* 859–878.

Warrington, E. K., & Shallice, T. (1984). Category specific semantic impairments. *Brain, 107,* 829–854.

Wells, F. L., & Reusch, J. (1945). *The mental examiner's handbook.* New York: Psychological Corporation.

Whitaker, H. (1976). A case of the isolation of the language function. In H. Whitaker & H. A. Whitaker (Eds.), *Studies in neurolinguistics, Vol. 2* (pp. 1-58). New York: Academic Press.

Whitaker, H. A., & Selnes, O. A. (1976). Anatomic variations in the cortex: Individual differences and the problem of the localization of language functions. *Annals of the New York Academy of Sciences, 280,* 844–854.

Wood, C. C. (1978). Variations on a theme by Lashley: Lesion experiments on the neural model of Anderson, Silverstein, Ritz, and Jones. *Psychological Review, 85,* 582–591.

Wood, C. C. (1982). Implications of simulated lesion experiments for the interpretation of lesions in real nervous systems. In M. A. Arbib, D. Caplan, & J. C. Marshall (Eds.), *Neural models of language processing* (pp. 485–509). New York: Academic Press.

Yamadori, A., & Albert, M. L. (1973). Word category aphasia. *Cortex, 9,* 112–125.

Yamadori, A., Osumi, Y., Ikeda, H., Kanazawa, Y. (1980). Left unilateral agraphia and tactile anomia. *Archives of Neurology, 37,* 88–91.

Yaqub, B. A., Gascon, G. G., Alsnosha, M., & Whitaker, H. (1988). Pure word deafness (acquired verbal auditory agnosia) in an Arabic speaking patient. *Brain, 111,* 457–466.

Zeki, S., & Shipp, S. (1988). The functional logic of cortical connections. *Nature, 335,* 311–317.

Zurif, E. B. (1980). Language mechanisms: A neuropsychological perspective. *American Scientist, 68,* 305–311.

Zurif, E. B., Caramazza, A., Myerson, R., & Galvin, J. (1974). Semantic feature representations for normal and aphasic language. *Brain and Language, 1,* 167–187.

3 Vocal Communication in Primates

Uwe Jürgens

BEHAVIORAL ASPECTS

Vocal communication in nonhuman primates differs from that in humans in that the motor patterns underlying vocal utterances do not have to be learned by imitation from conspecifics, but are more or less completely genetically determined. What is learned, at least to a large extent, is the meaning of the utterances. Cognition is thus restricted in nonhuman primate vocal communication to essentially two processes: a) auditory gestalt perception, that is, identification of vocal signals; b) learning to associate a particular call with a particular context.

Vocal Production

Squirrel monkey infants that are raised in an acoustic isolation room by mothers surgically muted during pregnancy develop all call types of the species' vocal repertoire within the first year of their life, that is, without ever having had an opportunity to hear another monkey's calls (Winter et al., 1973). Not all call types are present immediately after birth, and those which are often change in acoustic structure during ontogeny. We do not know at present whether these changes are purely maturational effects resulting from the successive increase in vocal fold length and lung capacity, the progressive myelination of intracerebral fiber tracts, et cetera or if some motor learning takes place in the sense that the animals know innately how the vocalizations should sound but need motor exercise (together with auditory feedback) to produce them correctly. Nevertheless, the fact remains that no external models are necessary for the development of the complete vocal repertoire.

Unfortunately, such Kaspar-Hauser experiments exist only for the squirrel monkey. Comparable experiments in other primates are therefore clearly needed. There are a few observations, however, that can be taken as supportive evidence that the genetic factor plays a role not only in the squirrel monkey. One such observation comes from gibbon hybrids. Geissman (1984), as well as Brockelman and Schilling (1984), found that the songs uttered by hybrids of Hylobates pileatus and Hylobates lar do not resemble the songs of their parental species but are somewhere in between despite the fact that the infants sing a lot in companionship with their mothers. Another observation stems from attempts to teach home-raised chimpanzees spoken words (Hayes & Hayes, 1951; Kellogg, 1968). The complete failure of these attempts, in view of a well-developed capacity of these animals for the acquisition of nonvocal communication signals (e.g., American Sign Language; Gardner & Gardner, 1969), points again to a genetic basis of vocal behavior, more specifically, to genetically determined limitations of vocal motor learning. Lieberman, Crelin, & Klatt (1972) drew attention to the fact that the larynx of the chimpanzee occupies a higher position within the neck than that of man, and, as a consequence, does not allow the production of as many vowels as in man—due to different resonant characteristics of the supralaryngeal tract. The study of Lieberman et al., however, also makes clear that the higher laryngeal position in the chimpanzee does not principally hinder the production of different vowels; it only limits it to a smaller group of less differentiated forms. As chimpanzees show a well-developed movability of lips and tongue (Van Hooff, 1976), that is, articulatory organs, the anatomical prerequisites for the production of at least a close approximation of spoken words nevertheless are met. The total inability to imitate speech thus cannot solely be explained by the different vocal organ anatomy.

The more or less complete inability of monkeys and apes to learn new vocal patterns does not mean, however, that there is a general lack of voluntary phonatory control in these animals. Vocal operant conditioning experiments in the rhesus monkey (Aitken & Wilson, 1979; Sutton, Larson, Taylor, & Lindeman, 1973) and capuchin monkey (Myers, Horel, & Pennypacker, 1965) have shown that these animals are able to increase their vocalization rate if vocalization is rewarded by either food or postponement of electric shock in an avoidance task. Sutton and co-workers (1978) succeeded in training their monkeys to utter a specific call type ("coo") during the presentation of a colored stimulus light, utter a second call type ("bark") during the presentation of a differently colored light, and refrain from vocalizing (to produce a nonvocal motor pattern) during presentation of a third stimulus light. This clearly shows that monkeys do have voluntary control of vocalization. The voluntary control, however, relates mainly to the initiation of vocalization, much less to its structure. Similar conclusions are suggested by a study of Cheney and Seyfarth (1985). These authors observed the warning behavior of vervet monkeys in their natural environment in East Africa. They found that adult females show a higher probability of uttering alarm calls in the presence of their own infants than in the presence of nonkin. Adult males utter warning calls more often in the presence of adult females than adult males. In vervet monkeys, predators thus do not automatically elicit warning calls: they do it dependent upon a learned context. That there is also control of the acoustic structure of the emitted calls has been shown by Sutton and co-workers (1973) for the rhesus monkey. In their vocal operant conditioning task, the animals were only food-rewarded when the emitted calls exceeded a certain intensity level and duration. It was found that during conditioning training there was an increase in average intensity and duration of the conditioned calls. These calls, however, always remained within the range of variability of spontaneously uttered calls; they, therefore, cannot be considered as newly acquired vocal patterns.

Genetically preprogrammed vocalizations do not only occur in monkeys and apes but also in humans. They can be found in essentially three forms:

1. Infant vocalizations. These include different cries (Truby & Lind, 1965; Wasz-Höckert, Lind, Vuorenkoski, Partanen, & Valanne, 1968), and five further call types expressing different emotional shades from uneasiness to satisfaction (Morath, 1979). As all these vocalizations are produced within the first weeks of life, long before vocal motor learning takes place, they must be considered as innate.

2. Nonverbal emotional vocal utterances beyond infancy. Laughing, whim-pering, pain shrieking, shouting for joy and moaning are emotional vocal ex-pressions that also occur in a more or less normal form in deaf-and-blind born, that is, in persons who do not have the opportunity to learn these patterns from others (Eibl-Eibesfeldt, 1973; Goodenough, 1932). They also must be consid-ered as innate, therefore.

3. Emotional intonation of speech. Transcultural comparisons of the emo-tional intonations used during anger, sadness, happiness or disgust reveal com-mon features for specific emotions across different languages, and thus suggest a genetic basis also for this type of vocal behavior (Beier & Zautra, 1972; Kramer, 1964).

From these observations, it may be concluded that nonhuman primate vo-calizations are closely related to human nonverbal emotional utterances and emotional intonations superimposed on verbal speech components. In the re-mainder of this chapter, whenever the neural mechanisms underlying monkey call production are discussed, it is with the understanding that monkey calls can serve as models for human nonverbal emotional vocal patterns but not for verbal ones.

Vocal Perception

In contrast to motor production, perception and adequate use of vocalizations are, to a greater extent, learned. The best documented examples are, again, the alarm calls of the vervet monkey (Seyfarth, Cheney, & Marler, 1980). Adult vervet monkeys use three different alarm calls against leopards, eagles and snakes, respectively. Leopard alarm calls elicit running to the next tree if the animals are on the ground, and climbing higher if they are already in a tree. Eagle alarm calls cause looking up; snake alarm calls cause looking down from a tree or, if the animals are on the ground, standing bipedally and scanning the ground. Vervet monkey infants (in the absence of their mothers) show an alerting reaction to these alarm calls but do not differentiate among them; that is, eagle alarm calls are not more likely to induce looking up than snake or leopard alarm calls. Infants thus seem to have a vague innate knowledge about the meaning of alarm calls in the sense that alarm calls mean danger. But their specific meaning—eagle alarm call means danger from above—must be learned.

This increase in reaction specificity to particular calls is parallelled by an increase in specificity of the situations eliciting such calls. While infant vervet monkeys react with eagle alarm calls not only to eagles but also to herons, geese, pigeons, hornbills and, occasionally, even to falling leaves, adult monkeys never do. Corresponding observations have been made in the squirrel monkey (Herzog & Hopf, 1984). Adult wild-caught squirrel monkeys react to dummy leopards with yapping calls. Monkeys raised from birth under social and acoustic isolation do not. In contrast to normal monkeys, they also do not avoid contact with such objects. Monkeys raised under social isolation but confronted occasionally with a dummy leopard together with yapping calls presented through a loudspeaker avoid the leopard. Again, there seems to be some innate knowledge about the meaning of yapping calls: yapping signals "potential predator." That moving objects with amber fur and black dots belong to the category "potential predator" must be learned, however.

In the case of the vervet and squirrel monkey alarm calls, the learning process consists of specifying the meaning of calls the motor production of which is already more or less perfect. This type of learning may be regarded as an intermediate form between a completely genetically determined vocal reaction, on the one hand, and a learned reaction to vocal sounds, which before learning had no meaning at all, on the other. Both extremes can be found among primates. An example of a completely genetically determined reaction is the warning call reaction against aerial predators in squirrel monkeys (Herzog & Hopf, 1984). Squirrel monkey infants raised under social isolation react to aerial predator warning calls with a prompt flight to their mother surrogate, similar as group-raised infants do with respect to their mothers. Moreover, presentation of a moving shadow of a specific size and angular velocity crossing a luminous background above the animal elicits the typical species-specific aerial predator warning call even in animals which never had an opportunity to hear this call before nor to observe the reaction of conspecifics to the call-eliciting stimulus. As an example of a completely learned reaction with no genetic predisposition, the speech-understanding chimpanzees of Savage-Rumbaugh, McDonald, Sevcik, Hopkins, & Rubert, 1986) may be mentioned. These authors trained pygmy chimpanzees to point to one photograph out of three presented simultaneously that showed an object the name of which had been given to the animal in form of a spoken word. Both animals trained succeeded in identifying more than 40 different words. This example makes clear that the perceptive speech capabilities of chimpanzees far outreach their motor speech capabilities. It also indicates that for physiological studies on speech, the perceptual processes underlying monkey vocal communication might represent a more adequate model than their motor counterparts.

PHYSIOLOGICAL ASPECTS

Vocal Production

Our knowledge about which brain structures are involved in the central control of monkey calls stems from four sources: electrical brain stimulation, lesioning, single unit recording, and neuroanatomical studies. In the following, we discuss the main findings of these approaches in this order.

Electrical Brain Stimulation Studies. Electrically elicited vocalizations have been reported in the marmoset (Lipp & Hunsperger, 1978), squirrel monkey (Jürgens & Ploog, 1970), rhesus monkey (Kaada, 1951; Magoun, Atlas, Ingersoll, & Ranson, 1937; Robinson, 1967), gibbon (Apfelbach, 1972) and chimpanzee (Brown, 1915). A more systematic investigation has been made, however, only in the rhesus and squirrel monkey. A comparison of the vocalization-eliciting electrode positions in rhesus and squirrel monkey is shown in Fig. 3.1. In both animals, positive sites are in the anterior limbic cortex but not in the frontal neocortex. Further posterior, both animals have positive sites in the septum, preoptic region, hypothalamus, amygdala and midline thalamus; both animals lack positive sites in the caudatum, putamen and globus pallidus. In the brain stem, finally, positive sites are concentrated in the periaqueductal gray and lateral pontine tegmentum; both the rhesus and squirrel monkey lack positive sites in the tectum and medial pontine tegmentum.

Apart from the close similarity in the distribution of vocalization-eliciting sites in both animals, representing such divergent forms as Old World monkeys, on the one hand, and New World monkeys, on the other, Fig. 3.1 demonstrates two further points. One is that the vocalization-eliciting substrate is not a small restricted area within the brain that could be interpreted as a "vocalization center"; it represents, on the contrary, an extensive, widely branching system reaching from the forebrain down to the lower brain stem. The second point concerns the close relationship between vocalization-eliciting areas and the

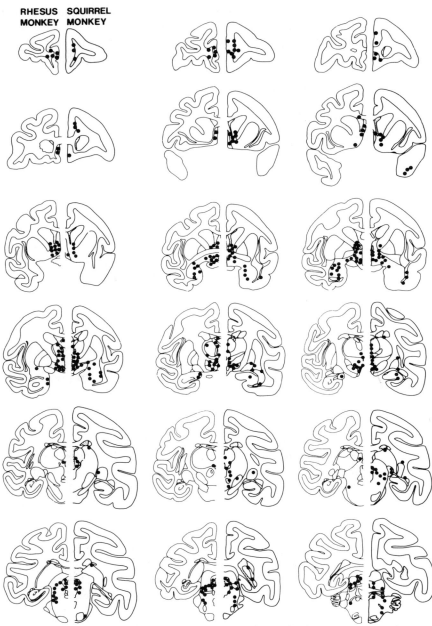

RHESUS   SQUIRREL
MONKEY   MONKEY

FIG. 3.1.   Distribution of sites yielding vocalization when electrically stimulated in the rhesus monkey (left side of brain diagrams) and squirrel monkey (right side).

limbic system, more specifically, the part of the limbic system that is related to motivation control. Such limbic vocalization-eliciting areas are, for instance, the anterior cingulate cortex, septum, amygdala, bed nucleus of stria terminalis, preoptic area, hypothalamus and midline thalamus. Interestingly, no vocalizations can be obtained from the classical motor areas, that is, the primary motor cortex, premotor cortex, basal ganglia, cerebellum, ventrolateral thalamus, nucl. ruber or inferior olive. Furthermore, those areas which do yield vocalization do not all produce the same call type. The midline thalamus, for instance, produces only aerial predator warning calls; the posterior periventricular hypothalamus yields exclusively cackling-like mobbing calls; the stria terminalis produces purring, a call normally uttered during huddling of group mates or suckling of infants. Some areas produce more than one call type, but these call types usually are functionally related.

This substrate specificity of the elicited call types, together with the close relationship between vocalization areas and motivation-controlling limbic structures suggest that the elicited calls probably do not represent primary, that is, pure motor responses, but represent secondary reactions to stimulation-induced motivational changes. In order to test this hypothesis, we have tried to find out whether elicitation of vocalization is accompanied by motivational effects. As it would have been illusory in an animal as highly evolved as the squirrel monkey to test for each possible motivation specifically, we looked for a more global indicator of motivational changes. In our opinion, a more general indicator is the positive or negative reinforcement associated with motivational changes or, in more subjective terms, the pleasurable or aversive states accompanying them. In other words, it is assumed that motivational changes strong enough to evoke vocalization are either pleasurable or aversive, and that a specific motivational effect is always accompanied by the same type of reinforcement. For instance, if an electrically elicited shriek were in fact a secondary reaction to stimulation-induced pain, and not a directly triggered pure motor response, we assume that this call would always be accompanied by aversive states.

The study (Jürgens, 1976) was carried out in such a way that squirrel monkeys were implanted with vocalization-eliciting electrodes and then placed into a cage consisting of two compartments. Presence in one compartment led automatically to stimulation of a vocalization-eliciting brain site; presence in the other compartment was devoid of stimulation. As the animal was free to move from one compartment to the other, it could switch on and off the vocalization-eliciting brain stimulation at will. The compartment in which the stimulation was given was not always the same, but changed every few minutes from one side of the cage to the other. In this way, it was possible to register whether the animal avoided stimulation by always changing into the stimulation-free compartment, or followed stimulation, or remained in one compartment irrespective of the presence or absence of stimulation. The procedure thus allowed the detection of aversive and pleasurable emotional states accompanying electrically elicited vocalizations.

The results of this study show:

1. In the majority of vocalization-eliciting brain areas vocalization is indeed accompanied by pleasurable or aversive states. Such areas are the hypothalamus, preoptic region, septum, amygdala, stria terminalis and midline thalamus.

2. These areas show a close correlation between elicited call type and accompanying emotional state. For instance, trilling calls elicitable from the septum and dorsolateral hypothalamus are always associated with positive self-stimulation. The same holds for purring calls elicitable from the amygdala and stria terminalis (Fig. 3.2). On the other hand, aerial alarm calls and shrieking, which are obtained from the midline thalamus and ventral hypothalamus, respectively, are always associated with avoidance behavior in the self-stimulation situation (Fig. 3.2).

3. Another point characterizing these brain areas is that the threshold for the elicitation of vocalization is higher than that for the emotional effects, that is, the stimulation current necessary for positive self-stimulation or avoidance behavior is below that necessary for making the animal vocalize. Taken together, these observations strongly suggest that the vocalizations elicitable from the majority of brain areas represent in fact expressions of stimulation-induced motivational effects rather than primary motor responses.

There are, however, two exceptions. These are the anterior cingulate cortex in the forebrain and the posterior periaqueductal gray and laterally bordering tegmentum in the midbrain. Here, one and the same vocalization type elicitable from neighboring electrode positions can be associated at one position with positive self-stimulation, at another with avoidance behavior, and at a third with neither of them (Fig. 3.3). In other words, in the anterior cingulate cortex and the posterior periaqueductal region electrically elicited vocalization and motivation are not correlated. This means that vocalization in these areas cannot be interpreted as a secondary reaction to stimulation-induced motivational effects. We therefore assume that the vocalizations elicited from these areas are triggered by the stimulation in a direct way.

Lesioning Studies.   The effects of brain lesions on vocal production can be of two kinds: they can change a) the acoustic structure of the calls or b) their rate. The most systematic study dealing with structural changes after brain lesions stems again from the squirrel monkey (Kirzinger & Jürgens, 1985). In this study, stereotaxically placed lesions were distributed throughout the brain stem and diencephalon in altogether 43 animals. The effects of these lesions on different call types elicited by electrical brain stimulation were investigated spectrographi-

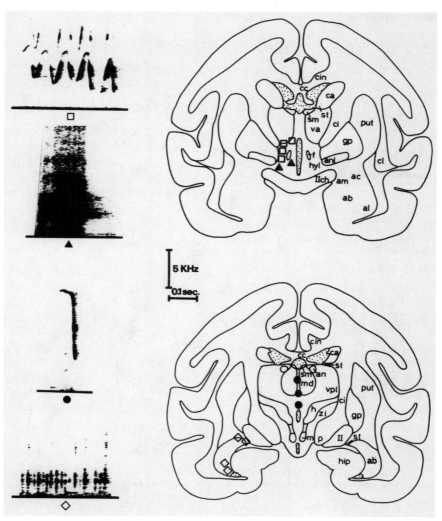

FIG. 3.2. Frontal sections of the squirrel monkey's brain with sites yielding trilling (square), shrieking (triangle), alarm peeping (circle) and purring (rhomb). The calls are represented in form of frequency–time diagrams (sonagrams) on the left side. All vocalization-eliciting sites yielding self-stimulation behavior are indicated by white symbols; those yielding escape/avoidance behavior are indicated in black. Abbreviations: ab nucl. basalis amygdalae, ac nucl. centralis amygdalae, al nucl. lateralis amygdalae, am nucl. medialis amygdalae, an nucl. anterior thalami, anl ansa lenticularis, ca nucl. caudatus, cc corpus callosum, ci capsula interna, cin cingulum, cl claustrum, f fornix, gp globus pallidus, h field H (Forel), hip hippocampus, hyl lateral hypothalamus, m mammillary body, md nucl. medialis dorsalis thalami, p pedunculus cerebri, put putamen, sm stria medullaris, st stria terminalis, va nucl. ventralis anterior thalami, vpl nucl. ventralis posterior lateralis thalami, zi zona incerta, ll n. opticus, ll ch chiasma opticum.

59

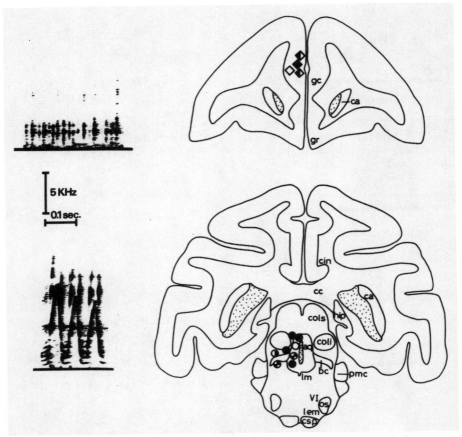

FIG. 3.3.   Frontal sections of the squirrel monkey's brain at the level of
the anterior cingulate cortex and posterior periaqueductal gray, respectively, with sites yielding purring (rhomb) and cackling (circle).
Sonagrams of both calls are shown on the left. Vocalization-eliciting
sites yielding self-stimulation are indicated by white symbols, sites
with escape/avoidance behavior by black symbols, neutral sites are
drawn half black, half white, sites yielding self-stimulation as well as
escape behavior, dependent on the stimulation parameters, are represented by black and white quadripartite symbols. Abbreviations: bc
brachium conjunctivum, ca nucl. caudatus, cc corpus callosum, cin
cingulum, coli colliculus inferior, cols colliculus superior, csp tractus
corticospinalis, gc gyrus cinguli, gr gyrus rectus, hip hippocampus,
lem lemniscus medialis, lm fasciculus longitudinalis medialis, os oliva
superior, pmc brachium pontis, VI n. abducens.

cally. Fig. 3.4 gives a summary of the results. It was found that deterioration of call structure occurred after lesions in the lateral midbrain and pontine tegmentum, as well as in large parts of the medulla. No deterioration occurred after lesions in the thalamus, hypothalamus, periventricular and rostral periaqueductal gray, superior and inferior colliculi, nucl. ruber, medial midbrain and pontine reticular formation, pontine gray, cerebellum, vestibular nuclei and raphe. This lack of an effect suggests that the latter structures do not play a crucial role in the motor coordination of monkey calls. A comparison with the human neurological literature reveals that some of these structures do play a role in speech production, however. Such structures are, for instance, the ventrolateral thalamus and cerebellum, both of which can cause severe articulatory disturbances when lesioned (Andrew, Fowler, & Harrison, 1983; Aronson, 1980; Bell, 1968; Kent & Rosenbek, 1982; Krayenbühl, Siegfried, & Yasargil, 1963). These findings suggest that there exist some brain areas that are essential for the motor coordination of learned vocal patterns (speech) but are dispensable for the production of genetically preprogrammed vocal utterances (monkey calls and, probably, human nonverbal emotional vocal utterances). Whether the reverse also holds, that is, there exist brain areas indispensable for innate vocal motor coordination but dispensable for learned vocal production, cannot be answered definitely at the moment but appears rather unlikely.

Lesions with an effect on vocalization rate rather than on acoustic structure have been described in two regions: one is the periaqueductal gray and laterally bordering tegmentum in the midbrain; the other is the mediofrontal cortex at the level of the genu of the corpus callosum, including anterior limbic cortex as well as overlying neocortex. Large lesions in the periaqueductal gray and laterally bordering tegmentum cause complete mutism, that is, such animals neither vocalize spontaneously nor react vocally to external stimuli, nor can be induced to vocalize by electrical brain stimulation (Jürgens & Pratt, 1979). The only exception to this concerns a restricted area within the pontine and medullary reticular formation that yields artificial calls when electrically stimulated. This area, the only one from which vocalizations with a highly abnormal acoustic structure can be produced, is also the only one not muted by periaqueductal lesions.

Smaller lesions within the periaqueductal regions have different effects on different call types. According to Newman and MacLean (1982), such lesions abolish spontaneous long-distance contact calls in isolated squirrel monkeys, but do not block long-distance contact calls made in response to calls of the same type played back from tape. In our own squirrel monkey experiments (Jürgens & Pratt, 1979), we found a complete block of the vocal alarm reaction against a dummy leopard, but a normal vocal reaction to grasping the animal. The failure of the visual stimulus to elicit vocalization was not due, in this case, to an impairment of visual recognition as the animal showed the typical flight reaction, with only vocalization lacking.

From these observations, it may be concluded that the periaqueductal gray and

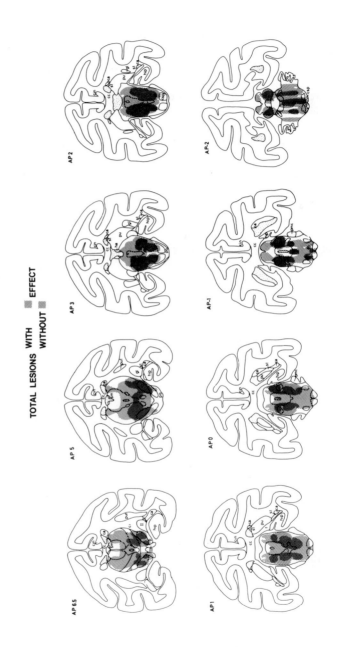

TOTAL LESIONS WITH EFFECT
WITHOUT

AP 2

AP-2

AP 3

AP-1

AP 5

AP 0

AP 6.5

AP 1

FIG. 3.4.   Summary of lesion effects on squirrel monkey vocalization. Hatching shows total lesion extent of all 43 squirrel monkeys studied. Hatching from the upper right corner to the lower left indicates brain areas destruction of which does not change the acoustic structure of vocalization; hatching from the upper left corner to the lower right shows lesion extent in animals which did show a change in vocalization. Abbreviations: ca nucl. caudatus, cc corpus callosum, ci capsula interna, cin cingulum, cr corpus restiforme, csp tractus corticosponalis, f fornix, gl nucl. geniculatus laterale, ha habenula, hip hippocampus, ns V nucl. spinalis n. trigemini, p pedunculus cerebri, pmc brachium pontis, po griseum pontis, pu pulvinar, put putamen, rl nucl. reticularis lateralis, sm stria medullaris, st stria terminalis, II n. opticus, III n. oculomotorius, VIII nucl. cochlearis.

laterally bordering tegmentum play a crucial role in the control of vocalization. As partial lesioning of this area leaves the acoustic structure of the remaining vocalizations intact, and electrical stimulation yields natural (not artificial) calls, it appears unlikely that this area is involved in the motor coordination of vocalization. Rather, its function seems to be to trigger vocalizations, that is, to couple motivation-controlling brain structures with vocal motor-coordinating ones.

As regards the mediofrontal cortex, lesion effects are less drastic. Destruction of the anterior limbic and bordering neocortex neither mutes the animal nor abolishes specific call types. In the case of the squirrel monkey, a decrease in vocalization rate of long-distance contact calls, but not of other calls, can be observed (Kirzinger & Jürgens, 1982; Newman & MacLean, 1985). In the rhesus monkey, there is a loss of the capability to master vocal operant conditioning tasks (Aitken, 1981; Sutton, Larson, & Lindeman, 1974, Sutton, Trachy, & Lindemann, 1985). The squirrel monkey's long-distance contact call differs from other calls of this species by being less dependent upon discrete external stimuli: it does not occur as a reaction to a predator like the alarm call, nor to an aggressive conspecific like the threatening call, nor to a huddling group mate like the purring call, but represents a self-initiated, active attempt to regain contact with group members out of sight. It therefore may carry a stronger volitional component than the other calls. If this were true, it would fit well with the rhesus monkey finding that anterior cingulate lesions interfere with the volitional production of vocalization (vocal operant conditioning), but not, or only to a minor degree, with their reactive production (vocal reaction against threatening stimuli; Sutton et al., 1974). The lesion findings thus suggest that the anterior limbic cortex and overlying mediofrontal cortex play an important role in the volitional initiation of vocalization.

Both periaqueductal region and mediofrontal cortex are also of importance for human speech production. Akinetic mutism is a well-known syndrome after diffuse midbrain lesions (Von Cramon, 1981). Mutism without akinesia has been reported by Botez and Carp (1968) in a patient with a lesion restricted to the left periaqueductal gray and immediately bordering tegmentum. The patient in this case was able to walk around and take his meals without help, but did not make a single vocal utterance until his death two months later. Lesions in the mediofrontal cortex, including the anterior limbic cortex, cause a syndrome called transcortical motor aphasia. This syndrome is characterized by an almost complete lack of spontaneous speech utterances. The patients, however, are able to repeat sentences spoken to them, and also to answer short questions; their articulation is normal (Rubens, 1975). Periaqueductal and mediofrontal lesions thus both cause a reduction of vocal behavior in monkey and man. While periaqueductal lesions affect the motivation for vocal behavior at the most elementary level, namely, that of reactive as well as self-initiated vocal utterances, mediofrontal lesions seem to interfere only with the latter.

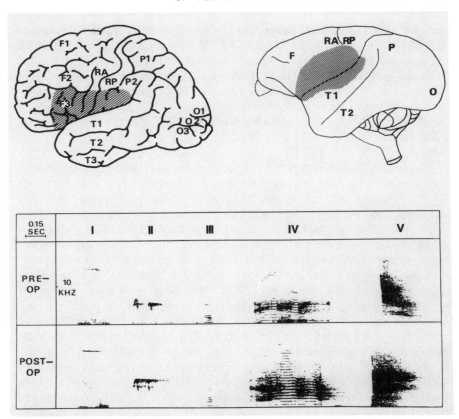

FIG. 3.5. Upper part: lesion extent in a human patient with a severe motor aphasia (left) and a squirrel monkey capable of producing all call types immediately after lesioning (right). The lesion was unilateral in the patient, bilateral in the monkey. Lower part: sonagrams of five different call types of the squirrel monkey recorded immediately before and after placing the lesion indicated above. Abbreviations: F,F1-3 frontal cortex; 0,01-3 occipital cortex; P,P1-2 parietal cortex; RA,RP anterior and posterior Rolandic cortex; T1-3 temporal cortex.

The cortical region that (since P. Broca 1861) is accepted to be the most important for speech production, the inferior peri-central and rostrally bordering premotor cortex (Broca's area), seems to play no role at all for the monkey's call production. In a comparative study in which we reduplicated the lesion of a patient with a severe motor aphasia in two squirrel monkeys, we could find neither a change in the acoustic structure of the monkeys' calls nor a decrease in vocalization rate (Jürgens, Kirzinger, & von Cramon, 1982). While the patient was not able to produce a single word for more than 10 weeks after the infarction, the monkey uttered all call types of its vocal repertoire within the first days after operation—despite the fact that the lesion in the monkey was a bilateral (symmetrical) one and in the patient was unilateral (left-sided) only. According to Sutton et al. (1974) and Aitken (1981), vocal operant conditioning also is not affected after similar lesions. These observations suggest that the lower pericentral and bordering premotor cortex is essential for the production of learned vocal patterns, but dispensable for the production of genetically preprogrammed vocalizations.

Single Unit Recording Studies.   Apart from the nucl. ambiguus, which contains the laryngeal motoneurons, there are at present only two areas for which vocalization-correlated activity has been reported: these are a) the anterior cingulate cortex and b) the periaqueductal gray. In the anterior cingulate cortex, a single unit recording study of Sutton and co-workers (1978) revealed that there are neurons changing their activity several hundred msec before vocalization in a vocal operant conditioning task. The activity could not be correlated with specific acoustic characteristics of the call, or laryngeal EMG activity. In the periaqueductal gray, Larson and Kistler (1984, 1986) described a greater number of neurons the activity of which also preceded vocalization. In contrast to the neurons of the anterior cingulate cortex, the neurons of the periaqueductal gray often showed a correlation in their activity with specific features of the call. Some cells were correlated with call intensity, some with fundamental frequency, others with call duration. There were cells firing during one call type but not another. Some cells reflected the activity of specific laryngeal muscles. These findings indicate that, within the vocal control system, the periaqueductal gray takes a position close to the motor output side. Together with the cingulate recordings, these findings underline the importance of the periaqueductal gray and anterior cingulate cortex for the control of primate vocal behavior.

Neuroanatomical Studies.   Autoradiographic tracing studies with tritium-labeled leucine have revealed that the anterior cingulate cortex is directly connected with the periaqueductal gray (Müller-Preuß & Jürgens, 1976). It also projects to the majority of secondary vocalization areas, that is, areas which, when electrically stimulated, yield motivation-correlated vocalization, such as the amygdala, preoptic region, septum, hypothalamus or midline thalamus (Jürgens & Müller-Preuß, 1977). The anterior cingulate cortex does not have any direct connections to the motoneuron pools involved in vocalization, such as the nucl. ambiguus, facial nucleus, hypoglossal nucleus, trigeminal motor nucleus or spinal respiratory motoneurons.

The periaqueductal gray receives direct projections from virtually all vocalization-eliciting areas in the brain (Jürgens & Pratt, 1979). It sends fibers to some (nucl. ambiguus, trigeminal motor nucleus), but not all phonatory motoneuron pools. The majority of fibers end in the lateral reticular formation of pons and medulla. This area in contrast to the periaqueductal gray, has direct connections with all phonatory motoneuron pools and thus, from an anatomical view point, is in an ideal position to coordinate the activity of the different muscles participating in vocalization (Thoms & Jürgens, 1987).

The anatomical findings, together with those gained from the stimulation, lesioning and recording studies mentioned previously, suggest the following hierarchical organization of the vocal motor system. The lowest level seems to be represented by the reticular formation of the lateral pons and medulla with its direct access to the phonatory motoneurons (Fig. 3.6, Level I). This level probably is responsible for the motor coordination of vocalization, that is, the integration of laryngeal, respiratory and articulatory activity. The structures at this level are not capable of producing vocalization on their own but need the facilitatory input from the next higher level (II), the periaqueductal gray and laterally bordering tegmentum of the caudal midbrain. This region seems to act as a mediator between sensory and motivation-controlling structures on the one hand and the motor-coordinating lower brain stem structures on the other. The region represents something like a bottleneck through which all vocalization-triggering stimuli must pass if vocalization is to occur. The periaqueductal region receives its input partly from limbic motivation-controlling structures, such as the amygdala, hypothalamus or midline thalamus (level III), partly via more direct sensory pathways, including collaterals from the spinothalamic tract and projections from superior and inferior colliculus, and partly from the anterior cingulate cortex (level IV). The latter seems to represent the highest level within the vocalization system, being responsible for the volitional initiation of monkey calls and, probably, human nonverbal emotional utterances.

Vocal Perception

Lesioning Studies.   There are two studies describing the effects of brain lesions on call recognition in monkeys. In the first study (Hupfer, Jürgens, & Ploog, 1977), squirrel monkeys were trained to discriminate species-specific calls from nonspecies-specific complex sounds in a go, no-go procedure with social contact as positive reinforcement. More specifically, animals were trained to jump from a perch to the bottom of the cage whenever they heard a species-specific call presented through a loudspeaker. Correct responses were reinforced by opening a window for 30 sec through which visual and tactual contact with a surgically muted group mate was possible. Jumps during the presentation of nonspecies-specific sounds (bird song, dog barking, human voice, bell ringing, etc), or between sound presentations were punished by mild electric shocks from the floor grid. The task thus required that the animals not only responded to a particular call but that they generalized to any squirrel monkey call, whether or not it had been presented previously in training. In other words, the task was not to discriminate two specific acoustic patterns, but to recognize sounds as belong-

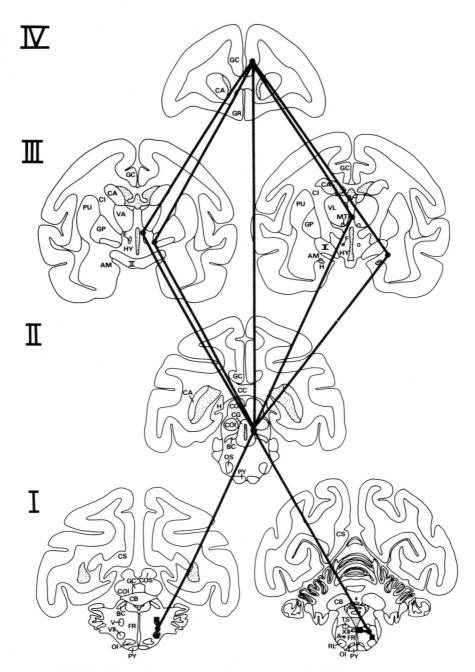

FIG. 3.6 Hierarchical scheme of vocal control. Black dots represent sites the electrical stimulation of which yields vocalization. Vocalization has a natural, species-specific structure at levels II to IV, but an artificial structure at level I. Squares indicate sites of cranial motor

ing to the animal's own vocal repertoire. After the animals had learned the task, they underwent auditory cortex ablation to varying extent. It was found that complete ablation of the primary and secondary auditory cortex rendered the animals unable to master the task. A simplified version, in which only one specific call had to be discriminated against white noise was no more possible. If the task was further simplified, so that the animals just had to detect a sound but not to discriminate it from others, they could master the task. This means that auditory cortex lesions do not deafen an animal but leave it unable to discriminate complex sounds. In the human neurological literature this deficit in auditory gestalt formation has been called auditory agnosia. Similar to the monkey, it is the result of large bilateral lesions in the superior temporal cortex (Adams, Rosenberger, Winter, & Zoellner, 1978; Lhermitte et al., 1971; Vignolo, 1969).

Auditory agnosia represents a perceptual deficit which concerns not only species-specific vocal utterances but all kinds of sounds. The question arises whether there are also brain regions specifically concerned with the decoding of conspecific vocal communication signals. In man, the Wernicke area, that is, the posterior-most part of the superior temporal gyrus of the left hemisphere, is regarded as such a region. Its destruction causes a deficit in speech comprehension with retained ability to identify animal voices, musical instruments, diverse noises, such as bell ringing, motor horn or water gurgling, and even emotional intonation (for review see Benson, 1979; Henschen, 1920; Luria, 1964). Heffner and Heffner (1984) investigated this problem in the Japanese macaque. They trained their animals to discriminate between two species-typical call types, both presented in form of different variants. The animals were water-deprived and had to learn that placing their mouth on a water spout was rewarded by a trickle of water during presentation of one of the two call types, as well as between call presentation; spout contact during presentation of the second call type was followed by a mild electric shock. After the animals had learned to avoid spout contact in the presence of the second call type, they underwent ablation of either

---

nuclei electrical stimulation of which yields fragmentary vocalization, such as isolated movements of the vocal folds, lips, tongue and jaw. Connecting lines between different dots, as well as between dots and squares, represent anatomically verified direct projections oriented from higher to lower levels. Further explanation see text. Abbreviations: A nucl. ambiguus, AM amygdala, BC brachium conjunctivum, CA nucl. caudatus, CB cerebellum, CC corpus callosum, CG periaqueductal gray, CI capsula interna, COI colliculus inferior, COS colliculus superior, CS cortex striatus, F fornix, FR formatio reticularis, GC gyrus cinguli, GP globus pallidus, GR gyrus rectus, H hippocampus, HY hypothalamus, MT tractus mammillo-thalamicus, OI oliva inferior, OS oliva superior, PU putamen, PY tractus pyramidalis, RL nucl. reticularis lateralis, TS nucl. tractus solitarii, VA nucl. ventralis anterior thalami, VL nucl. ventralis lateralis thalami, II chiasma opticum, V nucl. motorius n. trigemini, VII nucl. facialis, XII nucl. hypoglossus.

the temporo-parieto-preoccipital association cortex (Wernicke area) or the whole superior temporal gyrus (auditory cortex). It was found that bilateral ablation of the Wernicke area had no effect on the discrimination. Bilateral removal of the whole auditory cortex abolished the ability for call discrimination completely. This study agrees with the aforementioned squirrel monkey study (Hupfer et al., 1977) in attributing a crucial role to the auditory cortex in monkey call perception. Furthermore, it demonstrates that recognition of species-specific calls does not depend upon an intact Wernicke area. As both studies used a learned behavioral reaction in their discrimination training, it cannot be ruled out, however, that genetically determined behavioral reactions to specific call types, for instance, flight into cover in response to an aerial alarm call, can still take place without auditory cortex. In other words, it is not clear at present to what extent subcortical stations of the auditory system alone are able to mediate call-specific, genetically determined behavioral reactions.

In the Heffner study (Heffner & Heffner, 1984), it was found that unilateral ablation of the auditory cortex led to a transient impairment of call discrimination—but only if the ablation was left-sided. Right-sided ablations did not affect discrimination. A greater effect of left-sided than right-sided lesions on auditory perception was also reported by Dewson et al. (1975) in the rhesus monkey. In this study, however, pure tones instead of monkey calls were used as test stimuli, and the task of the animals was to decide whether two tones following each other within a few seconds were the same or different. A third study also points to a left hemisphere dominance. Petersen, Beecher, Zoloth, Moody, & Stebbins, (1978) trained Japanese macaques to discriminate two call types. The calls were presented by earphones either to the left or the right ear. The animals had to keep a lever depressed during presentation of one call type and between call presentations, and had to release the lever during presentation of the other call type. Correct release was food-rewarded. Evaluation of the reaction latencies and number of errors after presentation to the left and right ear revealed that the right ear is superior to the left in call type identification. As the auditory system is mainly crossed, this right-ear advantage indicates a left hemisphere superiority. Interestingly, the same animals did not show a right-ear advantage if the call discrimination had to be made according to fundamental frequency instead of call type. As fundamental frequency seems to be an acoustical feature largely irrelevant for the communicative meaning of a call, the authors concluded that decoding of the functional significance of monkey calls takes place predominantly in the left hemisphere.

In summarizing, these studies suggest that monkey call recognition takes place in the primary and secondary auditory cortex of the superior temporal gyrus—at least as learned aspects of vocal perception are concerned. Species-specific communicatory signals thus seem to be decoded in the same brain structures in which also nonspecies-specific sounds are processed. The fact that Wernicke area lesions severely affect speech recognition but not monkey call recognition probably is due to two factors: 1. The Wernicke area lies in the border zone between auditory, somatosensory and visual cortex and thus represents a multimodal association cortex. 2. Words seem to serve, much more than monkey calls, as multimodal representations of the external world—one and the same word (concept) can be perceived aurally (speech), visually (writing, sign language of deaf-mutes) or tactually (Braille reading of blind people), and all three types are disturbed by Wernicke-area lesions (Birchmeier, 1985; Douglass & Richardson, 1959; Iwata, 1984; Sarno, Swisher, & Sarno, 1969). With regard to lateralization, there is good evidence, at least in macaques, that there is a left hemisphere dominance for call perception. As such a dominance, however, is not only found in species-specific call recognition but also in certain other acoustic discrimination tasks (Dewson et al., 1975) and, furthermore, unilateral lesions never cause a permanent call recognition deficit (Heffner & Heffner, 1984), this clearly indicates that the hemispheric specialization in monkeys is much less advanced than in humans.

Single Unit Recording Studies.   In the squirrel monkeys, several studies have been carried out in which the neuronal activity within the auditory cortex was recorded during presentation of species-specific calls (Funkenstein, Nelson, Winter, Wollberg, & Newman, 1971; Manley & Müller-Preuß, 1978; Müller-Preuß & Ploog, 1981; Newman & Wollberg, 1973a, 1973b). It was hoped that such studies would reveal the principles of how the auditory cortex decodes species-specific calls. These expectations have not been fulfilled, however. Newman and Wollberg (1973a) found that 90% of the neurons in the auditory cortex could be activated by species-specific calls. Out of these, 89% reacted to more than six of the twelve different call types tested. Only one cell out of 75 reacted to a particular call type (out of the twelve tested); this cell, however, also reacted to a pure tone with no communicative meaning at all for the monkey. 96% of the cells responsive to species-specific calls were also responsive to pure tones. The frequency of the effective pure tone was not always identical with the frequency of the main energy of the effective call. Furthermore, many cells reacted to structurally very different call classes but did not react to all variants within one class—despite of the latter being much more similar to each other than the former. What makes the situation even more complicated is the fact that the responsiveness of a cell is not constant (Manley & Müller-Preuß, 1978). One and the same call type can elicit a vigorous response at one time and a very weak or no response at all at another. As the responsiveness often does not change for all call types to which a cell responds in the same direction—it may simultaneously decrease for one call type and increase for another—this change cannot be simply explained by a general shift of the arousal level. Even the pulse pattern with which a single neuron reacts to a specific call type is not constant. It may change, for instance, from a tonic "on" response to a phasic "on/off" response. A related observation was made by Newman and Wollberg (1973a). They reported that different cells reacting to the same call type often respond with completely different activity patterns.

From these studies, at least some negative statements can be made:

1. The neurons of the auditory cortex do not decode species-specific calls in a one-to-one fashion in the sense that specific call types are represented by specific cells.
2. Specific call types are not characterized by specific activity patterns of single neurons.
3. Single neurons probably are not able to detect specific acoustic features common to different call types, that is, to recognize features independent of their acoustic "environment." The only exception to this seems to be those few neurons having a stable, narrow best frequency.

Our understanding of call decoding thus still is at the very beginning. Two approaches appear promising to be followed in future research. One is to record the activity of neuronal ensembles instead of single units; the other is to look for much more complex features than hitherto tested in determining the response characteristics of single neurons.

Interrelations Between Vocal Perception and Production.   In humans, audition is necessary to develop normal speech production. The same holds for songbirds. Deafening immediately after hatching renders the birds unable to produce normal songs (Konishi, 1965). As both human speech and bird song are learnt, it is obvious that hearing is an indispensable prerequisite for their accomplishment. In the monkey, as we have seen above, vocal learning plays only a minor role and, in some species, possibly lacks any role at all. In agreement with this, deafening of adult squirrel monkeys does not change the acoustic structure of their calls, neither on the short nor on the long run (Talmage-Riggs, Winter, Ploog, & Mayer, 1972). In one case, a squirrel monkey infant was deafened immediately after birth. This animal survived only three months. Within that period, however, its vocalizations could not be distinguished from those of hearing infants of the same age (Winter, Handley, Ploog, & Schott, 1973). This suggests that the vocal motor control structures in monkeys are largely independent of an auditory input. On the other hand, neuroanatomical studies have revealed a number of direct connections between the auditory system and brain areas related to vocal motor production. Such connections are, for instance, from the auditory association cortex to the anterior cingulate cortex and the periaqueductal gray, or from the medial geniculate body and inferior colliculus to the periaqueductal gray (Müller-Preuß, 1988). Furthermore, single unit recording studies currently underway (Kirzinger & Jürgens, in preparation) show that, in a small zone of the reticular formation just between inferior colliculus and periaqueductal gray, there are neurons firing during external acoustic stimulations as well as just prior (30-100 msec) to self-produced vocalization. In other words, these cells seem to be involved in vocal motor control and auditory perception as well. Potentially, these cells are in a position to control vocal output according to auditory input. Whether this input, however, is actually used to shape the vocal output pattern or simply serves to trigger a call dependent upon specific external acoustic stimuli, or serves a completely different purpose, such as the initiation of the middle ear reflex, remains to be determined.

Control probably is exerted not only by the auditory system on the vocal motor system, but also the other way around. Single unit recording studies in the squirrel monkey have shown that there are numerous cells in the auditory cortex, medial geniculate body and, to a smaller extent, in peripheral parts of the inferior colliculus that do not react to self-produced vocalizations but react heavily if the same call is played back by a loudspeaker (Müller-Preuß & Ploog, 1981). In other words, these cells are activated by external acoustic stimuli but not by self-produced ones of more or less identical structure. This suggests that there are connections between the vocal motor and auditory system that inform the latter about ongoing activity in the former. By this feed-forward mechanism, the vocal motor system apparently blocks the reaction of certain auditory neurons to self-produced vocalizations. It is of interest that this inhibition does not cause a complete block of the cells' reactivity: if, during self-produced vocalization, a loudspeaker-produced call is presented, these cells show a normal reaction to the loudspeaker-produced call. The function of these cells thus may be interpreted as a selective attention mechanism, that is, to focus attention on external acoustic stimuli while ignoring simultaneous, self-produced ones. The neuroanatomical pathway underlying this effect still awaits elucidation.

REFERENCES

Adams, A. E., Rosenberger, K., Winter, H., & Zoellner, C. (1978). A case of cortical deafness. *Archiv für Psychiatrie und Nervenkrankheiten, 224,* 213–220.

Aitken, P. G. (1981). Cortical control of conditioned and spontaneous vocal behavior in rhesus monkeys. *Brain and Language, 13,* 171–184.

Aitken, P. G., & Wilson Jr., W. A. (1979). Discriminative vocal conditioning in rhesus monkeys: evidence for volitional control? *Brain and Language, 8,* 227–240.

Andrew, J., Fowler, C. J., & Harrison, M. J. G. (1983). Stereotaxic thalamotomy in 55 cases of dystonia. *Brain, 106,* 981–1000.

Apfelbach, R. (1972). Electrically elicited vocalizations in the gibbon Hylobates lar (Hylobatidae), and their behavioral significance. *Zeitschrift für Tierpsychologie, 30,* 420–430.

Aronson, A. E. (1980). *Clinical voice disorders. An interdisciplinary approach.* Stuttgart: Thieme.

Beier, E. G., & Zautra, A. J. (1972). Identification of vocal communication of emotions across cultures. *Journal of Consulting and Clinical Psychology, 39,* 166.

Bell, D. S. (1968). Speech functions of the thalamus inferred from the effects of thalamotomy. *Brain, 91,* 619–638.

Benson, D. F. (1979). *Aphasia, alexia and agraphia.* New York: Churchill Livingstone.

Birchmeier, A. K. (1985). Aphasic dyslexia of Braille in a congenitally blind man. *Neuropsychologia, 23,* 177–193.

Botez, M J., & Carp, N. (1968). Nouvelles données sur le probléme du mécanisme de déclenchement de la parole. *Revue Roumaine de Neurologie, 5,* 153–158.

Brockelman, W. Y., & Schilling, D. (1984). Inheritance of stereotyped gibbon calls. *Nature, 312,* 634–636.

Brown, T. G. (1915). Note on physiology of basal ganglia and midbrain of anthropoid ape especially in reference to act of laughter. *Journal of Physiology, 49,* 195–207.

Cheney, D. L., & Seyfarth, R. M. (1985). Vervet monkey alarm calls: manipulation through shared information? *Behaviour, 94,* 150–166.

Dewson, J. H., Burlingame, H., Kizer, K., Dewson, S., Kenney, P., and Pribram, K. H. (1975). Hemispheric asymmetry of auditory function in monkeys. *Journal of the Acoustical Society of America, 58* (Suppl. 1), 66.

Douglass, E., & Richardson, J. C. (1959). Aphasia in a congenital deaf-mute. *Brain, 82,* 68–80.

Eibl-Eibesfeldt, I. (1973). The expressive behaviour of the deaf-and-blind-born. In M. von Cranach & J. Vine (Eds.), *Social communication and movement* (pp. 163–194). London: Academic Press.

Funkenstein, H. H., Nelson, P. G., Winter, P., Wollberg, Z., & Newman, J. D. (1971). Unit responses in auditory cortex of awake squirrel monkeys to vocal stimulation. In M. B. Sachs (Ed.), *Physiology of the auditory system.* Baltimore: National Educational Consultants, Inc.

Gardner, R. A., & Gardner, B. T. (1969). Teaching sign language to a chimpanzee. *Science, 165,* 664–672.

Geissmann, T. (1984). Inheritance of song parameters in the gibbon song analysed in 2 hybrid gibbons (Hylobates pileatus x H. lar). *Folia Primatologica, 42,* 216–235.

Goodenough, F. L. (1932). Expression of the emotions in a blind-deaf child. *Journal of Abnormal and Social Psychology, 27,* 328–333.

Hayes, K. J., & Hayes, C. (1951). The intellectual development of a home-raised chimpanzee. *Proceedings of the American Philosophical Society, 95,* 105–109.

Heffner, H. E., & Heffner, R. S. (1984). Temporal lobe lesions and perception of species-specific vocalizations by macaques. *Science, 226,* 75–76.

Henschen, S. E. (1920). *Klinische und anatomische Beiträge zur Pathologie des Gehirns. 5. Teil: Über Aphasie, Amnesie und Akalkulie.* Stockholm: Nordiska Bokhandeln.

Herzog, M., & Hopf, S. (1984). Behavioral responses to species-specific warning calls in infant squirrel monkeys reared in social isolation. *American Journal of Primatology, 7,* 99–106.

Hupfer, K., Jürgens, U., & Ploog, D. (1977). The effect of superior temporal lesions on the recognition of species-specific calls in the squirrel monkey. *Experimental Brain Research, 30,* 75–87.

Iwata, M. (1984). Kanji versus Kana. Neuropsychological correlates of the Japanese writing system. *Trends in Neurosciences, 7,* 290–293.

Jürgens, U. (1976). Reinforcing concomitants of electrically elicited vocalizations. *Experimental Brain Research, 26,* 203–214.

Jürgens, U., & Müller-Preuß, P. (1977). Convergent projections of different limbic vocalization areas in the squirrel monkey. *Experimental Brain Research, 29,* 75–83.

Jürgens, U., & Ploog, D. (1970). Cerebral representation of vocalization in the squirrel monkey. *Experimental Brain Research, 10,* 532–554.

Jürgens, U., & Pratt, R. (1979). Role of the periaqueductal grey in vocal expression of emotion. *Brain Research, 167,* 367–378.

Jürgens, U., Kirzinger, A., & von Cramon, D. (1982). The effects of deep-reaching lesions in the cortical face area on phonation. A combined case report and experimental monkey study. *Cortex, 18,* 125–140.

Kaada, B. R. (1951). Somato-motor, anatomic and electrocorticographic responses to electrical stimulation of "rhinencephalic" and other structures in primates, cat and dog. *Acta Physiologica Scandinavica, 83,* 1–285.

Kellogg, W. N. (1968). Communication and language in the home-raised chimpanzee. *Science, 162,* 423–427.

Kent, R. D., & Rosenbek, J. C. (1982). Prosodic disturbance and neurologic lesion. *Brain and Language, 15,* 259–291.

Kirzinger, A., & Jürgens, U. (1982). Cortical lesion effects and vocalization in the squirrel monkey. *Brain Research, 233,* 299–315.

Kirzinger, A., & Jürgens, U. (1985). The effects of brain stem lesions on vocalization in the squirrel monkey. *Brain Research, 358,* 150–162.

Konishi, M. (1965). The role of auditory feedback in the control of vocalization in the white-crowned sparrow. *Zeitschrift für Tierpsychologie, 22,* 770–783.

Kramer, E. (1964). Elimination of verbal cues in judgment of emotion from voice. *Journal of Abnormal and Social Psychology, 68,* 390–396.

Krayenbühl, H., Siegfried, J., & Yasargil, M. G. (1963). Résultats tardifs des opérations stéréotaxiques dans le traitement de la maladie de Parkinson. *Revue Neurologique, 108,* 485–494.

Larson, C. R., & Kistler, M. K. (1984). Periaqueductal gray neuronal activity associated with laryngeal EMG and vocalization in the awake monkey. *Neuroscience Letters, 46,* 261–266.

Larson, C. R., & Kistler, M. K. (1986). The relationship of periaqueductal gray neurons to vocalization and laryngeal EMG in the behaving monkey. *Experimental Brain Research, 63,* 596–606.

Lhermitte, F., Chain, F., Escourolle, R., Ducame, B., Pillon, B., & Chedru, F. (1971). Etude des troubles perceptifs auditifs dans les lésions temporales bilatérales. *Revue Neurologique, 124,* 329–351.

Lieberman, P., Crelin, E. S., & Klatt, D. H. (1972). Phonetic ability and related anatomy of the newborn and adult human, Neanderthal man, and the chimpanzee. *American Anthropologist, 74,* 287–307.

Lipp, H. P., & Hunsperger, R. W. (1978). Threat, attack and flight elicited by electrical stimulation of the ventromedial hypothalamus of the marmoset monkey Callithrix jacchus. *Brain, Behavior and Evolution, 15,* 260–293.

Luria, A. R. (1964). Factors and forms of aphasia. In A. V. S. de Reuck & M. O'Connor (Eds.), *Disorders of language* (pp. 143–167). London: Churchill.

Magoun, H. W., Atlas, D., Ingersoll, E. H., & Ranson, S. W. (1937). Associated facial, vocal and respiratory components of emotional expression: an experimental study. *Journal of Neurology and Psychopathology, 17,* 241–255.

Manley, J. A., & Müller-Preuß, P. (1978). Response variability of auditory cortex cells in the squirrel monkey to constant acoustic stimuli. *Experimental Brain Research, 32,* 171–180.

Morath, M. (1979). Inborn vocalizations of the human baby and communicative value for the mother. *Experimental Brain Research* (Suppl. 2), 236–244.

Müller-Preuß, P. (1988). Neural correlates of audio-vocal behavior: properties of anterior limbic cortex and related areas. In J. D. Newman (Ed.), *The physiological control of mammalian vocalizations.* New York: Plenum Press, p. 245–262.

Müller-Preuß, P., & Jürgens, U. (1976). Projections from the "cingular" vocalization area in the squirrel monkey. *Brain Research, 103,* 29–43.

Müller-Preuß, P., & Ploog, D. (1981). Inhibition of auditory cortical neurons during phonation. *Brain Research, 215,* 61–76.

Myers, S. A., Horel, J. A., & Pennypacker, H. S. (1965). Operant control of vocal behavior in the monkey Cebus albifrous. *Psychonomic Science, 3,* 389–390.

Newman, J. D., & MacLean, P. D. (1982). Effects of tegmental lesions on the isolation call of squirrel monkeys. *Brain Research, 232,* 317–330.

Newman, J. D., & MacLean, P. D. (1985). Importance of medial frontolimbic cortex in production of the isolation call of squirrel monkeys. *Proceedings of the Society for Neuroscience,* p. 495.

Newman, J. D., & Wollberg, Z. (1973a). Multiple coding of species-specific vocalizations in the auditory cortex of squirrel monkeys. *Brain Research, 54,* 287–304.

Newman, J. D., & Wollberg, Z. (1973b). Responses of single neurons in the auditory cortex of squirrel monkeys to variants of a single call type. *Experimental Neurology, 40,* 821–824.

Petersen, M. R., Beecher, M. D., Zoloth, S. R., Moody, D. B., & Stebbins, W. C. (1978). Neural lateralization of species-specific vocalizations by Japanese macaques (Macaca fuscata). *Science, 202*, 324–327.

Robinson, B. W. (1967). Vocalization evoked from forebrain in Macaca mulatta. *Physiology and Behavior, 2*, 345–354.

Rubens, A. B. (1975). Aphasia with infarction in the territory of the anterior cerebral artery. *Cortex, 11*, 239–250.

Sarno, J. E., Swisher, L. P., & Sarno, M. T. (1969). Aphasia in a congenitally deaf man. *Cortex, 5*, 398–414.

Savage-Rumbaugh, S., McDonald, K., Sevcik, R. A., Hopkins, W. D., & Rubert, E. (1986). Spontaneous symbol acquisition and communicative use by pygmy chimpanzees (Pan paniscus). *Journal of Experimental Psychology: General, 115*, 211–235.

Seyfarth, R. M., Cheney, D. L., & Marler, P. (1980). Monkey responses to three different alarm calls: evidence of predator classification and semantic communication. *Science, 210*, 801–803.

Sutton, D., Larson, C., & Lindeman, R. C. (1974). Neocortical and limbic lesion effects on primate phonation. *Brain Research, 71*, 61–75.

Sutton, D., Larson, C., Taylor, E. M., & Lindeman, R.C. (1973). Vocalization in rhesus monkeys: conditionability. *Brain Research, 52*, 225–231.

Sutton, D., Samson, H. H., & Larson, C. R. (1978). Brain mechanisms in learned phonation of Macaca mulatta. In D. J. Chivers & J. Herbert (Eds.), *Recent advances in primatology*. Vol. I (pp. 769–784). New York: Academic Press.

Sutton, D., Trachy, R. E., & Lindeman, R. C. (1985). Discriminative phonation in macaques: effects of anterior medial cortex damage. *Experimental Brain Research, 59*, 410–413.

Talmage-Riggs, G., Winter, P., Ploog, D., & Mayer, W. (1972). Effect of deafening on the vocal behavior of the squirrel monkey (Saimiri sciureus). *Folia primatologica, 17*, 404–420.

Thoms, G., & Jürgens, U. (1987). Common input of the cranial motor nuclei involved in phonation in squirrel monkey. *Experimental Neurology, 95*, 85–99.

Truby, H. M., & Lind, J. (1965). Cry sounds of the newborn infant. In J. Lind (Ed.), *Newborn infant cry. Acta Paediatrica Scandinavica*, Suppl. 163.

Van Hooff, J. A. R. A. M. (1976). The comparison of facial expression in man and higher primates. In M. von Cranach (Ed.), *Methods of inference from animal to human behaviour* (pp. 165–196). Den Haag: Mouton.

Vignolo, L. A. (1969). Auditory agnosia: a review and report of recent evidence. In A. L. Benton (Ed.), *Contributions to clinical neuropsychology* (pp. 172–231). Chicago: Aldine.

Von Cramon, D. (1981). Traumatic mutism and the subsequent reorganization of speech functions. *Neuropsychologia, 19*, 801–805.

Wasz-Höckert, O., Lind, J., Vuorenkoski, V., Partanen, T. & Valanne, E. (1968). The infant cry. A spectrographic and auditory analysis. Clinics in Developmental Medicine, 29. Philadelphia: Lippincott.

Winter, P., Handley, P., Ploog, D., & Schott, D. (1973). Ontogeny of squirrel monkey calls under normal conditions and under acoustic isolation. *Behaviour, 47*, 230–239.

4 Bird Song

Heather Williams
Williams College and The Rockefeller University Field Research
Center for Ecology and Ethology

WHY STUDY BIRD BRAINS?

Because they mediate birdsong, which is a system of special interest to neuroscientists as well as to students of animal behavior. Here, packed into a very small brain, is a complex acoustic communication system with sophisticated attributes more often associated with large-brained mammals.

Bird songs are learned during development. Young birds (most often, young males) must first discriminate among the many songs they hear and select the appropriate conspecific model. The model is then stored, presumably as an auditory memory, for a period of up to several months. Once they begin to sing, the young males modify the output of their vocal motor program with reference to the stored auditory memory, and so come to sing a song that approximates that of their tutor (for a review of song learning, see Marler, 1981). This learned vocal output is broadcast to conspecifics; their responses are in turn heard and influence the listener (Falls, 1969, 1982; Catchpole, 1982).

Neural correlates of bird songs show parallels with song characteristics. Distinct nuclei of the forebrain control song production (see Fig. 4.8); this song system is lateralized (Nottebohm, 1977), sexually dimorphic (Nottebohm & Arnold, 1976), and portions of the system concentrate steroid hormones (Arnold, Nottebohm, & Pfaff, 1976). Developmental and seasonal changes within the brain's song system parallel developmental and seasonal changes in vocal output (Bottjer, 1987a, 1987b; DeVoogd, Nixdorf, & Nottebohm, 1981; Gurney, 1981; Herrman & Bischof, 1986; Nottebohm, 1981).

Bird song, as a communication system, requires its users to perform a number of cognitive functions. If we can ask the right questions, bird brains should tell us a great deal about how the acoustic signals used in conspecific communication are produced and perceived.

SONG STRUCTURE

Analysis of Song

What are a song's basic units? How are these units arranged? What are the boundaries that divide classes of units or sequences of those units? What variations within a set of songs are important to the birds? Before formulating questions about the brain mechanisms underlying the cognitive abilities represented in birds' song systems, we must build up a picture of the acoustic parameters that are likely to carry information. Because these acoustic parameters vary from species to species, the choice of subject is also important. Although many species' songs have been investigated, studies of the songbird brain have been primarily concentrated upon the canary, starling, zebra finch, and white-crowned sparrow. Among these select few, the zebra finch (*Poephila guttata*) is probably the subject of investigation in more behavioral neuroscience laboratories than any other songbird (e.g., Adkins-Regan, 1987; Arnold, 1980b; Balthazart, Schumacher, & Pröve, 1986; Bottjer, 1987a; Braun, Scheich, Schachner, & Heizmann, 1985; Harding, Sheridan, & Walters, 1983; Immelmann, 1969; Konishi & Akutagawa, 1985; Nordeen, Nordeen, & Arnold, 1986; Pohl-Apel & Sossinka, 1984; Vicario & Nottebohm, 1988).

Zebra finches are a small (10 gram) species native to the arid and semi-arid regions of Australia (Immelmann, 1965). These birds are not seasonal breeders, but maintain reproductive capabilities year-round so as to be ready for unpredictable rainfall (Farner & Serventy, 1960). Males sing and females do not (Arnold, 1974, 1975). Zebra finches are colonial nesters, and song is sung at close range, often "directed" by a courting male to a particular female listener from a distance of only a few centimeters (Sossinka & Böhner, 1980). Song learning is completed upon reaching sexual maturity at 90 days, after which songs do not change (Immelmann, 1969; Price, 1979). The song consists of a series of introductory notes followed by a set pattern of song "syllables" that is repeated with a characteristic order and rhythm (Sossinka & Böhner, 1980; see Fig. 4.2a). Although minor variations in the order of delivery of song syllables (Sossinka & Böhner, 1980) and in syllable phonology (Williams, unpublished data) occur after song learning is completed, the stereotypy of both syllable phonology and syllable order is marked; even in deafened birds, it remains constant over a period of several months (Price, 1979). Female zebra finches respond differently to familiar and unfamiliar songs, suggesting that song may be one of the bases of mate choice (Miller, 1979a, 1979b; Silcox & Evans, 1982).

Given that stereotyped zebra finch song carries information, certain variants of the sounds and temporal patterning in a song are likely to be significant to communicating zebra finches, while other variants may be ignored. Characterizing the variations within song that carry different messages is an essential first step in any study of song as a communication system. For the purpose of defining the characteristics of zebra finch song, I chose to consider syllable *phonology* (acoustic structure) and *syntax* (the order or sequence of syllables within a song) separately. This separation implies a definition of the song syllable as the unit of sound that is coherent when the order of delivery within a song is changed (either within a bird's song or when the song is transferred to another bird through learning). This definition of a zebra finch song syllable coincides with the definition of a song syllable as a sound unit separated from adjacent sound units by silence (see Böhner, 1983; Marler, 1981).

Syllable Phonology

The acoustic characteristics of a syllable are usually visualized as a sonogram, or plot of frequency against time. Such plots do not show amplitude information clearly and ignore the phase relationships of the frequency components within the sound. Other acoustic characteristics or patterns within syllables might also be obscured by this particular representation of song. In attempting to define the syllable characteristics that are important to the birds, possibilities may be discarded by a particular method of analysis; in the case of the sonogram, we rely upon the human eye and brain's processing of a partial visual representation of acoustic properties.

Evaluating the importance of observed variations in syllable phonology by means of visual plots poses another problem: do syllables varying along a particular dimension also vary in their perceptual significance to the birds? In attempting to define the importance of syllable variability along a given dimension, we can be guided by three general approaches:

1. testing the birds' discriminations of, or responses to, a variety of song syllables.
2. measuring the fidelity with which variations in the phonology of learned syllables are reproduced.
3. examining the role of central nervous control in the production of the acoustic characteristics of song syllables.

For example, if a syllable variant can be discriminated from other syllables, is accurately copied during song learning, or requires central control of the vocal organ for its production, it seems likely that the differences between that variant and other, similar syllables are important for communication using the song system.

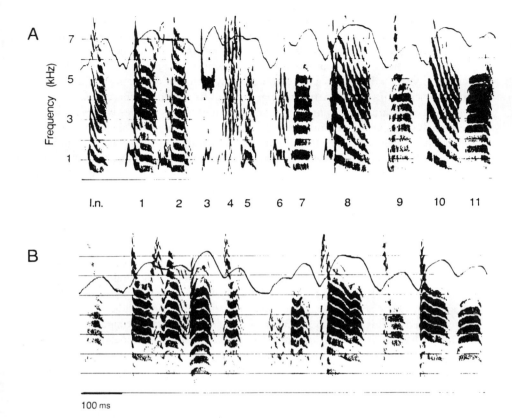

FIG. 4.1. Zebra finch song and motor control of the syrinx. A. Sono-gram of the song of an adult male zebra finch. Time runs along the horizontal axis, and frequency is represented on the vertical axis. The linear trace found above the 5 kHz mark is a plot of the instantaneous amplitude of the sounds being produced. Syllables are numbered. B. The song of the same adult male zebra finch after both tra-cheosyringeal nerves were cut. Although most details of the syllables phonology have been grossly altered, the amplitude plot and syllable timing remain largely unchanged except for the absence of syllable 5.

Zebra finch song consists of a series of introductory notes followed by a series of song syllables which lasts 1–2 seconds (Fig. 4.1a). This series of syllables, or phrase, is often repeated several times in the course of a song bout. Most zebra finch syllables consist of many frequency components, and the frequencies of these components are usually integer multiples of the fundamental frequency, forming a harmonic series. This structure contrasts sharply with the familiar whistles of many bird songs, and the richness of the harmonic structure in zebra finch song may be associated with the fact that it is sung at close range, and so is not subject to attenuation before reaching the hearer.

The basic harmonic structure of zebra finch song, the simple, unmodulated harmonic series (or "stack", for its appearance in a sonogram), is delivered with many variations. Acoustic dimensions along which these variations occur that carry information or may potentially be important are: time, frequency, frequency modulation, amplitude, amplitude modulation, amplitude envelope, timbre, phase, and number of voices.

Length and frequency are the most obvious parameters used in defining a syllable, and are replicated precisely in learned copies of songs (Böhner, 1983). Zebra finch syllables range between 15 and 100 msec long, with a median of approximately 35 msec. Fundamental frequencies range between 400 and 2000 Hz, although 90% of syllables fall between 500 and 700 Hz.

The most prominent frequency modulations are "downsweeps", which can vary in slope from click-like compression to slow downsweeps that maintain a constant amplitude (see syllables 4 and 6 in Fig. 4.1a). Syllables can presumably be grouped both by type of frequency modulation and by the timing of that modulation (see Marler & Pickert, 1984). With a better understanding of the set of motor commands, or vocal gestures, underlying syllables, a better classification (perhaps upon different lines) would be possible.

Among syllables with similar lengths, frequencies, and patterns of frequency modulation, a number of further acoustic variations may have consequences for communication. Rapid amplitude modulations, which produce frequency sidebands, are common in bird song (Greenewalt, 1968, Marler, 1969). Although amplitude modulation has not been studied in zebra finch song, sidebands do occur in some syllables (see syllable 3 in Fig. 4.3).

Syllables falling into the same frequency modulation class may vary in relative amplitude within one song. Such variations in amplitude can be large and fall well within the range of the zebra finch's ability to discriminate sound levels (as determined by Okanoya & Dooling, 1987).

Variations in the amplitude envelope of zebra finch song syllables with otherwise similar characteristics have not been systematically investigated. The underlying relationship between airflow and the fundamental frequency of the tympaniform membranes' vibration may impose limits upon the possible amplitude envelopes for a given time/frequency configuration. However, syllables with similar time/frequency structures often have different amplitude envelopes (e.g., syllable 2 in Fig. 4.1a and syllable 2 in Fig. 4.2). Again, the importance of syllables' amplitude envelopes to zebra finches is as yet unknown, though physiological evidence in other species suggests that this syllable attribute might affect responses. Neurons within a forebrain song nucleus in white-crowned sparrows and canaries are excited when conspecific song is presented as an auditory stimulus; these neurons do not respond or are inhibited when the song is played backwards (Margoliash, 1983; McCasland, 1983). In some cases, the most ob-

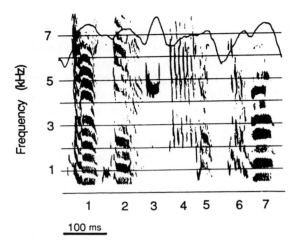

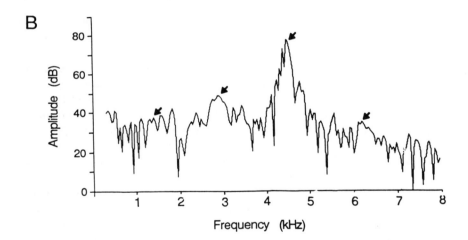

FIG. 4.2. Harmonic structure of a "high note." A. Sonogram of a portion of the song of an adult male zebra finch. In this representation, syllable 3 appears to be a single, high-frequency note centered at approximately 4.5 kHz. B. The power spectrum of syllable 3 from the song shown in A. This plot represents amplitude within the syllable as a function of frequency. There is a large peak at 4.5 kHz, corresponding to the black area seen in the sonogram, but smaller peaks at approximately 3 kHz and 6 kHz can also be seen, indicating that the syllable is actually a harmonic series with a fundamental frequency of approximately 1.5 kHz.

vious difference between backwards and forwards song syllables is the amplitude envelope, and Margoliash (1983) suggested that the configuration of the amplitude envelope might be the determinant of the observed difference in responses.

In sonograms, syllables may appear to lack certain harmonics (e.g., the 7th harmonic of syllable 1 in Fig. 4.2, and the 1st and 3rd harmonics of syllable 1 in Fig. 4.3 are "missing"). In some cases, only one frequency band remains in the sonogram, though plotting the power spectrum of such notes reveals that they are part of a harmonic series (Fig. 4.2). Syllables with the same fundamental frequency, length, and frequency modulation, can be delivered with different patterns of suppressed and emphasized harmonics, or "timbre". Timbre variants are learned (Williams, Cynx, & Nottebohm, in press); they can also be discriminated by zebra finches (Williams, Cynx, & Nottebohm, 1988) and so add an additional dimension of vocal diversity that carries information.

Phase relationships among the frequency components forming a syllable are another little-investigated syllable characteristic. Acoustic analysis of phase information is problematic, and normative data on the phase relationships within zebra finch song do not yet exist. Zebra finches' ability to perceive phase and use it to discriminate among song syllable variants is also unknown, but starlings, another songbird, show phase perception at frequencies of up to 4 kHz (Gleich & Narins, 1988). If phase relationships within song syllables do matter to zebra finches, they would constitute yet another dimension of signal diversity.

Zebra finches, like all songbirds, can potentially sing with two voices at once. The syrinx is located at the junction of the bronchi, and each syringeal half consists of a complete and independently innervated vocal organ. Chickadees, which produce vocalizations (the "dee" call) that are somewhat similar to zebra finch "stacks", use complex non-linear coupling of the two syringeal halves (Nowicki & Capranica, 1986); however, zebra finches may be able to use the two syringeal voices independently. Some syllables are clearly composed of two harmonic series with different frequency modulation, amplitude modulation, and fundamental frequency (Fig. 4.3). The phenomenon of two simultaneous or overlapping voices, however produced, poses a perceptual problem that has parallels to those encountered in human speech perception. Speech units, or phonemes, are coded by acoustic signals that overlap in time. This "coarticulation" is considered the main difficulty encountered when trying to extract meaning from the sound stream (Liberman, Cooper, Shankweiler, & Studdert-Kennedy, 1967). In zebra finches, two overlapping voices, phonating independently, may also pose a special problem for the perceptual apparatus.

The relative importance of each of the acoustic parameters considered here is unknown, and the list is almost certainly incomplete. Furthermore, these variables may interact in a manner that is not obvious to commonly used methods of acoustic analysis. Despite the limits inherent in this approach, describing variants of syllable phonology and their perceptual importance to the birds is essential: they guide the search for physiological correlates of song, and suggest organizing principles for the neural systems which produce the song.

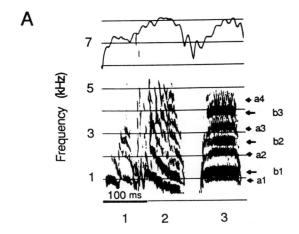

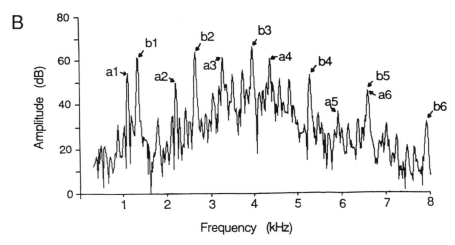

FIG. 4.3. Two voices contribute to one syllable. A. Sonogram of the
initial portion of an adult male zebra finch's song. Syllable 3 consists of
two sets of frequency components, one of which (a) is amplitude modulated and has an initial upsweep, while the other set (b) is not amplitude modulated and shows less frequency modulation. B. Syllable 3
shown in cross-section, as a power spectrum plot of amplitude as a
function of frequency. The frequency components can be clearly dis-
cerned as peaks on this plot. Each set of peaks is an independent
harmonic series, with fundamental frequencies of approximately 1.1
kHz (a) and 1.3 kHz (b).

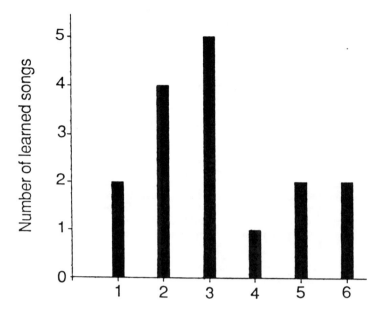

FIG. 4.4. Song models for learned songs. Sixteen songs sung by young male zebra finches were compared to the twelve available song models. Most young males copied song syllables from two or more adults.

Syllable Syntax

Zebra finch songs, once learned, are sung with a nearly invariant syllable order; changes in that order are few and predictable (Sossinka & Böhner, 1980). However, when young males learn songs, new permutations and combinations of syllables appear (Böhner, 1983). Most young zebra finch males (87.5%, $n = 16$) from one cohort raised in a group aviary environment (with the potential for physical contact with many adult males) learned syllables from more than one adult male (Fig. 4.4). The two exceptions were a bird that learned only syllables from one adult male's song (in a rearranged order) and another young male that sang an exact copy of an adult male's song.

In this group of 16 young males, song syllables were most often (92%, $n = 160$) learned in contiguous sequences, or chunks, derived from one adult male's song and retaining the order of the syllables in the tutor songs. Among the 13

TABLE 4.1
Size and Distributions of "Chunks" Learned From
Individual Song Models

	Chunk Size (Number of Syllables)								
	1	2	3	4	5	6	7	8	11
Total chunks	13	16	8	3	4	2	4	1	1
Initial chunks	1	1	2	3	2	2	4	0	1
Internal chunks	9	8	4	0	1	0	0	0	0
Terminal chunks	3	7	2	0	1	0	1	1	1*

Learned songs can be divided into chunks, or consecutive sequences of syllables, each learned from one song model. The distribution of the chunks within 16 learned songs is shown below. Initial chunks begin a song, terminal chunks end a song, and internal chunks neither begin nor end a song. One chunk (*) was both an initial and a final chunk.

syllables that were not part of chunks, 77% were judged not to have been copied from a tutor's song but to have been improvised. Table 4.1 shows the distribution of the sizes of learned chunks within the 16 birds' songs. The longest chunk within a song was most often the opening portion of the song: the median size of the 16 songs' initial chunks was 5 syllables, with middle and final chunks having median sizes of 2 syllables. Note that only two chunks were more than 7 syllables long; 24% of the chunks (including 35% of the syllables) were 2 or 3 syllables long (recall that an additional 13 syllables, or 8%, did not belong to chunks). Given a single syllable from one of these young males' songs and knowledge of the tutors' songs, it is possible to predict what syllables will follow. The first following syllable can be predicted with an accuracy of 69%, the second following syllable falls to 44% accuracy, and the third to 35%; by the 6th following syllable, the prediction's accuracy drops to 8%. The mean length of the average young male's song (excluding introductory notes and two cases of internal repeats that were counted only once in the chunking analysis) was 10 syllables. We can then define a typical sequence for a learned song: it is made up of three chunks of associated syllables, with a long initial chunk derived from the primary tutor's song followed by two shorter chunks (including one from a secondary tutor's song), plus one novel syllable inserted between chunks or at the end of the song.

The most comprehensive analysis of sequences within avian vocalizations to date deals with the "chick-a-dee" call (Hailman, Ficken, & Ficken, 1985, 1987). In this call system, the four different classes of notes (A, B, C, and D) follow each other in a semi-Markovian fashion: A can be followed by A, B, C, D, or silence; B can be followed by B, C, D, or silence; C by C, D, or silence; and D only by D or silence. In zebra finches, sequential rules are less restrictive, though

TABLE 4.2
Timing Intervals Within Zebra Finch Songs

	Syllable Position	Syllable Length	Intersyllable Interval (silence)
Syllable length	.336		
Intersyllable interval (silence)	−.141	−.089	
Syllable length + interval	.060	.762	.571

Correlations between syllable position within the song and three measures of timing relationships within the song. The only high *r* values occur when two measures containing some of the same information (e.g., syllable length and syllable length + interval) are compared.

some positional tendencies exist. In the sample of 28 males (12 adults and 16 young) described above, all introductory notes included downsweeps (though occasional relatively unmodulated downsweeps and two-parted introductory notes have been observed in the songs of birds from the Rockefeller University Field Center colony). The initial and final syllables of the songs and, for the young males, the song chunks, were also determined (Table 4.2). There is a significant tendency ($p < 0.001$) for the initial note in a song or a chunk to be a downsweep (e.g., Figs. 4.1a, 4.2a, and 4.3a, syllable 1) and the final note to be a "stack" (e.g., Fig. 4.1a, syllable 11), though these tendencies are slightly less marked in chunks than in the entire songs. Other syllable types are equally distributed among initial and final positions within chunks or songs ($p > .90$). Certain note types tend to occur in specific internal positions within the song sequence. In the songs of the 12 adult tutors, 19 syllables were classified as "high notes" (e.g., Fig. 4.1a, syllable 3) or "click trains" (e.g., Fig. 4.1a, syllable 4); 89.5% of these occurred in the 2nd, 3rd, or 4th position within the song. Many of these sequence biases may have arisen from a skewed song sample, (stacks have been observed occasionally as initial notes in other birds not used in this study), or be a species-wide trend. Because the positional biases recurred in the songs of young males raised in the colony, they may form a local syntactical dialect, similar to that of the swamp sparrow (Marler & Pickert, 1984).

A further characteristic of the delivery of sequences of zebra finch song syllables is cadence or rhythm. Unlike songs such as that of the canary, syllables are not repeated to fill roughly equivalent time slots. Syllables vary in length, as do the intersyllable silences and the intervals between the onset of syllables (see the songs and song segments in Figs. 4.1, 4.2 and 4.3). Timing intervals, as analyzed in six songs, do not follow any regular patterns. Syllable length and position are not correlated, and neither feature is related to the silent interval following the syllable (Table 4.2). However idiosyncratic they may seem, timing

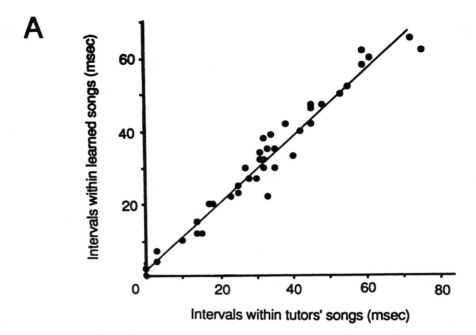

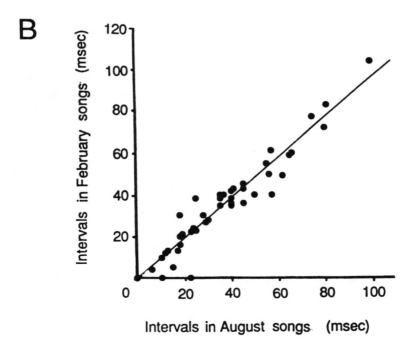

relationships are clearly important characteristics of zebra finch song: chunks of two different adult males' songs copied by a young male replicate the timing relationships within the tutor's song (Fig. 4.5a), and rhythm stereotypy persists to a remarkable degree in recordings made after an interval of 9 months (Fig. 4.5b).

The relationship between syllable amplitude and sequence (the equivalent of meter in poetry or accenting in speech), with some syllables being differentially emphasized by their delivery, is stereotyped and may also be important to zebra finches. A wide variety of amplitudes occurs within a single song (Fig. 4.2a), and amplitude level is not obviously related to syllable class (e.g., in Fig. 4.2a, compare syllable 9 to syllables 7 and 11). How this emphasis pattern is used by zebra finches is unknown, but "meter" seems likely to be an important feature of song.

Zebra finch song syntax seems then to be produced and learned according to the same general rules that govern the learning and production of individual syllables: most sequences are learned, most birds learn sequences from more than one source, and some sequences are improvised. Further, a syllable's phonology and syntax are often coupled during the learning process: single syllables inserted into or between copied song chunks tend to be improvised. This coupling is not entirely rigid. When chunks are spliced together during song learning, new sequences are generated using accurately copied syllables—implying that syllable phonology and syntax are separable.

Neuromuscular Correlates of Phonology and Syntax

The structure of the vocal organ, airways, and articulators places physical constraints upon the types and sequences of sounds that an animal can produce, defining the basic output of the vocal system. Similarly, the arrangement of vocal tract muscles and of the neural structures controlling those muscles defines how that basic output can be altered, determining what families of acoustic variations and sequences of syllables can be most easily produced.

FIG. 4.5. Temporal relationships within zebra finch songs are conserved. A. The length of each syllable, all intersyllable intervals, and the intervals between syllable onsets were measured 1) in the songs of two zebra finches and 2) in the models for those songs were copied. Temporal intervals in the learned songs were plotted against the corresponding intervals from the tutor's songs. The correlation between the two sets of intervals is extremely high ($r = .963$), implying that temporal relationships in song are learned. B. The relationship between the temporal intervals in the songs of two adult zebra finch males and the songs of the same two males recorded seven months later. The temporal intervals remain fixed, as is shown by the high correlation between the two sets of recordings ($r = .983$).

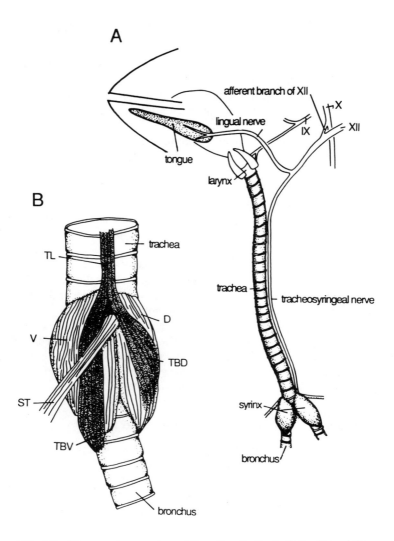

FIG. 4.6. The vocal apparatus of the zebra finch. A. Side view of the vocal tract and its innervation. The lower part of the trachea is rotated to show the two halves of the syrinx. Afferents from the tracheosyringeal nerve run in the small nerve branch leading from XII to X, and have cell bodies in the vagal ganglion (Bottjer & Arnold, 1984). The neck and mandibular muscles and their innervation presumably contribute to postural changes and the flaring of the beak during song, but are not shown here. After Nottebohm and Nottebohm, 1976. B. Left side view of the syrinx and its muscles (after Vicario & Nottebohm, 1988). Muscle designations: D: dorsal; ST: sternotracheal; TBD: dorsal tracheobronchal; TBV: ventral tracheobronchal; TL: tracheolateral; V: ventral.

The vocal instrument of the zebra finch, consisting of the syrinx and airways, is shown in Fig. 4.6. A complement of at least six sets of paired syringeal muscles are controlled by the tracheosyringeal motor nucleus (Vicario & Nottebohm, 1988). Syringeal muscles are thought to make their acoustic effects by altering the tension upon the internal tympaniform membranes, changing the frequencies produced or causing the onset and termination of vocalizations (Greenewalt, 1968; Nottebohm, 1975; Suthers & Hector, 1985; Warner, 1972).

In order to understand the manner in which central control can "play" the syrinx, the sounds produced by vocally denervated adult male zebra finches were compared to normal song. The syrinx was denervated by sectioning the two tracheosyringeal nerves (each innervating the muscles on one side of the syrinx), which are branches of the hypoglossal, or twelfth, nerve (abbreviated NXIIts). Birds will sing after this operation when presented with a female, and the song's amplitude envelope and timing are remarkably consistent with those in the intact bird's song (Fig. 4.2). Normal song is produced by a series of "mini-breaths" (Calder, 1970) which force air through the syrinx with timing corresponding to that of the song syllables' delivery. In birds with NXIIts transections, the respiratory musculature and its innervation, which control airflow through the syrinx, remain intact; the persistence of normal temporal patterning and amplitude envelopes in the songs of denervated birds may be due to appropriately timed airflow passing over and vibrating the tympaniform membranes (which are no longer under neural control). This interpretation is supported by the fact that the denervated birds produce audible "wheezes" with every expiration.

Unlike the temporal and amplitude patterns, the phonology of syllables within the denervated birds' songs is grossly altered. Each syllable is replaced by a series of harmonic components that are relatively unmodulated when compared to the intact bird's song. The frequency modulation that remains may be solely a function of respiratory airflow across the flaccid vocal membranes. As airflow increases, producing louder sounds (see Gaunt, Stein, & Gaunt, 1973; Gaunt, 1983), the fundamental frequency of the harmonic series rises. Figure 4.7 shows the relationship between fundamental frequency and syllable amplitude before and after cutting the tracheosyringeal nerves. The fundamental frequencies of syllables sung after nerve section were closely correlated to the amplitude of those syllables ($r = .84$; amplitude and frequency were not as closely related in the intact song ($r = .21$). Timbre variants disappear in song syllables produced by a denervated syrinx: each syllable has the same pattern of harmonic emphasis, with the highest amplitude harmonics having frequencies between 3 and 4 kHz, and the amplitudes of harmonics with higher and lower frequencies falling off smoothly (Williams et al., in press). The basic acoustic pattern produced by zebra finches' vocal apparatus is then a simply filtered harmonic series, with fundamental frequency dependent upon the amplitude.

Although we do not yet have an integrated picture of how the central nervous system controls the vocal musculature, the brain structures controlling many of

A

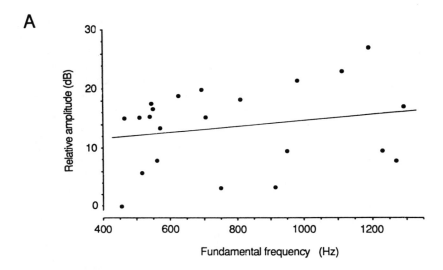

B

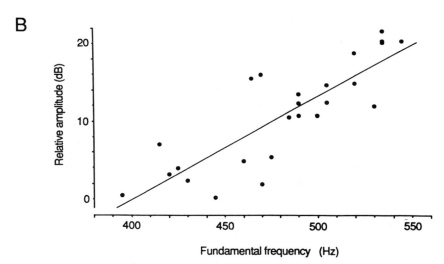

FIG. 4.7. Amplitude determines fundamental frequency in the denervated syrinx. A. The amplitudes of 12.8 msec segments of song syllables in an intact male's song are plotted as a function of the fundamental frequency of the syllable segment. There is only a slight positive correlation ($r = .21$) between frequency and amplitude. B. Relationship between amplitude and fundamental frequency in segments of syllables in the song of the same male after the vocal organ was denervated. Fundamental frequencies are now lower and fall within a narrower range. After vocal denervation, the correlation between fundamental frequency and amplitude is strong ($r = .84$).

the articulators and airflow sources are known. The motor neurons innervating five pairs of syringeal muscles lie in a roughly somatotopic arrangement within the tracheosyringeal motor nucleus (Vicario & Nottebohm, 1988). The size of the representation within the motor nucleus and the prominence of expiratory activity in the motorneurons (see Manogue & Paton, 1982) differ for each muscle. The largest sets of neurons within the motor nucleus innervate the dorsal and ventral syringeal muscles; these neurons have, respectively, the least and most expiratory-coupled activity (Vicario & Nottebohm, 1988). Because the ventral muscles contract with each expiration, keeping the airway through the syrinx from collapsing (Vicario, Williams, unpublished data), it may be that the dorsal syringeal muscles control much of the acoustic variation seen in zebra finch song while the ventral muscles are more important for regulating when sounds are produced.

The motor neurons controlling the muscles of the trachea, larynx, and tongue have been described (Nottebohm & Nottebohm, 1976; Nottebohm, Stokes, & Leonard, 1976; Nottebohm, Kelley, & Paton, 1982; Vicario & Nottebohm, 1988). The exact role of these potential articulators and their muscles in song is unknown, but Nowicki's (1987) observations of bird song in a helium atmosphere suggest that the vocal airways may form a variable acoustic filter, which could be controlled by the muscles affecting the conformation of the airway.

Pathways connecting midbrain and brainstem respiratory centers to midbrain vocal centers and tracheosyringeal motor neurons are known in the pigeon (Wild & Arends, 1987; see Fig. 4.8). These pathways presumably have homologs in songbirds. As noted previously, song as sung after syringeal denervation retains the intact temporal patterns and overall amplitude envelope, which are controlled by the respiratory system. In canaries, forebrain lesions of song nuclei affect phonology and syntax differently: removing HVc[1] disrupts both phonology and syntax, while birds with RA[2] lesions sing songs that have appropriate temporal structure but severe deficits in syllable phonology (Nottebohm, Stokes, & Leonard, 1976; Nottebohm, 1980b). Syllable phonology and syntax are then both represented within HVc, but separate at the next station in the motor pathway, with phonology being independently represented within RA; how syntax is transferred from HVc to the midbrain structures controlling vocal respiration is not known. The stereotyped and tightly coordinated delivery of song requires that the two branches of the vocal motor pathway (one associated with syringeal musculature and phonology, the other with respiratory musculature and

---

[1]The High vocal center of the neostriatum (Fig. 4.8). Formerly known as Hyperstriatum ventralis pars caudalis, this nucleus is the most extensively connected and one of the largest song nuclei. Some HVc neurons project directly to RA.

[2]Nucleus robustus of the archistriatum (Fig. 4.8). This nucleus sends projections directly to the tracheosyringeal motor neurons as well as to the midbrain regions associated with breath control during vocalization.

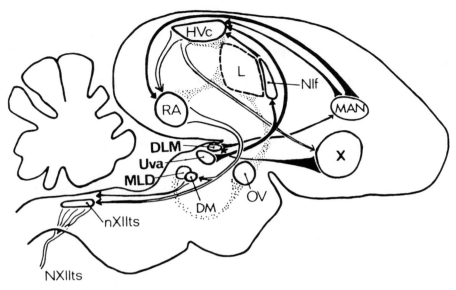

FIG. 4.8.   The zebra finch song system. A sagittal section through the
zebra finch brain, showing a composite view of the song system. Connections between nuclei associated with the descending branch of the
song system are shown with open arrows, other song nucleus connections are shown with solid arrows, and a portion of the ascending
auditory pathway is denoted by stippling. DLM: medial portion of the
dorso-lateral thalamic nucleus; DM: dorso-medial portion of the inter-
collicular nucleus; HVc: high vocal center of the neostriatum (formerly
hyperstriatum ventralis pars caudalis); L: field L, the primary telencephalic auditory projection; mMAN: medial portion of the magnocellular anterior nucleus of the neostriatum; lMAN: lateral portion of the
magnocellular anterior nucleus of the neostriatum; MLD: inferior colliculus; Nlf: nucleus interfacialis; OV: nucleus ovoidalis, the thalamic
auditory relay nucleus; nXIIts: tracheosyringeal motor nucleus, a portion of the 12th (hypoglossal) nucleus; NXIIts: tracheosyringeal nerve,
which innervates the muscles of the trachea and the syrinx (the avian
vocal organ); RA: nucleus robustus of the archistriatum; X: area X.

syntax) be regulated by input from a common center representing all the properties of a syllable.

SONG DEVELOPMENT AND LEARNING

Genetic Constraints

Some acoustic characteristics of vocalizations are defined by the structure of the
vocal tract, which is presumably genetically determined. For example, the con-

formation of the bronchi, syringes, and trachea within the vocal tract determine the characteristic spectral signature of oilbird calls (Suthers, unpublished data). Female zebra finch calls are also thought to be inherited and not learned (Zann, 1984, 1985). However, male zebra finches normally learn calls (Zann, 1984, 1985) and songs of adult males, assembling their songs from syllables drawn from the several songs while conserving the spectral characteristics of each tutor male's syllables (see "Syllable syntax"). Learning is not restricted to the songs of conspecifics: when young zebra finch males are fostered to Bengalese or strawberry finch parents, they learn to sing a song similar to that of their foster fathers (Clayton, 1987; Immelmann, 1969; Price, 1979). These data indicate that, although zebra finches' vocal apparatus presumably limits the types of sounds they can produce, their potential vocal repertoire far exceeds the normal range of any given male's song.

Within this large potential vocal repertoire, most songbird species show a preference for learning species-typical sounds when given a choice among taped tutor songs from several different species (Marler & Peters, 1977, 1981a; Thorpe, 1958). Further evidence for auditory predispositions is provided by the demonstration that young naive song sparrows' heart rates are affected differently by conspecific and heterospecific songs (Dooling and Searcy, 1980). An innate model of conspecific song, acting as a perceptual filter upon the songs heard by young songbirds and more restricted than the potential vocal output, must then be transmitted genetically (Marler, 1969, 1970). Understanding the neural mechanisms underlying species-specific auditory predispositions will have to await a better knowledge of the fine details of the brain's song circuitry. Another approach, that of searching for genetic differences corresponding to differences in vocalization, is still in its infancy (Clayton, Huecas, Sinclair-Thompson, Nastiuk, & Nottebohm, 1988), but may well prove fruitful, as it has in *Drosophila* (Kyriacou & Hall, 1986).

Stages of Song Development

The work of Peter Marler and his associates has defined discrete and sequential stages of song development (Konishi, 1965; Marler, 1970; Nottebohm, 1968). Some song birds, such as the canary, partially repeat the process of song learning during each breeding cycle, changing their songs from year to year. Others, such as the zebra finch, are closed-ended learners, passing through the stages of song development only once; when song learning is completed at three months, the song is fixed for life.

The normal song learning cycle is composed of four main stages (Marler, 1981; Marler & Peters, 1982a) and takes place as follows in zebra finch males:

1. *Song model acquisition,* choosing a tutor and storing a memory of his song, occurs during a "sensitive period" between days 15 and 35 after hatching (Immelmann, 1969).

2. *Subsong* consists of relatively soft, broad-band, unstructured sounds. This stage is thought to be the process by which a young bird calibrates his vocal instrument, akin to babbling in human infants (Nottebohm, 1975). In annual breeders, subsong is separated from the following stage, plastic song, by a period of silence. Subsong is not well described in zebra finches, which compress their song development into 3 months, but is thought to start at about day 25.

3. *Plastic song* is marked by the gradual approximation of the young male's vocal output to the stored song model (or models). Zebra finches sing plastic song between day 35 and day 80 (Price, 1979).

4. *Crystallization* is the fixing of the adult song in its permanent form, and takes place at approximately 90 days in zebra finches (Price, 1979). In some species, several songs are produced during plastic song and then dropped during crystallization (Marler & Peters, 1982b), but this does not seem to be the case for zebra finches.

It should be noted that although the stages of song learning are sequential and normally occur within narrowly defined periods, the process can be extended beyond the timetable described above if young males are deprived of a song model during early stages of development (Eales, 1985). However, the sequence of normal development, while subject to small variations between individuals, is constant enough to provide a good baseline for studying the neural bases of song learning.

Neural Correlates of Song Development

Morphology of Song Nuclei.   Developmental changes in song are paralleled by a number of changes in the morphology of the song system nuclei. The timing of increases in volume of HVc and RA, two forebrain nuclei that are necessary for normal song production (Nottebohm et al., 1976; see Fig. 4.8) is the most salient of these changes. Although the telencephalic volume of the zebra finch brain and the volume of nuclei associated with the visual system reach adult levels at approximately 30 days, both HVc and RA show substantial increases in volume during that period (Fig. 4.9a; Bottjer, Glaessner, & Arnold, 1985; Herr mann & Bischof, 1986). Canary HVc and RA also increase in volume relatively late in development, reaching their adult sizes at 6 months, during plastic song (Nottebohm, Nottebohm, & Crane, 1986). HVc volume increase is due to a corresponding increase in the number of neurons present in the nucleus, while increases in cell size (both soma and dendritic arbor) account for the volume change in RA (Bottjer, Miesner, & Arnold, 1986). Corresponding seasonal changes occur during successive years in adult male canaries, which relearn portions of their songs each breeding cycle: HVc and RA shrink during the summer, increasing again in volume during the fall (Nottebohm, 1981).

Another song system nucleus that changes size during song development is

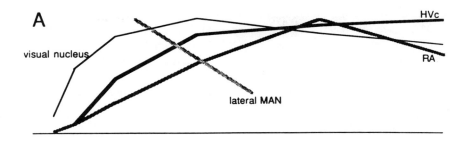

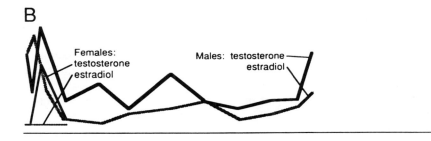

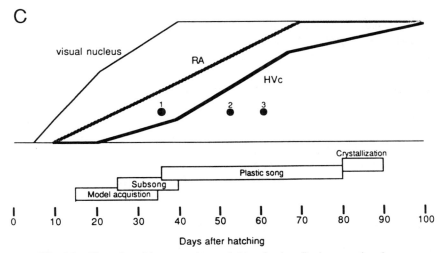

FIG. 4.9.   Neural and hormonal correlates of zebra finch song development. A. Changes in the volumes of song and visual nuclei during development (data from Bottjer et al., 1985; Herrman & Bischof, 1986). B. Circulating hormone levels during song development (data from Pröve, 1983 [after day 10] and Hutchison et al., 1984). C. The progress of myelination in song and visual nuclei during development. Specific changes in connectivity are marked by asterisks: 1. HVc fibers grow into RA; 2. DLM fibers enter IMAN; 3. Uva stimulation begins to inhibit auditory responses in HVc (data from Konishi & Akutagawa, 1985; Herrmann & Bischof, 1986; Williams, 1986; and Bottjer, 1987b).

the lateral portion of MAN (nucleus magnocellularis of the anterior neostriatum, or lMAN; see Fig. 4.9a). This nucleus is of particular interest because of its role specific to song development: lesioning lMAN between days 25 and 55 results in severe song deficits, but lMAN lesions do not affect song production in adult zebra finches (Bottjer, Miesner, & Arnold, 1984). Studies on the volume of lMAN during various stages of song development in zebra finches are subject to the problem of ambiguous boundaries for the nucleus in young birds. If the nucleus as seen in young birds corresponds to that in adults, the volume of lMAN peaks at about day 25, decreasing dramatically between days 25 and 50 (Fig. 4.9a); this decrease in size is thought to be due to cell loss and not neuronal atrophy or an increase in cell density (Bottjer et al., 1985).

Lateral MAN projects to RA (see Fig. 4.8, Nottebohm et al., 1982), and receives a projection from DLM (the medial portion of the dorso-lateral thalamic nucleus; Williams & Nottebohm, 1985); terminals from area X neurons are found in DLM (Bottjer, Halsema, Brown, & Miesner, 1988; Okuhata & Saito, 1987); area X in turn receives a projection from HVc neurons (Nottebohm et al., 1976). Lateral MAN is then part of a recurrent loop forming an indirect link between HVc and RA (Fig. 4.8). This parallel connectivity, coupled with MAN's role in early song development, suggests that the recurrent loop might form a neural substrate for comparisons, a process important in song learning.

Hormones and Sexual Dimorphism.   Adult female zebra finches do not sing (Arnold, 1974, 1975). Correspondingly, the song nuclei HVc and RA are much smaller in females (lower volume, fewer cells, smaller cells) than in males: females' RAs have smaller volumes, (Nottebohm & Arnold, 1976), fewer cells, and smaller cells (Gurney, 1981; Gurney & Konishi, 1980). This sexual dimorphism arises during development: the RA of female zebra finches follows the same development curve as in males until approximately day 30, after which neuronal death and atrophy reduce the RA volume in females (Fig. 4.9a; Konishi & Akutagawa, 1985). Sexual dimorphism in song, coupled with the sexual dimorphism in RA and HVc volume, suggests that changes in cell number and size within these song nuclei might be coordinated by steroid hormone levels during song learning.

Correlations between plasma E and T levels and stages of song development exist in canaries (E and T; Nottebohm, Nottebohm, Crane, & Wingfield, 1987; Weichel, Schwager, Heid, Guttinger, & Pesch, 1986), swamp and song sparrows, (E and T; Marler, Peters, & Wingfield, 1987; Marler, Peters, Ball, Dufty, & Wingfield, 1988) and zebra finches (T; Pröve, 1983). Testosterone may play a role during song crystallization in swamp and song sparrows (Marler et al., 1988) and in zebra finches (Korsia & Bottjer, 1988). However, castrated male swamp and song sparrows (Marler et al., 1988), marsh wrens (Kroodsma, 1986) and zebra finches (Arnold, 1975) learn songs normally. Castrated adult male zebra finches sing normal songs (Arnold, 1975, Harding et al., 1983). Hormone supplements (testosterone [T] and its active metabolites, estradiol [E] and 5α-dihydrotestosterone [5α-DHT]) given to adult females do not induce song or masculinize song nuclei (Arnold, 1974, 1975). Any organizing effects testosterone might have on the overall course of song learning must occur very early in development, before the age at which castration is possible (about 15–20 days). Castration does not reduce E levels appreciably (Hutchison, Wingfield, & Hutchison, 1984; Marler et al., 1988), making it difficult to evaluate the role estradiol plays during the later stages of song development from castration and replacement studies.

In male zebra finches, an early peak in plasma E levels occurs between days 3 and 9 after hatching; young female zebra finches show no such peak (Hutchison et al., 1984). Although circulating T levels are high immediately after hatching in females and testosterone could be aromatized to produce E (Hutchison et al., 1984), activity levels of 5β-reductase (which converts T to the inactive form of DHT, 5β-DHT) in the young females' brain are also extremely high at this stage of development (Balthazart et al., 1986). High levels of 5β-reductase would act as an inactivating shunt, preventing the circulating T from being converted to E.

Estradiol given to females in the first few days after hatching masculinizes song and song system nuclei (Gurney, 1981; Gurney & Konishi, 1980), but the effect upon singing and song nuclei decreases abruptly if the hormone is first administered more than 4 days after hatching (Pohl-Apel & Sossinka, 1984). These data suggest that estradiol plays a role in organizing brain centers controlling song during the early stages of development by preventing the cell loss and atrophy that occurs at about day 30 in normal female zebra finches (Konishi & Akutagawa, 1985). The disparity in timing between hormone administration (before day 10) and its effect upon cells in RA (seen at day 30) suggests that, in this case, estradiol serves to organize the tissue before song learning is initiated, preparing the song centers for inputs which arrive later in song development.

Steroid hormones affect target cells by binding to specific receptors (Goy & McEwen, 1980). Many of the zebra finch's forebrain song nuclei, including HVc, RA, and lMAN, contain large numbers of neurons that concentrate testosterone (Arnold et al., 1976). Estradiol receptors, although common in adult canary HVc neurons (Gahr, Flugge, & Guttinger, 1987), are not found in the RA of zebra finches, and can be found only at extremely low levels, if at all, in the HVc of the adult male zebra finches (Gahr et al., 1987, Gahr pers. comm.; Nordeen, Nordeen & Arnold, 1987b), adult female zebra finches, and young female zebra finches (Nordeen et al., 1987b). Paradoxically, the hormone that has the greatest effect upon song development is not bound or is bound only at low levels by the neurons which it is thought to affect.

Estradiol may affect testosterone receptor levels in song nuclei. During the period (between day 25 and 50) in which the number of lMAN neurons appears to decrease by approximately 50% (see Fig. 4.9a), the number of lMAN neurons that concentrate T remains constant (Bottjer, 1987a; Nordeen, Nordeen, & Arnold, 1987a). These T-concentrating neurons, which belong to the largest somal size class in lMAN (Bottjer, 1987a), may be preferentially rescued during a period of cell death or retained within the boundaries of what becomes lMAN in adults. The neurons with T receptors also concentrate more hormone at day 50 than at day 25 (Bottjer, 1987a). High levels of T-accumulating neurons in lMAN of adult male zebra finches are dependent upon E treatment in the period immediately after hatching (Nordeen, Nordeen, & Arnold, 1986). This result is also paradoxical: one effect of E administered early in development is to increase neuronal response to T—but, since castrated males develop normal song, (Arnold, 1975), effects upon testosterone response cannot account for the masculinizing effects of estradiol.

Steroid hormones, particularly estradiol, seem to play an organizing role in the development of song and associated brain structures. The early hormonal milieu influences the death, growth, and expression of hormone receptors in forebrain song nuclei. Because the changes in HVc, RA, and lMAN are effected by hormonal levels present before song learning starts, these changes cannot be a direct consequence of the auditory or vocal experiences that are critical to song learning. Changes in size and number of neurons occurring at day 30 affect opportunities for forming connections, and so might define the neural basis for the beginning or end of specific stages in song development. Yet we know that song learning is not a sequence of events that is completed on a developmental schedule; the process can be dramatically extended by manipulating the auditory environment (Eales, 1985). Hormonal effects upon song-related neurons seem most likely to provide a neural substrate, while auditory and motor experiences are the primary shapers of the song circuitry that underlies song learning.

Connectivity.   The trend towards late development of song-associated forebrain regions is paralleled by the formation of projections and the pattern of myelination. In zebra finches, myelination in two visual areas is completed before day 40, but in RA myelination continues until day 70, and in HVc it is delayed still longer, reaching adult levels at day 100 (Herrmann & Bischof, 1986; see Fig. 4.9c). Extremely late myelination would be expected if the formation of connections is prolonged and plastic during song development.

Further evidence of late formation of connections between song system nuclei is available in the case of the projection from HVc to RA. Most HVc-RA projection neurons are not born until days 20–40, relatively late in development, and new neurons are added well into adulthood (Alvarez-Buylla, Theelen, & Nottebohm, 1988; Nordeen, and Nordeen, 1988). In young zebra finch males, fibers from HVc surround RA at days 15 and 25, but no terminals can be observed within the nucleus until day 35 (Konishi & Akutagawa, 1985). In females, the ingrowth of fibers at day 35 does not occur (Konishi & Akutagawa, 1985), and the HVc-RA connection is not thought to be functional in adult females (Williams, 1985b; but see also Arnold, 1980b).

Loss of lMAN neurons (which also project to RA) may also occur at about day 30 (Bottjer, 1987a); ingrowth of HVc afferents and competition for terminal space on the dendrites of RA axons might initiate cell death in lMAN. In one class of canary RA neuron, synapses from HVc afferents outnumber those from lMAN by 20 to 1 (Canady, Burd, DeVoogd, & Nottebohm, 1988). HVc synapses occur predominantly on the dendritic spines of RA neurons while most of the synapses formed by lMAN afferents are on the shafts of the dendrites (Canady et al., 1988). A related observation, though in a different species and song system nucleus, is the reduction of dendritic spine density and the enlargement of the remaining spines in the mynah HVc during song development (Rausch and Scheich, 1982). If the number and location of synapses from lMAN and HVc neurons are reflections of competition for space on dendritic spines, the pattern described above might have resulted from a displacement of lMAN synapses by HVc synapses. Intriguingly, the relatively sudden ingrowth of HVc fibers into RA and the possible concurrent loss of lMAN neurons in zebra finches both occur at about 30–35 days after hatching, the age corresponding to the end of the sensitive period for the song model acquisition.

The formation of synapses upon lMAN neurons may also occur in a manner similar to the HVc-RA projection and at an age correlated to a stage in song development. In zebra finches, incoming fibers from DLM, which are the only neurons known to project to lMAN, grow up to and surround lMAN early in development (Bottjer, 1987a, 1987b). These incoming fibers remain outside the target nucleus for a period of at least several days before growing into lMAN at 50–55 days (Bottjer, 1987a, 1987b). Bottjer (1987a) suggested that this ingrowth of afferent fibers and the increase in T receptors within lMAN cells may be related, and that the inputs from DLM trigger the changes in androgen receptor number and activity. The formation of the DLM-lMAN connection may then be related to the change in lMAN's role in song production (Bottjer et al., 1984) that occurs at about day 50 after hatching.

Auditory Inputs.   The effect of auditory isolation on song development is well documented. Young zebra finch males placed in auditory isolation and thus deprived of a song model have extended sensitive periods for song model acquisition (Eales, 1985). Impoverished auditory environments also lead to the extension of sensitive periods in other songbird species (Baptista & Petrinovitch, 1986; Kroodsma & Pickert, 1980). Song learning is undeniably dependent upon the actions of steroid hormones and the progression of development in the neural substrate for song, but the neural key to normal song learning may be the effects and processing of auditory inputs in forebrain song nuclei during song learning.

The effects of T treatment on the volumes of RA and HVc in deafened canaries indicate the potential importance of auditory inputs to the development of these nuclei. Unlike zebra finch females, female canaries occasionally sing spontaneously (Pesch & Güttinger, 1985) and T treatment induces song (see

Herrick & Harris, 1957). Testosterone administered to female canaries also results in increased RA and HVc volumes (Nottebohm, 1980a) mainly due to lengthening of RA neurons' dendrites (DeVoogd & Nottebohm, 1981). However, in deafened birds, the increase in HVc volume after T treatment appears to be drastically reduced (Bottjer, Schoonmaker, & Arnold, 1986). Auditory inputs to HVc seem to be necessary to obtain the testosterone-associated increase in song nucleus volume, indicating that the sensory experiences of song learning may have major affects on the development of the brain structures that underlie the development of song.

As well as being necessary for song production, HVc neurons respond to auditory stimuli (Katz & Gurney, 1981; Margoliash, 1983). In adult birds, auditory responses in HVc are inhibited during and shortly after singing (Mc-Casland & Konishi, 1981). One input to HVc, that from Uva (nucleus uvaeformis; see Fig. 4.8), both activates the song motor system (HVc, RA, and the motor neurons) and inhibits auditory responses in HVc neurons (Williams, 1985a, 1986). However, in zebra finches less than 60 days old, Uva stimulation does not inhibit auditory responses in HVc neurons, though the stimulation is effective in eliciting activity in HVc, RA, and the tracheosyringeal motor neurons (Williams, 1986). The combination of these two results, the observation of auditory inhibition in HVc during singing and the age-dependent disparity in the effect of Uva stimulation on auditory responses in HVc neurons, suggests that simultaneous auditory and motor activity is possible in the HVc (and the nuclei to which it projects) of young male zebra finches during song development—but not in adults. The double loop of HVc efferents (directly to RA; to RA via area X, DLM, and lMAN)—or HVc itself—might serve as comparators in the process of matching vocalizations to an auditory model during plastic song. In such a model, Uva's role in blocking auditory responses in HVc at later stages of song development might serve to make the neurons' song system nuclei unresponsive to sounds produced by their motor activity. The song, now uninfluenced by comparisons to the stored auditory model, would become a fixed motor pattern.

ADULT NEUROGENESIS

Neurogenesis in adults is a special feature of the neural substrate for bird song. New neurons are born into the adult forebrain of canaries (Goldman & Nottebohm, 1983). Cell division in the ventricular walls of the forebrain gives rise to young neurons which then migrate along radial glia to sites in the forebrain up to 5 mm from the ventricle (Alvarez-Buylla & Nottebohm, 1988). The neostriatum, where most of the neurons born during adulthood are incorporated (Nottebohm, 1987) includes the song system nuclei HVc and NIf as well as field L, the primary auditory projection (see Fig. 4.8). Neurons born in adulthood form functional connections within HVc and respond to acoustic stimulation (Paton &

Nottebohm, 1984). Within the canary HVc, many new neurons are interneurons (Paton, O'Loughlin, & Nottebohm, 1985). Unlike many HVc interneurons, none of the neurons born in adulthood express GABA-like immunoreactivity (Paton, Burd, & Nottebohm, 1986). Of the two classes of projection neurons within HVc (projecting to RA or to area X) only RA-projecting neurons are produced in adulthood (Alvarez-Buylla et al., 1988). Neurons born in adulthood are then incorporated into a restricted set of song nuclei (among other brain areas), and within these nuclei, new neurons differentiate into only a few of the several known classes of neurons. Neurons are also incorporated into adult zebra finch forebrain song centers (Nottebohm, 1984; Nordeen & Nordeen, 1988). Because the size of song system nuclei does not increase after sexual maturity is reached (Nottebohm, Kasparian, & Pandazis, 1981), a continual turnover of particular classes of HVc neurons (including neurons responsive to auditory stimulation) must take place in adult songbirds: old neurons die, to be replaced by new neurons.

What function could neurons born in adulthood serve? In canaries that relearn portions of their songs every year, a role in song relearning seems indicated for new neurons. Yet in adult zebra finches song remains constant even after deafening (Price, 1979), implying that the newly born neurons do not play any role in adjusting song production according to external auditory stimuli. It is possible that newly produced neurons incorporated into the forebrain song centers of zebra finches merely take over the roles of existing neurons, or that they serve a purpose associated with auditory processing of song but unrelated to song production.

LATERALITY

Songbirds' bipartite syrinx (see Fig. 4.6) can potentially be used to sing with two voices at once (Greenewalt, 1968). Each syringeal half is a complete vocal organ, innervated by a separate nerve (Nottebohm, et al., 1976, 1982; Paton & Manogue, 1982). The phonating muscles associated with each half-syrinx are controlled by ipsilateral motorneurons, which in turn receive terminals from the ipsilateral song nucleus HVc via RA (Nottebohm, 1971; Paton & Manogue, 1982). Birds are acallosal, and forebrain song nuclei connections link only ipsilateral nuclei (Nottebohm et al., 1976; Nottebohm et al., 1982). To a large degree, the left and right song systems are separate.

The left or right syringeal half can be denervated by cutting the tracheosyringeal nerve on that side. Left and right nerve sections do not have equivalent effects upon song production; cutting one nerve results in more deleterious effects upon song than does cutting the other in all species examined to date, including the chaffinch, canary, white-crowned sparrow, white-throated sparrow, Java sparrow, and zebra finch (Crane, Price, & Nottebohm, 1984; Lemon, 1973;

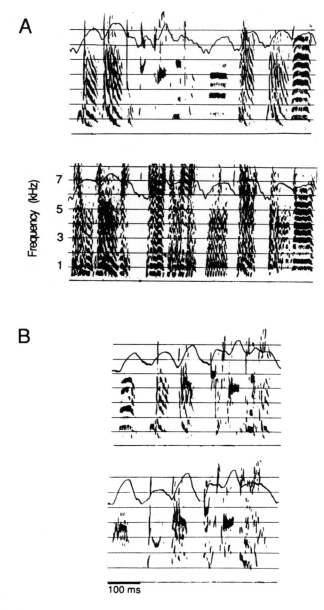

FIG. 4.10. Asymmetry in song deficits after left and right tracheosyringeal nerve section. A. Song of an adult zebra finch male as delivered
before and one day after surgical transection of the right tracheosyringeal nerve. Syllables in pre- and post-operative songs can be
matched by length, position, and amplitude profile (amplitude trace is

Nottebohm, 1971, 1972; Nottebohm & Nottebohm, 1976; Seller, 1979). Sectioning the right nerve has the greater effect upon the song of zebra finches, while the other species' songs are more affected by cutting the left nerve. The degree of difference in effect varies, as does the type of effect. In canaries, cutting the right nerve disrupts only a few components in a few syllables, while nearly all syllables are severely affected by cutting the left nerve (Nottebohm & Nottebohm, 1976). In zebra finches, cutting the right nerve results in a lower fundamental frequency and a reduction in frequency modulation for nearly all syllables, while the main effect of cutting the left is to emphasize higher-frequency elements within syllables (Fig. 4.10; Crane et al., 1984). Despite the interspecific variation in type of effect and side of the most prominent effect, the basic phenomenon is clear and constant: the innervation of one syringeal half is more important in the production of normal song.

Laterality is also seen in the central control of song production. Lesioning the left RA or HVc in canaries causes greater song deficits than does lesioning the corresponding nucleus on the right side (Nottebohm et al., 1976; Nottebohm & Nottebohm, 1976), and, as would be predicted from the results of nerve sections, this asymmetry occurs in the opposite direction in zebra finches (Crane et al., 1984). Central asymmetries are invariably less marked than the peripheral asymmetry: disparity in song deficits is greater after nerve cuts than after lesions of RA and HVc (Nottebohm, 1977). Stimulating HVc can result in weak responses in the contralateral tracheosyringeal nerve (Arnold, 1980b; Paton & Manogue, 1982); perhaps this slight bilaterality allows a bird with only one HVc to exert some control over the contralateral syringeal half, lessening the behavioral deficit relative to the complete loss of control that occurs when the nerve is cut.

Hemispheric dominance of song control can be reversed after surgical damage to the tracheosyringeal nerve or song nuclei on the dominant side (Nottebohm, Manning, & Nottebohm, 1979). Left nerve transections in young canaries result in right- rather than left-dominant song systems, and this result can be replicated in adult canaries that are allowed to survive for one full breeding cycle (or song learning cycle) after surgery (Nottebohm et al., 1979). Reversal of dominance after injury may depend upon the potential for continued learning. The relationship between the potential for central reorganization of hemispheric dominance and capacity for song learning could be tested in closed-ended learners such as the zebra finch.

---

shown by the plot between 5 and 8 kHz). After nerve section, syllable phonology is grossly altered, and fundamental frequency of most syllables has decreased. B. Song of a different adult male zebra finch before and one day after left tracheosyringeal nerve section. Deficits are much less marked than after right nerve section. The main effect upon phonology is a shifting of emphasis to higher-frequency components within a syllable.

These apparently clear-cut results showing asymmetry and lateralization of song production were called into question by the discovery that plugging one bronchus—stopping the air supply needed for phonation in one syringeal half—does not cause the marked song deficits seen after unilateral motor nerve section or song nucleus lesion (McCasland, 1983, 1987). In canaries, when airflow to either syringeal half is blocked, nearly all of the syllables are produced as in normal song, which can be interpreted as indicating that either the left and right song system alone is sufficient to produce normal song (McCasland, 1983, 1987).

This apparent contradiction can be resolved if the two-independent-voices model for song production is modified. Work in chickadees shows that many vocalizations are produced by using the physical coupling of the two syringeal halves; neither side alone can produce complete syllables, but the physical linkage of the two halves of the syrinx results in interactions between the motor commands sent along the left and right nerves (Nowicki & Capranica, 1986). This model has been tested in swamp sparrows by inserting bronchial plugs and subsequently cutting the opposite tracheosyringeal nerve (Nowicki, 1988). Either half of the syrinx is sufficient to produce a nearly intact song—but only if both halves are innervated (Nowicki, 1988). Firing patterns in the left and right tracheosyringeal nerves are different, but the resulting muscle contractions affect both sides of the syrinx, in some cases giving approximately the same vocal output from the left and right sides. Central neural asymmetry is then decreased in the periphery by the interactions of muscle contractions in physically linked syringeal halves.

Lateral asymmetry in the neural control of song production is revealed by analysis of the song, but no anatomical correlates of this asymmetry have yet been found. Although HVc volume is related to song repertoire size (Canady, Kroodsma, & Nottebohm, 1984; Nottebohm et al., 1981) left and right HVc and RA volumes are the same in canaries, zebra finches, and white-crowned sparrows (Arnold, 1980b; Baker, Bottjer, & Arnold, 1984; Nottebohm & Arnold, 1976; Nottebohm et al., 1981) and so do not reflect the hemispheric dominance of the behavior. Activity in HVc neurons during song production is equivalent in the left and right HVc (McCasland, 1983, 1987). The only known anatomical or physiological asymmetry is a 25-30% volume difference in the volume of the tracheosyringeal motor nucleus (Nottebohm and Arnold, 1976).

The coordination of the outputs from two systems for a single behavior is a problem for any incompletely lateralized behavior, such as birdsong, which is controlled to some degree by the non-dominant hemisphere. "Split-brain" patients provide extensive literature on an extreme example of the difficulties arising when two hemisphere cannot integrate activity or coordinate their output (see Sperry, 1974). Avian brains are acallosal, and song nuclei project only ipsilaterally (Nottebohm et al., 1976; Nottebohm et al., 1982). Yet song-related activity in the two hemispheres must be temporally matched so as to produce the

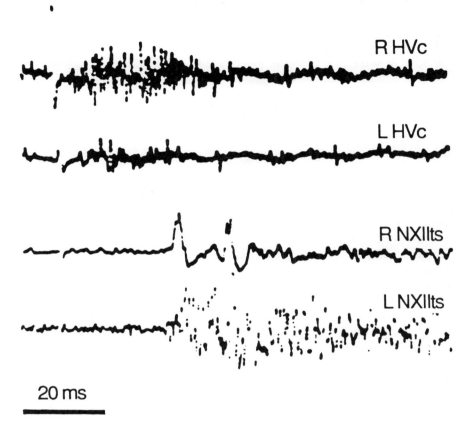

FIG. 4.11. Bilateral activation of the song system. Stimulating the right Uva elicits firing in the contralateral as well as the ipsilateral HVc. This activity is followed by volleys in both tracheosyringeal nerves.

exquisitely coordinated motor output. Input from Uva (see Fig. 4.8) may provide the timing signal which serves to coordinate song production: microstimulating Uva elicits activity in both ipsilateral and contralateral HVc neurons as well as in both tracheosyringeal motor nerves (Fig. 4.11; Williams, 1985a, 1985c). Again, there is no discernible difference in the effect of stimulating the left or the right Uva, except that latencies may differ slightly, reflecting a shorter ipsilateral pathway.

When laterality in the control of birdsong was first discovered, the avian brain seemed likely to provide a good model for studying questions such as the origins of cerebral dominance and its relationship with complex communication behaviors. Unlike the cerebral asymmetry associated with human speech (Geschwind & Levitsky, 1969), song lateralization has no obvious neural correlates, and all studies to date show only similarities in the left and right forebrain song nuclei. Perhaps the answer lies in more detailed study of the internal anatomy and connections of the song nuclei. Our understanding of the neural bases of lateralization in birdsong will remain limited until physical bases for asymmetry in the central song system are discovered.

MOTOR-AUDITORY INTERACTIONS

Auditory Responses in Song Nuclei

Song learning requires that the acoustic consequences of a motor output be matched to an auditory memory, a process that implicitly requires brain centers with access to both auditory and motor information. This line of reasoning guided the search for song control areas and led to the discovery of the HVc–RA–NXIIts pathway, the descending or motor branch of the song system (Nottebohm et al., 1976, see Fig. 4.8). Fibers from field L, the primary auditory area in the forebrain, terminate near HVc and RA (Kelley & Nottebohm, 1979), and HVc neurons fire in response to auditory stimuli (Katz & Gurney, 1981). HVc is necessary for song production, and so forms a link between the auditory and song motor systems.

Auditory responses can also be recorded from neurons in lMAN, DLM, area X, NIf, RA, as well as the tracheosyringeal motor nucleus, nXIIts (Fig. 4.12; Williams, 1985a, 1985b; Williams & Nottebohm, 1985). Auditory responsivity within song nuclei could result either from distinct auditory inputs to several song nuclei or from a restricted set of inputs, with dissemination of auditory information through projections within the song system.

Auditory units can be recorded in nuclei within the descending branch of the song system, NIf–HVc–RA–nXIIts (see Figs. 4.8 and 4.12) of awake as well as anesthetized animals (Williams, 1985a). Syringeal muscles as well as the motor neurons innervating those muscles show responses to auditory stimuli (Vicario, 1986). The timing of auditory response latencies within the descending branch of the song system is consistent with the hypothesis that auditory information cascades through the system (see Fig. 4.12). Lesion data support the same hypothesis: lesioning either HVc or RA eliminates the auditory responses downstream in the tracheosyringeal nerve (Fig. 4.13; Williams and Nottebohm, 1985).

There are two potential auditory inputs to HVc: a) the "shelf", an auditory area immediately underlying HVc and receiving inputs from field L (Kelley & Nottebohm, 1979), and b) NIf, a forebrain nucleus that projects to HVc, contains auditory units and might provide a second pathway for auditory input to HVc

Onset of tone burst

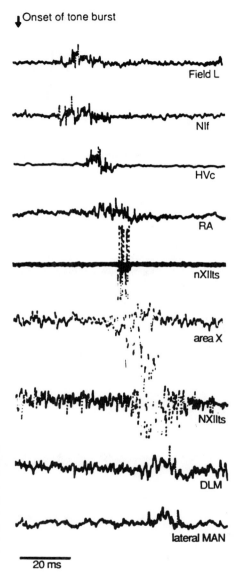

Field L

NIf

HVc

RA

nXIIts

area X

NXIIts

DLM

lateral MAN

20 ms

FIG. 4.12. Auditory responses in song nuclei. Responses to tone bursts as recorded at various locations in the song system (see Fig. 4.8). The traces are arranged according to the relationship among latencies, which remained constant between birds, though the absolute latencies varied.

(see Figs. 4.8 and 4.12). RA may also receive up to three auditory inputs. HVc neurons send terminals to RA; an area adjacent to RA, the "cup", is defined by anterograde tracers placed in field L (see Fig. 4.8; Kelley & Nottebohm, 1979); and neurons within lMAN, where auditory responses can be recorded (Fig. 4.12), synapse upon RA neurons (Canady et al., 1988; Nottebohm et al., 1982).

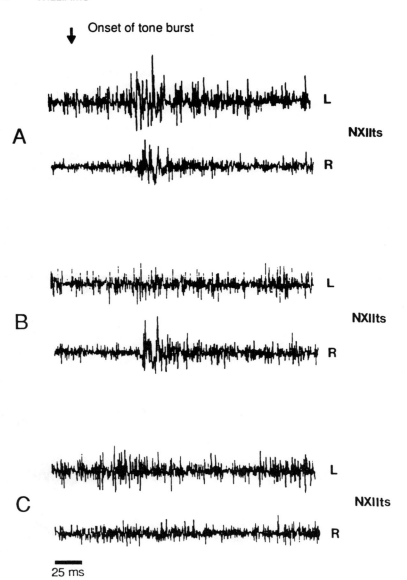

Onset of tone burst

FIG. 4.13.   HVc and RA lesions eliminate auditory responses in NXIIts. All traces shown in this figure represent the average of 10 stimulus presentations. Lesion sites were confirmed histologically. A. Auditory volleys are recorded in both tracheosyringeal nerves in the intact bird. B. After an electrolytic lesion in the left HVc, the auditory response in the ipsilateral NXIIts disappears. C. Subsequent to B, the right RA was lesioned, which eliminated the auditory response in the right NXIIts.

Because lesioning HVc eliminates auditory responses in the tracheosyringeal motor neurons (Fig. 4.13), the other two potential auditory inputs to RA are not sufficiently strong to transmit impulse to the tracheosyringeal motor neurons. However, secondary auditory inputs to RA could be inhibitory or weak relative to HVc inputs, and play a role in refining the selectivity of the auditory responses in RA projection neurons.

Neurons in nuclei of the recurrent loop of the song system, the HVc-area X-DLM-lateral MAN-RA pathway, also respond to auditory stimuli (Fig. 4.12). Latencies of auditory responses are longer at each succeeding nucleus in the pathway (see Figs. 4.8 and 4.12). Auditory responses within the recurrent branch of the song system are delayed with respect to those in the descending branch: for example, auditory activity is recorded in DLM in the song "motor" chain; auditory units in DLM fire after responses are recorded from the tracheosyringeal motor neurons.

Several loops, all responding to auditory stimulation, raise the possibility that multiple copies of auditory information exist. Each auditory stimulus might be split into several neural copies, processed by different pathways, and then converge upon the neurons within a single nucleus. One routing for auditory information would be the HVc-area X-DLM-lMAN-RA pathway; auditory neurons in HVc are thought to project to area X (Katz & Gurney, 1981) and auditory units can be recorded in all the nuclei in the pathway (Fig. 4.12). The long latency of auditory activity within DLM, a thalamic nucleus, raises the possibility that ascending afferents, either from collaterals within the motor nucleus[3] or from the syringeal muscles via spindle afferents (Bottjer & Arnold, 1984) might form a secondary loop, connecting auditory information as represented within descending branch of the song system to the thalamus, which could also receive auditory inputs from HVc via area X. Another possible auditory input to the recurrent loop would be secondary auditory projections from field L; such projections to areas in the anterior telencephalon, near lMAN, are known to exist in other species (Bonke, Bonke, & Scheich, 1979). Forebrain auditory connectivity is not well described beyond the secondary projections. Yet another point in the song system where multiple representations of song could coincide is RA. HVc sends a major input to RA which presumably carries information about both the auditory and motor aspects of song. Added to the HVc input is the potential auditory input from field L, as well as the projection from lMAN, which may also carry a complex auditory representation of song.

Comparisons of the latencies of auditory responses in the two main branches of the song system suggests that the two branches and their representations of auditory information may correspond to different functions. Characterizing the auditory information carried by each input to the song system and defining how

---

[3]Comparable to the connection between laryngeal motor neuron collaterals and Uva (Nottebohm et al., 1982).

those inputs are processed, compared, and converted to changes in motor output should provide important insights into the neural bases of memory-based learning.

Song-Specific Auditory Responses

The most intriguing work to date on the selectivity of the auditory units within the song system points to the bird's own song as a special stimulus. A small proportion of auditory neurons within HVc respond selectively to the frequency and timing characteristics of small segments of the bird's own song (Margoliash, 1983). Subsequent work recording multi-unit responses at many sites within HVc again showed a tendency for neurons to respond preferentially to the bird's own song as compared to a group of conspecific songs—although individual songs within that group were occasionally preferred to the bird's own song (Margoliash & Konishi, 1985; Margoliash, 1986).

Auditory processing may also take place at other sites within the song system, and forebrain centers that are not part of the song system may also have song-selective auditory neurons. No studies comparable to those of HVc auditory response specificity have been performed upon neurons in other song system nuclei, although recordings from the tracheosyringeal motor nucleus suggest that the degree of selectivity in the auditory responses recorded in HVc is at least maintained in the motor neurons (Williams & Nottebohm, 1985). The outlying portions of field L (L1 and L3) do not receive direct projections from the thalamic auditory relay nucleus and are thought to perform more complex auditory integration (Muller & Scheich, 1985). In starlings, mynahs, and Guinea fowl, some L1 and L3 neurons have auditory responses comparable in their specificity to the units described in HVc (Bonke, Scheich, & Langner, 1979; Langner, Bonke, & Scheich, 1981; Leppelsack, 1978; Leppelsack & Vogt, 1976; Scheich, Langner, & Bonke, 1979).

Developmental evidence supports the claim that song-specific responses are special to the song system. Selectivity for auditory stimuli that are similar to the bird's own song appears in HVc at the onset of plastic song (Volman & Konishi, 1987), when the process of matching an auditory model to vocal output begins. Circuits in HVc and, potentially, other song nuclei may perform specialized auditory processing functions specifically upon song stimuli. How neurons in these areas respond to a song stimulus would presumably depend upon the bird's vocal and auditory experience. The potential importance of a role in song learning for song-specific neurons that respond selectively to the bird's own song is obvious.

PRODUCTION OR PERCEPTION?

It is generally accepted that forming an auditory model for song and the subsequent matching of the vocal output to that auditory model is associated with changes in song-related brain structures. It has also been proposed that birds use the auditory circuitry within the song system in decoding song signals (Williams & Nottebohm, 1985; Margoliash, 1986). Such models define a second role for the song system—that of "special processor" for conspecific bird song (Marler & Peters, 1981b), forming the neural substrate for a motor theory of vocal perception (see Liberman et al., 1967). The argument for the use of the song system as an auditory processor is based upon three observations:

1. Auditory activity is found throughout the song system, including the motor neurons innervating the muscles of the vocal organ (Williams & Nottebohm 1985).

2. Auditory activity is inhibited within the song system of adult song birds during song motor activity—which means that singers cannot "hear" their own songs with their song system neurons (McCasland & Konishi, 1981; Williams, 1986).

3. New auditory neurons continue to be added to the adult male zebra finch HVc long after auditory feedback ceases to affect song production (Nottebohm, 1984; Nordeen & Nordeen, 1988).

Auditory responses in adult birds' song systems may merely be an epiphenomenon of the song learning process, but the inhibition of such activity specifically during song production (rather than the complete loss of auditory responsivity in the song system) and the continued incorporation of new auditory neurons into song system nuclei suggest that auditory responses in song system neurons continue to play some role in coordinating adults' behavior.

Two non-exclusive models for the song system as an auditory processor have been proposed.

1. Arguing from the preference of HVc neurons for auditory stimuli resembling the bird's own song, (Margoliash 1986; see also Margoliash & Konishi, 1985) suggested that a bird evaluates conspecific songs by comparing them to its own song. The bird's own song becomes the reference for evaluating all other songs.

2. The second model for the use of the song system as an auditory processor is more mechanistic. Auditory activity within the song system extends to the level of the tracheosyringeal motor neurons (Fig. 4.12, Williams & Nottebohm, 1985). These motor neurons are arranged in an orderly, somatotopic fashion within the motor nucleus (Vicario & Nottebohm, 1988). Auditory activity in the motor neurons causes contractions in the syringeal muscles; because these contractions are smaller than those that produce song and are not coupled with respiratory activity no vocalizations result (Vicario, 1986). Afferents from the syringeal muscles of zebra finches, possibly from muscle spindles, have cell bodies in the vagal ganglion and terminate upon nuclei of the ascending and descending trigeminal tract (Bottjer & Arnold, 1982). Reafference from the syringeal muscles is not necessary for song learning or for the maintenance of

song in adult zebra finches (Arnold and Bottjer, 1983; Bottjer & Arnold, 1984). It is possible, then, that this circuit (or a central collateral projection from nXIIts) serves to translate auditory information into a pattern of syringeal muscle contractions and so decode the acoustic stimulus into a series of vocal gestures. This model for the song system's function in song perception does not necessarily rely upon comparisons with the bird's own song. Instead, the bird could conceivably decode any sound for which his vocal apparatus has been calibrated. Calibration could be accomplished either by producing the sound (during subsong or plastic song) or by repeatedly "hearing" the sound with the song system. Newly born adult neurons might then play a role in recalibrating the system when new songs are heard during adulthood.

A combination of the two models is also possible; songs would be evaluated with respect to the bird's own song by being passed through the descending branch of the song system. Songs similar to the bird's own song would have particular salience for the system, but it could also evaluate a wide variety of conspecific song types. A bird's own song does seem to have special perceptual significance: in operant studies, zebra finches learn a song discrimination more rapidly if one of the songs is their own (Cynx & Nottebohm, 1989), and field studies of aggressive behavior in song sparrows, swamp sparrows, and redwinged blackbirds indicate that neighbors' songs, strangers' songs, and birds' own songs fall into distinct categories (MacArthur, 1986; Searcy, MacArthur, Peters, & Marler, 1981; Yasukawa, Bick, Wagman, & Marler, 1982). Yet some discriminations may require reference to standards other than the birds' own songs; zebra finches, although they only sing one song during their lifetime, live in an extremely varied song environment, and each breeding colony includes birds singing a diverse set of songs (Immelmann, 1969).

Special perception of song also predicts that lesioning central song nuclei should affect discrimination of song stimuli. Bilateral HVc lesions affect learning but not maintenance of a discrimination between two song syllables or songs (Cynx & Nottebohm, 1989). Testing zebra finches with lesions in other song nuclei on this song perception paradigm should show what regions of the song system are necessary for special perception of the bird's own song.

A model invoking the descending branch song system as a neural substrate for song perception predicts a sexual dimorphism in song perception. Auditory units occur in the HVcs of both male and female zebra finches (Fig. 4.14), but in females, the functional connection between HVc and RA is not made (Fig. 4.15; Konishi & Akutagawa, 1985; Williams, 1985b; but see also Arnold, 1980b). As a consequence, auditory information is not relayed to the syringeal motor neurons of adult female zebra finches (Williams, 1985b). If the descending motor pathway is used for song perception, male and female zebra finches should perceive conspecific song differently. Some evidence for sexual dimorphism in perception exists: female song sparrows attend more to the temporal structure of song than do males (Peters, Searcy, & Marler, 1980; Searcy, Marler, and Peters,

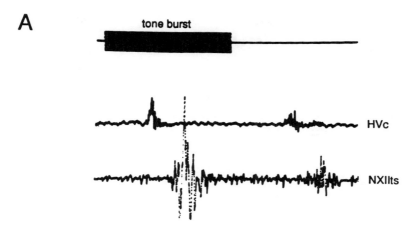

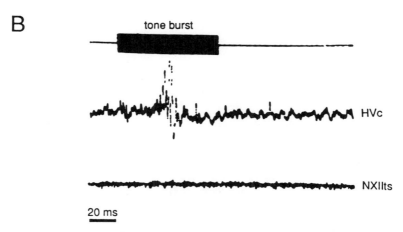

FIG. 4.14. Sexual dimorphism in auditory responses. A. "On" and "off" responses to a tone burst in the HVc and NXIIts of an adult male zebra finch. B. A tone burst played to an adult female zebra finch elicits a strong auditory response in HVc neurons, but no hint of an auditory response can be seen in the NXIIts recording. (After Williams, 1985b).

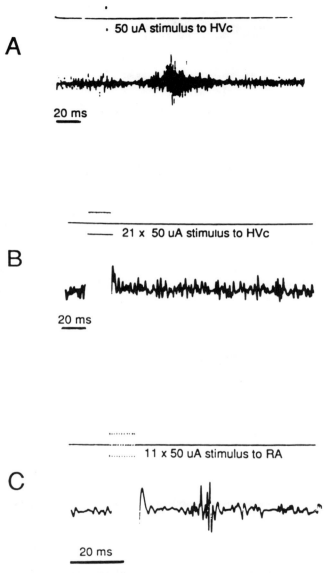

FIG. 4.15.   Sexual dimorphism in song system connectivity. A. A single 50 μA pulse delivered to HVc elicits a volley in the NXIIts of an adult male zebra finch. B. A stimulus train delivered to HVc in an adult female zebra finch fails to elicit any response to NXIIts. C. A stimulus train delivered to RA in the adult female zebra finch succeeds in generating a volley in NXIIts, indicating that the failure of HVc stimulation is due to the lack of a functional connection between HVc and RA in females. (After Williams, 1985b).

1981; Searcy, Balaban, Canady, Clark, Rumfeldt, & Williams, 1981), and female cowbirds are less flexible in their definition of conspecific song than are males (King & West, 1983, 1987; King, West, & Eastzer, 1986). Obtaining evidence for sexual dimorphism in perception has proven problematic. The difficulty may lie in finding suitable behavioral testing procedures or appropriate song parameters to test. A circularity which is basic to the problem complicates matters: we first need knowledge of how song is perceived by the birds so as to choose appropriate acoustic stimuli for testing how song is perceived by birds. A special processor for song implies perception using rules that will not be obvious to human researchers. Until we discover the mechanism birds' brains use in perceiving song, the organization of bird song and the information it carries may well remain opaque.

CONCLUSION

The extensive interdigitation of sensory and motor information in the bird brain's song system may reflect the special requirements a learned communication system makes upon neural circuitry. A sound signal transmitted by one individual and received by another has the same information content for both birds, but is represented in the brain of the sender as a series of motor commands and in the brain of the receiver as an acoustic waveform. Learning to produce a song that matches an auditory model is also a complex intertwining of sensory and motor functions. Thinking of "sensory" and "motor" systems in the context of the representation of bird song within the brain may not always be appropriate. Many neurons and most nuclei within the song system have both motor and sensory activity, and may best be thought of as coding for "song"—an entity which mingles both sets of properties.

However, the avian brain's representation of "song" is not an irreducible entity; it can be separated into components or modalities. Auditory inputs to the song system can be selectively and actively inhibited, making the descending branch of the song system, at least temporarily, a purely motor system. The song system can also become a purely auditory processor (activity in the syringeal motor neurons that is not appropriately coupled with respiratory activity does not yield a vocalization).

Interactions between auditory and motor modalities may form the basis for song learning. The overall course of song nucleus development is determined by the hormones present shortly after hatching, but auditory inputs shape the neural substrate to determine the form of the final song. A specific auditory input to a song nucleus at a given stage in development might trigger such neural events as expression of steroid receptors or axonal growth, or spare certain neurons from atrophy or death. Normal song development requires appropriate auditory inputs at appropriate stages, but is relatively independent of circulating hormones.

Intermingled auditory and motor modalities within the song system suggest a segmentation of song into components controlled by separate motor systems, perhaps in turn corresponding to perceptual components of song. The most basic distinction between separate song motor circuits is that between vocal organ and respiratory apparatus. Airflow through the vocal airway controls amplitude and syllable emphasis, defines the rhythm, and influences the fundamental frequency. The syringeal musculature defines frequency modulation and timbre and affects amplitude modulation, and upper airway articulators also influence timbre, helping to produce high notes. The left and right sides of the syrinx receive different motor commands. This plurality of song representations within motor circuits is most probably paralleled by multiple auditory representations, to some extent sharing the same song system circuitry.

What then might song's motor units tell us about its perceptual units? First, that each meaningful variation in syllable phonology may be controlled by a particular subset of vocal muscles or configuration of muscle contractions. Variation controlled by a discrete set of muscles or relationship among particular vocal muscles may then fall into a different perceptual category than a family of syllable variants controlled by a different set of muscles. Second, that song's sequence and timing are closely correlated with the pattern of airflow, which is controlled by an entirely different set of vocal muscles, and to some extent, by different neural circuits than those controlling phonology. Syllable order and temporal relationships between syllables would constitute a separate layer of motor control and hence of meaningful variation within bird song, and would be analyzed at a different level than the individual syllables.

Such a hierarchy of syllable and sequence, or phonology and syntax, recalls analyses of human language. In the avian brain, separate song systems exist within each hemisphere, and phonology and syntax are controlled by separate circuits. Motor and auditory modalities, however, are co-mingled throughout the song system. Perhaps the distinction between phonology and syntax is as salient to the neural circuitry for bird song as the distinction between production and perception. The neural substrate for song may be best seen as a special "communication" modality, encoding properties such as identity and intentionality rather than auditory and motor information.

ACKNOWLEDGMENTS

I thank Andrea de Majewski for help in assembling data and Patrick Dunlavey for assistance in figure preparation. Work reported here was supported by the Air Force Office of Scientific Research (AFOSR-86-0336) and P.H.S. award NS26825-01 supported the preparation of this manuscript.

REFERENCES

Adkins-Regan, E. (1987). Sexual differentiation in birds. *Trends in Neurosciences, 10,* 517–522.

Alvarez-Buylla, A., & Nottebohm, F. (1988). Migration of young neurons in the adult avian brain. *Nature, 335,* 353–354.

Alvarez-Buylla, A., Theelen, M., & Nottebohm, F. (1988). Birth of projection neurons in the higher vocal center of the canary forebrain before, during, and after song learning. *Proceedings of the National Academy of Sciences, 85,* 8722–8726.

Arnold, A. P. (1974). *Behavioral effect of androgen in zebra finches (Poephila guttata) and a search for its sites of action.* Unpublished doctoral dissertation, Rockefeller University, NY.

Arnold, A. P. (1975). The effects of castration and androgen replacement on song, courtship, and aggression in zebra finches (*Poephila guttata*). *Journal of Experimental Zoology, 191,* 309–326.

Arnold, A. P. (1980a). Effects of androgens on volumes of sexually dimorphic brain regions in the zebra finch. *Brain Research, 185,* 441–444.

Arnold, A. P. (1980b). Sexual differences in the brain. *American Scientist, 68,* 165–173.

Arnold, A. P. & Bottjer, S. W. (1983). Vocal learning in zebra finches: the role of hypoglossal afferent fibers. *Society for Neuroscience Abstracts, 9,* 537.

Arnold, A. P., Nottebohm, F., & Pfaff, D. W. (1976). Hormone concentrating cells in vocal control and other areas of the brain of the zebra finch (*Poephila guttata*). *Journal of Comparative Neurology, 165,* 487–512.

Baker, M. C., Bottjer, S. W., & Arnold, A. P. (1984). Sexual dimorphism and lack of seasonal changes in vocal control regions of the white-crowned sparrow brain. *Brain Research, 295,* 85–89.

Balthazart, J., Schumacher, M., & Pröve, E. (1986). Brain testosterone metabolism during ontogeny in the zebra finch. *Brain Research, 378,* 240–250.

Baptista, L. F., & Petrinovitch, L. (1986). Song development in the white-crowned sparrow: social factors and sex differences. *Animal Behaviour, 34,* 1359–1371.

Böhner, J. (1983). Song learning in the zebra finch (*Taenopygia guttata*): Selectivity in the choice of a tutor and accuracy of song copies. *Animal Behaviour, 31,* 231–237.

Bonke, B. A., Bonke, D., & Scheich, H. (1979). Connectivity of the auditory forebrain nuclei in the guinea fowl (*Numida meleagris*). *Cell and Tissue Research, 200,* 101–121.

Bonke, D., Scheich, H., & Langner, G. (1979). Responsiveness of units in the auditory neostriatum of the Guinea fowl (*Numida meleagris*) to species-specific calls and synthetic stimuli. I. Tonotopy and functional zones of field L. *Journal of Comparative Physiology A, 132,* 243–255.

Bottjer, S. W. (1987a). Ontogenetic changes in the pattern of androgen accumulation in song-control nuclei of male zebra finches. *Journal of Neurobiology, 18,* 125–139.

Bottjer, S. W. (1987b). Development of axonal connectivity in relation to a learned behavior. *Society for Neuroscience Abstracts, 12,* 1213.

Bottjer, S. W., & Arnold, A. P. (1982). Affeerent neurons in the hypoglossal nerve of the zebra finch (*Poephila guttata*): Localization with horseradish peroxidase. *Journal of Comparative Neurology, 210,* 190–197.

Bottjer, S. W., & Arnold, A. P. (1984). The role of feedback from the vocal organ. I. Maintenance of stereotypical vocalizations by adult zebra finches. *Journal of Neuroscience, 4,* 2387–2396.

Bottjer, S. W., Miesner, E. A., & Arnold, A. P. (1984). Forebrain lesions disrupt development but not maintenance of song in passerine birds. *Science, 224,* 901–903.

Bottjer, S. W., Glaessner, S. L., & Arnold, A. P. (1985). Ontogeny of brain nuclei controlling song learning and behavior in zebra finches. *Journal of Neuroscience, 5,* 1556–1562.

Bottjer, S. W., Miesner, E. A., & Arnold, A. P. (1986). Changes in neuronal number, size and density account for increases in volume of song-control nuclei during song development in zebra finches. *Neuroscience Letters, 67,* 263–268.

Bottjer, S. W., Schoonmaker, J. N., & Arnold, A. P. (1986). Auditory and hormonal stimulation interact to produce neural growth in adult canaries. *Journal of Neurobiology, 17*, 605–612.

Bottjer, S. W., Halsema, K. A., Brown, S. A., & Miesner, E. A. (1988). Axonal connections of a forebrain nucleus involved with vocal learning in zebra finches. *Journal of Comparative Neurology, 279*, 312–326.

Braun, K., Scheich, H., Schachner, M., & Heizmann, C. W. (1985). Distribution of parvalbumnin, cytochrome oxidase activity and 14C-2-deoxyglucose uptake in the brain of the zebra finch. I. Auditory and vocal motor system. *Cell and Tissue Research, 240*, 101–115.

Calder, W. A. (1970). Respiration during song in the canary (*Serinus canaria*). *Comparative Biochemistry and Physiology, 32*, 251–258.

Canady, R. A., Kroodsma, D. E., & Nottebohm, F. (1984). Population differences in complexity of a learned skill are correlated with the brain space involved. *Proceedings of the National Academy of Sciences, 81*, 6232–6234.

Canady, R. A., Burd, G. D., DeVoogd, T. J., & Nottebohm, F. (1988). Effect of testosterone on input received by an identified neuron type of the canary song system: a Golgi/EM/ degeneration study. *Journal of Neuroscience, 8*, 3770–3784.

Catchpole, C. K. (1982). The evolution of bird sounds in relation to mating and spacing behavior. In D. E. Kroodsma & E. H. Miller (Eds.), *Acoustic communication in birds: Vol. 1 Production, perception, and design features of sounds.* New York: Academic Press.

Clayton, D. F., Huecas, M. E., Sinclair-Thompson, E. Y., Nastiuk, K. L., & Nottebohm, F. (1988). Probes for rare mRNAs reveal distributed cell subsets in canary brain. *Neuron, 1*, 249–261.

Clayton, N. S. (1987). Song learning in cross-fostered zebra finches: a reexamination of the sensitive phase. *Behaviour, 102*, 67–81.

Crane, L. A., Price, P. H., & Nottebohm, F. (1984). *Right sided dominance for song control in the zebra finch.* Unpublished manuscript.

Cynx, J., & Nottebohm, F. (1989). Special processing in auditory perception: Song discrimination. *Association for Research on Otolaryngology Abstracts, 12*, 264.

DeVoogd, T. J., & Nottebohm, F. (1981). Gonadal hormones induce dendritic growth in the adult avian brain. *Science, 214*, 202–204.

DeVoogd, T. J., Nixdorf, B., & Nottebohm, F. (1985). Synaptogenesis and changes in synaptic morphology related to acquisition of a new behavior. *Brain Research, 329*, 304–308.

Dooling, R. J., & Searcy, M. (1980). Early perceptual selectivity in the swamp sparrow. *Developmental Psychobiology, 13*, 499–506.

Eales, L. A. (1985). Song learning in zebra finches: Some effects of song model availability on what is learnt and when. *Animal Behaviour, 33*, 1293–1300.

Falls, J. B. (1969). Functions of territorial song in the white-throated sparrow. In R. A. Hinde (Ed.), *Bird vocalizations.* Cambridge: Cambridge University Press.

Falls, J. B. (1982). Individual recognition by sound in birds. In D. E. Kroodsma & E. H. Miller (Eds.), *Acoustic communication in birds: Vol. 2. Song learning and its consequences.* New York: Academic Press.

Farner, D. S., & Serventy, D. L. (1960). The timing of reproduction of birds in the arid regions of Australia. *Anatomical Record, 137*, 354.

Gahr, M., Flugge, G., & Guttinger, H.-R. (1987). Immunocytochemical localization of estrogen-binding neurons in the songbird brain. *Brain Research, 402*, 173–177.

Gaunt, A. S. (1983). An hypothesis concerning the relationship of syringeal structure to vocal abilities. *Auk, 100*, 853–863.

Gaunt, A. S., Stein, R. C., & Gaunt, S. L. L. (1973). Pressure and air flow during distress calls of the Starling, *Sturnus vulgaris* (Aves: Passeriformes). *Journal of Experimental Zoology, 183*, 241–261.

Geschwind, N., & Levitsky, W. (1969). Human brain: left-right asymmetries in a temporal speech region. *Science, 161,* 186–187.

Gleich, O., & Narins, P. M. (1988). The phase response of primary auditory afferents in a songbird (*Sturnus vulgaris L.*) *Hearing Research, 32,* 81–92.

Goldman, S. A., & Nottebohm, F. (1983). Neuronal production, migration, and differentiation in a vocal control nucleus of the adult female canary brain. *Proceedings of the National Academy of Sciences, 80,* 2390–2394.

Goy, R. W., & McEwen, B. S. (1980). *Sexual differentiation of the brain.* Cambridge, MA: Massachusetts Institute of Technology Press.

Greenewalt, C. H. (1968). *Bird Song, acoustics, and physiology.* Washington, D.C.: Smithsonian Institution Press.

Gurney, M. E. (1981). Hormonal control of cell form and number in the zebra finch song system. *Journal of Neuroscience, 1,* 658–673.

Gurney, M. E. (1982). Behavioral correlates of sexual differentiation in the zebra finch song system. *Brain Research, 231,* 153–172.

Gurney, M. E., & Konishi, M. (1980). Hormone-induced sexual differentiation of brain and behavior in zebra finches. *Science, 208,* 1380–1383.

Hailman, J. P., Ficken, M. S., & Ficken, R. S. (1985). The 'chickadee' calls of *Pansatricapillus:* A recombinant system of animal communication compared with written English. *Semiotica, 56,* 191–224.

Hailman, J. P., Ficken, M. S., & Ficken, R. S. (1987). Constraints on the structure of combinatorial Chick-a-dee calls. *Ethology, 75,* 62–80.

Harding, C. F., Sheridan, K., & Walters, M. J. (1983). Hormonal specificity and activation of sexual behavior in male zebra finches. *Hormones and Behavior, 17,* 111–133.

Herrick, E. H., & Harris, J. O. (1957). Singing female canaries. *Science, 125,* 1299–1300.

Herrmann, K., & Bischof, H.-J. (1986). Delayed development of song control nuclei in the zebra finch is related to behavioral development. *Journal of Comparative Neurology, 245,* 167–175.

Hutchison, J. B., Wingfield, J. C., & Hutchison, R. E. (1984). Sex differences in plasma concentrations of steroids during the sensitive period for brain differentiation in the zebra finch. *Journal of Endocrinology, 103,* 363–369.

Immelmann, K. (1965). *Australian Finches in Bush and Aviary.* Sydney: Angus and Robertson.

Immelmann, K. (1969). Song development in the zebra finch and other estrildid finches. In R. A. Hinde (Ed.), *Bird vocalizations.* Cambridge: Cambridge University Press.

Katz, L. C., & Gurney, M. E. (1981). Auditory responses in the zebra finch's motor system for song. *Brain Research, 221,* 192–197.

Kelly, D. B., & Nottebohm, F. (1979) Projections of a telencephalic auditory nucleus—field L—in the canary. *Journal of Comparative Neurology, 183,* 455–470.

King, A. P., & West, M. J. (1983). Female perception of cowbird song: A closed developmental program. *Developmental Psychobiology, 16,* 335–342.

King, A. P., & West, M. J. (1987). Different outcomes of synergy between song production and song perception in the same subspecies (*Molothrus ater ater*). *Developmental Psychobiology, 20,* 177–187.

King, A. P., West, M. J., & Eastzer, D. H. (1986). Female cowbird song perception: Evidence for different developmental programs within the same subspecies. *Ethology, 72,* 89–98.

Konishi, M. (1965). The role of auditory feedback in the control of vocalizations in the white-crowned sparrow. *Zeitscrift für Tierpsychologie, 22,* 770–783.

Konishi, M., & Akutagawa, E. (1985). Neuronal growth, atrophy and death in a sexually dimorphic song nucleus in the zebra finch brain. *Nature, 315,* 145–147.

Korsia, S., & Bottjer, S. W. (1988). Chronic testosterone administration impairs vocal learning in male zebra finches. *Society for Neuroscience Abstracts, 14,* 285.

Kroodsma, D. E. (1986). Song development by castrated marsh wrens. *Animal Behaviour, 34*, 1572–1575.

Kroodsma, D. E., & Pickert, R. (1980). Environmentally dependent sensitive periods for avian vocal learning. *Nature, 288*, 477–479.

Kyriacou, C. P., & Hall, J. C. (1986). Interspecific genetic control of courtship song production and perception in *Drosophila. Science, 232*, 494–497.

Langner, G., Bonke, D., & Scheich, H. (1981). Neuronal discrimination of natural and synthetic vowels in field L of trained mynah birds. *Experimental Brain Research, 43*, 11–24.

Lemon, R. E. (1973). Nervous control of the syrinx in white-throated sparrows (*Zonotrichia albicollis*). *Journal of Zoology (London), 171*, 131–140.

Leppelsack, H. J. (1978). Unit responses to species-specific sounds in the auditory forebrain center of birds. *Federation Proceedings, 37*, 2336–2341.

Leppelsack, H. J., & Vogt, M. (1976). Responses of auditory neurons in the forebrain of a songbird to stimulation with species-specific sounds. *Journal of Comparative Physiology, 107*, 263–274.

Liberman, A. M., Cooper, F. S., Shankweiler, D. P., & Studdert-Kennedy, M. (1967). Perception of the speech code. *Psychological Reviews, 74*, 431–461.

MacArthur, P. D. (1986). Similarity of playback songs to self song as a determinant of response strength in song sparrows (*Melospiza melodia*). *Animal Behaviour, 34*, 199–207.

Manogue, K. R., & Paton, J. A. (1982). Respiratory gating of activity in the avian vocal control system. *Brain Research, 247*, 383–387.

Margoliash, D. (1983). Acoustic parameters underlying the responses of song-specific neurons in the white-crowned sparrow. *Journal of Neuroscience, 3*, 1039–1057.

Margoliash, D. (1986). Preference for autogenous song by auditory neurons in a song system nucleus of the white-crowned sparrow. *Journal of Neuroscience, 6*, 1643–1661.

Margoliash, D., & Konishi, M. (1985). Auditory representation of autogenous song in the song system of white-crowned sparrows. *Proceedings of the National Academy of Sciences, 82*, 5997–6000.

Marler, P. (1969). Tonal quality of bird songs. In R. A. Hinde (Ed.), *Bird vocalizations*. Cambridge: Cambridge University Press.

Marler, P. (1970). A comparative approach to vocal learning: Song development in white-crowned sparrows. *Journal of Comparative Physiology and Psychology, 71*, 1–25.

Marler, P. (1981). Birdsong: the acquisition of a learned motor skill. *Trends in Neurosciences, 4*, 88–94.

Marler, P., & Peters, S. (1977). Selective vocal learning in a sparrow. *Science, 198*, 519–521.

Marler, P., & Peters, S. (1981a). Sparrows learn adult song and more from memory. *Science, 213*, 780–782.

Marler, P., & Peters, S. (1981b). Birdsong and speech: Evidence for special processing. In P. Eimas & J. Miller (Eds.), *Perspectives on the study of speech*. Hillsdale, NJ: Lawrence Erlbaum Associates.

Marler, P., & Peters, S. (1982a). Structural changes during song ontogeny in the swamp sparrow *Melospiza georgiana. Auk, 99*, 446–458.

Marler, P., & Peters, S. (1982b). Developmental overproduction and selective attrition: New processes in birdsong epigenesis. *Developmental Psychobiology, 15*, 369–378.

Marler, P., & Pickert, R. (1984). Species-universal microstructure in the learned song of the swamp sparrow (*Melospiza georgiana*). *Animal Behaviour, 32*, 673–689.

Marler, P., Peters, S., & Wingfield, J. (1987). Correlations between song acquisition, song production, and plasma levels of testosterone and estradiol in sparrows. *Journal of Neurobiology, 18*, 531–548.

Marler, P., Peters, S., Ball, G. F., Dufty, A. M., & Wingfield, J. (1988). The role of sex steroids in the acquisition and production of birdsong. *Nature, 336*, 770–772.

McCasland, J. S. (1983). *Neuronal control of song production.* Unpublished doctoral dissertation, California Institute of Technology, Pasadena.

McCasland, J. S. (1987). Neuronal control of bird song production. *Journal of Neuroscience, 7,* 23–39.

McCasland, J. S., & Konishi, M. (1981). Interaction between auditory and motor activities in an avian song control nucleus. *Proceedings of the National Academy of Sciences, 78,* 7815–7819.

Miller, D. B. (1979a). The acoustic basis of mate recognition by female zebra finches (*Taenopygia guttata*). *Animal Behaviour, 27,* 376–380.

Miller, D. B. (1979b). Long-term recognition of father's song by female zebra finches. *Nature, 280,* 389–391.

Muller, S. C., & Scheich, H. (1985). Functional organization of the avian auditory field L. *Journal of Comparative Physiology A, 156,* 1–12.

Nordeen, K. W., & Nordeen, E. J. (1988). Projection neurons within a vocal motor pathway are born during song learning in zebra finches. *Nature, 334,* 149–151.

Nordeen, K. W., Nordeen, E. J., & Arnold, A. P. (1986). Estrogen establishes sex differences in androgen accumulation in zebra finch brain. *Journal of Neuroscience, 6,* 734–738.

Nordeen, E. J., Nordeen, K. W., & Arnold, A. P. (1987a). Sexual differentiation of androgen accumulation within the zebra finch brain through selective cell loss and addition. *Journal of Comparative Neurology, 259,* 393–399.

Nordeen, E. J., Nordeen, K. W., & Arnold, A. P. (1987b). Estrogen accumulation in the zebra song control nuclei: Implications for sexual differentiation and adult activation of song behavior. *Journal of Neurobiology, 18,* 569–582.

Nottebohm, F. (1968). Auditory experience and song development in the chaffinch, *Fringilla coe lebs. Ibis, 110,* 549–568.

Nottebohm, F. (1971). Neural lateralization of vocal control in a passerine bird. I. Song. *Journal of Experimental Zoology, 177,* 229–262.

Nottebohm, F. (1972). Neural lateralization of vocal control in a passerine bird. II. Subsong, calls, and a theory of vocal learning. *Journal of Experimental Zoology, 179,* 35–60.

Nottebohm, F. (1975). Vocal behavior in birds. In D. S. Farner & J. R. King, (Eds.), *Avian biology: Vol. 5.* New York: Academic Press.

Nottebohm, F. (1977). Asymmetries in neural control of vocalization in the canary. In S. Harnad, R. W. Doty, L. Goldstein, J. Jaynes, & G. Krauthamer (Eds.), *Lateralization in the nervous system.* New York: Academic Press.

Nottebohm, F. (1980a). Testosterone triggers growth of brain vocal control nuclei in adult female canaries. *Brain Research, 189,* 429–437.

Nottebohm, F. (1980b). Brain pathways for vocal learning in birds: A review of the first 10 years. In J. M. S. Sprague, & A. N. E. Epstein (Eds.), *Progress in Psychobiology and Physiological Psychology: Vol. 9.* New York: Academic Press.

Nottebohm, F. (1981). A brain for all seasons: Cyclical anatomical changes in song control nuclei of the canary brain. *Science, 214,* 1368–1370.

Nottebohm, F. (1984). Bird song as a model in which to study brain processes related to learning. *Condor, 86,* 227–236.

Nottebohm, F. (1987). Plasticity in adult avian central nervous system: possible relation between hormones, learning, and brain repair. In F. Plum (Ed.), *Section 1. Higher Functions of the Nervous System,* in V. Mountcastle (Chief Ed.), *Handbook of Physiology V. The Nervous System.* Washington, D.C.: The American Physiological Society.

Nottebohm, F., & Arnold, A. P. (1976). Sexual dimorphism in vocal control areas of the songbird brain. *Science, 194,* 211–213.

Nottebohm, F., & Nottebohm, M. (1976). Left hypoglossal dominance in the control of canary and white-crowned sparrow song. *Journal of Comparative Physiology, 108,* 171–192.

Nottebohm, F., Stokes, T. M., & Leonard, C. M. (1976). Central control of song in the canary, *Serinus canarius. Journal of Comparative Neurology, 165,* 457–486.

Nottebohm, F., Manning, E. & Nottebohm, M. (1979). Reversal of hypoglossal dominance in canaries following unilateral syringeal denervation. *Journal of Comparative Physiology, 134,* 227–240.

Nottebohm, F., Kasparian, S. & Pandazis, C. (1981). Brain space for a learned task. *Brain Research, 213,* 99–109.

Nottebohm, F., Kelley, D. B., & Paton, J. A. (1982). Connections of vocal control nuclei in the canary telencephalon. *Journal of Comparative Neurology, 207,* 344–357.

Nottebohm, F., Nottebohm, M., & Crane, L. (1986). Developmental and seasonal changes in canary song and their relation to changes in the anatomy of song-control nuclei. *Behavioral and Neural Biology, 46,* 455–471.

Nottebohm, F., Nottebohm, M., Crane, L., & Wingfield, J. C. (1987). Seasonal changes in gonadal hormone levels of adult male canaries and their relation to song. *Behavioral and Neural Biology, 47,* 197–211.

Nowicki, S. (1987). Vocal tract resonances in oscine bird sound production: Evidence from birdsongs in a helium atmosphere. *Nature, 325,* 53–55.

Nowicki, S. (1988). A comparison between the effects of syringeal denervation and airflow obstruction on songbird phonation. *Society for Neuroscience Abstracts, 13,* 89.

Nowicki, S., & Capranica, R. (1986). Bilateral syringeal interaction in vocal production of an oscine bird sound. *Science, 231,* 1297–1299.

Nowicki, S., & Marler, P. (1988). How do birds sing? *Music Perception, 5,* 391–426.

Okanoya, K., & Dooling, R. J. (1987). Hearing in passerine and psittacine birds: A comparative study of absolute and masked auditory thresholds. *Journal of Comparative Psychology, 101,* 7–15.

Okuhata, S., & Saito, N. (1987). Synaptic connections of thalamo-cerebral vocal nuclei of the canary. *Brain Research Bulletin, 18,* 35–44.

Paton, J. A., Burd, G. D., & Nottebohm, F. (1986). New neurons in an adult brain: Plasticity in an auditory–motor nucleus. In R. W. Ruben, E. Rubel, E., & T. van De Water (Eds.), *The biology of change in otolaryngology.* Amsterdam: Elsevier.

Paton, J. A., & Manogue, K. R. (1982). Bilateral interactions within the vocal control pathway of birds: Two evolutionary alternatives. *Journal of Comparative Neurology, 212,* 329–335.

Paton, J. A., & Nottebohm, F. (1984). Neurons generated in the adult brain are recruited into functional circuits. *Science, 225,* 1046–1048.

Paton, J. A., O'Loughlin, B. E., & Nottebohm, F. (1985). Cells born in adult canary forebrain are local interneurons. *Journal of Neuroscience, 5,* 3088–3093.

Pesch, A., & Güttinger, H. R. (1985). Der gesang des weiblichen Kanarienvogels. *Journal für Ornithologie, 126,* 108–110.

Peters, S. S., Searcy, W. A., & Marler, P. (1980). Species song discrimination in choice experiments with territorial male song and swamp sparrows. *Animal Behaviour, 28:* 393–404.

Pohl-Apel, G., & Sossinka, R. (1984). Hormonal determination of song capacity in females of the zebra finch: critical phase of treatment. *Zeitscrift für Tierpsychologie, 64,* 330–336.

Price, P. (1979). Developmental determinants of structure in zebra finch song. *Journal of Comparative Physiology and Psychology, 93,* 260–277.

Pröve, E. (1983). Hormonal correlates of behavioural development in male zebra finches. In J. Balthazart, E. Pröve, & R. Gilles (Eds.), *Hormones and behaviour in higher vertebrates.* Berlin, Heidelberg: Springer-Verlag.

Rausch, G., & Scheich, H. (1982). Dendritic spine loss and enlargement during maturation of the speech control system in the mynah bird (*Gracula religiosa*). *Neuroscience Letters, 29,* 129–133.

Searcy, W. A., Balaban, E., Canady, R. A., Clark, S. J., Runfeldt, S., & Williams, H. (1981). Responsiveness of male swamp sparrows to temporal organization of song. *Auk, 98,* 613–615.

Searcy, W. A., Macarthur, P. D., Peters, S. S., & Marler, P. (1981). Response of male song and swamp sparrows to neighbour, stranger, and self songs. *Behaviour, 77,* 152–163.

Searcy, W. A., Marler, P., & Peters, S. S. (1981). Species song discrimination in adult female song and swamp sparrows. *Animal Behaviour, 29,* 997–1003.

Seller, T. J. (1979). Unilateral nervous control of the syrinx in Java sparrows (*Padda oryzivora*). *Journal of Comparative Physiology, 129,* 281–288.

Scheich, H., Langner, G., & Bonke, D. (1979). Responsiveness of units in the auditory neostriatum of the guinea fowl (*Numida meleagris*) to species-specific calls and synthetic stimuli. II. Discrimination of iambus-like calls. *Journal of Comparative Physiology A, 132,* 257–276.

Silcox, A. P., & Evans, S. M. (1982). Factors affecting the formation and maintenance of pair bonds in the zebra finch, *Taenopygia guttata. Animal Behaviour, 30,* 1237–1243.

Sossinka, R., & Bohner, J. (1980). Song types in the zebra finch (*Poephila guttata castanotis*). *Zeitscrift für Tierpsychologie, 53,* 123–132.

Sperry, R. W. (1974). Lateral specialization in the surgically separated hemispheres. In F. O. Schmitt & F. G. Worden (Eds.), *The neurosciences. Third study program.* Cambridge, Ma.: Massachusetts Institute of Technology Press.

Suthers, R. A., & Hector, D. H. (1985). The physiology of vocalization by the echolocating oilbird. *Journal of Comparative Physiology A, 156,* 243–266.

Thorpe, W. H. (1958). The learning of song patterns by birds, with especial reference to the song of the chaffinch *Fringilla coelebs. Ibis, 100,* 535–570.

Vicario, D. (1986). Inputs to syringeal muscles in the zebra finch. *Society for Neuroscience Abstracts, 12,* 1538.

Vicario, D. S., & Nottebohm, F. (1988). Organization of the zebra finch song control system: I. Representation of syringeal muscles in the hypoglossal nucleus. *Journal of Comparative Neurology, 271,* 346–354.

Volman, S. F., & Konishi, M. (1987). Auditory selectivity in the song control nucleus HVc appears with the onset of plastic song. *Society for Neuroscience Abstracts, 12,* 870.

Warner, R. W. (1972). The anatomy of the syrinx in passerine birds. *Journal of Zoology, (London), 168,* 381–393.

Weichel, K., Schwager, G., Heid, P., Guttinger, H. R., & Pesch, A. (1986). Sex differences in plasma steroid concentrations and singing behaviour during ontogeny in canaries (*Serinus canaria*). *Ethology, 73,* 281–294.

Wild, J. M., & Arends, J. J. A. (1987). A respiratory-vocal pathway in the brainstem of the pigeon. *Brain Research, 407,* 191–194.

Williams, H. (1985a). *A motor theory for bird song perception.* Unpublished doctoral dissertation, The Rockefeller University, New York.

Williams, H. (1985b). Sexual dimorphism of auditory activity in the zebra finch song system. *Behavioral and Neural Biology, 44,* 470–484.

Williams, H. (1985c). Interhemispheric coordination of bird song. *Society for Neuroscience Abstracts, 11,* 871.

Williams, H. (1986). Modulation of the auditory and motor modes in the avian song system nucleus HVc. *Society for Neuroscience Abstracts, 12,* 315.

Williams, H., Cynx, J. & Nottebohm, F. (1988). "Timbre" control and discrimination in zebra finch song. *Society for Neuroscience Abstracts, 13,* 89.

Williams, H., Cynx, J., & Nottebohm, F. (in press). "Timbre" control in zebra finch song syllables. *Journal of Comparative Psychology.*

Williams, H., & Nottebohm, F. (1985). Auditory responses in avian vocal motor neurons: a motor theory for song perception in birds. *Science, 229,* 279–282.

Yasukawa, K, Bick, E. I., Wagman, D. W., & Marler, P. (1982). Playback and speaker-replacement experiments on song-based neighbor, stranger, and self discrimination in male red-winged blackbirds. *Behavioral Ecology and Sociobiology, 10,* 211–215.

Zann, R. (1984). Structural variation in the zebra finch distance call. *Zeitscrift für Tierpsychologie*, *66*, 328–345.

Zann, R. (1985). Ontogeny of the zebra finch distance call: I. Effects of cross-fostering to bengalese finches. *Zeitscrift für Tierpsychologie*, *68*, 1–23.

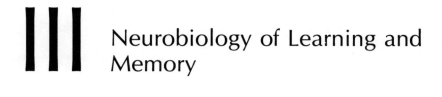

III Neurobiology of Learning and Memory

5 Representational Memory in Nonhuman Primates

Elisabeth A. Murray
National Institute of Mental Health

TWO INFORMATION STORAGE SYSTEMS

The modern era in the neuropsychology of primate learning and memory began 35 years ago with H.M., the patient who, in 1953, at the age of 27, underwent a bilateral resection of the medial temporal lobe in order to alleviate his intractable seizures (Milner, 1958; Scoville & Milner, 1957). The discovery that after surgery H.M. had an apparently pure and selective memory impairment, one affecting almost exclusively his ability to store new information, spurred research on the neural bases of memory in both human and nonhuman primates.

A wealth of data now indicates that damage to medial temporal lobe limbic structures in humans yields a global memory impairment, one that holds regardless of the sensory modality through which the information was perceived and the type of information to be remembered. Importantly, this memory deficit occurs in the absence of changes in perception or in other intellectual abilities, such as social skills and language.[1] Thus, the study of H.M. and other similar patients showed that a restricted set of brain structures was critical for information storage. In addition, however, amnesic patients were found to retain certain kinds of information, and it follows from these observations that there are at least two information storage systems in the primate brain. H.M. and other amnesic patients, while displaying rapid and near-complete forgetting of most events,

---

[1]This kind of deficit is quite different from those that might follow (a) neocortical damage, which characteristically produces material-specific memory impairments in addition to alterations in perception (see Newcombe & Ratcliff, 1979), or (b) damage to certain subcortical structures (see Cummings & Benson, 1984).

learn several tasks such as mirror drawing, mirror reading, eye-blink condition-ing, perceptual learning, and problem-solving tasks like the "Tower of Hanoi" at a normal rate (Cohen, Eichenbaum, DeAcedo, & Corkin, 1985; Corkin, 1968; Milner, 1962; Milner, Corkin, & Teuber, 1968; Weiskrantz, 1978). Furthermore, they exhibit normal cued recall and priming effects (Gordon, 1988; Warrington & Weiskrantz, 1970). Because the very same patients demonstrating the normal learning are unable to report *what* they have learned, and fail to recognize the experimenters and test situations, it has become clear that one of the memory systems can be accessed by the reporting systems of the brain, whereas the other(s) cannot (Cohen & Squire, 1980). In summary, one memory system is necessary for storing specific facts, episodes, and events, and is lost or severely compromised in amnesic patients, and the other system is critical for storing rules or procedures and is spared in amnesic patients.

The same two basic kinds of memory discussed above have also been de-scribed in nonhuman primates (Mishkin, Malamut, & Bachevalier, 1984; Mish-kin, Spiegler, Saunders, & Malamut, 1982; Zola-Morgan & Squire, 1984). For the purposes of this chapter, stored information about specific events and facts will be termed *representational memory* and stored information about rules will be referred to as *procedural memory*. Representational memory in other mne-monic frameworks has been identified as declarative, or simply (cognitive) "memory", whereas procedural memory in other frameworks has been labeled dispositional or skill memory, or habits (Cohen & Squire, 1980; Mishkin, Mal-amut, & Bachevalier, 1984; Thomas, 1984). These alternative labels are men-tioned in order to relate the present description of the organization of memory to that of others; the relative virtues of these various labels will not be discussed in detail. Representational memory in both human and nonhuman primates depends critically upon certain medial temporal lobe limbic structures, whereas pro-cedural memory does not. Other information storage systems may well exist (see Thompson et al., 1984; Tulving, 1987; Weiskrantz, 1987 for further discussion), but there is no consensus yet for a classification scheme that extends beyond that outlined previously.

Representational memory probably provides us with much of the meaning in our lives. For example, this kind of memory is employed when we plan future actions and when we associate the "what", "where", and "when" of events. So the medial temporal lobe limbic structures, by virtue of their critical role in forming representational memories, allow organisms to identify and attach meaning to objects in their environment. The remainder of this chapter focuses on the organization of representational memory.

NEURAL CIRCUITS SUBSERVING REPRESENTATIONAL MEMORY IN MONKEYS

A large number of experiments examining the neural basis of visual recognition memory in monkeys have indicated that many interconnected structures participate in memory processes. Combined removal of, or damage to, the amygdala and hippocampus, two limbic structures located in the medial temporal lobe, produces profound memory deficits in macaque monkeys, whereas removal of only one of these structures produces a milder impairment (Mishkin, 1978; Murray & Mishkin, 1984; Squire & Zola-Morgan, 1985). Furthermore, combined damage to the main thalamic targets of the amygdalar and hippocampal projections, the medial portion of the medial dorsal nucleus and the anterior nuclear complex, respectively, likewise leads to severe memory impairments, with damage to each thalamic region alone producing less severe impairment (Aggleton & Mishkin, 1983a, 1983b). It has been proposed, therefore, that two parallel limbo-diencephalic circuits, one an amygdalo-thalamic and one a hippocampo-thalamic circuit, support representational memory processes. Interruption of either of these circuits, either by removal of a structure or by interruption of the fibers that are interconnecting the limbic and diencephalic structures, will lead to a memory impairment. Disruption of both circuits leads to a more severe memory deficit than disruption of only one (Bachevalier, Parkinson, & Mishkin, 1985; Mishkin, 1982). Recently, these memory circuits have been found to include both the ventromedial prefrontal cortical targets of the medial dorsal nucleus, part of the amygdalar system, and the anterior group of thalamic nuclei, part of the hippocampal system (Bachevalier & Mishkin, 1986).

CLASSES OF REPRESENTATIONAL MEMORY

Despite the apparent ability of each structure to compensate for the loss of the other in certain tasks, the amygdalar and hippocampal contributions to representational memory in primates are beginning to be dissociated. This chapter considers three provisional categories of representational memory, each subserved by distinct neural mechanisms:

1. *Intramodal memory*—memories derived from a single sensory modality.
2. *Intermodal* or *crossmodal memory*—memories combining information from two or more sensory modalities.
3. *Supramodal memory*—memories of information derived from but not directly a reflection of any sensory modality.

Briefly, this classification scheme is derived from evidence that specific neural structures make independent contributions to memory, contributions that appear to fall into the categories proposed above.

Intramodal Memory

Intramodal memory refers to information storage/retrieval that concerns only the sensory modality in which the information was originally perceived. This kind of sensory memory may take the form of either stimulus recognition or stimulus–stimulus association. *Recognition memory* is reflected in the ability of subjects to judge familiarity of previously sensed stimulus material. The most common form of recognition occurs when the subject literally experiences again (or "knows" again) a stimulus or sensory event via the same sensory apparatus as before. Alternatively, the subject may recall previously perceived stimulus material. *Intramodal associative memory* involves the linking of two different stimulus items that are perceived in the same sensory modality. An example of this kind of memory would be the association formed between the appearance of a person and the color of the shirt they are wearing that day, or between the visual appearance of a walnut shell and the appearance of the walnut itself.

Recognition Memory.   Studies of the neural substrates of visual recognition memory in nonhuman primates have been carried out primarily in rhesus and cynomolgus macaques, and recognition memory is usually assessed through use of the delayed matching-to-sample (DMS) or delayed nonmatching-to-sample (DNMS) task employing trial-unique objects (see Gaffan, 1974; Mishkin & Delacour, 1975). In DNMS each trial is composed of two parts, a sample presentation and a choice test. For the sample presentation, the monkey displaces an object overlying the central well of a three-well test tray in order to obtain a food reward. Ten seconds later, on the choice test, the animal is confronted with the sample and a novel object, now overlying the lateral wells of the test tray, and the monkey must choose the novel object in order to obtain another food reward. The use of this task is based on the assumption that the subject stores information about the stimulus material over the delay that intervenes between the sample presentation and the choice test. At the time of the choice test, the subject is reinforced for discriminating the familiar from the novel item, and applying either the rule "approach the novel object" or "avoid the familiar object." Because new objects are used on every trial, cues based on reward history are unavailable, and because the left–right position of the correct object is randomized, position is irrelevant; the only relevant cues available to guide choice behavior are the familiarity/novelty of the items and the memory of the rule that led to reinforcement (nonmatching or novel stimulus rewarded) on previous trials.

As indicated earlier, combined but not separate removals of the amygdalar complex and hippocampal formation in monkeys yields a severe impairment on delayed nonmatching-to-sample when the delays between the sample presentation and choice test are more than 10 seconds or so. This memory impairment has been found for both the visual and tactual sensory modalities (Murray & Mishkin, 1984), a finding which suggests that the memory impairment in monkeys with damage to the medial temporal lobe structures, like that in humans with similar damage, transcends sensory modality. Although a number of experiments have suggested that the amygdala and hippocampus make roughly equal contri-

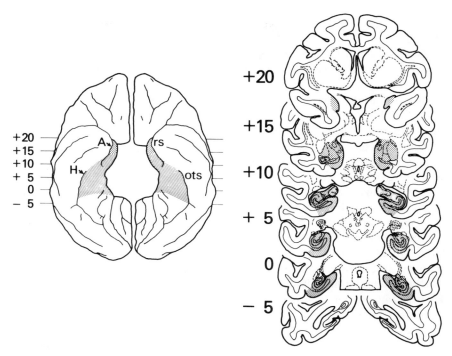

FIG. 5.1.   Schematic diagram of amygdalar removal (stipple) and hippocampal removal (oblique hatching) on a ventral view of a rhesus
monkey brain (left) and on standard coronal sections (right). Numerals
indicate the distance in mm from the interaural plane (0). Note that the
amygdalar removals include not only the amygdalar complex, but also
approximately the rostral half of the entorhinal cortex (tissue occupying the medial bank and lying medial to the rhinal sulcus). Similarly,
the hippocampal removals include not only the hippocampal formation, but also approximately the caudal half of the entorhinal cortex
and the parahippocampal gyrus (tissue medial to the occipitotemporal
sulcus). Abbreviations: A, amygdalar removal; H, hippocampal removal; rs, rhinal sulcus; ots, occipitotemporal sulcus.

butions to recognition memory (Mishkin, 1978; Murray & Mishkin, 1984; Saunders, Murray, & Mishkin, 1984) the lesions in those studies included not only the
structures of interest (e.g., the amygdalar complex and hippocampal formation),
but also small portions of the surrounding periallocortex and neocortex that are
removed to gain access to these structures. Thus, ever finer analyses will be
required to identify the contributions of the amygdalar complex and hippocampal
formation as distinct from those of the surrounding cortical areas such as the
entorhinal cortex, perirhinal cortex, periamygdalar cortex, and cortex of the
parahippocampal gyrus (see Fig. 5.1). Experiments examining these issues are

underway (Murray, Bachevalier, & Mishkin, 1985; Zola-Morgan, Squire, & Amaral, 1984, 1988).

One factor complicating the analysis of the hippocampal contribution to recognition memory is that Mahut, Zola-Morgan, & Moss (1982) and Zola-Morgan and Squire (1986; see also Squire & Zola-Morgan, 1985) have found an apparently more severe memory deficit in monkeys following hippocampectomy than have Mishkin (1978) and Murray and Mishkin (1984, 1986). This apparent difference in effects of hippocampal ablations across laboratories is accompanied by laboratory differences in test procedures, one of which (length of preoperative training) appears to be inversely correlated with the size of the impairment (see Murray & Mishkin, 1984; Zola-Morgan & Squire, 1986, for discussion). On average, monkeys without preoperative training on the nonmatching rule show larger differences in percent correct responses relative to controls than animals with preoperative training (see Table 5.1). Variables such as the species employed and the number of objects employed in testing may influence scores, but none appear so clearly related to the outcome as the amount of preoperative training. In addition, differences in surgical technique or extent of the lesion cannot account for the differences in results because monkeys operated by Mishkin and Murray but trained by Zola-Morgan and Squire performed about the same as animals operated on *and* trained by Zola-Morgan and Squire (1986). Furthermore, in support of the hypothesis concerning the relationship between extent of preoperative training and postoperative performance on recognition memory, experiments examining the effects of fornix transection yield a pattern of results similar to that seen following hippocampectomy. Again, animals with no preoperative training in visual recognition show larger differences in percent correct responses relative to controls than animals with such training (see Table 5.1). The use of a limited set of 200 or 300 objects is unlikely to account for the relatively poor scores of the fornix transected monkeys in Gaffan's (1974) study; in another study employing a small set size and hippocampectomy (Murray & Mishkin, 1984) the monkeys performed quite well. In addition, the poor scores of the fornix-transected monkeys in Gaffan's study are unlikely to be due to the use of the *matching* rule, because a direct comparison of the effects of fornix transection on performance in DNMS and DMS paradigms yielded no significant difference (Bachevalier, Saunders, & Mishkin, 1985).

Clearly, however, preoperative training is related to at least two phenomena. First, perhaps not surprisingly, it leads to higher overall scores for both operated and unoperated groups. Second, as already indicated, the amount of preoperative training appears to be inversely correlated to the magnitude of the experimental versus control differences in percent correct responses. Indeed, the study employing the most preoperative training (Murray & Mishkin, 1984) has the highest scores and the smallest difference between groups in percent correct responses; studies employing no preoperative training (Gaffan, 1974; Mahut, Zola-Morgan, & Moss, 1982; Zola-Morgan & Squire, 1986) have the lowest scores and the largest differences between groups in percent correct responses.

TABLE 5.1

Study	Species	Pre-op Training (Training History) Task	Test Condition	Performance Scores		Loss in %	Loss in d'
				Con	Expt		
Hippocampectomy vs. Control							
Mahut et al., 1982	M. mulatta	None (Sophisticated) DNMS[1]	60-70s 120-130s LL10	94 95 85	83 78 62	11 17 23	0.64 0.87 0.72
Zola-Morgan and Squire, 1986	M. fascicularis	None (Naive) DNMS[2]	60-70s 120-130s LL10	87 — —	76 — —	11 — —	0.39 — —
Mishkin, 1978	M. mulatta	Basic task, 10s delay (Naive) DNMS[2]	60-70s 120-130s LL10	99 97 92	94 91 81	5 6 11	0.80 0.60 0.55
Murray and Mishkin, 1984	M. fascicularis	Basic task plus longer delays (Naive) DNMS[3]	60-70s 120-130s LL10	"99.75" "99" —	99 95 —	0.75 4 —	0.48 0.68 —
Murray and Mishkin, 1986[4]	M. fascicularis	Basic task, 10s delay DNMS[2]	60-70s 120-130s LL10	95 94 85	86 85 75	9 9 10	0.52 0.59 0.36
Fornix Transection vs. Control							
Gaffan, 1974	M. mulatta	None (Naive) DMS[1]	60-70s 120-130s LL10	95 96 80	75 65 50	20 31 30	0.98 1.36 0.84
Mahut et al., 1982	M. mulatta	None (Sophisticated) DNMS[1]	60-70s 120-130s LL10	94 95 85	90 92 77	4 3 8	0.28 0.24 0.30
Bachevalier et al., 1985	M. mulatta	Basic task, 10s delays (Naive) DNMS[2]	60-70s 120-130s LL10	99 97 92	98 93 82	1 4 10	0.28 0.40 0.49

Summary of studies examining the effects of hippocampal-system damage on recognition memory.
Notes: Test conditions indicate delay between sample presentation and choice test in seconds (s) or list length (LL) of objects to-be-remembered. Con. = control group; Expt = experimental group. Numerals in quotations are estimates of what concurrently running control group might have achieved. d' values were obtained from Ringo (1988 and personal communication).
[1]Objects appeared in one trial per week
[2]Objects were trial unique
[3]Objects appeared in one trial per day
[4]Monkeys received ablations of hippocampal formation plus rhinal cortex.

As discussed by Ringo (1988), however, comparisons across different portions of the percentage scale are an inadequate method of comparing data from different laboratories. Ringo therefore reanalyzed the recognition memory data by converting differences in percent correct values to differences in detectability, the d' of signal detection theory, some of which are shown in Table 5.1. The mean detectability differences in the studies employing hippocampal ablations range from about .39 to .74, and do not differ significantly across laboratories (Ringo, 1988), a finding that indicates that the effects of hippocampal ablations on visual recognition are roughly equal across laboratories (Ringo, 1988). In Table 5.1, the only outlier in terms of detectability is the Gaffan study. In his study (Gaffan, 1974) the various delays were mixed within sessions whereas, in all the other studies, the delays were constant within a session. There is evidence from other work (D. Gaffan, E. A. Gaffan, & Harrison, 1984) that fornix-transected monkeys are more sensitive to changes of procedure than intact animals, so Gaffan's test methods may account for the poorer performance of the fornix-transected monkeys in his study relative to those in the other experiments listed in Table 5.1.

Recently, Zola-Morgan, Squire, and Amaral suggested that the amygdalar complex itself might not be contributing to recognition memory. Instead, they propose that the perirhinal and entorhinal cortical areas surrounding the amygdala are responsible for the behavioral effects of aspiration lesions of the amygdala (Zola-Morgan, Squire, & Amaral, 1989). This suggestion is based on the findings that: a) radiofrequency lesions of the amygdala, which spare the surrounding tissue, have little or no effect on DNMS performance (Zola-Morgan, Squire, & Amaral, 1989), whereas aspiration lesions of the amygdala, which do include such tissue, have a larger effect on DNMS performance (Mishkin, 1978; Murray & Mishkin, 1984), and b) radiofrequency lesions of the amygdala combined with hippocampectomy do not yield any greater impairment in recognition than hippocampectomy alone (Zola-Morgan, Squire, & Amaral, 1989). It is not yet clear whether differences in the lesions, the test procedures, or both might account for interlaboratory differences in effects of amygdalectomy on recognition memory, and resolution of these issues will require additional study.

For the remainder of this chapter, the cortex that surrounds the amygdala will be considered as if it were part of the amygdalar complex. The amygdalar removals discussed below thus include not only the amygdalar complex, but also roughly the rostral half of the entorhinal cortex, and the periamygdalar cortex as well (see Fig. 5.1). Behavioral effects may therefore be attributable to the removal of either the amygdalar complex itself, the surrounding cortical fields, or both. Similarly, the hippocampal removals include not only the hippocampal formation (hippocampus, dentate gyrus, and subfields of the subiculum), but also the caudal half of the entorhinal cortex and a large portion of the parahippocampal gyrus (see Fig. 5.1). Like the behavioral effects of amygdalectomy, those of hippocampectomy may be attributable to any one of the structures removed, or to some combination thereof.

Associative Memory.   One kind of task that has been successfully employed to examine associative memory in monkeys is the conditional discrimination (see D'Amato, Salmon, Loukas, & Tomie, 1985; Dewson & Burlingame, 1975). In tasks of this sort, cues must be used to guide choice behavior, and the animal must learn the correct cue–choice relations. For example, if *A* is present, or if *A* is a sample, choose *1* on a choice test where *1* and *2* are available. And if *B* is present, or if *B* is a sample, then choose *2* on the choice test instead of *1*. Conditional tasks of many types are possible if one varies the sensory modalities employed for cue and choice (e.g., visual–visual, visuo–motor, visuo–spatial, and auditory–visual conditional tasks, etc.). To evaluate intramodal associative memory, the sensory modality of the cue and choice must be one and the same, and to evaluate crossmodal associative memory, the sensory modalities of the cue and choice must be different. The latter kind of conditional task is discussed later, in the section on crossmodal memory.

The basic requirements of a conditional discrimination are that two or more pairs of stimuli are employed, and that the correct choice cannot be determined on the basis of its reward history (see Petrides, 1986, for discussion). In practice, this latter requirement means that the task must employ symmetrical reward. In order to evaluate the ability of an animal to link sensory events, which might be either arbitrary or naturally-occurring, one could measure the trials and errors required to learn a conditional task. In addition, pre-exposure to the correct sensory–sensory linkage may be employed. Clearly, an animal cannot use simple stimulus memory of the sample item (as in recognition memory) nor simple stimulus–response learning (as in traditional discrimination learning) to perform a conditional discrimination. Presumably, the only manner in which an animal can successfully perform this kind of task is to link specific stimuli with other stimuli (or responses) in memory. One possible alternative solution, however, is for the animal to learn a complex chain of sensory events and the response that produces reward in that situation. That is, the sequence of sample stimulus, say *A*, together with a particular set of choice stimuli, say *1* and *2*, would yield reward only if the animal chose stimulus *1*. This would reduce the solution of the task to a kind of complex discrimination learning. Although this solution is theoretically possible and cannot be ruled out as a potential learning mechanism, it would probably be very inefficient due to the animal's having to learn so many combinations of stimulus–stimulus–response chains. If a given brain lesion produces an impairment in acquisition of a conditional task, then one must still rule out deficits in perception, discrimination, and immediate memory as possible reasons for the impairment to arrive at the conclusion that the deficit is specifically in the animal's ability to link sensory stimuli with one another.

Although conditional tasks have often been employed to analyze the functions of the premotor and periarcuate cortex (Halsband & Passingham, 1985; Passingham, 1985; Petrides, 1982, 1987), only in the last few years have investigators attempted to train monkeys on conditional tasks for the purpose of analyzing the contributions of limbic structures to memory (Gaffan & Harrison, 1989a;

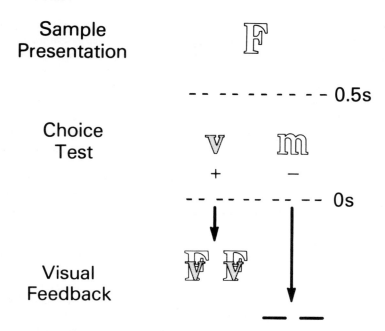

FIG. 5.2.   Schematic diagram of a trial in the visual–visual conditional task, which is run in an automated apparatus. The stimuli are 2-dimensional ASCII characters of various colors that appear on a monitor fitted with a touch-sensitive screen. When the monkey touches the sample stimulus, which is located in the center of the screen, it disappears. Half a second later two different stimuli appear on the sides of the screen for choice. Following a correct response, the monkey receives a food reward and positive visual feedback consisting of the superimposed visual–visual associates, whereas, following an incorrect response, the screen goes blank. *"v"* is the correct choice on this trial because the arbitrarily assigned paired associates for this task are: *F* and *v, m* and *l, ?* and *Y,* etc.

Murray, Davidson, Gaffan, Olton, & Suomi, 1989; Rupniak & Gaffan, 1987). Recently, visual–visual conditional discriminations have been employed to examine the neural substrates of intramodal associative memory in monkeys (Murray, Gaffan, & Mishkin, 1988). At the beginning of the experiment 20 different stimuli were arbitrarily divided into 10 pairs, which comprised the visual–visual associations that naive rhesus monkeys were required to learn. The experiment was run in an automated apparatus in which the monkeys viewed 2-dimensional stimuli on a color monitor. As illustrated schematically in Fig. 5.2, on any given trial, one of these 20 stimuli was presented as a sample and then, 0.5 seconds later, two stimuli that differed from the sample and from each other were presented for choice. One of these stimuli was the paired associate (correct choice) and the other was a distractor (incorrect choice). The distractor was always the member of another pair of visual–visual associates, and the presentation of the different stimuli was balanced within test sessions. Consequently, the two stimuli available for choice were approximately equally associated with reward. After the monkeys had learned the 10 visual–visual associations, they received ablations of either the amygdalar complex, the hippocampal formation, or both, and were then tested for retention of the preoperatively learned pairs and learning of new visual–visual pairs. The preliminary results suggest that combined but not separate ablations of the amygdala and hippocampus produce a severe deficit in retention of the associations (Murray, Gaffan, & Mishkin, 1988). Furthermore, combined removal of the two limbic structures severely compromises the monkeys' ability to learn new visual–visual associations, whereas removal of either structure alone has no effect. So it appears that for intramodal associative memory, as was the case for recognition memory, the amygdalar and hippocampal systems together are critically important, and that one of the systems can, to a large extent, compensate for loss of the other.

Crossmodal Memory

Crossmodal memory refers to the linking of stored sensory events that are perceived via two or more different sensory modalities. This kind of associative memory presumably is employed when we recall, upon hearing someone's voice, the appearance of that person, or when we imagine, upon smelling an odor, the possible source of that odor. For present purposes, crossmodal memories can be divided into two broad categories: (a) sensory–sensory associations, which are linkages of two or more sensory events derived from the different traditional senses (vision, touch, audition, etc.) and (b) sensory–affective associations, which are linkages of specific sensory events with affective qualities or states. Details concerning these two kinds of memory and how they may be evaluated are provided below.

Sensory–Sensory Associations.   Recent experiments have suggested that although the amygdalar and hippocampal systems together make essential contributions to intramodal memory, they may make selective contributions to other sorts of memory (Murray & Mishkin, 1985; Parkinson, Murray, & Mishkin, 1988). Specifically, it has been suggested that the amygdala but not the hippocampus is critical for crossmodal sensory–sensory associations. To evaluate the neural basis for crossmodal associative memory, monkeys were given a conditional discrimination, the form of which was described earlier, in which the sample and choice stimuli are presented in different sensory modalities. A typical trial is illustrated in Fig. 5.3. The monkeys were required to feel and displace a sample object in the dark, where only tactile cues could be obtained, and then, a few seconds later, were asked to choose, using vision only, between that same

Tactual to Visual DNMS

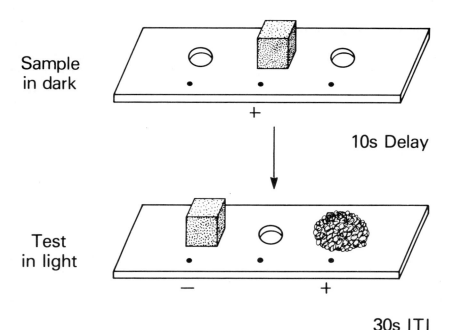

FIG. 5.3. Schematic diagram of a trial in the tactual–to–visual cross-modal nonmatching-to-sample task (Murray & Mishkin, 1985). The sample presentation (top) takes place in the dark, but the choice test (bottom) takes place in the light. To help orient the monkey in the dark, the location of the sample was indicated by a light-emitting diode that was recessed in the test tray in front of the object. See text for description of task.

object and another (Murray & Mishkin, 1985). The monkeys could obtain a food reward by choosing the object that was not the sample. Presumably the monkeys had learned, either during their long period of training with the limited set of objects, or by transfer from even earlier experience, to associate the visual and tactile qualities of these objects. When confronted with the crossmodal task they could then recall, given the tactile sample, the visual qualities of that object in order to avoid it on the choice test. Interestingly, monkeys that had received amygdalectomy performed extremely poorly on this task, whereas monkeys that had received hippocampectomy performed quite well (Fig. 5.4). Furthermore, both groups of monkeys demonstrated good intramodal performance when re-

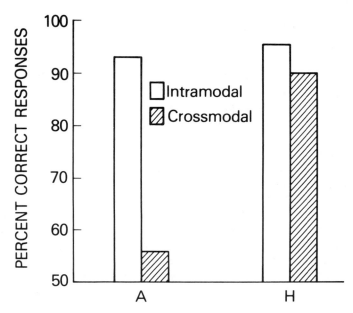

FIG. 5.4.   Effects of amygdalar removals alone and hippocampal removals alone on performance on the crossmodal task (shaded bars) compared with performance on the intramodal tasks (open bars: group mean scores on visual *and* tactile DNMS). All testing employed the same stimuli, test apparatus, and delay (10 sec) between sample presentation and choice test. Intramodal scores are based on 200 trials per monkey, and crossmodal scores are based on 500 trials per monkey. Abbreviations: A, amygdalectomized monkeys (*n*=3); H, hippocampectomized monkeys (*n*=3).

quired to remember the same stimuli for short periods of time, regardless of whether the to-be-remembered stimuli were presented for tactile recognition or visual recognition. Thus, the impairment of the amygdalectomized monkeys on this task cannot be attributed simply to an inability to discriminate the objects or to remember them for short periods of time, but must instead be due to an impairment in associative recall across sensory modalities. Gaffan et al. (1984) have found, consistent with the preceding, that monkeys with fornix transection are unimpaired in performing a conditional task employing auditory–visual associations, supporting the contention that the hippocampal system is unnecessary for the storage/retrieval of crossmodal associations.

Sensory–Affective Associations.   The experimental findings described above suggest that the amygdala may play a much broader role in memory than previously recognized. Because the amygdala is traditionally believed to participate in emotional and motivational processes, and to help generate appropriate emotional behavior, it is important to consider how the amygdala could be important for such seemingly disparate processes as crossmodal sensory–sensory associations, on the one hand, and emotional behavior, on the other. The amygdala is widely viewed as a critical relay for cortically processed sensory information to reach emotional centers via projections to the hypothalamus and midbrain, thereby allowing expression of emotional states appropriate to a given environmental stimulus (see Aggleton & Mishkin, 1986). In the same way, the amygdala may serve as a critical relay through which cortically processed sensory information elicits stored sensory representations in another modality, perhaps via the amygdalo-cortical projection system (Amaral & Price, 1984). In this view, amygdalar circuitry is seen as processing information about sensory modalities in the same manner as it processes information about emotional states, an assumption that reconciles the classification of affective behaviors within the concept of crossmodal associations. Given this assumption, many of the previously described alterations in behavior that follow amygdalar removal or damage can be interpreted as consistent with the hypothesis that the amygdala is critical for the storage/retrieval of crossmodal associations. For example, the classic Klüver–Bucy signs, which were originally described following bilateral temporal lobectomy in monkeys (Klüver & Bucy, 1938), but are now recognized as due mainly to removal of the amygdalar complex and underlying cortex (Iwai, Nishio, & Yamaguchi, 1986; Weiskrantz, 1956), can be accounted for by this hypothesis. That is, the indiscriminate grabbing and sniffing of objects by amygdalectomized monkeys may be due to the inability of these animals to recall, upon seeing an object, what it feels, tastes, or smells like. Similarly, the apparent lack of fear of these animals may be due to the failure of a familiar and previously feared environmental stimulus (e.g., a stick, net, or human being) to elicit the appropriate emotional response.

Learning about food reward also deserves comment. Gaffan has studied, perhaps more thoroughly and more elegantly than any other investigator, the various components of learning about food reward, and much of the following account is adapted from his analyses (see Gaffan & Harrison, 1987; Gaffan, Gaffan, & Harrison, 1989). Food rewards presumably have two main characteristics: (a) an intrinsic reward value that is sensed or monitored through an affective system, and (b) neutral sensory properties such as their appearance and taste that are monitored through traditional senses. Accordingly, when an animal is learning a behavioral task for food reward a number of associations involving the food reward, only some of which are crossmodal, may be learned. For most tasks, these associations would be between a stimulus object presented for visual inspection or choice and (a) the visual properties of the food reward, (b) the taste of the food reward, and (c) the hedonic or emotional aspects of food reward. Of the two medial temporal lobe limbic structures, it is the amygdala that appears to have a special or preferential role in learning about food reward (Phillips, Mal-amut, & Mishkin, 1983), a phenomenon which may reflect the fact that two of the three associations involved (b and c above) are *crossmodal* associations.

Learning about food reward may involve intramodal and crossmodal memories, and probably supramodal memories as well. By the present account, the extent to which the amygdala is found to contribute to learning about food reward should reflect the availability of crossmodal versus intramodal and supramodal cues in a given experimental paradigm. This view is consistent with the finding that amygdalectomy yields a less severe impairment in stimulus–reward association when measured in a manual testing apparatus such as the Wisconsin General Testing Apparatus (WGTA) than when measured in an automated apparatus. In the WGTA, the stimulus object overlies the foodwell and therefore the reward, so the visual properties of the stimulus and the visual properties of the reward may be associated (Phillips et al., 1983). In most automated apparatuses, by contrast, the stimulus and reward are not contiguous. Furthermore, except for the light given off by the video monitor, the test room is dark, so such a visual–visual association is unavailable (Gaffan, Gaffan, & Harrison, 1988).

The present view differs from some other prominent views concerning the role of the amygdala in memory processes. For example, Kesner (see Kesner, 1986; Kesner & DiMattia, 1987; Kesner, chap. 7, this volume) conceives of the amygdala as providing an affective component to cognitive memory, and Gaffan and his colleagues (Gaffan & Harrison, 1987; Gaffan, Gaffan, & Harrison, 1988; Gaffan, Gaffan, & Harrison, 1989) view the amygdala as critical for associating sensory stimuli with the intrinsic incentive value of food reward. The present view, however, suggests that the amygdalar complex is critical not only for associating environmental stimuli and events with affect or reward, as these alternative views stress, but also for the process of associating sensory stimuli with one another. In other words, the amygdalar complex may be critical for associative recall across the traditional sensory modalities such as vision, touch and audition, as well as quasimodalities such as affect.

Recency Memory.   Amygdalectomized but not hippocampectomized monkeys are markedly impaired on versions of the delayed matching- or nonmatching-to-sample with repeatedly used objects (Correll & Scoville, 1965; Mishkin & Oubre, unpublished observations; Murray & Mishkin, 1984). Murray and Mishkin (1984) suggested that the amygdala is required for *"recency" memory,* i.e, the ability to discriminate which of two highly familiar stimuli had just been seen (or touched).[2] Adequate categorization of this recency memory deficit as intra-

---

[2]This ability should not be confused with "recency" memory ability as used by Milner (1982); in her test, patients are required to judge the order of presentation of stimulus material that appeared once in a list, but were never required to make judgements concerning the relative recency of viewing of familiar items. Thus, the two tests of "recency" memory may be measuring different abilities.

modal or crossmodal will have to await determination of precisely what strategies normal monkeys use to perform this task. If their strategy is found to involve simple visual recognition memory or some sort of visual–visual associative memory, then the classification scheme proposed here would be violated. Alternatively, however, if the solution employs crossmodal associative memory, then it would strengthen the proposed classification scheme.

Can the impairment in recency memory be described in terms of an impairment in crossmodal memory? At the very least, it is clear that delayed nonmatching with repeatedly used objects cannot be performed by using cues of novelty or familiarity, as is usually the case for trial-unique DMS or DNMS, and must depend instead on use of some other cue. It will be argued here, for the sake of parsimony, that the critical cue is in a different sensory modality from the stimulus objects that are employed for sample and choice. For example, perhaps intact monkeys remember a highly familiar object as being recently experienced because the neural representation of this object is "enhanced" by the recent association with food reward that occurs during the sample presentation. If this mechanism is unavailable to amygdalectomized monkeys then they would be unable to perform the task. Alternatively, perhaps intact monkeys simply remember which object they have most recently displaced, and it is this process (the crossmodal association of stimulus objects with motor acts) that requires an amygdalar circuit. Both of these mechanisms rely on crossmodal associations. However speculative, they are consistent with the known anatomical projections of the amygdalar complex; amygdalo-inferior temporal cortical and amygdalo-premotor cortical projections (Amaral & Price, 1984; Avendaño, Price, & Amaral, 1983; Iwai & Yukie, 1987; Murray and Saunders, 1987) might subserve the functions proposed above, thereby permitting an enhanced neural representation of the stimulus and a stimulus–response association, respectively.

Supramodal Memory

Supramodal memory refers to the linking of stored sensory events in such a way that the memory transcends the sensory qualities per se of the perceived stimuli. The most common example of this type of memory is spatial mapping. Following only a single encounter with a new set of environmental stimuli (e.g. entering and exploring a new house), we can, if removed from the site, draw a map of the relative locations of objects. Because the spatial mapping involves a translation of perceived items, and does not depend on the items as having been viewed or otherwise sensed simultaneously, it can be identified as supramodal. For example, after experience with the relative locations of A with B, and of B with C, a spatial map allows an organism to navigate directly from A to C, even though there was no prior learning experience of going directly from A to C.

A vast array of data, much of it obtained from studies employing rodents, indicates that the hippocampal formation is critical for many kinds of spatial

One-Trial
Object-Place Association

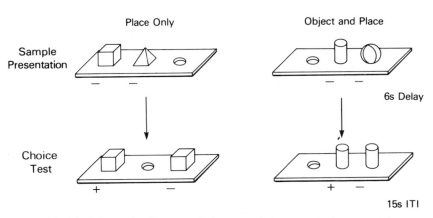

FIG. 5.5. Schematic diagram of the two trial types on the one-trial object–place association task (Parkinson et al., 1988). Note that the sample presentations for the two trial types are similar, and do not predict which trial type is being employed on any given trial. See text for description of task.

behaviors (see Chapters 7 and 13). In monkeys, hippocampal system damage disrupts spatial reversal learning (Jones & Mishkin, 1972; Mahut, 1972), performance on conditional tasks involving spatially directed responses (Gaffan & Harrison, 1989a; Rupniak & Gaffan, 1987), and spatial delayed nonmatching-to-sample in a T-maze (Murray, Davidson, Gaffan, Olton, & Suomi, 1989). A recent experiment examined whether the amygdala and hippocampus were making independent contributions to the ability to associate objects with their locations. Parkinson et al. (1988) trained monkeys on a version of indirect delayed response in which the monkeys were required to displace two different sample objects, neither of which was rewarded. Six seconds later, on a choice test, the monkeys could obtain a food reward by displacing the one of two identical objects that occupied the same location it had a few seconds earlier as a sample. As illustrated in Fig. 5.5, on half the trials (object and place) the monkeys were required to associate stimulus quality with place information in order to choose correctly on the choice test, but in the remaining trials (place only) information concerning place was sufficient. As it turned out, the hippocampectomized monkeys were equally severely impaired in performing both trial types, so the data for the two trial types have been combined in Fig. 5.6. Hippocampal ablations reduced choice accuracy to near chance levels on this task, whereas

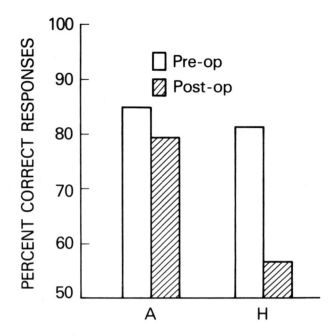

FIG. 5.6. Effects of amygdalar removals alone and hippocampal removals alone on performance on the one-trial object–place association task. Preoperative means are based on 600 trials per monkey, and
postoperative means are based on 1200 trials per monkey. Abbreviations: A, amygdalectomized monkeys (n=3); H, hippocampectomized
monkeys (n=3).

amygdalar ablations yielded a transient impairment followed by reattainment of
preoperative performance levels. Thus, in this one-trial object–place association
task, the hippocampus, but not the amygdala, was critical; this outcome is the
converse of that obtained with the crossmodal task. Furthermore, both amygdalectomized and hippocampectomized monkeys were able to recognize the
objects in a delayed matching-to-sample task (Parkinson et al., 1988). Since all
the animals were able to discriminate the objects and remember them for short
periods of time, the impairment of the hippocampectomized monkeys is clearly
related to the spatial requirements of the task.

    While these results demonstrate that the hippocampus is indeed critical for
associating objects and their locations, the hippocampectomized monkeys'
failure on both trial types suggests, in addition, that there may be a more fundamental impairment, one related to "place" alone. One alternative possibility,
however, is that the failure of the monkeys in the Parkinson et al. study was due
to interference from a strategy needed to remember the more difficult "object–
place" trials. To directly test this idea, naive rhesus monkeys were trained on the

"place" trials only. Preliminary results indicate that hippocampal removals severely disrupt performance even on the "place" trials alone (Angeli, Murray, & Mishkin, 1988). Stored information concerning the relative locations of objects in the environment, or "place only" memory, may in and of itself be a kind of associative memory (see McNaughton & Morris, 1987).

Because "place" and "movement" are usually confounded in studies examining the neural basis of spatial behaviors, the precise role of the hippocampal system in memory has resisted analysis. Nevertheless, most of the available data are consistent with the idea that the fundamental impairment that follows hippocampal system damage is due to either: (a) inability to learn the spatial relationships of objects (failure to form a spatial map), or (b) failure to associate spatially directed movements with environmental stimuli. Recent experiments employing spatial–visual conditional tasks (tasks in which spatial cues guide visual choices), however, fail to support the latter possibility. In Experiment 1 of Gaffan and Harrison (1989b) monkeys were confronted with two different objects, both of which appeared over a pair of foodwells located either on the left or right side of a test tray. When the objects appeared on the left, object A was rewarded whereas when the objects appeared on the right, object B was rewarded. Fornix transections yielded an impairment on this task. Because the task employed a spatial cue (both objects appearing on either the left or right side of the test tray) to guide a visual choice (object A or object B), the impairment cannot be classified as a deficit in making spatially directed responses (Gaffan & Harrison, 1989b). An even stronger argument against the spatially-directed movement hypothesis comes from yet another experiment carried out by Gaffan and Harrison (1989a). In their Experiment 1, monkeys were required to displace one of two objects on a test tray if their test cage was facing in one direction, but the other of the two objects if their test cage was facing in the opposite direction. The left–right position of the objects on the test tray was irrelevant. In addition, the room cues available for orientation were the same items regardless of whether the animal was in position 1 or position 2; that is, no environmental cues were specific to one position and not the other. Presumably, the monkeys had to use cues concerning the relative positions of the environmental stimuli with respect to themselves to discriminate the two locations. Fornix transection severely impaired the rate of learning on this task, again demonstrating that the deficits that follow hippocampal system damage are not restricted to instances in which the animal is making spatially directed movements. The data from these two experiments are consistent with the "spatial mapping" hypothesis, but only with the qualification that the "observer" is part of the spatial map.

Some recent experiments have helped define the nature of the deficit that follows hippocampal system damage by showing that certains kinds of spatial learning are unimpaired. For example, monkeys with fornix transection can discriminate "places" to which they have been passively transported, and can use this "place" information to guide their behavior (Murray, Davidson, Gaffan,

Olton, & Suomi, 1989). Thus the use of the term "spatial" must be carefully defined or qualified in any consideration of hippocampal function.

Theoretically, there could be other kinds of supramodal memories. For example, O'Keefe and Nadel (1978, 1979) have suggested that there is a relationship between spatial mapping and the process of "mapping" superficial structures or content of sentences onto their underlying deep structures. This idea will be discussed in more detail below. In addition, some investigators have suggested that the hippocampus might also be involved in temporal mapping. The latter proposal has arisen because at least a handful of impairments that follow hippocampal ablations cannot be accounted for by either "spatial mapping" or "spatially directed movement" hypotheses. The clearest examples are provided by Solomon and his colleagues (Solomon, 1977; Solomon & Moore, 1975), who have examined the classically conditioned nictitating membrane response in rabbits. Rabbits with hippocampal ablations, unlike intact rabbits, fail to exhibit either latent inhibition effects or blocking effects. Because these behavioral phenomena appear to depend on the rabbit's ability to "map" the temporal relationship of the conditioned stimulus, the unconditioned stimulus, and the conditioned response, the idea has been put forth that the hippocampus is responsible for this temporal mapping or coding (see Solomon, 1980). Although this remains an attractive hypothesis, our understanding is superficial. Further work needs to address: (a) precisely which sensory or motor events are being temporally related to produce the behavioral effects in normal rabbits, and (b) whether the so-called temporal mapping deficits are confined to instances of classically conditioned behaviors or extend to operantly conditioned behaviors as well.

HOW THE AMYGDALA AND HIPPOCAMPUS WORK TOGETHER IN MEMORY

As has been discussed elsewhere (Parkinson et al., 1988), the evidence suggests that the amygdala and hippocampus each contribute to at least two kinds of memory. Because each structure receives information from higher-order cortical processing areas subserving all the sensory modalities (with the exception of smell; Friedman, Murray, O'Neill, & Mishkin, 1986; Turner, Mishkin, & Knapp, 1980; Van Hoesen, 1981), either directly (amygdala) or indirectly via the entorhinal cortex (hippocampus), each structure is in a position to participate in intramodal sensory memory. For example, removal of one structure has relatively little effect on recognition memory, but removal of both structures results in an almost complete failure in recognition memory if the delays between sample presentation and choice are longer than about 10 seconds (Mishkin, 1978; Murray & Mishkin, 1984, 1986; Saunders, Murray, & Mishkin, 1984). And, as already discussed, preliminary evidence indicates that the formation of new intramodal associative memories is likewise critically dependent upon both structures (Murray, Gaffan, & Mishkin, 1988).

In addition, each structure makes a selective contribution to other kinds of memory, namely, crossmodal memory (amygdalar complex) and supramodal memory (hippocampal formation). The behavioral effects of either amygdalar removals alone or hippocampal removals alone on the associative memory tasks differ from those on recognition memory. On the recognition memory tasks, the lesion effects interact with delay, whereas on the associative memory tasks, the effects appear to be "all-or-none". That is, even animals with combined removal of the amygdala and hippocampus relearn delayed nonmatching-to-sample, a test of recognition memory. Furthermore, they display high levels of accuracy when short delays intervene between sample presentation and choice test; the impairment is evident only with the imposition of longer delays. By contrast, monkeys with either amygdalar or hippocampal removals alone show a near-complete inability to perform the tasks requiring tactual–to–visual crossmodal associations and one-trial object–place associations, respectively, even at short delays. These two different outcomes indicate that animals with the combined amygdalar and hippocampal ablations can still learn a rule, perhaps one based on an abstraction such as novelty (Weinstein, Saunders, & Mishkin, 1988). In situations where no such rule can guide behavior, however, as in conditional discriminations, the near-chance levels of performance obtained by monkeys with the selective amygdalar and hippocampal removals suggests that the critical associative link simply cannot be formed.

Although the amygdalar complex and hippocampal formation can be identified as contributing to more than one kind of memory, it is not clear whether these structures have functions that are partially redundant or completely separate. On the one hand, if recognition is a basic process common to both structures, then their functions can be identified as being partially redundant. On the other hand, each structure might carry out a unique function, one which yields the ability to perform DNMS simply as a by-product. For example, perhaps amygdalectomized monkeys perform DNMS by remembering the locations of sample objects, or the spatial relations of the sample object and the food reward, and perhaps hippocampectomized monkeys perform DNMS by remembering object–reward associations. There is presently no compelling evidence that argues in favor of either view, so further study is required to choose between these two possibilities.

REPRESENTATIONAL MEMORY
IN OTHER VERTEBRATES

Evidence from rodents (Olton, Becker, & Handelmann, 1979) and birds (Bingman, Ioale, Casini, & Bagnoli, 1987; Sherry & Vaccarino, 1989) suggests that the hippocampal system is critical for spatial behaviors in all vertebrates. Although we lack the theoretical foundation for a comprehensive comparative neuropsychology of learning and memory (see Macphail, 1982; cf. chapter 1, this book), some initial steps have been made. Because hippocampal function in rodents is usually assessed with spatial tasks requiring locomotion, and in monkeys with (nonspatial) object tasks requiring arm movement responses, some recent studies were undertaken to test rodents and nonhuman primates on the "other" kind of task for each order (Markowska, Olton, Murray, & Gaffan, 1989; Murray, Davidson, Gaffan, Olton, & Suomi, 1989). Rats were trained not only on spatial tasks requiring locomotion, but also on object tasks (requiring minimal locomotion), and monkeys were trained not only on object tasks, but also on spatial tasks that required locomotion. Interestingly, the rats learned the locomotor spatial task much faster than the monkeys, whereas the monkeys learned the object tasks faster than the rats. The main finding of the two studies taken together, however, was that the hippocampal system indeed contributes critically to spatial behaviors in both rodents and nonhuman primates (Markowska, Olton, Murray, & Gaffan, 1989; Murray, Davidson, Gaffan, Olton, & Suomi, 1989).

Recent work has indicated that the hippocampal system in rodents, like that in nonhuman primates, is contributing to nonspatial as well as to spatial behavior (Aggleton & Rawlins, 1986; Raffaele & Olton, 1988). Although the extent of the hippocampal contribution to nonspatial memory in rodents is unclear, the finding that this structure is participating in both spatial memory and in sensory (object) recognition memory again indicates that hippocampal function, at least in these two orders, is qualitatively similar.

Is the hippocampus preferentially involved in spatial memory as opposed to nonspatial memory? That may depend on the individual species and its life history. Perhaps with species with relatively poor vision and a dependence on locomotion through space, such as most rodents and nocturnal species generally, the hippocampal system is involved primarily with spatial memory. In other species, particularly the advanced primates with their highly developed visual systems, the ability to make limb projection movements and to manipulate objects in space, the hippocampal system participates not only in spatial mapping, but also in visuo-spatial functions and visual object recognition memory. And in humans, by contrast, where language is evident, the functions of the hippocampal system may extend beyond spatial or object memory to semantic mapping (O'Keefe & Nadel, 1978, 1979). Semantic mapping, like spatial mapping, allows an organism to arrive at new formulations of the available elements, only now the new relationships are for language content within framework rather than 3-dimensional objects within the environment. The recent finding that individual hippocampal (and amygdalar) neurons demonstrate word-specific firing is consistent with the concept of semantic mapping (Heit, Smith, & Halgren, 1988). Given the extent to which humans rely on language, the semantic mapping concept could account for the apparently more severe amnesic effects of hippocampal system damage in humans than in other species (see Zola-Morgan, Squire, & Amaral, 1986).

Less is known regarding amygdalar function in nonprimate vertebrates. In rodents and lagomorphs the amygdala plays a role in autonomic conditioning, such as heart-rate conditioning (Kapp, Gallagher, Frysinger, & Applegate, 1981; LeDoux, 1987) and fear conditioning (Davis, Hitchcock, & Rosen, 1987). For the reasons given earlier in discussing the relationship of emotional behavior to crossmodal memory, these data fit well with the hypothesis that the amygdala is critical for crossmodal associations. One might speculate, however, that just as has been suggested for the hippocampal formation, amygdalar function might be expressed differently in different species. According to Stephan and his colleagues (Stephan & Andy, 1977; Stephan, Frahm, & Baron, 1987), the basolateral amygdala (the portion of the amygdala with the most prominent anatomical projections to the hippocampal formation, the medial thalamus, and the neocortex), but not the centromedial amygdala, is relatively smaller (compared to brain or body weight) in primitive insectivores than in nonhuman primates, and in nonhuman primates than in humans. As these authors pointed out, these data indicate that the amygdala of primates is much more influenced by sensory neocortical areas than the amygdala of insectivora, which may be more influenced by structures mediating olfaction. These data strongly suggest that the basolateral amygdala has enlarged during the evolution of advanced primates, including humans; perhaps this enlargement reflects and is accompanied by an increased role for the amygdala in relating sensory stimuli to one another across sensory modalities.

SUMMARY

The amygdala and hippocampus both participate in vertebrate memory processes. Based on recent work on the neural substrates of memory in nonhuman primates, three provisional categories of representational memory have been proposed (Fig. 5.7). The amygdala and hippocampus together appear to be critically important for intramodal memory, the amygdala for crossmodal memory, and the hippocampus for supramodal (including spatial) memory. Although studies of animals in one order or another may lead investigators to draw narrower conclusions regarding amygdalar and hippocampal function than those suggested here, I have argued that the apparent behavioral differences of either amygdalar or hippocampal function across orders may reflect the life history and predisposition of the organism to use certain kinds of sensory input rather than species differences in amygdalar or hippocampal function. For example, the crossmodal concept for amygdalar function encompasses not only the learning of the relationships between sensory stimuli and emotional states, but also the learning of apparently nonaffective relationships between sensory stimuli of one modality and those of another. And, similarly, the supramodal concept for hippocampal function takes into account not only the spatial mapping processes so prominent

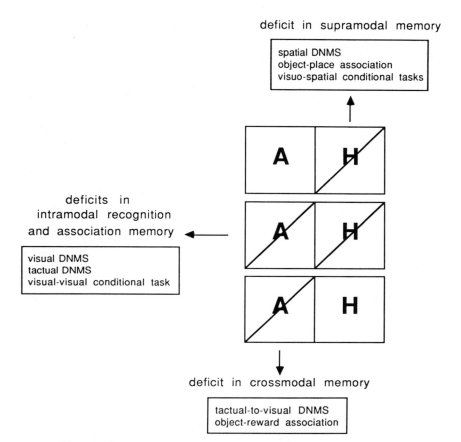

deficit in supramodal memory

spatial DNMS
object-place association
visuo-spatial conditional tasks

deficits in
intramodal recognition
and association memory

visual DNMS
tactual DNMS
visual-visual conditional task

deficit in crossmodal memory

tactual-to-visual DNMS
object-reward association

FIG. 5.7. Schematic diagram summarizing the effects of amygdalar and hippocampal system damage on representational memory in non-human primates.

in rodents, but also the possibility that humans may possess a semantic mapping process.

ACKNOWLEDGMENTS

I thank Mortimer Mishkin, David Gaffan, and Dragana Ivkovich for their helpful comments on an earlier version of this manuscript.

REFERENCES

Aggleton, J. P., & Mishkin, M. (1983a). Visual recognition impairment following medial thalamic lesions in monkeys. *Neuropsychologia. 21,* 189–197.

Aggleton, J. P., & Mishkin, M. (1983b). Memory impairments following restricted medial thalamic lesions in monkeys. *Experimental Brain Research, 52,* 199–209.

Aggleton, J. P., & Mishkin, M. (1986). The amygdala: sensory gateway to the emotions. In R. Plutchik & H. Kellerman (Eds.), *Emotion: Theory, research, and experience* (pp. 281–299). Orlando: Academic Press.

Aggleton, J. P., & Rawlins, J. N. P. (1986). The effects of single and combined lesions of the amygdala and hippocampus upon recognition memory in the rat. *Society for Neuroscience Abstracts, 12,* 977.

Amaral, D. G., & Price, J. L. (1984). Amygdalo-cortical projections in the monkey (*Macaca fascicularis*). *Journal of Comparative Neurology, 230,* 465–496.

Angeli, S. J., Murray, E. A., & Mishkin, M. (1988). The hippocampus and place memory in rhesus monkeys. *Society for Neuroscience Abstracts, 14,* 232.

Avendaño, C., Price, J. L., & Amaral, D. G. (1983). Evidence for an amygdaloid projection to premotor but not to motor cortex in the monkey. *Brain Research, 264,* 111–117.

Bachevalier, J., & Mishkin, M. (1986). Visual recognition impairment follows ventromedial but not dorsolateral prefrontal lesions in monkeys. *Behavioral Brain Research, 20,* 249–261.

Bachevalier, J., Parkinson, J. K., & Mishkin, M. (1985). Visual recognition in monkeys: effects of separate vs. combined transection of fornix and amygdalofugal pathways. *Experimental Brain Research, 57,* 554–561.

Bachevalier, J., Saunders, R. C., & Mishkin, M. (1985). Visual recognition in monkeys: effects of transection of fornix. *Experimental Brain Research, 57,* 547–553.

Bingman, V. P., Ioale, P., Casini, G., & Bagnoli, P. (1987). Impaired retention of preoperatively acquired spatial reference memory in homing pigeons following hippocampal ablation. *Behavioural Brain Research, 24,* 147–156.

Cohen, N. J., Eichenbaum, H., DeAcedo, B. S., & Corkin, S. (1985). Different memory systems underlying acquisition of procedural and declarative knowledge. In D. S. Olton, E. Gamzu, & S. Corkin (Eds.), *Memory dysfunctions: An integration of animal and human research from preclinical and clinical perspectives, Annals of the New York Academy of Sciences, 444* (pp. 54–71). New York: New York Academy of Sciences.

Cohen, N. J., & Squire, L. R. (1980). Preserved learning and retention of pattern-analyzing skill in amnesia: dissociation of knowing how and knowing that. *Science, 210,* 207–210.

Corkin, S. (1968). Acquisition of motor skill after bilateral medial temporal-lobe excision. *Neuropsychologia, 6,* 255–265.

Correll, R. E., & Scoville, W. B. (1965). Performance on delayed match following lesions of medial temporal lobe structures. *Journal of Comparative and Physiological Psychology, 60,* 360–367.

Cummings, J. L., & Benson, D. F. (1984). Subcortical dementia: Review of an emerging concept. *Archives of Neurology, 41,* 874–879.

D'Amato, M. R., Salmon, D. P., Loukas, E., & Tomie, A. (1985). Symmetry and transitivity of conditional relations in monkeys (*Cebus apella*) and pigeons (*Columba livia*). *Journal of the Experimental Analysis of Behavior, 44,* 35–47.

Davis, M., Hitchcock, J. M., & Rosen, J. B. (1987). Anxiety and the amygdala: pharmacological and anatomical analysis of the fear-potentiated startle paradigm. In G. H. Bower (Ed.), *Psychology of learning and motivation, Vol. 21* (pp. 263–305). San Diego: Academic Press.

Dewson, J. H. III, & Burlingame, A. C. (1975). Auditory discrimination and recall in monkeys. *Science, 187,* 267–268.

Friedman, D. P., Murray, E. A., O'Neill, J. B., & Mishkin, M. (1986). Cortical connections of the somatosensory fields of the lateral sulcus of macaques: evidence for a corticolimbic pathway for touch. *Journal of Comparative Neurology, 252*, 323–347.

Gaffan, D. (1974). Recognition impaired and association intact in the memory of monkeys after transection of the fornix. *Journal of Comparative and Physiological Psychology, 86*, 1100–1109.

Gaffan, D., Gaffan, E. A., & Harrison, S. (1984). Effects of fornix transection on spontaneous and trained nonmatching by monkeys. *Quarterly Journal of Experimental Psychology, 36B*, 285–303.

Gaffan, E. A., Gaffan, D., & Harrison, S. (1988). Disconnection of the amygdala from visual association cortex impairs visual reward–association learning in monkeys. *Journal of Neuroscience, 8*, 3144–3150.

Gaffan, D., Gaffan, E. A., & Harrison, S. (1989). Visual–visual associative learning and reward–association learning: The role of the amygdala. *Journal of Neuroscience, 9*, 558–564.

Gaffan, D., & Harrison, S. (1987). Amygdalectomy and disconnection in visual learning for auditory secondary reinforcement by monkeys. *Journal of Neuroscience, 7*, 2285–2292.

Gaffan, D., & Harrison, S. (1989a). Place memory and scene memory: effects of fornix transection in the monkey. *Experimental Brain Research, 74*, 202–212.

Gaffan, D., & Harrison, S. (1989b). A comparison of the effects of fornix transection and sulcus principalis ablation upon spatial learning by monkeys. *Behavioural Brain Research, 31*, 207–220.

Gordon, B. (1988). Preserved learning of novel information in amnesia: evidence for multiple memory systems. *Brain and Cognition, 7*, 257–282.

Halsband, U., & Passingham, R. E. (1985). Premotor cortex and the conditions for movement in monkeys (*Macaca fascicularis*). *Behavioural Brain Research, 18*, 269–277.

Heit, G., Smith, M. E., & Halgren, E. (1988). Neural encoding of individual words and faces by the human hippocampus and amygdala. *Science, 333*, 773–775.

Iwai, E., Nishio, T., & Yamaguchi, K. (1986). Neuropsychological basis of a K-B sign in Klüver-Bucy syndrome produced following total removal of inferior temporal cortex of macaque monkeys. In Y. Oomura (Ed.), *Emotion—neural and chemical control* (pp. 299–311). Tokyo: Japan Scientific Society Press.

Iwai, E., & Yukie, M. (1987). Amygdalofugal and amygdalopetal connections with modality-specific visual cortical areas in macaques (*Macaca fuscata, M. mulatta*, and *M. fascicularis*). *The Journal of Comparative Neurology, 261*, 362–387.

Jones, B., & Mishkin, M. (1972). Limbic lesions and the problem of stimulus–reinforcement associations. *Experimental Neurology, 36*, 362–377.

Kapp, B. S., Gallagher, M., Frysinger, R. C., & Applegate, C. D. (1981). The amygdala, emotion and cardiovascular conditioning. In Y. Ben-Ari (Ed.), *The amygdaloid complex* (pp. 355–366). Amsterdam: Elsevier/North-Holland Biomedical Press.

Kesner, R. P. (1986). Neurobiological views of memory. In J. L. Martinez, Jr., & R. P. Kesner (Eds.), *Learning and memory: A biological view* (pp. 399–438). Orlando: Academic Press.

Kesner, R. P., & DiMattia, B. V. (1987). Neurobiology of an attribute model of memory. In A. N. Epstein & A. R. Morrison (Eds.), *Progress in psychobiology and physiological psychology, Vol. 12* (pp. 207–277). Orlando: Academic Press.

Klüver, H., & Bucy, P. C. (1938). An analysis of certain effects of bilateral temporal lobectomy in the rhesus monkey, with special reference to "psychic blindness". *Journal of Psychology, 5*, 33–54.

LeDoux, J. E. (1987). Emotion. In *Handbook of physiology: Section 1, The nervous system, Vol. 5, Higher functions of the brain* In F. Plum (Ed.), (pp. 419–459). Bethesda: American Physiological Society.

Macphail, E. M. (1982). *Brain and intelligence in vertebrates*. Oxford: Oxford University Press.

Mahut, H. (1972). A selective spatial deficit in monkeys after transection of the fornix. *Neuropsychologia, 10*, 65–74.

Mahut, H., Zola-Morgan, S. & Moss, M. (1982). Hippocampal resections impair associative learning and recognition memory in the monkey. *Journal of Neuroscience, 2,* 1214–1229.

Markowska, A. L., Olton, D. S., Murray, E. A., & Gaffan, D. (1989). A comparative analysis of the role of fornix and cingulate cortex in memory: Rats. *Experimental Brain Research, 74,* 187–201.

McNaughton, B. L., & Morris, R. G. M. (1987). Hippocampal synaptic enhancement and information storage within a distributed memory system. *Trends in Neuroscience, 10,* 408–415.

Milner, B. (1958). Psychological defects produced by temporal lobe excision. *Research Publications of the Association for Nervous and Mental Disease, 36,* 244–257.

Milner, B. (1962). Les troubles de la memoire accompagnant des lesions hippocampiques bilaterales. In *Physiologie de l'hippocampe* (pp. 257–272). Paris: Centre National de la Recherche Scientifique.

Milner, B. (1982). Some cognitive effects of frontal-lobe lesions in man. *Philosophical Transactions of The Royal Society of London, 298,* 211–226.

Milner, B., Corkin, S., & Teuber, H.-L. (1968). Further analysis of the hippocampal amnesic syndrome: 14-year follow-up study of H.M. *Neuropsychologia, 6,* 215–234.

Mishkin, M. (1978). Memory in monkeys severely impaired by combined but not by separate removal of amygdala and hippocampus. *Nature, 273,* 297–298.

Mishkin, M. (1982). A memory system in the monkey. *Philosophical Transactions of The Royal Society of London, 298,* 85–95.

Mishkin, M., & Delacour, J. (1975). An analysis of short-term visual memory in the monkey. *Journal of Experimental Psychology: Animal Behavior Processes, 1,* 326–334.

Mishkin, M., Malamut, B., & Bachevalier, J. (1984). Memories and habits: two neural systems. In G. Lynch, J. L. McGaugh, & N. M. Weinberger (Eds.), *Neurobiology of learning and memory* (pp. 65–77). New York: The Guilford Press.

Mishkin, M., Spiegler, B. J., Saunders, R. C., & Malamut, B. L. (1982). An animal model of global amnesia. In S. Corkin, K. L. Davis, J. H. Growdon, E. Usdin, & R. J. Wurtman (Eds.), *Alzheimer's disease: A report of progress in research* (pp. 235-246). New York: Raven Press.

Murray, E. A., Bachevalier, J., & Mishkin, M. (1985). Rhinal cortex: a third temporal-lobe component of the limbic memory system. *Society for Neuroscience Abstracts, 11,* 461.

Murray, E. A., Davidson, M., Gaffan, D., Olton, D. S., & Suomi, S. (1989). Effects of fornix transection and cingulate cortical ablation on spatial memory in rhesus monkeys. *Experimental Brain Research, 74,* 173–186.

Murray, E. A., Gaffan, D., & Mishkin, M. (1988). Role of the amygdala and hippocampus in visual-visual associative memory in rhesus monkeys. *Society for Neuroscience Abstracts, 14,* 2.

Murray, E. A., & Mishkin, M. (1984). Severe tactual as well as visual memory deficits follow combined removal of the amygdala and hippocampus in monkeys. *The Journal of Neuroscience, 4,* 2565–2580.

Murray, E. A., & Mishkin, M. (1985). Amygdalectomy impairs crossmodal association in monkeys. *Science, 228,* 604–606.

Murray, E. A., & Mishkin, M. (1986). Visual recognition in monkeys following rhinal cortical ablations combined with either amygdalectomy or hippocampectomy. *The Journal of Neuroscience, 6,* 1991–2003.

Murray, E. A., & Saunders, R. C. (1987). Amygdaloid projections to premotor and supplementary motor areas in the rhesus monkey. *Anatomical Record, 218,* 95A.

Newcombe, F., & Ratcliff, G. (1979). Long-term psychological consequences of cerebral lesions. In M. S. Gazzaniga (Ed.), *Handbook of behavioral neurobiology, Vol. 2, Neuropsychology* (pp. 495–540). New York: Plenum Press.

O'Keefe, J., & Nadel, L. (1978). *The hippocampus as a cognitive map.* Oxford: Clarendon Press.

O'Keefe, J., & Nadel, L. (1979). Precis of O'Keefe and Nadel's *The hippocampus as a cognitive map. Behavioral Brain Sciences, 2,* 487–533.

Olton, D. S., Becker, J. T., & Handelmann, G. E. (1979). Hippocampus, space, and memory. *The Behavioral and Brain Sciences, 2,* 313–365.

Parkinson, J. K., Murray, E. A., & Mishkin, M. (1988). A selective mnemonic role for the hippocampus in monkeys: memory for the location of objects. *The Journal of Neuroscience, 8,* 4159–4167.

Passingham, R. E. (1985). Cortical mechanisms and cues for action. *Philosophical Transactions of the Royal Society of London, B, 308,* 101–111.

Petrides, M. (1982). Motor conditional associative-learning after selective prefrontal lesions in the monkey. *Experimental Brain Research, 5,* 407–413.

Petrides, M. (1986). The effect of periarcuate lesions in the monkey on the performance of symmetrically and asymmetrically reinforced visual and auditory go, no-go tasks. *The Journal of Neuroscience, 6,* 2054–2063.

Petrides, M. (1987). Conditional learning and the primate frontal cortex. In E. Perecman (Ed.), *The frontal lobes revisited* (pp. 91–108). New York: The IRBN Press.

Phillips, R. R., Malamut, B. L., & Mishkin, M. (1983). Memory for stimulus–reward associations in the monkey is more severely affected by amygdalectomy than by hippocampectomy. *Society for Neuroscience Abstracts, 9,* 638.

Raffaele, K. C., & Olton, D. S. (1988). Hippocampal and amygdaloid involvement in working memory for nonspatial stimuli. *Behavioral Neuroscience, 102,* 349-355.

Ringo, J. L. (1988). Seemingly discrepant data from hippocampectomized macaques are reconciled by detectability analysis. *Behavioral Neuroscience, 102,* 173–177.

Rupniak, N. M. J., & Gaffan, D. (1987). Monkey hippocampus and learning about spatially directed movements. *The Journal of Neuroscience, 7,* 2331-2337.

Saunders, R. C., Murray, E. A., & Mishkin, M. (1984). Further evidence that amygdala and hippocampus contribute equally to recognition memory. *Neuropsychologia, 22,* 785–796.

Scoville, W. B., & Milner, B. (1957). Loss of recent memory after bilateral hippocampal lesions. *Journal of Neurology, Neurosurgery, and Psychiatry, 20,* 11–21.

Sherry, D. F., & Vaccarino, A. L. (1989). The hippocampus and memory for food caches in Black-capped chicadees. *Behavioral Neuroscience, 103,* 308–318.

Solomon, P. R. (1977). Role of the hippocampus in blocking and conditioned inhibition of the rabbit's nictitating membrane response. *Journal of Comparative and Physiological Psychology, 91,* 407–417.

Solomon, P. R. (1980). A time and a place for everything? Temporal processing views of hippocampal function with special reference to attention. *Physiological Psychology, 8,* 254–261.

Solomon, P. R., & Moore, J. W. (1975). Latent inhibition and stimulus generalization of the classically conditioned nictitating membrane response in rabbits (*Oryctolagus cuniculus*) following dorsal hippocampal ablation. *Journal of Comparative and Physiological Psychology, 89,* 1192–1203.

Squire, L. R., & Zola-Morgan, S. (1985). The neuropsychology of memory: New links between humans and experimental animals. In D. S. Olton, E. Gamzu, & S. Corkin (Eds.), *Memory dysfunctions: An integration of animal and human research from preclinical and clinical perspectives, Annals of the New York Academy of Sciences, 444* (pp. 137–149). New York: New York Academy of Sciences.

Stephan, H., & Andy, O. J. (1977). Quantitative comparison of the amygdala in insectivores and primates. *Acta Anatomica, 95,* 130–153.

Stephan, H., Frahm, H. D., & Baron, G. (1987). Comparison of brain structure volumes in Insectivora and Primates, VII. Amygdaloid components. *Journal fur Hirnforschung, 28,* 571–584.

Thomas, G. J. (1984). Memory: Time binding in organisms. In L. R. Squire & N. Butters (Eds.), *Neuropsychology of memory* (pp. 374–384). New York: The Guilford Press.

Thompson, R. F., Barchas, J. D., Clark, G. A., Donegan, N., Kettner, R. E., Lavond, D. G., Madden, J. IV, Mauk, M. D., & McCormick, D. A. (1984). Neuronal substrates of associative learning in the mammalian brain. In D. L. Alkon & J. Farley (Eds.), *Primary neural substrates of learning and behavioral change* (pp. 71–99). Cambridge: The Cambridge University Press.

Tulving, E. (1987). Multiple memory systems and consciousness. *Human Neurobiology, 6*, 67–80.

Turner, B. H., Mishkin, M., & Knapp, M. (1980). Organization of the amygdalopetal projections from modality-specific cortical association areas in the monkey. *The Journal of Comparative Neurology, 191*, 515–543.

Van Hoesen, G. W. (1981). The differential distribution, diversity and sprouting of cortical projections to the amygdala in the rhesus monkey. In Y. Ben-Ari (Ed.), *The amygdaloid complex* (pp. 77–90). Amsterdam: Elsevier/North-Holland Biomedial Press.

Warrington, E. K., & Weiskrantz, L. (1970). Amnesic syndrome: consolidation or retrieval? *Nature, 228*, 628–630.

Weinstein, J. A., Saunders, R. C., & Mishkin, M. (1988). Temporo-prefrontal interaction in rule learning by macaques. *Society for Neuroscience Abstracts, 14*, 1230.

Weiskrantz, L. (1956). Behavioral changes associated with ablation of the amygdaloid complex in monkeys. *Journal of Comparative and Physiological Psychology, 49*, 381–391.

Weiskrantz, L. (1978). A comparison of hippocampal pathology in man and other animals. In Ciba Foundation (Eds.), *Functions of the septo-hippocampal system* (pp. 373–406). Amsterdam: North Holland: Elsevier/Excerpta Medica.

Weiskrantz, L. (1987). Neuroanatomy of memory and amnesia. *Human Neurobiology, 6*, 93–105.

Zola-Morgan, S., & Squire, L. R. (1984). Preserved learning in monkeys with medial temporal lesions: sparing of motor and cognitive skills. *The Journal of Neuroscience, 4*, 1072–1085.

Zola-Morgan, S., & Squire, L. R. (1986). Memory impairment in monkeys following lesions limited to the hippocampus. *Behavioral Neuroscience, 100*, 155–160.

Zola-Morgan, S., Squire, L. R., & Amaral, D. G. (1984). Performance of monkeys with separate and combined lesions of hippocampus and amygdala on delayed nonmatching to sample. *Society for Neuroscience Abstracts, 10*, 385.

Zola-Morgan, S., Squire, L. R., & Amaral, D. G. (1986). Human amnesia and the medial temporal region: enduring memory impairment following a bilateral lesion limited to field CA1 of the hippocampus. *The Journal of Neuroscience, 6*, 2950–2967.

Zola-Morgan, S., Squire, L. R., & Amaral, D. G. (1988). Amnesia following medial temporal lobe damage in monkeys: the importance of the hippocampus and adjacent cortical regions. *Society for Neuroscience Abstracts, 14*, 1043.

Zola-Morgan, S., Squire, L. R., & Amaral, D. G. (1989). Lesions of the amygdala that spare adjacent cortical regions do not impair memory or exacerbate the impairment following lesions of the hippocampal formation. *The Journal of Neuroscience, 9*, 1922–1936.

6 Brain Mechanisms of Learning in Reptiles

Alice Schade Powers
St. John's University

Studies of the role of the brain in learning in reptiles have been limited in number. Most of these studies have dealt with the role of the telencephalon, either whole or in part, in learning or memory. In 1980, Peterson compiled an excellent summary of the work on the telencephalon up to that time. Since then, research has indicated an important role for one particular region of the telencephalon, the dorsal cortex, in learning and memory in reptiles. This chapter concentrates on more recent work, emphasizing the role of the dorsal cortex in associative functions.

The class Reptilia has four extant orders: Chelonia, the turtles, Squamata, the snakes and lizards, Crocodilia, alligators and crocodiles, and Rhynchocephalia, which consists of one living species, the tuatara. Most of the work on the neural basis of learning in reptiles has been done with turtles, primarily for practical reasons: They are much easier to motivate for food than other reptilian groups, because they eat regularly. As it happens, this choice is a fortunate one for those of us who are interested in the evolution of the brain, because turtles are the best living representative of the ancient reptiles that gave rise to mammals. The common ancestors of present-day reptiles, birds, and mammals were the cotylosaurs, or stem reptiles, and turtles are the living order most closely related to that group (Romer, 1959). In this review, most of the work that is discussed deals with turtles.

Figure 6.1 shows a cross section through the telencephalon of a painted turtle, *Chrysemys picta*. The telencephalon of reptiles consists of a basal portion, consisting of the paleostriatum augmentatum (PA), globus pallidus (GP), and area d (d) in Fig. 6.1. It is anatomically equivalent to the basal ganglia of mammals (Reiner, Brauth, & Karten, 1984). The rest of the telencephalon, consisting of

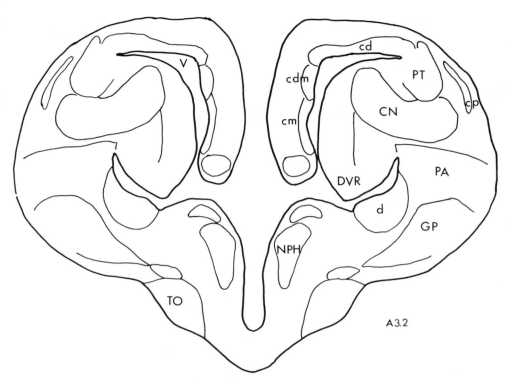

FIG. 6.1. A cross-section through the telencephalon of a turtle. Abbreviations are as follows: cd = dorsal cortex, cdm = dorsomedial
cortex, cm = medial cortex, cp = pyriform cortex, CN = core nucleus
of the dorsal ventricular ridge, d = area d, DVR = dorsal ventricular
ridge, GP = globus pallidus, NPH = periventricular hypothalamic nucleus, PA = paleostriatum augmentatum, PT = pallial thickening, TO =
optic tract, V = ventricle.

the areas dorsal to PA in Fig. 6.1, contains a number of termination areas for
sensory projections from the thalamus, and as such it has been compared to the
neocortex of mammals (Nauta & Karten, 1970; Powers & Reiner, 1979). No true
neocortex (i.e., six-layered cortex) exists in the nonmammalian brain, but individual regions resemble regions of the neocortex in receiving visual, somatosensory, and auditory projections from the thalamus (Balaban & Ulinski, 1981a,
1981b). These projections terminate in specific subdivisions of the telencephalon. Of these sensory pathways, the one of interest here projects from the
retina to the lateral geniculate nucleus of the thalamus, and from there to the
dorsal cortex (cd) and pallial thickening (PT) in turtles (Hall & Ebner, 1970;
Hall, Foster, Ebner, & Hall, 1977). (The pathway terminates solely in the pallial
thickening in lizards; Bruce & Butler, 1984).

Modern interest in the dorsal cortex probably arose out of curiosity about the role of the visual projection to the dorsal cortex in visual perception. An older, now discredited view (Crosby, 1917) that the dorsal cortex of reptiles was the precursor of the whole neocortex of mammals may also have contributed to interest in its function. One of the first studies to reveal an effect of lesions of the dorsal cortex was a study of habituation by Killackey, Pellmar, & Ebner (1972). These investigators studied habituation to a looming stimulus (a ball rapidly approaching the animal) in turtles (*Pseudemys scripta*). They measured head withdrawal in normal turtles and turtles with lesions of the dorsal cortex. The lesioned subjects showed slower habituation than normal, meaning that they responded *more* than normals to the visual stimulus. Increased responsiveness to visual stimuli would probably not result from a visual deficit; thus, this study suggested that the dorsal cortex might participate in some function other than vision.

Another early study (Morlock, 1972) examined the effects of lesions of the dorsal cortex on learning in two species of turtles: painted turtles (*Chrysemys picta*) and red-eared turtles (*Pseudemys scripta*). All testing was done postoperatively: Sham lesions and unoperated controls were included along with lesioned subjects. In addition to the learning task to be described below, two non-associative tasks were studied: latency to eat and open-field activity. Latency to eat was measured in an aquarium in which five cubes of ground beef were presented to the turtle, which had been deprived of food for 24 hours. Latency to the first bite of food was measured. Open-field activity was measured in a tank of water 10.2 cm deep, which had a grid of 25.4 cm squares on the floor. Number of squares entered in 10 minutes was measured in two sessions spaced 5 days apart. Neither of these measures showed any effect of lesions of the dorsal cortex.

Morlock also studied spatial discrimination in a discrimination apparatus for food reward. Only painted turtles were used in this part of the experiment. They were trained to choose one side, using five trials per day with an intertrial interval of one min. and a noncorrection procedure, to a criterion of 9 out of 10 correct trials or 100 total trials. The lesions in the operated group were small and spared the pallial thickening. One operated subject (out of five) failed to learn in 100 trials, and the mean number of trials to criterion was 75.5 for the other four, compared to 60.5 for the controls. Statistical comparisons of the data from the two groups were not presented. Although these findings were interpreted to mean that turtles with lesions of the dorsal cortex could learn a spatial discrimination, the data suggest that lesions of the dorsal cortex may disrupt spatial learning in turtles.

Lesions of the dorsal cortex in the lizard *Dipsosaurus dorsalis* impaired maze learning and serial reversal of a position habit in a T-maze (Peterson, 1980). In lizards, the dorsal cortex does not receive a visual projection (Bruce & Butler, 1984) and thus is not directly comparable to the dorsal cortex of turtles. For the maze learning study the lizards were trained preoperatively on two different Lashley mazes for heat reward. Following ablation of the dorsal cortex or sham or no lesions, they were retested on the mazes. Animals with lesions of the dorsal cortex were unable to perform the maze tasks postoperatively and did not relearn in twice as many trials as controls. The lesioned animals often entered a cul-de-sac and remained there for the duration of the trial period (3 min.), even though they were normally active and ate well in their home cages.

The same species was trained postoperatively on a series of position reversals in a T-maze (Peterson, 1980). Five lizards served as either intact or operated controls, and six had lesions of the dorsal cortex. The lesioned subjects did not differ from controls on their first position problem, but they showed deficits on the subsequent reversals relative to controls.

Lizards (*Dipsosaurus dorsalis*) with lesions of the dorsal cortex showed no elevation of brightness difference thresholds (Peterson, 1980). Operated and control subjects were trained to go to white in a black−white discrimination in a T-maze. The brightness of the negative arm was then varied from black to light gray and percent correct choice was measured. The lesioned animals were not impaired in learning the black−white discrimination originally nor did they show an elevation in brightness difference threshold. Thus in lizards, as would be expected in a species in which the dorsal cortex receives no visual projection, sensory function appears not to be affected by dorsal cortex lesions. This result is consistent with the habituation study described previously.

Thus, by the beginning of the 1980s a few studies suggested that the dorsal cortex might play a role in learning. Taken together, these studies had shown deficits on habituation, maze retention, and position reversal, and had shown no deficits on acquisition of a spatial or brightness discrimination or on brightness difference thresholds.

RETENTION OF VISUAL DISCRIMINATION

We began to investigate the function of the dorsal cortex in painted turtles (*Chrysemys picta*) out of an interest in the evolution of the visual system. As stated earlier, the dorsal cortex receives a projection from the lateral geniculate nucleus of the thalamus. As part of a larger series of studies on brain mechanisms of vision, we were interested in determining whether lesions of the dorsal cortex would disrupt performance on a visual discrimination learned preoperatively (Reiner & Powers, 1983). We therefore trained turtles to criterion on a pattern discrimination (horizontal vs. vertical stripes). We used a learning situation derived from one developed by Pert & Gonzalez (1974). The training chamber was made of black Plexiglas and contained water about 5 cm deep. Mounted side by side on one wall of the chamber were two response keys and, between them, a white disk with an opening in the middle through which the reinforcement, beef

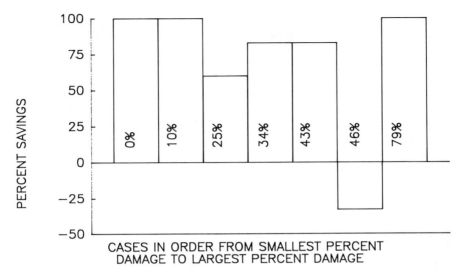

FIG. 6.2.   The savings score for each turtle trained on pattern discrimination in the experiment by Reiner & Powers (1983).

baby food, could be delivered by a syringe pump connected to a rubber tube. Projectors mounted behind the keys provide stimuli to be discriminated.

After the animals reached criterion on the discrimination, they were given ablations of the dorsal cortex. They were allowed to recover from surgery for 5 days and were then tested again on the same discriminations. Savings scores were calculated for each animal by subtracting the number of postoperative days required to reattain criterion from the number of days required to reach criterion preoperatively, dividing by the number of preoperative days to criterion, and multiplying times 100. Positive savings scores indicate that the animal did better postoperatively than it did preoperatively. The savings scores from the turtles trained on the pattern discrimination are shown in Fig. 6.2: Lesions of the dorsal cortex produced almost no deficits on the discriminations. Regardless of the amount of damage to the dorsal cortex, which ranged from 0 to more than 70% of each side, all the animals except one showed savings postoperatively.

To some extent, this result was expected. In birds, lesions of the area equivalent to the dorsal cortex, called the nucleus intercalatus hyperstriatii accessorii (IHA), also have been shown to produce no deficits on retention of brightness and pattern discriminations (Hodos, Karten, & Bonbright, 1973). In birds, however, such lesions do impair reversal learning (Benowitz & Lee-Teng, 1973; Macphail, 1976; Powers, 1969; Shimizu, 1986; Stettner & Schultz, 1967). Our next effort was directed at determining the effects of cortical lesions on reversal learning in turtles.

The experiment in which we studied reversal (Cranney & Powers, 1983) was designed to examine dimensional shifting as well. The turtles were trained to criterion on a series of 10 two-choice discrimination problems. The discriminanda consisted of horizontal and vertical stripes on red or green backgrounds. Either one of the two visual dimensions, pattern or color, could be relevant on a given problem, and the other irrelevant. Within each dimension, either of the two alternative stimuli could be correct. Thus, one of the four alternatives—red (R), green (G), horizontal stripes (H), or vertical stripes (V)—was correct on each problem. Each pattern appeared equally often on the red background and on the green (and on the left and right), so the turtle had to ignore one dimension to solve a problem on the other. The sequence of problems was as follows:

1—H 2—R 3—V 4—G 5—V 6—H
7—G 8—R 9—H 10—R

As can be seen, problems 6 and 8 were direct reversals of the previous problem (pattern and color respectively). Problems 2, 4, 7, and 10 were shifts from pattern to color; problems 3, 5, and 9 were shifts from color to pattern. The results are shown in Fig. 6.3: Turtles with lesions of the cortex were impaired only on problems 3 and 6. Each of these is a reversal of the previous pattern problem. Cortical lesions did not impair the acquisition of the original pattern discrimination or the learning of any color problem.

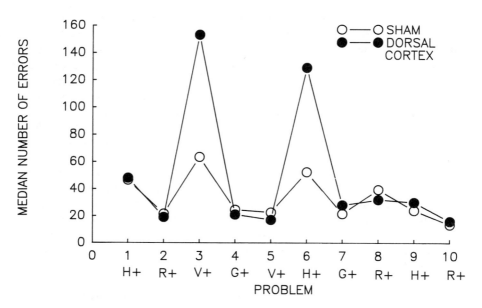

FIG. 6.3. The performance of the dorsal cortex and sham groups in the experiment by Cranney & Powers (1983).

Thus, lesions of the dorsal cortex impaired reversal learning, as was expected. They had no effect on the learning of the original discriminations. Two animals had lesions of the lateral or pyriform cortex instead of the dorsal cortex: These animals showed the same deficit as those with dorsal cortex lesions. This finding is not completely unexpected, because the lateral and dorsal cortices are extensively interconnected (Desan, 1984).

ACQUISITION OF A GO/NO-GO DISCRIMINATION

Our next set of experiments (Grisham & Powers, in press) was designed to examine the nature of the deficit found after lesions of the dorsal cortex. One possible explanation for the reversal deficit was that we had damaged the connections of the medial cortex, which run through the dorsal cortex (Desan, 1984). The medial cortex has long been considered to be the anatomical equivalent of the hippocampus in mammals (Humphrey, 1967; Johnston, 1913; Stensaas, 1967; Swanson, 1983), and hippocampal lesions frequently produce reversal deficits (O'Keefe & Nadel, 1978). We therefore made two types of lesions in these experiments: lesions of the dorsal cortex or of the medial cortex. If the effects of dorsal cortex lesions were due to damage to the projections to the medial cortex, then lesions of the medial cortex should produce deficits, too.

We wondered whether the reversal deficit was due to an inability to withhold a learned response. We therefore trained turtles with dorsal or medial cortex lesions on a go/no-go discrimination between horizontal and vertical stripes (Grisham & Powers, 1986; Grisham & Powers, in press). The stripes appeared on a black background in this experiment with no irrelevant color. The animals were first trained to press red keys, then given lesions, then trained to criterion on the discrimination. It turned out that many lesions damaged both dorsal and medial cortex instead of being restricted to only one. We therefore had to separate the effects of damage to one area or the other by statistical analysis. Damage to the dorsal cortex correlated significantly with days to criterion. No such correlation was found for damage to the medial cortex. Figure 6.4 shows the performance during the first 30 days of a turtle with damage to the dorsal cortex, which required 103 days to reach criterion (4 consecutive days with a difference in mean log latency of .7 or greater). The average number of days required by the control group was 18.8. This turtle was variable in response to the positive stimulus. It turned out that the animals with dorsal cortex lesions had no difficulty withholding response to the negative stimulus but showed a deficit because they were slower than normal to *acquire* the response to the positive stimulus.

RETENTION AND REVERSAL OF A GO/NO-GO DISCRIMINATION

We next attempted to determine whether lesions would disrupt the retention of a go/no-go discrimination (Grisham & Powers, 1985; Grisham & Powers, in

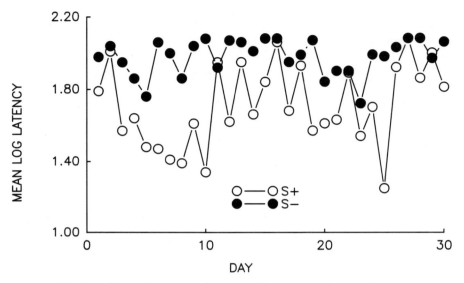

FIG. 6.4.   The performance of a turtle with a lesion of the dorsal cortex
on the first 30 days of a go/no-go discrimination.

press). For this experiment, we trained turtles to criterion preoperatively on the
go/no-go experiment, then tested them postoperatively on retention by retraining
them to criterion. Neither dorsal nor medial cortex damage affected retention of
the discrimination: All animals were at criterion when tested. This result showed
that the effect obtained on acquisition was not due to a sensory or motor loss or to
a lack of motivation. Any of these variables would be expected to affect retention
as well. The lack of an effect on retention was consistent with our earlier finding
(Reiner & Powers, 1983) that dorsal cortex lesions did not disrupt retention of a
simultaneous discrimination.

In order to determine whether reversal of a go/no-go discrimination was
affected in the same way as reversal of a simultaneous discrimination by lesions
of the cd, we reversed the animals in the retention experiment after they had
reached criterion (Grisham & Powers, 1987; Grisham & Powers, in press). In
this phase of the experiment, a number of turtles extinguished on the previously
positive stimulus without beginning to press the new positive (formerly negative)
one. When this occurred, we gave remedial training on the positive stimulus only
until the turtles were pressing well, and then we reintroduced the discrimination.
Animals with lesions of the dorsal cortex required more remedial training than

sham-operated controls. Again, because of overlap in lesions, we looked for correlations between damage to the dorsal cortex and deficit. The extent of damage to the dorsal cortex was correlated with the number of days in remedial training but not with the number of days in reversal training. Medial cortex damage was not correlated with either number of days in reversal training or number of days in remedial training. Thus, the turtles that had failed to show a deficit on retention of the go/no-go discrimination were impaired on reversal.

ACQUISITION OF A DISCRETE-TRIAL OPERANT

In order to examine the possibility that the dorsal cortex participates in learning, we decided to investigate the effects of dorsal and medial cortex lesions on the acquisition of a simple discrete-trial operant (Grisham & Powers, 1986; in press). In our previous experiments, we had trained turtles to press the response keys before we made lesions. Postoperatively, they had shown retention of the key-pressing response, as they had shown retention of simultaneous and successive visual discriminations in other experiments. Now for this experiment, we decided to teach the animals to eat from the food magazine preoperatively, then to remove the dorsal or medial cortex or to make sham lesions and to train them to press the key postoperatively. The postoperative training consisted of training on FR1 until the animals learned to press reliably (20 trials with a mean latency of less than 10 sec.). The response requirement was then raised to FR2 with a 60-sec. trial limit, and training continued until the mean latency across four successive sessions was 10 sec. or less.

As predicted, damage to the dorsal cortex was correlated with a deficit in acquiring the key-press response, whereas damage to the medial cortex was not. Some turtles with damage to the dorsal cortex required as many as 80 days to acquire the response; three turtles failed to reach the criterion in 80 days. The lesioned animals did press the key, but they did so erratically and with long latencies so that it took them much longer to achieve the criterion of stability.

After the turtles reached criterion on the original acquisition or had completed 80 days of training, we extinguished them and then retrained them to press the keys. Neither dorsal nor medial cortex damage had any effect on extinction or reacquisition. This result was important for us, because it suggested that the reversal deficit observed after dorsal cortex lesions in two experiments is not due to an inability of the lesioned turtles to extinguish a learned response tendency or to reacquire an extinguished response.

SUMMARY OF STUDIES ON THE FUNCTION
OF THE DORSAL CORTEX

This series of studies suggested that the dorsal cortex of reptiles participated in learning. Retention, whether of a go/no-go discrimination or a discrete-trial operant, was not disrupted by lesions of the dorsal cortex, but acquisition was.

How could these findings explain the reversal deficit that we had observed in the Cranney & Powers study? We concluded that reversal is especially sensitive to associative deficits; it is a task requiring acquisition of a new response. As such, it is difficult for turtles with lesions of the dorsal cortex, who seem to have deficits in their ability to learn.

Our results also showed that the reversal deficits seen after lesions of the dorsal cortex were not due to deafferentation of the medial cortex. We observed no effects of medial cortex damage on reversal or any other task in these experiments.

A BASAL FOREBRAIN CHOLINERGIC
SYSTEM IN TURTLES

In 1984, Mufson, Desan, Mesulam, Wainer, & Levey published a study of cholinergic neurons in turtles, in which they reported that cells in the basal forebrain react positively with an antibody for choline acetyltransferase (ChAT), the enzyme that is used as a marker for cholinergic cells. These cells, though small in number, resemble in their location and morphology the cholinergic cells in the basal forebrain of mammals. They extend from the medial septum to the ventral globus pallidus (termed in reptiles the *ventral paleostriatum*) to the horizontal limb of the diagonal band of Broca. These cells project in a systematic way to the surface of the hemisphere: The medial septum projects to the medial cortex, the horizontal limb of the diagonal band to the lateral cortex, and the ventral paleostriatum to the dorsal cortex (Desan, 1984; Ouimet, Patrick, & Ebner, 1985). Because of the resemblance between the ventral paleostriatum and the nucleus basalis of Meynert in mammals, we have called these cells the *nucleus basalis* in turtles. Bruce & Butler (1984) found a similar projection from the basal forebrain to the dorsal cortex in lizards. Thus, the basal forebrain of reptiles, like that of mammals, contains cholinergic cells that innervate the cortex. As explained earlier, the cortex of reptiles is not six-layered neocortex, but, in respect to cholinergic innervation, it appears to be similar to the neocortex of mammals.

Other findings, as well, suggest that the cholinergic cells of the basal forebrain of reptiles resemble those of mammals. The nucleus basalis of the rat receives a projection from nucleus accumbens (Nauta, Smith, Faull, & Domesick, 1978), and the nucleus basalis of reptiles receives a projection from a region equivalent to nucleus accumbens called area d (Brauth, personal communication; Powers, unpublished observation; Reiner, 1979). Both the nucleus basalis of the rat and that of the turtle are rich in substance P-containing fibers (Haber & Nauta, 1983; Ljungdahl, Hokfelt, & Nilsson, 1978; Reiner, Krause, Keyser, Eldred, & McKelvy, 1984), probably representing the terminations of a projection from the overlying striatal regions, area d in turtles and nucleus accumbens in mammals (Brauth, Reiner, Kitt, & Karten, 1983; Haber & Nauta, 1983). The striatal regions contain substance P-positive cell bodies in both turtles and rats (Ljungdahl et al., 1978; Reiner et al., 1984). The nucleus basalis in both classes contains a plexus of enkephalinergic fibers (Haber & Nauta, 1983; Reiner, 1987). These, too, may be the terminations of a projection from area d in turtles and nucleus accumbens in mammals, because both area d and nucleus accumbens contain enkephalinergic cell bodies (Haber & Nauta, 1983; Reiner, 1987). Thus the cholinergic neurons of nucleus basalis are anatomically equivalent in histochemistry, location, and known connections to those of the basal forebrain of mammals.

In mammals, of course, the nucleus basalis of Meynert has been implicated in learning and memory. It has been shown to degenerate in Alzheimer's disease (Johnston, McKinney, & Coyle, 1979; Whitehouse, Price, Clark, Coyle, & DeLong, 1981). Deficits in both learning and retention occur after lesions of the nucleus basalis in rats (Lerer, Warner, Friedman, Vincent, & Gamzu, 1985; Murray & Fibiger, 1985, 1986; for a review, see Olton & Wenk, 1987).

THE EFFECT OF BASAL FOREBRAIN LESIONS ON REVERSAL

The existence of an anatomical pathway in turtles so similar to that found in mammals led us to postulate that perhaps the learning deficits we saw following damage to the dorsal cortex in turtles were due to disruption of the cholinergic system projecting to the dorsal cortex. Accordingly, we decided to make lesions in the basal forebrain and examine the effects of these lesions on associative functions. Our first experiment (Blau & Powers, in press) examined the effects of dorsal cortex and basal forebrain lesions on the acquisition and reversal of a simultaneous pattern discrimination.

The subjects were trained preoperatively to eat from the food magazine and press the keys illuminated with red light on an FR2 schedule. They were then given lesions of either the dorsal cortex or nucleus basalis or sham lesions. No medial cortex lesions were included in this experiment. Dorsal cortex lesions were made by aspiration, and nucleus basalis lesions were made with ibotenic acid injections. After 5 days of postoperative recovery, the turtles were trained on a discrimination between horizontal and vertical stripes (approximately half had vertical-positive and half had horizontal-positive) to a criterion of 85% correct. On the day following achievement of criterion, they were reversed, so that those previously trained on horizontal-positive were now reinforced for going to vertical and vice versa, and again trained to criterion.

The results are shown in Fig. 6.5. Lesions of both the dorsal cortex and nucleus basalis disrupted both acquisition and reversal of the discrimination. The two lesioned groups did not differ on either phase, but both were significantly impaired relative to sham-operates. Thus, our hypothesis was confirmed: Damage to the basal forebrain in turtles produces deficits like those obtained with dorsal cortex lesions.

The deficit on acquisition after dorsal cortex lesions came as a surprise: We

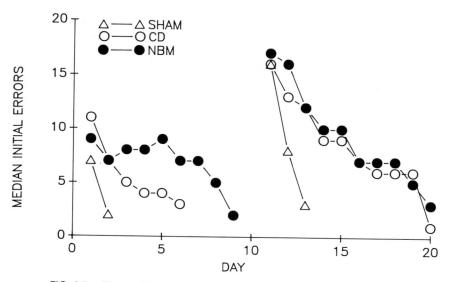

FIG. 6.5. The performance of three groups of turtles on acquisition and reversal of a simultaneous pattern discrimination. CD = dorsal cortex lesion; NBM = nucleus basalis lesion. (From Blau & Powers, in press, *Psychobiology,* reprinted by permission of Psychonomic Society, Inc.)

expected no deficit, because we had observed none in our previous investigation of the acquisition of a simultaneous discrimination (Cranney & Powers, 1983). Comparison of the lesions in that study and this one revealed, however, that the lesions in this study were considerably larger than those of Cranney & Powers and more similar in size to those in the Grisham & Powers study. The shams in this study also showed less variability on acquisition, so that any difficulty experienced by the lesioned animals would be detected as a deficit. The findings of this study thus extend the findings of Grisham and Powers that turtles with lesions of the dorsal cortex impair turtles' ability to learn a discrimination.

One of the questions we asked about these data was whether the deficits we observed were in learning or motivation. Although we cannot answer this question definitively, one way of approaching it is to ask whether the lesioned turtles were slower to respond than normals. Such a finding might suggest that they were less motivated for the food. Because the dorsal cortex animals in the go/no-go discrimination of Grisham & Powers were slower than shams, we expected to find the same result here. In this study, we recorded the overall session length in order to obtain an index of response latency. Although lesioned animals took longer to complete a session than shams, it turned out that all of the difference could be accounted for by the increased number of errors made by the turtles with lesions: The groups did not differ in time per trial. Thus, the experiment failed to provide evidence that dorsal cortex or basal forebrain lesions increase the latency of response in all situations and suggested, instead, that the lesioned subjects were as eager to eat as normal but had more difficulty learning to choose the correct stimulus, both in acquisition and in reversal.

EFFECTS OF BASAL FOREBRAIN LESIONS ON MAZE RETENTION

We wondered whether the deficit we observed after dorsal cortex lesions in the operant discrimination chamber might extend to learning or memory on other kinds of tasks. We therefore devised a maze for turtles and tested the effects of lesions on retention of the maze (Petrillo & Powers, 1987, in preparation). In mammals, lesions of the basal forebrain have been shown to affect retention of several different sorts of mazes (Olton & Wenk, 1987). The maze we used was in the shape of an X, with a start box at one end and a goal box with water in it at the end of the arm to the left of the start arm. The other two arms ended in wells that contained only dry gravel. The turtles were run for water reward, after 22 hr. of water deprivation. Three trials per day were given, with an intertrial interval of 5 min. On each trial, the experimenter placed the turtle in the start, waited 1 min. so that the animal could recover from handling, and opened a guillotine door to allow the turtle access to the maze. The experimenter was hidden from view during the trial. Trials lasted 5 minutes or until the turtle reached the water and drank for 15 sec. Latency and number of incorrect entries were recorded. For each day, a score was calculated by dividing the total number of goal entries (maximum = 3) by the total number of entries into all arms including the goal arm. Thus, an animal that went straight to the goal on all three trials of a day received a score of 1.0. Each animal was trained to a criterion of 2 consecutive days with a score of .67 or higher.

After achieving criterion, the turtles were given suction lesions of the dorsal cortex, ibotenic acid lesions of the basal forebrain, or sham lesions. Five days were allowed for postoperative recovery, and then the animals were again run in the maze to criterion or until they had been tested for three times as long as it took them to reach criterion preoperatively. Figure 6.6 shows the preoperative and postoperative performance of the three groups. Again, both dorsal cortex and basal forebrain lesions disrupted performance; the performance of both lesioned groups is significantly different from that of the shams. As can be seen, however, the performance of the lesioned groups in this experiment seemed to differ. All dorsal cortex subjects relearned the maze, but two out of four subjects with basal forebrain lesions did not. These two turtles tended to stop responding altogether and remain either in the start box or in one of the incorrect goal boxes on each trial. This behavior is identical to that described by Peterson (1980) for lizards with lesions of the dorsal cortex in her maze. It was rarely observed in turtles

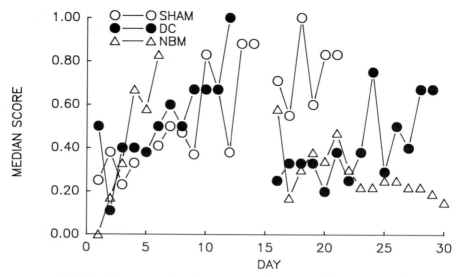

FIG. 6.6.   The pre- and postoperative performance of three groups of turtles trained on a maze for water reward. DC = dorsal cortex lesion; NBM = nucleus basalis lesion.

with dorsal cortex lesions in this experiment, however. In spite of this discrepancy in behavior between the two groups, the difference between the lesioned groups is not significant.

This was the first experiment in which retention was disrupted by lesions of the dorsal cortex. In our previous experiments, we had found only learning deficits. A possible resolution of this disparity is that a learning deficit might have impaired retention of a difficult task such as this one. As Fig. 6.6 shows, performance was not asymptotic preoperatively. It is possible that the lesioned subjects were still learning postoperatively and were disrupted because dorsal cortex lesions disrupt learning. If this analysis is correct, it predicts that if we had trained to a stricter criterion, we would have seen less of a deficit. In fact, the two turtles in the dorsal cortex group that had the most preoperative training showed the smallest effects postoperatively; one actually showed savings. Thus, these two animals, which may have been overtrained preoperatively, were less disrupted by the lesions than other subjects who had less preoperative training. The same relationship does not appear to hold for the subjects with nucleus basalis lesions; the nature of their deficit may be different from that caused by dorsal cortex lesions.

One question that must be asked about the results of this experiment, especially for the turtles with lesions of nucleus basalis, is whether the lesions disrupt an associative process or merely some aspect of performance, such as motivation. All subjects, even the two that never reached criterion, drank on those trials on which they reached the goal. Therefore, we believe that the lesioned turtles were not unmotivated for water but were, rather, impaired in remembering where the water was.

SOME CONCLUDING THOUGHTS

The results presented here show that in turtles the dorsal cortex and nucleus basalis, which together form part of a forebrain cholinergic system, participate in learning. Although some of our results suggest that there may be differences in function between these two structures, the similarity between the two in the effects of lesions is more marked.

Much work is, of course, yet to be done. We are in the process of attempting to demonstrate that the nucleus basalis lesions produced a loss of acetylcholine in the cortex. We would like to know the nature and limits of the deficit we observe in learning. Does it extend to habituation and classical conditioning? Can the function of the dorsal cortex and nucleus basalis be differentiated?

I have emphasized throughout this review that, in spite of the fact that the dorsal cortex receives a visual projection from the lateral geniculate nucleus, our results do not support the hypothesis that dorsal cortex lesions produce a visual deficit. When we started our investigation of dorsal cortex function, we were interested in seeing whether visual deficits might occur. The results showed that turtles with dorsal cortex lesions were not impaired on retention of a visual discrimination. Although we have since found deficits on acquisition of visual discriminations, we interpret the lack of a deficit on retention to mean that the deficits we observe are not due to sensory impairment. In turtles, it appears that lesions of the so-called tectofugal visual system result in sensory impairments (Reiner & Powers, 1978, 1983). Lesions of nucleus rotundus in the thalamus produce a clear visual deficit: an elevation of sensory threshold (Powers & Frank, 1983). Lesions of nucleus rotundus also cause a deficit on retention of simultaneous visual discriminations (Reiner & Powers, 1978). Thus, if dorsal cortex lesions produced a sensory impairment, they would be expected to affect retention of visual discriminations as well.

Table 6.1 presents a summary of the findings presented here and comparisons between them and studies of the IHA in birds and the hippocampus of mammals. A question still to be resolved is the relation of the medial and dorsal cortices and the relationship of them both to the hippocampus of mammals. Although the reptilian medial cortex is believed on anatomical grounds to be homologous with the mammalian hippocampus, we have obtained no evidence that the medial cortex plays a role in learning or memory. In fact, as described earlier and shown in Table 6.1, we have not observed any effects of medial cortex lesions in our experiments. Dorsal cortex lesions have, of course, generated such effects, and a

TABLE 6.1

	Reptilian Dorsal Cortex	Reptilian Medial Cortex	Reptilian Nucleus Basalis	Mammalian Hippocampus	Avian IHA or Wulst
Acquisition					
Key press	deficit (6)	no deficit (6)	—	—	—
Simultaneous visual discrimination	deficit (3) no deficit (5)	—	deficit (3)	no deficit (12)	no deficit (19)
Successive visual discrimination	deficit (6)	no deficit (6)	—	deficit (4)	deficit (26)
Spatial discrimination	no deficit (14)	—	—	deficit (12)	no deficit (8)
Retention					
Key press	no deficit (6)	no deficit (6)	no deficit (3)	—	no deficit (17)
Simultaneous visual discrimination	no deficit (21)	—	—	—	no deficit (7)
Successive visual discrimination	no deficit (6)	no deficit (6)	—	—	deficit (20)
Maze learning	deficit (15)	—	deficit (15)	deficit (12)	no deficit (18)
Reversal					
Simultaneous visual discrimination	deficit (3, 5)	—	deficit (3)	deficit (12)	deficit (2, 10, 16, 23, 24)

Successive visual discrimination	deficit (6)	no deficit (6)	—	deficit (25)	deficit (17)
Spatial discrimina- tion	deficit (14)	—	—	deficit (12)	deficit (8, 9)
Miscellaneous					
Brightness differ- ence threshold	no deficit (14)	—	—	—	no deficit (13)
Extinction	no deficit (6)	no deficit (6)	—	deficit (1, 22)	—

1. Amsel, Glazer, Lakey, McCullen, & Wong (1973)
2. Benowitz & Lee-Teng (1973)
3. Blau & Powers (in press)
4. Buerger (1970)
5. Cranney & Powers (1983)
6. Grisham & Powers (in press)
7. Hodos, Karten, & Bonbright (1973)
8. Macphail (1971)
9. Macphail (1975)
10. Macphail (1976)
11. Morlock (1972)
12. O'Keefe & Nadel (1978)
13. Pasternak & Hodos (1977)
14. Peterson (1980)
15. Petrillo & Powers (in preparation)
16. Powers (1969)
17. Powers (1989)
18. Powers, Caine, & Kaplan (1983)
19. Powers, Halasz, & Williams (1982)
20. Pritz, Mead, & Northcutt (1970)
21. Reiner & Powers (1983)
22. Schmaltz & Isaacson (1967)
23. Shimizu (1986)
24. Stettner & Schultz (1967)
25. Swanson & Isaacson (1967)
26. Zeigler (1963)

comparison of deficits obtained after dorsal cortex or hippocampal lesions (Table 6.1) reveals that the effects are similar although not identical. The dorsal cortex may function in a manner similar to that of the hippocampus of mammals, but there are enough discrepancies to warrant caution in making such an interpretation.

Another question of interest is the relationship of the dorsal cortex of reptiles to the IHA of the Wulst in birds. Many of the findings from studies of Wulst lesions match those found after dorsal cortex lesions in reptiles (see Table 6.1). The most robust finding is a deficit on reversal. Results have been mixed on acquisition and retention of discriminative learning. Pigeons with lesions of the Wulst do not have elevations of brightness difference thresholds. Thus, again in birds, the IHA is not functioning in an obviously visual capacity, but appears to be more associative in function. In spite of the differences between the results for birds and reptiles, I tend to think that the IHA of birds and the dorsal cortex of reptiles function in similar ways.

The findings described in this review suggest that the forebrain cholinergic system plays an important role in associative functions in reptiles. From an evolutionary standpoint, it is reasonable to surmise that the common ancestors of turtles and mammals, the cotylosaurs, possessed this system. The similarity of function in reptiles and mammals suggest that learning and (perhaps) memory in amniotes has long been mediated by such projections and that an understanding of their function in reptiles may allow us deeper insights into their role in associative function in mammals and humans.

REFERENCES

Amsel, A., Glazer, H., Lakey, J. R., McCullen, T., & Wong, P. T. P. (1973). Introduction of acoustic stimulation during acquisition and resistance to extinction in the normal and hippocampally damaged rat. *Journal of Comparative and Physiological Psychology, 84,* 176–186.

Balaban, C. D., & Ulinski, P. S. (1981a). Organization of thalamic afferents to anterior dorsal ventricular ridge in turtles. I. Projections of thalamic nuclei. *Journal of Comparative Neurology, 200,* 95–129.

Balaban, C. D., & Ulinski, P. S. (1981b). Organization of thalamic afferents to anterior dorsal ventricular ridge in turtles. II. Properties of the rotundo-dorsal nucleus map. *Journal of Comparative Neurology, 200,* 131–150.

Benowitz, L., & Lee-Teng, E. (1973). Contrasting effects of three forebrain ablations on discrimination learning and reversal in chicks. *Journal of Comparative and Physiological Psychology, 84,* 391–397.

Blau, A., & Powers, A. S. (in press). Discrimination learning in turtles after lesions of the dorsal cortex or basal forebrain. *Psychobiology.*

Brauth, S. E., Reiner, A., Kitt, C. A., & Karten, H. J. (1983). The substance P-containing striato-tegmental path in reptiles: An immunohistochemical study. *Journal of Comparative Neurology, 219,* 305–327.

Bruce, L. L., & Butler, A. B. (1984). Telencephalic connections in lizards. I. Projections to cortex. *Journal of Comparative Neurology, 229,* 585–601.

Buerger, A. A. (1970). Effects of preoperative training on relearning a successive discrimination by cats with hippocampal lesions. *Journal of Comparative and Physiological Psychology, 72,* 462–466.

Cranney, J., & Powers, A. S. (1983). The effects of core nucleus and cortical lesions in turtles on reversal and dimensional shifting. *Physiological Psychology, 11,* 103–111.

Crosby, E. C. (1917). The forebrain of *Alligator mississippiensis. Journal of Comparative Neurology, 27,* 325–402.

Desan, P. (1984). *The organization of the cerebral cortex of the pond turtle, Pseudemys scripta.* Unpublished doctoral dissertation, Harvard University, Cambridge, MA.

Grisham, W., & Powers, A. S. (1985). Effects of dorsal and medial cortex lesions on the acquisition and retention of a go–no go discrimination by turtles. *Society for Neuroscience Abstracts, 11,* 1113.

Grisham, W., & Powers, A. S. (1986). Effects of lesions of the dorsal and medial cortex on the acquisition, extinction, and reacquisition of a discrete-trial operant in turtles. *Society for Neuroscience Abstracts, 12,* 749.

Grisham, W., & Powers, A. S. (1987). Effects of lesions of the dorsal and medial cortex on the reversal of a go/no-go discrimination in turtles. *Society for Neuroscience Abstracts, 13,* 1067.

Grisham, W., & Powers, A. S. (in press). *Function of the dorsal and medial cortex of turtles in learning. Behaviorial Neuroscience.*

Haber, S. N., & Nauta, W. J. H. (1983). Ramifications of the globus pallidus in the rat as indicated by patterns of immunohistochemistry. *Neuroscience, 9,* 245–260.

Hall, W. C., & Ebner, F. F. (1970). Thalamotelencephalic projections in the turtle (*Pseudemys scripta*). *Journal of Comparative Neurology, 140,* 101–122.

Hall, J. A., Foster, R. E., Ebner, F. F., & Hall, W. C. (1977). Visual cortex in a reptile, the turtle (*Pseudemys scripta* and *Chrysemys picta*). *Brain Research, 130,* 197–216.

Hodos, W., Karten, H. J., & Bonbright, J. C., Jr. (1973). Visual intensity and pattern discrimination after lesions of the thalamofugal visual pathway in pigeons. *Journal of Comparative Neurology, 148,* 447–468.

Humphrey, T. (1967). The development of the human hippocampal formation correlated with some aspects of its phylogenetic history. In R. Hassler & H. Stephan (Eds.), *Evolution of the forebrain* (pp. 104–116). New York: Plenum.

Johnston, J. B. (1913). The morphology of the septum, hippocampus, and pallial commissures in reptiles and mammals. *Journal of Comparative Neurology, 23,* 317–478.

Johnston, M. V., McKinney, M., & Coyle, J. T. (1979). Evidence for a cholinergic projection from neurons in basal forebrain. *Proceedings of the National Academy of Science, 76,* 5392–5396.

Killackey, H., Pellmar, T., & Ebner, F. F. (1972). The effects of general cortex ablation on habituation in the turtle. *Federation Proceedings, 31,* 819.

Lerer, B., Warner, J., Friedman, E., Vincent, G., & Gamzu, E. (1985). Cortical cholinergic impairment and behavioral deficits produced by kainic acid lesions of rat magnocellular basal forebrain. *Behavioral Neuroscience, 99,* 661–677.

Ljungdahl, A., Hokfelt, T., & Nilsson, G. (1978). Distribution of substance P-like immunoreactivity in the central nervous system of the rat. I. Cell bodies and nerve terminals. *Neuroscience, 3,* 861–943.

Macphail, E. M. (1971). Hyperstriatal lesions in pigeons. Effects on response inhibition, behavioral contrast, and reversal learning. *Journal of Comparative and Physiological Psychology, 75,* 500–507.

Macphail, E. M. (1975). Hyperstriatal function in the pigeon: Response inhibition or response shift? *Journal of Comparative and Physiological Psychology, 89,* 609–618.

Macphail, E. M. (1976). Evidence against the response-shift account of hyperstriatal function in the pigeon. *Journal of Comparative and Physiological Psychology, 90,* 547–559.

Morlock, H. C. (1972). Behavior following ablation of the dorsal cortex of turtles. *Brain, Behavior, and Evolution, 5,* 256–263.

Mufson, E. J., Desan, P. H., Mesulam, M. M., Wainer, B. H., & Levey, A. I. (1984). Choline acetyltransferase-like immunoreactivity in the forebrain of the red-eared pond turtle (*Pseudemys scripta elegans*). *Brain Research, 323,* 103–108.

Murray, C. L., & Fibiger, H. C. (1985). Learning and memory deficits after lesions of the nucleus basalis magnocellularis: Reversal by physostigmine. *Neuroscience, 19,* 1025–1032.

Murray, C. L., & Fibiger, H. C. (1986). Pilocarpine and physostigmine attenuate spatial memory impairments produced by lesions of the nucleus basalis magnocellularis. *Behavioral Neuroscience, 100,* 23–32.

Nauta, W. J. H., & Karten, H. J. (1970). A general profile of the vertebrate brain with sidelights on the ancestry of cerebral cortex. In F. O. Schmitt (Ed.), *The neurosciences: second study program* (pp. 7–26). New York: Rockefeller University Press.

Nauta, W. J. H., Smith, G. P., Faull, R. L. M., & Domesick, V. B. (1978). Efferent connections and nigral afferents of the nucleus accumbens in the monkey. *Neuroscience, 3,* 385–401.

O'Keefe, J., & Nadel, L. (1978). *The hippocampus as a cognitive map.* Oxford: Clarendon.

Olton, D. S., & Wenk, G. L. (1987). Dementia: Animal models of the cognitive impairments produced by degeneration of the basal forebrain cholinergic system. In H. Y. Meltzer (Ed.), *Psychopharmacology: The third generation of progress* (pp. 941–952). New York: Raven.

Ouimet, C. C., Patrick, R. L., & Ebner, F. F. (1985). The projection of three extrathalamic cell groups to the cerebral cortex of the turtle *Pseudemys*. *Journal of Comparative Neurology, 237,* 77–84.

Pasternak, T., & Hodos, W. (1977). Intensity difference thresholds after lesions of the visual Wulst in pigeons. *Journal of Comparative and Physiological Psychology, 91,* 485–497.

Pert, A., & Gonzalez, R. C. (1974). The behavior of the turtle (*Chrysemys picta picta*) in simultaneous, successive, and behavioral contrast situations. *Journal of Comparative and Physiological Psychology, 87,* 526–538.

Peterson, E. (1980). Behavioral studies of telencephalic functions in reptiles. In S. O. E. Ebbesson (Ed.), *Comparative neurology of the telencephalon* (pp. 343–388). New York: Plenum.

Petrillo, M., & Powers, A. S. (1987). Disruption in maze performance after cortical lesions in turtles (*Chrysemys picta*). *Society for Neuroscience Abstracts, 13,* 1125.

Petrillo, M., & Powers, A. S. (in preparation). *Retention of maze performance after lesions of the dorsal cortex or nucleus basalis in turtles.*

Powers, A. S. (1969). *The role of the avian hyperstriatum in habit reversal.* Unpublished doctoral dissertation, Bryn Mawr College, PA.

Powers, A. S. (1989). Wulst lesions in pigeons disrupt go/no-go reversal. *Physiology and Behavior 46,* 337–339.

Powers, A. S., Caine, B., & Kaplan, L. (1983). The effects of lesions in telencephalic visual areas on stimulus generalization in pigeons. *Physiological Psychology, 11,* 147–153.

Powers, A. S., & Frank, R. (1983). The effects of lesions of nucleus rotundus on visual intensity difference thresholds in turtles (*Chrysemys picta*). *Brain Research, 264,* 47–56.

Powers, A. S., Halasz, F., & Williams, S. (1982). The effects of lesions in telencephalic visual areas of pigeons on dimensional shifting. *Physiology and Behavior, 29,* 1099–1104.

Powers, A. S., & Reiner, A. (1979). The central nervous system. In M. Harless & H. Morlock (Eds.), *Turtles: research and perspectives* (pp. 193–205). New York: Wiley.

Pritz, M. B., Mead, W. R., & Northcutt, R. G. (1970). The effects of Wulst ablations in color, brightness, and pattern discrimination in pigeons. *Journal of Comparative Neurology, 140,* 81–100.

Reiner, A. (1979). The paleostriatal complex in turtles. *Society for Neuroscience Abstracts, 5,* 146.

Reiner, A. (1987). The distribution of proenkephalin-derived peptides in the central nervous system of turtles. *Journal of Comparative Neurology, 259,* 65–91.

Reiner, A., Brauth, S. E., & Karten, H. J. (1984). Evolution of the amniote basal ganglia. *Trends in Neuroscience, 7,* 320–325.

Reiner, A., Krause, K. T., Keyser, W. D., Eldred, W. D., & McKelvy, J. F. (1984). The distribution of substance P in turtle nervous system: A radioimmunoassay and immunohistochemical study. *Journal of Comparative Neurology, 226,* 50–75.

Reiner, A., & Powers, A. S. (1978). Intensity and pattern discrimination in turtles following lesions of nucleus rotundus. *Journal of Comparative and Physiological Psychology, 92,* 1156–1168.

Reiner, A., & Powers, A. S. (1983). The effect of lesions in telencephalic visual structures on visual discriminative performance in turtles (*Chrysemys picta picta*). *Journal of Comparative Neurology, 218,* 1–24.

Romer, A. S. (1959). *The vertebrate story.* Chicago: University of Chicago Press.

Schmaltz, L. W., & Isaacson, R. L. (1967). FR, DRL, and discrimination learning in rats following aspiration lesions and penicillin injections into hippocampus. *Physiology and Behavior, 11,* 17–22.

Shimizu, T. (1986). *Reversal learning performance after selective lesions of the Wulst in pigeons* (*Columba livia*). Unpublished doctoral dissertation, University of Maryland.

Stensaas, L. T. (1967). The development of hippocampal and dorsolateral pallial regions of the cerebral hemisphere in fetal rabbits. I. Fifteen millimeter stage, spongioblast morphology. *Journal of Comparative Neurology, 129,* 59–70.

Stettner, L. J., & Schultz, W. (1967). Brain lesions in birds: Effects on discrimination acquisition and reversal. *Science, 155,* 1689–1692.

Swanson, A. M., & Isaacson, R. L. (1967). Hippocampal ablation and performance during withdrawal of reinforcement. *Journal of Comparative and Physiological Psychology, 64,* 30–35.

Swanson, L. W. (1983). The hippocampus and the concept of the limbic system. In W. Seifert (Ed.), *Neurobiology of the hippocampus.* New York: Academic Press.

Whitehouse, P. J., Price, D. L., Clark, A. W., Coyle, J. T., & Delong, M. R. (1981). Alzheimer's disease: Evidence for selective loss of cholinergic neurons in the nucleus basalis. *Annals of Neurology, 10,* 122–126.

Zeigler, H. P. (1963). Effects of endbrain lesions upon visual discrimination learning in pigeons. *Journal of Comparative Neurology, 120,* 161–182.

7

Learning and Memory in Rats with an Emphasis on the Role of the Hippocampal Formation

Raymond P. Kesner
University of Utah

The literature on the neurobiological basis of memory in rodents is voluminous. On the one hand there are a large number of theoretical approaches aimed at the understanding of the neurobiological basis of memory, and on the other hand there are many neural regions that have been implicated as critical substrates of memory. Therefore, this chapter emphasizes only one theoretical approach and only one neural region. Based on the idea that there might be multidimensional representations of memory, rather than a single or dual representation, and that specific localizable neural regions can mediate or code for these multidimensional representations, Kesner and DiMattia (1987) have proposed an attribute model of memory.

Based on earlier suggestions by Underwood (1969) and Spear (1976), the attribute model proposes that any specific memory is composed of a set of features or attributes that are specific and unique for each learning experience. In animal memory experiments, a set of at least five salient attributes characterize the structural organization of memory. These are labeled *space, sensory-perception, time, response,* and *affect.* A spatial attribute within this framework involves the coding and storage of specific stimuli representing places or relationships between places, which are usually independent of the subject's own body schema. It is exemplified by the ability to encode and remember maps and to localize stimuli in external space.

A sensory-perceptual attribute involves the encoding and storage of a set of sensory stimuli that are organized in the form of cues as part of a specific experience. A temporal attribute involves the encoding and storage of specific stimuli or sets of spatially or temporally separated stimuli as part of an episode marking or tagging its occurrence in time—that is, separating one specific epi-

179

sode from previous or succeeding episodes. A response attribute involves the encoding and storage of information based on feedback from responses that occur in specific situations as well as the selection of appropriate responses. An affect attribute involves the encoding and storage of reinforcement contingencies that result in positive or negative emotional experiences.

The organization of these attributes can take many forms utilizing both serial and parallel systems. There are critical interactions between attributes that can aid in identifying the underlying specific neural regions. For example, the interaction between spatial and temporal attributes can provide for external context of a situation, which is important in determining when and where critical events occurred. It is assumed that the hippocampal formation is critically involved in the coding of such spatial-temporal attributes. This latter assumption is in agreement with Winocur's (1980) views, who has suggested that the hippocampal formation codes the external context of specific situations. Another important interaction involves the temporal and affective attributes. In this case, the interaction can provide important information concerning the internal context (internal state of the organism), which is important in evaluating emotional experiences. It is assumed that the amygdala is critically involved in the coding of such affective-temporal attributes.

In the attribute model it is not only assumed that specific memories are represented by a set of attributes, but they are also processed in data-based and expectancy-based memory systems. The data-based memory system is biased toward the coding of incoming data concerning the present, with an emphasis on facts, data, and events that are usually personal and that occur within specific external and internal environmental contexts. In contemporary information processing theory terms, the emphasis of the data-based memory system is on "bottom-up" processing. During initial learning, there is a great emphasis on the data-based memory system, which will continue to be of importance even after initial learning in situations where trial-unique or novel information needs to be remembered. The data-based memory system is conceptually similar to Olton's working memory, but is not based on the requirement that the task only involve trial unique information. It is assumed that the hippocampal formation codes spatio-temporal attributes only within the data-based memory system.

The expectancy-based memory system is biased towards previously stored information and can be thought of as one's general knowledge of the world. It can operate in the abstract in the absence of critical incoming data. From an informational processing view, the emphasis of the expectancy-based memory system is on "top-down" processing.

Memories within the expectancy-based memory system are assumed to be organized as a set of cognitive maps and their interactions that are unique for each memory. The exact nature and organization of knowledge structures within each cognitive map needs to be determined. The cognitive maps are labeled *spatial (allocentric), spatial (egocentric), temporal, affect, response (somatic), response (autonomic), and sensory-perceptual* and are influenced by a set of attributes such as space, time, affect, response, and sensory-perception as well as interactions between attributes such as space and response. Note that the same attributes are also associated with the data-based memory system. It is assumed that the neocortex mediates different sets of cognitive maps. Support for this assumption can be found in Kesner and DiMattia (1987).

The expectancy-based memory system tends to be of greater importance after a task has been learned, given that the situation is invariant and familiar. In most situations, however, one would expect a contribution of both data-based and expectancy-based systems with varying proportion of involvement of one relative to the other.

Because the attribute model is very comprehensive and involves many neural regions, it is necessary because of space limitations to limit this presentation to the hippocampal formation. An attempt is made to illustrate with the use of a variety of behavioral paradigms its assumed role in subserving memory functions within the attribute model of memory.

A comprehensive review of the hippocampal formation in the rat has been detailed by Bayer (1985). A short summary emphasizing the different parts and connections of the hippocampal formation is presented hereafter.

The hippocampal formation in the rat occupies most of the ventroposterior and ventrolateral walls of the neocortex. It consists of six distinct structures: the entorhinal cortex, parasubiculum, presubiculum, subiculum proper, fields CA1–CA3 in Ammons horn, and dentate gyrus. The Ammons horn, which consists primarily of pyramidal cells, and dentate gyrus, which consists primarily of granule cells, form the hippocampus proper. There are other cell types (e.g., basket cells) within the hippocampus proper.

The major afferents into entorhinal cortex come from many areas of neocortex, olfactory bulb, CA1 and CA3 regions of Ammons horn, amygdala, basal forebrain areas, dorsal raphe, and locus coeruleus. The major efferents of the entorhinal cortex are to the hippocampus proper via the "perforant path," many areas of the neocortex, and amygdala.

The major afferents into subicular complex (parasubiculum, presubiculum, and subiculum) come from raphe nuclei, locus coeruleus, medial septum, vertical limb of diagonal band, amygdala, and CA1 region of Ammons horn. The major efferents of the subicular complex include anterior thalamic nuclei, mammillary body of the hypothalamus, neocortex, amygdala, and lateral septal nucleus.

The major afferents into Ammons horn include projections from raphe nuclei, locus coeruleus, entorhinal cortex, medial septum, and vertical limb of diagonal band. The major efferents of the Ammons horn include lateral septum, subicular complex, and entorhinal cortex. There are also intrinsic connections within the Ammons horn. The major afferents into dentate gyrus come from raphe nuclei, locus coeruleus, medial septum, vertical limb of diagonal band, and entorhinal cortex. The major efferents of the dentate gyrus include mossy fiber projections to CA3 in Ammons horn.

It is clear that there are a large number of neocortical, limbic, and diencephalic interconnections with the hippocampal formation as well as connections from raphe nuclei and locus coeruleus. There are also many intrinsic connections between the different components of the hippocampal formation. Thus, the hippocampal formation has the richness in anatomical organization and connections that are probably required for a critical role in mediating memory functions.

It should be noted that the majority of studies reported in this chapter have concentrated on the role of the hippocampus proper, but, based on the elaborate interconnections within the hippocampul formation, any lesion of the hippocampus proper probably also alters the function of the subicular complex and entorhinal cortex.

WHAT INFORMATION IS CODED IN THE HIPPOCAMPAL FORMATION

Does the hippocompal formation code all attributes or a subset of critical attributes associated with memory? The attribute model assumes that the hippocampus codes only spatio-temporal attribute (environmental context) information. An alternative view has been presented by O'Keefe and Nadel (1978). They proposed that the hippocampal formation exclusively codes and stores spatial information in the form of an allocentric spatial cognitive map (i.e., spatial maps that are independent of the body axes). This spatial cognitive map can be used for place recognition, navigation, and coding of context. The allocentric map is to be differentiated from egocentric or taxic and praxic orientations, which are subserved by different neural systems. This cognitive map model of hippocampal formation function suggests that the hippocampal formation only codes spatial attributes.

A somewhat different emphasis is provided by Rawlins' temporal context model of the hippocampal formation (Rawlins, 1985). The model states that the hippocampal formation serves as a multisensory, multistructural processor for temporally discontiguous data. The hippocampal formation is involved in processing information whenever two or more stimuli, regardless of sensory modality, are separated in time but must be associated in order to correctly solve a task. Thus, the hippocampal formation codes temporal attributes.

I review herein some, but not all, of the literature that pertains to the nature of information processing within the hippocampal formation.

Spatial Attribute

Support for the idea that the hippocampal formation codes spatial attribute information comes from a variety of sources. First, Kubie and Ranck (1983), Mc-

Naughton, Barnes, and O'Keefe (1983), O'Keefe (1979, 1983), and Olton, Branch and Best (1978) have shown that many hippocampal cells increase their firing rate when an animal is located in a specific place within a specific environment. These cells have complex spikes and are called "place" cells. Furthermore, O'Keefe & Speakman (1987) have shown that these "place" cells might indeed be related to spatial memory. They trained animals in a four-arm plus-shaped maze in order to obtain reward. During the study phase of a trial, an animal was allowed to enter a single goal arm. This arm was varied from trial to trial, but the extramaze spatial cues remained constant relative to the selected arm. During the test phase, these extramaze spatial cues remained in the same position ("perceptual trials") or the extramaze uses were removed ("memory trials"). They found that many CA1 pyramidal complex spike cells fired in a particular location in the maze for both perceptual and memory trials, given that the animal made the correct choice of goal arm.

Second, animals with hippocampal formation lesions have deficits in a variety of spatial tasks using a wide variety of procedures (for a review see Barnes, 1988). In particular, animals with hippocampal formation lesions are severely impaired in delayed spatial matching or nonmatching to sample tasks (Hunt, Kesner, & DeSpain, 1986; Kesner, Crutcher, & Beers, 1988; Olton, 1983, 1986). These tasks emphasize the importance of spatial memory.

Similar involvement in coding spatial information in monkeys and humans comes from the observation of "place" cells within the hippocampal formation of monkeys (Rolls et al., in press). Also, hippocampal formation lesions in monkeys produce severe deficits in spatial location memory tasks (Jones & Mishkin, 1972; Parkinson & Mishkin, 1982), and humans with presumed or demonstrated hippocampal damage show deficits in spatial memory tasks (Smith & Milner, 1981; Zola-Morgan, Squire, & Amaral, 1986).

Thus, there is good empirical evidence to suggest that the hippocampal formation plays an important role in coding spatial information and that memory for spatial attributes involves the hippocampal formation.

Sensory-Perceptual Attribute

To what extent does the hippocampal formation code nonspatial (sensory-perceptual) information? It should be noted that neither the attribute model nor the cognitive map or temporal context models predict that hippocampal formation lesions will yield a memory deficit for any sensory-perceptual attributes (e.g., visual, auditory, olfactory).

The majority of studies have shown that animals with hippocampal formation lesions are not impaired in sensory-perceptual discrimination tasks (O'Keefe & Nadel, 1978). However, a more recent experiment conducted by Olton and Feustle (1981) demonstrated that hippocampal formation lesions disrupt memory for visual cues. In this experiment, rats were placed in a plus-shaped maze with tunnel-like arms. Each arm was painted with a unique design. After allowing the animal to select and traverse one arm in exchange for food reward, the animal was confined, and the arms of the maze were rearranged. The animal was again allowed to select an arm but was rewarded only for traversing an arm containing a novel cue. The procedure was repeated until all four arms had been visited once. Note that spatial cues were eliminated from this experiment by rearranging the visual cues following each successful response. Thus, the visual cues were the only information available that could be used for solving the task. Animals were trained to a predetermined criteria before receiving lesions to the fimbria/-fornix (a primary hippocampal efferent/afferent system). Following these lesions, the rats' performance dropped to chance levels. These results indicate that the hippocampal formation is involved in the coding of visual cue information. In a slightly different task, Rafaelle and Olton (1988) pretrained rats on a one-item tactile and visual delayed matching-to-sample task using short delays. They found that large fimbria-fornix lesions resulted in a profound performance deficit, whereas small fimbria-fornix lesions only produced a mild impairment.

Further support for involvement of the hippocampus proper in coding of sensory-perceptual information can also be found in the single unit recording literature. Differential complex spike cell activity has been observed in those tasks that emphasize the importance of sensory-perceptual cue information (Eichenbaum & Cohen, 1988; Foster, Christian, Hampson, Campbell, & Dead-wyler, 1987; Wible et al., 1986). However, it appears that this differential firing is more related to a combination of visual (color) and spatial cues (Wible et al., 1986); olfactory and spatial cues (Eichenbaum & Cohen, 1988), and auditory and temporal cues (Foster et al., 1987).

In a somewhat different experiment within an eight-arm maze, Jarrard (1983), using somatosensory and visual cues, and Nadel and McDonald (1980), using only visual cues, found that large hippocampal formation lesions did not disrupt performance.

Aggleton, Hunt, and Rawlins (1986) also demonstrated that hippocampal formation damage affected neither the acquisition nor the retention of a visual, somatosensory, and object cue memory task. In this study, rats were trained in both immediate and delayed nonmatching-to-sample tasks on a Y-maze with many visual/tactile and object cue combinations. The correct choice for one trial served as the sample for the next trial. Rats received either complete hippocampectomies or cortical control lesions. Some rats received lesions following surgery to test for retention, whereas other rats received lesions prior to training to test for acquisition. No memory deficits were observed in either condition. Additionally, interstimulus delays of 20s and 60s were introduced following surgery. These delays, however, did not affect performance.

Thus, following hippocampal formation lesions, Aggleton, Hunt, and Rawlins (1986), Jarrard (1983), and Nadel and McDonald (1980) reported no deficits, whereas the Olton and Feustle (1981) and Rafaelle and Olton (1988) did find significant impairments. Based on lesion studies, it is currently difficult to determine whether the hippocampal formation codes visual-somatosensory information. The differences among the studies are too great to be able to discern clearly the critical variables. However, one important difference does emerge. Direct damage to the hippocampus proper does not produce deficits, whereas damage to the fimbria-fornix does. Further support for this idea comes from Jarrard (1986), who has shown that only lesions of the fimbria-fornix produce a permanent deficit for visual and somatosensory cue information in a working memory but not a reference memory task. In contrast, lesions of the total hippocampus proper, subiculum, CA3, or dentate gyrus produce no deficits on a visual and somatosensory cue working or reference memory task.

Additional evidence points to a lack of hippocampal formation involvement in coding olfactory cue information. Eichenbaum, Fagen, Mathews, and Cohen (1988) have shown that in rats with fimbria-fornix lesions there are no deficits in a successive cue go/no-go or a successive cue go left/go right olfactory discrimination task. Deficits are observed in a simultaneous cue go left/go right olfactory discrimination task. In this latter task, the olfactory cues were presented in spatially different locations requiring temporal processing of events prior to the selection of the appropriate response (see the Temporal Attribute section that follows).

It should also be noted that in monkeys tested in a delayed nonmatching to sample task for visual objects, hippocampal formation lesions do not produce large impairments. Performance is normal up to a 30-sec delay, some impairment is seen relative to controls with a 2- to 10-min delay, but performance is still better than chance (Squire 1987, p. 191). Also, humans with presumed hippocampal damage are not impaired in acquiring and remembering a variety of sensory-perceptual skills (Squire & Zola-Morgan, 1988).

Thus, it appears that at present the role of the hippocampal formation in coding nonspatial sensory-perceptual attributes in both rats, monkeys, and humans is unclear.

Temporal Attribute

The attribute model states that the hippocampal formation is involved in the coding of temporal information, regardless of sensory modality, within the data-based memory system. The hippocampus is believed to code the time in which a stimulus (e.g., a spatial or visual cue) occurred relative to the occurrence of other stimuli. Thus, the attribute model suggests that the hippocampal formation codes the sequential aspect of temporal information. Similar predictions are made by the temporal context model.

The attribute and temporal context models predict sequential memory deficits following hippocampal formation lesions, regardless of the sensory modality of the relevant cues. In contrast, the cognitive map model suggests that the hippocampal formation does not code temporal attributes unless the content of the sequential memory were spatial in nature. A deficit in memory for sequential information would be manifested following hippocampal formation lesions only because the spatial cognitive map would be eliminated, not because the hippocampal formation mediated sequential memory per se. This theoretical position states that sequential memory for nonspatial information, such as visual cues, would remain unaffected following damage to the hippocampal formation.

Experimental evidence to test each of the previously mentioned theories' predictions with respect to sequential memory is, to date, sparse. Kesner and Novak (1982) provided a test of spatial sequential memory, because the memory probe task required rats to remember the order in which spatial stimuli were presented. Rats in an eight-arm radial maze were allowed to traverse a randomly determined sequence of the eight arms. After a brief delay (approximately 20 sec), the rat was given a choice between either the first and second arms, the fourth and fifth arms, or the seventh and eighth arms in the sequence. The animal obtained a reward for returning to the arm visited first. Control animals demonstrated a serial position effect in that they performed at chance levels for the fourth versus fifth arm choice (the middle of the sequence), while performing significantly above chance on the first and last item pairs of the sequence. Following small lesions of the hippocampus proper, there were memory deficits only for items presented early in the sequence; memory for later items remained unaffected.

In a second experiment (Kesner, unpublished observations), rats were tested for memory for the frequency of occurrence of specific spatial locations. Temporal structuring of spatial information is required to remember that a specific spatial location has been repeated. In this task, the animals were tested on an eight-arm radial maze. On each trial (one per day), each animal was allowed to visit four arms to receive reinforcement in an order that was randomly selected for that trial. One of the arms was repeated with a *lag*[1] of one, two, or three arms in between a repetition. This constituted the *study phase*. Upon completion of the study phase, all doors were closed and a linoleum cover was placed over the eight doors in order to signify the beginning of the test phase and to ensure that the animal could not see which arm was reinforced. Within 20 seconds, the door in front of the repeated arm and a door in front of a nonrepeated arm were opened simultaneously, and the cover was removed. This constituted the *test phase*. The rule to be learned leading to an additional reinforcement was to choose the arm that had been *repeated* in the study phase sequence.

After about 60 trials of training, animals show excellent memory for the repetition with a lag of three arms between a repetition but poor performance for a lag of one or two arms, even when the data are analyzed for those trials on which the repetition occurred in the last serial position (see Fig. 7.1). The

---

[1]*Lag* refers to spacing of repeated items. When a spatial location is immediately repeated, the *lag* would be zero.

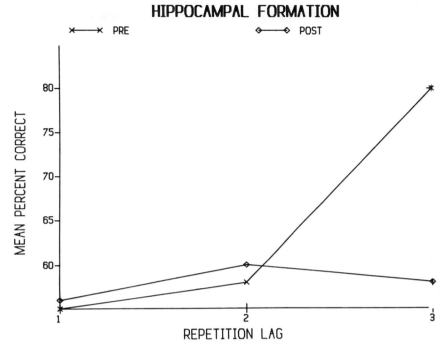

FIG. 7.1. Mean percent correct performance as a function of lag before (pre) and after (post) large hippocampal formation lesions.

animals then received large (dorsal and ventral) hippocampal formation lesions
and, following recovery from surgery, they were retested with eight tests of each
lag condition. Results are shown in Fig. 7.1 and indicate that the repetition lag
effect was impaired, that is, the animals performed poorly even with a lag of
three arms between a repetition. These results indicate that memory for temporal
sequencing of spatial events is mediated by the hippocampal formation.

Are there any experiments in which memory for sequential presentation of
nonspatial cues is critical for excellent performance within a task? In one experiment, rats were required to enter one arm of an eight-arm radial maze containing
a box with patterns painted on the walls and different somatosensory cues on the
floor. This procedure was repeated until three different patterns (visual and
somatosensory cues) had been presented for the trial. Each visual and somatosensory cue was presented in the same spatial location. Following the cue presentation phase, the rat was presented with an order memory probe. The probe
consisted of either the first and second, second and third, or first and third cues
presented. The animal was rewarded for entering the box containing the cue that
was presented earlier in the sequence. Most rats were capable of learning to

respond correctly consistently to at least one, and sometimes two, of the memory probes. Following large lesions of the hippocampal formation, the rats performed at chance levels (Kesner and Allen, unpublished observations).

The data from this experiment suggest that the hippocampal formation mediates some aspect of memory for sequential presentation of visual and somatosensory cues. One shortcoming of any experiment with a sequential memory component is that the sequence is inherently confounded with the type of cue (e.g., spatial, visual, somatosensory, auditory, etc.) that is used. Preliminary data suggest, however, that animals with hippocampal formation lesions are able to code visual and somatosensory information at least at short retention delays.

In a different experiment (Kesner, unpublished observations), animals were trained on a list of four conditional discriminations or paired associates. In this case, a unique food item that was presented in the center of an eight-arm maze was always paired with the opening of a door in one of four spatial coordinates (e.g., Froot Loops cereal was paired with North, Cocoa Puffs with South, etc.). The list of four paired associates was always presented sequentially but in a random order with a 15-sec intertrial interval in between presentations of each list. Prior to opening of the correct door leading to an additional piece of food, orienting responses (OR) were measured. A correct OR was defined as an orientation toward the appropriate door for the specific food that was presented. Based on a variety of manipulations (changing extramaze cues, rotating the maze), it is concluded that animals use intramaze (i.e., nonspatial) visual and egocentric cues. Performance in this task is shown in Fig. 7.2 as a function of serial order of presentation of each paired associate. Note that there is a clear temporal structure with better performance on the later items within the list. Chance performance on this task is 25%. Support for the importance of generating a temporal structure comes from the observation that 15-sec delays between each paired associate within the list attenuates the improved performance for the later items within the list. A retroactive analysis of relative frequency of errors revealed that animals make more errors the earlier the paired associate occurred within the list (Fig. 7.3). They make very few, if any, errors for the immediately preceding paired associate.

Animals with large (dorsal and ventral) hippocampal formation lesions do not show improved performance across serial positions, as shown in Fig. 7.2. This deficit pattern is permanent for at least 200 trials. A retroactive analysis of relative frequency of errors revealed that animals with lesions make many errors for paired associates that occurred earlier in the list, but make few if any errors for the immediately preceding paired associate (Fig. 7.3).

Thus, the hippocampal formation appears to play an important role in a task that is solved using nonspatial cues, but requires sequential memory for adequate performance. These lesioned animals, however, can learn the task if only one paired associate item (minimizing the need for temporal organization) was used, demonstrating that they can use appropriate OR strategies and that they can learn

HIPPOCAMPAL FORMATION

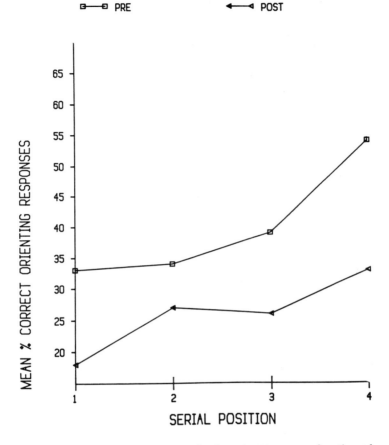

FIG. 7.2. Mean percent correct orienting responses as a function of serial position within the list of presentation of four paired associates before (pre) and after (post) large hippocampal formation lesions.

a single paired associate based on nonspatial cues. Thus, only when sequential coding of information is employed in this task does one observe impaired performance following large hippocampal formation lesions.

In a different experiment, Ross, Orr, Holland, and Berger (1984) showed that animals with hippocampal formation lesions were impaired in the acquisition of a conditional discrimination in which a tone following a light stimulus was reinforced, whereas a tone presentation in the absence of light was not reinforced. A nonconditional discrimination between a clicker and a noise was not affected by

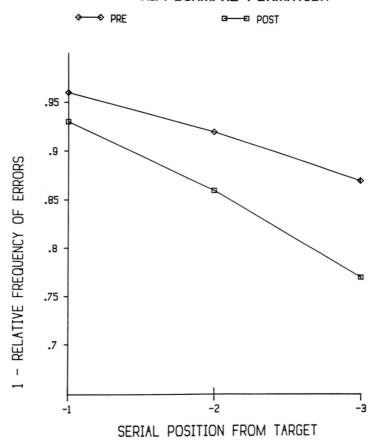

FIG. 7.3. Mean 1-relative frequency of errors as a function of serial position (distance) from target before (pre) and after (post) hippocampal formation lesions.

the lesion. Thus, the animals with lesions can learn to differentiate between nonspatial sensory cues, but they cannot perform well when temporal sequencing of two sensory cues are required for good performance.

In another experiment, Eichenbaum et al. (1988) have demonstrated that in olfactory discrimination tasks, animals with fimbria-fornix lesions are not impaired whenever a single odor presentation is directly related to response choice. However, when two odors are presented in spatially different locations requiring temporal sampling of specific cue information prior to a response choice, then fimbria-fornix lesions produce an impairment.

Thus, whenever temporal coding of spatial or nonspatial information is of importance to perform well in a task, animals with hippocampal formation lesions are impaired. These data provide excellent support for the attribute and temporal context models but cannot easily be handled by the cognitive map model.

Even though the hippocampal formation appears to play an important role in mediating temporal attributes, it does not markedly affect the ability to remember the duration of a single event as cued by an auditory stimulus (Meck, Church, & Olton, 1984). Only when the auditory stimulus is interrupted for a short duration and then started again do animals with fimbria-fornix lesions display a marked impairment in judgment of total duration of the auditory stimulus. It is likely that a normal animal will treat this "time gap" procedure as two similar sequential events that can be added together. However, animals with fimbria-fornix lesions have difficulty in coding sequential information (in this case nonspatial) and thus cannot very easily sum the two separate events (duration of an auditory stimulus).

Response Attribute

There are no published studies in rats in which the effect of hippocampal formation lesions on memory for a specific motor response has been investigated. Neither the attribute model nor the cognitive map model would predict deficits in response memory following hippocampal formation lesions. In order to test these predictions, rats were trained on a response memory task. In this task, there is a study and a test phase constituting a trial. In the study phase, a rat was placed at the end of a randomly assigned arm on an eight-arm maze or a modified six-arm plus maze. The animal was given the opportunity to make a right or left turn, which was accomplished by opening the right or left door. After making the appropriate turning response, the animal was given food reinforcement. The rat was then removed from the maze, and within 10 sec or 1 min the test phase was begun. During the test phase, the rat was placed at the end of an arm opposite the arm that was selected for the study phase. In this case, both right and left doors were opened, and the rat was given the opportunity to choose between the right and left doors. A repeat of the turn made during the study phase led to reinforcement. Thus, if the animal made a left turn during the study phase, it must also make a left turn during the test phase in order to receive reinforcement. Each animal was pretrained on one delay only. The animals received 6 trials per day, 5 days per week. After reaching criterion of 75% or better on a set of 24 trials, the animals either received large hippocampal formation, caudate nucleus, or cortical control lesions. Following recovery from surgery, the animals were retested. The results indicate that there is no deficit following large hippocampal formation or cortical control lesions. In contrast, animals with caudate nucleus lesions display a severe deficit. It should be noted that in a one-trial spatial delayed matching to sample task, animals with caudate nucleus lesions display no deficits, whereas animals with hippocampal formation lesions are permanently impaired (Kesner & Fuller, Hunt & Kesner, unpublished observations). These results are consistent with the findings that humans with presumed hippocampal formation damage can acquire and remember a variety of response-based motor skills (Squire, 1987). These data support the attribute and cognitive map models, because in contrast to its role in mediating spatial memory, the hippocampal formation does not appear to be critical for response memory.

Affect Attribute

The attribute model states that the hippocampal formation is probably not involved in coding and processing of affect information. Support for this idea can be found in a number of studies in which reinforcement manipulations, which are assumed to trigger the coding of affect information, do not alter the performance of animals with hippocampal formation lesions. For example, lesions or electrical stimulation of the hippocampal formation have no effect on taste aversion learning, manifestation of a frustration effect following reward ommission or change in magnitude of reinforcement (Best & Orr, 1973; Kesner & Berman, 1977; Swanson & Isaacson, 1969; Van Hartesveldt, 1973). A more detailed review of this literature can be found in Gray (1982). In contrast, lesions of another neural structure, namely the amygdala, produce deficits in tasks where memory for reinforcement is of great importance (Henke, 1977; Kemble & Beckman, 1970; Kesner & Andrus, 1982; Kesner, Berman, Burton, & Hankins, 1975; Nachman & Ashe, 1974).

Summary

It appears that the hippocampal formation codes spatial and temporal attributes, may or may not code sensory-perceptual attributes, but does not code response or affect attributes. The data support quite well the prediction of the attribute model, but to a lesser extent the predictions of the cognitive map and temporal context models. An alternative and perhaps more parsimonious way of viewing the nature of information coded in the hippocampal formation is to suggest that the hippocampal formation is involved in coding relational representations perhaps in the form of external contexts, configurations, or higher order representations, but certainly exemplified by the relational requirements of spatial and temporal attributes.

HOW INFORMATION IS
CODED IN THE HIPPOCAMPUS

The attribute model suggests that the hippocampal formation is directly involved in coding all new spatial-temporal incoming information that is likely to be relevant in trial unique situations but that could also be of importance for all trials within a learning task (data-based memory), but is not involved in coding information based on expected nonvarying information in the form of maps, rules, strategies, and procedures (expectancy-based memory).

A similar but slightly different view was proposed earlier by Olton (1983, 1986) and Olton, Becker, and Handelmann (1979). This view is labeled the "working memory model."

It posits that within every learning task there are two types of memories that organize all the critical information. Based on a distinction made by Honig (1978), the working memory model suggests that the specific, personal, and temporal context of a situation is coded in working memory. This translates into memory for events that occur on a specific trial in a task, biasing mnemonic coding towards the processing of incoming data. In contrast, information concerning rules and procedures (general knowledge) of situations is coded in reference memory. This translates into memory for events that happen on all trials in a task, biasing mnemonic coding toward the processing of expectancies based on the organization of the extant memory. The working memory model also states that both working and reference memory can operate independently of each other and that the hippocampal formation mediates working but not reference memory.

Possible differences between these two models are discussed later in this section. Compelling evidence for the data-based/expectancy-based or working/reference memory distinction and the role of the hippocampus as mediator for data-based (working) memory has been offered by Olton and Papas (1979). In this experiment, Olton and Papas trained rats to perform a task that required the animals to utilize both data-based (working) and expectancy-based (reference) components of their memories, in order to receive appropriate food rewards. Eight of 17 arms in a radial arm maze were baited, whereas the remaining 9 never contained food. Animals were trained to retrieve food from the eight baited arms without repetition and never enter one of the unbaited arms. Following complete transection of the fimbria-fornix, lesioned animals made both expectancy-based (reference) memory (entered constantly unbaited arms) and data-based (working) memory (repeated baited arms) errors. However, expectancy-based memory capacity quickly recovered, whereas data-based memory remained impaired. Somewhat different results were obtained in an eight-arm maze with four baited and four unbaited arms. In this situation, animals with hippocampal formation lesions displayed a deficit for both types of memory (Gage, 1985; Jarrard, 1986; Nadel & McDonald, 1980). In this same task, animals with parietal cortex lesions were impaired only on the expectancy-based but not the data-based memory component (Kesner, DiMattia, & Crutcher, 1987), providing for a dissociation of function between the hippocampal formation and parietal cortex.

There are a number of problems associated with this data-based/expectancy-based or working/reference memory task. First, the observed dissociation between the two types of memory might be a function of memory load (number of items to be remembered), although one would expect the dissociation to manifest itself more readily with a smaller number of remembered items. Second, in the eight-item expectancy-based/data-based memory task, the expectancy-based memory component is more difficult to learn than the data-based memory component. Third, because two different responses were required of the animal hippocampal formation lesions could have differentially affected these specific response requirements.

In order to overcome these problems, Olton (1986) devised a new procedure to test for data-based (working) and expectancy-based (reference) memory within a single task. In two T-mazes, the animal was given a right–left discrimination in the stem, which was divided in half by a barrier. In maze 1 the correct response was on the right, and in maze 2 the correct response was on the left. This component of the task never varied and was considered to engage primarily expectancy-based or reference memory. The second right–left discrimination was between the two arms of the T-maze and consisted of two runs. On the first run, the animal was forced to enter the right or left arm. On the second run, the animal could choose between the right or left arm but was rewarded for turning to the new arm (win-shift rule) in order to obtain a reinforcement. The animal needs to remember the critical information on the first run in order to perform well on the second run. This component of the task was considered to engage primarily data-based or working memory. After preoperative training, animals received fimbria-fornix, control, or amygdala lesions. There were no deficits for control animals and animals with amygdala lesions. However, animals with fimbria-fornix lesions performed very poorly for the data-based (working) memory component of the task without showing any deficits for the expectancy-based (reference) memory component.

In a somewhat different experiment Hunt et al. (1986) trained animals on one of two versions of a one-item delayed spatial matching to sample task. Half the animals were first trained in an eight-arm maze to enter a randomly selected arm in order to obtain reinforcement (study phase). Ten seconds after finding the food, the animal was removed from the maze for either a 0 sec, 1 min, or a 10-min delay period. Following the delay period, the animal was returned to the maze and given a retention test (test phase). Correct performance during the test phase required the animal to return to the previously reinforced arm (i.e., the animal had to use a "win-stay" rule in order to receive an additional reinforcement). This procedure was assumed to engage working or data-based memory. The remaining rats were also trained in an eight-arm maze, but during the study phase one arm was constant for all trials. All other procedures were identical. This procedure was assumed to engage reference or expectancy-based memory. After extensive training, rats made few errors. All rats received large (dorsal and ventral) hippocampal formation lesions following training. After a 1-week recovery period, the rats were retested at each delay. Because there was no effect of

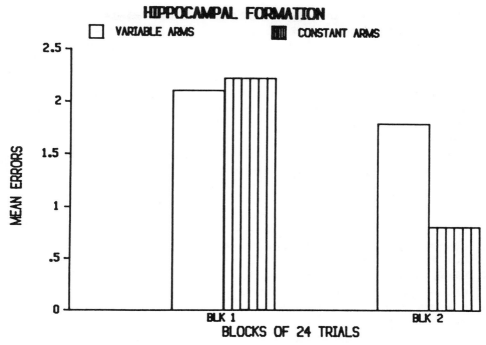

FIG. 7.4. Mean number of errors as a function of blocks of trials (24 trials per block) for animals with large hippocampal formation lesions within the variable arms (data-based memory) and constant arms (expectancy-based memory) tasks.

delay, all trials were combined. Performance as a function of blocks of trials, shown in Fig. 7.4, indicates that rats tested on a variable arm (data-based memory) task were unable to recall the targeted place after hippocampal formation lesions. However, rats tested on a constant arm (expectancy-based memory) task showed an initial deficit but recovered quickly. These last two experiments clearly support the working memory and attribute views of hippocampal formation involvement with data-based or working but not expectancy-based or reference memory.

Further support for noninvolvement of the hippocampal formation in expectancy-based or reference memory comes from a study by Walker and Olton (1984), who trained rats to enter a specific goal box from each of three different starting positions. After fimbria-fornix lesions, the rats were given transfer tests on a new starting position and tested for the selection of the same goal box. Successful selection of the goal box on the transfer tests requires the utilization of a cognitive map. Animals with fimbria-fornix lesions, as well as controls, performed the transfer tests without any difficulty.

However, in a number of other tasks that would be considered as expectancy-based or reference memory tasks, animals with hippocampal formation lesions do show deficits. For example, Morris (1983) found that rats with hippocampal formation lesions were impaired in learning a water maze. This task presumably involves primarily an expectancy-based or reference spatial memory. In this experiment, rats were trained in a large circular tub filled with water made opaque by the addition of milk. Their task was to find a platform that was hidden just below the surface of the cloudy water. Although the starting place was varied from trial to trial, nonlesioned animals learned this task quickly. Animals with large lesions of the hippocampal formation were impaired in learning the task, as indicated by long latencies to find the hidden platform. Thus, there appears to be a deficit in expectancy-based or reference memory in the lesioned animals. However, in a second study DiMattia and Kesner (1988) have replicated Morris' findings, but in addition, they trained animals first in the water maze. After training, the animals received either large (dorsal and ventral) hippocampal formation, parietal cortex, or control lesions. During the retention test, animals with parietal cortex lesions displayed a marked deficit, whereas animals with hippocampal formation lesions showed hardly any deficits compared to controls. Because animals with hippocampal formation lesions displayed praxic and taxic response strategies, it was difficult to assess the ability of these animals to retain the location of a hidden platform.

In order to avoid this problem, Kesner and Farnsworth (unpublished observations) have recently tested animals on a 177-hole cheese-board task using an analogous procedure as has been described for the water maze. In this case, the animals were food-deprived and, starting from different places, were given the opportunity to find food in one hole (spatial location). In this case, there were no clear stereotypic responses, but there were acquisition and retention deficits in animals with large (dorsal and ventral) hippocampal formation or parietal cortex lesions, yet hardly any deficits in animals with only dorsal hippocampal formation lesions.

In a somewhat different experiment, Ross et al. (1984) showed that animals with hippocampal formation lesions are impaired in a conditional discrimination task, and Eichenbaum et al. (1988) showed that animals with similar lesions are impaired in simultaneous go right/go left version of an olfactory discrimination task. Both tasks are expectancy-based memory tasks.

The last four studies provide difficulty for an exclusive hippocampal formation involvement with data-based or working memory. One problem, however, is that it is very difficult to characterize any one task as reflecting only data-based (working) or expectancy-based (reference) memory, because every task is more likely to support both memory components. In order to solve this problem, the attribute model has expanded somewhat on the meaning of working memory. It is suggested that the hippocampal formation is engaged in any task in which an animal needs to attend and remember *new incoming* (data-based) spatial-temporal information. The hippocampal formation is not engaged in the memory component of any task where information is expected (predictable) and nonvarying.

This new reformulation of working and reference memory can easily account for the Olton (1986) and Hunt et al. (1986) studies in which, following hippocampal formation lesions, a dissociation between data-based (working) memory and expectancy-based (reference) memory was found. In the nonvarying choice situation, the lesioned animals could perform the task based on expectancy-based memory, because on any one trial no new data needed to be processed. In contrast, in the varying-choice situation the lesioned animals were impaired, because on each trial the animal needed to attend and remember new spatial information.

In the case of the water-maze and cheese-board studies (Kesner & Farnsworth, unpublished observations; Morris, 1983), some new incoming spatial information needs to be processed on every trial, because the animal is placed in a different starting position relative to the goal. Thus, one would expect some (though not necessarily large) deficits in these tasks. In the case of the conditional light–tone discrimination (Ross et al., 1984) and olfactory discrimination (Eichenbaum et al., 1988) tasks, the impairment of animals with hippocampal formation lesions could have been due to the requirement to attend and remember temporally and spatially distinctive stimuli, which differed on any one trial and required a decision process based on new data information.

In order to demonstrate further the utility of data-based versus expectancy-based memory distinction, sham-operated and non-operated animals or animals with large (dorsal and ventral) hippocampal formation lesions were tested in a task that would be classified as an expectancy-based or reference memory task (Kesner & Beers, 1988). Animals were given 40 trials in an eight-arm radial maze. Each trial was divided into a study phase and a test phase. During the study phase of each trial, the animals were presented with a constant sequence of five arms on an eight-arm radial maze followed by a test phase in which a recognition test was given between an arm that was always in the study phase sequence and an arm that was never in the study phase sequence. The animal was reinforced for selecting the previously visited arm requiring a win-stay rule. Expectancy-based memory was measured during the study phase of the trials as a pattern of correct or incorrect orienting responses in anticipation of the ensuing doors in the constant sequence. Because the sequence of spatial locations did not vary from trial to trial, it was assumed that the emitted orienting responses reflected the operation of the expectancy-based memory component. Both groups of animals emitted the same pattern of correct orienting responses and made the same number and pattern of intralist and extralist intrusion errors. Data-based memory was measured during the test phase of the trial as correct recognition test performance. Because the test varied from trial to trial because the animals did not know which arm in the rewarded set (one of five) was to be compared with which arm in the nonrewarded set (one of three), it was assumed that recognition performance reflected the operation of the data-based memory component. During the test phase, the animals with hippocampal formation lesions were impaired relative to controls. These results suggest that the hippocampal formation might indeed mediate only data-based but not expectancy-based memory, and they imply a possible dissociation between expectancy-based and data-based memory systems.

It will be necessary in future studies to assess the contribution of the data-based and expectancy-based system for every memory task. The key to determine the involvement of the hippocampal formation lies in the degree to which an animal needs to process newly incoming spatial-temporal information requiring the operation of the data-based memory system. One approach is to select an appropriate task. For example, a variable spatial delayed matching-to-sample task clearly accentuates the importance of data input processing, whereas many spatial discrimination learning tasks do not rely on much new data input processing. Thus, one way to ensure hippocampal formation involvement is by selection of an appropriate memory task.

A second approach is to test animals with hippocampal formation lesions before or after training. There is clearly more data input processing during acquisition of new tasks (post-lesion training) compared to retention of most previously learned tasks (pre-lesion training). Thus, it is not surprising to discover that there are more likely to be deficits in a variety of spatial tasks with pre-lesion training compared to post-lesion training (Gage, 1985; Jarrard, 1986).

A third approach is to vary size of the hippocampal formation damage or lesion-specific subareas within the hippocampal formation. Assuming some equipotentiality of function within the hippocampal formation, it should be the case that the more data-based processing that is required, the greater the efficacy of hippocampal formation lesions to induce a memory deficit or the smaller the hippocampal formation lesions needed to produce an impairment in a specific task. Some support for these assertions come from a large number of studies. To mention only a few: Small lesions of the hippocampus proper produce mild or no impairment on a nonspatial cue working memory task, whereas fimbria-fornix lesions that affect the whole hippocampal formation do produce severe impairments (Jarrard, 1986; Rafaelle & Olton, 1988). In a one-item spatial delayed matching-to-sample task, only a small dorsal hippocampal lesion of CA1 of Ammons horn and subiculum is sufficient to produce a large and permanent deficit (Hunt et al., 1986), whereas this same lesion does not produce a deficit in learning the location of a single food source on a cheese board (Kesner & Farnsworth, unpublished observations).

Thus, it appears that the hippocampal formation plays an important role in processing of new spatial-temporal input but does not play a role in processing of extant information based on existing knowledge systems.

CROSS-SPECIES COMPARISONS

To what extent do the deficits in processing spatial-temporal attributes in rats with hippocampal formation lesions parallel those found in birds, monkeys, and humans with damage to the hippocampal formation? With respect to spatial attribute information, deficits have been reported in a variety of spatial location memory tasks in birds, monkeys, and humans with lesions of the hippocampal formation (See chap. 14 of this book; also Jones & Mishkin, 1972; Parkinson & Mishkin, 1982; Smith & Milner, 1981; Zola-Morgan et al., 1986). With respect to temporal attribute information, deficits have been reported for order recognition memory for a variety of stimuli in monkeys and humans with hippocampal formation lesions (Hirst & Volpe, 1984; Kimble & Pribram, 1963; Squire & Zola-Morgan, 1988). With respect to response attribute information, there are also parallels among rats, monkeys, and humans with hippocampal formation lesions in that memory appears to be intact for specific motor responses and motor skills (Kesner & Fuller, unpublished observations; Squire & Zola-Morgan, 1988; Zola-Morgan & Squire, 1984). With respect to sensory-perceptual attribute information, it is not clear whether there are any deficits in rats, monkeys, or humans (see the Sensory-Perceptual Attribute section, earlier in this chapter). With respect to affect attribute information, there are parallels between rats and monkeys with hippocampal formation lesions in that memory for affect appears to be intact (Kesner & DiMattia, 1987; Mishkin & Appenzeller, 1987).

In the monkey and human literature, the distinction between data-based (working) memory and expectancy-based (reference) memory has been labelled episodic versus semantic memory (Tulving, 1972), declarative versus procedural memory (Squire, 1987), recognition versus habit memory (Mishkin, Malamut, & Bachevalier, 1984), and implicit versus explicit memory (Schacter, 1987). Even though the meaning of these terms may vary somewhat with each distinction, the terms nevertheless capture the difference between forms of memory that involve the processing of new incoming versus the processing of extant knowledge information. Furthermore, it is assumed that episodic, declarative, recognition, or explicit memory is subserved by the hippocampal formation. Thus, it should be possible to discover parallels between rats and humans in terms of the afore-mentioned distinctions. In one experiment, Cohen and Squire (1981) showed that amnesic patients with hippocampal formation damage can learn and retain a mirror reading skill as well as normal subjects, but these subjects are impaired in recognizing the words that they had read previously. Squire has suggested that amnesic patients can learn procedures or build general knowledge (expectancy-based memory) concerning motor skills, but that new (data-based memory) information cannot be acquired. Kesner and Beers (1988) have shown that in an analogous experiment, animals with hippocampal formation lesions were able to acquire an orienting task based on specific information but were impaired on a subsequent recognition task based on the same information. Because the orienting task was assumed to reflect the operation of expectancy-based (reference, procedural, and implicit) memory, and the recognition task was assumed to reflect the operation of data-based (working, declarative, and explicit) memory, these data provide support for correspondence in hippocampal formation-databased memory function between rats and humans. Thus, in general, it appears that there are significant parallels across species in terms of hippocampal formation mediation of specific mnemonic functions.

SUMMARY

The hippocampal formation plays an important role in mediating mnemonic functions. Among four of the many views of hippocampal formation function (see Table 7.1) there are, however, no clear agreements concerning the exact nature of information that is processed within the hippocampal formation and how this information is processed.

With respect to the nature of information processing within the hippocampal formation, it can be concluded that the hippocampal formation codes spatial attributes, may or may not code sensory-perceptual attributes, appears to code temporal attributes based on spatial and sensory-perceptual cues, but does not code response or affect attributes. The involvement of the hippocampal formation with coding of spatial attributes supports the attribute and cognitive map models. The coding of temporal attributes based on spatial and sensory-perceptual cues supports the attribute and temporal context model views. The lack of hippocampal formation involvement with response attributes supports the attribute and cognitive map models. Thus, the data provide some support for each

TABLE 7.1
Theoretical Issues Associated with Hippocampal Formation Function

	Nature of Memory Coding	Working (Data-Based) Memory vs. Reference (Expectancy-Based) Memory	
Attribute Model	Temporal and Spatial Attributes	Data-Based Memory	Kesner
Cognitive Map Model	Spatial Attributes	—	O'Keefe & Nadel
Working Memory Model	—	Working Memory	Olton
Temporal Context Model	Temporal Attributes	—	Rawlins

theoretical view of hippocampal formation function but appear to be most consistent with the predictions made by the attribute model.

With respect to how information is coded within the hippocampus, it can be concluded that there is good support for hippocampal formation involvement in a working or data-based memory system but not a reference or expectancy-based memory system. These data support the attribute and working memory models.

In terms of cross-species comparisons, there appear to be significant parallels between rats, birds, monkeys, and humans with respect to the role of the hippocampal formation in mediating specific memory functions. Even though there are still many diverse theoretical views of hippocampal formation function, through the process of parallel operations across species there appears to be an ever-growing concensus concerning the role of the hippocampal formation in mediating specific mnemonic functions.

ACKNOWLEDGMENT

Support for this research was provided by NIH Grant No. R01NS20771-04.

REFERENCES

Aggleton, J. P., Hunt, P. R., & Rawlins, J. N. P. (1986). The effects of hippocampal lesions upon spatial and nonspatial tests of working memory. *Behavioral Brain Research, 19*, 133–146.

Barnes, C. A. (1988). Spatial learning and memory processes: The search for their neurobiological mechanisms in the rat. *Trends in Neurosciences, 11*, 163–169.

Bayer, S. A. (1985). Hippocampal region. In G. Paxinos (Ed.), *The rat nervous system, Vol. 1: Forebrain and midbrain,* (pp. 335–352). New York: Academic Press.

Best, P. J., & Orr, J., Jr. (1973). Effect of hippocampal lesions on passive avoidance and taste aversion conditioning. *Physiology & Behavior, 10*, 193–196.

Cohen, J. J., & Squire, L. R. (1981). Preserved learning and retention of pattern-analyzing skill in amnesia: Dissociation of knowing how and knowing that. *Science, 210*, 207–210.

DiMattia, B. V., & Kesner, R. P. (1988). Spatial cognitive maps: Differential role of parietal cortex and hippocampal formation. *Behavioral Neuroscience, 102*, 471–480.

Eichenbaum, H., & Cohen, N. J. (1988). Representation in the hippocampus: What do hippocampal neurons code? *Trends in Neurosciences, 11*, 244–248.

Eichenbaum, H., Fagan, A., Mathews, P., & Cohen, N. J. (1988). Hippocampal system dysfunction and odor discrimination learning in rats: Impairment or facilitation depending on representational demands. *Behavioral Neuroscience, 102*, 331–339.

Foster, T. C., Christian, E. P., Hampson, R. E., Campbell, K. A., & Deadwyler, S. A. (1987). Sequential dependencies regulate sensory evoked responses of single units in the rat hippocampus. *Brain Research, 408*, 86–96.

Gage, P. D. (1985). Performance of hippocampectomized rats in a reference/working-memory task: Effects of preoperative versus postoperative training. *Physiological Psychology, 13*, 235–242.

Gray, J. A. (1982). *The neuropsychology of anxiety: An enquiry into the functions of the septo-hippocampal system.* New York: Oxford University Press.

Henke, P. G. (1977). Dissociation of the frustration effect and the partial reinforcement extinction effect after limbic lesions in rats. *Journal of Comparative and Physiological Psychology, 91,* 1032–1038.

Hirst, W., & Volpe, B. T. (1984). Automatic and effortful encoding in amnesia. In M. S. Gazzaniga (Ed.), *Handbook of cognitive neuroscience* (pp. 369–386). New York: Plenum Press.

Honig, W. K. (1978). Studies of working memory in the pigeon. In S. H. Hulse, H. Fowler, & W. K. Honig (Eds.), *Cognitive processes in animal behavior* (pp. 211–248). Hillsdale, NJ: Lawrence Erlbaum Associates.

Hunt, M. A., Kesner, R. P., & DeSpain, M. J. (1986). The role of the hippocampus and the septohippocampal pathway on working (data-based) and reference (expectancy-based) memory in the rat. *Neuroscience Abstracts,* Vol. 12, Part 1, 744.

Jarrard, L. E. (1983). Selective hippocampal lesions and behavior: Effects of kainic acid lesions on performance of place and cue tasks. *Behavioral Neuroscience, 97,* 873–889.

Jarrard, L. E. (1986). Selective hippocampal lesions and behavior: Implications for current research and theorizing. In R. E. Isaacson & K. H. Pribram (Eds.), *The hippocampus* (Vol. 4, pp. 93–125). New York: Plenum Press.

Jones, B., & Mishkin, M. (1972). Limbic lesions and the problem of stimulus–reinforcement associations. *Experimental Neurology, 36,* 362–377.

Kemble, E. D., & Beckman, G. J. (1970). Runway performance of rats following amygdaloid lesions. *Physiology & Behavior, 5,* 45–47.

Kesner, R. P., & Andrus, R. G. (1982). Amygdala stimulation disrupts the magnitude of reinforcement contribution to long-term memory. *Physiological Psychology, 10,* 55–59.

Kesner, R. P., & Beers, D. R. (1988). Dissociation of data-based and expectancy-based memory following hippocampal lesions in rats. *Behavioral & Neural Biology, 50,* 46–60.

Kesner, R. P., & Berman, R. F. (1977). Effects of midbrain reticular formation, hippocampal and lateral hypothalamic stimulation upon recovery from neophobia and taste aversion learning. *Physiology & Behavior, 18,* 763–768.

Kesner, R. P., Berman, R. F., Burton, B., & Hankins, W. G. (1975). Effects of electrical stimulation of amygdala upon neophobia and taste aversion. *Behavioral Biology, 13,* 349–358.

Kesner, R. P., Crutcher, K., & Beers, D. R. (1988). Serial position curves for item (spatial) information: Role of the dorsal hippocampus and medial septum. *Brain Research, 454,* 219–226.

Kesner, R. P., & DiMattia, B. V. (1987). Neurobiology of an attribute model of memory. In A. N. Epstein & A. Morrison (Eds.), *Progress in psychobiology and physiological psychology* (Vol. 12, pp. 207–277). New York: Academic Press.

Kesner, R. P., DiMattia, B. V., & Crutcher, K. A. (1987). Evidence for neocortical involvement in reference memory. *Behavioral and Neural Biology, 47,* 40–53.

Kesner, R. P., & Novak, J. (1982). Serial position curve in rats: Role of the dorsal hippocampus. *Science, 218,* 173–174.

Kimble, D. P., & Pribram, K. H. (1963). Hippocampectomy and behavior sequences. *Science, 139,* 824–825.

Kubie, J. L., & Ranck, J. B. (1983). Sensory-behavioural correlates in individual hippoocampus neurons in three situations: Space and context. In W. Seifer (Ed.), *Neurobiology of the hippocampus* (pp. 433–447). London: Academic Press.

McNaughton, B. L., Barnes, C. A., & O'Keefe, J. (1983). The contributions of position, direction and velocity to single unit activity in the hippocampus of freely-moving rats. *Experimental Brain Research, 52,* 41–49.

Meck, W. H., Church, R. M., & Olton, D. S. (1984). Hippocampus, time, and memory. *Behavioral Neuroscience, 98,* 3–22.

Mishkin, M., & Appenzeller, T. (1987). The anatomy of memory. *Scientific American, 256,* 2–11.

Mishkin, M., Malamut, B. L., & Bachevalier, J. (1984). Memories and habits: Two neural systems. In J. L. McGaugh, G. Lynch, & N. M. Weinberger (Eds.), *Neurobiology of learning and memory* (pp. 65–77). New York: Guilford.

Morris, R. G. M. (1983). An attempt to dissociate "spatial-mapping" and "working-memory" theories of hippocampal function. In W. Seifert (Ed.), *Neurobiology of the hippocampus* (pp. 405–432). New York: Academic Press.

Nachman, M., & Ashe, J. H. (1974). Effects of basolateral amygdala lesions on neophobia, learned taste aversions, and sodium appetite in rats. *Journal of Comparative and Physiological Psychology, 87,* 622–643.

Nadel, L., & McDonald, L. (1980). Hippocampus: Cognitive map or working memory? *Behavioral & Neural Biology, 29,* 405–409.

O'Keefe, J. (1979). A review of the hippocampal place cells. *Progress in Neurobiology, 13,* 419–439.

O'Keefe, J. (1983). Spatial memory within and without the hippocampal system. In W. Seifert (Ed.), *Neurobiology of the hippocampus* (pp. 375–403). London: Academic Press.

O'Keefe, J., & Nadel, L. (1978). *The hippocampus as a cognitive map.* Oxford: Oxford University Press.

O'Keefe, J., & Speakman, A. (1987). Single unit activity in the rat hippoocampus during a spatial memory task. *Experimental Brain Research, 68,* 1–27.

Olton, D. S. (1983). Memory functions and the hippocampus. In W. Seifert (Ed.), *Neurobiology of the hippocampus* (pp. 335–373). New York: Academic Press.

Olton, D. S. (1986). Hippocampal function and memory for temporal context. In R. L. Isaacson & K. H. Pribram (Eds.), *The hippocampus* (Vol. 4, pp. 281–298). New York: Plenum Press.

Olton, D. S., Becker, J. T., & Handlemann, G. E. (1979). Hippocampus, space and memory. *Behavioral Brain Sciences, 2,* 313–365.

Olton, D. S., Branch, M., & Best, P. (1978). Spatial correlates of hippocampal unit activity. *Experimental Neurology, 58,* 387–409.

Olton, D. S. & Feustle, W. A. (1981). Hippocampal function required for nonspatial working memory. *Experimental Brain Research, 41,* 380–389.

Olton, D. S., & Papas, B. C. (1979). Spatial memory and hippocampal system function. *Neuropsychologia, 17,* 669–681.

Parkinson, J. K., & Mishkin, M. (1982). A selective mnemonic role for the hippocampus in monkeys: Memory for the location of objects. *Society for Neuroscience Abstracts, 8,* 23.

Rafaelle, K. C. & Olton, D. S. (1988). Hippocampal and amygdaloid involvement in working memory for nonspatial stimuli. *Behavioral Neuroscience, 102,* 349–355.

Rawlins, J. N. P. (1985). Associations across time: The hippocampus as a temporary memory store. *The Behavior and Brain Sciences, 8,* 479–496.

Rolls, E. T., Miyashita, Y., Cahusac, P. M. B., Kesner, R. P., Niki, H., Feigenbaum, J., & Bach, L. (in press). Hippocampal neurons in the monkey with activity related to the place in which a stimulus is shown. *Journal of Neuroscience.*

Ross, R. T., Orr, W. B., Holland, P. C., & Berger, T. W. (1984). Hippocampectomy disrupts acquisition and retention of learned conditional responding. *Behavioral Neuroscience, 98,* 211–225.

Schacter, D. L. (1987). Implicit memory: History and current status. *Journal of Experimental Psychology: Learning, Memory and Cognition, 13,* 501–508.

Smith, M. L., & Milner, B. (1981). The role of the right hippocampus in the recall of spatial location. *Neuropsychologia, 19,* 781–793.

Spear, N. F. (1976). Retrieval of memories: A psychobiological approach. In W. K. Estes (Ed.), *Handbook of Learning and Cognitive Processes* (Vol. 4, pp. 17–90). Hillsdale, NJ: Lawrence Erlbaum Associates.

Squire, L. R. (1987). *Memory and brain.* New York: Oxford University Press.

Squire, L. R., & Zola-Morgan, S. (1988). Memory: Brain systems and behavior. *Trends in Neurosciences, 11,* 170–175.

Swanson, A. M., & Isaacson, R. L. (1969). Hippocampal lesions and the frustration effect in rats. *Journal of Comparative and Physiological Psychology, 68,* 562–567.

Tulving, E. (1972). Episodic and semantic memory. In E. Tulving & W. D. Donaldson (Eds.), *Organization of memory* (pp. 382–403). New York: Academic Press.

Underwood, B. J. (1969). Attributes of memory. *Psychological Review, 76,* 559–573.

Van Hartesveldt, C. (1973). Size of reinforcement and operant conditioning in hippocampectomized rats. *Behavioral Biology, 8,* 347–356.

Walker, J. A. & Olton, D. S. (1984). Fimbria-fornix lesions impair spatial working memory but not cognitive mapping. *Behavioral Neuroscience, 98,* 226–242.

Wible, C. G., Findling, R. L., Shapiro, M., Lang, E. J., Crane, S., & Olton, D. S. (1986). Mnemonic correlates of unit activity in the hippocampus. *Brain Research, 399,* 97–110.

Winocur, G. (1980). The hippocampus and cue utilization. *Physiological Psychology, 8,* 280–288.

Zola-Morgan, S., & Squire, L. R. (1984). Preserved learning in monkeys with medial temporal lesions: Sparing of motor and cognitive skills. *Journal of Neuroscience, 4,* 1072–1085.

Zola-Morgan, S., Squire, L. R., & Amaral, D. G. (1986). Human amnesia and the medial temporal region: Enduring memory impairment following a bilateral lesion limited to field CA1 of the hippocampus. *Journal of Neuroscience, 6,* 2950–2967.

8 Fish in the Think Tank: Learning, Memory, and Integrated Behavior

J. B. Overmier
University of Minnesota

K. L. Hollis
Mount Holyoke College

This chapter emphasizes the relation between the fishes' brains and elementary cognitive processes, such as attention, learning, memory, the interactions of multiple learning experiences, and the integration of these into effective species typical behaviors (e.g., territorial defense). Books specializing in the analysis of learning and memory typically contain chapters with titles such as habituation, Pavlovian conditioning, instrumental learning, avoidance learning, and so on. These topics are addressed separately, because they involve different experimental operations or procedures in the study of each. A central question has been whether or not these different experimental procedures "access" fundamentally different learning mechanisms or behavioral systems. Indeed, this has been a hotly debated issue, one that is still not resolved (e.g., Hull, 1943; Rescorla & Solomon, 1967; Tolman, 1932).

Experiments have addressed this issue by ablating selected brain areas in fish and assessing the consequences for the various "forms" of learning or behaviors to be differentiated. The goal, of course, was to produce double dissociations: ablation *A* disrupting learning of form *X* but not that of form *Y* with ablation *B* disrupting learning of form *Y* but not that of form *X*. Dissociations have indeed been found, but not double dissociations (see Flood, Overmier, & Savage, 1976, for a review). In general, such experiments have been able to find disruption of selected complex forms of learning while leaving the lesser complex forms intact—for example, ablations that impair avoidance behavior leave escape behavior intact (Hainsworth, Overmier, & Snowden, 1967).

What do we make of this kind of finding? One possibility is that each "higher" form, though different from the lower, necessarily also makes use of the lower mechanism. Indeed, to the extent that the various forms of learning reflect anagenesis (Huxley, 1958) rather than independent emergence of separate processes, this is exactly the pattern of results that one would expect. Similarly, to the extent that selected species' typical behaviors are an integration of several anagenetically related, more basic processes (including motor reflexes, attentional processes, and forms of learning), then ablations that affect one or more component basic process—or the integration of these—will also disrupt the more complex species behaviors that are the species' "strategic" response to life's challenges.

FISH NEUROBIOLOGY AND COMPARATIVE COGNITION

In the 19th century, Herbert Spencer (1896) extended Darwin's doctrine of evolution to cognition—or the "involved forms of consciousness," as he referred to it—and argued in addition that, by study of the structure and function of less complex brains, one might come to a better understanding of the forms of cognitive processes of the highest order. Hypotheses such as Spencer's have provided one basis for a neurobiology of comparative cognition. Comparative psychologists typically speak of evolution, but one can look in detail only at the brains of contemporary creatures. One must make detailed comparisons of gross and micro-anatomy, of physiology, *and* of behavioral changes resulting from stimulation, lesions, and ablations (Bullock, 1984). Only after data from *all* of such sources are integrated, Campbell and Hodos (1970) argued, can one expect to make an accurate judgment about the homology and homoplasticity of neuroanatomical structures in modern species. Equally important is the question of the extent of functional analogy that exists among the structures at issue.

The present focus is on the behavioral functions of the teleost brain, primarily of the telencephalon, or forebrain, because it is the structure most studied.[1] The structure of the teleost forebrain is relatively simple, because it has no neocortex and only limited differentiation (Northcutt & Davis, 1983; Peter & Gill, 1975). Despite this apparent simplicity, its functions remain unclear. This apparent simplicity should not be attributed to the fish being primitive, because modern teleosts are evolutionarily advanced and far from their Devonian progenitors; no existing teleost can be regarded as representing a distinct stage in the development of other existing vertebrates (Nelson, 1969).

---

[1]Relatively little attention has been paid to the functional significance of the cerebellum of teleosts fish, although the recent work of McCormick and Thompson (1984), suggesting associative significance in mammals, stimulates new interest. Actually, a small number of studies have sought to determine if the teleost cerebellum plays a role in learning (Kaplan & Aronson, 1969; Karamyan, 1956; Tuge, 1934) but these used motor tasks, and the locus of any disturbed performance is unsure because it is clear that the teleost cerebellum does play a role in sensory-motor coordination (e.g., Behrend, 1984; Izower & Aronson, 1987).

The current interest in the functions of the fish forebrain directly reflects Spencer's hypothesis that these functions might relate to the structure of the cerebral hemispheres in higher vertebrates. Some anatomical similarities are certain (e.g., Echteler & Saidel, 1981).

The great bulk of studies to date have used the ablative technique. We should note that goals of ablation based research are not simple assertions about localizations of functions—assertions that are always suspect (Weiskrantz, 1968)—but rather to provide a basis for speculations about the modus operandi of the *system* in behavioral tasks. Any adequate characterization of the behavioral dysfunction consequent on telencephalon ablation in the teleost depends on a systematic fine-grain analysis of the behavioral dispositions in a wide variety of tasks—tasks that tap different cognitive and behavioral processes (e.g., Davis & Kassel, 1983; de Bruin, 1980; Flood et al., 1976; Overmier, in press; Savage, 1980; see Gray, 1985, for similar approach in mammals).

ANATOMICAL CONSIDERATIONS

The basic neuroanatomy of the fish telencephalon is described only briefly here. More complete descriptions have been presented elsewhere (Bernstein, 1970; Northcutt & Davis, 1983; Schroeder, 1980). Describing the anatomy and organizational structure of the fish telencephalon has been a vexing problem. The structure of the telencephalon is different from that of other vertebrates and is devoid of familiar neuroanatomical landmarks. The teleost telencephalon lacks a lateral ventricle and a prominent ventricular sulcus and has a uniquely extensive thin roof plate (Nieuwenhuys, 1967). This anatomy has been attributed by some to unusual embryonic development in which the neural tube and forebrain anlage undergo eversion resulting in a single common ventricle and an "inside-out" placement of neuronal complexes and their interconnections relative to that seen in other vertebrates. This characterization is shown in Fig. 8.1A. However, as Fig. 8.1B makes clear, anatomists are not yet in agreement about the topology of the telencephalic structure in the teleost. Indeed, even the labels given to these areas are not agreed on by all neuroanatomists because of the difficulty in delineating the structure of the teleost telencephalon (Droogleever-Fortuyn, 1961, versus Northcutt & Bradford, 1980). These areas are not highly differentiated, especially in those fish most studied behaviorally, such as goldfish, for example. The six major neuronal complexes of the telencephalon show divergent exaggerations and diminutions across species. Some choose to label these topologically (dorsalis paramedialis, dorsalis pars dorsalis, dorsalis pars lateralis, dorsalis pars centralis, ventralis pars dorsalis, and ventralis pars ventralis), whereas others choose labels that suggest homology with mammalian structures, as in Fig. 8.1. Schroeder (1980) provided a table for translating across several nomenclature systems.

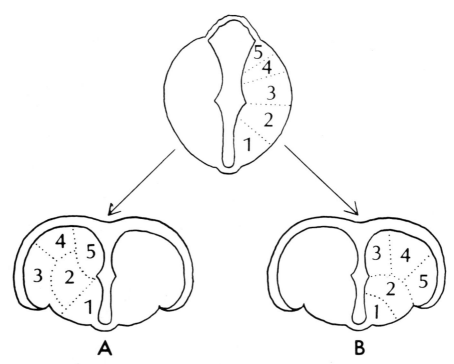

FIG. 8.1. Two hypothesized arrangements of basic divisions of the teleost telencephalon relative to the embryonic telencephalon anlage: A. after Schnitzlein (1968); B. after Scalia and Ebbesson (1971). See Schroeder (1980). Key: 1) septal area; 2) striatum; 3) pyriform area and amygdala; 4) general pallium; 5) hippocampal area.

These differentiated areas of the fish telencephalon are considered by some comparative neuroanatomists to have fields that are homologous with limbic formations of the more complex vertebrate brains (Bernstein, 1970; Scalia & Ebbesson, 1971; Schnitzlein, 1964, 1968), but this is a contested issue (Northcutt & Bradford, 1980). If the fields are primordial limbic structures, then our interest in them increases, because limbic structures such as the hippocampus are a central focus of the neurobiology of cognition—especially propositional and spatial memory (Gray, 1985; Lynch, 1986; Morris, 1984, Olton, Becker, & Handelmann, 1979).

Additionally, the very fact of the teleost telencephalon being different ontogenetically and organizationally has increased interest in its functional anatomy among comparative scientists. Specifically of interest are (a) the extent to which different anatomy leads to different functional solutions and (b) the extent to which common functional solutions can be the result of different neural structures—as a consequence, one presumes, of the common adaptive problems posed to organisms (e.g., Bitterman, 1988; MacPhail, 1982).

What functions does this telencephalon have? It was once thought to be exclusively olfactory in function (Prosser & Brown, 1961). Clearly, olfactory functions are the primary role of the ventral region of the telencephalon where most of the interconnections are with the olfactory tract (Bernstein, 1970). However, the dorsal region of the telencephalon shows a progressive development and differentiation, including increased connections with the ventral diencephalon, an increased thickness of the walls, and an increased differentiation of the basic neuronal areas. The result is that the dorsal region is a complex structure with diminished olfactory connections and increased diencephalic connections (Bernstein, 1970; Nieuwenhuys, 1967), which suggests subserving primary adaptive functions (Riss, Halpern, & Scalia, 1969; Vanegas & Ebbesson, 1976).

The role that the telencephalon plays in the mediation of teleost behavior has been elusive. Surprisingly, early investigations reported that total forebrain ablation in fish failed to produce any significant effects on behavior or learning (e.g., Janzen, 1933; Meader, 1939; Scharrer, 1928; Steiner, 1888; Vulpian, 1886). It is hard to imagine that the part of the brain that in other vertebrates has been shown to have such important functions—and even has been called "the organ of civilization" (Halstead, 1947)—would have no functional significance at all in the teleost. However, recent research has revealed that the fish forebrain is, in fact, involved in the mediation of complex adaptive behavior (e.g., Healy, 1957; Hollis & Overmier, 1978; Kaplan & Aronson, 1969; Segaar, 1961).

The present review focuses on behavioral phenomena; but, because these are complex, emergent phenomena, dependent on sensory-motor processes, we begin with a brief summary of the effects of telencephalon ablation on these.

BASIC SENSORY-MOTOR PROCESSES

Two major perceptual functions are affected by total forebrain ablation. Olfaction, as would be expected because of anatomical considerations, is permanently lost (Strieck, 1924). In contrast, taste and temperature perception seem unaffected (Berwein, 1941). Color vision is temporarily impaired by the surgical trauma but returns to normal within hours (Bernstein, 1961, 1962) or days (Sikharulidze, 1969).

No qualitative gross behavioral changes in topography of locomotion, posture (but, see Meyer, Heiligenberg, & Bullock, 1976), or feeding occur following forebrain ablation (e.g., Hale, 1956; Nolte, 1932). However, several important quantitative changes do occur. The most remarkable changes are reduction in response variability (Davis, Reynolds, & Ricks, 1978; Janzen, 1933) and a decrease in spontaneous locomotion (Hosch, 1936; Polimanti, 1913). Although the general activity levels of individual ablated fish decrease, those in schools show increased activity (Koshtoiants, Maliukina, & Aleksandriuk, 1960) with a mild disruption of schooling behavior (Hosch, 1936; Kumakura, 1928; Noble, 1936). Experiments suggest that this disruption of schooling may be an artifact of the loss of olfaction (Hemmings, 1966) or the method of testing (Berwein, 1941), rather than some effect on social behavior, per se.

Indeed, as we later consider other possible behavioral deficits, we must be alert to the possibility that the observed deficit is not a by-product of some disruption in olfaction, because olfaction plays an important role in species typical behavior fish just as it does in mammals (e.g., Kyle & Peter, 1982; Stacy & Kyle, 1983).

LEARNING AND MEMORY PROCESSES: PHYLETIC DIFFERENCES?

Researches with intact fish have been summarized elsewhere (Gleitman & Rozin, 1971), although this summary is somewhat dated now. More recent works touching on the topics do so within reviews of other vertebrate class' capacities with the aim of assessing whether evolution has resulted in divergences in associative and cognitive capacities (Livesey, 1986; MacPhail, 1982).

Although this book focuses on comparative neurobiology, consideration of whether the associative and cognitive processes of intact fish differ from mammals is relevant and potentially important to evaluating the meaning of the outcomes of neurobiological interventions. Like mammals, fish show habituation, Pavlovian conditioning, instrumental reward and escape learning, avoidance learning, and integration of separate learning experiences; often the similarities are striking (Flood, et al., 1976). Indeed, it was the existence of such similarities across several phyla that led the major learning theorists, such as Thorndike and Hull, to adopt general theories of learning. Hull's formalization of simple stimulus–response (S–R) reinforcement theory (1943) soon foundered upon new mammalian data (e.g., Crespi, 1942), and new theories replaced it (e.g., Spence's incentive theory). Nonetheless, the old Thorndikian-Hullian theory seemed to account perfectly well for virtually all learning and performance data obtained with fish in the laboratory—so well, in fact, that the fish has been described as a prototypical Thorndikian animal (Bitterman, 1968, 1975). Such a description is to claim some important fundamental differences in the capacities of fish as contrasted with other vertebrates; but this claim has been challenged as vigorously as it has been put forth (Mackintosh, 1969; MacPhail, 1982), although the challenges have relied heavily on speculation about possible mechanisms. At present, we tend to give more weight to the observed differences than to the speculations as to why such differences should not be taken seriously, but we also recognize that the apparent absence of a given learning/performance phenomenon in fish may only mean that the right experiments have not yet been done. For example, one may teach an animal a stimulus discrimination in a simple choice task and, upon mastery of the discrimination, require the animal to learn the opposite; upon mastery, the animal is required to learn the reverse again, and so on—the so-called serial reversal problem. Across successive reversals, mammals typically make fewer and fewer errors in mastering each reversal (variously characterized as a form of learning sets by some, as developing a win-stay/lose-shift strategy by others, etc.), but over several experiments fish did not do so (see Bitterman, 1968, for a review). Later, however, it was demonstrated that fish can, under limited circumstances, manifest such improvement across successive reversals (Englehardt, Woodard, & Bitterman, 1973), thus illustrating the dangers in accepting the null hypothesis. This caution aside, let us look briefly at the claims of difference.

Basic S–R theory (Thorndike, 1911) hypothesizes that when in the presence of a stimulus (S) a given act (R) produces a reward, the reward acts as a catalyst to establish an association between the stimulus and the act, the S–R association. But according to the S–R theory, the reward itself does not enter into association with S or R, just as a catalyst in chemistry promotes bonding but does not itself bond in compounds. To the extent, then, that the fish is the perfect Thorndikian animal, the tenets of S–R theory suggest that the kind of learning tasks in which fish differ from mammals involve "learning about" reinforcers and "expectations." These include, in addition to the aforementioned successive reversal learning, tasks involving shifts in magnitude of reinforcement whereupon mammals show contrast effects but fish do not, and spaced trials partial reinforcement tasks wherein mammals show more persistence after intermittent large rewards than after consistent large rewards whereas fish show the opposite (reviewed by Bitterman, 1968; Gleitman & Rozin, 1971; MacPhail, 1982). These findings are taken by many to imply that fish do not form cognitive representations and expectations of response-contingent outcome events and that absence of such expectations constitutes a lower level of cognitive functioning attributable to the differences in brain organization and development.

Evidence consonant with the hypothesis that such differences may be attributable to differences in brain structure are the findings of Amsel and his associates (Amsel, 1986) of an identical behavioral deficiency in the immature rat and the emergence of behavioral "expectancy" phenomena as the hippocampus matures. Additionally, extreme forebrain ablations in rats eliminate their capacity to show improvements over successive reversals and result in "fish-like" behavior. A controversial experiment by Bressler and Bitterman (1968) sought to show the obverse: The brain tissue of fish was *supplemented* by grafting embryonic brain tissue into a host. Of six attempted grafts, four appeared successful and, critically, these four and only these four showed error reductions across the successive reversals—that is, "rat-like" behavior![2] Hence, marked behavioral-cognitive differences are directly relatable to differences in brain structure.

---

[2]One serious criticism of this study is that the grafting was of tectal tissue, and there is little evidence that the tectum plays a role in learning *per se* by teleost fish.

BRAIN LESIONS AND LEARNING

Let us now address directly the effects of telencephalon lesions on learning. In most cases hereafter we review studies in which the lesion is ablation of the total telencephalon; few studies have explored more limited lesions, in part because, early on, there was no evidence of any effect and, later, because the anatomy was not yet worked out. In any case, total telencephalon ablation should not generally be thought of as equivalent to removal of the cerebral hemispheres in mammals but rather as more like removal of limbic structures, because the teleost telencephalon is essentially prelimbic and also lacks neocortex. Our review of the experimental literature here provides an analytic overview of the general pattern of results obtained.

Habituation

Habituation is the reduction in response engendered by repeated presentations of, or prolonged exposure to, a stimulus. It is a phenomenon of interest not only because of the variety of proffered theoretical accounts—both nonassociative and associative (Tighe & Leaton, 1976), but also because of its putative relation to attention and its use as an index of information processing and memory (e.g., Olson, 1976). Habituation is often used to indicate that the features of a stimulus have been processed, dismissed as noninformative, and remembered. From this point of view, habituation, essentially, is the waning of attention.

Habituation in telencephalon-ablated fish has been studied using a variety of stimuli and responses. For example, 10-min exposures to prey as the stimulus result in equal rates of habituation of the elicited feeding response on day 1 for ablated and sham-operated control fish; however, only the control fish retained this reduction between daily sessions; the ablated fish did not (Peeke, Peeke, & Williston, 1972). Thus, ablation of the telencephalon impairs long-term but not short-term habituation of feeding responses. Within-session differences have also been noted; upon repeated exposures to various "startle" stimuli (looming or a plunger), ablated fish were impaired on habituation both within as well as across daily sessions (Laming & Ennis, 1982, Laming & McKee, 1981). Control experiments showed that this impairment was not a by-product of the olfactory bulbectomy that necessarily accompanies telencephalon ablation (Rooney & Laming, 1984).

The effects of more limited lesions are reported to have mixed effects. Whereas it has been reported that lesions in the posterior telencephalon produced effects similar to those of total ablation (Rooney & Laming, 1986), dorsomedial lesions lateral to the dorsal commissure resulted in facilitation of habituation (Marino-Neto & Sabbatini, 1983). Such a mixed pattern suggests that the behavior changes observed to repeated stimulus presentations may well be the product of interacting opposite processes, as suggested by the theory of Thompson and Spencer (1966).

Pavlovian Conditioning

Pavlovian conditioning generally is taken as the simplest form of associative learning. Descriptively, when a "neutral" stimulus and a hedonically powerful stimulus are presented repeatedly in an arrangement such that the neutral stimulus (CS) predicts the hedonic one (US), then the CS acquires behavior-controlling properties (CR). Virtually all studies of the effects of total telencephalon ablation on Pavlovian conditioning have used an aversive US. (Some Russian experiments, like those by Kholodov, that are cited as appetitive Pavlovian conditioning are really instrumental paradigms; the Russian literature traditionally has not made our Western distinction.).

The effect of telencephalon ablation on Pavlovian conditioning is summarized easily: Across a wide variety of procedures using a variety of associative indices and even a range of delays *between* CSs and USs, total telencephalon ablation has had *no* effects on the Pavlovian conditioning process (e.g., Bernstein, 1961; Overmier & Curnow, 1969; Overmier & Savage, 1974). In fact, even more "complex forms" of Pavlovian conditioning, such as higher-order conditioning in which a former CS is used as a "US" to condition a new CS, proceeds unimpaired in telencephalon-ablated fish (Farr & Savage, 1978)! One implication of this would seem to be that fish can learn readily that stimuli signal other hedonically important stimuli and that this process is unimpaired by the ablation. Important but unanswered is whether this learning means that fish develop "expectancies" of the US or whether the learning is of the S–R type. We readdress this issue later.

Instrumental Learning

In instrumental learning tasks, reinforcers such as the presentation of hedonically positive events (e.g., food or sexual partner) or the *termination* of hedonically negative events (e.g., electric shock) are made contingent upon performance of designated behaviors. The usual consequent of this arrangement is that the designated behavioral response becomes more probable and more vigorous. In general, when the reward is delivered promptly upon completion of the response, total telencephalon ablation has no deleterious effects on learning (e.g., Kholodov, 1960; Savage, 1969a, Exp 1 and 2; 1969b).

However, it would be wrong to conclude that instrumental learning is totally spared following telencephalon ablation, because instrumental learning—especially discriminative, choice learning—is impaired under special conditions. Impairment results when the response to be learned and the reinforcer are separated either temporally or spatially (Flood & Overmier, 1971; Savage, 1969b; see analyses by Overmier & Hollis, 1983). If, however, appropriate cues are presented concurrently with the reinforcer so as to reinstate the stimulus conditions present at the time of choice response initiation, then the impairment is eliminated (Overmier & Patten, 1982). This finding is likely related to the fact that even normal animals typically suffer some deficit in learning when there is a delay between response and reinforcer unless secondary reinforcing stimuli are present *during* the delay to bridge the temporal interval (Grice, 1948). The difference between the two findings is the method of "bridging" the delay: continuing the choice stimuli or representing them after the temporal/spatial delay when the reinforcer is presented. One interpretation of this result with ablated fish is that the deficit originally observed is one of poor retrospective memory—that the fish cannot remember at the time of reward what response they made to obtain the reward. An alternative interpretation is that the deficit arises at the time of response initiation—that the stimuli before the fish do not elicit conditioned expectancies of the reinforcer to facilitate and guide choice responding. The latter is suggested because the method of representing the choice stimuli at the time of reinforcement allows for conditioning of expectancies but not secondary reinforcement of choices.

This sensitivity of ablated fish to separation between the events to be associated in the instrumental paradigm but not in the Pavlovian paradigm suggests that these two paradigms differ to some degree in the neural substrates that subserve these forms of learning. Further evidence for this independence of Pavlovian and instrumental learning mechanisms comes from the study of avoidance learning, a task that involves both Pavlovian and instrumental learning processes.

Avoidance Learning

Avoidance learning paradigms have long held a special place in the analysis and development of learning theory (e.g., Mowrer, 1947). This is because typical avoidance learning tasks involve components of both Pavlovian conditioning and instrumental training and, yet, cannot be "explained" simply by invoking accounts of either one of them. In a typical avoidance task, events are arranged so that a few seconds after the presentation of a brief CS comes on a US is scheduled to occur, and such Pavlovian pairing will occur unless the animal makes a designated response, in which case the US (typically electric shock, but see Kovačević, 1978) is omitted. On early trials, the procedure is one of Pavlovian CS–US pairings; the animal typically responds to terminate (escape) the US. After a few such trials, the animal comes to make the response when the CS first comes on and, hence, instrumentally prevents the US; this response is learned, becoming reliable and vigorous. The conundrum of avoidance learning is how the *omission* of an event can function to reinforce avoidance behavior; after all, if the animal makes the designated response, nothing happens! The nonoccurrence of an event can be meaningful only if the animal *expected* the event, and hence avoidance learning forced animal behavior theorists to deal with the problem of expectancies—clearly a cognitive construct—in animals.

Normal fish readily learn to make avoidance responses, and this facility has been demonstrated under a wide variety of circumstances (Gleitman & Rozin, 1971). That they do so must imply that fish have the capacity to learn to expect noxious events or have some proactive representations of such events. This is important in considering the basis of the differences between fish and mammal behavior in appetitive instrumental experiments involving shifts in reward magnitude to which we alluded earlier. Those differences have been attributed to the inability of the fish to develop *or use* expectations of rewards in the control of their behavior. Successful avoidance learning by fish means either that the difference between fish and mammals in appetitive instrumental tasks has a basis other than the inability to develop representations of the rewards, or that in fish this capacity to develop expectancies and representations is limited to aversive events. Resolution of this issue will be important to both comparative psychologists and learning theorists.

Given that fish readily master avoidance tasks, we may ask: What are the consequences of telencephalic ablations for such learning? The question can be treated in two ways: (a) the effect on initial acquisition and (b) the effect on performance once the task is mastered. The answer to the first is very consistent, whereas the latter is a bit more controversial.

Despite the fact that, as described earlier, total telencephalon ablation has no effect on Pavlovian conditioning nor upon instrumental escape performance (preceding sections), such ablations dramatically impair instrumental avoidance learning in all species tested (Hainsworth, Overmier & Snowden, 1967; Kaplan & Aronson, 1969; Overmier & Gross, 1979; Savage, 1969a). Although learning of the avoidance response is not completely blocked by ablation, the response is very slow to develop, unstable, and extinguishes very rapidly. Of possible interpretive significance is that massing of avoidance trials appears to aid the ablates in learning the avoidance task, whereas massing has the opposite effect on normal fish (Savage, 1968). Savage attributed the improvement to a priming of short-term memory in the massed group, but we suspect that an equally plausible account not yet tested is that the massed trials procedure results in more frequent shocks, increasing arousal, which is known to be low in telencephalon-ablated fish (Aronson & Kaplan, 1968).

If intact fish are trained to asymptote in an avoidance task and then undergo the ablation, the effect is virtually to eliminate the avoidance response (Hainsworth, et al., 1967; Savage, 1969a). Retraining these fish reveals little, if any, savings. These results suggest a separation between learning processes, on the one hand, and retention or retrieval processes, on the other. The degree of savings in retraining the ablated fish seems to be independent of the amount of preablation training but not of motivational level (Overmier & Papini, 1986); increases in motivation, by using a stronger US, result in improved post-ablation relearning. Whether this later effect is associatively based or motivationally based is yet to be determined.

In any case, the dissociation of effects of telencephalon ablations on avoidance as contrasted with simple Pavlovian and instrumental learning suggests that avoidance behavior is dependent on brain mechanisms that are different from those of simple Pavlovian and instrumental learning. One simple hypothesis about how telencephalon ablation disrupts avoidance learning without disrupting its component elements of Pavlovian conditioning and instrumental response learning is that the neural damage prevents the integration of these two components—that the poor fish just can't "get it together." The hypothesis has its origins in the "two-process" theory of avoidance (Mowrer, 1947). One test of this idea uses what is called a transfer of control design, in which the component processes are separately established followed by tests for their integration into coherent, adaptive behavior. Consider a specific example: In the three phases of this experiment, ablated and control fish were (a) trained—albeit with some difficulty—to perform an avoidance response when given an auditory cue; (b) removed to a novel place and given Pavlovian aversive conditioning to a visual cue; and (c) returned to the original avoidance apparatus and tested for the visual CS's ability to control the previously learned avoidance response (Overmier & Starkman, 1974). The behavior of the ablated fish in this test was identical to that of normal fish; for both, the visual cue immediately evoked the avoidance response previously trained to the tone. Control treatments established that this immediate transfer of control was not some form of generalized responding but specific to Pavlovianly conditioned CSs. This observation suggests that ablated fish do learn to expect the US after the CS and that they can integrate this information into control of a *previously learned* avoidance response. So the problem seems to be that the telencephalon is critical to the avoidance acquisition process, per se. Hollis and Overmier (1978) have offered a hypothesis about just what role in the learning process the telencephalon mediates: It is that ablated fish are impaired in utilizing either the eliciting or the reinforcing properties of stimuli that are not themselves primary reinforcers but have been associated with reinforcers. The hypothesis remains to be tested vigorously.

Avoidance behavior is, of course, not merely a laboratory curiosity but an important defensive behavior integral to survival. Animals must learn what to flee (active avoidance) or where not to go because harm might result (passive avoidance). Just as telencephalon ablation impairs active avoidance, so too does it impair passive avoidance (Overmier & Flood, 1969). An especially interesting form of passive avoidance learning is learning not to prey upon species that result in illness if eaten, and this form of passive avoidance ("toxiphobia") is also impaired by telencephalon ablation (Gordon, 1979).

Spatial Learning

Surprisingly little research with fish has focused on spatial learning, especially as modulated by brain lesions. This is especially unfortunate for two reasons. First, fish of at least several species exhibit excellent spatial learning and long-term memory for this learning (Gleitman & Rozin, 1971; Hasler, 1956). Second, tests of spatial learning ability following various CNS insults have become a powerful tool in the armamentarium of the cognitive neurobiologist (Morris, 1984; O'Keefe & Nadel, 1978; Olton et al., 1979). Two experiments have explored simple spatial learning in a two-choice maze (Frank, Flood, & Overmier, 1972; Warren, 1961). Both obtained similar results. They, of course, confirmed in a spatial task the already noted observation that fish—in contrast to mammals—do not seem to improve when they are required repeatedly to reverse successively the previously trained response. Additionally, total telencephalon ablation or ablation of the anterior lobes resulted in impairment of the fish's ability to learn such successive reversals: whereas normal fish did not reduce errors over successive reversals, ablated fish actually got worse across successive reversals. The meaning of these results is, at this point, unclear, and several additional variations are needed. A number of investigators working with mammals have developed procedural variations that could be profitably explored in elucidating the neurobiology of fish learning (e.g., Morris, 1983). Indeed, spatial tasks have proved to be very important tools in the neurobiology of cognition in animals (e.g., Olton, 1979), and it is known that at least normal fish can master these tasks both in the laboratory (Roitblat, Tham, & Golub, 1982) and in the natural environment (Aronson, 1951). Following their lead would allow us to begin to bridge the gap between the cognitive neuroscience of fish and that of mammals.

Long-Term Memory

The distinction between short-term memory and long-term memory has been a traditional one that is useful in the study of the neurobiology of learning, although other distinctions are now proving useful as well (e.g., working memory vs. reference memory, Morris, 1983). We have already seen that telencephalon ablation results in deficits in appetitive instrumental learning with delayed reinforcers that may imply a short-term memory deficit. However, few studies have investigated the effects of telencephalic lesions on long-term memory in learning tasks.

To answer the question of whether forebrain ablation modulates long-term retention of an appetitive instrumental learning, both normal and ablated fish were first trained on a shape discrimination choice task. After both groups reached a high criterion of accuracy, an 8-day delay was imposed, followed by tests for choice accuracy. Neither group showed any reduction in choice accuracy, indicating that the ablation had no effect on long-term memory (Flood,

1975). Our review has found no parallel studies using the other learning paradigms, indicating that the area of long-term memory is yet to be explored.

One strategy for the study of the neurobiology of memory is the transfer of RNA brain extracts from trained fish to untrained fish. There are numerous reports that this manipulation results in the transfer of "learning" from one animal to the other (Bryant, 1972; Fjerdingstad, 1969). Typically, those experiments report a facilitation in the acquisition of avoidance behavior by fish that are recipients of brain RNA extracts from avoidance-trained fish relative to those fish that are recipients of brain RNA extracts from naive fish or stressed but untrained fish (Braud & Hoffman, 1973a). Some experiments have demonstrated highly specific transfer effects, such as intersubject transfer of training to perform the avoidance response on presentations of specific colors—to avoid blue but not green or vice versa (Ungar, Galvin, & Chapouthier, 1972)! Nearly all of these experiments have been restricted to the use of active avoidance tasks, although there is an occasional exception using appetitive procedures (e.g., Braud & Hoffman, 1973b).

Despite the excitement that these experiments generate, considerable caution seems in order, based on a concatenation of other observations. The line of cautionary argument goes as follows. During fishes' learning, there are changes in *brain* RNA but not, say, in liver RNA (Shashoua, 1976). Furthermore, brain RNA is distinctively different from liver RNA (Tano, Mizuno, & Shirahata, 1970), and these distinctive RNAs show preferential uptake by the respective organ of the recipient (Stillwell, Porter, & Byrne, 1971). Yet, despite all this localization of change, specificity, and selective uptake, experimenters are reporting that extracts of *liver* RNA from trained animals result in intersubject transfer of training (Frank, Stein, & Rosen, 1970; Miller & Holt, 1977)! Do we conclude that memories are stored in the liver? Clearly, something is amiss, and perhaps more creative uses of the available array of learning paradigms will aid in achieving resolution on this important issue by ruling out types of nonspecific behavioral alteration.

Of course, that RNA plays some role in learning and memorial processes of fish, as well as the other vertebrates, is widely accepted (e.g., Shashoua, 1968, 1985). If the consolidation of long-term memory from short-term memory is achieved through RNA-modulated protein synthesis, then disruption of this protein synthesis process should have deleterious effects on long-term retention. A number of experimenters have been following just this logic and using intracranial injections of protein synthesis inhibitors to study habit fixation in fish (e.g., Agranoff, 1970, 1971; but see Uphouse, MacInnes, & Schlesinger, 1974, for a critical review). A wealth of data has been amassed showing that intracranial injections into goldfish of puromycin, glutaramides, and camptothectin—all of which inhibit RNA-modulated protein synthesis, albeit by different mechanisms—result in retention deficits if the injections are timed so as to yield their inhibition during the consolidation period (e.g., Neale, Klinger, & Agranoff,

1973; Springer, Schact, & Agranoff, 1976). A serious interpretive problem exists for all this data as to the site of action. Is it upon the telencephalon, upon the tectum, or elsewhere? The question arises because no effort has been taken to localize the site of functional impact. Would properly timed doses of puromycin augment further the deficit in avoidance learning of telencephalon-ablated fish?

Once again though, this mass of data obtained with fish and presumed to apply to all learning and memory phenomena has been based almost exclusively on the active avoidance paradigm. Deviations from this particular learning paradigm suggest that the effects may be specific to active and passive avoidance learning tasks and not obtainable with, say, Pavlovian conditioning tasks, the learning of which also presumably involves memory (Potts & Bitterman, 1967; Huber & Longo, 1970). But most important are recent data that suggest that the deficit is not one of memory at all, but one of retrieval (Barraco & Stettner, 1976); it seems that these "lost" memories can be made functional by selected treatments prior to testing.

THEORETICAL ANALYSIS

Learning by fish is claimed by some to be best accounted for by Thorndikian S–R principles—principles different from those that are invoked to account for mammalian learning. The two sets of principles differ in that the former does not provide for any learning about, or associations with, the reward or reinforcing event. Associations with the reinforcing event are the basis for *expectancies,* and such associations (and the consequent expectancies play a prominent role in contemporary accounts of mammalian behavior, e.g., Colwill & Rescorla, 1986, 1988; Dickinson, 1980).

The data reviewed suggest to us that this hypothesized difference between *normal* fish and mammals is incorrect. Normal fish can learn to (a) initiate responses leading to temporally and contextually remote goals (Overmier & Patten, 1982), (b) avoid signalled but absent noxious events and sustain that behavior under extinction conditions (Overmier & Papini, 1986), and (c) use separately established signals for noxious events as a basis for initiating previously learned avoidance responses (Overmier & Starkman, 1974). Taken together, they suggest that fish do learn associative expectancies of reinforcing events and that these expectancies are not mere S–R associations. These expectancies play a key role in bridging temporal gaps, eliciting or motivating behavior, and reinforcing behavior in the absence of primary (unlearned, "need-based") reinforcers.

Although we believe it incorrect to describe normal fish as "Thorndikian S–R" animals, we do believe that this label correctly characterizes the telencephalon-ablated teleost fish. The ablation does impair the fish on exactly those tasks that we use to suggest that expectancies normally operate: Telencephalon-ablated fish cannot (a) reliably initiate prompt responses leading to temporally or contextually remote goals (Overmier & Patten, 1982) nor (b) reliably avoid signalled but absent noxious events (Overmier & Papini, 1986) nor sustain such behaviors in extinction (Hainsworth et al., 1967). That ablated fish can use separately established signals for noxious events as a basis for initiating a *previously* learned avoidance response—although at longer latency (Overmier & Starkman, 1974) but not for the learning of a new response (Farr & Savage, 1978) suggests that it is the *secondary* reinforcing functions of expectancies that are most impaired.[3] Secondary reinforcers are weak reinforcers that have acquired their power through direct association with primary reinforcers. Such secondary reinforcers can function not only to strengthen completed *acts* but can also serve discriminative and response-evoking functions (Dinsmoor, 1950), presumably by virtue of their power to elicit expectancies of the primary reinforcers. Because the Pavlovian conditioning relationship is the basis for learning of expectancies (Overmier & Lawry, 1979; Trapold & Overmier, 1972) and because Pavlovian conditioning is not impaired by telencephalon ablation, it is likely the case that ablation impairs not expectancy *learning* but rather *utilization* of expectancies for control of various acts.

Learning, of course, is a biological adaptation to enable an animal to cope flexibly with the varying demands of the environment (viz. Bitterman, 1988). To the extent that complex integrated behaviors build upon basic learning processes, those integrated behaviors that involve expectancies directly in their learning or maintenance should be substantially impaired. To anticipate or understand the effects of telencephalon ablation on complex integrated behaviors, we must analyze these behaviors to uncover the imbedded forms of learning. If the imbedded forms identified in a given situation involve forms that we know are disrupted by telencephalon ablation, such as those that involve the conditioned reinforcing properties of expectancies, then we should find the emergent complex adaptive behavior also impaired. Thus, looking to the effects of ablation on the complex integrated behaviors provides us with tests of the hypotheses that these behaviors involve the basic learning processes and that those learning processes that rely on utilization of expectancies are causal in any observed deficits in the integrated behaviors.

We do not believe that the telencephalon plays *only* one role in the mediation of complex behaviors. However, the other potential functions of arousal and short-term memory have been emphasized elsewhere without notable explanatory success (see Flood et al., 1976, for review). Hence, here we have emphasized the expectancy/secondary reinforcement hypothesis as a heuristic. Let us see how well it fares.

---

[3]The careful reader will note that we seem to have ignored habituation in this analysis. However, we note that one currently popular model of habituation (Wagner, 1976) essentially accounts for habituation as the result of learning to expect an event.

THE ROLE OF LEARNING IN INTEGRATED BEHAVIOR

The involvement of learning and memory processes in the species-specific integrated behavior of vertebrates is commonly taken for granted by ethologists and psychologists alike. However, the actual role of such learning is not often investigated experimentally. Rare indeed are naturalistic studies of learning in fish. A few notable exceptions, however (e.g., Baerends, 1957; Losey, 1982; Peeke & Peeke, 1982), have documented the importance to species-specific behavior of several of the learning processes reviewed earlier in this chapter. When taken together with the animal learning literature, these studies suggest that learning and conditioning are an integral part of the expression of adaptive phenotypic behaviors, including foraging, territoriality, reproduction, and parental care. We conclude from this observation that the largest gains in understanding of telencephalic function may derive from attempts to integrate the results of laboratory learning studies with those of naturalistic observation. In the remainder of this chapter, we attempt to bridge these two areas of research.

For example, many species of territorial fish behave as if they are able to recognize potential competitors for the resource that they are guarding. Members of other species that pose a threat to the security of that resource are driven away, whereas members of noncompetitive species, even when they cannot be recognized individually, are permitted to remain within the territory. Experiments with damselfish (Losey, 1982) suggest that such interspecific aggression toward competitors is learned. Moreover, individuals not only learn to distinguish between species that represent a threat and species that do not, but they are capable of making fine discriminations between different species of the same genera. Although these data suggest that some process of learning is operating here—and, perhaps, in other instances of interspecific aggression—the particular characterization of the form(s) of learning involved, as habituation, Pavlovian, or instrumental conditioning, remains unresolved. However, we next review studies of naturalistic behavior in which the role and the form of learning seems clear.

Habituation and Sensitization

Laboratory studies of *intra*specific aggression in convict cichlids suggest the operation of habituation and sensitization processes (Peeke & Peeke, 1973, 1982). Aggression between territorial neighbors is initially both intense and frequent but, over time, wanes to a point where their aggressive interactions are both fewer in number and relatively mild. This habituation is what permits the fish to engage in other behavior and to proceed to subsequent phases of the reproductive cycle uninterrupted by unnecessary aggressive gestures. Yet, despite the detente that comes to exist between territorial neighbors throughout a breeding cycle, a *strange* male is not at all spared from a full-blown aggressive attack. These observations suggest that, like many other studies of habituation

221

that psychologists have studied in the laboratory (see Groves & Thompson, 1970, for a review), habituation of intraspecific aggression is stimulus-specific and of long-term duration.

Also like laboratory studies of habituation, the waning of interspecific aggression in convict cichlids is thought to result from the interaction of underlying opposing processes, one decremental (habituation) and the other incremental (sensitization). Opposing incremental sensitization processes are hypothesized to manifest themselves in the abrupt increases in aggressiveness that mark transitions between one stage of the reproductive cycle to the next (Peeke & Peeke, 1982). Of particular interest to our study of the function of the teleost telencephalon is the observation that such transitions are modulated by forebrain-controlled neurohumoral state (Kyle & Peter, 1982).

Pavlovian Conditioning

Briding the gap somewhat between naturalistic studies of aggression and traditional learning investigations are demonstrations that aggressive behavior itself can be conditioned. For example, Siamese fighting fish will charge and display aggressively to stimulus events paired with the presentation of a rival male in a standard Pavlovian conditioning procedure (Thompson & Sturm, 1965b). This conditional aggressive response, which can be elicited by learned visual signals, also can be evoked by learned spatial signals, such as a geographical area in which territorial contests were waged in the past (Bronstein, 1986). The adaptive significance of this conditional aggressive response is suggested by experiments with a close relative of fighting fish, namely the blue gourami: Males that attempted to defend their territory in an encounter signaled by a Pavlovian CS were able to deliver significantly more bites and tailbeatings and won more of the territorial contests than males that were denied the benefit of such signaling (Hollis, 1984a, 1984b; see Hollis, in press, for a review).

Winning an aggressive encounter may provide added benefits: Compared to the losers of an aggressive encounter, swordtail fish that win aggressive contests exhibit significantly lower levels of circulating corticoids, or stress hormones, whereas losers, which exhibit extremely elevated levels of these hormones far above control fish, remain in the stressed state for as long as 14 days after the contest is over (Hannes, Frank, & Liemann, 1984). The comparative psychologist will note that similar findings have been obtained with mice (Bronson, 1973) and rats (Militzer & Reinhard, 1982; van de Poll, Smeets, van Oyen, & van der Zwan, 1982) and infer that, whatever the species, losers appear to suffer from a defeat "stress syndrome." Thus, the ability to modify aggressive behavior through conditioning may be an integral part of a male's territorial aggressive strategy and facilitate coping with the stress of combat.

Courtship behavior in fish also has been conditioned with Pavlovian procedures and, like the conditioning of aggression, such modification of reproductive behavior appears to have adaptive consequences (Hollis, Cadieux, & Colbert, 1989). When, following Pavlovian conditioning pairings of a visual CS and a female US, Pavlovian-trained males encountered a receptive female announced by that same CS, they performed significantly more courtship behavior—and significantly less aggressive behavior—than control males that encountered females without the benefit of a prior signaling. The adaptive advantage of such signaling in the wild may be that territorial males are able to relax their territorial aggression without jeopardizing territory ownership—a prerequisite for mating—and, at the same time, to begin courting the female sooner.

Instrumental Learning

Reward-based instrumental learning may be yet another way that behavior can be modified in naturalistic sequences. In the case of territorial aggression, for example, detection of intruders is of paramount importance. Any mechanism that enhances a male's ability to detect an invasion will convey a territorial advantage and, thus, increase fitness. Learning mechanisms can result in the fish restricting territorial patrol to specific areas where intruders have appeared in the past. Approach and patrol behavior, as we saw earlier, can be elicited by spatial landmarks via Pavlovian conditioning. A male's approach and patrol behavior also might be modified, via instrumental conditioning, if at least some components of a male's aggressive behavior are followed by reinforcing stimuli. Such reinforcement seems very likely indeed. Numerous studies have shown that the opportunity to display aggressively to a conspecific (or to a model or mirror image) can be a potent reinforcer for a variety of simple locomotor instrumental responses and choice among alternatives (Hogan, 1961, 1967, Sevenster, 1973; Thompson, 1963, 1966; Thompson & Sturm, 1965a; see Hogan & Roper, 1978, for a review).

Similarly, the ability to locate available females or to establish territories where females have been encountered at a favorable rate in the past might be shaped by instrumental conditioning. Studies with sticklebacks have shown that male fish will perform an instrumental response to gain access to a receptive female (Sevenster, 1968, 1973). Again, however, we are left with the question of whether a male's behavior in the wild is shaped by this type of instrumental reward. Although our interpretation of this research is highly speculative, we suggest that Pavlovian conditioning and instrumental reinforcement may serve to hone a fish's aggressive and courtship behavior so that the behavior appears preparatory, cognitively strategic, and purposively efficient. Studies of the effect of telencephalon ablation on naturalistic behavior suggest that habituation, Pavlovian conditioning, and instrumental reward training, as forms of learning, do in fact contribute to integrated behavior. In the next section we review these data.

BRAIN LESIONS AND INTEGRATED BEHAVIOR

Given the pattern of impairment and sparing of learned behaviors following telencephalon ablation—in which habituation and instrumental responses based on expectancies are impaired whereas Pavlovian conditioning and simple instrumental tasks are not—and given our assumption that the processes underlying these learning tasks contribute to naturalistic integrated behavior, we ought to find impairments in naturalist behavior wherever habituation processes and/or expectancies are thought to contribute in substantial ways to that behavior. In the following sections, we assess these assertions and predictions by looking at the effects of telencephalon ablation on two types of integrated behavior, namely aggressive and reproductive behavior.

Aggressive Behavior

Across a broad range of subject species, the effects of ablation on aggressive behavior reveal a consistent pattern. Following ablation, marked decrements in territorial aggressive behavior have been observed in sticklebacks (Schonherr, 1955; Segaar, 1961, 1965; Segaar & Nieuwenhuys, 1963), jewel fish, swordtails (Noble, 1936; Noble & Borne, 1941), sunfish (Hale, 1956), and fighting fish (de Bruin, 1977). Once fighting behavior is elicited in ablates, however, it does not differ in any way from that exhibited by normal fish (Fiedler, 1967, 1968; Hale, 1956; Karamyan, Malukova, & Sergeev, 1967). In fighting fish, for example, the frequency of aggressive gill cover displays decreases, but neither the duration nor the form of this display is affected by complete ablation (Shapiro, Schuckman, Sussman, & Tucker, 1974).

Interestingly, a similar pattern of aggressive deficits follow limbic lesions in mammals. Lesions of the amygdala, hippocampus, and cingulate disrupt threat behavior, overt aggression, and social dominance (e.g., Bard, 1950; Dicks, Myers, & Kling, 1969; Rosvold, Mirsky, & Pribaum, 1954). Paralleling these similarities in aggressive deficits are interesting theoretical similarities as well. For example, the behavioral deficits of limbic lesioned mammals are said to result from disruption of general arousal (e.g., Kaada, 1960), short-term memory (e.g., Scoville & Milner, 1957), and motivational and reinforcer processes (e.g., Gloor, 1960; Vanderwolf, 1971).

The latter theory, that mammalian limbic structures participate in motivational and reinforcer processes, attributes aggressive behavior deficits following limbic lesions to the failure of inherently reinforcing species-specific events to maintain normal levels of responding. More recent studies provide a measure of additional support for such a hypothesis: Limbic areas have been discovered that participate in the modification of behavior through conditioning (Rolls, 1987). Thus, the limbic system, seemingly important to both learned and species-specific behavior, may function to integrate behavior in ways that are similar to those described previously.

The weak or secondary reinforcement hypothesis account of telencephalic function assumes that performance of species-specific events is reinforcing, as has been demonstrated for intraspecific displays. Thus, according to both mammalian and teleostian reinforcement theories, the disruption of inherently reinforcing properties of individual acts or components within the sequence of aggressive-territorial behaviors should disrupt the integrated behavior; however, the components themselves should remain intact. Indeed, this is exactly the pattern that Segaar (1961) observed in his study of the effect of ablation on the full reproductive cycle. But the reinforcement hypothesis suggests more: If some aspect of aggressive behavior serves as a reinforcer *in situ*, as seems likely, then ablated fish should show impaired learning of a simple instrumental task when that supposed reinforcer is made contingent upon the instrumental behavior.

Some recent experiments have made the familiar observations of impaired integration of behaviors in the reproductive cycle while the elemental acts remain intact. Importantly for the reinforcement hypothesis, however, tests for reinforcing efficacy of the elemental behaviors was also included. Using the paradise fish, telencephalon ablation reduced males' display and attack, nest building, and spawning, and the sequential integration of these acts was also disrupted (Schwagmeyer, Davis, & Kassel, 1977). The "operant" reinforcing properties of the display-attack component was assessed, as well (Davis, Kassel, & Schwagmeyer, 1976; Kassel, Davis, & Schwagmeyer, 1976), and found a marked reduction in the reinforcing properties of the display-attack act that were parallel to the disruptions in the reproductive cycle.

Despite this promising beginning, more recent tests of the telencephalic reinforcement hypothesis with Siamese fighting fish have not been equally supportive. Telencephalon ablation had no effect on the learning of an instrumental tunnel-swimming response reinforced by mirror presentation (Hollis & Overmier, 1982). This seems to contradict the previous experiments with paradise fish. However, those earlier experiments did not assess the effect of the reinforcement contingency per se using the more powerful yoked-control procedure. The yoked-control procedure provides better control for activity differences and the eliciting properties of seeing an opponent as contrasted with the reinforcing properties of the opportunity to display. Consistent with the observation that ablates' motor activity typically is depressed, reinforcer presentations in yoked-control groups elicited fewer responses in ablates than in normal and sham-operated control fish. Relative to this reduced level of elicited responding, those ablated fish for which the conspecific image was contingent upon responding showed significant and substantial increases in operant responding. Thus, the opportunity to respond *was* an effective reinforcer—a finding that challenges the hypothesis that the telencephalon mediates the efficacy of weak and secondary reinforcers.

Reproductive Behavior

The effects of telencephalon ablation on reproductive behavior are similar to its effects on aggressive behavior, namely a marked decline in the frequency, but not usually total elimination, of such activities as nest building, spawning, and parental behavior (see Hollis & Overmier, 1978, for a review). This pattern of ablation-produced impairment has been observed in several cichlid species (Aronson, 1948, 1949; Ribbink, 1972; Overmier & Gross, 1974), as well as sticklebacks (Noble, 1936, 1937, 1939; Noble & Borne, 1941), swordtails (Kamrin & Aronson, 1954), and paradise fish (Davis et al., 1976; Kassel et al., 1976; Schwagmeyer et al., 1977). And in reproductive behavior, as in aggressive behavior, we find a parallel between teleost telencephalon ablation and mammalian limbic lesions: Although limbic lesions impair and disorder mammalian reproductive and parental behaviors, all components seem available (Kimble, Rogers, & Hendrickson, 1967; Michal, 1965; Slotnick, 1967).

The similarity between the effects of telencephalon ablation on aggressive and reproductive behavior suggests that similar mechanisms may underlie the disruption seen in each. One hypothesis is that reproductive behavior sequences, too, are integrated or held together as behavioral chains, each component of which is weakly or secondarily reinforced, and that the telencephalon mediates such secondary reinforcers. Of particular interest would be experiments in which the opportunity to court a female was made contingent upon an instrumental response. Were the findings of such an experiment to reveal a difference between ablates and normals, the secondary reinforcement hypothesis' account of naturalistic deficits would at least seem tenable. The similar patterns of ablation-produced deficits in aggressive and reproductive behavior do suggest disruption of a common underlying mechanism; investigations that address the potentially similar role of learning in aggression and reproduction may well reveal how these mechanisms operate.

CONCLUSIONS

The study of the effects of telencephalon ablation on the behavior of fish has been able to inform the study of learning theory in general, as well as the study of how that learning might be incorporated into the species-specific behavior of animals, especially fish. We have seen that learning under Pavlovian conditioning and instrumental training procedures are not similarly affected by telencephalon ablation. From this, we conclude that these forms of learning must be different processes, because they do not rely on common underlying brain mechanism. If this conclusion is accurate, it is of fundamental importance to animal learning theory because it confirms an assertion of multiple learning processes that has been challenged (Rescorla & Solomon, 1967). Also of importance to learning

226

theory is the finding that avoidance behavior is severely impaired following ablation, despite the fact that the individual components of that behavior, namely Pavlovian conditioning and simple instrumental escape learning, are spared such disruptive effects. Thus, avoidance behavior cannot be merely the additive product of Pavlovian conditioning and simple instrumental escape behavior, as it is often claimed to be (e.g., Kimble, 1961). Taken together, these summarized findings suggest a modularity of cognitive function. Understanding this cognitive modularity is the key to understanding the problem-solving capabilities of the brain (see Rumelhart, 1988).

Researchers commonly assert that learning underlies many complex integrated behaviors of animals. We see reason to believe that, to the extent that animals' integrated behavior seems purposive and strategic to a human observer, this probably reflects the operation of underlying learning processes. Telencephalon ablation, we have seen, clearly disrupts learned behavior that depends on one of the functional properties of expectancies—likely the reinforcement property. And, ablation also disrupts directed purposive naturalistic behavior—behavior that exhibits those features that might be called strategic, or cognitive, or purposive. One conclusion is that the impairments in species-specific behavior following telencephalon ablation are essentially disruptions of selected learning mechanisms. If this conclusion is correct, then we should observe impairments in species-specific behavior whenever, say, habituation is involved but not when the behavior is primarily a Pavlovian conditional response. Also, we should observe impairments whenever the occasions for naturally reinforcing, species-specific behavior are delayed or whenever the response is a naturally occurring avoidance behavior, but not when the behavior depends on simple instrumental locomotor escape responses. In short, we should observe disruptions in naturalistic integrated behavior that parallel the disruptions that have been observed in laboratory learning experiments. We suggest that future tests of this assertion of the role of learning in integrated behavior not only will provide a better understanding of the function of the teleost telencephalon but will further the efforts of animal behavior researchers to reconcile laboratory studies of learning with ethologically important, integrated behavior.

ACKNOWLEDGMENTS

Preparation of this chapter was supported in part by grants to J. Bruce Overmier and the Center for Research in Learning, Perception, and Cognition (MH-07151) and a grant to K. L. Hollis from the Dana Foundation.

REFERENCES

Agranoff, B. W. (1970). Protein synthesis and memory formation. In A. Lajtha (Ed.), *Protein metabolism in the nervous system* (pp. 533–541). New York: Plenum.

Agranoff, B. W. (1971). Effects of antibiotics on long-term memory formation in the goldfish. In W. K. Honig & P. H. R. James (Eds.), *Animal memory* (pp. 243–258). New York: Academic Press.

Amsel, A. (1986). Developmental psychobiology and behaviour theory: Reciprocal influences. *Canadian Journal of Psychology, 40,* 311–342.

Aronson, L. R. (1948). Problems in the behavior and physiology of a species of African mouth-breeding fish (*Tilapia macrocephala*). *Transactions of the New York Academy of Sciences, 11,* 33–42.

Aronson, L. R. (1949). An analysis of reproductive behavior in the mouthbreeding cichlid fish, *Tilapia macrocephala* (Bleeker). *Zoologica, 34,* 133–158.

Aronson, L. R. (1951). Orientation and jumping behavior in the gobiid fish *Bathygobius soporator*. *American Museum Novitates, 1486,* 1–22.

Aronson, L. R., & Kaplan, H. (1968). Function of the teleostean forebrain. In D. Ingle (Ed.), *The central nervous system and fish behavior* (pp. 107–126). Chicago: University of Chicago Press.

Baerends, G. P. (1957). The ethological analysis of fish behavior. In M. E. Brown (Ed.), *The physiology of fishes* (Vol. 2, pp. 229–270). New York: Academic Press.

Bard, P. A. (1950). Central nervous mechanisms for the expression of anger in animals. In M. L. Reymert (Ed.), *Feelings and Emotions: The Moosehart Symposium* (pp. 211–237). New York: McGraw Hill.

Barraco, R. A., & Stettner, L. J. (1976). Antibiotics and memory. *Psychological Bulletin, 83,* 242–302.

Behrend, K. (1984). Cerebellar influence on the time structure of movement in the electric fish *Eigenmannia*. *Neuroscience, 13,* 171–178.

Bernstein, J. J. (1961). Loss of hue discrimination in forebrain ablated fish. *Experimental Neurology, 3,* 1–17.

Bernstein, J. J. (1962). Role of the telencephalon in color vision of fish. *Experimental Neurology, 6,* 173–185.

Bernstein, J. J. (1970). Anatomy and physiology of the central nervous system. In W. S. Hoar & D. J. Randall (Eds.), *Fish physiology, Vol. 4: The nervous system, circulation, and respiration* (pp. 2–90). New York: Academic Press.

Berwein, M. (1941). Beobachtungen und Versuche uber das gesellige Leben von Elritzen. *Zeitschrift für Vergleichende Physiologie, 28,* 402–420.

Bitterman, M. E. (1968). Comparative studies of learning in the fish. In D. Ingle (Ed.), *The central nervous system and fish behavior* (pp. 257–270). Chicago: University of Chicago Press.

Bitterman, M. E. (1975). The comparative analysis of learning. *Science, 188,* 699–709.

Bitterman, M. E. (1988). Vertebrate-invertebrate comparisons. In H. J. Jerison & I. L. Jerison (Eds.), *Intelligence and evolutionary biology* (pp. 251–276). Berlin: Springer-Verlag.

Braud, W. G., & Hoffman, R. B. (1973a). Specificity of process, response, and stimulus in behavioral bioassays. *Journal of Comparative & Physiological Psychology, 84,* 304–312.

Braud, W. G., & Hoffman, R. B. (1973b). Response facilitation and response inhibition produced by intracranial injections of brain extracts from trained donor goldfish. *Physiological Psychology, 1*(2), 169–173.

Bressler, D. E., & Bitterman, M. E. (1969). Learning in fish with transplanted brain tissue. *Science, 163,* 590–592.

Bronson, F. H. (1973). Establishment of social rank among grouped male mice: Relative effects on circulating FSH, LH and corticosterone. *Physiology and Behavior, 10,* 947–951.

Bronstein, P. M. (1986). Socially mediated learning in male *Betta splendens*. *Journal of Comparative Psychology, 100,* 279–284.

Bryant, R. C. (1972). Dark-avoidance transfer activity in brain extract from trained goldfish. *Journal of Biological Psychology, 14*(2), 3–9.

Bullock, T. H. (1984). Understanding brains by comparing taxa. *Perspectives in Biology and Medicine, 27,* 510–524.

Campbell, C. B. G., & Hodos, W. (1970). The concept of homology and the evolution of the nervous system. *Brain, Behavior, and Evolution, 3,* 353–367.

Colwill, R. M., & Rescorla, R. A. (1986). Associative structures in instrumental learning. In G. H. Bower (Ed.), *The Psychology of Learning and Motivation* (vol. 20, pp. 55–104). New York: Academic Press.

Colwill, R. M., & Rescorla, R. A. (1988). Associations between the discriminative stimulus and the reinforcer in instrumental learning. *Journal of Experimental Psychology: Animal Behavior Processes, 14,* 155–164.

Crespi, L. P. (1942). Quantitative variation of incentive and performance in the white rat. *American Journal of Psychology, 55,* 467–517.

Davis, R. E., & Kassel, J. (1983). Behavioral functions of the teleostean telencephalon. In R. E. Davis & R. G. Northcutt (Eds.), *Fish neurobiology. Vol. 2: Higher brain areas and functions* (pp. 237–263). Ann Arbor: University of Michigan Press.

Davis, R. E., Kassel, J., & Schwagmeyer, P. (1976). Telencephalic lesions and behavior in the teleost *Macropodus opercularis:* Reproduction, startle reaction, and operant behavior in the male. *Behavioral Biology, 18,* 168–178.

Davis, R. E., Reynolds, R., & Ricks, A. (1978). Suppression behavior increased by telencephalic lesions in the teleost, *Macropodus opercularis. Behavioral Biology, 18,* 165–177.

de Bruin, J. P. C. (1977). *Telencephalic functions in the behavior of the Siamese fighting fish, Betta splendens Regan.* Published doctoral dissertation, University of Amsterdam.

de Bruin, J. P. C. (1980). Telencephalon and behavior in teleost fish: A neuroethological approach. In S.O.E. Ebbesson (Ed.), *Comparative neurology of the telencephalon* (pp. 175–202). New York: Plenum.

Dickinson, A. (1980). *Contemporary animal learning theory.* Cambridge: Cambridge University Press.

Dicks, D., Myers, R. E., & Kling, A. (1969). Uncus and amygdala lesions: Effects on social behavior in the free-ranging rhesus monkey. *Science, 165,* 69–71.

Dinsmoor, J. A. (1950). A quantitative comparison of the discriminative and reinforcing properties of a stimulus. *Journal of Experimental Psychology, 40,* 458–472.

Droogleever-Fortuyn, J. (1961). Topographical relations in the telencephalon of the sunfish, *Eupomotis gibbosus. Journal of Comparative Neurology, 116,* 249–263.

Echteler, S. M., & Saidel, W. M. (1981). Forebrain connections in the goldfish support telencephalic homologies with land vertebrates. *Science, 212,* 683–685.

Englehardt, F., Woodard, W. T., & Bitterman, M. E. (1973). Discrimination reversal in the goldfish as a function of training conditions. *Journal of Comparative and Physiological Psychology, 85,* 144–150.

Farr, E. J., & Savage, G. E. (1978). First- and second-order conditioning in the goldfish and their relation to the telencephalon. *Behavioral Biology, 22,* 50–59.

Fiedler, K. (1967). Ethologische und neuroanatomische Auswirkungen von Vonderhirn exstirpationen bei Meer brassen (*Diplodus*) und Lippfischen (*Crenilabrus, Perciformes, Teleostei*). *Journal für Hirnforschung, 9,* 481–563.

Fiedler, K. (1968). Verhaltenswirksame Strukturen im Fischgehirn. *Zooligischer Anzeiger, 31,* 601–616.

Fjerdingstad, E. J. (1969). Memory transfer in goldfish. *Journal of Biological Psychology, 11,* 20–25.

Flood, N. C. B. (1975). Effect of forebrain ablation on long-term retention of a food reinforced shape discrimination. *Psychological Reports, 86,* 783–786.

Flood, N. C. B., & Overmier, J. B. (1971). Effects of telencephalic and olfactory lesions on appetitive learning in goldfish. *Physiology & Behavior, 6,* 35–40.

Flood, N. C. B., Overmier, J. B., & Savage, G. E. (1976). The teleost telencephalon in learning: An interpretive review of data and hypotheses. *Physiology & Behavior, 16,* 783–796.

Frank, A. H., Flood, N. B., & Overmier, J. B. (1972). Reversal learning in forebrain ablated and olfactory tract sectioned teleost, *Carassius auratus. Psychonomic Science, 26,* 149–151.

Frank, B., Stein, P. G., & Rosen, J. (1970). Interanimal memory transfer results from brain and liver homogenates. *Science, 169,* 399–402.

Gleitman, H., & Rozin, P. (1971). Learning and memory. In W. S. Hoar & D. J. Randall (Eds.), *Fish Physiology, Vol. VI: Environmental relations and behavior* (pp. 191–278). New York: Academic Press.

Gloor, P. (1960). Amygdala. *Handbook of Physiology, Sect. 1: Neurophysiology, 2,* 1395–1420.

Gordon, D. (1979). Effects of forebrain ablation on taste aversion in goldfish (Carassius auratus). *Experimental Neurology, 63,* 356–366.

Gray, J. A. (1985). A whole and its parts: Behaviour, the brain, cognition and emotion. *Bulletin of the British Psychological Society, 38,* 99–112.

Grice, G. R. (1948). The relation of secondary reinforcement to delayed reward in visual discrimination learning. *Journal of Experimental Psychology, 38,* 1–16.

Groves, P. M., & Thompson, R. F. (1970). Habituation: A dual-process theory. *Psychological Review, 77,* 419–450.

Hainsworth, F. R., Overmier, J. B., & Snowden, C. T. (1967). Specific and permanent deficits in instrumental avoidance responding following forebrain ablation in the goldfish. *Journal of Comparative and Physiological Psychology, 63,* 111–116.

Hale, E. B. (1956). Effects of forebrain lesions on the aggressive behavior of green sunfish. *Lepomis cyancellus. Physiological Zoology, 29,* 107–127.

Halstead, W. C. (1947). *Brain and intelligence, Vol. 13.* Chicago: University of Chicago Press.

Hannes, R. P., Frank, D., & Liemann, F. (1984). Effects of rank-order fights on whole-body and blood concentration of androgens and corticoids in the male swordtail (*Xiphophorus belleri*). *Zeitschrift für Tierpsychologie, 65,* 53–65.

Hasler, A. D. (1956). Influence of environmental reference points on learned orientation in the fish (*Phoxinus*). *Zeitschrift für Vergleichende Physiologie, 38,* 303–310.

Healey, E. G. (1957). The nervous system. In M. E. Brown (Ed.), *The physiology of fishes* (Vol. 2, pp. 1–119). New York: Academic Press.

Hemmings, C. C. (1966). Olfaction and vision in fish schooling. *Journal of Experimental Biology, 45,* 449–464.

Hogan, J. A. (1961). Motivational aspects of instinctive behavior in *Betta splendens.* Unpublished doctoral dissertation, Harvard University, Cambridge, MA.

Hogan, J. A. (1967). Fighting and reinforcement in the Siamese fighting fish (*Betta splendens*). *Journal of Comparative & Physiological Psychology, 64,* 356–359.

Hogan, J. A., & Roper, T. J. (1978). A comparison of the properties of different reinforcers. In J. S. Rosenblatt, R. A. Hinde, C. Beer, & M. C. Bresnell (Eds.), *Advances in the study of behavior* (Vol. 8, pp. 156–255). New York: Academic Press.

Hollis, K. L. (1984a). The biological function of Pavlovian conditioning: The best defense is a good offense. *Journal of Experimental Psychology: Animal Behavior Processes, 10,* 413–425.

Hollis, K. L. (1984b). Cause and function of animal learning processes. In P. Marler & H. S. Terrace (Eds.), *The biology of learning* (pp. 357–371). Berlin: Springer-Verlag.

Hollis, K. L. (in press). The role of Pavlovian conditioning in territorial aggression and reproduction. In D. A. Dewsbury (Ed.), *Contemporary issues in comparative psychology.* Sunderland, MA: Sinauer.

Hollis, K. L., Cadieux, E. L., & Colbert, M. M. (1989). The biological function of Pavlovian conditioning: A mechanism for mating success. *Journal of Comparative Psychology, 103,* 115–121.

Hollis, K. L., & Overmier, J. B. (1978). The function of the teleost telencephalon in behavior: A reinforcement mediator. In D. I. Mostofsky (Ed.), *The behavior of fishes and other aquatic animals* (pp. 137–195). New York: Academic Press.

Hollis, K. L., & Overmier, J. B. (1982). Effect of telencephalon ablation on the reinforcing and eliciting properties of species-specific events in *Betta splendens*. *Journal of Comparative & Physiological Psychology, 96*, 574–590.

Hosch, L. (1936). Untersuchungen uber Grosshirnfunktionen der Elritze (*Phoxinus laevis*) und des Grundlings (*Gobio fluviatilis*). *Zoologische Jahrbucher abteilung für Allgemeine Zoologie und Physiologie der Tiere, 57*, 57–98.

Huber, H., & Longo, H. (1970). The effect of puromycin on classical conditioning in the goldfish. *Psychonomic Science, 18*, 279–280.

Hull, C. L. (1943). *Principles of behavior.* New York: Appleton-Century-Crofts.

Huxley, J. S. (1958). Evolutionary processes and taxonomy with special reference to grades. *University of Uppsalla Arsskrift* (pp. 21–39). Uppsalla: University of Uppsalla.

Izower, J., & Aronson, L. R. (1987). Behavioral correlates of cerebellar ablations in the teleost fish, *Aquidens latifrons. International Journal of Comparative Psychology, 1*, 28–49.

Janzen, W. (1933). Untersuchungen uber Grosshirnfunktionen des Goldfisches (*Carassius auratus*). *Zoologische Jahrbucher abteilung für Allgemeine Zoologie und Physiologie der Tiere, 52*, 591–628.

Kaada, B. R. (1960). Cingulate, posterior orbital, anterior insular and temporal pole cortex. *Handbook of Physiology Section I: Neurophysiology, 2*, 1345–1372.

Kamakura, S. (1928). Versuche an Goldfischen, denen beide Hemisphären des Grosshirns exstirpiert worden waren. *The Nagoya Journal of Medical Science, 3*, 19–24.

Kamrin, R. P., & Aronson, L. R. (1954). The effects of forebrain lesions on mating behavior in the male playfish, *Xiphophorus maculatus. Zoologica, 39*, 133–140.

Kaplan, H., & Aronson, L. R. (1969). Function of the forebrain and cerebellum in learning in the teleost, *Tilapia heudelottis macrocephala. Bulletin of the American Museum of Natural History, 142*, 141–208.

Karamyan, A. I. (1956). "Evolutsiya funktsii mozzhechka i bol'shikh polusharii golovnogo mozga." [Evolution of the function of the cerebellum and cerebral hemispheres.] Leningrad: Medgiz. (Translated by National Science Foundation, Washington, D.C., 1962, OTS TT 61-31014)

Karamyan, A. I., Malukova, I. V., & Sergeev, B. F. (1967). Participation of the telencephalon of bony fish in the accomplishment of complex conditioned-reflex and general behavior reactions. In *Behavior and Reception in Fish*. Academy of Science, USSR, Moscow. (transl. by Bureau of Sport Fisheries and Wildlife, OTS no. PB 184929T).

Kassel, J., Davis, R. E., & Schwagmeyer, P. (1976). Telencephalic lesions and behavior in the teleost, *Macropodus opercularis:* Further analysis of reproductive and operant behavior in the male. *Behavioral Biology, 18*, 179–188.

Kholodov, Y. A. (1960). Simple and complex food-obtaining conditioned reflexes in normal fish and in fish after removal of the forebrain. *Proceedings of Institute of Higher nervous Activity(Academy of Sciences USSR). Physiological Series, 5*, 194–201.

Kimble, D. P., Rogers, L., & Hendrickson, C. W. (1967). Hippocampal lesions disrupt maternal, not sexual, behavior in the Albino rat. *Journal of Comparative & Physiological Psychology, 63*, 401–407.

Kimble, G. A. (1961). *Hilgard and Marquis' conditioning and learning.* New York: Appleton-Century-Crofts.

Koshtoiants, K. S., Maliukina, G. A., & Aleksandriuk, S. P. (1960). The role of the forebrain in the "group effect" in fish. *Fiziologicheskii Zhurnal SSSR imeni I. M. Sechenov, 46*, 1038–1043. (Journal translated by the National Science Foundation.)

Kovacevic, N. S. (1978). Fish avoidance conditioning with tactile reinforcement. *Bollettino di Zoologica, 45*, 41–44.

Kyle, A. L., & Peter, R. E. (1982). Effects of forebrain lesions on spawning behavior in the male goldfish. *Physiology & Behavior, 28*, 1103–1109.

Laming, P. R., & Ennis, P. (1982). Habituation of fright and arousal responses in the teleosts

Carassium auratus and *Rutilus rutilus. Journal of Comparative & Physiological Psychology, 96,* 460–466.

Laming, P. R., & McKee, M. (1981). Deficits in habituation of cardiac arousal responses incurred by telencephalic ablation in goldfish, *Carassius auratus,* and their relation to other telencephalic functions. *Journal of Comparative & Physiological Psychology, 95,* 460–467.

Livesey, P. J. (1986). *Learning and emotion: A biological synthesis, Vol. 1: Evolutionary processes.* Hillsdale, NJ: Lawrence Erlbaum Associates.

Losey, G. S. (1982). Ecological cues and experience modify interspecific aggression by the damselfish, *Stegastes faxciolatus. Behaviour, 81,* 14–37.

Lynch, G. (1986). *Synapses, Circuits, and the Beginnings of Memory.* Cambridge, MA: MIT Press.

Mackintosch, N. J. (1969). Comparative studies of reversal and probability learning: Rats, birds, and fish. In R. M. Gilbert & N. S. Sutherland (Eds.), *Animal discrimination learning* (pp. 137–162). New York: Academic Press.

MacPhail, E. M. (1982). *Brain and intelligence in vertebrates.* Oxford: Clarendon.

MacPhail, E. M. (1987). The comparative psychology of intelligence. *Behavioral and Brain Sciences, 10,* 645–656. (And commentary, pp. 657–695.)

Marino-Neto, J., & Sabbatini, R. M. (1983). Discrete telencephalic lesions accelerate the habituation rate of behavioral arousal responses in Siamese fighting fish (*Betta splendens*). *Brazilian Journal of Medicine & Biological Research, 16,* 271–278.

McCormick, D. A., & Thompson, R. F. (1984). Cerebellum: Essential involvement in the classically conditioned eyelid response. *Science, 223,* 296–299.

Meader, D. J. (1965). Notes on the functions of the forebrain in teleosts. *Zoologica, 24,* 11–14.

Meyer, D. L., Heiligenberg, W., & Bullock, T. H. (1976). The ventral substrate response, a new postural control mechanism in fishes. *Journal of Comparative Physiology, 109,* 59–68.

Michal, E. K. (1965). *The effects of lesions in the limbic system on courtship and mating behavior of male rats.* Unpublished doctoral dissertation, University of Illinois, Urbana.

Militzer, K. & Reinhard, H.-J. (1982). Rank positions in rats and their relations to tissue parameters. *Physiological Psychology, 10,* 251–260.

Miller, B. E., & Holt, G. L. (1977). Memory transfer in rats by injection of brain and liver RNA. *Journal of Biological Psychology, 19,* 4–9.

Morris, R. G. M. (1983). An attempt to dissociate "spatial mapping" and "working memory" theories of hippocampal function. In W. Seifert (Ed.), *Neurobiology of the hippocampus* (pp. 405–432). New York: Academic Press.

Morris, R. G. M. (1984). Developments of a water-maze procedure for studying spatial learning in the rat. *Journal of Neuroscience Methods, 11,* 47–60.

Mowrer, O. H. (1947). On the dual nature of learning—a re-interpretation of "conditioning" and "problem-solving." *Harvard Educational Review, 17,* 102–148.

Neale, J. H., Klinger, P. D., & Agranoff, B. W. (1973). Camptothecin blocks memory of conditioned avoidance in the goldfish. *Science, 179,* 1243–1245.

Nelson, G. J. (1969). Origin and diversification of teleostean species. *Annals of the New York Academy of Sciences, 167,* 18–30.

Nieuwenhuys, R. (1966). The interpretation of the cell masses in the teleostean forebrain. In R. Hassler & H. Stephan (Eds.), *Evolution of the forebrain* (pp. 32–39). Stuttgard: Georg Thieme Verlag.

Noble, G. K. (1936). The function of the corpus striatum in the social behavior of fishes. *Anatomical Record, Supplement, 64,* 34. (Abstract No. 76).

Noble, G. K. (1937). Effect of lesions of the corpus striatum on the brooding behavior of cichlid fishes. *Anatomical Record, Supplement, 70,* 58. (Abstract No. 53).

Noble, G. K. (1939). Neural basis of social behavior in vertebrates. *Collecting Net, 14,* 121–124.

Noble, G. K. & Borne, R. (1941). The effect of forebrain lesions on the sexual and fighting behavior of *Betta splendens* and other fishes. *Anatomical Record, Supplement, 79,* 49. (Abstract No. 138).

Nolte, W. (1932). Experimentelle untersuchungen zum Problem der Lokalisation des Assoziation-suermogens in Fischgehirn. *Zeitschrift für Vergleichende Physiologie, 18,* 255–279.

Northcutt, R. G., & Bradford, M. R. (1980). New observations on the organization and evolution of the telencephalon of actinopterygian fishes. In S. O. E. Ebbesson (Ed.), *Comparative neurology of the telencephalon* (pp. 41–98). New York: Plenum.

Northcutt, R. G., & Davis, R. E. (1983). Telencephalic organization in ray-finned fishes. In R. E. Davis & R. G. Northcutt (Eds.), *Fish neurobiology, Vol. 2: Higher brain areas and functions* (pp. 203–236). Ann Arbor: University of Michigan Press.

O'Keefe, J., & Nadel, L. (1978). *The Hippocampus as a cognitive map.* Oxford: Clarendon.

Olson, G. M. (1976). An information-processing analysis of visual memory and habituation in infants. In T. J. Tighe & R. N. Leaton (Eds.), *Habituation* (pp. 239–278). Hillsdale, NJ: Lawrence Erlbaum Associates.

Olton, D. S. (1979). Mazes, maps, and memory. *American Psychologist, 34,* 583–596.

Olton, D. S., Becker, J. T., & Handelmann, G. E. (1979). Hippocampus, space, and memory. *Behavioral and Brain Sciences, 2,* 313–322.

Overmier, J. B. (1989). Sparing, loss, and recovery of function in the telencephalon ablated teleost fish. In J. Schulkin (Ed.), *Preoperative events: Their effects on behavior following brain damage* (pp. 191–211). Hillsdale, NJ: Lawrence Erlbaum Associates.

Overmier, J. B., & Curnow, P. (1969). Classical conditioning, pseudoconditioning, and sensitization in "normal" and forebrainless goldfish. *Journal of Comparative & Physiological Psychology, 68,* 193–198.

Overmier, J. B., & Flood, N. B. (1969). Passive avoidance in the forebrain ablated teleost fish (*Carassius auratus*). *Physiology & Behavior, 4,* 791–794.

Overmier, J. B., & Gross, D. (1974). Effects of telencephalic ablation upon nest-building and avoidance behaviors in East African mouthbreeding fish, *Tilapia mossambica. Behavioral Biology, 12,* 211–222.

Overmier, J. B., & Hollis, K. L. (1983). The teleostean telencephalon in learning. In R. E. Davis & R. G. Northcutt (Eds.). *Fish neurobiology, Vol. II: Higher brain areas and functions* (pp. 265–284). Ann Arbor: University of Michigan Press.

Overmier, J. B., & Lawry, J. A. (1979). Pavlovian conditioning and the mediation of behavior. In G. Bower (Ed.), *The psychology of learning and motivation* (Vol. 13, pp. 1–55). New York: Academic Press.

Overmier, J. B., & Papini, M. R. (1986). Factors modulating the effects of teleost telencephalon ablation on retention, relearning, and extinction of instrumental avoidance behavior. *Behavioral Neuroscience, 100,* 190–199.

Overmier, J. B., & Patten, R. L. (1982). Teleost telencephalon and memory for delayed reinforcers. *Physiological Psychology, 10,* 74–78.

Overmier, J. B., & Savage, G. E. (1974). Effects of telencephalic ablation on trace classical conditioning of heart rate in goldfish. *Experimental Neurology, 42,* 339–346.

Overmier, J. B., & Starkman, N. (1974). Transfer of control of avoidance behavior in normal and telencephalon ablated goldfish (*Carassius auratus*). *Physiology & Behavior, 12,* 605–608.

Peeke, H. V. S., & Peeke, S. C. (1973). Habituation in fish with special reference to intraspecific aggressive behavior. In H. V. S. Peeke & M. J. Herz (Eds.), *Habituation: behavioral studies* (Vol. 1, pp. 59–83). New York: Academic Press.

Peeke, H. V. S., & Peeke, S. C. (1982). Parental factors in the sensitization and habituation of territorial aggression in the convict cichlid (*Cichlasoma nigrofasciatum*). *Journal of Comparative & Physiological Psychology, 96,* 955–966.

Peeke, H. V. S., Peeke, S. C., & Williston, J. S. (1972). Long term memory deficits for habituation of the predatory behavior in the forebrain ablated goldfish, *Carassius auratus. Experimental Neurology, 36,* 288–294.

Peter, R. E., & Gill, V. E. (1975). A stereotaxic atlas and technique for forebrain nuclei of the goldfish, *Carassius auratus. Journal of Comparative Neurology, 159,* 69–102.

Polimanti, O. (1913). Contributions a la physiologie due systeme nerveux central et du mouvement des poissons. *Archives Italiennes de Biologie, 59,* 383–401.

Potts, R., & Bitterman, M. E. (1967). Puromycin and retention in goldfish. *Science, 158,* 1594–1596.

Prosser, C. L., & Brown, F. A. (1961). *Comparative animal physiology.* Philadelphia: Saunders.

Rescorla, R. A., & Solomon, R. L. (1967). Two-process learning theory: Relationships between Pavlovian conditioning and instrumental learning. *Psychological Review, 74,* 151–182.

Ribbink, A. J. (1972). The behavior and brain function of the cichlid fish, *Hemihaplochromis philander. Zoologica Africanis, 7,* 21–41.

Riss, W., Halpern, M., & Scalia, F. (1969). Anatomical aspects of the evolution of the limbic and olfactory systems and their potential significance for behavior. *Annals of the New York Academy of Science, 159,* 1096–1111.

Roitblat, H. L., Tham, W., & Golub, L. (1982). Performance of *Betta splendens* in a radial arm maze. *Animal Learning & Behavior, 10,* 108–114.

Rolls, E. T. (1987). Information representation, processing, and storage in the brain: Analysis at the single neuron level. In J.-P. Changeux & M. Konishi (Eds.), *The neural and molecular bases of learning* (pp. 503–540). New York: John Wiley & Sons.

Rooney, D. J., & Laming, P. R. (1984). Effects of olfactory bulb ablation on cardiac and ventilatory arousal responses and their habituation in the goldfish. *Behavioral & Neural Biology, 42,* 120–126.

Rooney, D. S., & Laming, P. R. (1986). Localization of telencephalic regions concerned with habituation of cardiac and ventilatory responses associated with arousal in the goldfish. *Behavioral Neuroscience, 100,* 45–50.

Rosvold, H. E., Mirsky, A. F., & Pribram, K. H. (1954). Influence of amygdalectomy on social behavior in monkeys. *Journal of Comparative Physiological Psychology, 47,* 173–178.

Rumelhart, D. (1988). The relevance of neuroscience to network models of cognition. *Bulletin of the Psychonomic Society, 26,* 511.

Savage, G. E. (1968). Temporal factors in avoidance learning in normal and forebrainless goldfish (*Carassium auratus*). *Nature* (London), *218,* 1168–1169.

Savage, G. E. (1969a). Telencephalic lesions and avoidance behavior in the goldfish, *Carassium auratus. Animal Behavior, 17,* 362–373.

Savage, G. E. (1969b). Some preliminary observations on the role of the telencephalon in food reinforced behavior in the goldfish, *Carassius auratus. Animal Behavior, 17,* 760–772.

Savage, G. E. (1980). The fish telencephalon and its relation to learning. In S. O. E. Ebbesson (Ed.), *Comparative neurology of the telencephalon* (pp. 129–174). New York: Plenum.

Scalia, F., & Ebbesson, S. O. E. (1971). The central projections of the olfactory bulb in a teleost (*Gymnothorax funebris*). *Brain, Behavior, and Evolution, 4,* 376–399.

Scharrer, E. (1928). Die Lichtempfindlichkeit blinder Elritzen. *Zeitschrift für Vergleichende Physiologie, 1,* 1–21.

Schnitzlein, H. N. (1964). Correlation of habit and structure in the fish brain. *American Zoologist, 4,* 21–32.

Schnitzlein, H. N. (1968). Introductory remarks on the telencephalon of fish. In D. Ingle (Ed.), *The central nervous system and fish behavior* (pp. 97–100). Chicago: University of Chicago Press.

Schonherr, J. (1955). Uber die Abhangigkeit der Instinkthandlungen vom Vorderhirn und Zwischenhirn (Epiphyse) bei *Gasterosteus aculeatus* L. *Zoologische Jahrbucher (Physiologie), 65,* 357–386.

Schroeder, D. M. (1980). The telencephalon of teleosts. In S. O. E. Ebbesson (Ed.), *Comparative neurology of the telencephalon* (pp. 99–115). New York: Plenum.

Schwagmeyer, P., Davis, R. E., & Kassel, J. (1977). Telencephalic lesions and behavior in the teleost *Macropodus opercularus:* The effects of telencephalon and olfactory bulb ablation on sparing and foam nest building. *Behavioral Biology, 20,* 463–470.

Scoville, W. B., & Milner, B. (1957). Loss of recent memory after bilateral hippocampal lesions. *Journal of Neurology, Neurosurgery & Psychiatry, 20*, 11–21.

Segaar, J. (1961). Telencephalon and behavior in *Gasterosteus aculeatus. Behaviour, 18*, 256–287.

Segaar, J. (1965). Behavioural aspects of degeneration and regeneration in fish brain: A comparison with higher vertebrates. *Progress in Brain Research, 14*, 143–231.

Segaar, J., & Nieuwenhuys, R. (1963). New etho-physiological experiments with male *Gasterosteus aculeatus,* with anatomical comment. *Animal Behavior, 11*, 331–344.

Sevenster, P. (1968). Motivation and learning in sticklebacks. In E. Ingle (Ed.), *The central nervous system and fish behavior* (pp. 233–245). Chicago, IL: University of Chicago Press.

Sevenster, P. (1973). Incompatibility of response and reward. In R. A. Hinde & J. Stevenson-Hinde (Eds.), *Constraints on learning: Limitations and predispositions* (pp. 265–283). London: Academic Press.

Shapiro, S., Schuckman, H., Sussman, D., & Tucker, A. M. (1974). Effects of telencephalic lesions on the gill cover response in Siamese fighting fish. *Physiology & Behavior, 13*, 749–755.

Shashoua, V. (1968). RNA changes in goldfish during learning. *Nature, 217*, 238–240.

Shashoua, V. (1976). Brain metabolism and the acquisition of new behaviors: 1. Evidence for specific changes in the pattern of protein synthesis. *Brain Research, 111*, 347–364.

Shashoua, V. E. (1985). The role of extracellular proteins in learning and memory. *American Scientist, 73*, 364–370.

Sikharulidze, N. I. (1969) K izucheniiu roli perednego mozga v povedenii ryb. *Bulletin of the Academy of Sciences of the Georgian SSR, 53*, 193–196.

Slotnick, B. M. (1967). Disturbances of maternal behavior in the rat following lesions of the cingulate cortex. *Behaviour, 29*, 204–236.

Spencer, H. (1896). *Principles of psychology.* New York: Appleton & Co.

Springer, A. D., Schacht, J., & Agranoff, B. W. (1976). The effect of memory blocking antibiotics and their analogs on acetylcholinesterase. *Pharmacology, Biochemistry and Behavior, 5*, 1–3.

Stacy, N. E., & Kyle, A. L. (1983). Effects of olfactory tract lesions on sexual and feeding behavior in the goldfish. *Physiology & Behavior, 30*, 621–628.

Steiner, J. (1888). *Die Funktionen des Zentral-Nervensystems und ihre Phylogenese, Vol. 2: Die Fische.* Braunschweig: Vieveg & Sohn.

Stillwell, E. F., Porter, R. J., & Byrne, W. L. (1971). Membrane specificity and memory transfer: The fate of 3H-leucine-labelled homogenates inject intraperitoneally into rats. In G. Adam (Ed.), *Biology of memory* (pp. 163–170). Budapest: Akademiai Kiado.

Strieck, F. (1925). Untersuchungen uber den Geruchs und Geschmackssin der Elritze (*Phoxinus laevis A.*). *Zeitschrift für Vergleichende Physiologie, 2*, 122–154.

Tano, S., Mizuno, S., & Shirahata, S. (1970). Organ specificity of RNA and identity of DNA in the salmon brain. *Biochimica et Biophysica Acta, 213*, 45–54.

Thompson, R. F., & Spencer, W. A. (1966). Habituation: A model phenomena for the study of neuronal substrates of behavior. *Psychological Review, 73*, 16–43.

Thompson, T. (1963). Visual reinforcement in Siamese fighting fish. *Science, 141*, 55–57.

Thompson, T. (1966). Operant and classically conditioned aggressive behavior in Siamese fighting fish. *American Zoology, 6*, 629–641.

Thompson, T., & Sturm, T. (1965a). Visual-reinforcer color, and operant behavior in Siamese fighting fish. *Journal of the Experimental Analysis of Behavior, 8*, 341–344.

Thompson, T., & Sturm, T. (1965b). Classical conditioning of aggressive display in Siamese fighting fish. *Journal of the Experimental Analysis of Behavior, 8*, 397–403.

Thorndike, E. L. (1911). *Animal intelligence: Experimental studies.* New York: Macmillan.

Tighe, T. J., & Leaton, R. N. (1976). *Habituation.* Hillsdale, NJ: Lawrence Erlbaum Associates.

Tolman, E. C. (1932). *Purposive behavior in animals and men.* New York: Appleton-Century-Crofts.

Trapold, M. A., & Overmier, J. B. (1972). The second learning process in instrumental learning. In

A. H. Black & W. F. Prokasy (Eds.), *Classical conditioning II: Current theory and research* (pp. 427–452). New York: Appleton-Century-Crofts.

Tuge, H. (1934). Studies on cerebellar functions in the teleost fish. I. Reactions resulting from cerebellar ablation. *Journal of Comparative Neurology, 60,* 201–224.

Ungar, G., Galvan, L., & Chapouthier, G. (1972). Evidence for chemical coding of color discrimination in goldfish brain. *Experientia, 28,* 1026–1027.

Uphouse, L. L., MacInnes, J. W., & Schlesinger, K. (1974). Role of RNA and protein in memory storage: A review. *Behavior Genetics, 4,* 29–81.

Vulpian, A. (1986). Sur la persistance des mouvements volontaires chez les poissons osseux a la suite de l'ablation des lobes cerebraus. *Comptes Rendus Academie Science, 102,* 1526–1530.

van de Poll, N. E., Smeets, J., van Oyen, H. G., & van der Zwan, S. M. (1982). Behavioral consequences of agonistic experience in rats: Sex differences and the effects of testosterone. *Journal of Comparative and Physiological Psychology, 96,* 893–903.

Vanderwolf, C. H. (1971). Limbic-diencephalic mechanisms of voluntary movement. *Psychological Review, 78,* 83–113.

Vanegas, H., & Ebbesson, S. O. E. (1976). Telencephalic projections in two teleost species. *Journal of Comparative Neurology, 165,* 181–196.

Wagner, A. R. (1976). Priming in STM: An information processing mechanism for self-generated or retrieval-generated depression in performance. In T. J. Tighe & R. N. Leaton (Eds.), *Habituation* (pp. 95–128). Hillsdale, NJ: Lawrence Erlbaum Associates.

Warren, J. M. (1961). The effects of telencephalic injuries on learning by Paradise fish, *Macropodus opercularis. Journal of Comparative and Physiological Psychology, 54,* 130–132.

Weiskrantz, L. (1968). Treatments, inferences, and brain function. In L. Weiskrantz (Ed.), *Analysis of behavior change* (pp. 400–414). New York: Harper & Row.

9 Learning, Memory, and "Cognition" in Honey Bees

Randolf Menzel
Universität Berlin

THE MIND OF THE COMMUNITY AND THE MIND OF THE INDIVIDUAL

Are bees reflex machines? This poignant question was prompted by Buttel-Reepen in the title of his book on honey bee behavior at the turn of this century, in which he concluded that bees are neither stupid reflex automata nor super intelligent beasts guided by insight into the complex relationships of the world. Instead, bees are animals that are able to learn and behave according to the memory of earlier experience. In his words (Buttel-Reepen 1900):

> On the basis of my observations I believe that bees either lack a mind or possess it at a low level of complexity. The question of whether an animal enjoys a conscious mind is left up to subjective opinion, but the question of whether an animal learns and stores experience in a memory can be decided objectively. We have seen that bees possess a perfect memory both during their orientation and other activities. Furthermore, I believe to have given evidence that bees recognize colors and patterns and are able to communicate through a rich "sound language." I also showed that they collect experience, and learn from associations between sensory impressions. (p. 75)

These sentences were written decades before the great discoveries of Karl von Frisch and his students on the sensory capacities and social behavior of honey bees. Although our knowledge of many aspects of behavior in bees has dramatically increased since those early days, one is still forced to express a sense of wonder when one considers the capabilities of a brain that has a volume of less than one cubic millimeter and that consists of only 950,000 neurons. For example, the ability of individual bees to learn and their control of orientation in space and time are impressive, but even more astonishing are the communication between tens of thousands of animals in one colony, social learning, and the effectiveness of such cooperative behavior. The "secret" behind this success is a combination of the concerted action of two sources of information that govern the behavior of all animals, the species' memory and the individual memory. The species' phylogenetic memory is carried in the genome and expressed in the body structure and neuronal wiring, and the memory resulting from individual experience modulates and selects existing neural connections, thus producing new connections and new behaviors.

The honey bee is a particularly suitable animal for the study of the interaction between innate and acquired sources of information (Lindauer, 1959, 1963, 1970). As with other insects, the stereotyped behavioral patterns, with their relatively inflexible stimulus–response connections, occupy a considerable proportion of the total behavioral repertoire. This applies not only to simple behaviors such as taxes, reflexes, and fast servo-control mechanisms, but also to more complex routines like escape, attack, feeding, and behaviors concerned with social communication and orientation.

Unlike most insect species, the honey bee is a social insect that lives in a highly organized and intensively cooperating community. The "superorganism" of the community adapts to the changing environment, regulates its members according to social requirements, stores information, and acts as a complete unit (Lumsden, 1982; Seeley 1985a, 1985b; Seeley & Levin, 1987; von Frisch, 1967; Wilson, 1985). Indeed, this superorganism gives the impression that it is capable of cognitive functions without possessing a unifying nervous system (Markl, 1985, 1987). The "knowledge" of the colony superorganism is a kind of "artificial intelligence" with strong cognitive components, where the whole represents more than the summed knowledge of the total members because cooperative interactions produce properties that do not exist in any single member.

Consider, for example, the process of colony reproduction and swarming. When the size of a colony becomes too large, a new queen is raised, and the old queen leaves the hive with a portion of the experienced foragers (Lindauer, 1955). This swarm first settles at a convenient resting place (e.g., a branch), and from here bees scout for a new hive site. These bees must erase the habit of flying back to the old hive but continue to use their knowledge of landmarks and celestial cues for effective orientation. Furthermore, they must activate a completely new search image when searching for a potential hive site, such as a tree hole. The suitability of such a site is evaluated by close inspection (Seeley 1977), and the information is encoded and communicated by each respective scout bee in the vigour of its waggle dance. As a consequence, many scouts may dance on the surface of the swarm at the same time and each may point to different nest sites. Lindauer (1955) observed individual bees who danced for one particular site, observed comrades dancing for another site, which they then inspected, and if the new site was more favorable, gave up the old site and recruited for the new one. The questions of whether bees can "change their mind" without "personal" inspection, whether some bees act as opinion-makers and others as passive followers, and which general factors regulate the flow of information are just some questions that are worthy of further studies.

It is, therefore, important to remember that the social nature of honey bees and the continuous life of the "superorganism" have formed an extremely important framework in which learning and memory have been shaped during the evolution of the species (Lindauer 1955, 1963). Because we concentrate later on more obvious stimulus–response relationships of the individual bee in an attempt to search for underlying mechanisms, it should be realized now that learning in the social context is an indication of the high degree of plasticity and adaptiveness at the individual *and* collective levels.

Bees are not tightly programmed robots. In the words of Karl von Frisch (1967): "Life in the bee colony is governed by strict rules but not in a rigid fashion. Individual differences in skills and performances characterize the complex." The studies I refer to in this chapter have ignored individual differences and interpreted interindividual deviations as statistical fluctuations. Although such assumptions are convenient, they nevertheless remain approximations, particularly in the context of the social life of honey bees.

The first part of this chapter summarizes behavioral tests that demonstrate the sophistication of natural learning abilities. The central question is whether an animal with such a small brain is, by necessity, bound to stereotyped behavior and tightly programmed learning. We see that this is by far not the case. The second part of the paper concentrates on a particular learning set: the olfactory conditioning of movement of the mouth parts. This preparation allows us to address questions related to the localization of memory consolidation and specific actions of aminergic drugs in particular parts of the bee brain. A model of sequential memory processing is presented, which helps to bridge the behavioral and cellular level of the analysis of memory mechanisms.

OPERANT LEARNING IN A NATURAL CONTEXT

Concise experimentation with honey bees started with a famous controversy between the young Karl von Frisch and the influential physiologist von Hess, in which von Hess denied that bees can see colors, whereas von Frisch had compelling evidence in favor of color vision (von Frisch, 1914; von Hess, 1913, 1918). In retrospect, we know that both competitors were correct and at the same time incorrect, although von Hess undoubtedly was more wrong than von Frisch! The solution to the puzzle lies in the fact that bees discriminate and learn colors as signals for food reward and indicators for the hive entrance, but behave as if they were color blind and do not learn any visual stimuli in the context of escape behavior (Menzel & Greggers, 1985; see Menzel & Backhaus, 1989a, 1989b for further discussion). Von Hess tested the bees in the latter context and generalized his findings to all behaviors, whereas von Frisch trained bees at the feeding station or at the hive entrance (von Frisch, 1919), and he generalized this, although much more carefully, to apply to all other behaviors. The answer to the question of color vision in bees was a crucial one, because the "unrevealed mystery of nature in the construction and fertilization of flowers" (the title of a book published by K. C. Sprengel in 1793) was that the flower signals—their morphology and the production of sweet nectar—are directed towards the insect pollinators to improve cross-fertilization (Darwin, 1877).

The perception and learning of floral signals, and particularly their coloration and smell, was taken for granted by many entomologists of the last century (Buttel-Reepen, 1900; Fabre, 1879; Forel, 1910; Lubbock, 1883; Müller, 1882), but proof came with von Frisch's elegant experiments. Furthermore, in the context of the controversy with von Hess, von Frisch's experiments gave the first hint of the context-specific limitations of the perceptual and learning processes involved. Later, von Frisch (1922) described this relationship as follows: "The bees' high intelligence and their excellent learning ability appears to be lost in the moment they are asked to perform tasks which are not part of their usual behavior" (p. 157).

In the honey bee, adaptive predispositions to learning may form a particularly tight framework, especially when one considers the limited neuronal capacity of the brain. It is often assumed, though with little experimental verification, that nervous systems that are comprised of relatively few neurons are more effective with a higher portion of stereotyped connections and less adaptability. In other words, sensory cues may be preordained, motor programs flexible and adjustable only within certain behavioral contexts, reinforcing conditions may be preprogrammed so that associations can be formed quickly and selectively, and internal memory processes necessary for the fine tuning of memory may run under the tight control of automatic storage routines. These points are discussed in turn in the following sections.

Learning and Preordained Sensory Cues

Visual Signals.   An extreme case of preparedness for learning is the situation where signals are perceived but not learned. For example, the polarized light pattern, perceived by the bee as a guide post for far-distance orientation in flight, is quickly learned as a celestial cue to guide the foraging bee on its flights between the hive and a patch of rewarding flowers. Polarized light, however, is not learned as a substrate signal for food. Also, flashing light stimuli or slowly rotating vertical sectors or moving grids presented to a bee approaching a feeding place are hardly or not at all learned (Erber, 1982; Fischer, 1973; Vogt, 1969). Furthermore, moving black-and-white stripes are learned differently, depending on whether they are arranged vertically or horizontally on a vertical screen. The intensity of a colored stimulus (its subjective brightness) is a parameter that is probably not learned in appetitive training experiments (Backhaus, Werner, & Menzel, 1987b; Daumer, 1956; Hertz, 1939; Hörmann, 1934; Menzel, 1967), and the small discrimination values found in these studies are most likely due to residual differences in hue and/or saturation. Quantitative perceptual models of the color vision system in bees are consistent with the assumption that honey bees have a two-dimensional color vision system that lacks the perceptual dimension of brightness (Backhaus & Menzel, 1987; Backhaus, Menzel & Kreißl, 1987a). Because bees are extremely sensitive to brightness differences of signals in other behavioral contexts (phototaxis, optokinetic response, scanning behavior, depth perception, land mark orientation), they perceive these signals at the feeding place but do not learn them as food signals.

Exclusion of stimuli or stimulus parameters from learning is a rare and extreme case of preparedness. Because the honey bee is able to learn many different sorts of visual stimuli, studies that test for "preordained" visual cues require stringent quantitative control. In the past few years, six different procedures have been applied with varying degrees of success: spontaneous choice, rate of acquisition, duration of memory, generalization, reversal, and multireversal learning (see Menzel, 1985). The results of these attempts to uncover prepared visual stimuli and stimulus–response associations are consistent with the interpretation that genetic predispositions build a relatively loose framework for the perception and association of stimuli in certain behavioral contexts. The visual stimuli at the feeding place are a particularly interesting problem, because it prompts the question of whether bees are innately prepared for flower-type patterns when they search for food. Bees learn all colors they can see, but violet is learned fastest and bluish-green slowest (blue, yellow, bee-purple, and ultraviolet rank in between) (Menzel, 1967). Sensory properties of the visual system are not responsible for this difference; rather, a kind of central nervous evaluation on the basis of a phylogenetically acquired rank order prepares the animals for certain associations more than for others. Pattern recognition in bees is known to be different from human pattern recognition, insofar as geometric patterns in the human sense are of little importance for perception (see Wehner, 1981, for an exhaustive review). Instead, the discrimination of patterns depends on the density of contrast lines and their orientation and distribution between the upper and lower parts of the visual field. All kinds of geometrical patterns are associated with food, irrespective of whether or not they resemble floral pattern. The question of preordained patterns has, unfortunately, not yet been properly addressed experimentally, and Gould's experiments (1985, 1986b) are interesting in this context. He generalized that "bees recognize flower-like objects instinctively: they land spontaneously on small, brightly colored objects that have a high spatial frequency . . ." (Gould & Marler, 1987, p. 76). I must admit that in 20 years of work with bees, I have not seen a single bee behaving like this, and in fact Gould's own results do not support this conclusion (see also Wehner, 1971). In Gould's experiments, where bees learned many patterns irrespective of their floral-like shape, it was not possible to determine any preference when discriminability was used as a parameter. This indicates a major problem with most studies on pattern recognition, in that discriminability is not an adequate parameter to measure associability, preparedness, or salience.

Olfactory Stimuli.   Von Frisch (1921) already observed, in his first olfactory training experiments, that certain odorants are harder to train than others. Such an odorant is "patchouli oil," for which the sensory threshold does not seem very different when compared to other odorants. However, in von Frisch's experiment, the bees gave the distinct impression of not "liking" the odor (von Frisch, 1922). Many experiments have shown (Koltermann 1969, 1971; Kriston 1971, 1973; von Frisch 1967) that odors that are pleasant for humans also seem to be "pleasant" for bees. Furthermore, bees learn "pleasant" odors faster. This is particularly interesting in the context of coevolution between insects and flowers, in that it has been demonstrated that insects learn odors from insect-pollinated flowers better than odors from bird-pollinated flowers (von Aufsess, 1960). However, the story is more complicated than it first appears. Lysol, for example, is used by bee keepers to prevent bees from approaching a location, and yet bees eagerly choose a feeding place marked with lysol when they are rewarded there. The same is true for propanol, which acts as a repellent (antennae are withdrawn) but which nevertheless is easy to condition (Menzel & Sugawa, 1986). Iso-amylacetate, the pheromone that initiates sting-releasing attack behavior in bees, is also easily conditioned when paired with sucrose solution, and the same is true for CO_2 (which bees avoid at higher concentration), and water vapor (Hertz, 1934; Kuwabara & Takeda, 1956). Thus, all perceived olfactory stimuli can be associated with a food reward, despite some graduation in the acquisition rate.

Other procedures have been used to test predispositions or saliency of odorants, such as generalization tests and reversal learning (Koltermann 1969, 1973a, 1973b). As one might expect, the different tests give different rank orders for the same set of odorants.

Mechanosensory Stimuli.   Bees are extremely sensitive to substrate vibration, and this tends to be an important technique for extensive social communication (see Markl, 1973, 1974; von Frisch, 1967). Such vibration is brought about by shaking the body and is sensed by the mechanoreceptors in the tarsi of other bees.

Airborne sound is produced during the waggling phase of the recruitment dance and is detected with the antennae (Esch, 1961; Michelsen, Towne, Kirchner, & Kryger, 1987). It is already well established that bees following the dance routine obtain information relating to the distance, direction, and quality of a food source (von Frisch, 1967). Whereas stereotyped behaviors (e.g., feeding and begging) are released by substrate vibration through mechanoreceptors whose axons project from the legs to the ganglia of the ventral chord, mechanosensory input for sophisticated learning processes in the ritualized dance behavior is provided by the antennae, whose mechanoreceptors send their axons to the deutocerebral part of the brain, which is tightly connected with the higher centers of the bee's brain (see *The Amnestic Syndrome,* beginning on p. 269). Whether or not the feeding of bees after the waggle dance routine is an essential component of learning behavior during dance communication is still unknown. Thus, it is still unclear if recruited bees learn the features of an indicated food source via an associative process or as a consequence of pure observation. If the food exchanges between the dancing and following bees are not essential, then one should investigate whether body vibration acts as an unconditioned stimulus.

Surface texture is also sensed with the mechanoreceptors on the antennae. Kalmus (1937) succeeded in training bees to discriminate a cardboard surface from tin, and similar experiments were undertaken by Martin (1965), who used holes and grooves in plastic sheets, and Mühlen (1987), who tested sand papers with different grain sizes. Kevan and Lane (1985) have successfully trained bees to discriminate the orientation of a microtexture on the florets of the sun flower, *Helianthus annus,* and also observed that bees were able to successfully differentiate between *Helianthus* and *Xylorhiza* on the basis of texture differences. In a situation where both odor and surface structure stimuli are simultaneously presented, the first stimulus always overrides the second one (Martin, 1965). Furthermore, training to a coarse surface structure alone (holes or differently oriented grooves of 1 mm depth and 1 mm width) is very slow, whereas training to the odor is very fast. It still remains unclear whether fine structures, such as those investigated by Kevan and Lane (1985), are more salient signals than coarse structures. If the surface structure can be sensed with both the antennae and tarsae, then learning is faster, and discrimination is better (Mühlen, 1987).

Orientation of the body with respect to gravity is sensed with a large number of external hair cells and internal proprioreceptors (Markl, 1974), and bees are able to learn a certain angle relative to gravity when no other cues are available (Markl, 1966a, 1966b).

Learning of Motor Skills

To what extent do motor programs adapt as a result of learning? In attempting to answer such a question, one should first remember the number of extremely sophisticated and impressive maneuvres performed by a variety of appendages on this somewhat mechanical-looking body. Let us first consider comb building, a process that involves thousands of bees working in virtual darkness to a great degree of precision: The floor of each cell in the comb is tilted by 13° to the vertical, the cells are exactly 5.2 mm wide in diameter (drone cells 6.2 mm), and the thickness of the walls is 0.073 ± 0.002 mm (drone cells 0.094 mm). Such exactness is the consequence of a stereotyped behavior that is unlikely to be influenced by individual learning (Martin & Lindauer 1966; von Frisch and von Frisch, 1974). Nevertheless, in a general sense, learning is involved, because each bee emerges from a comb that is then used as a reference with respect to the dimensions and arrangements of the cells (von Oelsen & Rademacher, 1979) and also the earth's magnetic field (De Jong, 1982; Lindauer & Martin, 1972). De Jong's paper is particularly interesting because he reported that swarms lose the memory of comb orientation relative to the magnetic field if they are kept 9 days or longer in a bait hive that does not permit comb building.

Dance behavior also involves many components of stereotyped patterns, although a few essential components are modulated by learning, and increasing experience improves the precision with which distance and direction are indicated (von Frisch, 1967). Also, the chances of recruited bees finding a new food source increases with the number of waggle dances they observe (Mautz, 1971).

Foraging generally requires a large range of motor skills that are adaptable by learning, and this is of vital importance to the efficiency of the colony. For example, when one considers that an individual bee generally averages a total flight distance of 2,000 km during its lifetime, then it is clear that unnecessary detours and ineffective foraging are costly errors in terms of energy expenditure. Von Frisch and his students described a range of experiments that demonstrate how flight distance and energy consumption is minimized by path integration and several other strategies (Heran, 1963; Lindauer, 1963; von Frisch, 1967).

Flowers are often complicated structures that require special handling skills for nectar extraction. The evolution of such structures was determined by several factors: protection of the nectar from rain, sun, wind, and from other insects less effective in species-specific cross-fertilization. Therefore, flowers have selected pollinators in two directions: "stupid" specialists that are equipped with the proper mechanical parts and neuronal programs to handle a complicated structure, and "intelligent" generalists that use the all-purpose machinery of their body extremeties and learn quickly how to reach the nectar. For example, Laverty and Plowright (1988) have compared two bumble bee generalists (*Bombus fervidus* and *B. pensylvanicus*) and one specialist (*B. consobrinus*) in their effectivenss to manipulate the morphologically complex flowers of *Aconitum* (monkshood). The specialist species is not only much faster, but the rate of success is close to 100% for the first trial, as opposed to 50% for the generalists. Learning improves the handling skills in the generalist species until there is no difference between the specialist and the generalists. More examples of motor learning in hymenopteran pollinators are described in Heinrich (1976, 1979a, 1979b), Laverty (1980), and Waser (1983). When specialists and generalists are compared, the costs of learning become apparent. Because the net gain of a specialist on the rich nectar source of jewelweed is 110 calories/min at the beginning, the generalist has to forage for a longer period to compensate for its initial deficit. However, the generalists are better equipped to deal with changes of the environment, and this is their advantage over the specialists.

An indication of the relationship between prepared motor routines and learned motor skills in handling flowers comes from Daumer's (1958) observation that bees apply certain stereotyped movements when landing on a new flower. He observed that bees, who for many generations had no experience with natural flowers, extended their proboscides when they walked on a surface that changed from shorter wavelength reflection to longer wavelength reflection. Furthermore, bees learned radial color patterns better if the UV-absorbing part was in the middle rather than in the periphery. It is tempting to speculate that there exists a prepared motor program that is adapted to the general feature of most flowers, namely that the position of the nectaries is always marked with a UV-absorbing pigmentation and is somewhere close to the center of the flower where the petals converge. This view is supported by the observation of Laverty and Plowright (1988) where the two generalist bumble bees, when initially confronted with the monkshood, mistakenly probed in the center of the flower. It has been argued (Gould, 1986a; Gould & Marler, 1984) that flower handling procedures involve innate subroutines that are linked together by experience. Although this may be an important aspect of the nature–nurture relationship in motor skills, insufficient experimental evidence exists for definite conclusions. The large range of different procedures used by individuals from the same colony to "handle" an artificial food source is also not in line with this view. Again, it appears that the capacity to learn by individual trial and error is the most important factor for general pollinators such as the honey bee.

Temporal Organization of Learned Behavior

Ontogenetic Development of Learning.   Honey bees spend the first 2 weeks of their adult life within the colony, where they are responsible for feeding the larvae, cleaning the hive, building new combs, processing the stored nectar to honey, receiving the foragers and distributing the nectar, and guarding the entrance of the hive. The first learned signals are of a chemosensory and topographical nature, because the positions of the food store and different larvae (worker, drone, queen) at various stages of development change continously. Are bees, therefore, capable of olfactory learning immediately after emergence? It appears not, because we found that olfactory conditioning is retarded within the first day after emergence and reaches its final level only during the second and third day. The maturation of learning of the attraction pheromone component geraniol is faster than that of the chemical propionic acid, a chemical to which bees show signs of spontaneous aversion before conditioning. Discrimination between odors further improves after the second day. Most of the reduced learning shortly after emergence is probably due to developmental processing in the antennal lobe, because it has been shown that the electrical activity in the chemosensory pathway and the structural maturation within the antennal glomeruli does not reach an adult stage before the second to fourth day (Masson & Arnold, 1987).

Visual learning starts when bees perform their "play flights" with which they familiarize themselves with the visual appearance of the hive, its relative location to landmarks, and the landmarks relative to the celestial cues. At the same time, bees also learn the movement of the sun and trigger their internal clock to the sun's azimuth (see von Frisch, 1967, for details). The visual cues close to the hive entrance and the landmarks surrounding it are learned at a moment shortly before further excursions, when the bee turns towards the hive after take-off. Solitary bees and wasps follow the same strategy (Baerends, 1941; Tinbergen, 1932; van Iersel & van dem Assem, 1965). The learning involved cannot be considered to be "irreversible imprinting," because bees can learn new cues that guide to the hive entrance and actually do this under natural conditions when the experienced bees and the old queen leave the hive and swarm. However, reversal learning at the hive entrance is much slower than at the feeding place if one compares similar visual cues and considers each visit at the feeding place and each return to the hive as a learning trial.

Time-Linked Learning.   Forel (1910) knew that bees must have an accurate sense of time, because they arrived every morning punctually at his breakfast table. Indeed, bees are accurate to within a few minutes during a period of 24 hours. In a biological sense, they require a high temporal accuracy for celestial orientation and a time sense for specific flowers where nectar flow is limited to short periods during the day. The internal clock is normally triggered by external signals, such as the sun (Beier, 1968; Beier & Lindauer, 1970; Beling, 1929; Frisch, 1987; Frisch & Aschoff, 1987; Kleber, 1935; Moore & Rankin, 1983; Wahl, 1932), but a circadian rhythm of food supply can also be a time-setting stimulus under otherwise constant conditions. Experiments have shown that the circadian periodicity deviates from the 24-hr circle by only about 1 hour.

Bees learn to associate a specific time with an odor if they are fed with this odor at this particular time, and are given no further odor stimuli with continuous feeding during the rest of the day (Koltermann, 1971). Furthermore, if the odorant appears for 15 min. in regular intervals of 45 min., the bees learn to choose the odorant more frequently every 45 min.

Bees easily learn to select, for example, a yellow target at a feeding place in the *south,* and a blue target in the east. If the two places provide food only at a certain time, say in the *south* from 10:00–11:00, in the east from 13:00–14:00, then the bees choose the right color at the right time. Bees arriving at the feeding place at the wrong time choose the color that is correct for the place but not for the time. Similarly, Gould (1988b) trained bees to land on a particular part of a vertically arranged target during 9:30–11:00 and on another part of the same target between 11:00–12:30. Again, the bees preferred the correct part of the target at the corresponding times after a long period of differential training. These experiments do not imply, however, that the conditioned stimuli are learned in a time-linked fashion per sec., because time-linked behavior occurs only after differential conditioning over an extended period of time. Memory without differential conditioning is not organized in a circadian way (see the following).

Bogdany (1978) used compounds of color, shape, and odor for time-linked differential training and likewise found a preference for the particular compound at the correct time. If the compounds were rearranged in such a way that other color/odor combinations were rewarded, the bees behaved as if the odor was the prominent cue and overshadowed the memory of the other cues. The consequence of this effect is that the new composition has to be learned anew.

Memory for the time and direction of a feeding place is very stable. Lindauer (1963, p. 373) reported an experiment in which bees performed dances 6 weeks after they were brought into a flight room. Despite this time interval, the bees still correctly indicated the direction of the last feeding place in the open field.

In summary, it is clear that the time of the day can also be trained appetitively, whereby two constraints are important: circadian periodicity and temporal resolution. If compounds of food signals are trained differentially over extended periods of time, then time can be linked to a certain composition of the stimuli. Memory is content-addressable, and time of the day does not rank very high in the hierarchy of cues. In fact, there is no evidence of any further function of time, such as an automatic circadian rhythm of memory formation or memory retrieval.

Sequential Learning, Reversal Learning, and Overlearning.   Long-distance orientation, as observed in the honey bee, requires the learning of sequences of cues and the correct retrieval of context-dependent memories. There is already a wealth of literature that describes the capacity of the honey bee to establish and retrieve such memories (see von Frisch 1967). In an elegant study, Collett and Kelber (1988) have recently shown that landmarks trigger the memory specific for that particular feeding place.

Learning of sequences was also observed with running bees and wasps in simple mazes, where the animals learned to associate a right or left turn with color, odor, or surface structure (Kalmus, 1937; Mühlen, 1984, 1987; Weiss, 1953, 1954, 1957). Up to seven turns towards the feeding place have been mastered by the bee, although the task becomes more difficult for increasing distances from the feeding place. If the bees have to continue to run in the same direction after feeding, they must learn the cues anew. Learning of a simple maze with three successive turns indicated by three different types of cues (e.g., a visual pattern, an odor, a surface structure) again demonstrated that odorants are particularly salient cues, followed by colors and patterns, and finally surface structures that are particularly difficult to associate with a turn (Mühlen, 1987).

Under natural conditions, a general pollinator must be able to adapt to changes in the provision of nectar and pollen. Because 95% of foraging bees tend to visit only one kind of flower, it is especially important that bees are able to switch to other types of flower if the availability of the usual food source decreases. For this reason, reversal learning is frequently observed in honey bees. Bumble bees, in contrast, tend to be more "individualistic" in food collecting and lack the efficient social communication structure of the honey bee, and thus are less flower constant and less prepared to switch to a new flower. Instead, they adapt by slightly altering the proportion of their visits to different kinds of flowers. Bumble bees are even resistant to such adaptations if they are rewarded for a long time with only one kind of flower (Heinrich, 1976, 1984) or are "imprinted" with one flower species—a condition that has never been observed in honey bees.

Honey bees readily reverse learned preferences in dual choice experiments, and systematic studies of reversal learning for color stimuli have revealed a few general features similar to those observed in vertebrate studies. For example, in a first phase of learning, reversal learning is retarded with an increasing number of initial learning trials, and strongest resistance to reversal learning is reached after 5 or 10 trials. Continued training to the initial color increases the readiness to reverse to the new color, a situation that is termed the *overlearning-reversal effect* (Menzel, 1969). Multiple reversal schedules with fixed performance schedules reveal a learning strategy that, after many reversals, leads to a decrease in the number of reversed learning trials. This would seem to indicate an acquired strategy to learn reversal learning (Meineke, 1978).

Schedules of Sequential Reinforcement.   Even under the best ecological conditions, only a fraction of the flowers on which a bee alightens provide nectar and/or pollen. Experimental procedures that test the ability of an animal and its strategy to evaluate its performance relative to the reward schedules are Skinner's (1938) continuous, fixed-ratio, and fixed-interval reinforcement schedules (CRF, FR, and FI, respectively). Experiments (Grossmann, 1973) have shown that bees develop a higher resistance to extinction in a FR (1 out of 5 trials reinforced) than a CRF schedule, where resistance was orderly graded with a ratio of reinforcement of up to 2. Bees on a FI schedule of reinforcement gave lower response rates than those that were given FR reinforcement. FR schedules of up to 1 reinforcement out of 30 trials and FI schedules of up to 90 sec. between reinforcements were reached after several days of training. Bitterman (1988) added the numbers FR-80 (one of 3 μl sucrose reinforcement out of 80 responses in a FR schedule), and FI-40 sec. (every 40 sec. reinforcement in a FI schedule).

Reinforcement

Floral Rewards and Matching of Choice.   It was common sense to the pollination biologists of the last century that flowers with more nectar and/or pollen are visited more frequently than those with less (Buttel-Reepen, 1900; Forel, 1910; Kugler, 1943; Müller, 1873, 1882). Later, Pankiew (1967) observed the frequency of visits on alfalfa flowers and found a linear relationship between mg nectar per floret and the degree of visitation. Bees fly faster between nectar sources (artificial or natural) if these sources provide more or higher quality nectar per visit, and they increase the sample size before returning to the hive (Nunez, 1966, 1979, 1982; Seeley, 1985b). The flight path between florets is modulated accordingly, in that higher quality rewards result in more turns in successive flights and lower rewards in more straight flights (Heinrich, 1979a; Schmid-Hempel, 1984; Waddington, 1980). As a consequence, bees are able to concentrate foraging in nectar-rich areas (Inouye, 1978; Pleasants, 1981). Likewise, patches with higher reward variance are avoided by flying in a generally straighter direction and for longer distances after experiencing larger variance ("risk avoidance behavior"; Waddington, Allen, & Heinrich, 1981). The learning and memory aspects of such behavior have, unfortunately, not yet been studied.

From a learning point of view, one might argue that the strength of an association is a function of the number of rewards and the amount of reward per learning trial (Couvillon & Bitterman, 1985). However, this is an over-simplistic interpretation. For example, the acquisition function for the first 10 learning trials on colored targets is independent of the amount of reward (Menzel & Erber, 1972), and rewards lasting for only 1 sec. (which corresponds to approx. 1 µl sucrose solution) are equally as effective as 60-sec. long rewards. However, resistance to extinction, as opposed to rate of acquisition, may be a better parameter with which to measure associative strength. Menzel (1968) already demonstrated that extinction after one single short reward (2 or 5 sec.) is much stronger than after one long reward (15 sec. or longer). Also, the motivation to search for the food source increases with the amount of reward per learning trial—even within the first learning trials (Menzel & Erber, 1972).

Other Primary Positive Reinforcers.   Other materials that act as positive reinforcers are pollen for pollen foragers, water for water collectors (when the colony is in danger of overheating), and resin for resin collectors (when the hive has to be insulated). Certain behaviors may also play a role as positive reinforcers: successful homing for foragers (during the whole lifetime, but particularly when leaving the hive for the first time), appropriate parameters of a potential new nest site (for scouts of a swarm), following dances (possibly the sound pulse of the dancing bee). Unfortunately, none of these reinforcing signals have been carefully studied with respect to learning and memory perspectives. For example, although it is known that the odor of a food source sticks to the hairs on the body of a dancing bee, and that this odor is then learned by recruited bees during dance observation (Koltermann, 1969), it is still unknown whether this learning process actually requires the reinforcement by food transfer.

Aversive Reinforcers, Conditioned Inhibition and Differential Conditioning.
The anthers of alfalfa flowers are strongly pushed against the bodies of potential pollinators, with the consequence that small insects like the honey bee are

knocked down. Honey bees learn to avoid this flower or alternatively collect nectar from the side. Another interesting example is the soldier's lungwort (*Borraginacea pulmonaria*), where fertilized florets change from red to blue, and where these blue flowers fall off if a bee still happens to land on them (Kugler, 1943, p. 224). Gould (1988b) has trained bees to avoid landing on certain parts of a star-like pattern by flicking them off when they land on these parts. When they land on the correct parts of the pattern, they are trained to walk towards the center where they receive a sucrose reward. No acquisition functions are reported, but it appears that they learn this task quite readily.

Pure water is a strong aversive stimulus when the bee expects a sucrose solution. In some experiments, it has been suggested that quinine has aversive properties, but the negative reinforcing reported here is probably due to water. Several substances are known to be poisonous to bees, but these are not avoided and do not seem to act as aversive reinforcers (e.g. monosaccharids, $FeSO_4$, Ca-arsenate; Kunze, 1933). LiCl used in aversive training experiments with vertebrates does not seem to act as a negative reinforcer when added to a weak sucrose solution (Menzel, personal observation), and taste aversion conditioning as in vertebrates has yet to be performed with bees.

Electrical shock as a reinforcer is rarely used in honey bee studies. Nunez and Denti (1970) and Balderama, Diaz, Sequeda, Nunez, and Maldonado (1987) delivered an electric current to the proboscis of bees in order to inhibit sucking of a sucrose solution and succeeded in training bees for particular durations of drinking periods. The bees consequently learned to avoid the shock by retracting the proboscis shortly before its onset. Walker and Bitterman (1985) used a differential training technique (sucrose solution and electric shock with 5 VAC) to demonstrate that bees perceive the magnetic field and associate it with a feeding place, and Michelsen et al. (1987) reported an experiment where one of the co-authors trained bees to airborne sound by electric shock.

The combination of positive and negative reinforcing stimuli leads in general to better discrimination and increasing associative strength. This is particularly true for stimuli that are learned relatively slowly.

As mentioned earlier, several species of flowers are known to change their color after they have been fertilized. These old flowers do not usually produce any more nectar and may also change their orientation so that the interior of the flower is not so well protected against rain or dew. Bees learn quickly to avoid these older florets (e.g., Kugler's 1943 observations on chest-nut flowers, *Aesculus hippocastanum*; for more examples, see Vogel, 1950, p. 86). Indeed, flowers probably only retain their old florets in order to improve their detection by insects, especially with respect to far distance recognition. This is a particularly favorable situation, because the old florets no longer compete for insect visitation with other florets on the same plant, and self-fertilization is already excluded. Thus, the aversive conditioning combined with the changed color (or/and odor, pattern) facilitates the concentration of the bees on the remaining unfertilized flowers.

Selective Associations of Natural Sequences. A foraging flight follows a natural sequence of exposures to stimuli that guide the bee to a food source and that have to be learned anew every time a fresh patch of flowers is chosen. At which time do bees learn the relevant signals during the approach flight, the feeding on the flower, the orientation flight after take off, and the return flight? In response to these questions, Opfinger (1931) performed a series of classic experiments that were later confirmed and extended by Menzel (1968) and by Grossmann (1970, 1971) (Fig. 9.1). The visual signals in the immediate surround of the food site ("close signals") have to be perceived a few seconds before the onset of feeding, and a period of 3 seconds (in the case of uncued delay) or even up to 7–8 sec. (cued delay) may elapse between the last exposure to the visual stimulus and the onset of reward. Effective cues for delay are the contextual stimuli that characterize the feeding place. There is no learning during the entire period of feeding (50–80 sec. uninterrupted sucking). The close signals are not learned during the take-off and circling orientation flights, which the bee performs for about 10 sec. before flying straight back to the hive. Landmarks (i.e., larger objects that are a few meters away from the food source) are principally learned during the orientation flight, weakly learned during the whole approach flight, but not learned at all during feeding. The association of the close signals follows a forward (trace) conditioning procedure, whereas the learning of landmarks during orientation flights incorporates either (a) backward conditioning (if food reward is the reinforcer), (b) long delay reinforcement (if successful homing is the reinforcer), or (c) latent learning.

Memory

Associative and latent learning leads to a stable and lasting memory that is retained throughout the lifetime of the adult bee. Lindauer (1963) observed that the properties of a feeding place (e.g., its distance and direction from the hive, landmarks, or close signals such as color and odor) are remembered over periods of up to several months. A stable memory for a color signal lasting for at least 2 weeks is already established after 3 learning trials (Menzel, 1968).

Programmed Sequential Memory Retrieval. Foraging under natural conditions is structured into four distinct sequential phases: approach flight (hive to flower patch), foraging at several to many flowers, return flight, and time in the hive. Successive foraging bouts are separated by intervals of a few minutes; for example, an average of 4.3 minutes was observed during a large number of foraging bouts at an artificial feeding place 100 m from the hive. Landings on flowers during foraging depends on flower density and the availability of nectar or pollen. For example, an average interval of 5.5 sec. was recorded for four different kinds of flowers blooming during springtime in a dense population (Menzel, 1987). Memory with respect to flower features is, therefore, necessary at two distinct temporal periods, first in the range of seconds during one foraging

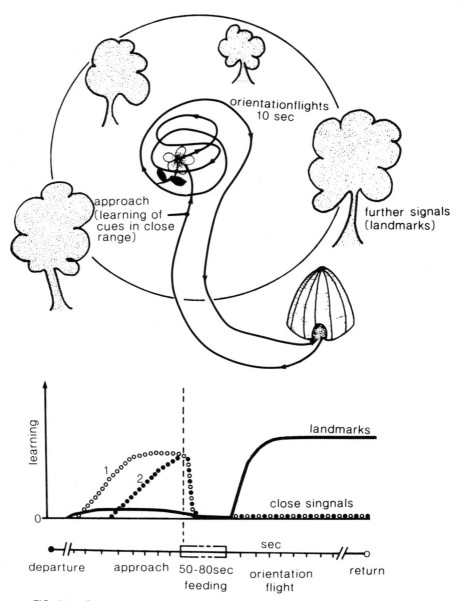

FIG. 9.1.   Sequence of learning under natural conditions. A bee flies
out from the hive to a flower and learns the landmarks on its way.
Close to the flower, it associates the close signals that are perceived
within 3 sec. (uncued delay) or up to 7–8 sec. (cued delay) before onset
of feeding. No signals are learned during feeding. Further signals are
learned during the orientation flight after feeding (summary of results
by Grossmann, 1970, 1971; Menzel, 1968; Opfinger, 1931).

bout (i.e., flights between flowers) and second in the range of several minutes between successive foraging bouts. Choice behavior after a single learning trial is very accurate immediately after the learning trial, decreases dramatically after 2–3 minutes but then rises again to form a high and stable plateau, which slowly drops to a lower level over the following 4–6 days. This characteristic time course is independent of the amount of sucrose imbibed and the duration of the reward, and this suggests that a single learning trial may be considered as being one unit of association—at least with respect to the control of choice behavior. Reversal learning and sensitivity to extinction are, however, dependent on the *amount* of reward (Menzel, 1968, 1979; see also above). Furthermore, although the new memory immediately after the learning trial principally controls the ensuing choice behavior, it is nevertheless still labile, because it is effectively erased by a new and different learning experience (Menzel, 1979, 1987). It appears from these results that memory resulting from an appetitive experience runs through a set of programmed stages that resemble the time course of the natural sequence of behaviors at a foraging bout.

Mental Operations?

Before concluding this section on the natural learning behavior of bees, let me shortly discuss the question: How complex is the "mind" of the honey bee? Are there indications of mental operations that, in the absence of behavioral acts, may be interpreted as internal operations of learned representations? Rather than approach such questions from an abstruse philosophical point of view, let us reflect upon existing experimental evidence that suggests mental operations. Social interactions have already reached a high level of sophistication in honey bees; consider, for example, the social consensus reached in swarm bees. However, even this complex pattern of behaviors is not indicative of anything more than stimulus–response relationships, symbolic ritualized movements, fast latent learning, and a perfect memory, although such a high level of complexity surely includes important features of "general intelligence." Let us consider here two other cases—the assumption of a "cognitive map" and of "arithmetic" operations.

Experienced foragers recognize the landmarks surrounding the hive very well and return easily and quickly to the hive when they are transported to a release site within the experienced foraging area (about 2 km radius) (Forel, 1910; von Frisch, 1967). Gould (1986a) described an experiment where bees were trained to an artificial feeding station set up at a certain distance from the hive. On leaving the hive, the bees were then caught and released from a third site, which was within this foraging area. Gould claimed that the bees flew directly to the artificial feeder when released, and that this indicates that bees are capable of "mental triangulation." However, this result is contradictory to the experiments of Karl von Frisch and his coworkers, who observed that bees always follow the same compass direction when the sun (or blue sky) is visible, or fly along

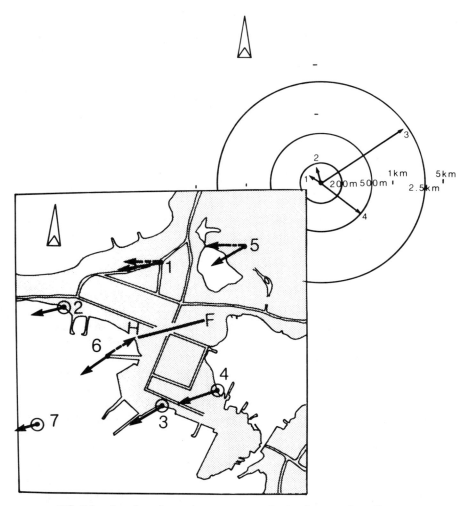

FIG. 9.2.   A series of experiments to test whether bees perform "mental" operations within a map-like representation of the landscape. The experiments were carried out in the town of Woods Hole (MA, USA). The bees of the test colony (hive: H) were familiar with the closer surround in the north and northeast, and with two areas further away: 2,5 km away in the northeast and 500 m away in the southeast (see upper arrows 1, 2, 3, and 4, which indicate the average direction and distance of places to which 127 dances were directed at the same time when the experiments were performed). Bees were trained to collect sucrose solution at the feeding station F, 190 m northeast from the hive H. Seven release sites (1–7) were selected—Nos: 1 and 5 were in areas that were familiar to the bees as judged from the dance behavior, whereas all the other sites (2, 3, 4, 6, 7) were in unfamiliar areas. Site 6 is very close to the hive but still unfamiliar. The flight direction

obvious landmarks if they appear similar to those already learned. To check Gould's hypothesis, we performed a series of similar experiments, but we did not find any signs of this "internal triangulation" or "mental operation within a cognitive map" (Menzel, 1989; see also Wehner & Menzel, in press). In these experiments, which are summarized in Fig. 9.2, bees were caught at an artificial feeder (F) just as they were preparing to fly back to the hive (H) and were transported to several different release sites that were either unfamiliar (Nos. 2, 3, 4, 6, 7) or in an area known to the bees from earlier foraging flights (Nos. 1, 5). If the sun was visible, the displaced bees departed along the compass direction that they would have taken, had they flown from the feeder to the hive (irrespective of whether the area was known or unfamiliar; black arrows in Fig. 9.2). If the sun was obscured (dotted arrows in Fig. 9.2), bees that knew the area chose the same direction by using landmarks to reconstruct the compass direction (release sites 1 and 5) (see also von Frisch, 1967, for many other examples). Bees released in an unknown area when the sun was obscured were either completely disoriented (indicated by a circle around the release site in Fig. 9.2, Nos. 2, 3, 4), or—if the hive was directly visible from the release site (as at release site No. 6)—flew straight towards the hive. On the basis of these observations and others (see Wehner & Menzel, in press), it seems that Gould's assumptions are unjustified.

The "arithmetic" assumption refers to the apparent ability of bees to "foresee" the next location of a feeding place if the feeder is moved in a stepwise fashion from the hive, whereby each step is a multiple factor of the last step. If bees were able to foresee the next location, they would have to be able to calculate the constant factor from the earlier positions and multiply the current distance with that factor. Gould and Gould (1982) commented: "If anything, this seems a more impressive intellectual feat than potato washing (in monkeys)" (p. 281). Bicker and Hertel (in personal communication) carried out several experiments to test this possibility but were not able to confirm Gould's conclusion or

---

taken by the bees when released at any of the seven sites were determined by the direction at which the experimenter lost sight of the individually released bee (vanishing direction). Each bee was released only once and not included in any further experiment. The average directions of vanishing points at the various sites are indicated with arrows. A solid arrow indicates releases on sunny days, a dotted arrow on overcast days. Circles around the release site mark random directions of vanishing points for experiments on overcast days. More details about this experiment are reported in Menzel (1989) and Wehner & Menzel (in press). The number of bees released at any site ranged from 20 to 60. The average directions indicated by the arrows are highly significant (Batschelet circular statistics).

(I am grateful to three students of the course "Neural systems and behavior", Linda Rinaman, Richard Born, Frederic Libersat, and my children, Julia, Rebecca, and Simon, who were all actively engaged in this experiment).

verify von Frisch's impression. Bees certainly do increase their circling flight paths when the distance increases, but they always continue to search more at the old feeding place than at the next place to which the feeder should move. Therefore, and perhaps unsurprisingly, bees do not apply arithmetic in controlling their behavior. Similarly, they do not learn that a feeder moves with the sun in a circle around the hive, but they constantly adjust their foraging trips to the new position of the feeder (Lindauer, 1963).

The sophisticated skills involved in the ritualized dance behavior and the orientation during long-distance flights appear as motor expressions of memory chains, which are hooked up and activated by simple rules. There is no well-documented observation that forces us to assume any flexible handling of memory chains or internal operations of representations as suggested by Griffin (1984). However, we are forced to conclude that the volume and complexity of the memory chains are impressive—by large. Such memories, obviously, do not result from restricted or instinctive learning processes, as claimed by Gould (1984; see also Gould & Marler, 1984). Rather, the honey bee's learning is characterized by large freedom and only guided loosely by preordained cues and prepared associations. It thus appears that its small brain does not limit the amount of memory storage or the richness of the learning strategies, but it excludes the innovative handling of the memories.

So, where in the brain are these memories stored, and what are the neural mechanisms? Obviously, such questions cannot be approached with behavioral experiments using bees under natural conditions. It is necessary to simplify the questions, develop experimental paradigms that still include the essence of associative learning and allow the application of physiological methods. The second part of this chapter describes a suitable preparation and addresses questions related to the physiological mechanisms of learning and memory in bees.

REFLEX CONDITIONING AND THE SEARCH FOR NEURAL MECHANISMS

Time of Input

When the tip of the front legs or the antennae are touched with a drop of sucrose solution, the bee extends its proboscis. Minnich (1932) and von Frisch (1934) used this proboscis extension reflex (PER) to localize and study the sensitivity of sucrose receptors at the antennae and tarsae. Both researchers were quite surprised to find that after a period of time the bees also responded to pure water, which led von Frisch to become suspicious about the extremely high sensitivity to sucrose molecules (von Frisch, 1967). In fact, Minnich and von Frisch's student, Kautner, had inadvertently conditioned the bees to water vapor, as was shown later by Kuwabara (1957). Kuwabara also succeeded in establishing a conditioned reflex to a light stimulus by pairing it with a sucrose stimulus presented to the tarsae; the antennae were cut off in this experiment to avoid any interference with the strong conditioning to water vapor. Frings (1944) had already realized that the proboscis extension reflex can easily be conditioned to odorants (he used cumarin), and Takeda (1961) determined the associative nature of this olfactory conditioning using several odorants (citral, hydroxycitronellal, and aromatic aldehyde). These early studies differed from all later experiments in that the tarsae of the frontlegs were stimulated with the sucrose solution to release the PER, whereas in all other studies the antennae were stimulated with sucrose (Vareschi, 1971; Masuhr & Menzel, 1972; Menzel, Erber, & Masuhr, 1974; Bitterman et al., 1983). The reason for this is that the PER is more reliable with antennal stimulation. Although olfactory PER-conditioning is the most frequently used technique, conditioning of mechanical stimuli to the antennae is equally effective

---

FIG. 9.3. (See pages 258–259) Basic phenomena of olfactory PER-conditioning. a: Trace conditioning: A 2-sec. odor puff as the CS is presented at nine different times (grey bars at the abscissa) before (+) or after (−) the onset (at 0) of the US (dotted column, 2 sec. of feeding with sucrose solution). The conditioned response (CR) is tested for each of the nine different groups of bees 20 min. after the single presentation of CS and US. The ordinate gives the proportion of the bees responding to the CS only. The CR is successfully established if the CS precedes the US by up to 5 sec. Because the CS lasts only for 2 sec., a CS trace lasting over 3 sec. can be associated with the US. Backward conditioning is uneffective. b: Acquisition function for CS–US pairing (o). The CS (carnation) preceded the US by 2 sec. Two control groups were tested (unpaired presentation of CS and US, and US presentation alone). In the latter group, the animals were tested whether they responded to contextual stimuli. This is not the case (see Bitterman et al., 1983, for more details). c: Motivational factors. Dependence of the sucrose (US) reflex, the conditioned reflex after 1 or 3 olfactory conditioning trials (1 and 3 l.t.), and spontaneous response to an odor stimulus (sp) on hunger-induced motivation. The ordinate gives the proportion of the animals in the respective groups that respond with the PER to stimulation of the antenna with sucrose solution (reflex), to the CS (one learning trial: 1 l.t., three learning trials: 3 l.t.), or the presentation of the odor without prior pairing with the US (spontaneous response: sp). Each of the four groups consists of 40 animals. Satiated animals do not show the reflex, nor do they learn. The reflex develops about equally fast as the conditioned reflex. Spontaneous responding to an odor stimulus develops particularly slowly. d: Correlation between the spontaneous response level (sp, ordinate) and the conditioned response (CR, abscissa) after one conditioning trial. The regression line 1 is for geraniol (sp spontaneous response to geraniol, CR to geraniol after one conditioning trial; $n = 23$, corr. coeff. $r = 0,73$). The dotted line 2 for propionacid ($n = 14$, $r = 0,77$). The high correlation between spontaneous response level and rate of conditioning for both odorants is indicative for "α-conditioning" (Hull, 1943).

a

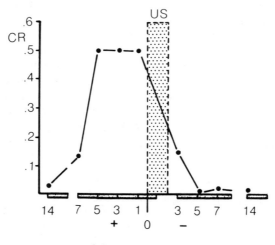

CS/US interval (sec)

b

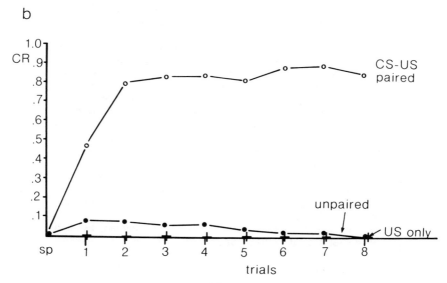

FIG. 9.3.

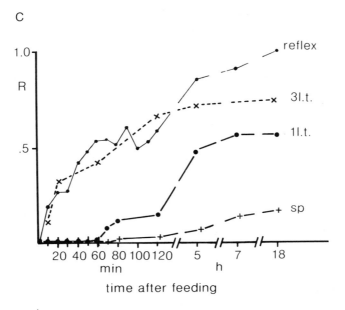

time after feeding

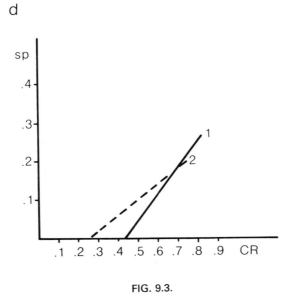

FIG. 9.3.

(Salisbury, in personal communication). PER-conditioning of visual stimuli is very slow and is only effective in about 30% of bees (Kuwabara, 1957; Masuhr & Menzel, 1972).

The associative nature of PER-conditioning is well established (Bitterman, Menzel, Fietz, & Schäfer, 1983), and the temporal window for optimal trace conditioning is precisely defined (3–0 sec. before the onset of the unconditioned stimulus (US). The change in behavior is so strong that even a single learning trial can significantly change the behavior (50–80% of the bees show the conditioned response [CR] after one learning trial depending on the conditions described below). Some basic phenomena of PER-conditioning are summarized in Fig. 9.3. Fig. 9.3a documents the narrow temporal window of trace conditioning. Conditioned acquisition occurs only in those animals that were stimulated with the CS before onset of the US (Fig. 9.3b, CS–US pairing), specifically unpaired presentations of CS and US or presentations of CS alone (not shown in Fig. 9.3b) or US alone do not change the behavior.

Non-Associative Components

Hungry animals are more readily conditioned appetively than satiated animals, and Fig. 9.3c shows how the reflex, and the spontaneous (not conditioned) and conditioned response to odorants, increases with greater hunger. The repeated release of the PER without feeding has a pronounced effect on the recovery rate of the reflex, indicating habituation or inhibitory learning by repeated stimulation with sucrose (not shown in the figure). Furthermore, acquisition of a CR rises with increasing hunger-induced motivation (1 l.t. and 3 l.t. in Fig. 9.3c). The rate of spontaneous (unconditioned) extension of the proboscis to an odor stimulus is low even in very hungry animals. This rate depends also on hunger (Fig. 9.3c, curve for the spontaneous response). Similarly, one finds a correlation between the level of spontaneous responses to the odorant used afterwards in conditioning and the CR after one conditioning trial (Fig. 9.3d). In the particular experiments of Fig. 9.3d, all bees were fed to satiation the day before conditioning. The reasons for the different levels of spontaneous responses are unknown, but differences in the status of satiation cannot be excluded. Because the two odorants used in the tests, geraniol and propionic acid, differ considerably with respect to their ecological significance, an effect through prelearning is not likely. Thus, the motivational effect on improved conditioning is unlikely to depend on earlier experience with the CR. Hull (1943) has coined the term "α-conditioning" to describe conditioning where the CS releases the response at a low level already previous to conditioning. Olfactory PER-conditioning appears to belong to this category, whereas mechanical PER-conditioning (CS: touching the antennae) or visual PER-conditioning may be considered as β-conditioning, because the proboscis is never extended to the CS before conditioning.

The reflex to repeated stimulation with sucrose habituates if the animal is not fed. However, if the animal is stimulated only once with sucrose solution on the antennae (or on the antennae plus the proboscis), the response probability to other stimuli (e.g., odorants, mechanical stimuli, water vapor) is sensitized. The sensitization effect after a single presentation of sucrose solution is even stronger if only the antennae are stimulated. This is in marked contrast with the action of sucrose solution as an US: stimulation of the antennae alone is a weak US (Bitterman et al., 1983). The time-course of the sucrose induced sensitization is discussed hereafter.

Information in Olfactory PER-Conditioning

The predictive value of the conditioned stimulus (CS) should depend on the reliability with which it is causally related to the US. Several paradigmatic experiments from vertebrate studies (Rescorla, 1988), have been successfully transferred to PER-conditioning in bees. For example, repeated exposure to an odorant in unpaired trials reduces its acquisition in subsequent conditioning (Bitterman et al., 1983). The results shown in Fig. 9.4 present new experiments that quantify the effect in two different ways. In differential conditioning, the reversal to the initially unpaired stimulus is more strongly retarded for more initial exposures than for less preexposures. The same applies for US-only preexposures. Similar results were found in aversive conditioning of freely flying bees (Abramson & Bitterman, 1986). Unconditioned presentations of the CS during its acquisition (partial reinforcement schedules) do not, however, have an effect on the initial acquisition or the resistance to extinction (Salisbury, in personal communication). This is a familiar observation in both vertebrate and invertebrate studies, and it highlights the differences between operant and classical conditioning.

Blocking and overshadowing experiments are widely used to characterize the informational content of conditioned stimuli (Kamin, 1968; Rescorla & Wagner, 1972; Rescorla, 1988). When we conditioned compounds of olfactory and mechanical stimuli, the odorant overshadowed the mechanical stimulus, but blocking effects did not occur (Fig. 9.5). These results are in general agreement with those collected from operant conditioning experiments (Couvillon, Klosterhalfen, & Bitterman, 1983). In other words, blocking has no or little effect in PER-conditioning. This would suggest that attentiveness is not a limiting factor in PER-conditioning, and that salience or the "associability" of a stimulus (olfactory over mechanical) are more important factors.

Second-order conditioning is a technique that tests whether a CS can acquire the potential of an US. Bitterman et al. (1983) reported the positive outcome of a second-order conditioning experiment. Stronger effects were found in new experiments in which the more salient stimulus citral was used as the acquired US. (Fig. 9.6 describes an experiment in which octanal (Fig. 9.6a) or citral (Fig.

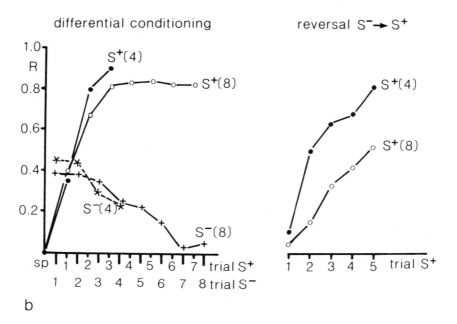

differential conditioning   reversal S⁻ → S⁺

retardation of acquisition : effect of unpaired trials

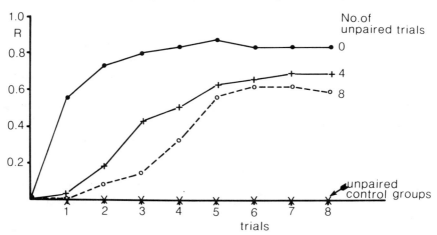

FIG. 9.4.   a: The effect of differential conditioning on the acquisition of a stimulus after reversal. An odor stimulus (S⁺) was appetitively reinforced four times (S⁺4), or eight times (S⁺8), and a different stimulus (S⁻) was equally often presented without US. Initially, the response to S⁻ is high, due to generalization effects, and differential conditioning depresses the response to S⁻. After reversal of S⁻ to S⁺, the acquisition is retarded when compared to the initial acquisition, and more strongly for more S⁻ presentations. b: Retardation of ac-

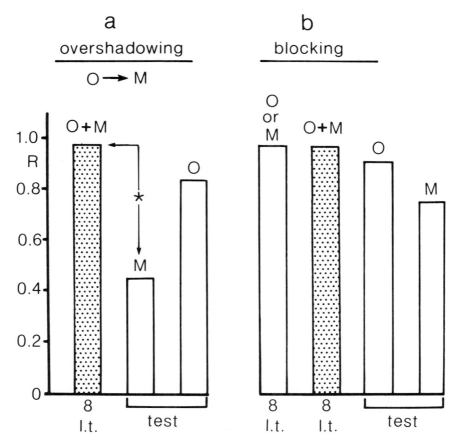

FIG. 9.5.   a: Overshadowing experiment with the PER-conditioning paradigm. A group of bees is conditioned to a compound of olfactory and mechanical stimuli (O = carnation, M = touching of the antenna with filter paper). The grey column gives the proportion of CR (ordinate R) to the compound after eight conditioning trials (8 l.t.) Afterwards, the CR is separately tested for each stimulus component. CR to M is significantly reduced (* $p \leq 0.01$, χ^2-test), but not CR to O. The odor stimulus overshadows the mechanical stimulus. b: In a blocking experiment, a group of bees is either conditioned to O or M, and then to the compound O + M. Afterwards, the initial O-group is tested for its CR to M-stimulation, and the initial M-group to its CR to O-stimulation. No significant blocking is found.

quisition by unpaired presentations of CS and US. CS and US were either not presented before (group 0) or four times (group 4) or eight times (group 8). The control group (unpaired control group) did also not receive any CS/US presentations before.

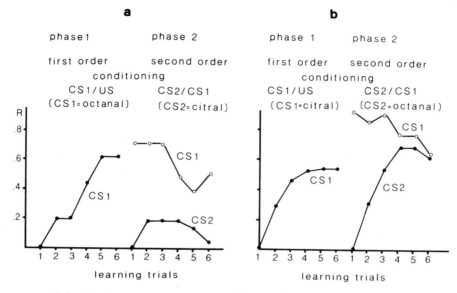

FIG. 9.6. Second-order olfactory PER-conditioning. a: A group of bees is conditioned by six trials to octanal (= CS1; US = sucrose solution; phase 1). Afterwards, (phase 2) CS1 is paired with citral (CS2), and the response to CS1 and CS2 is determined in six trials. Only a weak second-order conditioning effect is found. (The sum of CR in trials 2, 3, and 4 is just significantly different from the sum of the CR from trials 1, 5, and 6, $p = 0.04$, χ^2-test). b: A similar experiment as in a but with the reversed order of CS1 and CS2. The acquisition function for CS2 shows strong second-order conditioning, the extinction function to CS1 shows the expected reduction over repeated nonreinforced presentations. Citral is a more effective acquired US, because second-order conditioning in experiment b: gives highly significant effects, but only weak effects in experiment (Courtesy B. Smith).

9.6b) was the initially conditioned stimulus CS1, which was paired afterwards with the other of the two odors. As in Bitterman et al.'s (1983) experiment, octanal acquires only a weak potential as an US, whereas citral becomes a strong acquired US.

Sequential Memory Processing

One of the most striking results of both operant and classical conditioning experiments is that the weakest response to a conditioned stimulus is at around 2–4 min. after the learning trial, whereas the best responses are immediately after the learning trial and then later after a period of more than 10 min. (Menzel, 1968). This observation gave rise to an extended series of experiments that increasingly

substantiated also for the honey bee Ebbinghaus' (1885) and Müller and Pilzecker's (1900) notions of memory consolidation. If the time dependence of the
performance after a single learning trial is measured, with no other factor than
time laps interfering, one finds a dual-phase time course with high performance
immediately after learning and 10 or more min. later. These two phases are
separated by a minimum at 2–4 minutes. At longer intervals, the memory fades
after a few days, in the case of a single trial operant color learning, and after 1 or
more days in single trial olfactory conditioning. If training consists of several
learning trials, the performance saturates at a high level immediately during
training, and time dependence disappears even if the massed learning trials are
performed within the same time (30–40 sec.) as a single learning trial. This is
true for both olfactory conditioning of PER and instrumental learning of colors.
A memory established by three or more trials lasts for the lifetime of a bee.

The early memory after a single learning trial is particularly sensitive to
extinction and reversal learning, whereas the consolidated memory is much more
resistant (Menzel, 1968; 1979). We shall now discuss whether these memory
phases indicate distinct forms of memory. One approach to this question assumes
a sequence of at least three stages of the memory trace, a short-term memory
(STM), an intermediate-term memory (ITM), and a long-term memory (LTM),
whereby a single learning trial initiates only the first two memory phases, and the
LTM is only reached after multiple learning trials. To test these assumptions, I
examine the following questions: (a) Is the content of the various memory forms
the same? (b) Are nonassociative components involved in STM? (c) Is the
memory trace sensitive to experimental interference, and at which stages? Experiments with genetic lines of good- and poor-learning bees have shown that
these lines differ with respect to their STM–ITM consolidation, and this is
discussed in the light of the preceding considerations. In the context of these
results, I present a more profound hypothetical model of memory formation in
the honey bee.

The Content of STM and ITM.   Consolidation is most likely an active process
that allows for the incorporation of a new memory into an already acquired or
innately existing memory. Thus, it is possible that the information remembered
after consolidation differs from that before termination of the consolidation process. Smith and Menzel (in preparation) approached this question by conditioning a group of bees with a single learning trial to an odorant, and testing
subgroups to one out of four odorants, either in the STM-range (30 sec. after
conditioning) or in the ITM-range (15 min.). Fig. 9.7 gives two examples from a
series of experiments. If citral is conditioned, consolidation leads to a sharpening
of the generalization profile, whereas if geraniol is conditioned, the four odorants
are reevaluated during the process of consolidation. In this case, geraniol initiates
the highest response in STM, whereas in ITM the preference is shifted and the
nonconditioned odorant citral is responded to highest. The time-courses of condi-

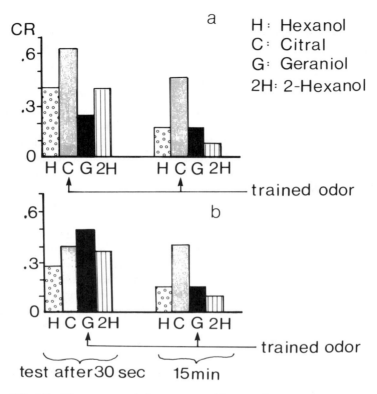

FIG. 9.7. The content of short-term and intermediate-term memory. The PER was conditioned to citral (in a:) or geraniol (in b:) by one conditioning trial. Each of the two groups were devided into two sub-groups, one of which was tested 30 sec. after conditioning (short-term memory) and the other 15 min. after conditioning (intermediate-term memory). Each of the four subgroups was again devided into four further groups with respect to the four odorants to be tested. If citral is trained (a) the consolidation of the short-term into the intermediate-term memory sharpens the generalization profile in favor of the trained stimulus, whereas after training to geraniol the generalization profile changes drastically indicating a reevaluation of the memory during consolidation. Statistics: the χ^2-test reveals that differences in CR exceeding 18% are significant with $p \leq 0.01$ (540 animals in all 16 test groups).

tioned responses after a single learning trial provide additional evidence for differences in internal processing. Citral follows the well-known biphasic time-course, whereas the CR to geraniol declines but shows no sign of consolidation. In fact, the consolidation process favors citral, even though geraniol has been conditioned. These results indicate that the memory has been interpreted and rerouted in the case of geraniol. Thus, the consolidation process does indeed change the content of the STM and ITM, with the consequence that the animal is able to discriminate more precisely between conditioned and nonconditioned stimuli. In certain cases, however, the content is drastically and qualitatively changed in favor of an already existing or preordained memory trace.

Time-course of the Nonassociative and Associative Components in STM. Sucrose stimulation of the chemoreceptors of the antennae and/or mouthparts acts as a US *and* sensitizes the animal in a general sense. Obviously, the response after conditioning is comprised of sensitizing (pseudoconditioning, positive non-associative) and conditioning (associative) components. Fig. 9.8 shows the results of an experiment designed to test how these two components act together to control conditioned responses. Let us first compare the time courses after a single sensitization or conditioning trial. Initially, the response probability after the sensitization trial is very high. Because the response probability after the conditioning trial should depend on the sum of both the nonassociative and associative components, the associative component is initially small and the nonassociative component large. But, during the process of consolidation, the associative component rises and the nonassociative component falls drastically, reaching a zero value 5 min. later. Because sensitization fades faster than the rise of the associative memory, the compound of both effects produces the familiar biphasic time-course of the conditioned response. A consequence of this interpretation is that a weak associative memory already exists immediately after a single learning trial, which becomes stronger over a time period of minutes. After three conditioning trials, the associative component is much stronger already immediately after conditioning, whereas the nonassociative component after three sensitization trials is even weaker than after a single sensitization trial. Therefore, the associative component dominates the response probability after three conditioning trials, and the temporal dynamic is reduced. Most importantly, repeated sensitizations produce a qualitatively different effect than conditioning: The habituating effect of repeated US-only exposures are not seen in repeated conditioning trials.

This experiment clearly shows that conditioning is in no sense a stronger sensitization, but rather qualitatively different, because (a) the consolidation after a single conditioning trial is not triggered by repeated trials with US only, and (b) the speed-up of the consolidation process, as is the case for multiple trials, occurs only for associative trials and not for nonassociative trials. One may argue, therefore, that contiguity of CS and US necessitates a physiological mechanism that is qualitatively different from the up- or down-regulation caused by unpaired stimuli. From this approach, one might favor a "contiguity dependent" mechanism of neuromodulation rather than an "activity dependent" mechanism (Kandel, 1976; Byrne, 1987). Such contiguity dependent mechanisms are essentially what Hebb (1949) was referring to when he proposed a cellular mechanism for

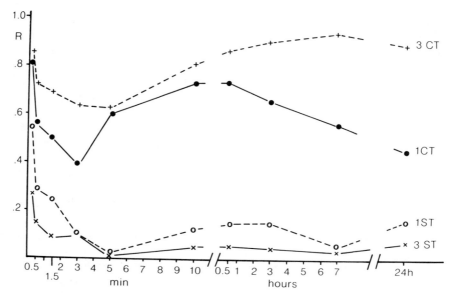

FIG. 9.8.   Time-course of the memory trace after one or three olfactory PER-conditioning trials (one CT, three CT), and after one or three sensitization trials (one ST, three ST). In the case of conditioning, the CS (carnation) preceded immediately the US (sucrose solution on antennae and proboscis for 2 sec.), in the case of sensitization the CS and US were separated by several minutes. Seventy-two (18 × 4) test groups, each with 20 to 30 animals were run in parallel: four different treatments (one and three CT, one and three ST) and 18 intervals between treatment and test. Each animal was exposed to the odor stimulus (carnation) three times: (1) in the spontaneous response test performed with all animals before the specific treatment, (2) during the specific treatment (one or three CT, one or three ST) and (3) during the single test (presentation of the odorant) at varying intervals (abscissa). The three tests at longer intervals are exceptions to this rule (3, 7, and 24 hours). In these groups each animal was tested three times, 3, 7, and 24 hours after the conditioning or sensitization. The ordinate gives the probability of the PER in the tests excluding the animals that responded to the odorant in the spontaneous response test. The spontaneous response rate was below 15% for all four treatment groups. The experiment allows to dissociate the nonassociative and associative components that interact in controlling the time course after one or three conditioning trials, and favors the interpretation of qualitative different mechanisms for associative learning (see text).

associative learning. However, as we see hereafter, activity-dependent neuromodulation could equally well account for such mechanisms.

Genetic Lines of Good and Poor Learners Differ in Memory Consolidation. Additional evidence for successions of memory phases has come from experiments dealing with the analysis of genetic lines. Such experiments were undertaken by Brandes (1985, 1988), who tested selected genetic lines of honey bees that differed in their learning ability. The poorly learning bees were inferior in olfactory PER-conditioning, in extinction after PER-conditioning, in compound visual and mechanical PER-conditioning, and in various aspects of visual operant learning both at the feeding place and at the hive entrance. When these lines were examined for the time-course of memory formation, similar to that described in Fig. 9.9a, it became clear that the difference between the lines did not result from their ability to learn but rather in the processes leading to a stable memory (Brandes, Frisch, & Menzel, 1988). The good learners showed all the characteristics described earlier (compare Fig. 9.8 with Fig. 9.9a, and notice the different time scale): high sensitization immediately after a single learning trial, a minimum of conditioned performance followed by a prominent consolidation phase, and a long-lasting memory. The poor learners were only weakly sensitized and lacked the consolidation phase, although their conditioned response was not significantly lower than that of the good learners at the minimum of CR (dotted line in Fig. 9.9a).

These results resemble those from experiments with single gene memory mutants in *Drosophila* (review Tully, 1988; see Fig. 9.9b, solid line). The mutants amnesiac, rutabaga, dunce, and turnip are less sensitized by strong stimuli and lose their memory for aversively or appetitively reinforced olfactory stimuli much faster than the wild type fly. Experiments similar to those described previously for the bee showed that differences in the time-courses between the normal and impaired learners were optimal between 0.5–3 hr. This corresponds surprisingly well with those results from the honey bee, even though the flies were trained with 12 pairings of an odorant and an aversive stimulus (electric shock) spaced over 60 sec., whereas the bees were conditioned by a single appetitive trial lasting just 3–4 seconds. Unfortunately, the time-course of the sensitization effect is unknown in *Drosophila,* and the temporal resolution of conditioned performance could not be tested within the first few minutes. Nevertheless, the results from both the honey bee and the fruit fly suggest a specific impairment of an intermediate memory phase that is responsible for the consolidation of an early or short-term memory trace into an intermediate memory.

The Amnestic Syndrome. Experimentally induced retrograde amnesia in bees was already described by Buttel-Reepen (1900), who wrote: "If bees are narcotized with chloroform, ether, bovist, etc., they lose their memory for land-

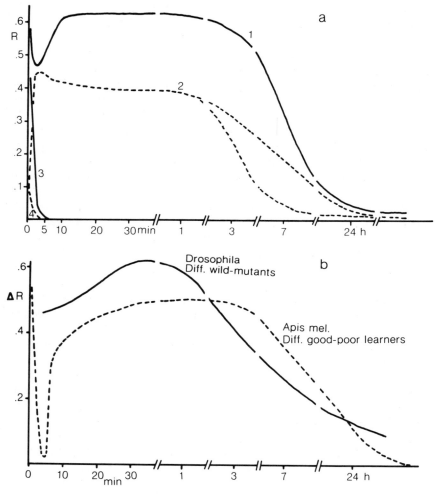

FIG. 9.9.   a: Time-course of the memory trace after one olfactory PER-conditioning trial or one sensitization trial in two different genetic lines of honey bees. The test procedure was similar to that described in Fig. 9.8. Curve 1: Line of good learners, one conditioning trial; curve 2: line of poor learners, one conditioning trial. Curve 3: line of good learners, one sensitization trial; curve 4: line of poor learners, one sensitization trial. The good learners behave like the normal bees with a high sensitization (curve 3) and a biphasic memory phase (curve 1). The bad learners show little sensitization (curve 4, left corner), a reduced CR within the first few minutes, and a reduced and shorter intermediate memory phase. b: Comparison of *Drosophila* memory mutants and *Apis* genetic lines: The ordinate (ΔR) gives the difference of the conditioned performance between wild type and memory mutants (*Dros-*

marks completely and forever. They can be introduced into a foreign colony after recovery from narcosis, and they do not fly back to the place of their own colony. . . . They have lost all what they have learned before . . . their memory is erased" (p. 38). He also observed (p. 46) that cooling or shock treatment by immersing the bees for a short time in water resulted in partial retrograde amnesia. Von Frisch repeated some of Buttel-Reepen's experiments (von Frisch, 1922, p. 159) and observed that most of the bees had not lost their memory. Several authors supported Buttel-Reepen's original findings (Brunskill & Rankin 1952; Tirala, 1923), whereas others rejected his observations (Jordan, 1952; Medugorac, 1967; Ribbands, 1950; Rösch-Berger, 1933) or claimed that the effect was dependent on the type of narcosis (Gontarski,. 1950). We now know that a well-established memory is resistant to experimental manipulations such as narcosis, cooling, or electroshock, but that recently acquired memory is erased and does not recover with time (Beckmann, 1974; Erber, 1975a, 1975b; Menzel, 1968; Schmid, 1964). The single learning paradigm provides us once again with a favorable means with which to study the time-course of retrograde amnesia, and olfactory PER-conditioning permits localization of sensitive regions in the brain. The latter is achieved by reversible and local cooling of small brain regions for a short period of time (30 sec., 1°C) (Erber, Masuhr, & Menzel, 1980; Masuhr, 1976; Menzel et al., 1974), or local electrical stimulation with weak alternating currents at different intervals after the single learning trial (Sugawa & Menzel, 1986; Menzel, 1987).

The memory trace is not susceptible to narcosis, electroshock, or cooling after more than 7 min. following a single learning trial, and not susceptible at all if the animal is trained by three or more trials (Fig. 9.10). The formation of a stable memory trace is accelerated by learning trials, rather than sole repetition of the CS or US, and results in a faster transfer of the susceptible memory into a stable memory (Menzel & Sugawa, 1986). Therefore, the susceptible and stable memory traces are necessarily sequential, and the transfer between the two forms is dependent on both time and associative events. The time-course of susceptibility to the various amnestic treatments is independent of the learning paradigm (operant conditioning of colors, classical conditioning of odorants). These experimental treatments (cooling, narcosis, and electroshocks) do not seem to act as inhibitory reinforcers, because a pairing with a CS does not reduce the response to the stimulus. Furthermore, the normal conditioning to the stimulus after an amnestic

ophila) or good and poor learners (*Apis*). *Drosophila* was trained with 12 pairings of an odorant and an aversive stimulus (from Tully, 1988), and *Apis* was conditioned with one trial in the PER-conditioning paradigm (see Fig. 9.7). The data from three different memory mutants of *Drosophila* were pooled and the average subtracted from those of the wild type. In the honey bee, the data from three different lines of poor learners were pooled. The genetic lines of poor learners in both species are specifically deficient in an intermediate memory phase.

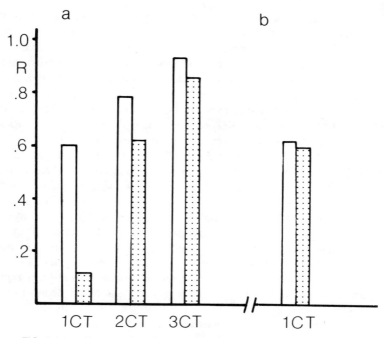

FIG. 9.10.   a: The effect of weak electrical stimulation of the brain on memory formation after 1, 2, or 3 olfactory PER-conditioning trials (1 CT, 2 CT, 3 CT). The electric stimulation was applied to the animals of the experimental groups (grey bars) 20 sec. after the last conditioning trial. Each of the six groups consisted of 35 animals. The control groups (open bars) were sham-treated. The ordinate gives the CR probability as measured 30 min. after the treatment. A statistically highly significant amnestic effect is found only after a single learning trial ($p \leq .01$, χ^2-text). b: The same experiment as in a but the interval between the single learning trial is 7 minutes. Electric stimulation of the brain does not cause an amnestic effect. The same is true after two or three conditioning trials and 7 min. interval (not shown).

treatment is not reduced. Retrograde amnesia appears as a permanent memory loss, at least over about 24 hours.

These results are better understood when one considers various structures of the bee brain. For this reason, the reader has to be introduced to the basic organization of the bee brain.

The brain consists of two major parts (Fig. 9.11): (a) the supraoesophageal ganglion (brain) with the optic lobes, the protocerebrum with the paired mushroom bodies and the unpaired central body, the deutocerebrum with the paired antennal lobes and the tritocerebrum, and (b) the suboesophageal ganglion, which is composed of the three neuromeres belonging to the three segments of

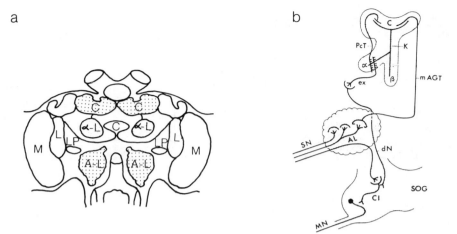

FIG. 9.11.   The basic organization of the bee brain as it is relevant for the neural circuits underlying the olfactory conditioning of the PER. a: Diagram of the major neuropils in the supraoesophageal ganglion (= brain). M (medulla) and L (lobula) are the two inner visual ganglia, AL (antennal lobe) the primary olfactory neuropiles, C (calyx) and α-L (α-lobe) belong to the mushroom bodies, LP (lateral protocerebrum) is an unstructured neuropile ventro-lateral to the mushroom bodies at the output region of the protocerebrum, C (central body). b: Major pathways that are involved in PER-conditioning. SN = antennal sensory nerve; Mn = motorneurons controlling the mouthparts; mAGT = median antenno-glomerularis tract, a major relay pathway to the chemosensory input region of the mushroom bodies; Kn = Kenyon cells, the intrinsic neurons of the mushroom body; α and β are the two output lobes of the mushroom body; Pct = protocerebro-calycal tract, a feedback tract between the α-lobe and calyx; SOG = suboesophageal ganglion, Cl = premoter and central interneurons that relay the decending commands to the motorneurons.

the mouthparts. The essential neuropiles involved in olfactory conditioning are the antennal lobes (afferent projections of the chemoreceptors on the antennae and first stage of sensory processing), suboesophageal ganglion (motor control of the movements of the mouthparts—the SOG also receives afferent input from the antennae), and the pair of mushroom bodies in the protocerebrum (higher order processing of sensory input from the eyes, the antennae, and other receptor systems). The mushroom bodies have long been suspected as being the centers of insect "intelligence," because they are larger in social insects, and their size appears to correlate with the number of skills of various species of bees and wasps (Armbruster, 1919; Erber, Homberg, Gronenberg, 1987; Howse, 1974; von Alten, 1910). If the connections between the antennal lobes and the protocerebrum are cut, then olfactory conditioning and retrieval of formerly estab-

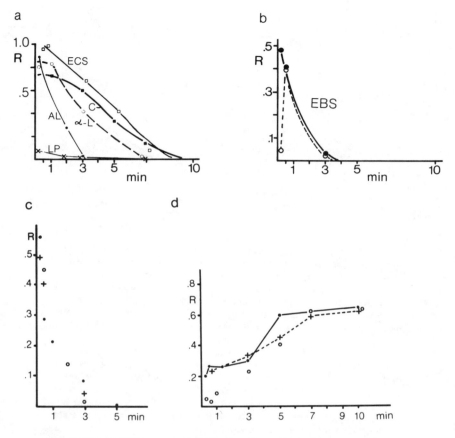

FIG. 9.12.   a: Time-courses of local cooling that lead to amnestic effects in olfactory PER-conditioning. In all cases, both antennae were exposed to the CS, and the animals were conditioned by one trial. The indicated paired structures (see Fig. 9.11a) were cooled to 1°C for 10 sec. (for experimental details, see Erber et al., 1980). The abscissa gives the time interval between the conditioning trial and the ontset of cooling. The ordinate gives the sensitivity to the amnestic treatment. The latter is the inverse of the proportion of animals responding to the CS 20 min. after the amnestic treatment, at a time when the animals have fully recovered. (redrawn from Erber et al., 1980). b: Time-course of the amnestic effect of local electric brain stimulation (EBS). The animals perceived the olfactory CS with only one antenna. The α-lobe ipsi (————) or contralateral (--------) to the antenna was stimulated at various intervals (abscissa) after the single conditioning trial. The ordinate gives the sensitivity to the amnestic treatment as in a:. c: The time-courses of amnestic sensitivity in the antennal lobe to cooling (○), and electric stimulation of the ispsilateral α-lobe (+) are compared with the time course of sensitization after a single sensitizing trial (●)

lished olfactory memory is lost, whereas the sucrose-induced reflex is not impaired (Masuhr, 1976; Michelsen, 1987; Turanska, 1973; Voskreskenskaya, 1957).

Reversible blocking of neural activity in selected brain areas with thin, cooled needles revealed the time courses of amnestic effects after single trial olfactory PER-conditioning (Erber et al., 1980; Masuhr, 1976; Menzel et al., 1974; see Menzel, 1987, for review) (Fig. 9.12a). It was found that cooling induces retrograde amnesia within a short time period (2 min.) following conditioning if the antennal lobes are treated, and for extended periods of time (up to 7 min.) if the mushroom bodies are treated. The output regions of the mushroom bodies (α-lobes) have a faster time-course of susceptibility than the input regions (calyx). If only one antenna is stimulated with the CS, retrograde amnesia results from a cooling of the antennal lobe ipsilateral to the CS input. The antennal lobe contralateral to the CS input is not involved, because cooling of the contralateral antennal lobe causes no retrograde amnesia. However, cooling of the ipsi- or contralateral mushroom bodies results in amnesia with about equal effect. If localized electric brain stimulation is used instead of cooling, the time course of successful impairment is the same for the ipsilateral antennal and α-lobes, and resembles the short retrograde amnestic effects observed from cooling of the ipsilateral antennal lobe. Electrical stimulation of the contralateral α-lobe initially has no effect but interferes 30 sec. after conditioning (Fig. 9.12b; Sugawa, 1986). This means that the susceptible memory trace is restricted to the ipsilateral side of the brain only for less than 30 seconds.

If one compares the time-courses of sensitization with that of the susceptibility of the memory trace in the ipsilateral antennal and α-lobe (Fig. 9.12c), one finds a close correspondence. Similarly, one finds a close correspondence between the time-course of susceptibility of the memory trace in the mushroom bodies (ipsi- and contralateral calyces) and the calculated associative component after a single conditioning trial (Fig. 9.12d). The associative component was calculated from the results shown in Fig. 9.8 by subtracting the sensitization component (curve 1ST in Fig. 9.8) from that of conditioning (curve 1CT in Fig. 9.8), which should reflect the combined effects of sensitization and associative learning. This procedure should only be taken as a first-order approach to qualitatively characterize

---

(see text). d: The time-courses of the effect of amnestic treatments of the whole animal (○, electroconvulsive shock after Erber (1975a) and cooling of the calyces (--- + ---). These two time courses are compared with the time course of the calculated associative memory component as described in the text (———●———). The similarities in the respective time courses are interpreted to indicate that the neural substrate of sensitization resides predominantly in the sensory input (antennal lobe) and premotor output (α-lobe) regions, whereas that of the associative memory component resides in the calyx neuropil of the mushroom bodies.

the time-course of the associative component. It is tempting to conclude that the memory trace erased by cooling the antennal lobes corresponds to that initiated by the US alone (sensitization), whereas the memory trace erased by cooling the calyces corresponds to that which results from the consolidation of associative memory. The first phase, short-term memory (STM), is obviously necessary for the establishment of an associative memory trace, because in this particular experiment the bees were tested for the conditioned response 15–30 min. after the local cooling period of 30 seconds. This component of the STM must reside in the antennal lobes (and α-lobes?). The second phase, the intermediate-term memory (ITM), rises with the time-course of the improvement of learned behavior and lasts for up to about 24 hr (see Fig. 9.8). The ITM is probably located within the mushroom bodies, because cooling of these structures and particularly the input regions, prevents the formation of ITM. The locus and functional properties of the permanent memory (LTM) are not yet known, because experimental procedures have not been found to selectively interfere with its formation.

The Concept of Elementary Memory Processes as a Cellular Basis of Sequential Memory Phases. Memory needs time to develop—and it changes with time. The wealth of information accummulated on this issue since Ebbinghaus' (1885) pioneering discoveries on human learning is concisely summarized in models that assume a sequence of stages that are partly characterized by (a) duration (stability in time), (b) sensitivity to new experience, (c) susceptibility to experimental interference, and (d) differential injury in pathological cases (Agranoff, 1980; Goelet, Castellucci, Schacher, & Kandel, 1986; Klatzky, 1980; Squire & Cohen, 1982; Weiskrantz, 1970). Data from the honey bee and *Drosophila* also fit into this general scheme, although it is still unknown how these different characterizations of memory phases may indicate a unified and coherent model of the underlying cellular mechanisms. The data on *Drosophila* and *Apis* suggest that a common cellular mechanism may be at work with two major properties. Firstly, each memory phase is not just an extension of the previous memory, in that long-term memory is not just extended short-term memory, and associative memory is not an extension or strengthening of sensitization. Secondly, it appears that specific events *and* time drive the system to branching points that are arranged in sequence and that cause the memory trace to change qualitatively by a process called *consolidation*. The experiments outlined previously indicate that the time-courses, the control over behavior, and the content and the susceptibility of the memory trace behind each branch point are different for each respective branch.

A summary of the arguments based on the time-dependent processes involved in memory formation is presented in Fig. 9.13. The model assumes three temporal memory phases and two consolidation processes (I, II). Short-term memory (STM) is highly dominated by the nonassociative memory component (sensitization curve 1) but includes an initially weak and rapidly growing associative

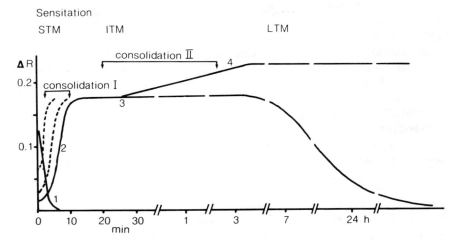

FIG. 9.13. Model of sequential memory processing as derived from the experiments described in Fig. 9.8, 9.9a, and 9.12. Curve 1: Time course of sensitization, describing the rapid decline of a non-associative memory. Curve 2: The rising phase of the associative component after a single conditioning trial. This function is the result of subtracting the sensitization component from that after an associative trial, and it describes the first kind of consolidation (I). Consolidation I is thought to reflect an automatic internal process that stablizes the associative memory trace. Rapid repetitions of associative trials speed up consolidation I to such an extent that consolidation II is reached immediately (dotted lines). Curve 3: Time course of the intermediate memory (ITM). Curve 4: Consolidation II, a process that leads to a permanent memory trace and is initiated by repeated associative learning trials.

component (curve 2). The transition to a pure associative memory (curve 3) is called consolidation I and establishes a temporarily limited intermediate-term memory (ITM). A permanent memory trace (LTM) is only reached by several learning trials. If these trials are spaced in time, the transition to LTM, called consolidation II, starts at the ITM phase (curve 4 in Fig. 9.13). Massed associative learning trials (dotted lines in Fig. 9.13) may speed up the consolidation processes so much that the distinction between consolidation I and II is lost. The latter assumption is the most speculative component of the model, because so far it is unknown whether the LTM reached by multiple massed and spaced learned trials is functionally the same.

The experimentally best supported scheme of a cellular basis of memory is the one developed for sensitization and conditioning in the marine slug, *Aplysia* (Byrne, 1987; Carew & Saley, 1986; Goelet et al., 1986). How does our model of the sequential processing of memory phases compare with this model? This question is particularly relevant, because it has already been shown that the cellular deficits of *Drosophila* memory mutants do, in fact, fit quite well into this *Aplysia* scheme (Quinn, 1984; Tully, 1988), which is termed *activity-dependent neuromodulation*. The most important features of this include continuation between nonassociative and associative learning, plasticity in existing neural circuits, and the involvement of secondary messenger systems and their synergistic interactions. Can such a cellular mechanism account for the succession of qualitatively different memory traces, or is it necessary to assume complex network properties?

Qualitative changes in the form of branch points are not a serious problem if one assumes additional synergistic processes, such as that of thresholding and switching to novel molecular reactions as a consequence of cooperation between component reactions. Crick (1984), Goelet et al. (1986), Lisman (1985), and others have pointed out several conceivable mechanisms based on known molecular properties. The important step is always a cellular event (e.g., the intracellular accumulation of Ca^{2+} after stimulation with the CS) interacting with an activated molecular process (e.g., the synthesis of cAMP, and consequently the phosphorylation of key molecules). This cooperative process leads to an increase in the molecular turnover, with the consequence that the activity of key molecules rises above a threshold, thus enabling further reactions such as autocatalytic phosphorylation or the phosphorylation of proteins. The latter may adopt the role of internal messengers for novel reactions, such as the activation of RNA or DNA. When applying such a concept to behavioral or neurophysiological studies, it is important to note that the key molecules (e.g., cAMP) serve two functions at the same time. The first function is readily detectable by appropriate techniques (behavioral performance measures, ion currents through cell membranes), whereas the second is initially "hidden," requires time for expression, and appears after a delay as a new property. In behavioral studies, this latter function corresponds to the process of "consolidation." In other words, consolidation reflects both a qualitatively new property of the system but is, at the same time, based on the properties of the lower (or preceding) level in the sequence of stages.

In relating a behavior to cellular processes, the ultimate performance is the result of more complex neural activities, including the parallel processing of cellular plasticity at multiple sites with different time-courses, synergistic effects at both the cellular and network level, and formation of new connectivities. Indeed, plasticities at multiple sites have been postulated for even simple conditioning paradigms (Byrne, 1987; Frost, Clark, & Kandel, 1988), and new connectivities as an expression of plasticity are already documented for nonassociative learning (Bailey & Chen 1983). Also, synergistic network properties have been assumed for certain basic properties of conditioning (Frost et al., 1988; Hawkins & Kandel, 1984). In the bee, cellular reactions underlying memory formation are distributed throughout the brain in a specific hierarchical pattern. For example, the sensory neuropil and antennal lobes appear to contain only those components that lead to nonassociative plasticities (Fig. 9.12d), whereas the input side and the neurons of the mushroom bodies contain those components responsible for the associative plasticity that are necessary for the ITM and most likely also for the LTM. Therefore, as in other animals, serial and parallel processing at multiple sites with qualitative different properties also appears to be a major neural strategy in the formation of memory traces in bees.

Pharmacology of Performance, Learning, and Memory Retrieval

Pharmacological studies on learning and memory are concerned with a variety of fundamental questions. Which transmitters, neuromodulators, and neurohormones are involved in memory formation and retrieval? Which brain parts, nuclei, neuropils, classes of neurons, or individual neurons are modulated by these substances so that memory formation and/or retrieval is improved or reduced? How are the two processes "memory formation" and "memory retrieval" separable from each other and from the sensory and motor components of reflex and learned performance? These questions have been studied in the bee using the olfactory PER-conditioning paradigm. The test substances were injected into the brain in nl quantities before, during, or after the single learning trial, and the effects were tested at various time intervals after the injection.

Two experimental procedures were used to study the effect of injected drugs:

1. The retrieval test: A group of bees were first tested for their spontaneous responses to an odor, and the nonresponding animals were conditioned once to this odor by pairing the odor with sucrose solution (Fig. 9.14a line acquisition after one learning trial [LT]). After conditioning, approximately 70% of the animals extended their proboscides to the presentation of the odor alone. The drug was then injected into the brain, and the animals were tested afterwards by repeatedly presenting the odor stimulus alone. The control group (the same amount of saline was injected) showed a small extinction effect due to the repeated testing. The experimental group responded transiently much less, but the drug effect disappeared at longer intervals. The example given in Fig. 9.14a is for DA (10^{-6}M, 100nl injected into the protocerebrum), which inhibits conditioned responding maximally at 20–30 min. after injection. Other drugs have much faster time-courses.

2. Storage test: This procedure tested whether a drug interferes with the formation of memory. The example given in Fig. 9.14b shows the effects after an injection of 5 nl of 5-HT (10^{-8}) into each α-lobe of the mushroom bodies. The drug (or saline, control group) was injected, and the animals were conditioned by one trial (LT) at the time of optimal action of the drug as determined in the retrieval test. The dotted curved line in Fig. 9.14b indicates the time-course as

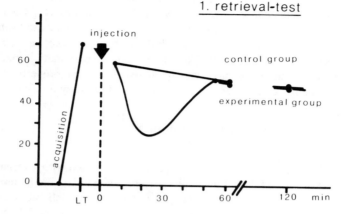

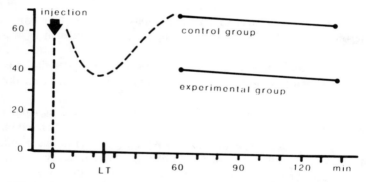

FIG. 9.14. Two procedures were used in the pharmacological experiments to separate between storage and retrieval processes: a: Retrieval test: The animals were injected after a single learning trial—the control group with saline, the experimental group with the drug. Tests for conditioned responding started shortly after injection. Repeated tests cause a small extinction effect in the control group. If the animals of the experimental group are injected with 10^{-6} M dopamine, as in this example, conditioned responding is transiently reduced but recovers to the same response level as the control group. b: Storage test: The animals were injected before the single learning trial (control group, saline; experimental group, drug, in this example 10^{-8} M serotonin). The single learning trial was given at the time of optimal action of the drug (here, 25 min. after injection). The tests for conditioned responding started when the drug had no effect anymore. Serotonin causes a permanent memory deficit, indicating an inhibitory effect on memory formation. It also reduces retrieval as shown in the dotted line, which gives the result of a different experiment. The retrieval effect is fully reversible, but the storage effect is not.

measured in separate retrieval tests. The animals were tested for the conditioned response at a time when the drug had no effect anymore. In the case of 5-HT, the experimental animals showed a persistent reduction of conditioned responding. This indicates that 5-HT injected into the α-lobe interferes disruptively with the formation of the memory trace. Other drugs, such as OA or NA, may persistently improve the memory when injected before the conditioning trial (see following).

Biogenic amines have been tested with these two procedures, because they are thought to act as neuromodulators in both vertebrate and invertebrate brains (Dunn, 1986; Evans, 1980; Martinez, 1986). The bee brain contains the two catecholamines dopamine (DA) and noradrenaline (NA), the indolamine serotonin (5-HT), and the phenolamine octopamine (OA) (Mercer, Mobbs, Evans, & Davenport, 1983). The distribution of DA (Schäfer & Rehder, 1989) and 5-HT (Schäfer & Bicker, 1986) has been evaluated by immunocytochemical procedures (Bicker, Schäfer, & Rehder, 1987). The retrieval of stored olfactory memory is drastically reduced if DA, NA, or 5-HT are injected in physiological concentrations (10^{-6}-10^{-8} M), but relatively large quantities (about 200 nl) into the bee brain via the thick neuron tract of the median ocellus. Similarly, at the level of the antennal lobes, DA transiently reduces the retrieval of stored information (MacMillan & Mercer, 1987). The application of OA in the same way has no effect on the retrieval test (Mercer & Menzel, 1982). Because the sensory and motor components of the reflex appeared to be normal, some selective action on the memory system was suspected. This was confirmed for DA when injected into the protocerebrum, in that bees learned normally when conditioned at the time of optimal action of DA (Michelsen, 1988).

Local injections (2–5 nl) of biogenic amines, and their agonists and antagonists, reveal a pattern of pharmacological actions in the bee brain (Bicker & Menzel, 1989; Menzel, Michelson, Rüffer, & Sugawa, 1988) (Fig. 9.15). For example, 5-HT (10^{-4}–10^{-8} M) injected into the mushroom bodies (5 nl in each structure) transiently blocks memory retrieval (optimal action at 3 min. after injection). If 5-HT is injected into the mushroom bodies 3 min. before the learning trial, the CR is permanently reduced, but not if 5-HT is injected into the antennal lobe.

OA, and its agonist synephrine, exerts an arousing action in the bee irrespective of whether it is injected into the hemolyph, the median brain (in larger quantities—0.5 μl), or locally into the mushroom bodies (in nl quantities). Thus, we concluded that OA enhances not only the CR but also the formation of new memory when injected before conditioning, because satiated animals, which do not show the reflex to sucrose stimulation and do not learn, show a 90% response to sucrose after OA injection. They also imbibe double the normal amount of sucrose solution and learn normally, even though they are satiated.

More examples and a summary of site-specific pharmacological actions are described in Fig. 9.15. The right side of the figure summarizes the action of

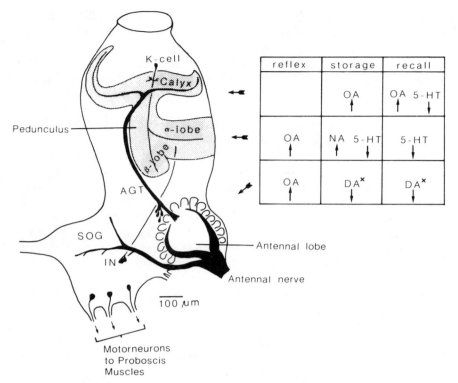

reflex	storage	recall
	OA ↑	OA ↑ 5-HT ↓
OA ↑	NA ↑ 5-HT ↓	5-HT ↓
OA ↑	DA* ↓	DA* ↓

FIG. 9.15. Summary of the effect of local injections on the reflex, storage, and retrieval during olfactory learning in honey bees. The left side of the figure presents a schematic side view of the main pathways in the brain and suboesophageal ganglion (SOG) mediating the proboscis extension reflex (compare with Fig. 9.11a, which shows a front view, from Bicker and Menzel, 1989). The chemosensory afferents of the antennal nerve project to the glomeruli of the antennal lobe (AL) and into the suboesophageal ganglion (SOG) and other brain parts. Relay neurons (AGT) transmit olfactory information through the antenno-glomerular tract into the calyces of the mushroom body (stippled neuropile). The mushroom body contains about 170,000 intrinsic Kenyon cells (K-cell), which project to the two output regions of this neuropile, the α-lobe and β-lobe, which are connected with the suboesophageal ganglion via interneurones (IN). The suboesophageal ganglion contains the motor circuits and motor neurons (MN) responsible for the extension of the proboscis. OC: ocelli. The right side summarizes the action of locally injected amines on the three behavioral components: reflex (to sucrose stimulation of the antennae), storage (in PER-conditioning, see Fig. 9.14b), and recall (after PER-conditioning, see Fig. 9.14a). The procedure is described in the text and in Fig. 9.14. Arrows pointing upwards indicate a facilitatory effect on the respective behavior, those pointing downwards an inhibitory effect. The data for dopamine (DA*) come from MacMillan and Mercer (1987).

locally injected amines on the three behavioral components of reflex, storage, and retrieval. The substances were injected into either both antennal lobes, or both α-lobes, or both pendunculi (PD) of the mushroom bodies. The volume in each case was 2–5 nl, and concentrations were in the range of 10^{-6}–10^{-8} M. The volume of the brain, for comparison, is approx. 1 μl. The drug effects were compared with control animals that were injected at the same sites with the same volumes of saline as explained in Fig. 9.14. Several hundred animals were tested (Menzel et al., 1988; data for DA from MacMillan & Mercer, 1987). The arrows pointing upwards indicate a facilitatory effect on the reflex or conditioning response, those pointing downwards an inhibitory effect. Arrows pointing towards the diagram mark the injection site. OA mimicks the sensitizing action of the US (sucrose stimulus) and stimulates feeding behavior, suggesting a role of OA in reinforcement. If OA is injected into the pendunculus of the mushroom bodies (mb) close to the calycal input synapses of the chemosensory relay neurons, no changes were found for the reflex components, but both components of learning—namely, memory formation and retrieval—were enhanced. OA has no effect when injected into the output regions of the mb, the α-lobes, whereas NA injections into this region enhance memory formation particularly in animals that have lower learning rates. 5-HT, on the other hand, antagonizes the facilitatory action of OA and NA in the mb but does not affect the nonassociative modulation of the reflex.

In short, it appears that the DA-containing neurons of the median protocerebrum may specifically control the "read-out" of memory. 5-HT inhibits memory formation and memory retrieval, whereas OA and NA facilitate these two processes. Other transmitters have been found to be either not involved in learning or memory (e.g., GABA; Michelsen, 1987) or have not been studied carefully enough even though their distribution is well known, such as acetylcholine (Kreißl & Bicker, in press) and glutamate (Bicker, Schäfer, Ottersen, & Storm-Mathisen, 1988).

CONCLUSION

This review has, of course, only touched upon the subject of learning, memory, and "cognition" in honey bees. How can an insect with a brain of less than 1 mm³ and with less than 10^6 neurons (1/1000 of the number of neurons of our retina) accomplish such an astonishing variety of behavioral tasks? Certainly, specific design features of the neural substrate have shown a trend towards simplifing neural operations. Color vision, for example, is not a general visual capacity, but is limited to certain well-defined behaviors, such as feeding or returning to the hive, and is excluded from a large range of other visually guided behaviors. The capacity of bees to orientate to a pattern of polarized light in the sky is another good example of a design principle, in that perfect solutions are compromised for reduced neural investment, thus permitting the application of simple "rule of thumb" guidelines. Orientation to landmarks is also an example of "good approximation." Bees certainly do not carry a mental map around that allows them to calculate the shortest-distance flights or foresee the movement of a feeding place. Instead, they follow a hierarchy of rules that serve as back-up systems that enable the bees to handle different natural conditions. Still, the number of images stored for landmark orientation must be impressively high.

Preordained cues and facilitated associations are applied in a broad sense and do not appear as exclusive, but rather inclusive, principles. Separation between behavioral routines including plasticity and others excluding plasticity is another fundamental principle. For example, bees are helplessly "stupid" when trying to escape from a room, and will readily crash into a window, but are surprisingly "inventive" in handling a flower to extract nectar or collect pollen.

Perhaps the most elusive neural design principle is that which controls the storage of large memories and with the least number of neurons. Are associative matrices appropriate models or rather labeled lines and designated neural assemblies (Menzel & Bicker, 1987). Further speculation would be too premature at this point, and one can only hope that further studies with honey bees will continue to provide the solutions to these and many other questions. Indeed, it would certainly be difficult to find a more cooperative and exciting research animal with which to tackle such problems.

ACKNOWLEDGMENTS

I am most grateful to Mirko Whitfield for many discussions and help with the English text, Sabine Funke for typing various versions of the manuscript, and Astrid Klawitter for drawing the figures. Editha Salisbury provided the unpublished data in Figures 9.4 and 9.5. These data are part of her Ph.D. thesis. Dr. B. Smith collected the data of Figure 9.6, and Uta Schneider, Mishirŭ Sugawa, and Martin Hammer collaborated in the experiments reported in Figure 9.8. I am grateful to all co-workers for allowing me to include unpublished data. The research work referred to in the text was kindly supported by the Deutsche Forschungsgemeinschaft.

REFERENCES

Abramson, C. I. & Bittermann, M. E. (1986). The US-pre-exposure effect in honeybees. *Animal Learning and Behavior, 14,* 374–379.

Agranoff, B. W. (1980). Biochemical events mediating the formation of short-term and long-term memory. In Y. Tsukada & B. W. Agranoff (Eds.), *Neurobiological basis of learning and memory.* New York: John Wiley.

von Alten, H. (1910). Zur Phylogenie des Hymenopterengehirns. *Zeitschrift für Naturwissenschaft, 46,* 511–590.

Armbruster, L. (1919). Bienen und Wespengehirne—Meßbare phänotypische und genotypische Instinktveränderungen. *Archiv für Bienenkunde, 5,* 145–184.

von Aufsess, A. (1960). Geruchliche Nahorientierung der Biene bei entomophilen und ornitophilen Blüten. *Zeitschrift für vergleichende Physiologie, 43,* 469–498.

Backhaus, W. & Menzel, R. (1987). Color distance derived from a receptor model of color vision in the honeybee. *Biological Cybernetics, 55,* 321–331.

Backhaus, W., Menzel, R., Kreißl, S. (1987a). Multidimensional scaling of color similarity in bees. *Biological Cybernetics, 56,* 293–384.

Backhaus, W., Werner, A. & Menzel, R. (1987b). Color vision in honeybees, metric, dimensions, constancy and ecological aspects. In R. Menzel & A. Mercer (Eds.), *Neurobiology and behaviour of honeybees* (pp. 172–190). Berlin: Springer Verlag.

Baerends, G. P. (1941). Fortpflanzungsverhalten und Orientierung der Grabwespe *Ammophila campestris. Tijdschrift Entomologie, 84,* 71–248.

Bailey, C. H. & Chen, M. (1983). Morphological basis of long-term habituation and sensitization in Aplysia. *Science, 220,* 91–93.

Balderama, N., Diaz, M., Sequeda, A., Nunez, J. & Maldonado, H. (1987). Behavioural and pharmacological analysis of the stinging response in africanized and italian bees. In Menzel, R. and Mercer, A. (Eds.) *Neurobiology and Behavior of Honeybees,* pp. 121–129. Berlin-Heidelberg-New York: Springer Verlag.

Beckmann, H. E. (1974). Beeinflussung des Gedächtnisses der Honigbiene durch Narkose, Kühlung und Streß. *Journal of Comparative Physiology, 94,* 249–266.

Beier, W. (1968). Beeinflussung der inneren Uhr der Bienen durch Phasenverschiebung des Licht-Dunkel-Zeitgebers. *Zeitschrift für Bienenforschung, 9,* 356–378.

Beier, W. & Lindauer, M. (1970). Der Sonnenstand als Zeitgeber für die Biene. *Apidologie, 1,* 5–28.

Beling, I. (1929). Über das Zeitgedächtnis der Bienen. *Zeitschrift für vergleichende Physiologie, 9,* 260–338.

Bicker, G. & Menzel, R. (1989). Chemical codes for the control of behaviour in arthropods. *Nature, 337,* 33–39.

Bicker, G., Schäfer, S. & Rehder, V. (1987). Chemical neuroanatomy of the honeybee brain. In R. Menzel & A. Mercer (Eds.), *Neurobiology and behavior of honeybees* (pp. 202–224). Berlin: Springer Verlag.

Bicker, G., Schäfer, S., Ottersen, O. P. & Storm-Mathisen, J. (1988). Glutamate-like immunoreactivity in identified neuronal populations of insect nervous systems. *Journal of Neuroscience, 8,* 2108–2122.

Bitterman, M. E. (1988). Vertebrate-invertebrate comparisons. *Evolutionary Biology, 17,* 251–275.

Bitterman, M. E., Menzel, R., Fietz, A. & Schäfer, S. (1983). Classical conditioning of proboscis extension in honeybees (*Apis mellifica*). *Journal of Comparative Psychology, 97,* 107–119.

Bogdany, F. J. (1978). Linking of learning signals in honey bee orientation. *Behavioral Ecology and Sociobiology, 3,* 323–336.

Brandes, C. (1985). Unterschiede von verschiedenen Bienen eines Volkes bei der Suche nach Futterplatz. *Apidologie, 16,* 203–208.

Brandes, C. (1988). Estimation of heritability of learning behaviour in honeybees (*Apis mellifera capensis*). *Behavioral Genetics, 18,* 119–132.

Brandes, C., Frisch, B. & Menzel, R. (1988). Time-course of memory formation differs in honey bee lines selected for good and poor learning. *Animal Behavior, 36,* 981–985.

Brunskill, W. & Rankin, I. G. (1952). The use of nitrous oxide for moving bees in the active season. *Bee World, 33,* 173–179.

Buttel-Reepen, H. (1900). Sind die Bienen Reflexmaschinen?. *Experimentelle Beiträge zur Biologie der Honigbiene, 20,* 1–84.

Byrne, J. H. (1987). Cellular analysis of associative learning. *Physiological Review, 67,* 329–439.

Carew, T. J. & Sahley, C. L. (1986). Invertebrate learning and memory, from behavior to molecules. *Annual Review of Neuroscience, 9*, 435–487.

Collett, T. S. & Kelber, A. (1988). The retrieval of visuo-spatial memories by honeybees. *Journal of Comparative Physiology, 163*, 145–150.

Couvillon, P. A. & Bitterman, M. E. (1985). Analysis of choice in honey bees. *Animal Learning and Behavior, 13*, 246–252.

Couvillon, P. A., Klosterhalfen, S. & Bitterman, M. E. (1983). Analysis of overshadowing in honeybees. *Journal of Comparative Physiology, 97*, 154–166.

Crick, F. (1984). Memory and molecular turnover. *Nature, 286*, 100–101.

Darwin, C. (1877). The effects of cross and self fertilisation in the vegetable kingdom (2nd Ed). London: John Murray.

Daumer, K. (1956). Reizmetrische Untersuchung des Farbensehens der Bienen. *Zeitschrift für vergleichende Physiologie, 38*, 413–478.

Daumer, K. (1958). Blumenfarben wie sie die Bienen sehen. *Zeitschrift für vergleichende Physiologie, 41*, 49–110.

De Jong, D. (1982). Orientation of comb building by honeybees. *Journal of Comparative Physiology, 147*, 495–501.

Dunn, A. J. (1986). Biochemical correlates of learning and memory. In J. L. Martinez & R. P. Kesner (Eds.), *Learning and memory* (pp. 165–201). Orlando, Florida: Academic Press.

Ebbinghaus, M. (1885). Über das Gedächtnis. K. Büchler, Leipzig.

Erber, J. (1975a). The dynamics of learning in the honeybee (*Apis mellifera carnica*). I. The time dependence of the choice reaction. *Journal of Comparative Physiology, 99*, 231–242.

Erber, J. (1975b). The dynamics of learning in the honeybee (*Apis mellifica carnica*). II. Principles of information processing. *Journal of Comparative Physiology, 99*, 243–255.

Erber, J. (1982). Movement learning of free flying honeybees. *Journal of Comparative Physiology, 146*, 273–282.

Erber, J., Homberg, U. & Gronenberg, W. (1987). Functional roles of the mushroom bodies in insects. In A. P. Gupta (Ed.), *Arthropod brain, its evolution, development, structure, and functions* (pp. 485–511). New York: John Wiley & Sons.

Erber, J., Masuhr, T. & Menzel, R. (1980). Localization of short-term memory in the brain of the bee, *Apis mellifera. Physiological Entomology, 5*, 343–358.

Esch, H. (1961). Über die Schallerzeugung beim Werbetanz der Honigbiene. *Zeitschrift für vergleichende Physiologie, 45*, 1–11.

Evans, P. D. (1980). Biogenic amines in the insect nervous system. In M. J. Berridge, J. E. Treherne & V. B. Wigglesworth (Eds.), *Advances in insect physiology*—Vol. 15 (pp. 317–473). New York: Academic Press.

Fabre (1879). Souvenirs entomologiques (Paris).

Fischer, J. (1973). Verhaltensphysiologische Untersuchungen zur Frage der dynamischen Übertagungseigenschaften der Photorezeptoren bei der Honigbiene. Staatsexamensarbeit Zoologie, TH Darmstadt.

Forel, A. (1910). Das Sinnesleben der Insekten. München, Reinhardt.

Frings, H. (1944). The loci of olfactory end-organs in the honey-bee, *Apis mellifera* Linn. *Journal of Experimental Zoology, 88*, 65–93.

Frisch, B. (1987). Articipation of feeding time in honey bees. In J. Eder & H. Rembold (Eds.), *Chemistry and Biology of Social Insects*. München, J. Peperny.

Frisch, B. & Aschoff, J. (1987). Circadian rhythms in honeybees, entrainment by feeding cycles. *Physiology and Entomology, 12*, 41–49.

Frost, W. N., Clark, G. A. & Kandel, E. R. (1988). Parallel processing of short term memory for sensitization in *Aplysia. Journal of Neurobiology, 19*, 297–334.

Goelet, P., Castellucci, V. F., Schacher, S. & Kandel, E. R. (1986). The long and the short of long-term memory—a molecular framework. *Nature, 322*, 419–422.

Gontarski, H. (1950). Betäubungsmittel und ihre Wirkung auf Königinnen und Arbeitsbienen. *Bienenzucht, 3*, 393–401.

Gould, J. L. (1984). The natural history of honey bee learning. In P. Marler & H. Terrace (Eds.), *The biology of learning* (pp. 149–180). Berlin: Springer Verlag.

Gould, J. L. (1985). How bees remember flower shapes. *Science, 227*, 1492–1494.

Gould, J. L. (1986a). The biology of learning. *Annual Review of Psychology, 37*, 163–192.

Gould, J. L. (1986b). Pattern learning by honey bees. *Animal Behavior, 34*, 990–997.

Gould, J. L. (1986c). The local map of honey bees, Do insects have cognitive maps?. *Science, 232*, 861–863.

Gould, J. L. & Gould, C. G. (1982). The insect mind: physics or metaphysics? In D. R. Griffin (Ed.), *Animal Mind*, Dahlem-Konferenzen (pp. 269–298). Berlin: Springer Verlag.

Gould, J. L. & Marler, P. (1984). Ethology and the natural history of learning. In P. Marler & H. S. Terrace (Eds.), *The biology of learning* (pp. 47–74). Berlin: Springer Verlag.

Gould, J. L. & Marler, P. (1987). Learning by instinct. *Scientific American, 255*, 74–85.

Griffin, D. R. (1984). Animal Thinking. Cambridge, Harvard University Press.

Grossmann, K. (1970). Erlernen von Farbreizen an der Futterquelle durch Honigbienen während des Anfluges und während des Saugens. *Zeitschrift für Tierpsychologie, 27*, 553–562.

Grossmann, K. E. (1971). Belohnungsverzögerung beim Erlernen einer Farbe an einer künstlichen Futterstelle durch Honigbienen. *Zeitschrift für Tierpsychologie, 29*, 28–41.

Grossmann, K. E. (1973). Continuous, fixed-ratio, and fixed-interval reinforcement in honey bees. *Journal of Experimental Analysis of Behavior, 20*, 105–109.

Hawkins, R. D. & Kandel, E. R. (1984). Is there a cell-biological alphabet for simple forms of learning? *Psychological Review, 91*, 375–391.

Hebb, D. (1949). The organization of behaviour. New York: John Wiley.

Heinrich, B. (1976). The foraging specializations of individual bumblebees. *Ecological Monograph, 46*, 105–128.

Heinrich, B. (1979a). Resource heterogeneity and patterns of movement in foraging bumblebees. *Öcologia, 40*, 235–245.

Heinrich, B. (1979b). "Majoring" and "minoring" by foraging bumblebees, *Bombus vagans*, an experimental analysis. *Ecology, 60*, 245–255.

Heinrich, B. (1984). Learning in invertebrates. In P. Marler & H. S. Terrace (Eds.), *The biology of learning* (Dahlem Konferenzen) (pp. 135–147). Berlin: Springer Verlag.

Heran, H. (1963). Wie beeinflußt eine zusätzliche Last die Fluggeschwindigkeit der Honigbiene?. *Verhandlungen der Deutschen Zoologischen Gesellschaft Wien, 26*, 346–354.

Hertz, M. (1934). Eine Bienendressur auf Wasser. *Zeitschrift für vergleichende Physiologie, 21*, 463–467.

Hertz, M. (1939). New experiments on color vision in bees. *Journal of experimental Biology, 16*, 1–8.

Hörmann, M. (1934). Über den Helligkeitssinn der Bienen. *Zeitschrift für vergleichende Physiologie, 21*, 188–219.

Howse, P. E. (1974). Design and function in the insect brain. In L. Barton-Brown (Eds.), *Experimental Analysis of Insect Behaviour* (pp. 180–194). Berlin, New York: Springer Verlag.

Hull, C. L. (1943). Principles of behaviour. New York: Appleton-Century-Crofts.

Inouye, D. W. (1978). Resource partitioning in bumblebees, experimental studies of foraging behavior. *Ecology, 59*, 672–678.

Jordan, R. (1952). Erfahrungen mit Lachgas. *Alpenländer Bienenzeitschrift, 38*, 367–370.

Kalmus, H. (1937). Vorversuche über die Orientierung der Biene im Stock. *Zeitschrift für vergleichende Physiologie, 24*, 166–187.

Kamin, L. J. (1968). Attention-like processes in classical conditioning. In M. R. Jones (Ed.), *Miami Symp. Predictability, Behavior and Aversive Stimultion* (pp. 9–32). Miami: University Miami Press.

Kandel, E. R. (1976). Cellular basis of behavior—an introduction to behavioral neurobiology (pp. 1–727). San Francisco: W. H. Freeman.

Kevan, P. G. & Lane, M. A. (1985). Flower petal microtexture is a tactile cue for bees. *Proceedings of the National Academy of Science, 82,* 1203–1206.

Klatzky, R. L. (1980). Human Memory—Structures and Processes (2nd ed.). San Francisco: W. H. Freeman.

Kleber, E. (1935). Hat das Zeitgedächtnis der Bienen biologische Bedeutung?. *Zeitschrift für vergleichende Physiologie, 22,* 221–262.

Koltermann, R. (1969). Lern- und Vergessensprozesse bei der Honigbiene—aufgezeigt anhand von Duftdressuren. *Zeitschrift für vergleichende Physiologie, 63,* 310–334.

Koltermann, R. (1971). 24-Std-Periodik in der Langzeiterinnerung an Duft- und Farbsignale bei der Honigbiene. *Zeitschrift für vergleichende Physiologie, 75,* 49–68.

Koltermann, R. (1973a). Retroaktive Hemmung nach sukzessiver Informationseingabe bei *Apis mellifica* und *Apis cerana* (Apidä). *Journal of Comparative Physiology, 84,* 299–310.

Koltermann, R. (1973b). Rassen- bzw. artspezifische Duftbewertung bei der Honigbiene und ökologische Adaptation. *Journal of Comparative Physiology, 85,* 327–360.

Kreißl, S. & Bicker, G. (in press). Histochemistry of acetylcholine-esterase and immunocytochemistry of an acetylcholine receptor—like immunoreaction in the honey bee brain. *Journal of Comparative Neurology.*

Kriston, I. (1971). Zum Problem des Lernverhaltens von *Apis mellifica L.* gegenüber verschiedenen Duftstoffen. *Zeitschrift für vergleichende Physiologie, 74,* 169–189.

Kriston, I. (1973). Zum Zusammenhang zwischen Signalbewertung und Lernprozeß, Die Bewertung von Duft- und Farbsignalen an der Futterstelle durch *Apis mellifica. Journal of Comparative Physiology, 84,* 77–94.

Kugler, H. (1943). Hummeln als Blütensucher. Ein Beitrag zur experimentellen Blütenökologie. *Ergebnisse der Biologie, 19,* 143–323.

Kunze, G. (1933). Einige Versuche über den Antennengeschmackssinn der Honigbiene. *Zoologisches Jahrbuch, 52,* 389–560.

Kuwabara, M. (1957). Bildung des bedingten Reflexes von Pavlovs Typus bei der Honigbiene, *Apis mellifica. Journal of the Faculty of Science,* Hokkaido University, Serie VI Zool., *13,* 458–464.

Kuwabara, M. & Takeda, K. (1956). On the hygroreceptor of the honeybee. *Physiology and Ecology, 7,* 1–6.

Laverty, T. M. (1980). Bumble bee foraging, floral complexity and learning. *Canadian Journal of Zoology, 58,* 1324–1335.

Laverty, T. M. & Plowright, R. C. (1988). Acquisition of handling skills on a complex flower, behavioural differences between specialist and generalist bumble bee species. *Animal Behavior, 36,* 733–740.

Lindauer, M. (1955). Schwarmbienen auf Wohnungssuche. *Zeitschrift für vergleichende Physiologie, 37,* 263–324.

Lindauer, M. (1959). Angeborene und erlernte Komponenten in der Sonnenorientierung der Bienen. *Zeitschrift für vergleichende Physiologie, 42,* 43–62.

Lindauer, M. (1963). Allgemeine Sinnesphysiologie. Orientierung im Raum. *Fortschritte der Zoologie, 16,* 58–140.

Lindauer, M. (1970). Lernen und Gedächtnis—Versuche an der Honigbiene. *Naturwissenschaften, 57,* 463–467.

Lindauer, M. & Martin, H. (1972). Magnetic effect on dancing bees. In S. R. Galler (Ed.), Symposium NASA SP-262, *Animal Orientation and Navigation* (pp. 559–567). Washington D.C., US Government Printing Office.

Lisman, J. E. (1985). A mechanism for memory storage insensitive to molecular turnover. A bistable autophosphorylating kinase. *Proceedings of the National Academy of Science, 82,* 3055–3057.

Lubbock, J. (1883). Ameisen, Bienen und Wespen. Leipzig.

Lumsden, C. J. (1982). The social regulation of physical caste. The superorganism revived. *Journal of theoretical Biology, 95,* 749–781.

MacMillan, C. S. & Mercer, A. R. (1987). An investigation of the role of dopamine in the antennal lobes of the honey bee. *Journal of Comparative Physiology, 160,* 359–366.

Markl, H. (1966a). Schwerkraftdressuren an Honigbienen II. Die Rolle der schwererezeptorischen Borstenfelder verschiedener Gelenke für die Schwerekompassorientierung. *Zeitschrift für vergleichende Physiologie, 53,* 353–371.

Markl, H. (1966b). Schwerkraftdressuren an Honigbienen I. Die geomenotaktische Fehlorientierung. *Zeitschrift für vergleichende Physiologie, 53,* 328–352.

Markl, H. (1973). Leistungen des Vibrationssinnes bei wirbellosen Tieren. *Fortschritte der Zoologie, 21,* 100–120.

Markl, H. (1974). The perception of gravity and of angular acceleration in invertebrates. In H. H. Kornhuber (Ed.), *Handbook of sensory physiology* (pp. 17–74). Berlin: Springer Verlag.

Markl, H. (1985). Manipulation, modulation, information, cognition, some of the riddles of communication. *Experimental Behavioral Ecology, 31,* 163–194.

Markl, H. (1987). Soziale Systeme als kognitive Systeme—Zur Anpassungsleistung sozialer Organisation bei Tieren. *Rheinische Westfälische Akademie der Wissenschaften*—Vorträge, *354,* 35–71.

Martin, H. (1965). Leistungen des topochemischen Sinnes bei der Honigbiene. *Zeitschrift für vergleichende Physiologie, 50,* 254–292.

Martin, H. & Lindauer, M. (1966). Sinnesphysiologische Leistungen beim Wabenbau der Honigbiene. *Zeitschrift für vergleichende Physiologie, 53,* 372–404.

Martinez, J. L. (1986). Memory, drugs and hormones. In J. L. Martinez & R. P. Kesner (Eds.), *Learning and memory—A biological view* (pp. 127–164). Orlando: Academic Press.

Masson, C. & Arnold, G. (1987). Organization and plasticity of the olfactory system of the honeybee, *Apis mellifera.* In R. Menzel & A. Mercer (Eds.), *Neurobiology and behavior of honeybees* (pp. 280–295). Berlin: Springer Verlag.

Masuhr, T. (1976). Lokalisation und Funktion des Kurzzeit-gedächtnisses der Honigbiene, *Apis mellifica,* Dissertation, TH Darmstadt.

Masuhr, T. & Menzel, R. (1972). Learning experiments on the use of sidespecific information in the olfactory and visual system in the honeybee of *Apis mellifica.* In R. Wehner (Ed.), *Information processing in the visual systems of Arthropods* (pp. 315–322). Berlin: Springer Verlag.

Mautz, D. (1971). Der Kommunikationseffekt der Schwänzeltänze. *Zeitschrift für vergleichende Physiologie, 72,* 197–220.

Medugorac, I. (1967). Orientierung der Bienen in Raum und Zeit nach Dauernarkose. *Zeitschrift für Bienenforschung, 9,* 104–119.

Meineke, H. (1978). Umlernen einer Honigbiene zwischen gelb- und blau-Belohnung im Dauerversuch. *Journal of Insect Physiology, 24,* 155–163.

Menzel, R. (1967). Das Erlernen von Spektralfarben durch die Honigbiene. *Zeitschrift für vergleichende Physiologie, 56,* 22–62.

Meznel, R. (1968). Das Gedächtnis der Honigbiene für Spektralbarben. I. Kurzzeitiges und langzeitiges Behalten. *Zeitschrift für vergleichende Physiologie, 60,* 82–102.

Menzel, R. (1969). Das Gedächtnis der Honigbiene für Spektralfarben. II. Umlernen und Mehrfachlernen. *Zeitschrift für vergleichende Physiologie, 63,* 290–309.

Menzel, R. (1979). Behavioural access to short-term memory in bees. *Nature, 281,* 368–369.

Menzel, R. (1985). Learning in honey bees in an ecological and behavioral context. In B. Hölldobler & M. Lindauer (Eds.), *Experimental behavioral ecology* (pp. 55–74). Stuttgart: Gustav Fischer Verlag.

Menzel, R. (1987). Memory traces in honeybees. In R. Menzel & A. Mercer (Eds.), *Neurobiology and behavior of honeybees* (pp. 310–325). Berlin: Springer Verlag.

Menzel, R. (1989). "Bee-havior" in the course Neural System and Behavior. In T. J. Carew & D. Kelley (Eds.), *Perspectives in Neural Systems and Behavior*, New York: A. R. Liss.

Menzel, R. & Bicker, G. (1987). Plasticity in neuronal circuits and assemblies of invertebrates. In J. P. Changeux & M. Konishi (Eds.), *The neural and molecular basis of learning* (Dahlem-Konferenzen) (pp. 433–472), John Wiley.

Menzel, R. & Erber, J. (1972). The influence of the quantity of reward on the learning performance in honeybees. *Behavior, 41*, 27–42.

Menzel, R., Erber, J. & Masuhr, T. (1974). Learning and memory in the honeybee. In L. Barton-Browne (Ed.), *Experimental analysis of insect behaviour* (pp. 195–217). Berlin: Springer Verlag.

Menzel, R., Michelsen, B., Rüffer, P. & Sugawa, M. (1988). Neuropharmacology of learning and memory in honey bees. In G. Herting & H. C. Spatz (Eds.), *Synaptic transmission and plasticity in nervous systems* (pp. 335–350). Berlin: Springer Verlag.

Menzel, R. & Sugawa, M. (1986). Time course of short-term memory depends on associative events. *Naturwissenschaften, 73*, 564–565.

Mercer, A. & Menzel, R. (1982). The effect of biogenic amines on conditioned and unconditioned responses to olfactory stimuli in the honey bee, *Apis mellifica. Journal of Comparative Physiology, 145*, 363–368.

Mercer, A., Mobbs, P. G., Evans, P. D. & Davenport, A. (1983). Biogenic amines in the brain of the honey bee, *Apis mellifera. Cell and Tissue Research, 234*, 655–677.

Michelsen, A., Towne, W. F., Kirchner, W. H. & Kryger, P. (1987). The acoustic near field of a dancing honeybee. *Journal of Comparative Physiology A, 161*, 633–643.

Michelsen, D. B. (1987). Neuropharmakologische Untersuchungen zum Lernverhalten der Honigbiene *(Apis mellifera)*. Dissertation, Freie Universität Berlin.

Michelsen, D. B. (1988). Catecholamines affect storage and retrieval of conditioned odour stimuli in honey bees. *Comparative Biochemistry and Physiology, 91c*, 479–482.

Minnich, D. E. (1932). The contact chemoreceptors of the honey bee *Apis mellifera. Journal of Experimental Zoology, 61*, 375–393.

Moore, D. & Rankin, A. A. (1983). Diurnal changes in the accuracy of the honey bee foraging rhythm. *Biological Bulletin, 164*, 471–482.

Mühlen, W. (1984). Untersuchungen zur Lernkapazität von *Apis mellifera* L. für Farben. *Verhandlungen der Deutschen Zoologischen Gesellschaft, 77*, 252–252.

Mühlen, W. (1987). Untersuchungen zum visuellen, olfaktorischen und haptischen Unterscheidungslernen bei der Orientierung von *Apis mellifera*. Dissertation, University Münster (pp. 145).

Müller, G. E. & Pilzecker, A. (1900). Experimentelle Beiträge zur Lehre vom Gedächtnis. *Zeitschrift für Psychologie, 1*, 1–288.

Müller, H. (1873). Die Befruchtung der Blumen durch Insekten und die gegenseitigen Anpassungen beider. Leipzig.

Müller, H. (1882). Versuche über die Farbenliebhaberei der Honigbiene. *Kosmos, 12*, 273–299.

Nunez, J. A. & Denti, A. (1970). Repuesta de abejas recolectoras a un estimulo nociceptive. *Acta Physiologica Latimo Americana, 20*, 140–146.

Opfinger, E. (1931). Über die Orientierung der Biene an der Futterquelle. *Zeitschrift für vergleichende Physiologie, 15*, 432–487.

Pankiew, P. (1967). Study of honey bee preference and behaviour on normal and standardless alfalfa flowers. *Journal of Apicultural Research, 6*, 105–112.

Pleasants, J. M. (1981). Bumblebee response to variation in nectar availability. *Ecology, 62*, 1648–1661.

Quinn, W. G. (1984). Work in invertebrates on the mechanisms underlying learning. In P. Marler & H. S. Terrace (Eds.), *The biology of learning* (pp. 197–246). Heidelberg, New York, Springer Verlag.

Rescorla, R. A. (1988). Behavioral studies of pavlovian conditioning. *Annual Review of Neuroscience, 11*, 329–352.

Rescorla, R. A. & Wagner, A. R. (1972). A theory of classical conditioning, variations in the effectiveness of reinforcement and non-reinforcement. In A. H. Black & W. F. Prokasy (Eds), *Classical conditioning II, Current research and theory*, (pp. 64–99). New York: Appleton-Century-Crofts.

Ribbands, C. R. (1950). Changes in the behaviour of honey-bees following their recovery from anesthesia. *Journal of experimental Biology, 27*, 302–310.

Rösch-Berger, K. (1933). Das Gedächtnis der Bienen nach der Narkose. *Zeitschrift für vergleichende Physiologie, 18*, 474–480.

Schäfer, S. & Rehder, V. (1989). Dopamine-like immunoreactivity in the brain and suboesophageal ganglion of the honey bee. *Journal of Comparative Neurology* (in press).

Schäfer, S. & Bicker, G. (1986). Common projection areas of 5-HT- and GABA Like immunoreactive fibres in the visual system of the honeabee. *Brain Research, 380*, 368–370.

Schmid, J. (1964). Zur Frage der Störung des Bienengedächtnisses durch Narkosemittel, zugleich ein Beitrag zur Störung der sozialen Bindung durch Narkose. *Zeitschrift für vergleichende Physiologie, 47*, 559–595.

Schmid-Hempel, P. (1984). The importance handling time for the flight directionality in bees. *Behavioral Ecology and Sociobiology, 15*, 303–309.

Seeley, T. (1977). Measurement of nest cavity volume by the honey bee (*Apis mellifera.*) *Behavioral Ecology and Sociobiology, 2*, 201–227.

Seeley, T. D. (1985a). The information-center strategy of honeybee foraging. *Fortschritte der Zoologie, 31*, 75–90.

Seeley, T. D. (1985b). Honeybee ecology. A study of adaptation in social life. Princeton University Press.

Seeley, T. D. & Levin, R. A. (1987). Social foraging by honeybees, how a colony tracks rich sources of nectar. In R. Menzel & A. Mercer (Eds.), *Neurobiology and behavior of honeybees* (pp. 38–53). Berlin: Springer Verlag.

Skinner, B. F. (1938). The behavior of organisms. New York, Appleton-Century-Crofts.

Smith, B. H. & Menzel, R. (in preparation). The content of short-term and long-term memory of odorants in the honey bee.

Sprengel, C. K. (1793). Das entdeckte Geheimnis der Natur im Bau und in der Befruchtung der Blumen. Berlin.

Squire, L. & Cohen, N. (1982). Remote memory, retrograde amnesia, and the neuropsychology of memory. In L. S. Cermak (Ed.), *Human memory and amnesia*. Hillsdale: Lawrence Erlbaum.

Sugawa, M. (1986). Zeitliche Dynamik und Lokalisation des Engrammes im Honigbienengehirn (*Apis mellifera*)—Diploma Thesis, TU Berlin Berlin.

Sugawa, M. & Menzel, R. (1986). Zeitliche Dynamik und Lokalisation der Gedächtniskonsolidierung bei der Biene. In N. Elsner & W. Rathmayer (Eds.), *Sensomotorik identifizierter Neuronen* (pp. 174–174). Stuttgart: Thieme Verlag.

Takeda, K. (1961). Classical conditioned response in the honey bee. *Journal of Insect Physiology, 6*, 168–179.

Tinbergen, N. (1932). Über die Orientierung des Bienenwolfes. *Zeitschrift für vergleichende Physiologie, 16*, 305–334.

Tirala, L. (1923). Über den Einfluß der Äthernarkose auf die Heimkehrfähigkeit der Bienen. *Naunyn-Schmiedebergs Archiv für experimentelle Pathologie und Pharmakologie, 97*, 433–440.

Tully, T. (1988). On the road to a better understanding of learning and memory in Drosophila melanogaster. In G. Herting & H. Spatz (Eds.), *Modulation of synaptic transmission and plasticity in nervous systems* (pp. 401–417). Berlin: Springer Verlag.

Turanska, V. M. (1973). The brain and behaviour of the bees. *Pcelovodstov, 9*, 17–19.

Vareschi, E. (1971). Duftunterscheidung bei der Honigbiene-Einzelzell-Ableitungen und Verhaltensreaktionen. *Zeitschrift für vergleichende Physiologie, 75*, 143–173.

Vogt, P. (1969). Dressur von Sammelbienen auf sinusförmig moduliertes Flimmerlicht. *Zeitschrift für vergleichende Physiologie, 63*, 182–203.

van Iersel, J. J. & van Assem, J. den (1965). Aspects of orientation in the diggerwasp Bembix rostrata. *Animal Behavior, 1,* 145–162.

von Frisch, K. (1914). Der Farbensinn und Fomensinn der Biene. *Zoologisches Jahrbuch Teil Physiologie, 35,* 1–188.

von Frisch, K. (1921). Über den Sitz des Geruchssinnes bei Insekten. *Zoologisches Jahrbuch Teil Physiologie, 38,* 1–68.

von Frisch, K. (1922). Methoden sinnesphysiologischer und psychologischer Untersuchungen an Bienen. In E. Abderhalden (Ed.), *Handbuch der biologischen Arbeitsmethoden,* Abt. VI, Teil D. Berlin, Wien, Urban und Schwarzenberg.

von Frisch, K. (1934). Über den Geschmackssinn der Bienen. *Zeitschrift für vergleichende Physiologie, 21,* 1–156.

von Frisch, K. (1967). The dance language and orientation of bees. Cambridge, Harvard University Press.

von Frisch, K. & von Frisch, O. (1974). Tiere als Baumeister. Frankfurt, Ullstein.

von Hess, C. (1913). Experimentelle Untersuchungen über den angeblichen Farbensinn von Bienen. *Zoologisches Jahrbuch Teil Physiologie, 34,* 81–106.

von Hess, C. (1918). Beiträge zur Frage nach einem Farbensehen bei Bienen. *Archiv der gesamten Physiologie, 170,* 337–366.

von Oelsen, G. & Rademacher, E. (1979). Untersuchungen zum Bauverhalten der Honigbiene (*Apis mellifera*). *Apidologie, 10,* 175–209.

Voskresenskaya, A. K. (1957). On the role played by the fungoid bodies of the supräsophageal ganglion in conditioned reflexes of the honeybee. *Dokl. Akad. Nank. SSSR, 112,* 964–967.

Waddington, K. D. (1980). Flight patterns of foraging bees relative to density of artificial flowers and distribution of nectar. *Öcologia, 44,* 199–204.

Waddington, K. D., Allen, T. & Heinrich, B. (1981). Floral preferences of bumblebees (*Bombus Edwardsii*) in relation to intermittent versus continuous rewards. *Animal Behavior, 29,* 779–784.

Wahl, O. (1932). Neue Untersuchungen über das Zeitgedächtnis der Bienen. *Zeitschrift für vergleichende Physiologie, 16,* 529–589.

Walker, M. M. & Bitterman, M. E. (1985). Conditioned responding to magnetic fields by honeybees. *Journal of Comparative Physiology, 157,* 67–71.

Waser, N. M. (1983). The adaptive nature of floral traits, Ideas and evidence. In L. A. Real (Ed.), *Pollination biology* (pp. 241–285). New York: Academic Press.

Wehner, R. (1971). The generalization of directional visual stimuli in the honey bee, *Apis mellifera*. *Journal of Insect Physiology, 17,* 1579–1591.

Wehner, R. (1981). Spatial vision in arthropods. In H. Autrum (Ed.), *Handbook of Sensory Physiology* VIc (pp. 287–616). Berlin, Heidelberg, New York: Springer Verlag.

Wehner, R. & Menzel, R. (in press). Maps and orientation in bees. *Annual Revies of Neuroscience.*

Weiskrantz, L. (1970). A long-term view of short-term memory in psychology. In G. Horn & R. A. Hinde (Eds.), *Short-term memory in psychology* (pp. 63–74). London: Cambridge University Press.

Weiss, K. (1953). Versuche mit Bienen und Wespen in farbigen Labyrinthen. *Zeitschrift für Tierpsychologie, 10,* 29–44.

Weiss, K. (1954). Der Lernvorgang bei einfachen Labyrinthdressuren von Bienen und Wespen. *Zeitschrift für vergleichende Physiologie, 36,* 9-20-531-542.

Weiss, K. (1957). Zur Gedächtnisleistung von Wespen. *Zeitschrift für vergleichende Physiologie, 39,* 660–693.

Wilson, E. O. (1985). The principles of caste evolution. *Experimental Behavioral Ecology, 31,* 307–324.

10 Learning and Memory in *Aplysia* and Other Invertebrates

John H. Byrne
University of Texas Medical School at Houston

Invertebrates are particularly useful for analyzing the neural and molecular events underlying learning. The nervous systems of many invertebrates contain only several thousand cells (compared with the billions of cells in the vertebrate nervous system). Despite the small number of cells, an invertebrate ganglion can control a variety of different behaviors. A given behavior may therefore be mediated by 100 neurons or less, and this small size of the circuit makes complete description easier. Moreover, many neurons are relatively large and can be repeatedly identified as unique individuals, permitting one to examine the functional properties of an individual cell and to relate those properties to a specific behavior mediated by the cell. Changes in cellular properties that occur when a behavior is modified by learning can then be related to specific changes in behavior. Molecular and biophysical events underlying the changes in cellular properties can then be determined.

Many investigators interested in a cellular analysis of learning have employed both nonassociative and associative learning paradigms. Associative learning involves a wide range of behavioral modifications, and two that have been extensively studied are classical conditioning and operant conditioning. In both, two events are temporarily paired. In contrast, nonassociative learning is not dependent on pairing. Examples of this form of learning are habituation and sensitization. Habituation, perhaps the simplest form of nonassociative learning, refers to a decrement of responsiveness due to repetition of a stimulus. It is generally distinguished from simple fatigue because responsiveness can be rapidly restored (dishabituated) by the presentation of a novel stimulus to the animal. Sensitization is also a form of nonassociative learning and refers to the enhancement of a behavioral response as a result of applying a novel stimulus to the animal. One example of associative learning that has been examined extensively is classical or Pavlovian conditioning. In classical conditioning, a test stimulus (known as the conditioned stimulus, CS) becomes effective in eliciting a response (the conditioned response, CR) when the CS is paired with another stimulus (the reinforcing or unconditioned stimulus, US) that reliably produces a response (the unconditioned response, US). Operant conditioning, or instrumental conditioning, is also a form of associative learning, but it differs from classical conditioning in that during this training procedure the reinforcing stimulus is contingent on the performance of a behavior produced by the animal rather than on a CS delivered by the experimenter. As a result, the animal learns the consequences of its own behavior and alters that behavior as a result of training.

This chapter surveys briefly the capabilities of several selected invertebrates for nonassociative and associative learning. The selection was somewhat arbitrary but was guided, at least in part, by their suitability for mechanistic analyses. A detailed description of cellular studies is provided for one invertebrate, the marine mollusc *Aplysia,* for which significant progress has been made in elucidating the neural and molecular mechanisms underlying simple examples of nonassociative and associative learning.

ASSOCIATIVE AND NONASSOCIATIVE MODIFICATIONS OF DEFENSIVE SIPHON AND TAIL WITHDRAWAL REFLEXES IN APLYSIA

The neuronal mechanisms contributing to nonassociative and associative learning have been analyzed extensively in two defensive behaviors of *Aplysia*; the siphon and gill withdrawal reflex elicited by stimulation of the siphon, and the siphon and tail withdrawal reflex elicited by stimulation of the tail (for reviews, see Byrne, 1985, 1987; Carew, 1987; Hawkins, Clark & Kandel, 1986b; Kandel & Schwartz, 1982). Of the various sites in the neural circuits for these behaviors, the sensory neurons that mediate these reflexes appear particularly susceptible to modulation through a variety of cellular mechanisms. I first review some of the behavioral studies and then discuss the current understanding of the underlying neuronal mechanisms.

Behavioral Studies

Non-Associative Learning.   A tactile stimulus to the siphon (a protruding funnel-like structure on the dorsal surface of the animal) causes a reflex withdrawal of the siphon and gill that presumably serves a defensive role to protect the sensitive gill and siphon from potentially harmful stimuli. With repeated stimulation, the reflex undergoes both short- and long-term habituation (Carew, Pinsker, & Kandel, 1972; Pinsker, Kupfermann, Castellucci, & Kandel, 1970).

Restoration of a habituated response or sensitization of a nonhabituated response can be produced by applying a noxious stimulus to the head or tail (Carew, Castellucci, & Kandel, 1971; Pinsker et al., 1970). Short-term sensitization, lasting minutes to hours (Pinsker et al., 1970), and long-term sensitization, lasting days to weeks (Pinsker, Hening, Carew, & Kandel, 1973), have been demonstrated.

Scholz and Byrne (1987) examined the effects of long-term sensitization training on withdrawal of the siphon elicited by stimulation of the tail. Both sides of each *Aplysia* were initially tested by the delivery of weak electric shock to the posterior part of the body wall. The test stimuli produced a coordinated set of defensive responses, including reflex withdrawal of the tail and siphon. Changes in the siphon response relative to pretest responses were used as a measure of sensitization. Immediately after initial testing, one randomly chosen side of the animal was subjected to sensitization training over a 2-hour period. The reflex on the side that received the training procedure was significantly enhanced for at least 24 hours after training.

Associative Learning.   Carew, Walters, and Kandel (1981) examined associative learning of the reflex withdrawal of siphon elicited by stimulation of the siphon. The CS was a brief weak tactile stimulus to the siphon, which by itself produced a small siphon withdrawal. The US was a short-duration strong (noxious) electric shock to the tail, which by itself produced a large withdrawal of the siphon. Paired stimuli were presented every 5 minutes. After 15 pairings, the ability of the CS to produce siphon withdrawal (the CR) was enhanced beyond that produced by presentations of the US alone (sensitization control) or explicitly unpaired or random presentations of the CS and US (Carew et al., 1981). The conditioning persisted for as long as 4 days. Carew, Hawkins, and Kandel (1983) also found that this reflex exhibited differential classical conditioning. Differential associative learning could be produced by delivering one CS to the siphon and another to the mantle region, or by delivering the CS+ and CS− to different parts of the siphon (Carew et al., 1983). As in the previous studies, the US was an electric shock delivered to the tail. Additional parametric features of the associative conditioning have been analyzed (Hawkins, Carew, & Kandel, 1986a). Associative learning of the gill-withdrawal reflex has also been demonstrated in a reduced preparation consisting of the isolated siphon, mantle, gill, and abdominal ganglion (Lukowiak, 1986; Lukowiak & Sahley, 1981).

Neural Mechanisms of Short-Term Nonassociative Learning in *Aplysia:* Habituation, Dishabituation, and Sensitization

Short-term habituation (lasting minutes) of the withdrawal of the gill and siphon elicited by stimulation of the siphon is paralleled by a decrease in the amount of neurotransmitter release from the presynaptic terminals of the sensory neurons. Because the amount of transmitter release determines the level of excitatory drive to the motor neurons, a decrease in the release of transmitter leads to progressively less activation of the motor neurons and a decremented behavioral response (Byrne, 1982; Byrne, Castellucci, & Kandel, 1978; Castellucci & Kandel, 1974; Castellucci, Pinsker, Kupferman, & Kandel, 1970; Kupfermann, Castellucci, Pinsker, & Kandel, 1970). (For an introductory discussion of synaptic transmission, see Byrne & Schultz, 1988.) At the mechanistic level, synaptic depression is due at least in part to cumulative inactivation of the sensory neuron Ca^{2+} current (Klein, Shapiro, & Kandel, 1980) and depletion of neurotransmitter (Bailey & Chen, 1988b; Gingrich & Byrne, 1985, 1987). Thus, there is both less Ca^{2+} to cause the release of transmitter and less transmitter available to be released.

The sensory neurons are also a cellular locus for dishabituation and sensitization. Dishabituation and sensitization have been associated with increased transmitter release from the presynaptic terminals of the sensory neurons (presynaptic facilitation) (Carew et al., 1971; Castellucci & Kandel, 1976; Castellucci et al., 1970). Presynaptic facilitation is due at least in part to a cAMP-dependent reduction in a membrane K^+ currents (Fig. 10.1) (Baxter & Byrne, 1987, 1989; Klein & Kandel, 1978, 1980; Klein et al., 1980; Walsh & Byrne, 1989). Because K^+ currents are reduced, the action potential in the sensory neurons will be broader, allowing Ca^{2+} influx to occur for a longer period of time. Enhanced Ca^{2+} influx leads to enhanced release of transmitter. Mobilization of transmitter also appears to occur as a result of sensitizing stimuli (Gingrich & Byrne, 1985, 1987; Gingrich, Baxter, & Byrne, 1988; Hochner, Klein, Schacher, & Kandel, 1986). Thus, release is enhanced not only because of the greater Ca^{2+} influx but also because more transmitter is available to be released as a consequence of mobilization. The enhanced release leads to enhanced activation of motor neurons and an enhanced behavioral response. The presynaptic facilitation produced by sensitizing stimuli can be mimicked by application of the neurotransmitter serotonin (Kandel & Schwartz, 1982).

Neural Mechanisms of Long-Term Habituation and Sensitization in *Aplysia*

A neural analogue of long-term habituation training was used as a first step to study the mechanisms underlying long-term habituation of the siphon- and gill-withdrawal reflex elicited by stimulation of the siphon (Carew & Kandel, 1973). The complex excitatory postsynaptic potential (EPSP) in gill motor neurons was used as an analogue of the behavioral response, whereas repeated electrical stimulation of a peripheral nerve was used as an analogue of stimulation of the siphon. Twenty-four hours after the training, the EPSPs from the stimulated nerve were significantly reduced compared with those from a control nerve that did not

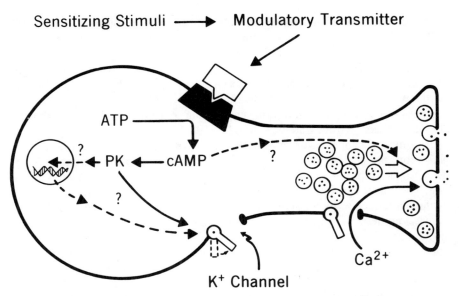

FIG. 10.1. Model of heterosynaptic facilitation that contributes to short- and long-term sensitization in *Aplysia* (see text for details).

receive the habituation training. These results indicate that long-term habituation, like short-term habituation, is due to decreased synaptic drive in motor neurons. In addition to these *in vitro* analog experiments, electrophysiological and morphological correlates of the long-term habituation and sensitization have been found. Castellucci, Carew, and Kandel (1978) examined the connections between sensory neurons and motor neurons in abdominal ganglia taken from *Aplysia* that received long-term habituation training. They found that such training procedures produced a profound depression in the efficacy of synaptic transmission compared with controls. Frost, Castellucci, Hawkins, and Kandel (1985) found that long-term sensitization was correlated with an enhancement of the connections between sensory neurons and motor neurons. These results indicate that the same plastic site (i.e., the sensory neuron) that is modified during short-term habituation and sensitization is also modified during long-term habituation and sensitization. Ultrastructural studies indicate that at least part of the change in synaptic efficacy is due to changes in the structure of the sensory neuron synapse (Bailey & Chen, 1983). For example, the number, size, and vesicle complement of active zones of sensory neurons were larger after long-term sensitization training than in controls. In addition, the total number of varicosities is also increased (Bailey & Chen, 1988a). Conversely, these parameters were smaller in animals after long-term habituation training. Thus, structural changes are correlated with the behavioral modifications, and these changes can be detected at critical synapses involved in the learning.

Long-term sensitization of the tail- and siphon-withdrawal reflex elicited by tail stimulation have also been described (Scholz & Byrne, 1987; Walters, 1987). Stimulation of the tail activates sensory neurons that have receptors in the tail and somata in the pleural ganglia. This stimulation leads to reflex withdrawal of both the tail and the siphon. These tail sensory neurons serve as the first central relay of the response pathway, and they had been shown to be a cellular locus for the changes that accompany short-term sensitization of the reflex (Walters & Byrne, 1983a; Walters, Byrne, Carew, & Kandel, 1983b).

In order to gain insights into the locus and mechanisms for long-term sensitization, tail sensory neurons were voltage-clamped, and the current–voltage (I–V) relationship of each cell was examined 24 hours after sensitization training. The consequences of long-term sensitization training in the sensory neurons include a reduction in net outward membrane current (Scholz & Byrne, 1987). Thus, long-term sensitization, like short-term sensitization (Klein & Kandel, 1978, 1980), is correlated with a reduction of net outward membrane current in the sensory neurons. Reduction of outward currents would contribute to broadening of the action potential and enhancing the excitability of the cell. The currents modulated by serotonin (5-HT) in the short-term (Klein & Kandel, 1980; Baxter & Byrne, 1987, 1989) are similar to the currents altered in a long-term fashion by sensitization. These results parallel similar findings on the sensory neurons in the abdominal ganglion and indicate that the tail sensory neurons in the pleural ganglia are not only a cellular locus for short-term sensitization, but they also serve as a cellular locus for long-term sensitization.

Although many of the cellular changes that contribute to short-term sensitization in both the sensory neurons in the abdominal and pleural ganglia are triggered by an elevation of cAMP, a major unresolved question is the identity of the intracellular signal that triggers the long-lasting cellular changes. A number of studies indicate that cAMP, in addition to promoting protein phosphorylation through the activation of a protein kinase, may also participate in the regulation of protein synthesis (Schacher, Castellucci, & Kandel, 1988; Scholz & Byrne, 1988). Thus, one hypothesis for the induction of long-term sensitization is that the transient elevation of cAMP during training may trigger protein synthesis or other biochemical events that produce the long-lasting changes in the sensory neurons. An alternative hypothesis is that the induction of long-term sensitization is mediated by a different second messenger system. To begin to test the hypothesis that cAMP is involved in the induction of long-term sensitization, cAMP was injected directly into sensory neurons in order to mimic the effects of sensitization training at the level of single sensory neurons (Scholz & Byrne, 1988). Long-lasting effects were found. Furthermore, the effects of cAMP injection were similar to those changes produced 24 hours after sensitization training.

These findings, together with those showing that sensitization training elevates cAMP in sensory cells (Ocorr, Tabata, & Byrne, 1986), suggest that cAMP is one of the critical intracellular signals that triggers the long-lasting cellular changes that underly long-term sensitization. Additional support for this conclusion comes from the work of Schacher et al. (1988). These studies have shown that bath application of permeable analogues of cAMP leads to an enhancement of the synaptic connections between cultured sensory and motor neurons 24 hours after treatment.

An important remaining question is how cAMP mediates these long-term effects. Studies by Montarolo et al. (1986), Dale, Kandel, and Schacher (1987), and Schacher et al. (1988) point to a critical role for cAMP, 5-HT, and protein synthesis in producing long-term synaptic facilitation and increases in excitability of sensory neurons in culture. Treatments that mimic sensitization training have been used to begin to examine the role of specific proteins in long-term sensitization. Using two-dimensional polyacrylamide gel electrophoresis (2D-PAGE), it was found that prolonged (2- to 3-hr.) exposure to serotonin (5-HT) led to changes in incorporation of labeled amino acid into several proteins from isolated clusters of tail sensory neurons (Barzilai, Kennedy, Kandel, & Sweatt, 1988; Eskin, Byrne, & Garcia, 1988; Eskin, Garcia, & Byrne, 1989). The same proteins that were affected by treatment with 5-HT were also altered by the adenylate cyclase activator, forskolin, and analogues of cAMP.

In addition, Castellucci, Kennedy, Kandel, and Golet (1988) have identified changes in incorporation of labeled amino acids in sensory neurons of abdominal ganglia 24 hours after sensitization training. At least some of these proteins appear to be different from the ones described previously. Thus, different proteins may be affected at different times after training. These results suggest the intriguing hypothesis that some proteins may be involved in the induction of long-term sensitization, whereas others may be involved in its maintenance (for discussion see Goelet, Castellucci, Schacher, & Kandel, 1986).

A model that summarizes some of the neural and molecular mechanisms contributing to short- and long-term sensitization is illustrated in Fig. 10.1. Sensitizing stimuli lead to the activation of facilitatory neurons that release a modulatory neurotransmitter, such as serotonin. The modulatory transmitter acts on the sensory neurons to increase the levels of cAMP, which in turn leads to closure of membrane K^+ channels through protein phosphorylation (Brunelli, Castellucci, & Kandel, 1976; Siegelbaum, Camardo, & Kandel, 1982). Closure of these K^+ channels leads to membrane depolarization and an enhancement of the excitability of the sensory neurons. An additional consequence of reduced K^+ channel activity is a reduction of the repolarizing current during an action potential. Thus, action potentials initiated in the sensory neurons are broader. This broadening may serve to enhance Ca^{2+} influx in the presynaptic terminal and increase transmitter release from the sensory neurons (Klein & Kandel, 1978). Recent results also indicate that modulatory transmitters (e.g., 5-HT) affect a second subcellular process referred to as mobilization (Gingrich & Byrne, 1985, 1987; Gingrich et al., 1988; Hochner et al., 1986), perhaps by causing the translocation of vesicles from a storage pool to a readily releasable pool.

The mechanisms for the long-term changes are not yet fully understood.

However, it appears that the same intracellular messenger that leads to the expression of the short-term changes also triggers cellular processes that lead to long-term changes. One possible mechanism for this action is through the regulation of protein synthesis by cAMP (Montarolo et al., 1986; Schacher et al., 1988). It is also possible that long-term changes in membrane currents could be due, at least in part, to changes in the ratio of subunits of the cAMP-dependent protein kinase (Greenberg, Castellucci, Bayley, & Schwartz, 1987). Thus, both short- and long-term sensitization are associated with a number of cellular alterations that appear to act in concert to increase the excitability of the sensory neurons and enhance transmitter release, thereby producing an enhanced withdrawal response.

Neural Mechanisms of Associative Conditioning in *Aplysia*

A cellular mechanism called *activity-dependent neuromodulation* (Hawkins, Abrams, Carew, & Kandel, 1983; Walters & Byrne, 1983a) may contribute to associative learning in *Aplysia* (Carew et al., 1983; Hawkins et al., 1986a). A general cellular scheme of activity-dependent neuromodulation is illustrated in Fig. 10.2. Two sensory neurons (1 and 2), which constitute the pathways for the conditioned stimulus (CS), make weak subthreshold connections to a response system (e.g., a motor neuron). Delivering a reinforcing or unconditioned stimulus (US) alone has two effects. First, the US activates the response system and produces the unconditioned response (UR). Second, the US activates a diffuse modulatory system that nonspecifically enhances transmitter release from all the sensory neurons. This nonspecific enhancement contributes to sensitization. Temporal specificity, characteristic of associative learning, occurs when there is pairing of the CS, spike activity in one of the sensory neurons (sensory neuron 1), with the US, causing a selective amplification of the modulatory effects in that specific sensory neuron (Hawkins et al., 1983; Walters & Byrne, 1983a). Unpaired activity does not amplify the effects of the US in sensory neuron 2. The amplification of the moduatlry effects in the paired sensory neuron leads to an enhancement of the ability of sensory neuron 1 to activate the response system and produce the conditioned response (CR).

As indicated earlier, experimental analyses of sensitization of defensive reflexes in *Aplysia* have shown that the neuromodulator released by the reinforcing stimulus acts, at least in part, by reducing potassium currents in the sensory neurons. Consequently, action potentials elicited after the reinforcing stimulus are broader (due to less repolarizing K^+ current), causing an enhanced influx of Ca^{2+}. Enhanced influx of Ca^{2+} triggers greater release of transmitter from the sensory neurons, which causes increased activation of motor neurons and, thus, sensitization of the reflex. The pairing specificity in the associative conditioning is due, at least in part, to an enhancement of cAMP levels beyond that produced

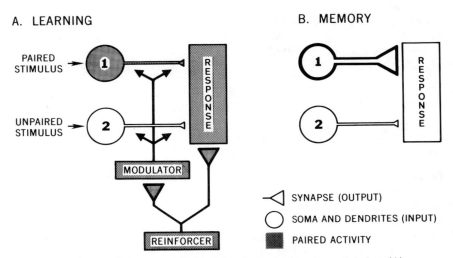

FIG. 10.2.   General model of activity-dependent neuromodulation. (A) Learning. Stippling indicates temporally contiguous activity. A motivationally potent reinforcing stimulus activates a neural response system and a modulatory system that regulates the efficacy of diffuse afferents to the response system. Increased spike activity in the paired afferent (1) immediately before the modulatory signal amplifies the degree and duration of the modulatory effects, perhaps through the Ca^{2+} sensitivity of the modulatory evoked second messenger. The unpaired afferent neuron (2) does not show an amplification of the modulatory effects. (B) Memory. The amplified modulatory effects cause long-term increases in transmitter release and/or excitability of the paired neuron, which in turn strengthens the functional connection between the paired neuron (1) and the response system.

by the modulator alone (Abrams, Bernier, Hawkins, & Kandel, 1984; Ocorr, Walters, & Byrne, 1985). Furthermore, it appears that influx of Ca^{2+} associated with the CS (spike activity) amplifies the US-mediated modulatory effect (Abrams, Carew, Hawkins, & Kandel, 1983) by interacting with a Ca^{2+}-sensitive component of the adenylate cyclase (Abrams, Eliot, Dudai, & Kandel, 1985; Schwartz et al., 1983; Weiss & Drummond, 1985). A critical role for Ca^{2+}-stimulated cyclase is also provided by studies of *Drosophila* where it has been shown that the particulate adenylate cyclase of a mutant deficient in associative learning exhibits a loss of Ca^{2+}/calmodulin sensitivity (Aceves-Pina et al., 1983; Dudai, 1985; Livingstone, 1985).

An important conclusion is that this mechanism for associative learning is simply an elaboration of mechanisms already in place that mediate a simpler form of learning: sensitization. This finding raises the interesting possibility that even more complex forms of learning may be achieved by using these simpler forms as building blocks, an idea that has been suggested by some psychologists for many years, but one that, until now, has not been testable at the cellular level.

SELECTED EXAMPLES OF LEARNING
IN APLYSIA AND OTHER INVERTEBRATES

Associative Modification of Phototactic Behavior in *Hermissenda*

Hermissenda exhibit a positive phototaxis and thus respond to a gradient of illumination by movement toward an illuminated area. When illumination (conditioned stimulus, CS) was paired with high-speed rotation (unconditioned stimulus, US), the normal positive phototactic behavior was suppressed (Crow & Alkon, 1978). A three-step procedure was utilized. In the first phase, *Hermissenda* were placed at one end of glass tubes filled with seawater, and base-line (pretraining) measurements of the time necessary to locomote to the illuminated end of the tube were determined. In the second phase, *Hermissenda* received 150 pairings (50/day) of light and rotation. Control procedures consisted of random presentations of rotation, random light, explicitly unpaired light and rotation, random light and rotation, and no light or rotation. In the third phase, the phototactic responses were retested by presenting light alone. Immediately after training, all groups showed some suppression of phototactic behavior (i.e., nonassociative effects), but *Hermissenda* that received paired presentations showed more suppression than any of the control groups. Retention tests conducted at 24 hr after training showed no statistically significant nonassociative components to the behavioral modification; thus, nonassociative components exhibited only short-term changes in phototactic behavior (Crow, 1983). Significant suppression of phototactic behavior was retained for at least 3 days after training was terminated. Studies by Crow and Offenbach (1983) and Farley and Alkon (1982) have revealed that the change in phototactic behavior after conditioning can be explained by an increase in the latency to initiate locomotion in the presence of light. Once locomotion is initiated, it occurs at a relatively constant rate that is unchanged by the conditioning procedure. Parametric features of the behavioral modifications have been analyzed (Crow, 1984; Farley, 1987; Richards, Farley, & Alkon, 1984).

Other measurements of phototactic behavior have also been examined. Crow (1985) showed that conditioned *Hermissenda* remain in an illuminated area significantly less than random controls. In addition, Lederhendler, Gart, and Alkon (1986) showed that in response to light onset (the CS) the foot lengthens, whereas rotation (US), when presented alone, leads to a shortening of the foot (unconditioned response, UR). After training, random and control groups continue to show light-elicited lengthening of the foot, but *Hermissenda* receiving the paired presentations of light and rotation show a shortening in response to the CS (Lederhendler et al., 1986). Thus, as a result of training, the light produces a response (conditioned response, CR) resembling that of the UR.

Significant advances have been made in the cellular analysis of associative learning in *Hermissenda*. At least one critical site of the plasticity is the photoreceptors on which extensive biophysical and biochemical analyses have been performed (for reviews see Alkon, 1984; Crow, 1988). The plasticity is associated with changes in membrane currents, and the learning-induced changes can be mimicked by transmitters such as serotonin as well as by second messengers. Long-term changes are dependent on protein synthesis.

Food-Avoidance Conditioning in *Limax*

Food-avoidance conditioning procedures are roughly analogous to the initial conditioning procedures described earlier for *Hermissenda*. In the *Limax* studies, a noxious US is used to modulate or suppress some aspect of feeding behavior (CR) normally produced or triggered by an olfactory or gustatory CS. The ability of *Limax* to learn various tasks has been extensively examined (Gelperin, 1975; Sahley, Gelperin, & Rudy, 1981; Sahley, Rudy, & Gelperin, 1981). These include classical conditioning, blocking, and second-order conditioning.

Limax is an herbivore that locomotes toward desirable food odors. The animal's normal attraction (CR) to a preferred food odor, however, can be reduced significantly following a single pairing of that odor with a bitter taste (US). A two-phase training and testing procedure was utilized by Sahley, Gelperin, & Rudy (1981). On the training day, *Limax* were allowed to feed on potatoes for a 2-min. period. The experimental group then received a 20-min. exposure to quinidine sulfate, whereas the control group received saline. The effectiveness of the training procedure was assessed by utilizing an odor-preference test on the following day. In comparison with control *Limax,* trained *Limax* showed a marked reduction in their preference for the odor that had been paired with quinidine (Sahley, Gelperin, & Rudy, 1981). The suppression was not due to a nonspecific effect of exposure to quinidine (Sahley, Gelperin, & Rudy, 1981). Sahley, Rudy, and Gelperin (1981) have extended these studies by examining second-order conditioning, blocking, and the effects of transient US preexposure.

Rapid taste-aversion learning occurs in the isolated central nervous system (Chang & Gelperin, 1980). This, coupled with the recent identification of neural elements controlling feeding (Gelperin, Tank, & Tesauro, 1989), will facilitate subsequent cellular analyses of learning in *Limax*.

Avoidance Conditioning in *Pleurobranchaea*

Pleurobranchaea exhibit a characteristic bite-strike response when they are exposed to food. If a food stimulus in the form of squid homogenate (the CS) is paired with strong electric shock to the oral veil (US), the bite-strike response is modified. Indeed, after training, the CS, instead of eliciting a bite-strike response, elicited withdrawal and suppression of feeding responses (CR). Mpitsos and Collins (1975) delivered the US for 60 sec. contingent on the response to the food stimulus. If the CS elicited a bite response, the US was presented immediately thereafter. If *Pleurobranchaea* did not bite, the US was given 180 sec. after the CS. Control procedures included explicitly unpaired CS and US presentations, random presentations, and controls for backward conditioning. The learned task is acquired rapidly (within a few trials separated by 1 hr.) and retained for up to 4 weeks (Davis et al., 1980; Mpitsos & Collins, 1975; Mpitsos, Collins, & McClellan, 1978). Control procedures distinguish the learning from nonassociative behavioral modifications (Davis et al., 1980; Mpitsos & Collins, 1975; Mpitsos et al., 1978).

A good deal is known about the neural circuit that controls feeding behavior, and specific neural correlates of the learning have been identified (e.g., Kovac, Davis, Matera, Morielli, & Croll, 1985; London & Gillette, 1984; Morielli et al., 1986). Some neurons in the circuit have enhanced excitability, presumably due to modulation of membrane currents, whereas other neurons show decreased sensitivity to ACh, a putative neurotransmitter released by presynaptic neurons.

Lymnaea Stagnalis

An example of nonaversive conditioning in the freshwater gastropod, *Lymnaea stagnalis,* was demonstrated by Audesirk, Alexander, Audesirk, and Moyer (1982). A neutral chemostimulus (CS) was paired with a solution of a strong phagostimulant (US). After five trials per day over a 3-day period, *Lymnaea* receiving the paired training showed significantly greater levels of feeding movements than *Lymnaea* receiving random presentations of the CS and US, explicitly unpaired presentations of the CS and US, the US alone, or the CS alone. Additional features of the behavior, such as the effects of forward, backward, and simultaneous pairings of the CS and US, were analyzed (Alexander, Audesirk, & Audesirk, 1982). One-trial learning of the response, which persists for 19 days, was demonstrated by Alexander, Audesirk, & Audesirk (1984). *Lymnaea* may prove a valuable preparation for the cellular analysis of this nonaversive conditioning, because much is presently known about the neural control of feeding in this animal (e.g., Elliott & Benjamin, 1985a, 1985b).

Leech

The leech has proven to be a valuable preparation for the cellular analysis of simple neural circuits (for reviews, see Kuffler, Nichols, & Martin, 1984; Muller, Nichols, & Stent, 1981), but has received little attention as a model system for analyzing neural mechanisms underlying associative behavioral modifications.

The possibility for this type of analysis now exists, however, with the demonstration of associative learning in the leech (Henderson & Strong, 1972; Sahley & Ready, 1988). For example, Sahley and Ready (1988) conditioned leeches by pairing light touch to the head (CS) with an electric shock to the tail (US). The CS normally produced a shortening response, but the response was enhanced following 30 pairings of the CS and US. The learning persisted for at least 24 hours. In contrast, leeches that received explicitly unpaired presentations of the CS and US, CS alone, or US alone exhibited decreased responses to touch over trials.

Sahley and Ready (1988) also demonstrated associative learning of stepping behavior. A light touch to the midbody region (the CS) normally results in a small local bending. Following 20 pairings of the touch (CS) with an electric shock to the tail (US), which leads to stepping behavior (UR), the CS when presented alone elicited stepping responses (CR). Training with the CS alone, US alone, and explicitly unpaired presentations of CS and US produced no learning.

Examples of nonassociative learning, such as habituation and sensitization, have also been demonstrated in the leech (Boulis & Sahley, 1988; Lockery, Rawlins, & Gray, 1985).

Conditioning in *Drosophila*

Although the neural circuitry in *Drosophila* is both complex and relatively inaccessible, these difficulties are compensated by the ease with which genetic analyses of behavior can be performed. A variety of conditioning procedures have been utilized, but only one is described here in which training consists of a two-stage differential odor-shock avoidance conditioning procedure. Populations of about 150 flies were placed on a chamber lined with a conductive grid for delivering electric shocks (the US) (Tully, 1987; Tully & Quinn, 1985). *Drosophila* were exposed to two different odors. One of the odors was paired with shock (CS+), and the other was explicitly unpaired (CS−). The CS+ and US were delivered simultaneously for 60 sec. with an intertrial interval of 180 sec. An odor-choice procedure tested the effectiveness of conditioning. Specifically, flies were transferred to the center of a T-maze where they encountered the CS+ and CS− odors coming from opposite sides of the maze. Typically, 95% of the flies moved into the T-maze containing the CS− odor, thereby avoiding the odor that was paired with the shock. Little or no differential effects were obtained with presentations of shock alone, odor alone, or explicitly unpaired odor and shock (Tully & Quinn, 1985). Learning was typically retained for several hours (Quinn, Sziber, & Booker, 1979; Tully & Quinn, 1985).

A variety of mutants have rather specific deficiencies in their ability to learn and remember (for reviews, see Aceves-Pina et al., 1983; Dudai, 1985, 1988; Tully, 1987). The striking feature of these mutations is that they appear to affect some aspect of a monoamine pathway and its associated intracellular biochemical cascade. Two of the mutants affect specific aspects of the cAMP cascade and therefore may affect the ability of extrinsic signals to activate the cAMP cascade.

The results from genetic studies on *Drosophila* support the hypothesis that monoamines and alterations in second messenger systems are critically involved in learning and memory, and parallel similar conclusions derived from the studies on *Aplysia*. They also support the hypothesis that a mechanism for associative learning can be an elaboration of mechanisms already in place that mediate sensitization, a simple example of nonassociative learning. For example, Duerr and Quinn (1982) found that mutants that were defective in associative learning also exhibited similar defects in sensitization.

Operant Conditioning of Leg Position in Arthropods

In a paradigm first developed by Horridge (1962), either a cockroach or a locust was suspended over a liquid surface. In such a preparation, the legs initially make many movements, including those that caused the leg to come in contact with the liquid surface. Two animals were arranged in a "yoked controlled" fashion. One animal received the training and was referred to as the Positional (P). The other was referred to as the Random (R). Electric shock, the negative reinforcer, was delivered to the P animal each time its leg contacted the surface. The R animal (not suspended over the liquid) received a shock each time the P animal did, but the shocks were uncorrelated with any particular position of the leg. The training lasted for 45 minutes, during which time there was a progressive decrease in the number of shocks delivered. As a result of training, the P animal learned to avoid positioning its legs in the liquid. After the training phase, a testing phase was utilized in which both the P and R animals were placed over a liquid surface, and shocks were delivered independently to each animal if its leg contacted the liquid. Initially, the number of shocks received by the P group was significantly fewer than those received by the R group. With time, however, the R group also received fewer shocks, as these animals learned to associate leg position with the negative reinforcer.

Hoyle (1965) and Tosney and Hoyle (1977) extended Horridge's procedure by automating it and by conditioning the frequency of action potentials of an identified motor neuron innervating the musculature of the leg, rather than leg position itself. Preparations with decreased rates of motor neuron activity received a negative reinforcer that caused firing rates to increase. In addition to this "up" conditioning, "down" conditioning was also demonstrated. Here, spontaneous increases in motor neuron frequency could be reduced by delivering the reinforcing stimulus. The conditioned changes in the firing of the motor neurons seems to be due to an intrinsic change in the membrane properties of the motor neuron rather than a change in its synaptic input (Woollacott & Hoyle, 1976, 1977).

Conditioned Modification of Feeding Behavior in *Aplysia*

Feeding behavior in *Aplysia* can be modified by pairing feeding with negative reinforcement. In the presence of food wrapped in a tough plastic net, *Aplysia* bite and attempt to swallow the food (Susswein & Schwarz, 1983). However, netted food cannot be swallowed and is eventually pushed out of the buccal cavity. The inability to consume food appears to be an aversive stimulus that modifies the prior feeding behavior, because trained animals do not attempt to bite netted food. Moreover, training does not produce a generalized inhibition of feeding behavior, because feeding was restored when the food in the net was replaced with an alternate food, or when texture of the food was changed by presenting the food out of a net. A differential learning paradigm was used to demonstrate that the behavioral change is specific to pairing: When aversive stimuli were explicitly unpaired with feeding responses, no behavioral change was seen (Susswein & Schwarz, 1983; Susswein, Schwartz, & Feldman, 1986). Susswein et al. (1986) also found learned increases in feeding behavior. For example, when a hole was cut in the net, allowing *Aplysia* to pull food out and consume it, *Aplysia* learned that netted food was edible. Pairing successful food consumption with feeding behavior produced changes opposite to those produced by failed attempts to consume food (Susswein et al., 1986).

When the esophageal nerves were cut bilaterally, all behavioral changes due to associative learning were abolished. Thus, the esophageal nerves innervating the gut were necessary for learning. This result suggests that these nerves carry information about whether or not an attempt to consume food is successful (Schwarz & Susswein, 1986).

Recently, putative command neurons controlling feeding behavior have been identified (Rosen, Miller, Weiss, & Kupfermann, 1988; Susswein & Byrne, 1988). Thus, it may be possible to identify elements in the circuit that are modified by the conditioning procedure and examine the underlying mechanisms.

Operant Conditioning of Head Waving in *Aplysia*

Head waving is a natural behavior exhibited by *Aplysia,* and it can be studied experimentally by suspending animals by their parapodia. Cook and Carew (1986) punished head waving toward one side or the other by the presentation of aversive bright lights. Experiments consisted of a 5-min. base-line phase, 10 min. of training, and a 5-min. testing phase. After training, *Aplysia* that received contingent reinforcement spent significantly more test time on the nonreinforced ("safe") side compared with their own behavior during the base-line phase and compared with yoked controls in which illumination was unrelated to the behavioral response to the animal. When contingencies of reinforcement were subsequently reversed (safe side punished and vice versa), the contingent group showed a marked decrease in turning toward the now-punished side. When trained *Aplysia* were an additional 10 min. of training in which no light was present, they exhibited significant retention. Cook and Carew have begun to analyze the cues used as feedback to determine where the head is located with respect to light. To distinguish between visual cues in the environment and internally derived ones (e.g., proprioceptive or efference copy), they repeated the training procedure but disrupted visual cues by rotating animals 180° before testing. The contingent group still showed significant learning, whereas yoked controls once again did not learn. These results indicate that internal cues are used to code the operant response.

Because neurons controlling neck muscles have been identified (Cook & Carew, 1988), the cellular mechanisms of this example of operant conditioning in *Aplysia* can begin to be analyzed.

CONCLUSIONS

One of the key findings to emerge from recent studies on invertebrates is their capacity to exhibit various forms of associative learning. Of particular significance is the finding that at least some molluscs, such as *Limax,* exhibit higher order features of classical conditioning such as second-order conditioning and blocking. Context learning, conditioned discrimination learning, and contingency learning have been described in *Aplysia* (Colwill, Absher, & Roberts, 1988a, 1988b; Hawkins et al., 1986a). Such higher order features can be viewed in a cognitive context and raise the interesting possibility that other cognitive-like phenomena will be identified as the behavioral capabilities of these animals are investigated further. Because many of the invertebrates reviewed in this chapter are amenable to cellular analysis, an examination of cognitive properties at the cellular level may be possible.

The possibility of relating cellular changes to complex behavior in invertebrates is encouraged by the progress that has already been made in examining the neural mechanisms of simple forms of nonassociative and associative learning. The results of these analyses on *Aplysia* have shown that: (a) learning involves changes in existing neural circuitry (one does not need the growth of new synapses and the formation of new circuits for learning and memory to occur); (b) that learning involves the activation of second messenger systems; (c) that the second messenger affects multiple subcellular processes to alter the responsiveness of the neuron (at least one locus for the storage and read-out of memory is the alteration of specific membrane currents); and (d) that long-term memory requires new protein synthesis, whereas short-term memory does not.

Although the results in *Aplysia* are consistent with those of simple forms of learning in other invertebrate and vertebrate model systems, there is, as yet, no complete mechanistic analysis available for any single example of simple learning. Many of the technical obstacles are being overcome, however, and within the next few years it is likely that the analyses of several examples of learning will be fairly complete.

For the near future, major questions to be answered include the following:

1. To what extent are mechanisms for classical conditioning common both within any one animal and between different species?

2. What is the relationship between the initial induction of neuronal change (acquisition of learning) and the maintenance of the associative change (retention of learning)?

3. What are the relationships between different forms of learning, such as sensitization, classical conditioning, and operant conditioning?

More ambitious questions include the analysis of cognitive phenomena and whether such learning involves processes and mechanisms that are fundamentally different from those underlying classical conditioning. Interestingly, much theoretical work has shown that artificial neural networks based on relatively simple learning rules have interesting computational capabilities and cognitive-like properties. Thus, it is interesting to speculate that the critical distinction between simple and complex cognitive examples of learning will be found not at the level of basic cellular mechanisms, but rather at the level of the neural network and the specificity of neuronal connections.

ACKNOWLEDGMENTS

I thank L. Cleary and T. Crow for their comments on a previous draft of the manuscript. Supported by National Institute of Mental Health Award K02 MH00649, National Institutes of Health Research Grant NS 19895 and Air Force Office of Scientific Research grant 87-0274.

REFERENCES

Abrams, T. W., Bernier, L., Hawkins, R. D., & Kandel, E. R. (1984). Possible roles of Ca^{++} and cAMP in activity-dependent facilitation, a mechanism for association learning in *Aplysia*. *Society for Neuroscience Abstracts, 10,* 269.

Abrams, T. W., Carew, T., Hawkins, R. D., & Kandel, E. R. (1983). Aspects of the cellular mechanism of temporal specificity in conditioning in *Aplysia:* Preliminary evidence for Ca^{2+} influx as a signal of activity. *Society for Neuroscience Abstracts, 9,* 168.

Abrams, T. W., Eliot, L., Dudai, Y., & Kandel, E. R. (1985). Activation of adenylate cyclase in

Aplysia neural tissue by Ca^{2+}/calmodulin, a candidate for an associative mechanism during conditioning. *Society for Neuroscience Abstracts, 11,* 797.

Aceves-Pina, E. O., Booker, R., Duerr, J. S., Livingston, M. S., Quinn, W. G., Smith, R. F., Sziber, P. P., Tempel, B. L., & Tully, T. P. (1983). Learning and memory in *Drosophila,* studied with mutants. *Cold Spring Harbor Symposium of Quantitative Biology, 48,* 831–840.

Alexander, J. E., Jr., Audesirk, T. E., & Audesirk, G. J. (1982). Rapid, nonaversive conditioning in a fresh-water gastropod. II. Effects of temporal relationships on learning. *Behavioral and Neural Biology, 36,* 391–402.

Alexander, J. E., Jr., Audesirk, T. E., & Audesirk, G. J. (1984). One-trial reward learning in the snail *Lymnaea stagnalis. Journal of Neurobiology, 15,* 67–72.

Alkon, D. L. (1984). Calcium-mediated reduction of ionic currents: A biophysical memory trace. *Science, 226,* 1037–1045.

Audesirk, T. E., Jr., Alexander, G. J., Jr., Audesirk, T. E., & Moyer, C. (1982). Rapid, nonaversive conditioning in a fresh water gastropod. I. Effects of age and motivation. *Behavioral and Neural Biology, 36,* 379–390.

Bailey, C. H. & Chen, M. (1983). Morphological basis of long-term habituation and sensitization in *Aplysia. Science, 220,* 91–93.

Bailey, C. H., & Chen, M. (1988a). Long-term memory in *Aplysia* modulates the total number of varicosities of single identified sensory neurons. *Proceedings of the National Academy of Sciences of the United States of America, 85,* 2373–2377.

Bailey, C. H., & Chen, M. (1988b). Morphological basis of short-term habituation in *Aplysia. Journal of Neuroscience, 8,* 2452–2459.

Barzilai, A., Kennedy, T. E., Kandel, E. R., & Sweatt, J. D. (1988). Serotonin (5-HT) causes changes in protein synthesis in pleural sensory neurons from *Aplysia. Society for Neuroscience Abstracts, 14,* 909.

Baxter, D. A., & Byrne, J. H. (1989). Serotonergic modulation of two potassium currents in the pleural sensory neurons of *Aplysia. Journal of Neurophysiology, 62,* 665–679.

Baxter, D. A., & Byrne, J. H. (1987). Modulation of membrane currents and excitability by serotonin and cAMP in pleural sensory neurons of *Aplysia. Society for Neuroscience Abstracts, 13,* 1440.

Boulis, N. M., & Sahley, C. L. (1988). A behavioral analysis of habituation and sensitization of shortening in the semi-intact leech. *Journal of Neuroscience, 8,* 4621–4627.

Brunelli, M., Castellucci, V., & Kandel, E. R. (1976). Synaptic facilitation and behavioral sensitization in *Aplysia:* Possible role of serotonin and cyclic AMP. *Science, 194,* 1178–1181.

Byrne, J. H. (1982). Analysis of the synaptic depression contributing to habituation of gill-withdrawal reflex in *Aplysia californica. Journal of Neurophysiology, 48,* 431–438.

Byrne, J. H. (1985). Neural and molecular mechanisms underlying information storage in *Aplysia:* Implications for learning and memory. *Trends in Neuroscience, 8,* 478–482.

Byrne, J. H. (1987). Cellular analysis of associative learning. *Physiological Reviews, 67,* 329–439.

Byrne, J. H., Castellucci, V., & Kandel, E. R. (1978). Contribution of individual mechanoreceptor sensory neurons to defensive gill-withdrawal reflex in *Aplysia. Journal of Neurophysiology, 41,* 418–431.

Byrne, J. H., & Schultz, S. G. (1988). *An Introduction to membrane transport and bioelectricity.* New York: Raven.

Carew, T. J. (1987). Cellular and molecular advances in the study of learning in *Aplysia.* In J.-P. Changeux and M. Konishi (Eds.), *The neural and molecular bases of learning* (pp. 177–204). Chichester: John Wiley and Sons.

Carew, T. J., Castellucci, V. F., & Kandel, E. R. (1971). An analysis of dishabituation and sensitization of the gill-withdrawal reflex in *Aplysia. International Journal of Neuroscience, 2,* 79–98.

Carew, T. J., Hawkins, R. D., & Kandel, E. R. (1983). Differential classical conditioning of a defensive withdrawal reflex in *Aplysia californica. Science, 219,* 397–400.

Carew, T. J., & Kandel, E. R. (1973). Acquisition and retention of long-term habituation in *Aplysia:* Correlation of behavioral and cellular processes. *Science, 182,* 1158–1160.

Carew, T. J., Pinsker, H. M., & Kandel, E. R. (1972). Long-term habituation in *Aplysia. Science, 175,* 451–454.

Carew, T. J., Walters, E. T., & Kandel, E. R. (1981). Classical conditioning in a simple withdrawal reflex in *Aplysia californica. Journal of Neuroscience, 1,* 1426–1437.

Castellucci, V. F., Carew, T. J., & Kandel, E. R. (1978). Cellular analysis of long-term habituation of the gill-withdrawal reflex of *Aplysia californica. Science, 202,* 1306–1308.

Castellucci, V. F., & Kandel, E. R. (1974). A quantal analysis of the synaptic depression underlying habituation of the gill-withdrawal reflex in *Aplysia. Proceedings of the National Academy of Sciences of the United States of America, 71,* 5004–5008.

Castellucci, V. F., & Kandel, E. R. (1976). Presynaptic facilitation as a mechanism for behavioral sensitization in *Aplysia. Science, 194,* 1176–1178.

Castellucci, V. F., Kennedy, T. E., Kandel, E. R., & Golet, P. A. (1988). Quantitative analysis of 2-D gels identifies proteins in which labeling is increased following long-term sensitization in *Aplysia. Neuron, 1,* 321–328.

Castellucci, V. F., Pinsker, H., Kupfermann, I., & Kandel, E. R. (1970). Neuronal mechanisms of habituation and dishabituation of the gill-withdrawal reflex in *Aplysia. Science, 167,* 1745–1748.

Chang, J. J., & Gelperin, A. (1980). Rapid taste aversion learning by an isolated molluscan central nervous system. *Proceedings of the National Academy of Sciences of the United States of America, 77,* 6204–6206.

Colwill, R. M., Absher, R. A., & Roberts, M. L. (1988a). Context-US learning in *Aplysia californica. Journal of Neuroscience, 8,* 4434–4439.

Colwill, R. M., Absher, R. A., & Roberts, M. L. (1988b). Conditional discrimination learning in *Aplysia californica. Journal of Neuroscience, 8,* 4440–4444.

Cook, D. G., & Carew, T. J. (1986). Operant conditioning of head waving in *Aplysia. Proceedings of the National Academy of Sciences of the United States of America, 83,* 1120–1124.

Cook, D. G., & Carew, T. J. (1988). Operant conditioning identified neck muscles and individual motor neurons in *Aplysia. Society for Neuroscience Abstracts, 14,* 607.

Crow, T. (1983). Conditioned modification of locomotion of sensory adaptation in *Hermissenda crassicornis:* Analysis of time dependent associative and nonassociative components. *Journal of Neuroscience, 3,* 2621–2628.

Crow, T. (1984). Cellular neurophysiological and behavioral studies of learning in molluscs. In L. R. Squire & N. Butters (Eds.), *Neuropsychology of memory* (pp. 608–721). New York: Guilford.

Crow, T. (1985). Conditioned modification of phototactic behavior in *Hermissenda.* I. Analysis of light intensity. *Journal of Neuroscience, 5,* 209–214.

Crow, T. (1988). Cellular and molecular analysis of associative learning and memory in *Hermissenda. Trends in Neuroscience, 11,* 136–142.

Crow, T., & Alkon, D. L. (1978). Retention of an associative behavioral change in *Hermissenda. Science, 201,* 1239–1241.

Crow, T., & Offenbach, N. (1983). Modification of the initiation of locomotion in *Hermissenda:* Behavioral analysis. *Brain Research, 271,* 301–310.

Dale, N., Kandel, E. R., & Schacher, S. (1987). Serotonin produces long-term changes in the excitability of *Aplysia* sensory neurons in culture that depend on new protein synthesis. *Journal of Neuroscience, 7,* 2232–2238.

Davis, W. J., Villet, J. J., Lee, D., Rigler, M., Gillette, R., & Prince, E. (1980). Selective and differential avoidance learning in the feeding and withdrawal behavior of *Pleurobranchaea californica. Journal of Comparative Physiology A, 138,* 157–165.

Dudai, Y. (1985). Genes, enzymes and learning in *Drosophila. Trends in Neuroscience, 8,* 18–21.

Dudai, Y. (1988). Neurogenetic dissection of learning and short-term memory in *Drosophila. Annual Review of Neuroscience, 11,* 537–563.

Duerr, J. S., & Quinn, W. G. (1982). Three *Drosophila* mutations that block associative learning also affect habituation and sensitization. *Proceedings of the National Academy of Sciences of the United States of America, 79,* 3646–3650.

Elliott, C. J. H., & Benjamin, P. R. (1985a). Interactions of pattern-generating interneurons controlling feeding in *Lymnea stagnalis. Journal of Neurophysiology, 54,* 1396–1411.

Elliott, C. J. H., & Benjamin, P. R. (1985b). Interactions of the slow oscillator interneurons with feeding pattern-generating interneurons in *Lymnaea stagnalis. Journal of Neurophysiology, 54,* 1412–1421.

Eskin, A., Byrne, J. H., & Garcia, K. (1988). Identification of proteins that may mediate sensitization in *Aplysia. Society for Neuroscience Abstracts, 14,* 838.

Eskin, A., Garcia, K. S., & Byrne, J. H. (1989). Information storage in the nervous system of *Aplysia:* Specific proteins affected by serotonin and cAMP. *Proceedings of the National Academy of Sciences of the United States of America, 86,* 2458–2462.

Farley, J. (1987). Contingency learning and causal detection in *Hermissenda:* I. Behavior. *Behavioral Neuroscience, 101,* 13–27.

Farley, J., & Alkon, D. L. (1982). Associative neural and behavioral change in *Hermissenda:* Consequences of nervous system orientation for light and pairing specificity. *Journal of Neurophysiology, 48,* 785–807.

Frost, W. N., Castellucci, V. F., Hawkins, R. D., & Kandel, E. R. (1985). Monosynaptic connections made by the sensory neurons of the gill- and siphon-withdrawal reflex in *Aplysia* participate in the storage of long-term memory for sensitization. *Proceedings of the National Academy of Sciences of the United States of America, 82,* 8266–8269.

Gelperin, A. (1975). Rapid food-aversion learning by a terrestrial mollusk. *Science, 189,* 567–570.

Gelperin, A., Tank, D. W., & Tesauro, G. (1989). Olfactory processing and associative memory: Cellular and modeling studies. In J. H. Byrne & W. O. Berry (Eds.), *Neural models of plasticity* (pp. 133–159). Orlando, FL: Academic Press.

Gingrich, K. J., Baxter, D. A., & Byrne, J. H. (1988). Mathematical model of cellular mechanisms contributing to presynaptic facilitation. *Brain Research Bulletin, 21,* 513–520.

Gingrich, K. J., & Byrne, J. H. (1985). Simulation of synaptic depression, posttetanic potentiation, and presynaptic facilitation of synaptic potentials from sensory neurons mediating gill-withdrawal reflex in *Aplysia. Journal of Neurophysiology, 53,* 652–669.

Gingrich, K. J., & Byrne, J. H. (1987). Single-cell neuronal model for associative learning. *Journal of Neurophysiology, 57,* 1705–1715.

Goelet, P., Castellucci, V. F., Schacher, S., & Kandel, E. R. (1986). The long and short of long-term memory—a molecular framework. *Nature, 322,* 419–422.

Greenberg, S. M., Castellucci, V. F., Bayley, H., & Schwartz, J. H. (1987). A molecular mechanism for long-term sensitization in *Aplysia. Nature, 329,* 62–65.

Hawkins, R. D., Abrams, T. W., Carew, T. J., & Kandel, E. R. (1983). A cellular mechanism of classical conditioning in *Aplysia:* Activity-dependent amplification of presynaptic facilitation. *Science, 219,* 400–405.

Hawkins, R. D., Carew, T. J., & Kandel, E. R. (1986a). Effects of interstimulus interval and contingency on classical conditioning of the *Aplysia* siphon withdrawal reflex. *Journal of Neuroscience, 6,* 1695–1701.

Hawkins, R. D., Clark, G., & Kandel, E. R. (1986b). Cell biological studies of learning in simple vertebrate and invertebrate systems. In *Handbook of physiology. The nervous system. Higher functions of the brain* (Sec. 1, Vol. 6, Chap. 2, pp. 25–83). Bethesda, MD: *American Physiology Society.*

Henderson, T. B., & Strong, P. N., Jr. (1972). Classical conditioning in the leech *Macrodbella ditera* as a function of CS and UCS intensity. *Conditional Reflex, 7,* 210–215.

Hochner, B., Klein, M., Schacher, S., & Kandel, E. R. (1986). Additional component in the cellular mechanism of presynaptic facilitation contributes to behavioral dishabituation in *Aplysia. Proceedings of the National Academy of Sciences of the United States of America, 83,* 8794–8798.

Horridge, G. A. (1962). Learning of leg position by the ventral nerve cord in headless insects. *Proceedings of the Royal Society of London. Series B: Biological Sciences, 157,* 33–52.

Hoyle, G. (1965). Neurophysiological studies on "learning" in headless insects. In J. E. Treherne & J. W. L. Beament (Eds.), *Physiology of insect central nervous system* (pp. 203–232). New York: Academic Press.

Kandel, E. R., & Schwartz, J. H. (1982). Molecular biology of learning: modulation of transmitter release. *Science, 218,* 433–443.

Klein, M., & Kandel, E. R. (1978). Presynaptic modulation of voltage-dependent Ca^{2+} current: Mechanism for behavioral sensitization in *Aplysia californica. Proceedings of the National Academy of Sciences of the United States of America, 75,* 3512–3516.

Klein, M., & Kandel, E. R. (1980). Mechanism of calcium current modulation underlying presynaptic facilitation and behavioral sensitization in *Aplysia. Proceedings of the National Academy of Sciences of the United States of America, 77,* 6912–6916.

Klein, M., Shapiro, E., & Kandel, E. R. (1980). Synaptic plasticity and the modulation of the Ca^{2+} current. *Journal of Experimental Biology, 89,* 117–15.

Kovac, M. P., Davis, W. J., Matera, E. M., Morielli, A., & Croll, R. P. (1985). Learning: Neural analysis in the isolated brain of a previously trained mollusc, *Pleurobranchaea californica. Brain Research, 331,* 275–284.

Kuffler, S. W., Nichols, J. G., & Martin, A. R. (1984). *From neuron to brain* (2nd ed.). Sunderland, MA: Sinauer.

Kupfermann, I., Castellucci, V., Pinsker, H., & Kandel, E. R. (1970). Neuronal correlates of habituation and dishabituation of the gill-withdrawal reflex in *Aplysia. Science, 167,* 1743–1745.

Lederhendler, I., Gart, S., & Alkon, D. L. (1986). Classical conditioning of *Hermissenda:* Origin of a new response. *Journal of Neuroscience, 6,* 1325–1331.

Livingstone, M. S. (1985). Genetic dissection of *Drosophila* adenylate cyclase. *Proceedings of the National Academy of Sciences of the United States of America, 82,* 5992–5996.

Lockery, S. R., Rawlins, J. N. P., & Gray, J. A. (1985). Habituation of the shortening reflex in the medicinal leech. *Behavioral Neuroscience, 99,* 333–341.

London, J. A., & Gillette, R. (1984). Functional roles and circuitry in an inhibitory pathway to feeding command neurones in *Pleurobranchaea. Journal of Experimental Biology, 113,* 423–446.

Lukowiak, K. (1986). In vivo classical conditioning of a gill withdrawal reflex in *Aplysia:* Neural correlates and possible neural mechanisms. *Journal of Neurobiology, 17,* 83–101.

Lukowiak, K., & Sahley, C. (1981). The in vitro classical conditioning of the gill withdrawal reflex in *Aplysia californica. Science, 212,* 1516–1518.

Montarolo, P. G., Golet, P., Castellucci, V. F., Morgan, J., Kandel, E. R., & Schacher, S. (1986). A critical period for macromolecular synthesis in long-term facilitation in *Aplysia. Science, 234,* 1249–1254.

Morielli, A. D., Matera, E. M., Kovac, M. P., Shrum, R. G., McCormack, K. J., & Davis, W. J. (1986). Cholinergic suppression: A postsynaptic mechanism of long-term associative learning. *Proceedings of the National Academy of Sciences of the United States of America, 83,* 4556–4560.

Mpitsos, G. J., & Collins, S. D. (1975). Learning: Rapid aversive conditioning in the gastropod mollusk *Pleurobranchaea. Science, 188,* 954–957.

Mpitsos, G. J., Collins, S. D., & McClellan, A. D. (1978). Learning: A model system for physiological studies. *Science, 199,* 497–506.

Muller, K. J., Nichols, J. G., & Stent, G. S. (1981). (Editors). *Neurobiology of the leech.* Cold Spring Harbor, NY: Cold Spring Harbor.

Ocorr, K. A., Walters, E. T., & Byrne, J. H. (1985). Associative conditioning analog selectively increases cAMP levels of tail sensory neurons in *Aplysia. Proceedings of the National Academy of Sciences of the United States of America, 82,* 2548–2552.

Ocorr, K. A., Tabata, M., & Byrne, J. H. (1986). Stimuli that produce sensitization lead to elevation of cyclic AMP levels in tail sensory neurons of *Aplysia. Brain Research, 371,* 190–192.

Pinsker, H., Hening, W. A., Carew, T. J., & Kandel, E. R. (1973). Long-term sensitization of a defensive withdrawal reflex in *Aplysia. Science, 182,* 1039–1042.

Pinsker, H., Kupfermann, I., Castellucci, V., & Kandel, E. R. (1970). Habituation and dishabituation of the gill-withdrawal reflex in *Aplysia. Science, 167,* 1740–1742.

Quinn, W. G., Sziber, P. P., & Booker, R. (1979). The *Drosophila* memory mutant *amnesiac. Nature, 277,* 212–214.

Richards, W. G., Farley, J., & Alkon, D. L. (1984). Extinction of associative learning in *Hermissenda:* Behavior and neural correlates. *Behavioral Brain Research, 14,* 161–170.

Rosen, S. C., Miller, M. W., Weiss, K. R., & Kupfermann, I. (1988). Activity of CBI-2 of *Aplysia* elicits biting-like responses. *Society of Neuroscience Abstracts, 14,* 508.

Sahley, C., Gelperin, A., & Rudy, J. W. (1981). One-trial associative learning modifies food odor preference in a terrestrial mollusc. *Proceedings of the National Academy of Sciences of the United States of America, 78,* 640–642.

Sahley, C. L., & Ready, D. L. (1988). Associative learning modifies two behaviors in the leech *Hirudo medicinalis. Journal of Neuroscience, 8,* 4612–4620.

Sahley, C. L., Rudy, J. W., & Gelperin, A. (1981). An analysis of associative learning in the terrestrial mollusc. I. Higher-order conditioning, blocking, and a transient US-preexposure effect. *Journal of Comparative Physiology A, 144,* 1–8.

Schacher, S., Castellucci, V. F., & Kandel, E. R. (1988). Cyclic AMP evokes long-term facilitation in *Aplysia* sensory neurons that requires new protein synthesis. *Science, 240,* 1667–1669.

Scholz, K. P., & Byrne, J. H. (1987). Long-term sensitization in *Aplysia:* Biophysical correlates in tail sensory neurons. *Science, 235,* 685–687.

Scholz, K. P., & Byrne, J. H. (1988). Intracellular injection of cAMP induces a long-term reduction of neuronal K+ currents. *Science, 240,* 1664–1666.

Schwartz, J. H., Bernier, L., Castellucci, V. F., Polazzolo, M., Saitoh, T., Stapleton, A., & Kandel, E. R. (1983). What molecular steps determine the time course of the memory for short-term sensitization in *Aplysia? Cold Spring Harbor Symposium on Quantitative Biology, 48,* 811–819.

Schwarz, M., & Susswein, A. J. (1986). Identification of the neural pathway for reinforcement of feeding when *Aplysia* learn that food is inedible. *Journal of Neuroscience, 6,* 1528–1536.

Siegelbaum, S. A., Camardo, J. S., & Kandel, E. R. (1982). Serotonin and cyclic AMP close single K+ channels in *Aplysia* sensory neurons. *Nature, 299,* 413–417.

Susswein, A. J., & Byrne, J. H. (1988). Identification and characterization of neurons initiating patterned neural activity in the buccal ganglia of *Aplysia. Journal of Neuroscience, 8,* 2049–2061.

Susswein, A. J., & Schwartz, M. (1983). A learned change of response to inedible food in *Aplysia. Behavioral and Neural Biology, 39,* 1–6.

Susswein, A. J., Schwartz, J. M., & Feldman, E. (1986). Learned changes of feeding behavior in *Aplysia* in response to edible and inedible foods. *Journal of Neuroscience, 6,* 1513–1527.

Tosney, T., & Hoyle, G. (1977). Computer-controlled learning in a simple system. *Proceedings of the Royal Society of London. Series B: Biological Sciences, 195,* 365–393.

Tully, T. (1987). *Drosophila* learning and memory revisited. *Trends in Neuroscience, 10,* 330–335.

Tully, T., & Quinn, W. G. (1985). Classical conditioning and retention in normal and mutant *Drosophila Melanogaster. Journal of Comparative Physiology, 157,* 263–277.

Walsh, J. P., & Byrne, J. H. (1989). Modulation of a steady-state Ca²+-activated, K+ current in tail sensory neurons of *Aplysia:* Role of serotonin and cAMP. *Journal of Neurophysiology, 61,* 32–44.

Walters, E. T. (1987). Site-specific sensitization of defensive reflexes in *Aplysia:* A simple model of long-term hyperalgesia. *Journal of Neuroscience, 7,* 400–407.

Walters, E. T., & Byrne, J. H. (1983a). Associative conditioning of single sensory neurons suggests a cellular mechanism for learning. *Science, 219,* 405–408.

Walters, E. T., & Byrne, J. H. (1983b). Slow depolarization produced by associative conditioning of *Aplysia* sensory neurons may enhance Ca^{2+} entry. *Brain Research, 280,* 165–168.

Walters, E. T., Byrne, J. H., Carew, T. J., & Kandel, E. R. (1983a). Mechanoafferent neurons innervating tail of *Aplysia*. I. Response properties and synaptic connections. *Journal of Neurophysiology, 50,* 1522–1542.

Walters, E. T., Byrne, J. H., Carew, T. J., & Kandel, E. R. (1983b). Mechanoafferent neurons innervating tail of *Aplysia*. II. Modulation by sensitizing stimulation. *Journal of Neurophysiology, 50,* 1543–1559.

Weiss, S., & Drummond, G. I. (1985). Biochemical properties of adenylate cyclase in the gill of *Aplysia californica. Comparative Biochemistry and Physiology. B: Comparative Biochemistry, 80,* 251–255.

Woollacott, M., & Hoyle, G. (1976). Membrane resistance changes associated with single, identified neuron learning. *Society for Neuroscience Abstracts, 2,* 339.

Woollacott, M., & Hoyle, G. (1977). Neural events underlying learning in insects: Changes in pacemaker. *Proceedings of the Royal Society of London. Series B: Biological Sciences, 195,* 395–415.

IV   Neurobiology of Spatial Organization

11 Frameworks for the Study of Human Spatial Impairments

Frances J. Friedrich
University of Utah

The neurologist Oliver Sacks (1985) has described the fascinating case of Dr. P., a musician who was referred to Sacks because of occasional "visual problems." Sacks noted that Dr. P.'s acuity was good—he could see a pin on the floor—but that his attempt to describe a picture revealed the nature of his visual problem:

> His eyes would dart from one thing to another, picking up tiny features, individual features. . . A striking brightness, a colour, a shape would arrest his attention and elicit comment—but in no case did he get the scene-as-a-whole. . . He had no sense whatever of a landscape or scene. (p. 9)

Sacks went on to examine the nature of Dr. P.'s "inner" visual world:

> Was it possible that his visual memory and imagination were still intact? I asked him to imagine entering one of our local squares from the north side, to walk through it, in imagination or in memory, and tell me the buildings he might pass as he walked. He listed the buildings on his right side, but none of those on his left. I then asked him to imagine entering the square from the south. Again he mentioned only those buildings that were on the right side, although these were the very buildings he had omitted before. Those he had "seen" internally before were not mentioned now; presumably, they were no longer "seen". It was evident that his difficulties . . . were as much internal as external, bisecting his visual memory and imagination. (p. 14)

Dr. P.'s deficits included difficulty recognizing familiar faces and objects; at various points he mistook his bare foot for a shoe and his wife's head for his hat. His visual-spatial deficits are particularly striking in the face of his seemingly intact visual acuity, linguistic and musical abilities, and general intellectual functioning. What was it that had gone awry in how Dr. P. saw the world? What is the relation between the spatial deficits he showed, such as an inability to attend to one side of space, and his other visual recognition problems? In short, how are we to characterize and understand the nature of his deficits and the nature of the brain injury that could produce such striking dissociations?

Dr. P.'s deficits, although dramatic, are not unique; indeed, there are a wide variety of visual and spatial deficits reported in the clinical literature. For example, the problem of getting lost in familiar surroundings has become a hallmark of progressive degenerative diseases such as Alzheimer's dementia. Although the clinical literature relating to visuo-spatial deficits has increased considerably over the last 30 years, however, the problem of defining the nature of these impairments and their relation to underlying brain structures remains a significant challenge.

Three distinct, although related, frameworks for investigating spatial abilities and deficits can be identified in the literature, and these frameworks provide the basis for the organization of this chapter. Analyses at the level of *hemispheric specialization* emphasize the superior capability of the nondominant hemisphere, generally the right hemisphere, in the performance of nonverbal tasks. From this view, the processing of spatial information falls within the domain of the right hemisphere, although other nonverbal tasks, such as music perception, are subserved by the right hemisphere as well. In its most extreme form, this approach reflects the assumption that each hemisphere is a self-contained, independently functioning brain and that tasks that involve a specific type of material (e.g., verbal vs. spatial) or a particular type of processing (e.g., analytic vs. holistic, sequential vs. simultaneous) are carried out by one hemisphere.

A second level of analysis focuses on the nature of the spatial task and *dissociable spatial skills,* rather than hemispheric differences in processing. The emphasis here is on different types of spatial representations, such as distinctions among body space, grasping space, and action space (Kolb & Whishaw, 1985), or between personal and extrapersonal space (Semmes, Weinstein, Ghent, & Teuber, 1963). From this view, the localization of spatial skills does not depend on a verbal–nonverbal distinction but on the nature of the spatial representation needed to perform the task.

A third framework for understanding the neural substrates of cognitive functions has recently emerged; this approach reflects a component *process analysis* of cognitive tasks and attempts to relate neural systems to the cognitive subsystems that underlie the processing of spatial information. From this view, a particular task can be broken down into more basic operations; for instance, an imagery task might involve a number of dissociable abilities, including the generation of the image, the retention of the image over time, inspection, decision processes defined by the task at hand, and response production (Farah, 1984; Kosslyn, 1987). Each of these basic operations may be mediated by different brain structures, and any given task may require a different combination of these basic operations. In many respects, the process analysis approach appears to be the most promising, both in terms of understanding the nature of normal cognitive functioning and in terms of clarifying the often inconsistent neuropsychological evidence concerning the localization of spatial processing impairments.

The following section provides an overview of the types of spatial deficits described in the clinical literature and how they have been studied. The subsequent section discusses in more detail the three frameworks described previously and some of the basic issues involved in the analysis of spatial abilities.

SPATIAL IMPAIRMENTS: AN OVERVIEW

A very broad range of deficits appear under the general heading of "spatial impairments," including disorders of visual perception and localization, spatial attention, left–right confusion, directional sense, maze learning, and motor deficits such as misreaching and constructional disorders. It is not within the scope of this chapter to review all the possible varieties of visuo-spatial deficits, and there are a number of reviews available that deal with portions of this vast literature. De Renzi's (1982) book provides one of the most comprehensive reviews of the range of impairments of spatial cognition, and a number of other reviews focus on one or more specific topics, such as visuo-perceptual disorders (e.g., Benton, 1982, 1985b; Ratcliff, 1982), disorders of body schema and right–left confusion (e.g., Benton, 1985a; Frederiks, 1969), constructional deficits (e.g., Benton, 1985b; McFie & Zangwill, 1960; Warrington, 1969), spatial attention disorders (e.g., Heilman, Watson, & Valenstein, 1985; Weinstein & Friedland, 1977), and visual imagery impairments (e.g., Farah, 1984).

Although a comprehensive review of all of these disorders is not attempted here, it is useful to get a sense of the range of deficits considered in the literature, the types of tasks used to identify the deficits, and the location of the brain injuries associated with specific impairments. Selected references are summarized in Tables 11.1 and 11.2, with an indication of the type of task on which impaired performance was found and the associated lesion sites. The entries are grouped according to some general categories reflecting the focus of the study, that is, whether the emphasis was on perceptual processes, memory processes, orientation in space, or constructional processes.

The first group of deficits listed in Table 11.1 reflect *perceptual or attentional* impairments. The tasks used in these studies generally involve the identification or matching of material that is presented in a nonverbal form. For example, in a visual-tactile shape matching task, blindfolded patients run their fingers along the edges of wooden blocks cut into meaningless shapes. They are then asked to identify the shape on a multiple-choice visual display (De Renzi & Scotti, 1969).

TABLE 11.1
Types of Spatial Impairments

Task	Representative Reference	Lesion Producing Impairment
PERCEPTION/ATTENTION		
Visual-tactile shape matching	DeRenzi & Scotti, 1969	R-hemisphere L-hemisphere
Tactile form board	DeRenzi, Faglioni, & Scotti, 1968	R-posterior
Face identification	Newcombe & Russell, 1969	R-frontal R-posterior
Incomplete figure identification	Warrington & James, 1967	R-posterior
Localization	Hannay, Varney, & Benton, 1976	R-hemisphere
Picture matching (unusual orientations)	Warrington & Taylor, 1978	R-posterior
Target detection	Posner et al., 1984	R-parietal L-parietal
Misreaching, simultaneous agnosia	Holmes, 1919	Bilat-posterior
ORIENTATION		
Visual rod orientation	DeRenzi et al., 1971	R-posterior
Locomotion through space	Semmes et al., 1963	L-posterior Bilat-posterior
	Ratcliff & Newcombe, 1973	Bilat-posterior
Body schema	Semmes et al., 1963	L-frontal R-frontal L-posterior
Right–left confusion	Benton, 1985a	L-posterior R-posterior
Mental rotation	Ratcliffe, 1979	R-posterior
	Butters & Barton, 1970	R-parietal L-parietal
	Butters et al., 1972	R-parietal L-frontal
Directional sense	Butters et al., 1972	L-frontal R-parietal L-temporal

Other studies require the identification of visually presented figures or detection of a visual target. One characteristic common to all of the tasks in this category is that the memory requirements of the task are minimized; that is, the visual or tactile stimulus remains available for inspection until a response is made.

Even though these deficits appear to be perceptually based, they cannot be

TABLE 11.2
Types of Spatial Impairments (cont.)

Task	Representative Reference	Lesion Producing Impairment
IMMEDIATE MEMORY		
Location (spatial span)	DeRenzi, Faglioni, & Previdi, 1977	R-posterior L-posterior
	DeRenzi & Nichelli, 1975	R-posterior L-posterior
Abstract pattern recognition	Gianotti, Caltagirone, & Miceli, 1978	R-posterior L-posterior
Face recognition	Milner, 1968	R-temporal Frontal
LEARNING		
Stylus maze learning	Milner, 1965	R-temporal R-frontal
	Ratcliff & Newcombe, 1973	R-posterior Bilat-posterior
	Newcombe & Russell, 1969	R-frontal R-posterior
	DeRenzi, Faglioni, & Villa, 1977	R-posterior
Block arrangement	DeRenzi et al., 1968	R-posterior L-posterior
Topographical amnesia	DeRenzi, Faglioni, & Villa, 1977	R-posterior
Location (superspan)	DeRenzi, Faglioni, & Previdi, 1977	R-posterior L-posterior
CONSTRUCTION		
Block design (WAIS subtest)	Benton, 1969	R-hemisphere L-hemisphere
	Piercy & Smith, 1962	R-parietal L-parietal
Drawing	Warrington et al., 1966	R-hemisphere L-hemisphere
	Piercy & Smith, 1962	R-parietal L-parietal

accounted for on the basis of a loss of sensory information alone, although in some cases a visual field deficit may be present. In the case of simultaneous agnosia, for instance, a patient may accurately identify a series of objects when each is presented singly but be unable to see more than one object at a time, even when two objects overlap a single spatial location. Such deficits appear to reflect higher order perceptual impairments that involve the organization and grouping of perceptual information or the localization of information in space.

The tasks that are grouped under the heading of *orientation* in Table 11.1 are distinct from the perceptual tasks in that an analysis of a specifically spatial element of the stimulus is required to perform the task. In this respect, these tasks seem to tap into more genuinely "spatial" processes than the perceptual tasks, which may be considered spatial primarily by virtue of the nonverbal nature of the stimulus materials. Even so, a wide assortment of deficits falls into this category, ranging from impairments in the judgment of line orientation (De Renzi, Faglioni, & Scotti, 1971) to map reading (Ratcliff & Newcombe, 1973) to mental rotation of inverted figures (Ratcliff, 1979). Moreover, the response requirements of the different tasks vary considerably; a spatial locomotion task requires that the patient use a map to walk through a maze, whereas the directional sense task requires the use of verbal labels, such as the identification of "right" versus "left."

The spatial tasks grouped under the first two categories in Table 11.2 all have a distinct memory requirement inherent to the task, although the nature of the memory demand may differ from task to task. Entries listed under *immediate memory* reflect tasks in which spatial information must be maintained for a brief period of time. For example, the Corsi block test (e.g., De Renzi, Faglioni, & Previdi, 1977) evaluates memory for location and provides a spatial analog to the verbal digit span test. The Corsi block test consists of a board with small cubes scattered about it at nine locations; in the immediate memory test, the examiner taps a number of blocks in a given order and the patient must immediately replicate the sequence.

The Corsi block test is explicitly spatial, in that a sequence of spatial locations must be recalled; however, other immediate memory tasks may be considered spatial to the extent that nonverbal material is used. In the face recognition task, for instance, patients studied a set of 12 photographed faces for 45 seconds and were then asked to identify those studied from a set of 25 photographs (Milner, 1968). This task does not require a judgment of spatial features, such as location or orientation; nevertheless, it has generally been assumed to reflect nonverbal processes that are similar to those used in more explicitly spatial tasks, such as maze learning.

Tasks listed under the heading of *learning* differ from the immediate memory tasks in several respects. In general, the information is acquired over a series of repeated trials and must be retained for a longer period of time. For example, the Corsi block test, described earlier as a measure of immediate memory for location, can also be used to evaluate the acquisition of longer sequences of locations over a series of trials. Interestingly, these two types of spatial memory impairments are dissociable; some patients, most often those with parietal lobe involvement, show an impairment on an immediate memory task but not a long-term memory task (De Renzi & Nichelli, 1975), whereas others, right temporal lobe patients in particular, have a normal immediate spatial memory span but are unable to acquire longer sequences over repeated trials (Milner, 1971).

The *constructional* tasks listed in Table 11.2 generally require an organized motor performance, involving either the assembly of blocks to match a model design or graphomotor skills, such as copying or drawing. Quantitative evaluation of graphomotor performance is often difficult, although efforts have been made to systematically rate the quality of drawings and the types of errors that occur (Warrington, James, & Kinsbourne, 1966). Performance on assembly tasks may be somewhat easier to evaluate; the block design task, for example, is both timed and graded in difficulty, which allows for more quantitive measurement. The patient is shown a model of a design constructed from colored blocks and is asked to reproduce the design; difficulty is varied by the complexity of the design and the number of blocks required to produce it. Although constructional disorders are correlated with visuo-perceptual disturbances (Piercy & Smyth, 1962), they are generally thought to represent an impairment of the integration of perceptual and motor skills (Benton, 1985b). The broad category of constructional disorders may, in fact, consist of at least two distinct subclasses of impairment, one reflecting a primary disorder of spatial perception and another resulting from a disturbance of complex motor planning (Benton, 1982; Warrington et al., 1966).

At this point, it should already be clear that the first step in understanding the nature of spatial impairments—that of defining what constitutes a spatial task—is in itself a difficult issue. Should the critical feature be the nature of the material, so that presentation of pictoral stimuli, by definition, provides a measure of spatial abilities? Certainly many types of visual nonverbal material can be labeled, and many seemingly spatial tasks can be performed using verbal strategies. Should only those tasks that explicitly assess the spatial aspects of a stimulus be treated as measures of spatial ability? This definition would leave out whole classes of perceptual deficits, such as neglect of one side of space or simultaneous agnosia, that are based on detection or recognition performance. Even excluding those tasks that do not require an explicitly spatial analysis, a number of apparently different types of spatial abilities remain. The mental rotation, map-reading, and stylus maze tasks, for instance, seem to tap into different kinds of spatial representations.

The lesions associated with spatial impairments also vary widely, as Tables 11.1 and 11.2 demonstrate. Performance on a particular task may be generally associated with a specific lesion site; visual line orientation judgments, for instance, most frequently result from posterior lesions in the right hemisphere. Across the whole range of spatial impairments, however, lesions in virtually every area of the brain have been implicated, including both anterior and posterior, and left- as well as right-hemisphere lesions.

From this overview, any effort to identify a single deficit or a single lesion location common to all spatial impairments seems doomed to failure. However, the existing literature can be organized in various ways in order to clarify the nature of the brain mechanisms that underlie spatial abilities. The next section reviews the most important frameworks that have emerged, the assumptions that underlie them, and how well they appear to account for spatial deficits.

FRAMEWORKS FOR THE ANALYSIS
OF SPATIAL IMPAIRMENTS

The problems inherent in defining a spatial task have already been noted, and in some sense the frameworks for understanding spatial impairments that have emerged reflect an attempt to identify a few organizing principles that implicitly define and account for a wide range of factors that affect performance on spatial tasks. Some of the factors that may be important to keep in mind when evaluating the different approaches include the following:

1. Task Demands.   A range of important considerations fall under this heading. As indicated earlier, tasks may differ in terms of memory demands, in specific response requirements, or in the types of material used; these aspects of the task essentially define the spatial problem and how performance will be measured. In addition, strategy selection or the nature of the process carried out on that space may vary; some tasks may make a heavy demand on the ability to generate a visual image, whereas others may require a reorientation or transformation of spatial information.

2. Individual Differences.   There is an extensive literature on individual differences indicating that a range of spatial abilities exists within the normal population (e.g., Horn, 1978; McGee, 1979; Pellegrino & Kail, 1982). In the case of a patient who is assessed after an acute brain injury, of course, the prior ability level of that individual may be difficult to determine. Moreover, spatial abilities appear to decline more rapidly than verbal abilities in the course of normal aging (Berg, Hertzog & Hunt, 1982; Schaie, 1979). Such a decline has consequences not only for the absolute level of performance that an individual might display, but also for the strategies that are used to perform a task.

3. Consequences of Aphasic Disorders.   A related issue concerns the role of a language disturbance in poor performance on a spatial task. The possible impact of impaired language function is an obvious consideration in tasks that require verbal responses, such as right–left orientation tasks. Some efforts have been made to evaluate the role of aphasia in these tasks (Benton, 1985a), and in general the spatial impairments shown by left-hemisphere patients can not be completely accounted for on the basis of a language disturbance. Determining whether verbal *mediation* is used to solve a spatial problem even when a verbal response is not required is a more difficult problem, however. Any given task may be performed with either a spatial or a verbal strategy, even those that are designed to be more amenable to the use of spatial representations, such as mental rotation (Just & Carpenter, 1985) and cognitive map tasks (Berg, 1988). Consequently, patients with left-hemisphere lesions could show impairments on spatial tasks either because of the contribution of the left hemisphere to spatial processing or because some individuals attempt to use a verbal strategy and fail.

4. Consequences of Low-Level Impairments on Higher Level Functions. Dissociations within an individual, such as better performance on perceptual tasks than orientation tasks, lend support to the argument that many high-level cognitive impairments cannot be accounted for on the basis of subtle low-level deficits. However, as spatial tasks become more complex, the effects of low-level deficits may become more apparent. For example, certain types of reading errors produced by patients with left parietal lesions have been associated with subtle spatial attention deficits that are often not reflected in standard clinical assessment procedures (Friedrich, Walker & Posner, 1985).

No theory currently exists that addresses and accounts for all of these factors; nevertheless, these considerations provide a guide in evaluating the frameworks that have emerged in recent years.

Hemispheric Specialization

The most basic organizing principle that has been applied to the study of spatial impairments is the notion that the two hemispheres perform distinctly different functions. The idea that the right hemisphere in humans is specialized for nonverbal functions dates back at least to the late 19th century, when John Hughlings-Jackson suggested lateralization of visual-perceptual abilities (Jackson, 1874/ 1915). More widespread acceptance of this notion, however, did not occur for several decades, bolstered by studies of large groups of patients analyzed on the basis of lateralization of lesions. For example, two types of visual recognition disorders associated with injury to the two hemispheres have been distinguished (Hecaen & Albert, 1978). From this view, deficits in the recognition of objects, colors, and letters tend to occur following left-hemisphere lesions, whereas spatial agnosia and face recognition deficits are associated with right-hemisphere lesions.

Similarly, epileptic patients who have had portions of the temporal lobe surgically removed show dissociations between verbal and nonverbal material. Deficits in maze learning and in the recognition and recall of complex nonverbal material occur subsequent to right temporal excisions, whereas deficits for verbal material occur after left temporal excisions (Corkin, 1965; Milner, 1965, 1968, 1971). Deficits in perceptual tasks involving nonverbal material, such as dot estimation and contour discrimination, have also been found following right temporal excisions, although these impairments may be relatively subtle (Kimura, 1963; Meier & French, 1965).

The hemispheric specialization of high-level spatial cognition has received further support from the "split-brain" work, in which the commissures connecting the two hemispheres have been cut in an effort to control intractible epilepsy. This procedure allows the functioning of a single, intact hemisphere to be evaluated independently of the other hemisphere. While work with patients with cortical lesions has demonstrated differential deficits in the processing of verbal and nonverbal material, the split-brain work has shown that the right hemisphere is not only capable of functioning independently of the left hemisphere but is also superior to the left hemisphere in the performance of certain nonverbal tasks (see Springer & Deutsch, 1985).

For example, in a delayed matching to sample task, split-brain patients were asked to tactilely explore a meaningless wire figure and then identify it among several alternatives (Milner & Taylor, 1972). These patients were generally unable to match-to-sample even at the zero delay with the right hand (left hemisphere), whereas the left hand (right hemisphere) was successful at delays ranging from 15 seconds to 2 minutes. Similarly, after commissurotomy, right-handed patients were strikingly better at performing a variety of tasks with the left hand than with the right hand, including copying geometric designs, performing a block design task, and sorting block sizes and shapes into categories (e.g., Gazzaniga & Le Doux, 1978; Sperry, 1982). Right hemisphere superiority also occurs in more perceptually based tasks, such as face recognition (e.g., Levy, Trevarthen, & Sperry, 1972), perception of part–whole relations (Nebes, 1978), and visuo-tactile matching of abstract shapes (Franco & Sperry, 1977).

Both the temporal excision data and the split-brain research demonstrate that the nondominant hemisphere has important spatial capabilities; these findings have been particularly important in the context of the previously held belief that the right hemisphere was passive, mute, and essentially "retarded" with respect to high-level cognition (Sperry, 1982). Even so, the use of a lateralization framework for understanding spatial deficits that result from natural lesions has severe limitations. Very often, the verbal or nonverbal nature of the material is assumed to determine which hemisphere will be engaged to perform the task, and questions of task demands or strategies for performing the task are not addressed. As a result, this approach does not fare well in accounting for lesion sites producing spatial impairments. Although the general consensus is that a right-hemisphere lesion is more often associated with spatial deficits of greater severity than is a left-hemisphere lesion, a variety of spatial deficits also result from left-hemisphere lesions. In fact, deficits in seemingly nonverbal tasks are apparent in patients with left-hemisphere lesions on tasks ranging from complex visual discrimination (Benton, Hamsher, Varney, & Spreen, 1983) and spatial short-term memory (DeRenzi & Nichelli, 1975; De Renzi, Faglioni, & Previdi, 1977) to mental rotation (Butters & Barton, 1970) and constructional tasks (Benton, 1985b).

One possible reason that spatial deficits resulting from left-hemisphere lesions were initially overlooked involves the methodology used. In many studies, the comparison of interest has been the relative performance of patients with left- versus right-hemisphere lesions, and very often the right-hemisphere patients have a significant deficit compared to left-hemisphere patients. When a normal control group is included, however, left-hemisphere patients frequently show some degree of impairment relative to the controls. In a task requiring subtle visual discriminations, for example, patients with right temporal excisions were 46% worse than patients with left temporal excisions; however, the left temporal patients were also significantly impaired relative to normal controls (Meier & French, 1965). Similarly, in a review of patients with unilateral lesions, 58% of the right-hemisphere patients and 47% of the left-hemisphere patients were im- paired in complex form discrimination relative to normal controls (Benton et al., 1983).

Investigations of spatial short-term memory deficits reveal a similar pattern, in which posterior lesions in either hemisphere produce some degree of impair- ment, but with relatively more severe deficits resulting from right posterior lesions (see De Renzi, 1982, for a review). For example, both right and left posterior patients have a significantly reduced spatial short-term memory span relative to normal controls, but these two patient groups did not differ from one another (De Renzi, Faglioni, & Previdi, 1977). When either a filled or unfilled delay was introduced into the span test, both patients and controls showed a decline in performance, but the failure of retention was worse for the right posterior patients than for any other group. De Renzi et al. also looked at performance in a learning-to-criterion task, in which a patient was given 50 trials to learn a spatial sequence two items longer than his or her span. All control subjects reached criterion, within 13 trials on the average; however, 30% of the left posterior patients and 65% of the right posterior patients failed to reach the criterion at all. Although the right hemisphere does seem to play a dominant role under certain memory conditions, damage to either hemisphere can disrupt spa- tial short-term memory.

Given evidence of this sort, which shows that a hemispheric specialization scheme based on a strict verbal–nonverbal dichotomy will not hold up, other bases for specialization have been suggested. For example, Levy (1974) argued that the hemispheres are specialized on the basis of the type of processing performed, with the right hemisphere making use of holistic strategies and the left hemisphere performing analytic functions. Hemispheric specialization has also been linked to the simultaneous or sequential nature of a given task (see Moscovitch, 1979, for a review). However, neither the analytic-holistic hypoth- esis nor the sequential-processing hypothesis succeeds in fully accounting for functional differences between the hemispheres (Gazzaniga & Le Doux, 1978; Moscovitch, 1979). Indeed, Moscovitch (1979) suggested that there may not be only one organizing principle at work:

Depending on the demands of the task, the organization of the system at the time the task is attempted, and a host of other internal and external factors, the operation of different structures will be emphasized, which in turn will bias the operation of the entire system now in one way, now in another. According to this view, the organizing principle, to some extent, is situationally determined. (p. 417)

Overall, then, although the right hemisphere is important in the performance of many spatial tasks, attempts to dichotomize the left and right hemispheres as specialized for verbal and spatial systems, respectively, fail to account for the diversity of spatial deficits found in brain-injured patients. However, some consistent patterns of dissociation *within* the spatial domain have emerged that may provide a useful framework for understanding spatial impairments.

Dissociable Spatial Skills

Attempts to dichotomize cognitive functions on the basis of hemispheric specialization have proved to be oversimplistic; the verbal–nonverbal processing distinction, in particular, makes little headway in terms of defining what constitutes a spatial task. The notion that multiple dissociable spatial skills can be identified addresses this problem more directly and represents somewhat of a shift in level of analysis. That is, rather than attempting to look at brain-behavior relations on the basis of the verbal or nonverbal nature of the stimulus materials, this framework requires that task demands be considered in more detail.

A good example of the importance of this type of task analysis can be seen in the case of spatial orientation tasks. Attempts to localize spatial orientation ability have been made difficult by a lack of converging evidence across different tasks. Topographical orientation is often evaluated using a visually guided stylus maze learning task, in which a patient learns, over repeated trials, to move a stylus in a certain path through a maze. Patients with right parietal lesions are impaired in this type of maze learning, whereas left parietal patients perform at normal levels (Newcombe & Russell, 1969; Ratcliff & Newcombe, 1973); impairments on this task have also been related to right temporal/hippocampal excision (Milner, 1965), and left or right frontal lesions (Corkin, 1965; Milner, 1965).

In contrast, tasks that require changes in body orientation or an environmental scale produce a different pattern of results. In a locomotor task, for instance, a pattern of disks is laid out on the floor, and the patient must use a map in order to follow the correct path. Lesions involving either the right or left posterior regions of the brain produce impairments in this type of map-reading task (Semmes, Weinstein, Ghent, & Teuber, 1955, 1963; Hecaen, Tzortzis, & Masure, 1972, cited in De Renzi, 1982). A third measure of orientation, relating specifically to a topographical representation of the body, produces yet another pattern of results: Left posterior lesions and anterior lesions of either hemisphere, particularly of the left hemisphere, produce deficits when the task involves pointing to body parts, whereas right posterior patients perform at normal levels (Semmes et al., 1963).

Thus, although the maze learning, locomotor map-reading, and body part tasks all fall within the general category of spatial orientation, no single lesion site is associated with deficits on these tasks. Dissociations among these tasks within individual patients have helped to clarify the situation somewhat. The maze learning task makes demands on memory that the other tasks do not, and selective impairments of topographical memory occur in patients who appear to be intact in terms of other visual perceptual and spatial tasks (DeRenzi, Faglioni, & Villa, 1977; Whiteley & Warrington, 1978). Poor performance on the maze learning task could, therefore, result from a specific memory deficit (with no generalized spatial disorientation) in the case of right temporal lesions, but from a specific spatial impairment in the case of right posterior lesions (Newcombe & Russell, 1969).

The dissociation of maze learning and other spatial tasks with minimal memory requirements highlights the importance of analyzing tasks in terms of general categories of cognitive processes, such as the perceptual, memory, and response requirements. Another important distinction that has emerged concerns the nature of the spatial information itself (see, e.g., O'Keefe & Nadel, 1978). One theoretical approach distinguishes three functionally different types of space, including body space, grasping space, and action space, each of which might have a different neural representation (Kolb & Whishaw, 1985). Body space basically consists of the surface of the body and the ability to localize points on that surface, although it may also include the ability to recognize objects external to the body by touch. The area immediately surrounding the body, within reach of the individual, can be considered grasping space. Disorders of reaching, of localizing auditory information, and of eye movements reflect impairments in this type of spatial representation. Action space consists of space on a larger environmental scale; knowledge of action space is needed in order to generate a mental representation that will allow an individual to get from one place to another.

Although attempts to specify the nature of space in this way are intuitively appealing, the value of these distinctions in terms of associating different brain regions with different types of spatial representation is less clear. For example, damage to either the right or left parietal lobe may produce a deficit in tactile object recognition, which requires a body space representation according to this framework. However, unilateral parietal lobe damage is also associated with misreaching and disorders of eye movements, which fall within the scope of action space, and with disorders of route-walking and left–right orientation, which require action space representations (Kolb & Whishaw, 1985).

A somewhat different approach is based on the idea that types of space can be distinguished in terms of the point of reference used in orientation. Personal, or egocentric, space uses the body as the point of reference, and the position of an object in space (e.g., left vs. right) relative to an individual will change as body position changes. In contrast, extrapersonal, or allocentric, space makes use of absolute spatial positions that remain fixed irrespective of body position (e.g., the location of New York on a map).

The various orientation deficits described earlier have been discussed in terms of dissociations between impairments of personal space and extrapersonal space (e.g., Butters, Soeldner, & Fedio, 1972; Semmes et al., 1963). According to this view, frontal lesions produce impairments on tasks that require a body schema or in which the body is used as a reference point in space, whereas posterior lesions interfere with representations of extrapersonal space. For example, in a task that required patients to look at a diagram of a body and to point to corresponding parts of their own bodies, both left and right anterior lesions resulted in significant impairments (Semmes et al., 1963). In contrast, the route-walking (extrapersonal) task revealed no impairment in anterior patients but significant loss for left and bilateral posterior lesion patients (Semmes et al., 1963).

Although this dissociation between performance on personal and extrapersonal spatial tasks is relatively clear and is consistent with other findings (e.g., Butters et al., 1972), the argument that these tasks reflect anatomically separable spatial representations has not been well supported (DeRenzi, 1982; Kolb & Whishaw, 1985). One problem is that performance on other right–left orientation tasks, which should reflect orientation in personal space, do not converge with the results of body schema studies. Left–right confusion frequently results from posterior damage and is, in fact, one component of Gerstmann's syndrome, associated with left parietal lesions (Hecaen & Albert, 1978). On the other hand, frontal lesions have been shown to produce deficits in maze learning (Corkin, 1965; Milner, 1965), which should reflect the use of extrapersonal rather than personal space. Overall, after reviewing the literature, De Renzi (1982) concluded that disorders of orientation in personal space are not clearly distinguishable from disorientation in extrapersonal space.

Process Analyses

Although efforts to identify a set of dissociable spatial skills with separate neural substrates have not been completely successful at this point, that approach reflects a greater awareness of the importance of different task requirements. The component process approach takes this type of analysis one step further. From this view, any given task can be analyzed in terms of more basic operations that can be isolated and measured; tasks that are related, such as two different orientation tasks, might be similar in requiring many of the same basic operations but differ in other required processes.

A process analysis has clear applications for the study of cognitive deficits resulting from brain injury; in fact, this approach may allow us to think about complex cognitive functions at a level that is more compatible with the "language" of the neural system (Posner, 1987). Whereas the hemispheric specialization framework focuses on the type of material to be processed and the spatial representation framework considers the type of spatial task to be performed, a process level analysis attempts to identify the component operations *within* a task and the brain mechanisms that underlie those processes. A lesion at a particular location, then, might be manifested in different ways, depending on the specific task and the component operations required. Alternatively, lesions in several different areas of the brain might each produce a deficit on the same task if different component processes are impaired by the various lesions.

This approach has recently been applied to the study of spatial attention impairments. A patient with unilateral visual neglect or extinction shows a lack of awareness for information on the side of space opposite the lesion, even when visual acuity in that field remains intact. Evidence of such deficits can be seen in a wide variety of tasks, ranging from visual discrimination and recognition tasks to tasks that do not require complex visual perception, such as drawing pictures from memory, describing visual images, and tactile maze exploration (Bisiach & Luzzati, 1978; De Renzi, Faglioni & Scotti, 1970). Some form of spatial attention deficit can result from injury to several different areas of the brain, including the posterior parietal lobe (e.g., Bisiach, Luzzatti & Perani, 1979; Heilman et al., 1985), the frontal lobe (e.g., Heilman & Valenstein, 1972; Morrow & Ratcliff, 1987), and the thalamus (Watson & Heilman, 1979). Overall, however, the right parietal lobe is most frequently associated with severe spatial attention deficits (De Renzi, 1982; Weinstein & Friedland, 1977).

How can a component process analysis be applied to the study of spatial attention deficits? The first step involves identifying possible subcomponent processes within a specific task. The cued target detection task has been shown to be sensitive to spatial attention impairments and has been used with several neurological populations (Baynes, Holtzman, & Volpe, 1986; Morrow & Ratcliffe, 1987; Posner, Cohen, & Rafal, 1982; Posner, Walker, Friedrich, & Rafal, 1984; Posner, Inhoff, Friedrich & Cohen, 1987; Rafal & Posner, 1987; Rafal, Posner, Friedman, Inhoff, & Bernstein, 1988). In a typical experiment of this type, simple response time to detect a target (e.g., an asterisk) is measured; the target can appear at one of two or more locations in the visual field. Prior to the target, a cue is presented to let the subject know where to expect the target. On 80% of the trials, the cue is valid, accurately indicating where the target would appear; on the remaining trials, however, the cue is invalid. The difference in detection time on the valid and invalid trials serves as a marker of attentional orienting. That is, targets are detected more quickly if they occur at the cued location than at an uncued location; this relative facilitation is an indication that attention has been shifted to the cued location.

Although this type of detection task seems extremely simple, a number of operations within the attentional system are required to carry it out. Three elementary processes in particular have been identified as needed in order to shift attention to a new spatial location: An individual must **disengage** attention from the current focus, **move** attention through space, and then **engage** attention at the new spatial location (Posner, 1980: Posner, Cohen, & Rafal, 1982).

Recent evidence suggests that each of these operations can be selectively impaired by lesions to different brain structures. For example, unilateral parietal lobe lesions produce a deficit that is specific to the "disengage" operation (Baynes et al., 1986; Morrow & Ratcliff, 1987; Posner et al., 1982; Posner et al., 1984; Posner, Inhoff, Friedrich, & Cohen, 1987; Posner, Walker, Friedrich, & Rafal, 1987; Rafal & Posner, 1987). These patients detect the target more quickly on valid than invalid trials, demonstrating that they can shift attention to the cued location, which in turn facilitates target detection at that location. However, on invalid trials they have unusually long response times for targets contralateral to the lesion; that is, once attention is cued to the "good," ipsilateral field, they have a great deal of trouble disengaging attention from that location to shift to a target in the "bad," contralateral field. This pattern of impairment occurs in both left and right parietal patients, although the effect is generally more evident in the right parietal patients (Posner et al., 1984).

Additional studies using this cued target detection task indicate that the "engage" and "move" operations may be selectively impaired by damage to other locations. Patients with midbrain lesions resulting from progressive supranuclear palsy (PSP) appear to be impaired in the "move" operation, resulting in unusually slow movement of attention across space (Posner, Choate, Rafal, & Vaughan, 1985; Rafal et al., 1988). It should be noted that the target detection task itself does not require eye movements; in fact, patients are instructed to keep their eyes directed to a central fixation point. Nevertheless, the spatial attention impairment in these midbrain patients appears to be a deficit in an internal attention-shifting operation that is linked to the overt eye-movement system. Finally, an impairment in the "engage" operation appears to be associated with thalamic lesions (Rafal & Posner, 1987). Even though these patients are able to shift attention through space, they seem to have difficulty using attention to facilitate target detection.

An impairment in any of these operations may affect not only simple target detection but a variety of spatial cognition functions, to the extent that the impaired process plays an important role in a particular task. For example, in parietal patients, even a mild spatial attention impairment can have consequences for higher level pattern recognition, such as visual matching or reading (Friedrich et al., 1985; Sieroff, Pollatsek, & Posner, 1988). The picture is a complex one, however; even within the same task, evidence of a deficit can depend on the nature of the visual stimulus materials. Thus, in a visual matching task, a spatial attention deficit has a greater effect on unfamiliar letter strings than on highly familiar words (Friedrich et al., 1985; Sieroff et al., 1988), suggesting that the two types of materials make different demands on the spatial attention system.

CONCLUSIONS

Although we have yet to achieve a unified theory of spatial cognition, the emergence of increasingly complex levels of analysis marks progress toward that goal. Each of the frameworks discussed here focuses on important factors that must be incorporated into a unified theory. The hemispheric specialization approach emphasizes external factors, such as the nature of the stimulus material. Although the notion that the two hemispheres operate independently and on different types of materials is overly simplistic, this approach nevertheless provides a starting point for identifying differences among tasks and their processing requirements. The emphasis on dissociable spatial skills shifts the focus to more specific task demands and to internal factors, such as different ways that space can be internally represented. This approach demands a more careful consideration of how a "spatial" task is defined and has resulted in attempts to categorize tasks and abilities in terms of processing similarities.

Rather than categorizing tasks with respect to global spatial abilities, the component process approach tends to focus on one particular task and identify the underlying cognitive operations required. This approach opens up the possibility of considering alternative strategies in task performance and of specifying more precisely the similarities and differences among various types of spatial tasks. Both internal and external factors affecting the cognitive system must necessarily be taken into account in this type of task analysis.

As a result of the increasing attention to specific task requirements, a number of basic operations have been identified that function together to carry out spatial processing. New tasks have been created in order to isolate and selectively measure these operations. In the case of impairments in visual imagery and in orienting of spatial attention, deficits in the different component processes appear to be associated with lesions to different brain structures. The fact that several different brain lesions can produce an impairment on a given task becomes more comprehensible in this context; appropriate testing can reveal that the nature of the deficit will differ, depending on the specific brain structure, and the specific component operation, affected.

The task of identifying the neural mechanisms underlying spatial cognition in humans remains a considerable challenge, despite the progress in this area. Ideally, as we continue to identify basic processes underlying individual spatial tasks, we will come to a better understanding of the similarities across spatial tasks as well. For example, in the case of spatial attention deficits, higher level tasks such as reading, scanning a visual image, or constructing a spatial representation based on tactile information, will be affected by a deficit in one of these processes to the extent that the higher level task, and the individual's strategy for performing the task, requires that operation. At this point, however, our understanding of the components of complex tasks does not readily permit predictions about how high-level functions will be affected by lower level deficits. So, although the potential is great, so is the complexity inherent in such a detailed level of analysis. As Moscovitch (1979) pointed out, there are a number of internal and external factors that may influence the organization of the cognitive system at any given time; the challenge is to identify some simplifying principles to create a coherent framework for understanding spatial impairments without losing sight of the complexity of cognitive functions and of brain–behavior relationships.

ACKNOWLEDGMENTS

The author thanks Jean Walker for her assistance in conducting the literature review and Dr. Cindy Berg for her helpful comments on an earlier version of this chapter.

REFERENCES

Baynes, K., Holtzman, J., & Volpe, B. (1986). Components of visual attention: Alterations in response patterns to visual stimuli following parietal lobe infarction. *Brain, 109,* 99–114.

Benton, A. L. (1969). Disorders of spatial orientation. In P. J. Vinken & G. W. Bruyn (Eds.) *Handbook of clinical neurology* (Vol. 3, pp. 212–228). Amsterdam: North Holland.

Benton, A. L. (1982). Spatial thinking in neurological patients: Historical aspects. In M. Potegal (Ed.), *Spatial abilities: Developmental and physiological foundations* (pp. 253–275). New York: Academic Press.

Benton, A. (1985a). Body schema disturbances: Finger agnosia and right–left disorientation. In K. Heilman & E. Valenstein (Eds.), *Clinical neuropsychology* (pp. 115–130). New York: Oxford University Press.

Benton, A. L. (1985b). Visuoperceptual, visuospatial, and visuoconstructive disorders. In K. M. Heilman & E. Valenstein (Eds.), *Clinical neuropsychology* (pp. 151–185). New York: Oxford University Press.

Benton, A., Hamsher, K., Varney, N., & Spreen, O. (1983). *Contributions to neuropsychological assessment.* New York: Oxford University Press.

Berg, C. (1988, April). *Individual differences in strategies for verifying cognitive maps.* Paper presented at the Cognitive Aging Conference, Atlanta, GA.

Berg, C., Hertzog, C. & Hunt, E. (1982). Age differences in the speed of mental rotation. *Developmental Psychology, 18,* 95–107.

Bisiach, E., & Luzzatti, C. (1978). Unilateral neglect of representational space. *Cortex, 14,* 129–133.

Bisiach, E., Luzzati, C. & Perani, D. (1979). Unilateral neglect, representational schema and consciousness. *Brain, 102,* 609–618.

Butters, N., & Barton, M. (1970). Effect of parietal lobe damage on performance of reversible operations in space. *Neuropsychologia, 8,* 205–214.

Butters, N., Soeldner, C., & Fedio, P. (1972). Comparison of parietal and frontal lobe spatial deficits in man: Extrapersonal vs. personal (egocentric) space. *Perceptual and Motor Skills, 34,* 27–34.

Corkin, S. (1965). Tactually-guided maze learning in man: Effects of unilateral cortical excisions and bilateral hippocampal lesions. *Neuropsychologia, 3,* 339–351.

De Renzi, E. (1982). *Disorders of space exploration and cognition.* New York: John Wiley.

De Renzi, E., Faglioni, P., & Previdi, P. (1977). Spatial memory and hemispheric locus of lesion. *Cortex, 13,* 424–433.

De Renzi, E., Faglioni, P., & Scotti, G. (1968). Tactile spatial impairment and unilateral cerebral damage. *Journal of Nervous and Mental Disease, 146,* 468–475.

De Renzi, E., Faglioni, P. & Scotti, G. (1970). Hemispheric contribution to the exploration of space through the visual and tactile modality. *Cortex, 6,* 191–203.

De Renzi, E., Faglioni, P., & Scotti, G. (1971). Judgment of spatial orientation in patients with focal brain damage. *Journal of Neurology, Neurosurgery & Psychiatry, 34,* 489–495.

De Renzi, E., Faglioni, P., & Villa, P. (1977). Topographical amnesia. *Journal of Neurology, Neurosurgery and Psychiatry, 40,* 498–505.

De Renzi, E. & Nichelli, P. (1975). Verbal and non-verbal short-term memory impairment following hemispheric damage. *Cortex, 11,* 341–354.

De Renzi, E. & Scotti, G. (1969). The influence of spatial disorders in impairing tactual discrimination of shapes. *Cortex, 5,* 53–62.

Farah, M. J. (1984). The neurological basis of mental imagery: A componential analysis. *Cognition, 18,* 245–272.

Franco, L. & Sperry, R. (1977). Hemisphere lateralization for cognitive processing of geometry. *Neurospcyhologia, 15,* 107–114.

Frederiks, A. (1969). Disorders of the body schema. In P. J. Vinken & G. W. Bruyn (Eds.), *Handbook of clinical neurology* (pp. 207–240). Amsterdam: North-Holland.

Friedrich, F. J., Walker, J., & Posner, M. I. (1985). Effects of parietal lesions on visual matching: Implications for reading errors. *Cognitive Neuropsychology, 2,* 253–264.

Gainotti, G., Caltagirone, C., & Miceli, G. (1978). Immediate visual-spatial memory in hemisphere-damaged patients & impairments of verbal coding and of perceptual procession. *Neuropsychologia, 16,* 501–507.

Gazzaniga, M. S., & Le Doux, J. E. (1978). *The integrated mind.* New York: Plenum.

Hannay, H. J., Varney, N. R., & Benton, A. L. (1976). Visual localization in patients with unilateral brain disease. *Journal of Neurology, Neurosurgery and Psychiatry, 39,* 307–313.

Hecaen, H., & Albert, M. (1978). *Human neuropsychology.* New York: Wiley and Sons.

Hecaen, H., Tzortzis, C., & Masure, M. (1972). Troubles de l'orientation spatiale dans une éperuve de recherche d'intineraire lors des lésions corticales unilaterales. *Perception, 1,* 325–330.

Heilman, K. & Valenstein, E. (1972). Frontal lobe neglect in man. *Neurology, 22,* 660–664.

Heilman, K. M., Watson, R. T., & Valenstein, E. (1985). Neglect and related disorders. In K. M. Heilman & E. Valenstein (Eds.), *Clinical neuropsychology* (pp. 243–294). New York: Oxford University Press.

Holmes, G. (1919). Disturbances of visual space perception. *British Medical Journal, 2,* 230–233.

Horn, J. (1978). Human ability systems. In P. B. Baltes (Ed.), *Life-span development and behavior* (Vol. 1, pp. 211–256). New York: Academic Press.

Jackson, J. H. (1915). On the duality of the brain. *Brain, 38,* 80–103. (Originally published in 1874.)

Just, M. & Carpenter, P. (1985). Cognitive coordinate systems: Accounts of mental rotation and individual differences in spatial ability. *Psychological Review, 92,* 137–172.

Kimura, D. (1963). Right temporal lobe damage. *Archives of Neurology, 8,* 264–271.

Kolb, B. & Whishaw, I. (1985). *Fundamentals of human neuropsychology.* New York: Freeman & Co.

Kosslyn, S. (1987). Seeing and imagining in the cerebral hemispheres: A computational approach. *Psychological Review, 94*(2), 148–175.

Levy, J. (1974). Psychobiological implications of bilateral asymmetry. In S. Diamond & S. Beaumont (Eds.), *Hemispheric function in the human brain.* New York: Halstead Press.

Levy, J., Trevarthen, C., & Sperry, R. (1972). Perception of bilateral chimeric figures following hemispheric disconnection. *Brain, 95,* 61–78.

McFie, J., & Zangwill, O. L. (1960). Visual-constructive disabilities associated with lesions of the left cerebral hemisphere. *Brain, 83,* 243–260.

McGee, M. (1979). Human spatial abilities: Psychometric studies and environmental, genetic, hormonal, and neurological influences. *Psychological Bulletin, 86,* 889–918.

Meier, M. & French, L. (1965). Lateralized deficits in complex visual discrimination and bilateral transfer of reminiscence following unilateral temporal lobectomy. *Neuropsychologia, 3,* 261–272.

Milner, B. (1965). Visually-guided maze learning in man: Effects of bilateral hippocampal, bilateral frontal, and unilateral cerebral lesions. *Neuropsychologia, 3,* 317–338.

Milner, B. (1968). Visual recognition and recall after right temporal lobe excision in man. *Neuropsychologia, 6,* 191–209.

Milner, B. (1971). Interhemispheric differences in the localization of psychological processes in man. *British Medical Bulletin, 27,* 272–277.

Milner, B. & Taylor, L. (1972). Right hemispheric superiority in tactile pattern-recognition after cerebral commissurotomy: Evidence for nonverbal memory. *Neuropsychologia, 10,* 1–15.

Morrow, L. & Ratcliff, G. (1987). Attentional mechanisms in clinical neglect. *Journal of Clinical and Experimental Neuropsychology, 9*(1), 74. (Abstract).

Moscovitch, M. (1979). Information processing and the cerebral hemispheres. In M. Gazzaniga (Ed.), *Handbook of behavioral neurobiology Vol. 2: Neuropsychology* (pp. 379–446). New York: Plenum.

Nebes, R. (1978). Direct examination of cognitive function in the right and left hemispheres. In M. Kinsbourne (Ed.), *Asymmetrical function of the brain* (pp. 99–137). Cambridge: Cambridge University Press.

Newcombe, F., & Russell, W. R. (1969). Dissociated visual perceptual and spatial deficits in focal lesions of the right hemisphere. *Journal of Neurology, Neurosurgery and Psychiatry, 32,* 73–81.

O'Keefe, J. & Nadel, L. (1978). *The hippocampus as a cognitive map.* London: Oxford University Press.

Pellegrino, J. & Kail, R. (1982). Process analysis of spatial aptitude. In R. J. Sternberg (Ed.), *Advances in the psychology of human intelligence* (pp. 311–365). Hillsdale, NJ: Lawrence Erlbaum Associates.

Piercy, M. & Smith, V. (1962). Right hemisphere dominance for certain non-verbal intellectual skills. *Brain, 85,* 775–790.

Posner, M. I. (1980). Orienting of attention. *Quarterly Journal of Experimental Psychology, 32,* 3–25.

Posner, M. I. (1987, August). *Structure and functions of selective attention.* Master lecture given at the annual meeting of the American Psychological Association, New York.

Posner, M. I., Choate, L. S., Rafal, R. D., & Vaughan, J. (1985). Inhibition of return: Neural mechanisms and function. *Cognitive Neuropsychology 2,* 211–228.

Posner, M. I. & Cohen, Y. (1984). Components of attention. In H. Bouma & D. Bowhuis (Eds.), *Attention and performance, X,* 55–66. Hillsdale, NJ: Lawrence Erlbaum Associates.

Posner, M. I., Inhoff, A. W., Friedrich, F. J., & Cohen, A. (1987). Isolating attentional systems: A cognitive-anatomical analysis. *Psychobiology, 5*(2), 107–121.

Posner, M., Cohen, Y., & Rafal, R. (1982). Neural systems control of spatial orienting. *Philosophical Transactions of the Royal Society, London, 298,* 187–198.

Posner, M. I., Walker, J. A., Friedrich, F. J., & Rafal, R. D. (1984). Effects of parietal lobe injury on covert orienting of visual attention. *Journal of Neuroscience, 4,* 1863–1874.

Posner, M. I., Walker, J. A., Friedrich, F. J., & Rafal, R. D. (1987). How do the parietal lobes direct covert attention? *Neuropsychologia, 25*(1), 135–145.

Rafal, R. D. & Posner, M. I. (1987). Deficits in visual spatial attention following thalamic lesions. *Proceedings of the National Academy of Sciences, Vol. 84,* 7349–7353.

Rafal, R., Posner, M. I., Friedman, J., Inhoff, A., & Bernstein, E. (1988). Orienting of visual attention in progressive supranuclear palsy. *Brain, 111,* 267–280.

Ratcliff, G. (1979). Spatial thought, mental rotation and the right cerebral hemisphere. *Neuropsychologia, 17,* 49–54.

Ratcliff, G. (1982). Disturbances of spatial orientation associated with cerebral lesions. In M. Potegal (Ed.), *Spatial abilities: Developmental and physiological foundations* (pp. 301–331). New York: Academic Press.

Ratcliff, G., & Newcombe, F. (1973). Spatial orientation in man: Effects on the left, right, and bilateral posterior cerebral lesions. *Journal of Neurology, Neurosurgery, and Psychiatry, 36,* 448–454.

Sacks, O. (1985). *The man who mistook his wife for a hat.* New York: Summit Books.

Schaie, K. W. (1979). The primary mental abilities in adulthood: An exploration in the development of psychometric intelligence. In P. B. Baltes & O. G. Brim, Jr. (Eds.), *Life span development and behavior* (Vol. 2, pp. 69–117). New York: Academic Press.

Semmes, J., Weinstein, S., Ghent, L., & Teuber, H. L. (1955). Spatial orientation in man after cerebral injury: I. Analysis by locus of lesion. *Journal of Psychology, 39,* 227–244.

Semmes, J., Weinstein, S., Ghent, L., & Teuber, H. L. (1963). Correlates of impaired orientation in personal and extra-personal space. *Brain, 86,* 747–772.

Sieroff, E., Pollatsek, A., & Posner, M. I. (1988). Recognition of visual letter strings following injury to the posterior visual spatial attention system. *Cognitive Neuropsychology, 5(4),* 427–450.

Sperry, R. (1982). Some effects of disconnecting the cerebral hemispheres, *Science, 217,* 1223–1226.

Springer, S. P., & Deutsch, G. (1985). *Left brain, right brain.* San Francisco: Freeman.

Warrington, E. K. (1969). Constructional apraxia. In P. J. Vinken & G. W. Bruyn (Eds.), *Handbook of clinical neurology* (pp. 67–83). Amsterdam: North-Holland.

Warrington, E. K., & James, M. (1967). Disorders of visual perception in patients with localized cerebral lesions. *Neuropsychologia, 5,* 253–266.

Warrington, E. K., James, M., & Kinsbourne, M. (1966). Drawing disability in relation to laterality of cerebral lesions. *Brain, 89,* 53–82.

Warrington, E. K., & Taylor, A. M. (1978). Two categorical stages of object recognition. *Perception, 7,* 695–705.

Watson, R. & Heilman, K. (1979). Thalamic neglect. *Neurology, 29,* 690–694.

Weinstein, E. & Friedland, R. (1977). *Hemi-inattention and hemispheric specialization: Advances in neurology 18.* New York: Raven Press.

Whiteley, A. & Warrington, E. (1978). Selective impairment of topographical memory: A single case study. *Journal of Neurology, Neurosurgery and Psychiatry, 41,* 575–578.

12 Functions of the Primate Hippocampus in Spatial Processing and Memory

Edmund T. Rolls
University of Oxford

The aims of this chapter are to consider which spatial functions are performed by the primate hippocampus, how these are related to the memory functions performed by the hippocampus, and how it performs these functions. In addition to the evidence that is available from anatomical connections, the effects of lesions to the system, and recordings of the activity of single neurons in the system, neuronal network models of hippocampal function are also introduced, as they have the promise of enabling one to understand what and how the hippocampus computes, and thus the functions being performed by the hippocampus. The spatial functions performed by other brain regions are considered elsewhere (e.g., parietal cortex: P. Andersen, 1987; Sakata, 1985; prefrontal cortex: Gaffan & Harrison, 1989a; Goldman-Rakic, 1987). Many of the studies described have been performed with macaque monkeys in order to provide information as relevant as possible to understanding amnesia in humans. Effects on memory are produced by damage to the hippocampus or to some of its connections, such as the fornix, and these structures are collectively referred to hereafter as the hippocampal system.

DAMAGE TO THE HIPPOCAMPAL SYSTEM AND SPATIAL FUNCTION

Damage to the hippocampus or to some of its connections, such as the fornix in monkeys, produces deficits in simple left–right discrimination learning in which, for example, food is hidden consistently on the right or the left under one of two identical objects, and the monkey must learn whether to displace the left or the right object in order to find food (Mahut, 1972). Fornix lesions also impair conditional left–right discrimination learning, in which the visual appearance of an object specifies whether a response is to be made to the left or the right (Gaffan, Saunders, et al., 1984; Rupniak & Gaffan, 1987; and in humans— Petrides, 1985). (An example of such a conditional spatial response task is this: If two objects shown are red, then the object on the left must be chosen to obtain a reward, and if the two objects shown are green, then the object on the right must be chosen to obtain a reward.) Two possible interpretations of these spatial learning impairments produced by fornix section are as follows.

First, it is possible that the learning system disrupted is only for the acquisition of map-like knowledge about the environment, such as that there is food in a certain place. This is not the case, in that lesioned monkeys were impaired in learning to make a response to one side when one picture was shown and to the other side when a different picture was shown (Rupniak & Gaffan, 1987), that is, in conditional spatial response learning, as just described. The spatial environment was held constant, and thus damage to the hippocampal system does not impair only the ability to acquire map-like knowledge of the environment. The experiment does show, on the other hand, that there is an impairment when monkeys must learn to make spatial responses on the basis of nonspatial stimuli.

Second, it is possible that the hippocampal learning system is only for the control of spatially directed movements, such as go left and go right. This is not the case; fornix sectioned monkeys are impaired in learning, on the basis of a spatial cue, which object to choose (e.g., if two objects are on the left, choose object A, but if the two objects are on the right, choose object B) (Gaffan & Harrison, 1989a). Thus, the deficit is not just in learning spatial responses; in this task, the response was not spatial. The spatial aspect of this task was in the spatial position of the stimuli.

These findings suggest that fornix damage can impair learning about both the places of objects and the places of responses. Gaffan and Harrison (1989) have analyzed further what it is that characterizes the spatial learning deficit of monkeys with damage to the hippocampal system, in experiments in which the monkey was moved to different positions in a room. Impairments were found when which of two or more objects the monkey had to choose depended on the position of the monkey in the room, provided that the same parts of the room were in view from both positions of the monkey, so that the relative positions of room cues had to be remembered in order to solve the task (Gaffan & Harrison, 1989b, experiment 1). This requirement is referred to as "whole scene analysis." If the parts of the room visible from the monkeys' testing positions were different, then there was no impairment in learning which object to choose (Gaffan & Harrison, 1989b, experiment 2). However, if the monkeys had to make a spatial response to one of two identical objects that depended on different environmental cues (whether room-based or local), then fornix-sectioned monkeys displayed a learning impairment (Gaffan & Harrison, 1989b, experiments 3 and 5). These experiments suggest that fornix-sectioned monkeys can predict which of two different objects is rewarded based on a conjunction of background items in the environment and the object displaced. Accordingly, they can thus choose one of two (visually) different objects in a scene provided that the scene has different items visible in it, whether locally or distantly. However, a deficit is produced by fornix section when the monkey has to store the spatial relations of the background items and of identical objects in a scene. Accordingly, the fornix-sectioned monkeys are impaired in learning to select different objects depending on the spatial relations of items in the scene, or to make spatial responses to identical objects in a scene, as these involve storing the relative positions of places to which to respond (Gaffan & Harrison, 1989b).

Another spatial task that is impaired by damage to the hippocampal system in monkeys (Gaffan & Saunders, 1985; Parkinson, Murray, & Mishkin, 1988) and in humans (Smith & Milner, 1981) is an object–place memory task. In this task, not only *which* objects have been seen before, but *where* in space each object was located, must be remembered. The task has been run with macaques by showing a picture in each of four positions on a screen twice (Rolls, Miyashita, Cahusac, Kesner, Niki, & Feigenbaum, 1989). The first time the monkey saw the picture in a particular position, he had to withold a lick response (in order to avoid saline). The second time a picture appeared in a given position on the screen, the monkey could lick to obtain fruit juice. Each picture was shown in each position twice, once as novel and once as familiar for that position, and many different pictures were used in sequence. Thus, in order to perform the task, the monkey had to remember not only which pictures had been seen before but also the position on the screen in which the picture had been seen. In humans, the object–place task was run by showing the subjects a tray containing a set of objects, and then asking later not only which objects had been seen before, but where they were on the tray (Smith & Milner, 1981). Such object–place tasks require a whole-scene, or snapshot-like, memory in which spatial relations in a scene must be remembered. It is not sufficient just to be able to remember the objects that have been seen before. The deficit in the object–place memory task is thus analogous to the deficit in the spatial tasks described previously, in that the deficit is fully apparent when not just objects, but objects and their spatial relations to each other, must be remembered.

NONSPATIAL ASPECTS OF THE FUNCTION OF THE HIPPOCAMPUS IN PRIMATES: ITS ROLE IN MEMORY

In addition to the spatial deficits described earlier that are produced by damage to the hippocampal system in primates, there are also deficits in nonspatial memory tasks. For example, the anterograde amnesia that is associated with damage to the hippocampus in humans is evident as a major deficit in learning to recognize new stimuli, and the recognition memory deficit encompasses nonspatial items (e.g., objects and people) as well as places (Milner, 1972; Scoville & Milner, 1957; Squire, 1966; Squire & Zola-Morgan, 1988). Recognition memory is also impaired in monkeys with damage to the hippocampal system (Gaffan, 1974, 1977; Gaffan & Weiskrantz, 1980; Owen & Butler, 1981; Zola-Morgan & Squire, 1986), although it is possible that severe deficits on recognition memory are found only when there is also damage to the amygdala (Mishkin, 1978, 1982, 1989; Murray and Mishkin, 1984). In a typical recognition memory task in the monkey, a stimulus is shown to the monkey and, when it is shown again later, the monkey can choose it to obtain a reward. If no other stimuli intervene between the first and second presentations of a given stimulus, then the task is described as a match-to-sample task. If other stimuli intervene between the first (novel) and second (familiar) presentations of a stimulus, then the task is described as a serial or running recognition task. A serial recognition task is often used when analyzing the role of the hippocampus in memory, because a memory task with intervening stimuli is more difficult than a delayed match-to-sample task, and may therefore be a more sensitive indicator of an effect on memory (Gaffan, 1974, 1977).

It is interesting that the impairment produced by damage to the hippocampal system in recognition memory tasks as usually implemented (e.g., choose or respond to objects seen before, that is delayed match-to-sample, perhaps with intervening stimuli) is much less clear if delayed non-match-to-sample is used (choose the novel stimulus) (Gaffan, Gaffan, & Harrison, 1984). The impairment is also much less severe if the monkeys are trained initially with the long (and therefore difficult) intervals between stimuli with which they are tested later (Gaffan, Gaffan, & Harrison, 1984). The implication of these findings is that the deficit produced by the fornix section is not simply due to an inability to distinguish novel from familiar stimuli, but is due perhaps just as much to a difficulty that these lesioned animals have in altering their instrumental response strategies (e.g., so that they respond to familiar stimuli when the natural tendency is to respond to novel stimuli, and so that they start responding at long memory intervals when they have been trained previously to respond with short memory intervals; see Gaffan, Gaffan, & Harrison, 1984). However, although the deficit usually found in recognition memory tasks may not strictly be due to an inability to distinguish novel from familiar stimuli, there is nevertheless a nonspatial impairment apparent in recognition memory tasks. Another nonspatial impairment produced by fornix section in monkeys is a deficit in learning the unnatural instrumental response rule "Choose the object not previously paired with reward" (sometimes called a win–shift rule) (Gaffan, Saunders, et al., 1984). (Fornix section did not impair use of the natural instrumental rule, "Choose the object previously associated with reward," sometimes called the win–stay rule—Gaffan, Saunders, et al., 1984). Thus, in monkeys, hippocampal function is not only involved in some types of spatial learning, but also in some aspect of nonspatial learning, even if this latter may not be pure novelty versus familiarity learning but is instead related in some way to organizing flexibly adaptive instrumental responses.

There is also the evidence from human primates that the hippocampus is involved in nonspatial (as well as spatial) memory, for example in paired (word) associate learning, and in episodic memory, such as the memory of events that happened and people met on previous days.

RELATION BETWEEN SPATIAL AND NONSPATIAL ASPECTS OF HIPPOCAMPAL FUNCTION

One way of relating the impairment of spatial processing to other aspects of hippocampal function is to note that this spatial processing involves a snapshot type of memory, in which one whole scene must be remembered. This memory may then be a special case of episodic memory, which involves an arbitrary association of a set of events that describe a past episode. Further, the nonspatial tasks impaired by damage to the hippocampal system may be impaired because they are tasks in which a memory of a particular episode, rather than of a general rule, is involved. Thus, the learning of tasks with nongeneral rules, such as choose the object not previously rewarded (i.e. win–shift, lose–stay) may be impaired, because to solve them the particular pairing in the particular context (of performing with this special rule) must be remembered in order to choose the correct object later. (The natural rule, which, in the natural environment, usually leads to reward, is to choose the object previously associated with reward.) Another example is that choosing familiar rather than novel objects in a recognition memory task may be particularly difficult for monkeys with damage to the hippocampal system, because it involves a special rule—choose the familiar object, in this task—rather than what may be a more general tendency, to choose the novel rather than the familiar object. The latter rule is what normally guides behavior, as this rule is more likely to lead to reward for objects without an explicit reward association already in the natural environment. Further, recognition memory may be particularly impaired when this involves the memory of particular and arbitrary associations between parts of the image, especially when the same elements may occur in different combinations in other images. Also, the deficit in paired-associate learning in humans may be especially evident when this involves arbitrary associations between words, for example window–lake. I suggest here that the reason why the hippocampus is used for the spatial and nonspatial types of memory described previously, and the reason that makes these two types of memory so analogous, is that the hippocampus contains one stage, the CA3 stage, which acts as an autoassociation memory. (The structure, operation, and properties of autoassociation memories are described in the next section.) It is suggested that an autoassociation memory implemented by the CA3 neurons equally enables whole (spatial) scenes or episodic memories to be formed, with a snapshot quality that depends on the arbitrary associations that can be made and the short temporal window that characterizes the synaptic modifiability in this system (see next section and Rolls, 1987, 1989a, 1989b). The way in which the architecture of the hippocampus is specialized to perform these functions in spatial snapshot and episodic memory are described next, in order to lead towards a deeper understanding of hippocampal function in these types of learning.

THE COMPUTATIONAL SIGNIFICANCE OF THE FUNCTIONAL ARCHITECTURE OF THE HIPPOCAMPUS

The internal connections of the hippocampus, and the learning rules implemented at its synapses, are described first to delineate its functional architecture, which provides the basis for a computational theory of the hippocampus.

Schematic diagrams of the connections of the hippocampus are shown in Figs. 12.1 and 12.2. In primates, major input connections are from the association areas of the cerebral cortex, including the parietal cortex (which processes spatial information), the temporal lobe visual and auditory areas, and the frontal cortex. Within the hippocampus, there is a three-stage sequence of processing, consisting of the dentate granule cells (which receive from the entorhinal cortex via the perforant path), the CA3 pyramidal cells, and the CA1 pyramidal cells. Outputs return from the hippocampus to the cerebral cortex via the subiculum, entorhinal cortex, and parahippocampal gyrus.

The CA3 Pyramidal Cells

One major feature of hippocampal neuronal networks is the recurrent collateral system of the CA3 cells, formed by the output axons of the CA3 cells having a branch that returns to make synapses with the dendrites of the other CA3 cells, as shown in Figs. 12.1 and 12.2. Given that the region of the CA3 cell dendrites on which the recurrent collaterals synapse is long (approximately 11.5 mm), and that the total dendritic length is approximately 15 mm and has approximately 10,000 spines (D. G. Amaral, in personal communication; Squire, Shimamura, & Amaral, 1989), approximately 7,700 synapses per CA3 pyramidal cell could be devoted to recurrent collaterals; with 180,000 CA3 neurons in the rat, this makes the probability of contact between the CA3 neurons 4.3% (Rolls, 1989a, 1989b). It is remarkable that the contact probability is so high, and also that the CA3 recurrent collateral axons travel so widely in all directions that they can potentially come close to almost all other CA3 neurons (D. G. Amaral, in

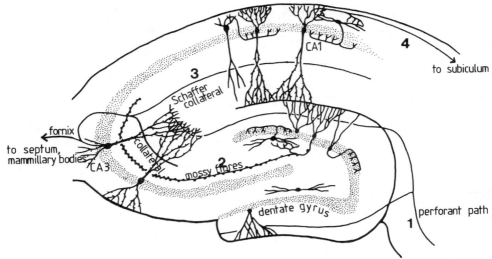

FIG. 12.1.   Representation of connections within the hippocampus. In-puts reach the hippocampus through the perforant path (1), which makes synapses with the dendrites of the dentate granule cells and also with the apical dendrites of the CA3 pyramidal cells. The dentate granule cells project via the mossy fibers (2) to the CA3 pyramidal cells. The well-developed recurrent collateral system of the CA3 cells is indicated. The CA3 pyramidal cells project via the Schaffer collaterals (3) to the CA1 pyramidal cells, which in turn have connections (4) to the subiculum.

personal communication; Squire, Shimamura, & Amaral, 1989; Rolls, 1989a, 1989b). The connectivity of these CA3 cells is even more remarkable than this, for in addition there is a commissural system in which CA3 neurons on one side of the brain send axons to end primarily on the dendrites of the CA3 neurons of the other side of the brain. The terminals are made on the same stretch of the CA3 dendrites as the recurrent collaterals, so that the contact probability calcu-lated before must be reduced (with the lower limit being perhaps 2.15%, repre-senting 7,700 synapses shared among 360,000 CA3 neurons). The remarkable effect achieved by this is that the CA3 neurons provide one interconnected network of neurons for both sides of the brain, with a reasonably high probability that any CA3 neuron will be connected to any other CA3 neuron, irrespective of the side of the brain, as illustrated in Fig. 12.3. Although connectivity across the midline is likely to be high in the rat, as implied in Fig. 12.3, the two sides of the hippocampus are probably not fully interconnected in humans, as indicated by the evidence that damage to the right temporal lobe affects spatial tasks (such as conditional spatial response learning) more than nonspatial memory tasks, whereas damage to the left temporal lobe affects nonspatial tasks, such as paired

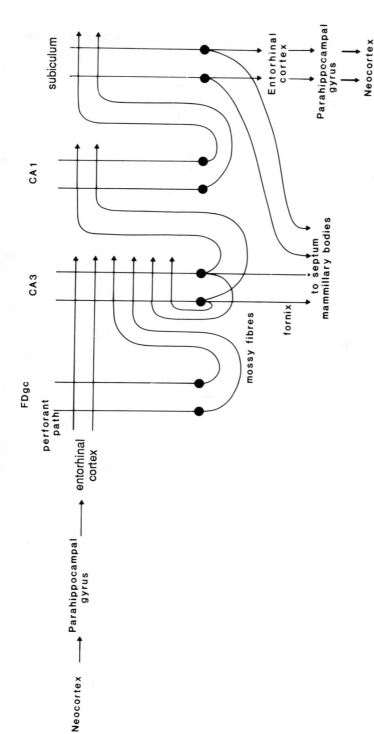

FIG. 12.2. Schematic representation of the connections of the hippocampus, showing also that the cerebral cortex (neocortex) is connected to the hippocampus via the parahippocampal gyrus and entorhinal cortex, and that the hippocampus projects back to the neocortex via the subiculum, entorhinal cortex, and parahippocampal gyrus. FDgc = dentate granule cells.

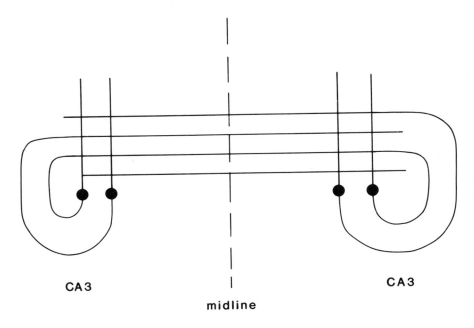

CA3   CA3

midline

CA3 recurrent collateral system

FIG. 12.3.   Schematic representation of the connections of the CA3 neurons, showing that they are interconnected across the midline by commissural connections, as well as on each side of the brain via the recurrent collateral axons.

word associate learning, more than nonspatial tasks (Milner, 1982; Kolb & Whishaw, 1985).

There is evidence from studies of long-term potentiation (Bliss & Lomo, 1973; P. Andersen, 1987; Wigstrom, Gustaffson, Huang, & Abraham, 1986; Kelso, Ganong, & Brown, 1986) that the synapses in this recurrent collateral system are Hebb-modifiable; that is, that they become stronger when there is strong conjunctive postsynaptic and presynaptic activity (Miles, 1988).

An Autoassociation Memory Implemented by the CA3 Recurrent Collateral System

This functional anatomy of the CA3 pyramidal cells immediately suggests that this is an autoassociation (or autocorrelation) matrix memory. The autoassociation arises because the outputs of the CA3 cells are fed back by the recurrent collateral axons to make Hebb-modifiable synapses with the dendrites of the

INPUT STIMULUS

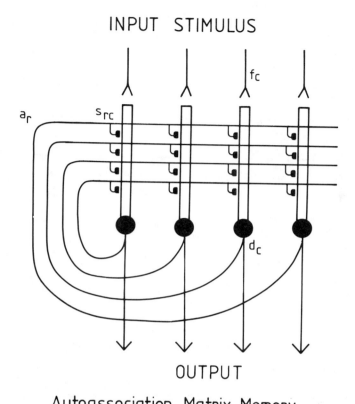

OUTPUT

Autoassociation Matrix Memory

FIG. 12.4. An autoassociation matrix memory. The dendrites, d_c, have recurrent collateral axons, a_r, which make Hebb-modifiable synapses, s_{rc}, with the other neurons in the population.

other CA3 neurons. The result of implementation of the Hebb rule in this architecture is that any strongly activated cell or set of cells becomes linked by strengthened synapses with any other conjunctively strongly activated cell or set of cells. During learning, the matrix of synaptic weights that link the cells together (see Fig. 12.4) comes to reflect the correlations between the activities of the CA3 cells. Because the matrix of synaptic weights stores the correlations between the activities of the cells of the memory, this type of memory is called an *autocorrelation or autoassociation matrix memory.* During recall, presentation of even a part of the original pattern of activity of the CA3 cells, which might represent one part of or key to the memory, comes to elicit the firing of the whole set of cells that were originally conjunctively activated. This important property of this type of memory is termed *completion,* and it is fundamental to any biological memory system. During recall, if a pattern similar to one learned by the system is presented, then, insofar as some of the neurons active in the key stimulus were also part of a pattern stored previously in the memory, the previously stored pattern is recalled. This property, which is also fundamental to biological memory, is termed *generalization.* Another property of this type of memory is that it continues to function moderately well if it is partially damaged, or if, for example, not every synapse in the matrix is present, either because of limitations of fan in of individual neurons, or because of limitations of the precision of development. This property is also important for a biological memory system, and it is termed *graceful degradation or fault tolerance.* More extensive descriptions of the properties of autoassociation matrix memories are given by Kohonen, Oja, and Lehtio (1981), Kohonen (1988), and Rolls (1987). The suggestion made here is that the output of the CA3 pyramidal cells is fed back along the horizontally running recurrent collateral axons that make Hebb-modifiable synapses with other CA3 dendrites so that the pattern of activity in the CA3 pyramidal cells is associated with itself.

For this autoassociation to work correctly, it is important that a depolarization produced by synaptic input on one part of the dendrite is effective on other parts of the dendrite, so that even distant active synapses experience the post-synaptic term required for the Hebb rule to be implemented. This condition does appear to be met, as shown by the short electrical length of the dendrites and by the cooperation that occurs between inputs that synapse on different parts of the dendrite in setting up the postsynaptic depolarization required for long-term potentiation (P. Andersen, 1987; McNaughton, 1984). This cooperativity between active synapses made at different positions along the postsynaptic membrane, so that active synapses onto a neuron alter their strength only when other synapses are active on the same dendrite and produce postsynaptic activation, enables associations to be formed based on temporal conjunctions that occur between any set of conjunctively active afferents. In a sense, the large number of synapses of these CA3 cells devoted to the recurrent collaterals allows correlations of firing across a large information space to be detected. Consistent with this suggestion about the computational role of the CA3 system of the hippocampus, it is known that the probability of contact of the neurons in an autoassociation matrix memory must not be very low if it is to operate usefully (see Gardner-Medwin, 1976; Marr, 1971, 1970). The synaptic modifiability implemented in the CA3 recurrent collateral system may utilize NMDA receptors, which allow synaptic modifiability only when the postsynaptic membrane is strongly activated. This interesting nonlinearity of the learning rule means that only correlations between strongly activated CA3 pyramidal cells are stored, which may help to maximize the storage capacity of the system and to minimize interference.

It is suggested hereafter that the systems level function of this autoassociation memory is to enable events occurring conjunctively in quite different parts of the association areas of the cerebral cortex to be associated together to form a memory that could well be described as episodic. Each episode would be defined by a conjunction of a set of events, and each episodic memory would consist of the association of one set of events (such as where, with whom, and what one ate at lunch on the preceding day). It is suggested that the "snapshot, whole-scene" spatial memory in which the hippocampus is implicated, as shown before, is what the hippocampus can achieve for spatial information processing, by allowing all the parts of a whole scene to be associated together to provide a memory of the whole scene. The importance of the hippocampus in episodic memory and "whole-scene" memory may arise from the fact that in one part of it, the CA3 region, there is one association matrix with a relatively high contact probability that receives information originating in many different areas of the cerebral cortex and from both sides of the brain. One reason why there may not be more cells in the CA3 region is that it is important that the connectivity be kept relatively high so that any event represented by the firing of a sparse set of CA3 cells can be associated with any other event represented by a different set of CA3 cells firing. Because each CA3 pyramidal cell has a limited fan in or number of synapses (perhaps 10,000, see p. 344), the total number of cells in the auto-association memory can not be increased beyond the limit set by the fan in and the connectivity. The advantages of sparse encoding and a well-interconnected matrix are that a large number of different (episodic) memories can be stored in the CA3 system, and that the advantageous emergent properties of a matrix memory, such as completion, generalization, and graceful degradation (see Kohonen, 1988; Kohonen et al., 1977, 1981; Rolls, 1987), are produced efficiently. Completion may operate particularly effectively here with a sparse representation, because it is under these conditions that the simple autocorrelation effect can reconstruct the whole of one pattern without interference, which would arise if too high a proportion of the input neurons was active.

The Dentate Granule Cells and the CA1 Pyramidal Cells

The theory is developed elsewhere that the dentate granule cell stage of hippocampal processing that precedes the CA3 stage acts in two ways to produce the sparse yet efficient (i.e., nonredundant) representation in CA3 neurons that is required for the autoassociation to perform well (Rolls, 1989a, 1989b). The first way is that the perforant path–dentate granule cell system, with its Hebb-like modifiability, is suggested to act as a competitive learning matrix to remove redundancy from the inputs, producing a more orthogonal and categorized set of outputs. The second way arises because there is a very low (0.008% in the rat) contact probability in the mossy fibre–CA3 connections, which achieves by pattern separation relatively orthogonal representations (compared to those on the dentate granule cells, and within the limits set by the relative numbers of dentate granule and CA3 cells—see Rolls, 1989a), that are required if the auto-association matrix memory formed by the CA3 cells is to operate with usefully large memory capacity and with minimal interference (see Kohonen et al., 1977, 1981; Rolls, 1987). As the neurons have positive firing rates, the only way in which relatively orthogonal representations can be formed is by making the number of neurons active for any one input stimulus relatively low (see e.g. Jordan, 1986), and this sparse representation is exactly what can be achieved by the low contact probability pattern separation effect of the mossy fibers (Rolls, 1989a, 1989b). The pattern separation effect refers to the point that input patterns that are correlated produce output patterns that are less correlated with each other.

The function of the CA1 stage that follows the CA3 cells (see Figs. 12.1 and 12.2) is also considered to be related to the CA3 autoassociation effect, in which several arbitrary patterns of firing occur together on the CA3 neurons and become associated together to form an episodic, or "whole-scene," memory. It is essential for this operation that several different sparse representations are present conjunctively in order to form the association. Moreover, when completion operates in the CA3 autoassociation system, all the neurons firing in the original conjunction can be brought into activity by only a part of the original set of conjunctive events. For these reasons, a memory in the CA3 cells consists of several different simultaneously active ensembles of activity. It is suggested that the CA1 cells, which receive these groups of simultaneously active ensembles, can detect the conjunctions of firing of the different ensembles that represent the episodic memory and allocate, by competitive learning, relatively few neurons to represent each episodic memory. The episodic memory would thus consist in the CA3 region of ensembles of active cells, each ensemble representing one of the subcomponents of the episodic memory (including context), whereas the whole episodic memory would be represented not by its parts, but as a single collection of active cells, at the CA1 stage. It is suggested on p. 358 that one role that these economical (in terms of the number of activated fibers) and relatively orthogonal signals in the CA1 cells have is to guide information storage or consolidation in the cerebral cortex. To understand how the hippocampus may perform this function for the cerebral cortex, it is necessary to turn to a systems level analysis to show how the computations performed by the hippocampus fit into overall brain function. It may be noted that, by forming associations of events derived from different parts of the cerebral cortex (the CA3 stage) and by building new economical (i.e., less redundant) representations of the conjunctions detected (the CA1 stage), the hippocampus provides an output that is suitable for directing the long-term storage of information.

SYSTEMS LEVEL ANALYSIS OF HIPPOCAMPAL FUNCTION, INCLUDING NEURONAL ACTIVITY IN THE PRIMATE HIPPOCAMPUS

We have just utilized the functional architecture (internal anatomy and physiology) of the hippocampus to suggest a computational theory of how it operates. In order to understand what these computations are used for and how they contribute to the information processing being performed by other parts of the brain, we now turn to a systems level analysis in which we consider the connections of the hippocampus with the rest of the brain, and the activity of single neurons in the hippocampus when it is performing its normal function, as assessed by the effects of selective damage to the hippocampus as described previously.

Systems Level Anatomy

The primate hippocampus receives inputs via the entorhinal cortex (area 28) and the parahippocampal gyrus from many areas of the cerebral association cortex, including the parietal cortex, which is concerned with spatial functions, the visual and auditory temporal association cortical areas, and the frontal cortex (Van Hoesen, 1982; Amaral, 1987; Rolls, 1985, 1989a,c). In addition, the entorhinal cortex receives inputs from the amygdala. There are also subcortical inputs from, for example, the amygdala and septum. The hippocampus, in turn, projects back via the subiculum, entorhinal cortex, and parahippocampal gyrus (area TF-TH), to the cerebral cortical areas from which it receives inputs (Van Hoesen, 1982), as well as to subcortical areas such as the mammillary bodies (see Figs. 12.1 and 12.2).

Systems Level Neurophysiology

The information processing being performed by the primate hippocampus while it is performing the functions for which lesion studies have shown it is needed has been investigated in studies in which the activity of single hippocampal neurons has been analyzed during the performance and learning of these (and related) spatial tasks. Watanabe and Niki (1985) analyzed hippocampal neuronal activity while monkeys performed a delayed spatial response task. In a delayed spatial response task, a stimulus is shown on, for example, the left, there is then a delay period, and after this the monkey can respond by, for example, touching the left stimulus position. They reported that 6.4% of hippocampal neurons responded differently while the monkey was remembering left as compared to right. The responses of these neurons could reflect preparation for the spatial response to be made, or they could reflect memory of the spatial position in which the stimulus was shown. To provide evidence on which was important,

Cahusac, Miyashita, and Rolls (1989) analyzed hippocampal activity in this task, and in an object–place memory task. In the object–place memory task, the monkey was shown a sample stimulus in one position on a video screen, there was a delay of 2 seconds, and then the same or a different stimulus was shown in the same or in a different position. The monkey remembered the sample and its position, and if both matched the delayed stimulus, he licked to obtain fruit juice. 3.8% of the 600 neurons analyzed in this task responded differently for the different spatial positions, with some of these responding differentially during the sample presentation, some in the delay period, and some in the match period. Thus, some hippocampal neurons (those differentially active in the sample or match periods) respond differently for stimuli shown in different positions in space, and some (those differentially active in the delay period) respond differently when the monkey is remembering different positions in space. In addition, some of the neurons responded to a combination of object and place information, in that they responded only to a novel object in a particular place. These neuronal responses were not due to any response being made or prepared by the monkey, for information about which behavioral response was required was not available until the match stimulus was shown. Cahusac et al. (1989) also found that the majority of the neurons that responded in the object–place memory task did not respond in the delayed spatial response task. Instead, a different population of neurons (5.7% of the total) responded in the delayed spatial response task, with differential left–right responses in the sample, delay, or match periods. Thus, this latter population of hippocampal neurons had activity that was related to the preparation for or initiation of a spatial response, which, in the delayed response task, could be encoded as soon as the sample stimulus was seen. These recordings showed that there are some neurons in the primate hippocampus with activity that is related to the spatial position of stimuli or to the memory of the spatial position of stimuli (as shown in the object–place memory task), and that there are other neurons in the hippocampus with activity that is related not to the stimulus or the memory of the stimulus, but instead to the spatial response that the monkey is preparing and remembering (as shown in the delayed spatial response task).

The responses of hippocampal neurons in primates with activity related to the place in which a stimulus is shown was further investigated, using a serial multiple object–place memory task. The task required a memory for the position on a video monitor in which a given object had appeared previously (Rolls, Miyashita, et al., 1989). This task was designed to allow a wider area of space to be tested than in the previous study and was chosen also because memory of where objects had been seen previously in space was known to be disrupted by hippocampal damage (Gaffan & Saunders, 1985; Gaffan, 1987). In the task, a visual image appeared in one of four or nine positions on a screen. If the stimulus had been seen in that position before, the monkey could lick to obtain fruit juice, but if the image had not appeared in that position before, the monkey had not to lick in order to avoid the taste of saline. Each image appeared in each position on the screen only twice—once as novel and once as familiar. The task thus required memory not only of which visual stimuli had been seen before but also of the positions in which they had been seen, and is an object–place memory task. It was found that 9% of neurons recorded in the hippocampus and parahippocampal gyrus had spatial fields in this and related tasks, in that they responded whenever there was a stimulus in some but not in other positions on the screen. 2.4% of the neurons responded to a combination of spatial information and information about the object seen, in that they responded more the first time a particular image was seen in any position. Six of these neurons were found that showed this combination even more clearly, in that they responded, for example, only to some positions and only provided that it was the first time that a particular stimulus had appeared there. Thus, not only is spatial information processed by the primate hippocampus, but it can be combined, as shown by the responses of single neurons, with information about which stimuli have been seen before (Rolls, Miyashita, et al., 1989).

The ability of the hippocampus to form such arbitrary associations of information, probably originating from the parietal cortex, about position in space with information originating from the temporal lobe about objects may be important for its role in memory. Moreover, these findings provide neurophysiological support for the computational theory described earlier, according to which such arbitrary associations should be formed onto single neurons in the hippocampus.

These "space" neurons (Rolls, Miyashita, et al., 1989; Cahusac et al., in press) may be compared with "place" cells recorded in the rat hippocampus (see O'Keefe, 1984; McNaughton, Barnes, & O'Keefe, 1983). The "place" cells that have been described in the rat respond when the rat is in a particular place in the environment as specified by extra-maze cues, whereas the cells described here respond to particular positions in space, or at least when stimuli are shown in particular positions in space (see further Feigenbaum, Rolls, Cahusac, & Bach, in preparation).

These studies showed that some hippocampal neurons in primates have spatial fields. In order to investigate how space is represented in the hippocampus, Feigenbaum, Cahusac, and Rolls (1987) and Feigenbaum et al. (in preparation) investigated whether the spatial fields use egocentric or some form of allocentric coordinates. This was investigated by finding a neuron with a space field and then moving the monitor screen and the monkey, relative to each other and to different positions in the laboratory. For 7% of the spatial neurons, the responses remained in the same position relative to the monkey's body axis when the screen was moved or the monkey was rotated or moved to a different position in the laboratory. These neurons thus represented space in egocentric coordinates. For 61% of the spatial neurons analyzed, the responses remained in the same position on the screen or in the room when the monkey was rotated or moved to a different position in the laboratory. These neurons thus represented space in allocentric coordinates. Evidence for two types of allocentric encoding was found. In the first type, the field was defined by its position on the monitor screen independently of the position of the monitor relative to the monkey's body axis and independently of the position of the monkey and the screen in the laboratory. These neurons were called "frame of reference" allocentric, in that their fields were defined by the local frame provided by the monitor screen. The majority of the allocentric neurons responded in this way. In the second type of allocentric encoding, the field was defined by its position in the room and was largely independent of position relative to the monkey's body axis or to position on the monitor screen face. These neurons were called "absolute" allocentric, in that their fields were defined by position in the room. These results provide evidence that, in addition to neurons with egocentric spatial fields, which have also been found in other parts of the brain (Sakata, 1985; R. Andersen, 1987), there are neurons in the primate hippocampal formation that encode space in allocentric coordinates.

In another type of task for which the primate hippocampus is needed, conditional spatial response learning, in which the monkeys had to learn which spatial response to make to different stimuli (that is, to acquire associations between visual stimuli and spatial responses), 14% of hippocampal neurons responded to particular combinations of stimuli and responses (Miyashita, Rolls, Cahusac, Niki, & Feigenbaum, 1989). The firing of these neurons could not be accounted for by the motor requirements of the task, nor wholly by the stimulus aspects of the task, as demonstrated by testing their firing in related visual discrimination tasks. These results showed that single hippocampal neurons respond to combinations of the visual stimuli and the spatial responses with which they must become associated in conditional response tasks, and are consistent with the computational theory described previously, according to which part of the mechanism of this learning involves associations between visual stimuli and spatial responses learned by single hippocampal neurons. In a following study, it was found that during such conditional spatial response learning, 22% of this type of neuron analyzed in the hippocampus and parahippocampal gyrus altered their responses so that their activity, which was initially equal to the two new stimuli, became progressively differential to the two stimuli when the monkey learned to make different responses to the two stimuli (Rolls, Cahusac, Miyashita, & Niki, in preparation). These changes occurred for different neurons just before, at, or just after the time when the monkey learned the correct response to make to the stimuli. In addition to these neurons, which had differential responses that were sustained for as long as the recordings continued, another population of neurons (45% of this type of neuron analyzed) developed differential activity to the two stimuli, yet showed such differential responses transiently for only a small number of trials at about the time when the monkey learned. These findings are consistent with the hypothesis that some synapses on hippocampal neurons modify during this type of learning so that some neurons come to respond to particular stimulus–spatial response associations that are being learned. Further, the finding that many hippocampal neurons started to reflect the new learning, but then stopped responding differentially (the transient neurons), is consistent with the hypothesis that the hippocampal neurons with large sustained changes in their activity inhibited the transient neurons, which then underwent reverse learning, thus providing a competitive mechanism by which not all neurons are allocated to any one learned association or event. These transient modifications are consistent with the computational theory outlined earlier in this chapter and elsewhere (Rolls, 1989a, 1989b), inasmuch as the return of the neuronal activity to nondifferential responsiveness is consistent with an implementation of competitive networks using reverse learning when the postsynaptic neuron is inhibited conjunctively with active afferents (see Rolls, 1989b).

The activity of hippocampal neurons in nonhuman primates has also been analyzed during the performance of nonspatial tasks for which the hippocampus is needed, such as recognition memory tasks (Rolls, Miyashita, Cahusac, & Kesner, 1985; Rolls, Cahusac, Feigenbaum, & Miyashita, in preparation). It has been found that, in the macaque hippocampus, some neurons do respond differently to novel and familiar stimuli in a serial recognition memory task, with those that did respond differentially typically responding more to novel than to familiar visual stimuli. It was notable that the proportion of hippocampal neurons that responded in this way was small (2.3%), but that this is not inconsistent with the hypothesis that the hippocampus is involved in episodic memory. It might be of interest in future studies of recognition memory and hippocampal function to investigate whether there are hippocampal neurons that are tuned to respond to only rather few of a set of stimuli being remembered, and whether the representation found is sparse, as would be useful if the CA3 neurons are to store many different stimuli using an autoassociation network. Brown (1982) has also found context-sensitivity of hippocampal neurons recorded during a delayed match-to-sample memory task (which is consistent with a role in episodic memory, in which context is important), but the task also included a conditional response component that may have contributed to the neuronal responses found.

Systems Level Theory

The effects of damage to the hippocampus indicate that the very long-term storage of information is not in the hippocampus, at least in humans, in that the retrograde amnesia produced by damage to the hippocampal system in humans is not always severe, and in that very old memories (e.g., for events that occurred 30 years previously) are not destroyed (Squire, 1986; Squire & Zola-Morgan, 1988). On the other hand, the hippocampus does appear to be necessary for the storage of certain types of information (characterized by the description declarative, or knowing that, as contrasted with procedural, or knowing how, which is spared in amnesia). Declarative memory includes what can be declared or brought to mind as a proposition or an image. Declarative memory includes *episodic memory,* which is memory for particular episodes, and *semantic memory,* which is memory for facts (Squire & Zola-Morgan, 1988; Squire, Shimamura, & Amaral, 1988).

These computational and systems level analyses suggest that the hippocampus is specialized to detect the best way in which to store information and then, by the return paths to the cerebral cortex, to direct memory storage there. The hypothesis is that the CA3 autoassociation system is ideal for remembering particular episodes, because (perhaps uniquely in the brain) it provides a single autoassociation matrix that receives from many different areas of the cerebral association cortex. It is thus able to make almost any arbitrary association, including incorporation by association of the context in which a set of events occurred. This autoassociation type of memory is also what is required for paired-associate learning, in which arbitrary associations must be made between words, and an impairment of which is almost a defining test of anterograde amnesia. Impairment of this ability to remember episodes by using the CA3 autoassociation matrix memory may also underly many of the memory deficits produced by damage to the hippocampal system. For example, conditional spatial response learning (see Miyashita et al., 1989) may be impaired by hippocampal damage, because a monkey or human cannot make use of the memory of the episode of events on each particular trial—for example, that a particular stimulus and a particular response were made, and reward was received. Similarly, object–place memory tasks, also impaired by hippocampal damage, require associations to be made between particular locations and particular objects—again a natural function for an autoassociation memory. Further, the difficulty with memory for places produced by hippocampal damage (see Barnes, 1988) may be because a place is normally defined by a conjunction of a number of features or environmental cues or stimuli, and this type of conjunction is normally made by the autoassociation memory capability of the hippocampus (see further Rolls, Miyashita et al., 1989). Clearly, the hippocampus, with its large number of synapses on each neuron, its potentiation type of learning, and its CA3 autoassociation system, is able to detect when there is conjunctive activation of arbitrary sets of its input fibers and is able, as indicated both theoretically and by recordings made in the behaving monkey, to allocate neurons economically (i.e., with relatively few neurons active) to code for each complex input event (by the output or CA1 stage). Such output neurons could then represent an efficient way in which to store information, in that complex memories with little redundancy would have been generated. It should be noted that this theory is not inconsistent with the possibility that the hippocampus provides a working memory, in that in the present theory the hippocampus sets up a representation using Hebbian learning, which is useful in determining how information can best be stored in the neocortex, and this representation could provide a useful working memory. It may be that by understanding the operations performed by the hippocampus at the neuronal network level, it can be seen how the hippocampus could contribute to several functions that are not necessarily inconsistent.

The question of how the hippocampal output is used by the neocortex (i.e. cerebral cortex) is considered next. Given that the hippocampal output returns to the neocortex, a theory of backprojections in the neocortex is needed; this is developed elsewhere (Rolls, 1989a, 1989b). By way of introduction to this, it may be noted that which particular hippocampal neurons happen to represent a complex input event is not determined by any teacher or forcing (unconditioned) stimulus. Thus, the neocortex must be able to utilize the signal rather cleverly. One possibility is that any neocortical neuron with a number of afferents active at the same time as hippocampal return fibers in its vicinity are active modifies its responses so that it comes to respond better to those afferents the next time those afferents are active. This learning by the cortex would involve a Hebb-like learning mechanism. It may be noted that one function served by what are thus, in effect, backprojections from the hippocampus is some guidance for or supervision of neocortical learning. It is a problem of unsupervised learning systems that they can detect local conjunctions efficiently, but that these are not necessarily those of most use to the whole system. It is exactly this problem that it is proposed that the hippocampus helps to solve, by detecting useful conjunctions globally (i.e., over the whole of information space) and then directing storage locally at earlier stages of processing, so that filters are built locally that provide representations of input stimuli which are useful for later processing. It is also suggested (Rolls, 1989a, 1989b) that the backprojections are used for recall, for dynamic adjustment of the processing of earlier stages to facilitate the optimal satisfaction of multiple constraints, and for attention.

CONCLUSION

A computational theory of the hippocampus that has as a key feature the ability to implement an autoassociation memory using the CA3 pyramidal cells has been proposed. It is proposed that the hippocampus is involved in both spatial and episodic memory as a result of its ability to form arbitrary associations between input stimuli, so that whole spatial scenes or all the events that comprise a single episodic memory can be associated together. Recordings from single neurons in the primate hippocampus are consistent with the theory that inputs to the hippocampus originating from different parts of the cerebral cortex are brought together onto single neurons within the hippocampus, and that synaptic modifications within the hippocampus implement the associations, although further work is needed to test the detailed predictions of the theory.

ACKNOWLEDGMENTS

The author has worked on some of the experiments and neuronal network modelling described here with A. Bennett, P. Cahusac, D. Cohen, J. D. Feigenbaum,

R. P. Kesner, G. Littlewort, Y. Miyashita, H. Niki, and R. Payne, and their collaboration is sincerely acknowledged. Discussions with David G. Amaral of the Salk Institute, La Jolla, California were also much appreciated. This research was supported by the Medical Research Council.

REFERENCES

Amaral, D. G. (1987). Memory: Anatomical organization of candidate brain regions. In *Handbook of neurophysiology, Section 1: The nervous system. Vol. V, Part 1* (pp. 211–294). Washington, DC: American Physiological Society.

Andersen, P. O. (1987). Properties of hippocampal synapses of importance for integration and memory. In G. M. Edelman, W. E. Gall, & W. M. Cowan, (Eds.), *New insights into synaptic function* (pp. 403–429). New York: Neuroscience Research Foundation/Wiley.

Andersen, R. A. (1987). Inferior parietal lobule function in spatial perception and visuomotor integration. In *Handbook of physiology, Section 1: The nervous system. Vol. V. Higher functions of the brain. Part 2* (pp. 483–518). American Physiological Society, Bethesda, Md.

Barnes, C. A. (1988). Spatial learning and memory processes: the search for their neurobiological mechanisms in the rat. *Trends in Neurosciences, 11,* 163–169.

Bliss, T. V. P. & Lomo, T. (1973). Long-lasting potentiation of synaptic transmission in the dentate area of the anaesthetized rabbit following stimulation of the perforant path. *Journal of Physiology, 232,* 331–356.

Cahusac, P. M. B., Miyashita, Y., & Rolls, E. T. (1989). Responses of hippocampal neurons in the monkey related to delayed spatial response and object–place memory tasks. *Behavioural Brain Research, 33,* 229–240.

Feigenbaum, J., Cahusac, P. M. B., & Rolls, E. T. (1987). The coding of spatial information by neurons in the primate hippocampal formation. *Society for Neuroscience Abstracts, 13,* 608.

Feigenbaum, J. D., Rolls, E. T., Cahusac, P. M. B., & Bach, L. Allocentric and egocentric spatial information processing in the hippocampal formation of the behaving primate. In preparation.

Gaffan, D. (1974). Recognition impaired and association intact in the memory of monkeys after transection of the fornix. *Journal of Comparative Physiological Psychology, 86,* 1100–1109.

Gaffan, D. (1977). Monkey's recognition memory for complex pictures and the effects of fornix transection. *Quarterly Journal of Experimental Psychology, 29,* 505–514.

Gaffan, D. (1987). Amnesia, personal memory and the hippocampus: Experimental neuropsychological studies in monkeys. In S. M. Stahl, S. D. Iversen, & E. C. Goodman, *Cognitive neurochemistry* (pp. 46–56). Oxford: Oxford University Press.

Gaffan, D., Gaffan, E. A., & Harrison, S. (1984). Effects of fornix transection on spontaneous and trained non-matching by monkeys. *Quarterly Journal of Experimental Psychology, 36B,* 285–303.

Gaffan, D. & Harrison, S. (1989a). A comparison of the effects of fornix section and sulcus principalis ablation upon spatial learning by monkeys. *Behavioural Brain Research, 31,* 207–220.

Gaffan, D., & Harrison, S. (1989b). Place memory and scene memory: Effects of fornix transection in the monkey. *Experimental Brain Research, 74,* 202–212.

Gaffan, D. & Saunders, R. C. (1985). Running recognition of configural stimuli by fornix transected monkeys. *Quarterly Journal of Experimental Psychology, 37B,* 61–71.

Gaffan, D., Saunders, R. C., Gaffan, E. A., Harrison, S., Shields, C., & Owen, M. J. (1984). Effects of fornix transection upon associative memory in monkeys: Role of the hippocampus in learned action. *Quarterly Journal of Experimental Psychology, 26B,* 173–221.

Gaffan, D. & Weiskrantz, L. (1980). Recency effects and lesion effects in delayed non-matching to randomly baited samples by monkeys. *Brain Research, 196,* 373–386.

Gardner-Medwin, A. R. (1976). The recall of events through the learning of associations between their parts. *Proceedings of the Royal Society, London, B, 194,* 375–402.

Goldman-Rakic, P. S. (1987). Circuitry of primate prefrontal cortex and regulation of behavior by representational memory. In F. Plum & V. Mountcastle (Eds.), *Handbook of physiology* (Vol. 5, pp. 373–417). Bethesda, MD: American Physiological Society.

Jordan, M. I. (1986). An introduction to linear algebra in parallel distributed processing. In D. E. Rumelhart & J. L. McClelland (Eds.), *Parallel distributed processing Vol. 1: Foundations* (pp. 365–442). Cambridge, MA: MIT Press.

Kelso, S. R., Ganong, A. H., & Brown, T. H. (1986). Hebbian synapses in the hippocampus. *Proceedings of the National Academy of Science, 83,* 5326–5330.

Kohonen, T. (1988). *Self-organization and associative memory.* Berlin: Springer-Verlag. 2nd Edn.

Kohonen, T., Lehtio, P., Rovamo, J., Hyvarinen, J., Bry, K., & Vainio, L. (1977). A principle of neural associative memory. *Neuroscience, 2,* 1065–1076.

Kohonen, T., Oja, E., & Lehtio, P. (1981). Storage and processing of information in distributed associative memory systems. In G. E. Hinton & J. A. Anderson (Eds.), *Parallel models of associative memory* (pp. 105–143). Hillsdale, NJ: Lawrence Erlbaum Associates.

Kolb, B. & Whishaw, I. Q. (1985). *Fundamentals of human neuropsychology* (2nd ed.). New York: Freeman.

Mahut, H. (1972). A selective spatial deficit in monkeys after transection of the fornix. *Neuropsychologia, 10,* 65–74.

Marr, D. (1970). A theory for cerebral cortex. *Proceedings of the Royal Society, B, 176,* 161–234.

Marr, D. (1971). Simple memory: A theory for archicortex. *Philosophical Transactions of the Royal Society, B, 262,* 23–81.

McNaughton, B. L. (1984). Activity dependent modulation of hippocampal synaptic efficacy: Some implications for memory processes. In W. Seifert (Ed.), *Neurobiology of the hippocampus* (pp. 233–252). London: Academic Press.

McNaughton, B. L., Barnes, C. A., & O'Keefe, J. (1983). The contributions of position, direction, and velocity to single unit activity in the hippocampus of freely-moving rats. *Experimental Brain Research, 52,* 41–49.

Miles, R. (1988). Plasticity of recurrent excitatory synapses between CA3 hippocampal pyramidal cells. *Society for Neuroscience Abstract, 14,* 19.

Milner, B. (1972). Disorders of learning and memory after temporal lobe lesions in man. *Clinical Neurosurgery, 19,* 421–446.

Milner, B. (1982). Some cognitive effects of frontal lobe lesions in man. *Philosophical Transactions of the Royal Society, London, B, 298,* 211–226.

Mishkin, M. (1978). Memory severely impaired by combined but not separate removal of amygdala and hippocampus. *Nature, 273,* 297–298.

Mishkin, M. (1982). A memory system in the monkey. *Philosophical Transactions of the Royal Society, B, 298,* 85–95.

Miyashita, Y., Rolls, E. T., Cahusac, P. M. B., Niki, H., & Feigenbaum, J. D. (1989). Activity of hippocampal formation neurons in the monkey related to a conditional spatial response task. *Journal of Neurophysiology. 61,* 669–678.

Murray, E. A. & Mishkin, M. (1984). Severe tactual as well as visual memory deficits follow combined removal of the amygdala and hippocampus in monkeys. *Journal of Neuroscience, 4,* 2565–2580.

O'Keefe, J. (1984). Spatial memory within and without the hippocampal system. In W. Seifert (Ed.), *Neurobiology of the hippocampus* (pp. 375–403). Academic Press: London.

Owen, M. J. & Butler, S. R. (1981). Amnesia after transection of the fornix in monkeys: Long-term memory impaired, short-term memory intact. *Behavioural Brain Research, 3,* 115–123.

Parkinson, J. K., Murray, E. A., & Mishkin, M. (1988). A selective mnemonic role for the hippo-campus in monkeys: Memory for the location of objects. *Journal of Neuroscience, 8,* 4059–4167.

Petrides, M. (1985). Deficits on conditional associative-learning tasks after frontal- and temporal-lobe lesions in man. *Neuropsychologia, 23,* 601–614.

Rolls, E. T. (1985). Connections, functions and dysfunctions of limbic structures, the prefrontal cortex, and hypothalamus. In M. Swash & C. Kennard (Eds.), *The scientific basis of clinical neurology* (pp. 201–213). London: Churchill Livingstone.

Rolls, E. T. (1987). Information representation, processing and storage in the brain: analysis at the single neuron level. In J. P. Changeaux & M. Konishi (Eds.), *The neural and molecular bases of learning* (pp. 503–540). Chichester: Wiley.

Rolls, E. T. (1989a). Functions of neuronal networks in the hippocampus and neocortex in memory. In J. H. Byrne & W. O. Berry (Eds.), *Neural models of plasticity: Theoretical and empirical approaches* (pp. 240–265). New York: Academic Press.

Rolls, E. T. (1989b). The representation and storage of information in neuronal networks in the primate cerebral cortex and hippocampus. In R. Durbin, C. Miall, & G. Mitchison (Eds.), *The computing neuron* (pp. 125–159). Wokingham, England: Addison-Wesley.

Rolls, E. T. (1989c). Visual information processing in the primate temporal lobe. In M. Imbert (Ed.), *Models of visual perception: From natural to artificial.* Oxford: Oxford University Press.

Rolls, E. T., Miyashita, Y., Cahusac, P., & Kesner, R. P. (1985). The responses of single neurons in the primate hippocampus related to the performance of memory tasks. *Society for Neuroscience Abstracts, 11,* 525.

Rolls, E. T., Miyashita, Y., Cahusac, P. M. B., Kesner, R. P., Niki, H., Feigenbaum, J., & Bach, L. (1989). Hippocampal neurons in the monkey with activity related to the place in which a stimulus is shown. *Journal of Neuroscience, 9,* 1835–1845.

Rolls, E. T., Cahusac, P. M. B., Miyashita, Y., & Niki, H. (In preparation). Modification of the responses of hippocampal neurons in the monkey during the learning of a conditional spatial response task.

Rolls, E. T., Feigenbaum, J. D., Cahusac, P. M. B. & Miyashita, Y. (1989). Responses of single neurons in the hippocampus of the macaque related to recognition memory. In preparation.

Rupniak, N. M. J. & Gaffan, D. (1987). Monkey hippocampus and learning about spatially directed movements. *Journal of Neuroscience, 7,* 2331–2337.

Sakata, H. (1985). The parietal association cortex: Neurophysiology. In M. Swash & C. Kennard (Eds.), *The scientific basis of clinical neurology* (pp. 225–236). London: Churchill Livingstone.

Scoville, W. B. & Milner, B. (1957). Loss of recent memory after bilateral hippocampal lesions. *Journal of Neurology, Neurosurgery and Psychiatry, 20,* 11–21.

Smith, M. L. & Milner, B. (1981). The role of the right hippocampus in the recall of spatial location. *Neuropsychologia, 19,* 781–793.

Squire, L. (1986). Mechanisms of memory. *Science, 232,* 1612–1619.

Squire, L. R., Shimamura, A. P., & Amaral, D. G. (1989). Memory and the hippocampus. In J. Byrne & W. O. Berry (Eds.), *Neural models of plasticity: Theoretical and empirical approaches* (pp. 208–239). New York: Academic Press.

Squire, L. R. & Zola-Morgan, S. (1988). Memory: Brain systems and behavior. *Trends in Neuro-sciences, 11,* 170–175.

Van Hoesen, G. W. (1982). The parahippocampal gyrus. New observations regarding its cortical connections in the monkey. *Trends in Neurosciences, 5,* 345–350.

Watanabe, T. & Niki, H. (1985). Hippocampal unit activity and delayed response in the monkey. *Brain Research, 325,* 241–254.

Wigstrom, H., Gustaffson, B., Huang, Y.-Y., & Abraham, W. C. (1986). Hippocampal long-term potentiation is induced by pairing single afferent volleys with intracellularly injected depolarizing currents. *Acta Physiologica Scandinavia, 126,* 317–319.

Zola-Morgan, S., Squire, L. R. (1985). Medial temporal lesions in monkeys impair memory on a variety of tasks sensitive to human amnesia. *Behavioral Neuroscience, 99,* 22–34.

Zola-Morgan, S., Squire, L. R., & Amaral, D. G. (1986). Human amnesia and the medial temporal region: enduring memory impairment following a bilateral lesion limited to field CA1 of the hippocampus. *Journal of Neuroscience, 6,* 2950–2957.

13

Spatial Representation in the Rat: Conceptual, Behavioral, and Neurophysiological Perspectives

B. Leonard and B. L. McNaughton
University of Colorado

> *"Now it happens that the visual activity of lower species is dominated by the perception of place. This turns out experimentally to mean a dominance of cues from remote objects instead of near ones; and remote objects provide the most stable and constant stimulation of the animal's environment."*
>
> —D. O. Hebb (1949), *The organization of behavior*

Rats, like many other animals, can use a variety of sources and kinds of information to localize both themselves and desired places in space (e.g., Honzik, 1936; Potegal, 1982; Sutherland & Dyck, 1984; Zoladek & Roberts, 1978). Thus, a noisy fan could be a source of auditory directional information that might specify which way to turn in order to find food. The velocity, duration, and angular components of walking from a fixed starting point would be a different source and kind of spatial information—information that could, for example, inform the rat about distance from its nest (Mittelstaedt & Mittelstaedt, 1980; Mittelstaedt & Mittelstaedt, 1982). One could also imagine that a given source might simultaneously provide different kinds of information that could be useful for spatial localization.

A given source of spatial information might have a different navigational status for the rat at different times (Collett, Cartwright, & Smith, 1986; Whishaw & Mittleman, 1986). At one time, a distant landmark might act as a visual source that is co-localized with a goal of navigation, such as a place of refuge. At a different time, this same landmark might provide little spatial information on its own; but in combination with other landmarks it might contribute to the unique localization of a previously hidden food source.

363

The ability of rats to return repeatedly and efficiently to a goal that is not immediately perceptible (e.g., Barnes, 1979; Morris, 1981) or to avoid accurately places that have recently been visited (Olton & Samuelson, 1976) suggests that impinging spatial information becomes organized and meaningful as the rat experiences its environment. In short, it acquires an internal model, or representation, of its environment.

The goal of this chapter is to consider the manner in which such internal models may be constructed in the rat's nervous system, and to begin to develop some ideas about how such representations may be manipulated so that adaptive behaviors, such as the computation of novel spatial trajectories, might occur. It is our belief that, ultimately, the consideration of the neural and cognitive processing involved in spatial behavior in the rat will lead to a more general understanding of operations in human cognition, specifically those involving the internal manipulation of representations of past experience in order to predict the consequences of actions within a given context or to select an appropriate set of actions to accomplish an internally represented desired outcome.

Some of the clearest data obtained from human cognitive studies that indicate that internal manipulation of representations does, in fact, occur comes from the elegant studies of Shepard and his colleagues on "mental rotation" (e.g., Cooper & Shepard, 1973; Shepard & Metzler, 1971). Briefly, these studies showed that the time required to identify whether two objects (presented with random relative orientations) are the same or mirror images of each other is a linear function of the degree of rotation necessary to bring the objects into congruence. As we hope will become clear, cognitive operations, not too dissimilar from those involved in such phenomena, may also be implemented in the nervous system of the rat, in the course of interacting with and learning about spatially extended environments.

This chapter consists of five main sections. The first section discusses some fundamental aspects about the general construct of representation and compares and contrasts two hypotheses about the nature of spatial representation. The second section defines terms and concepts and presents a brief summary of the sensory abilities of the rat. Because spatial representations contain information about environments and guide spatial behavior, we need to define what we mean by "spatial" information, "spatial" behavior, and "environment." Also, it is our belief that in order to understand the nature of spatial representations in the rat— or in any species, for that matter—one first needs to consider what sensory information is available to the organism. The third section reviews some fundamental studies on spatial behavior in the rat. Consideration of these studies provides some insights into the organization of the rat's spatial representation. The fourth section reviews neurophysiological studies of spatial encoding and memory in the rat. These kinds of data can potentially provide direct information on the nature and organization of spatial information processing and representation. The final section presents a simple conceptual model of how spatial information might be neurally encoded when a rat is learning about its environment and how this information could be used for adaptive behavior.

SPATIAL REPRESENTATION

Though not always explicitly appreciated, the concept of a representation logically implies the existence of two worlds, or two sets, that are related to each other by some unique transfer function or mapping (Palmer, 1978). The representing world preserves or carries information about the represented world. The mapping function specifies how features in the two worlds are related. Such a mapping need not imply that properties of the representation must actually resemble properties of what is represented, a point upon which we dwell at some length. Moreover, not all aspects of the represented world need to be contained in the representation. For example, there is no *necessary* reason for adjacent locations in an environment to be represented in an adjacent manner in neural circuitry, and just because absolute differences in the heights of landmarks in the environment might exist does not necessarily mean that this aspect will be preserved internally. Although all external information may not be explicitly represented, it is important to keep in mind the possibility that "absent" information could be reconstructed or derived if the requisite processing mechanisms exist.

Following a tradition that traces its origin at least back to Tolman (1948), O'Keefe and Nadel (1978) proposed that spatial relationships in the world are represented internally by a cognitive structure that, although it may not be isomorphic with a two-dimensional geographical map, is sufficiently similar to one in its logical implications that useful inferences about the neural representation of space might be drawn from the analogy. The essence of such a structure is the existence of a global representation of objects within some manifold or coordinate system from which their mutual spatial relationships can be derived, but that is, to some extent, independent of the objects themselves. For example, if the distances and directions from A to B and from A to C are known, then the directed distance from B to C can be extracted from the coordinate framework, and the animal might thus generate a novel trajectory from B to C, even if the features of C are not immediately perceptible. The fundamental implication of the theory of "cognitive mapping" is the existence of an internal representation of such an absolute space existing independently of objects or sensory events, but within which such experiences can be located. Such an internal model does not depend on body orientation but is assumed, in some abstract way, to maintain its orientation with respect to the external world with rotation of the animal. O'Keefe and Nadel (1978) proposed that the hippocampal formation constitutes the physical medium within which this abstract coordinate framework is constructed. The general hypothesis was that, once a particular object or location was specified, the entire metrical structure of the corresponding environment was somehow globally activated (see also Nadel, Wilner, & Kurz, 1985; O'Keefe, 1988).

There is an alternative to this general view that differs from the cognitive map idea in a manner that is similar to the difference between modern and classical gravitational theory. With the alternative view, one foregoes a coordinate system altogether. A point in space (or space-time) is described purely on the basis of the event, or "intersection of world lines" that occurs there. A spatial framework is nothing more than a listing of completely independent events and the *local* relations that connect them (see for example, Misner, Thorne & Wheeler, 1973). The cognitive structure of such a representation of space would be essentially one in which spatial relationships are derived by tracing or recreating, on a sequential basis, the paths in memory by which local events are connected. A location is nothing more than a set or constellation of sensory/perceptual experiences, joined to others by specific movements. To the extent that such a constellation recurs in a relatively constant form from experience to experience, it provides a basis for predicting the outcome of particular movement sequences. A movement is specified purely on an egocentric basis with the added "context" of the current local exteroceptive input. The notion that space is represented as such a linked list of events we refer to as the "local view" hypothesis (McNaughton, 1987, 1988a, 1988b).

Both hypotheses are similar to the extent that they postulate a dominant role of autoassociative memory, that is, the ability to recreate a complete representation from a current experience of a restricted subset of the usual local view. They differ in that the completed representation that is activated at one moment includes, in the map hypothesis, many features that are not within the current range of the animal's sensorium. These features are somehow assigned to a coordinate framework from which their relational structure can be derived. In the local view hypothesis, only those features that are (or were previously) within sensory range, as defined by the animal's current location and orientation within its environment, are recreated by such an autoassociative process. The hidden features, those that are not accessible in the current "local view," are not simultaneously activated. Rather, they are only recalled through an interaction with the representation of the movement (or chain of movements and local views) that link them to the current view. The cognitive map hypothesis assigns such an egocentrically based system of movements both a subordinate, and somewhat superfluous role with respect to navigation, and a likewise weakly connected anatomical system for its implementation. The local view hypothesis requires that the two systems must be inextricably linked; allocentric space is derived from an egocentric representation.

Concepts about the general construct of representation and the application of these concepts to the problem of spatial representation have only been touched on here. A more comprehensive treatment of the general subject of representation can be found in Palmer (1978). An analysis of the representation of space using "location instances," to which some of the fundamental ideas presented here can be traced, can be found in Zipser (1983).

Spatial Behavior, Sensory Capacities, and Spatial Cues

Spatial Behavior

In the broadest sense, all behavior occurs in space and so could be considered spatial. A more focused definition, however, would emphasize movements of an animal's body or body parts, which are orderly and self-generated (Schöne, 1984). In this chapter, we focus primarily on those behaviors of rodents that are actively ordered in space and that involve body displacements through environments that cannot be perceived in their entirety from a single local view or vantage point. Furthermore, our focus is mainly on spatial behaviors that reflect the rodent's knowledge, or acquisition of knowledge, about its own positions and movements and about positions of objects in space.

Sensory Capacities of the Rat

Before discussing spatial cues, it is useful to mention briefly some particular aspects about the rat's sensory capacities. Although consideration of this topic is central to the study of spatial representation, our purpose here is only to outline broadly what sensory aspects of the rat's spatial world might influence the nature of its spatial representation.

The rat is widely believed to process very poor visual capacities, yet, in the laboratory at least, it uses vision predominantly to guide its spatial behavior (Honzik, 1936; Zoladek & Roberts, 1978). Perhaps this belief derives, in part, from the fact that the rat possesses low visual acuity compared to other mammals. The maximum spatial frequency (at a mean luminance level of 3.4 cd/m^2) that the albino rat can resolve behaviorally is about 0.38 cycles/degree (Birch & Jacobs, 1979). Pigmented rats are not much better, at 1.2 cycles/degree, when compared to the human spatial contrast sensitivity function, which displays a maximum cutoff of about 60 cycles/degree.

However, although this property of our visual system allows us to detect sharp edges, it turns out that most natural scenes exhibit power spectra that are dominated by low spatial frequencies (1/f^2; Field, 1987), where the contrast sensitivity of the rats is, in fact, superior to humans and other primates. This may explain in part why rats tend to use vision when navigating in space rather than other, relatively more acute sensory abilities. Also, visual information allows discriminations to be made at a distance, whereas tactile information permits very local discriminations only, and olfactory information in the typical laboratory maze situation tends to be expressed in nonlocalized gradients, again allowing only local discriminations.

Another sensory capacity of the rat that certainly influences its spatial navigation and the nature of the underlying spatial representation is its auditory spectral sensitivity and sound localization threshold. The albino rat has a range of hearing from 250 Hz to 80 kHz (70 dB cutoff). Although its hearing is most sensitive at 8 kHz, it is only slightly less so at 38 kHz (Kelly & Masterton, 1977). Like visual information, auditory information can be a source for spatial localization. Information on auditory localization of pure tones in their "best" frequency is not available for the albino rat, but it is known that rats can localize a noise source within about 10 degrees (Kelly & Glazier, 1978). Although it has not been given much experimental attention, rats apparently can use this sound localization ability in conjunction with echolocation to navigate through a maze (Riley & Rosensweig, 1957).

Finally, we should mention what little is known about the ability of the rat to use tactual sensory information, derived from its vibrissae, to guide spatial behavior. To our knowledge, no recent behavioral work has been done on describing the range of sensitivity of the rat's vibrissae in making discriminations. However, results from systematic studies on the role of the rat's vibrissae in behavior done at the beginning of the century and inferences from a more recent study suggest the importance for the rat of environmental information gained from these organs. Briefly, rats with vibrissae present unilaterally negotiate walled mazes in a manner that keeps them in constant contact with their intact vibrissae (Vincent, 1912). In the same study, a gross measure of the rat's ability to discriminate surfaces with its vibrissae was also provided. Vibrissae*less* rats can acquire a spatial discrimination in which one alleyway of three is distinguished by corrugated walls in about the same number of trials as normal rats, *but* their average trial time is five times as long at criterion performance (Vincent, 1912).

In a depth discrimination task in which conflicting tactual and visual information is present, normal rats rely on information from their vibrissae to guide their behavior, whereas vibrissaeless rats rely on vision (Schiffman, Lore, Passafiume, & Neeb, 1970). This task took advantage of the rat's known preference to step down from a high support onto the shallow side of a visual cliff instead of the deep side. A low support was used in this experiment to provide the opportunity to use tactual information in addition to visual information. Vibrissaeless rats showed the usual preference for the shallow side, whereas the normal rats showed equal preference for both sides. Presumably, the rats with intact vibrissae could detect the presence of the glass surface and therefore were not influenced by the differential visual depth information about the two surfaces under the glass. This prepotence of tactual information over visual information in this context suggests the possibility that spatial representations and their neurobiological organization may be different for environments that have few accessible vertical boundaries compared to those that do.

Spatial Cues

As implied in the foregoing sections, a necessary step in understanding any form of cognitive representation is the identification of the kinds and dimensions of information to which an organism is sensitive. Information that is used by the organism to guide spatial behavior is termed a *spatial cue*. Spatial cues provide information about the external world in terms of distance, direction, or both (Schöne, 1984). Some consideration of the various types of spatial cues should lead to a better understanding of the organization of the representation of large-scale space. In particular, appreciation of the fact that the availability of certain cue types results in predictable types of spatial behaviors allows one to infer what kinds of spatial information are preserved in the rat's internal representation, if it is known what types of spatial cues are available.

Rats become knowledgeable about their position in space and about the relative position of both visible and hidden objects through the detection of spatial cues. While spatial cues are definable in terms of the sensory modality (or modalities) in which they are detected, they can also be classified according to their arrangement and distribution in space (Schöne, 1984).

Landmarks. Landmarks are one type of spatial cue (Schöne, 1984). Consisting of discrete, fixed objects, they can be further grouped into three classes according to the type of spatial behavior they can support (Collett et al., 1986).

The first class consists of **beacons,** which are objects that are so close to a goal of navigation that the animal simply has to orient and approach. Functionally, the goal and beacon are co-localized. Although knowledge about direction and distance to a goal is unnecessary for navigation with this type of cue, this does not mean that this information is not encoded in the rat's spatial representation.

The second class of landmark consists of **singular distal landmarks.** These are fixed singular objects that are further away from a goal of navigation than a beacon but still close enough to provide some information about distance to the goal (Collett et al., 1986). However, these single, symmetrical landmarks cannot define a second point in space (e.g., a hidden goal) without the use of other spatial cues. Navigation based solely on this type of landmark can only localize an imperceptible goal to a circle of fixed radius around the landmark. Unless additional information is available, such as a fixed starting location, additional landmarks, or an internal direction sense, singular distal landmarks cannot uniquely localize a point in space.

The third class of landmark consists of **compass-marks** (Collett et al., 1986). These are singular objects that are so far from a goal of navigation that they appear to remain stationary as the animal traverses the accessible environment. Unlike the second class, compass-marks can only provide directional information on their own, leaving distance information about the location of a goal unspecified (Schöne, 1984).

Arrays. A second type of spatial cue consists of **arrays.** Complete spatial information about a location, which is not co-localized with a landmark, requires the presence of at least two featurally distinct points. Individual objects or points of an array do not provide both distance and direction about a location (except in the cases of a fixed starting point and absolute directional sense), but in relation to the other objects or points of the array, precise distance and direction information is available. A single nonsymmetrical object can really be considered to be such an array of spatial stimulus points.

Distributed Cues. Beacons, singular distal landmarks, and arrays of objects are discretely localized in space and therefore can potentially provide relatively accurate information for spatial localization. However, other types of cues that are widely distributed in space can provide a measure of spatial localization. In the laboratory, the most prominent of these spatially extended cues are boundaries of the test apparatus. For example, the walls of a circular arena can provide radial distance information about locations but not about angular information. Other types of distributed cues include olfactory density gradients, illumination gradients (i.e., shadows), and distributed gradients of texture. In general, the precision of localization provided for by a spatial cue is related to its distribution in space and to its distance from the observer.

Motion Cues. The types of spatial cues discussed to this point exist external to the animal. A fourth kind of spatial cue cannot be strictly classified according to its arrangement and distribution in space, but nonetheless, in combination with other types of cues, provides information that can be used to localize objects or places in space. Vestibular, kinesthetic, motor "efference copy," and visual motion cues are derived from internally generated information about movements in relation to a goal (Potegal, 1982). Specifically, knowledge about movement velocity and/or the period of time or number of the relevant motor cycles required to travel between two locations can provide distance information. Similarly, angular head movements in the horizontal plane provide information about relative direction, whereas vertical head movements and rearing very likely provide distance information as a result of parallax (Ellard, Goodale, & Timney, 1984). Finally, the possibility must be emphasized that rats, like humans, may be capable of learning, from experience with the results of various motor sequences, that certain sets of movements may have spatially equivalent consequences (motor equivalence). This may form the basis of a kind of geometrical sense, which would enable the computation of novel trajectories between familiar locations.

Although this classification scheme is probably incomplete and certainly could be modified, it brings attention to the fact that the available spatial information in the typical experimental environment is considerably richer than previous classifications of spatial cues might imply. Traditionally, features of the environment have been operationally divided into "proximal" cues, which include the physically accessible features of the test apparatus, and "distal" cues, which include features that are not proximal. As the foregoing discussion suggests, however, this dichotomy may not adequately capture the qualities of spatial information available in the environment and thus the potential kinds of information that might be encoded.

SPATIAL BEHAVIOR IN THE RAT

Our intent in this section is to present a selected survey of studies of spatial behavior in the rat, studies that we believe illustrate the computational power and flexibility of the rat's spatial representation. To set the stage for the consideration of the underlying neuronal operations, in the course of this survey we make passing reference to the extent to which the performance of particular spatial tasks is affected by damage to the hippocampal formation (see Barnes, 1988 for a review). This brain region is believed to play a central role in at least the primary stages of the establishment of spatial representations in the rat (see O'Keefe & Nadel, 1978, for a comprehensive treatment of this subject).

Exploration

There are many behaviors that are loosely called "spatial," and many experimental situations in which the components of such behaviors may be, to varying degrees, isolated and studied. It is instructive, however, to consider first a simple, unstructured behavioral situation that illustrates how the rat's environment acquires meaning and becomes organized during exploration.

A small group of laboratory rats, reared in the typical, spatially restricted environment of small colony cages, was released each night for several nights into a large room filled with a variety of "junk" objects. Food and water were located at various places, and the floor was marked with 1-foot grid squares (Sharp, Barnes, & McNaughton, 1987). Behavioral observations and counts of grid crossings were made during 15-minute periods in the evenings (under dim red lighting) and the mornings (under normal room lighting).

During the first few minutes following the first release, the animals made few movements, and these were restricted to small excursions away from their initial location, followed immediately by return to that spot. After 1 or 2 hours, however, there was considerable movement about the room, with an average of about 25–30 grid crossings per animal per 15 minutes. During the second and third evenings, this number had increased substantially to 50–70. The maximum morning activity was about half of the maximum evening activity.

There was a clear progression of behaviors observed during the three evening sessions. In the first, the animals made excursions from some single place of cover, such as a tunnel or box, to other parts of the room, always returning to the point of origin. During the second evening, the animals were engaged primarily in collecting the food from the various deposit sites and caching it in specific places. During the third evening, aggressive social/territorial interactions, characterized by rearing, pushing, and submissive posturing were observed. Recovering the animals was relatively easy during the first morning, whereas during subsequent mornings recovery was considerably more difficult because the animals would dash rapidly and directly from one inaccessible location to another. By the third day, there were signs of nest building, always within some enclosed space, and there had developed a clear pattern of collections of rat droppings at specific locations other than the nest areas.

A number of nontrivial conclusions can be drawn from these and similar observations. Rats, even if reared in restricted spaces, have a natural propensity to explore, and a 222-sq.-ft-room by no means approaches the limit of this propensity. During this exploration, certain regions are assigned attributes such as food source, safety, and latrine. Other areas are designated as "home" territory and are defended aggressively. Open spaces are avoided, somewhat less so in darkness. Some form of "patrolling" or exploratory activity appears to continue even after the animals have become highly familiar with the environment, although the routes may become more stereotyped. Finally, the significance attached to particular locations changes dynamically, for example, the likelihood of finding the rat in an open area changes according to illumination conditions and how recently the experimenter entered the room, and locations from which food has been removed are not soon revisited. Although the effects of hippocampal damage were not assessed in this study, numerous other studies have noted a general increase in activity characterizable as exploratory following such damage (e.g., Jarrard & Bunnell, 1968). One interpretation of this observation is that, with a damaged hippocampus, animals are unable to form a cognitive representation of their environment, with the result being that the environment appears novel with each introduction.

Incidental Learning and the Spatial Habit

One of the earliest studies on the nature of the rat's spatial ability was conducted by Tolman and Honzik (1930). The experiment examined the rats' ability to use alternative paths to a goal when a well-practiced one was blocked. The results of this experiment suggest that rats acquire incidental knowledge of spatial relationships during exploration and are able to "query" this knowledge to predict the spatial consequences of a future behavioral choice.

An elevated runaway maze was used, which had three alternative pathways to a food box. The pathways varied in their length and directness (see Fig. 13.1).

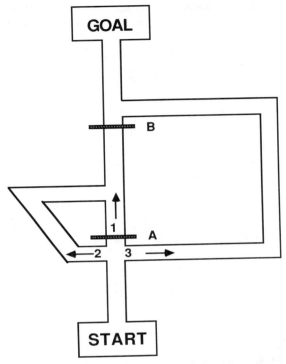

FIG. 13.1.   Illustration of the apparatus used in early investigations of "spatial inference" by Tolman and Honzik (1930). The maze consisted of an elevated runway maze, open to the laboratory. In the first phase of the study, the animals were allowed to explore the maze and freely choose their routes to the goal box, where they received food reward. After some exploration, the direct route was reliably chosen over the two longer routes. In the second phase, a barrier was placed at point A. The animals reliably selected the shorter of the two routes on over 90% of trials. Finally, the block was moved to point B. In this case, on encountering the block, the animals returned to the choice point and selected the long path. The inference from these results was that the animals had, in some way, represented the fact that the routes 1 and 2 had an intersection before the block, whereas 1 and 3 had an intersection beyond the block.

An important design feature of the maze was that paths 1 and 2 had a common end segment leading to the food. The experiment consisted of two phases. Preliminary training assessed the rats' relative preference for the three pathways in navigating to the goal. Not surprisingly, the rats chose path 1 most frequently, and chose path 2 over path 3 on over 90% of the trials when a block was placed at point A. By placing a block at point B, the test phase of the experiment assessed whether the rats had internally represented the fact that paths 1 and 2 had a common end segment. That is, when the rats encountered the block at point B would they return to the start point and choose the highly preferred path 2, or would they know that this also would lead to the block and thus choose the only open path to the food? On the very first test trial, 14 of 15 rats took path 3 after reaching the block at B in spite of the strong preference for path 2. Taken together with the finding in the same study that rats do not display this sort of inference behavior in a maze with high walls (Tolman & Honzik, 1930), these results suggest that rats acquire a cognitive representation of their distant surroundings and are able to use it to plan future spatial behaviors. Tolman's and Honzik's results also imply that the rat's spatial representation can be flexible in the sense that it is not linked to particular motor sequences that have a high probability of reinforcement.

As indicated by the quotation at the beginning of this chapter, rats are not only capable of exhibiting rather sophisticated spatial behaviors, but in fact, space appears to play a dominant role in their behavior. In his discussion of this fact, Hebb (1949) described how this position habit or spatial hypothesis (Kretchevsky, 1932) is "a constant nuisance" during visual discrimination training in rats, something that has to be overcome "by repeated discouragement" before anything else can be learned. Hebb illustrated this point with several experiments that show clearly that when a rat is required to move from one discrete location to another, the movement is guided by the remote sensory cues, rather than cues local to the target (see Fig. 13.2).

In considering why the "spatial hypothesis" should be so predominant, Hebb (1949) was drawn to the conclusion that "the animal perceives, and responds to, the least-variable objects in its environment, which are the ones at the greatest distance from the observer. The stimulation received from any object varies with the animal's movements, but there are important differences that depend on the distance of that object. When the animal turns around, excitation is changed equally from near and far objects; but not when he moves from one place to another. Changes of position affect retinal locus, extent, and intensity only slightly when the stimulus is remote, very greatly when it is near. Even with body rotation, the order in which nearby objects is seen has no constancy, unless the animal always turns at precisely the same point. But the order in which distant objects is seen is the same, no matter where the animal is in the experimental apparatus.

Strategy Redundancy

In many situations in which spatial behavior in rats has been studied (i.e., mazes), the task can be solved on the basis of more than a single mode of behavior. There are generally three different behavioral modes, or "strategies," that are available (O'Keefe & Nadel, 1978): (a) the "place" strategy, (b) the

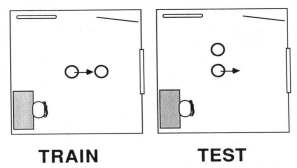

TRAIN   TEST

FIG. 13.2.   Diagram of experiments described by Hebb (1949) that il-lustrate the dominance of distal visual cues in guiding goal-directed spatial behavior. In one study, the animals were trained to jump from one platform to another in order to obtain food reward. After training, the goal platform was moved to a position 90° away from its training location. The animals jumped into empty space in the direction of the original location.

"cue" strategy, and (c) the "response" strategy. The place strategy refers to a plan of behavior in which the only guiding influence for localization is the use of remote sensory cues. With the cue strategy, either the use of some sequence of local cues leading to the goal, or the minimization of distance from a single beacon is the means for localization. The response strategy employs a specific sequence of motor acts, largely independently of the distribution of sensory cues, to attain a goal of navigation. Of course, these strategies may not be independent and, where no conflict is involved, may form a redundant or complementary set, all of which may be used for navigation in a single situation (see Whishaw & Mittleman, 1986). Furthermore, different components may predominate at differ-ent stages of training (Mackintosh, 1965), during which the nature of the spatial representation is probably changing.

In some situations, these strategies can be distinguished experimentally. A good illustration is one in which young and aged animals were trained to obtain water reward at one branch of a T-maze (Barnes, Nadel, & Honig, 1980). The goal arm was distinguished from the unbaited arm by its spatial location, by the presence of a discriminable tactile cue (a mat inserted into the arm), and by the direction of body turn required by the animal at the choice point. Following training, a series of probe trials, in which the maze configuration was systemat-ically altered, was interspersed with regular trials. The alterations were struc-tured so as to enable an assessment of the relative strategy bias exhibited by the animals (see Fig. 13.3). There was no difference between the groups on the number of trials required to reach criterion on the task, but there was a significant difference in the probability of exhibiting particular strategies on probe trials. Young animals exhibited a strategy distribution of about 30% "place," 25%

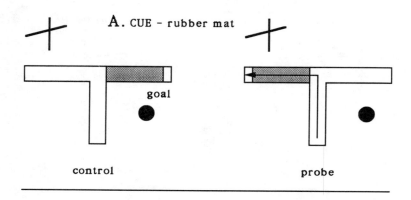

A. CUE – rubber mat

goal

control   probe

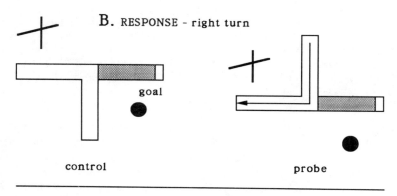

B. RESPONSE – right turn

goal

control   probe

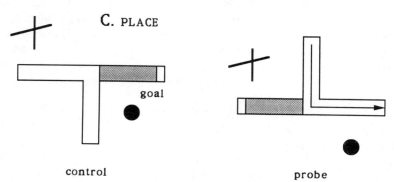

C. PLACE

goal

control   probe

FIG. 13.3.   Illustration of the manner in which Barnes et al. (1980) were able to determine the relative contributions of the "cue," "place," and "response" strategies used by rats in solving a simple T-maze problem. The animals were first well trained to find food located at the end of the right arm of the T. This arm was, coincidentally, also distinguished by a rubber mat of distinct texture and was located at a fixed place in relation to the distal sensory cues. Subsequently, "probe" trials were introduced occasionally in which the three types of strategies could be disambiguated. Arrows in each panel indicate the type of strategy used in the probe.

"cue," and 45% "response." Old animals showed significantly less use of the place strategy, and proportionally more use of the response strategy. It is interesting to note that hippocampal damage has little effect on the acquisition of the T-maze task, probably due to the predominance of the use of the response strategy.

The "Purely Spatial" Paradigm

In an effort to devise a task in which only the place strategy could be used for successful localization, the pronounced tendency of rats to avoid brightly illuminated open spaces has been used as a motivator (Barnes, 1979). Animals were placed in a random orientation in the center of a brightly illuminated, white, circular platform (1.2 m diameter), around the circumference of which were 18 equally spaced holes large enough to admit a rat (Fig. 13.4a). At one point only, the hole led to a dark tunnel, located underneath the platform. The platform itself could be rotated randomly from trial to trial, independently of the tunnel, which remained fixed relative to the remote spatial cues. Thus, the random starting orientation and the rotation of the maze surface precluded the use of response and cue strategies, respectively.

With one trial per day, 7 to 10 days were required for the animals to reach asymptotic performance on this task. During this acquisition period, an interesting progression of behaviors was observed (see Fig. 13.4b): The first trial was characterized by small excursions from the central starting point with many animals never finding the tunnel or even reaching the periphery within the alotted 5 minutes (in which case they were placed by the experimenter next to the tunnel, which they immediately entered); the next phase was characterized by many, apparently random traverses of the maze, each traverse passing near the center, until the tunnel was located; this phase was superceded gradually by direct movement, in an apparently random direction to the maze periphery, followed by systematic hole-to-hole search; finally, the initial heading error was minimized such that the initial trajectory brought the animal to the correct hole directly.

A conceptually similar task that also requires the predominant use of a place strategy has been extensively used to study spatial behavior in rodents. The essential feature of the task is that rats are placed into a large circular pool of water from which they can escape by swimming to a small hidden platform (Morris, 1981). The platform is hidden by placing it just below the water surface, which is rendered opaque. Thus, the only spatial cues that ultimately define the platform's location are distal landmarks and arrays of objects in the room, and the distributed cue presented by the walls of the pool.

Rats rapidly learn to take escape paths directly to the hidden platform, although during acquisition they display a sequence of search behaviors somewhat similar to that observed in the circular platform task. In a pool 1.3 or 1.5 meters in diameter, escape latencies approach asymptotic times of about 10 sec after about 8–10 trials (Morris, 1981; Sutherland & Dyck, 1984). Trajectory headings

A

B

1

2

3

4

also are accurate, averaging less than 20 degrees of error at asymptotic performance. Response or cue strategies do not appear to be a predominant basis for accurate navigation in the water pool task (cf. Whishaw & Mittleman, 1986), because direct trajectories are still observed when the rats are started from a variety of start locations (Morris, 1981).

The finding that rats in both the circular platform and water pool tasks learn to take direct paths to an imperceptible goal that cannot be located efficiently on the basis of a consistent motor response or local sensory cues confirms that rats navigate on the basis of a stored representation of some aspects of their distal surroundings. Furthermore, because they learn to do this with very little experience, their nervous systems must be organized in a way that permits the rapid encoding and organization of this information.

Perhaps the strongest evidence that the rat hippocampal formation is necessary for processing spatial information comes from the effects of hippocampal lesions on the acquisition of the Morris water pool task. Although rats with hippocampal damage can accurately navigate to a *visible* platform, thus showing that visuoperceptual and motor processes necessary for the task are unimpaired, they cannot learn to navigate directly or efficiently to a hidden platform (Morris, Garrud, Rawlins, & O'Keefe, 1982; Sutherland, Whishaw, & Kolb, 1982).

In addition to processing the capacity to generate efficient spatial trajectories to an imperceptible goal, rats are also able to keep track dynamically of where they have recently been. The ability of rats to avoid recently visited locations and to approach unvisited ones was first assessed systematically by Olton and Samuelson (1976). They examined this ability using an apparatus consisting of an elevated central octagonal platform from which eight arms radiated outward for about a meter. Food pellets were placed at the ends of the arms, and the task of the rat was to traverse each arm until all the food was obtained. The primary finding was that the rats learned to visit each arm with a low probability of

---

FIG. 13.4.   A: Barnes (1979) used a brightly illuminated circular platform in order to assess spatial learning under conditions in which neither the "cue" nor the "response" strategies could be used successfully. The animals were placed, in a random orientation, into a false-bottomed start chamber that initially rested in the center of the platform and was subsequently raised to start a trial. Motivated by bright overhead lights, the rat's task was to escape into a dark tunnel, located below the maze surface, that was accessible through only one of the 18 holes surrounding the platform periphery. Because the platform surface was rotated from trial to trial (leaving the tunnel fixed in place), any cues local to the maze surface (e.g., odor trails) were likewise of no navigational use. B: Schematic representation of the progression of behaviors exhibited by the animals in the course of acquiring the circle platform task when given one trial per day (see text). Tunnel location indicated by arrow and lines reflect movement paths of the rat.

repeating entrances into arms in which food was already eaten. After 20 days of training, the rats entered an average of 7.8 different arms on the first eight choices (Olton & Samuelson, 1976). One explanation for this accurate performance was that the rats had acquired a cognitive representation of the maze and its relationship to the room surroundings during training and had used this spatial representation to "keep track" of which arms had been entered during a trial (Olton, 1977).

That this ability to keep track of places is truly one that depends on a cognitive representation of the environment, and is not simply an expression of a non-spatial response strategy or the detection of discrete local cues, is supported by numerous control experiments. When many spatially distributed objects are present external to the maze, rats do not tend to enter the arms in a fixed order (Olton & Samuelson, 1976). Rather, their order of entry approaches randomness, and from day to day they display different orders, suggesting that an egocentric motor algorithm is not being used. The possibilities of odor labels being deposited by the rats at the entrance of visited arms or food scents being emitted from the ends of unvisited arms were also ruled out as a basis of accurate performance by rotating the maze during the trial. Although Olton and his colleagues originally characterized this task as depending on "working memory," this does not necessarily mean that it is of short duration. For example, delays of up to 8 hours on the eight-arm maze (Beatty & Shavalia, 1980) and 4 hours on the 12-arm maze (Mizumori, Rosensweig, & Bennet, 1985) can be interposed between the selection of the first set of arms and the completion of the trial without substantial disruption of performance. It is also interesting to note that, during the course of performance of this task, the animals frequently make false entries into previously visited arms, followed by withdrawal and selection of an unvisited one. One implication of this "vicarious trial and error" (Muenzinger, 1938) is that rats store images of local views of the environment and can use these images to distinguish visited from unvisited places.

What is Encoded and How are Spatial Representations Used?

The foregoing studies indicate that the rat uses for navigation representations of space that involve different computations and largely different neural substrates than those used for remembering simple associations between specific objects and reward, or between specific motor acts and reward. They shed relatively little light, however, on exactly what elements of the spatial array of cues are encoded, or on the computations (manipulations) that can be performed on these data. In this section, we discuss several relatively recent studies that we feel begin to address these questions.

In a study aimed at investigating stimulus control of accurate spatial navigation, the circular platform apparatus described earlier was placed inside of a cue-controlled environment. The environment was a circular area partitioned with grey drapery, on which was mounted a set of discrete and removable visual cues (Barnes, et al., 1980). After acquisition, navigation to the hole was unimpaired when the two cues nearest the goal were removed during probe trials. On the other hand, removal of the complete set caused performance to deteriorate to near chance. This led the authors to the conclusion that the animals were solving the task by learning the spatial relations among the objects in the environment, rather than learning to approach a specific distal cue. Although the latter part of the conclusion is clearly correct, it is not so clear exactly what is meant by the former conjecture. It is one thing to suppose that the animal's associative memory allows it to fill in or "complete" images of the particular local view of the environment in the direction of the goal, given some subset of the corresponding features. It is quite another to infer that the mutual distance relations among features of the environment have been globally and explicitly encoded (e.g., as some form of map).

A similar conceptual distinction applies to a study done with the radial eight-arm maze in a similar cue-controlled environment (Suzuki, Augerinos, & Black, 1980). Seven different spatial cues (e.g., a fan, 5-watt light bulb, etc.) were suspended from the ceiling of the otherwise visually homogeneous environment, just beyond seven of the arms. The positions of the cues could be transposed relative to each other, changing the spatial relationships among the cues and the maze, or could be rotated as a group, leaving the configuration intact but changing the relationship of the configuration to particular physical locations. Before cue manipulations were performed, the rats learned about the environment with the cues in a constant configuration. Learning consisted of a two-part task. The rats were forced to "choose" three arms, a delay was imposed, and then they were allowed to freely choose the five correct (unvisited) arms out of eight presented. After the rats learned to make four or five correct choices, either transposition or rotation of the cues was made during the delay (the rat was not allowed to see these manipulations), and choice accuracy during the free choice period was assessed. Although transpositions and rotations changed some spatial aspects of the cues, these manipulations still left individual cues just beyond the ends of the arms after the change. It should also be noted that the transposition bore little resemblance to the original configuration of cues.

If the rats had represented the maze in terms of associating each arm with a particular distal cue, then transposition or rotation should not have affected choice accuracy. If, however, their spatial representation preserved information about spatial relationships, then transposition should affect accuracy, and rotation should not. In fact, transposition, and not rotation, of the spatial cues severely disrupted the rats' accuracy. This suggests that, for some conditions, rats do not represent locations in their environments in terms of a series of beacons or singular distal cues, but in terms of spatial relationships. However, as we indicated in the discussion of the Barnes, et al. (1980) study, this result does not *necessarily* imply a map-like representation. We return to this point later.

Another experiment that addresses the issue of the structure of the rat's spatial representation was conducted with the radial eight-arm maze in a similar cue-controlled environment (Pico, Gerbrandt, Pondel, & Ivy, 1985). Rats were trained to find food on four arms of the maze, which was located within a partitioned-off enclosure. Four distinct visual or auditory cues defined the extra-maze space. The relative position of the cues and the correct four arms remained constant throughout the experiment, but the maze and the cues were rotated as a group between trials to ensure that the controlled cues were the only features that were spatially invariant. After training, the effects of removing subsets of the cues on choice accuracy was examined. Either one, two, or three cues were removed. The presence of any two of the four-cue set was sufficient to maintain high accuracy in avoiding the unbaited arms and visiting the baited arms only once. When three cues were absent, accuracy declined to chance levels. If the spatial representation had encoded the relationships among the cues as some form of map, then one cue should have been sufficient for accurate performance. The fact that at least two were required suggests that the animal's coding involved "images" of the sensory conditions that correspond to orientation towards correct arms. Although these images might be completed from fractional information in the local view, the relationships of these local views to each other appears not to have been encoded in this situation.

Accurate navigation in the water pool task is also degraded when the environment is impoverished of spatial cues. When the only discrete spatial cue present is a black arc subtending 100 degrees of the pool perimeter, rats are able to learn to navigate to a hidden platform (Pellymounter, Smith, & Gallagher, 1987), but their knowledge of the platform's location may be less precise when compared to rats trained in the same pool but with many spatial cues present (Rapp, Rosenberg, & Gallagher, 1987). During a 90-sec probe trial in which the platform was removed from the pool, rats in the cue-poor environment (Pellymounter, et al., 1987) made about half the number of swim trajectories (about three) over the platform's former location than rats in the cue-rich environment (Rapp, et al., 1987). Also, the initial heading errors of the rats in the cue-poor environment were about 10 degrees larger than typically observed in a pool of comparable size. The rats in the cue-poor environment did show that they possessed some global knowledge about the platform's location, because they spent most of their swim time in the correct quadrant of the tank during the probe. However, this information was not, apparently, precise enough to restrict their trajectories over the precise location of the platform.

Most experiments that have investigated which aspects of the rat's environment might be preserved in its spatial representation have assessed the effects on spatial behavior of manipulating landmarks. However, another fundamental question is whether, or to what extent, rats make use of what could loosely be referred to as the geometrical features, or distributed cues, of the environment. This problem was addressed by Cheng (1986) in a series of experiments in which rats were required to learn the location of food that was buried in a black, rectangular box (120 × 60 cm). A small unique feature panel was located at each corner of the box, and in some experiments, a white panel covered one of the long walls. In one series of experiments, the target was changed from day to day, and the animals were given a "free" trial in which the food was not covered, and then a test trial. On the test trial, the animals searched about equally in the correct location and in the location that was 180° rotated from it. In other words, they chose the two *geometrically* equivalent locations with respect to the shape of the box, in spite of the fact that there were other featural cues that distinguished the locations, and that, as further studies showed, could be discriminated by the animals. Surprisingly, even when one entire wall was made white, there was no significant bias for the correct location over its rotational equivalent. This result bears directly on our interpretation of some of the physiological data to be discussed presently. In tests of long-term spatial memory, in which the reward site remained fixed, the animals continued to make systematic rotational errors. These results suggest that, in environments that are relatively small and bounded by walls, the rat's spatial navigation, and presumably its spatial representation, are dominated by the geometric characteristics of the environment, and that information about color, brightness, texture, and smell is subordinate.

A recent study carried out in this laboratory (McNaughton, Elkins, & Meltzer; unpublished) addressed the question of whether rats make use of distal sensory cues merely as beacons to be approached for reward, or whether the geometrical relation between the distal cues and reward was somehow encoded. Rats were given five trials per day on a task in which only one arm of the radial maze was baited. The maze was located in one of two partitioned-off areas in a large room. With two exceptions, within each partitioned area the distal spatial cues were completely different, and the rats were trained on alternate days in one of the two partitions. The baited arm was changed randomly from day to day, and the first trial of each day was a free presentation of the baited arm only. Once the animals had mastered this, a second phase was initiated in which, between the fourth and fifth trials, the animals were removed from the testing room, the maze itself was physically translocated (without rotation) to the other partition, and the fifth trial was instated in which the same physical arm was baited as in trials 1–4. Also, a single 40-watt lamp, pointing toward one corner of the partition, and the experimenter and experimenter's recording station (a small stainless steel tray mounted on a stand) were shifted between partitions, thus constituting the only distal sensory cues in common between the two configurations. The difference, however, was that the relative locations of the lamp and the experimenter were mirror images in the two configurations (see Fig. 13.5).

Because the distal cues were different in the two configurations, except for the mirror-reversed locations of experimenter and the lamp, it was possible to assign a strategy category to the animal's trial-5 choice on the basis of whether it was consistent with navigation relative to the lamp (L), the experimenter (E), the absolute compass direction (D; the correct choice), or to some intermediate

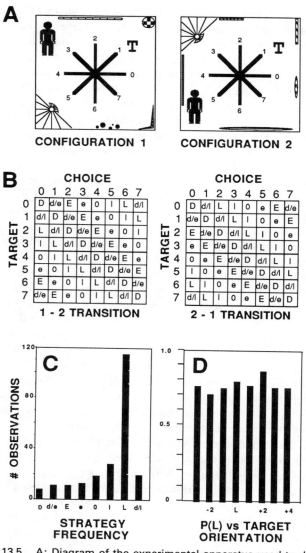

FIG. 13.5.   A: Diagram of the experimental apparatus used to determine the manner in which a prominent visual landmark (a single 40W
lamp) is incorporated into the rats representation of space. On each
day, the rats were initially trained either in configuration 1 or 2 to
locate the one arm that contained food reward (T). A different arm was
chosen at random on each day. After four trials in the starting configuration, by which time the target arm was reliably selected, the animals
were tested in the alternate configuration. Only two visual landmarks
were common to the two configurations (the experimenter and the

combination of these (indicated by lowercase letters in Fig. 13.5). The assignment of strategies on the basis of the combination of target and choice arms is illustrated in Fig. 13.5b. For example, for the transition from configuration 1 to configuration 2, a target of arm 4 and a choice of arm 2 indicated a choice on the basis of the lamp position (45° to the left of the target). Notice that in this case, use of the experimenter as a landmark would have led to a choice of arm 6, which is 180° away from the position determined on the basis of the light. Figure 13.5c shows that the lamp was selected as the basis for orientation well in excess of any other spatial cue. Indeed, the animals never learned the correct solution to this problem (which was to use either or both of absolute direction and some cue local to the maze itself). Moreover, this selection occurred independently of whether the target arm was initially pointing toward or away from the lamp, or at some intermediate location. These data thus lead to the conclusion that rats tend to encode the geometrical relation between a singular distal landmark and a goal, rather than the simple fact that approach to a particular beacon is to be rewarded.

Collett et al. (1986) conducted a series of experiments aimed at clarifying what specific aspects of the geometry of various configurations of proximal visual landmarks were encoded by gerbils in the course of learning to find a buried food item. The apparatus was a 3.5-m-diameter circular arena located in a black-painted room, and illuminated from above by a single lamp. The animals were trained to locate a buried sunflower seed in proximity to a set of one or

---

lamp), and the positions of these landmarks were mirror reversed in the two configurations. This permitted an assessment of the relative degree to which these landmarks had been incorporated into the spatial representation in the original training configuration. B: The transition tables used to assess choice strategy. L, E, D, and 0 refer to "navigational strategies" based on the lamp, the experimenter, the absolute direction, or no discernable cue, respectively. Lowercase letters refer to choices in which the strategy was ambiguous but could be restricted to some combination of the principal strategies. For example, if the target in configuration 1 was arm 1 and, in configuration 2, the rat chose arm 7, then it could be inferred that the animal was orienting in a direction directly away from the lamp. If, however the animal chose arm 3, then the conclusion would be that its orientation was based on the selection of the arm that was located 2 positions clockwise to the experimenter. Because the two landmarks are mirror reversed, the two orientation strategies are dissociable. C: The percent of observations on which particular strategies were chosen by the animals following the transition to the alternate configuration. Clearly the animal's spatial behavior was dominated by the use of the lamp as the principal, most salient landmark. D: The probability of using the lamp as the principal landmark was independent of whether the original target arm was located toward the lamp, away from it, or at some intermediate orientation. Thus, landmarks are used in a more sophisticated fashion than merely as objects of approach.

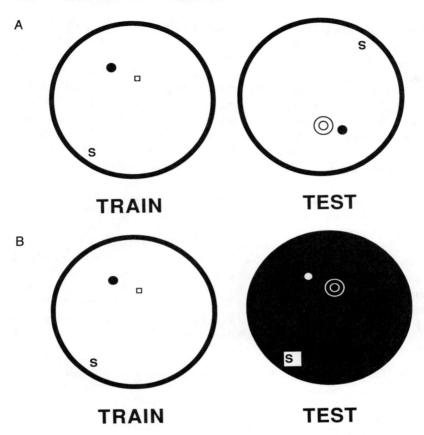

FIG. 13.6.   Schematic summary of landmark learning in gerbils (Collett, et al., 1986). Very-well-practiced gerbils were trained to find a buried sunflower seed on the floor of a circular arena (3.5 m diameter) at a spot defined, in different experiments, by a landmark or an array of landmarks also placed on the floor. Animals were usually trained with constant environmental conditions and subsequently tested with some environmental change. In all figures, a small filled circle represents a landmark (white cylinder, 40 cm in height and 6.3 cm in diameter), an open square represents the location of the buried sunflower seed, S indicates where the gerbil was released to start a trial, and concentric circles indicate the foci of search time during a test trial. (These figures have been schematized for simplicity and do not accurately represent the actual experimental apparatus used by the authors.) A. The relation between a fixed starting point and a goal is encoded by gerbils. With the sunflower seed buried at a constant distance (50 cm) from a single landmark and holding a constant relationship to the start point, gerbils

C

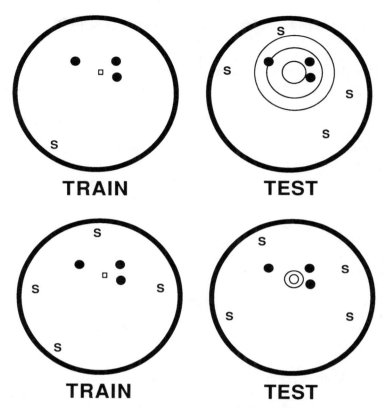

accurately restrict their search patterns to the correct region of space. B. Gerbils' spatial representations contain distance information. This experiment consisted of two phases. First, animals were trained with full illumination to find the seed placed in a constant position with respect to a landmark. Second, the lights were switched off soon after the animal was released. The animals took direct paths to the correct location, showing that they could plan trajectories based on current and stored sensory information and execute these trajectories in the absence of visual feedback. If the lights were extinguished before releasing the animals, the trajectories were essentially random. C. If trained from a variety of starting locations, the animals were capable of using information about the geometry of the cue array to successfully locate the hidden food (lower panel). However, if the animals were trained from a constant start location (upper panel), this relationship was either not encoded or was replaced with a simple "response" coding. This resulted in inaccurate search if the animals were released from a different starting point.

more cylindrical posts (landmarks). Several of the specific experiments and the general pattern of their results are summarized schematically in Fig. 13.6.

A number of important conclusions developed from these studies. First, rodents are able to preplan a trajectory toward a goal and execute the trajectory even if the lights are extinguished in the interval between seeing the landmarks and running. Thus, distance information must be encoded. Within a certain range, the size of the retinal image (apparent size) of a landmark can be used to encode distance. Second, if trained with a constant relation between the start location and a landmark array, the animals do not appear to learn much about the geometrical relations among the components of the array; their search becomes inaccurate when the start location is changed. If trained with a variety of start locations, the animals' search patterns are determined strongly by the geometry of the array. Finally, it seems that the animals plan a trajectory by computing separate vectors for each landmark (see Fig. 13.7). When two equidistant identical landmarks are separated such that they each lead to different predictions, the search pattern splits into two fields rather than shifting so as to find the "best-fitting solution." If only one of three equidistant landmarks is moved, however, such that two landmarks lead to the same prediction and one leads to a different prediction, the correct location is searched. This again suggests that the vectors are computed independently for each landmark, and the aberrant one is rejected. Other factors also apparently contribute, in cases of conflict, to the selection of single vectors. These include relative proximity and probably salience when these are not equivalent among the landmarks.

These findings carry the strong implication that, in rodents, spatial encoding of a particular goal does not involve the formation of a topological map, if by this we mean a representation that would be globally distorted by stretching or shrinking the coordinate framework. Rather, the representation appears to consist of a set of remembered "local views" of the environment in which the direction and distance to individual reference points is encoded, coupled with the ability to compute a resultant vector, given the perceived set of distance and heading pairs and a remembered set from the position of the target. Of course, implicit in such a hypothesis is the assumption that the circle of position ambiguity associated with singular "point" landmarks can be resolved. There are two ways that this could be achieved. The first would be to search the set of all possible resultant vectors for two (or more) landmarks for the unique point of intersection. This might become computationally expensive, although it is certainly possible using a variety of minimization algorithms. The alternative would be to endow the system with some form of inertial guidance system or magnetic compass, so that directional information was maintained independently of particular landmarks. In such a case, a singular landmark would be sufficient to compute the trajectory from any start location to any previously visited target when both are within the range of visibility of the landmark. As we shall see, there is good evidence, both

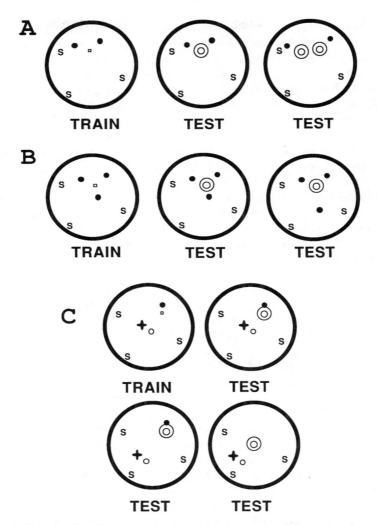

FIG. 13.7. Gerbils appear to encode separate heading vectors for each element of a landmark array, rather than the topological relations among the elements. A. If the animals are trained using an array of two equivalent landmarks, and then the array is stretched, two search foci develop, rather than a single focus at the topologically correct location. B. If, however, an array of three landmarks is distorted such that two of the three still provide a correct solution, then the single correct site is searched. Again, the hypothesis of a topological representation would have predicted a shift in search focus. C. Finally, proximity and/or salience relations among landmarks also bias which of the separate relation vectors are used by the animals in selecting their search focus.

from behavioral and from neurophysiological studies, that the rat indeed possesses a kind of inertial direction sense that is updated by its own movements.

Considerable insight into the properties of this directional sense derives from studies of homing behavior and pup retrieval in female gerbils (Mittelstaedt & Mittelstaedt, 1980). The apparatus consisted of a circular arena (1.3 m in diameter). The nest was placed at a point on the periphery of the arena. Preliminary studies showed that if a pup was displaced to a small cup at various angles and distances (up to about ten times the animal's length) from the nest, the female was able to retrieve the pup after a circuitous search and then return on a direct path to the nest *in complete darkness*. It was then demonstrated that the animal could correct for angular but not linear displacements of the arena so long as the angular acceleration was sufficiently great. Slow, smooth angular displacements, presumably below the sensitivity of the vestibular system, were not compensated for. The authors concluded that homing by path integration involved two sources of input: inertial directional information provided by the vestibular system, and "idiothetic" linear information involving proprioception and/or efference copy from the animal's self-generated motion (see Fig. 13.8).

A more recent study investigated the role of the hippocampal formation in this inertial directional sense. Rats were subjected to various rotations and were then required to indicate whether their direction sense had been perturbed (Matthews, Campbell, & Deadwyler, 1988). The apparatus consisted of a "+" maze with a rotatable central platform on which was a set of four intersecting enclosed alleyways, one of which served as a start chamber.

The animals were first allowed several sessions of free exploration of the apparatus with the cover to the alleys and the black curtains at their exit points removed. Next, they were trained to locate food at the end of the arm directly opposite the start chamber, while the alleys were covered and the external view was obscured by the curtains at the ends. Thus, the animals learned to run straight out of the start chamber to a goal that was fixed in space. Once this problem was learned, the animals were subjected to various rotations while in the start chamber and were required to chose which alley led to the goal, that might now be located either to the left or to the right or straight ahead. The rotational velocity was approximately 180° per sec. Choice accuracy by normal animals was unaffected by rotations of less than 360°, and fell to chance only after 10 revolutions. Animals with damage to the hippocampal formation were seriously impaired by rotation.

The results discussed to this point suggest that, during learning about locations in an environment, rats construct an internal model based on some aspects of the distal cues, and that during accurate performance they translate this knowledge into direct and efficient motor patterns. However, these results suggest little about the computational "power" of the rat's spatial representation. The water pool task has been a useful tool in examining the nature of the computations that are possible with the spatial information that rats encode. Starting the rats from a

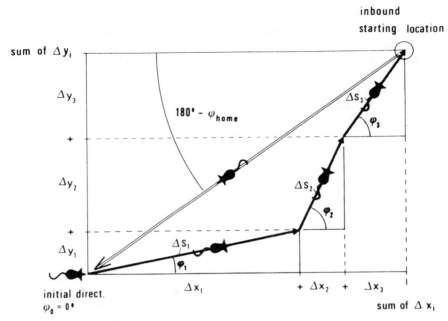

FIG. 13.8. Schematic illustration of homing to show geometrical basis of path integration based on idiothetic and inertial information sources. If the path segments δs_i and the orthogonal components of the azimuth, $\sin\psi_i$ and $\cos\psi_i$ are known, the coordinate values of the animal's location may be computed as $\Sigma\delta y_i = \Sigma\delta s_i\sin\psi_i$ and $\Sigma\delta x_i = \Sigma\delta s_i\cos\psi_i$. For the homing task described in the text, information about the orthogonal components of the azimuth is available from output from the vestibular system. (reproduced with permission from Mittelstaedt, 1983).

novel point in the pool, from which the view of the distal spatial cues is presumably different from the view obtained during training from a constant start point, apparently does not affect the rats' ability to navigate efficiently to the platform (Morris, 1981). This seems to indicate that, using the learned trajectory from the usual starting location, and possibly the memory of the appearance of the environment from the platform, rats can calculate completely novel routes. However, this interpretation has been challenged. It has been suggested that rats performing the water pool task experience a large number of different views and final approach trajectories through their initial random search patterns during training. Thus, no potential start point is truly novel for the well-trained rat (Sutherland, Chew, Baker, & Linggard, 1987). In this interpretation, the task reduces to a simple recognition problem, and little or no computation on the encoded spatial information would be involved.

A clearer experiment that transcends the interpretive problems of Morris' original observation on the generation of novel search paths, and that suggests that completely novel trajectories can indeed be computed was conducted by Keith and McVety (1988). Rats were trained and tested in two separate rooms. They first received training to a fixed, hidden platform in one room until they had mastered the procedural aspects of the water pool task. In a transfer test, conducted in a second room to which they had never been exposed, one group of rats was placed on the platform and allowed to view the room for 120 sec *before* they were released from the wall of this second pool. Thus, all views of the second environment were novel, except for the view from the surface of the hidden platform.

This single viewing experience was sufficient for the rats to execute a direct trajectory to the platform from a completely novel start location. As concluded by Keith and McVety (1988), this striking example of latent learning strongly suggests that the rat's spatial representation is independent of the behavior the rats must engage in to locate the platform. A more global conclusion might be that rats possess a general knowledge of how visual scenes are transformed as a result of their own movements and are capable of computing the movement trajectory necessary to bring about a desired transformation. Alternatively, if the animals possessed an internal sense of direction and were also able to discern distance relationships to distal landmarks on the basis of apparent size, then this information should be sufficient to compute the required heading.

One of the most striking illustrations of the power of the rat's spatial memory system derives from a series of experiments (O'Keefe & Conway 1980), in which rats were required to remember the configuration of spatial cues across a considerable temporal gap. The apparatus consisted of a four-arm "+" maze located within a circular curtain. An array of spatial cues was distributed within the curtain. This array was rotated at random, from trial to trial, with respect to the external world (laboratory frame). Rats were trained to locate a particular goal arm defined by its relation to the internal cue array, when started at random from one of the other three arms. O'Keefe and Conway designated such trials as "perceptual" trials, indicating that the cue array was available for use in selecting the goal. As might be expected, the animals had no difficulty learning this phase of the problem. During subsequent "memory" trials, the animals were placed in the start arm and allowed to view the cue array for 10 seconds, after which the entire array was removed from the enclosure, leaving only the maze and the featurally homogeneous circular curtain. The animals were confined to the start arm for various periods up to 30 minutes before being allowed to make their choice. For all intervals, choice accuracy was close to 100% and not different from perceptual trials. On control trials, during which the rats were introduced into the environment with the cues already absent, choice accuracy fell to chance. Unlike previous experiments, O'Keefe and Conway's studies show that well-trained rats can either "maintain," or internally generate, a spatial representation in the absence of immediate sensory stimulation. O'Keefe and Speakman (1987) have extended these behavioral studies to examine how hippocampal neurons behave during this task. These experiments are discussed in the next section.

In summary, if given the opportunity, rats appear to construct cognitive representations of their environments based on the available distal cues. This is true even when a goal of navigation is entirely defined by a beacon. Hebb (1938), and more recently Whishaw and Mittleman (1986), demonstrated this by showing that when rats are trained to navigate toward a beacon in a room that is rich with distal spatial cues, and then the beacon is displaced on some trials, the rats still approach the location that the beacon formerly occupied. Other experiments already discussed also support the notion that aspects of distal landmarks and arrays of objects are stored and used to guide spatial behavior. However, when these aspects of an environment are de-emphasized (cf., Cheng, 1986), distributed cues appear to become predominant.

The nature of the encoding of the spatial cues appears to depend on what the animal was required to do in the environment. When trained to navigate from a constant start location, geometrical relations among an array of distal objects appear not to be encoded. This, however, may merely reflect the secondary development of a "response" strategy, as distance and direction information about individual objects *are* apparently encoded when the animal is trained to navigate to a goal from a variety of start locations. Beyond these specifics, the rat's representation of space may be organized in terms of a list of local views, activation of which does not necessarily depend on immediate sensory stimulation.

NEUROPHYSIOLOGICAL MECHANISMS OF SPATIAL ENCODING AND MEMORY

Behavioral studies such as those just discussed provide one effective means of drawing inferences about the nature of the rat's spatial representation, particularly when careful attention is paid to dissociation of the multiple components or strategies that invariably participate in most uncontrolled behavioral situations. Indeed, there are many who would argue that such studies can, at least in principle, lead to a complete understanding of spatial behavior, in the sense that accurate predictions might be derived for any given situation. The fallacy of this view resides, at least in part, in the fact that without understanding the physical substrate of the representational system, it is not always possible to deduce its computational capabilities. The arguments supporting the interdependence of computational algorithms and the physical architecture in which they are implemented have recently been summarized by Churchland (1988), and it is not our purpose to delve deeply into such fundamental issues here. Rather, we believe that a discussion of recent findings concerning the neurophysiological bases of spatial representation and memory in the rat will illustrate clearly how such data not only provide much needed constraints on hypotheses about spatial computation, but also lead rather directly either to the generation of new conceptual frameworks or at least to the selection, from what would otherwise be a lengthy list, of those possible algorithms most likely actually to be implemented.

Apart from behavioral and lesion studies of the sort just discussed, which indicate that damage to the hippocampal formation in rats leads to a profound, and to some extent selective, impairment in their ability to develop new spatial representations, the most fundamental insight into the neural substrates of these operations has come from the observation that hippocampal pyramidal cells, recorded from conscious, unrestrained rats, display a striking selectivity of their discharge in relation to where the animal is in its environment (O'Keefe, 1976; O'Keefe & Dostrovsky, 1971). This fundamental observation is now one of the most robust findings in the literature of single-unit recording. Given a recording environment with a minimum of spatial extension, it is virtually as likely to find spatially selective discharge in hippocampal pyramidal cells as it is to find visually responsive neurons in the primary visual cortex (see for example Jones Leonard, McNaughton, & Barnes, 1987). The issues in the field have shifted from debates about whether "place cells" have firing preferences that are determined by where the animal is, rather than, for example, by some particular behavior that is nonuniformly distributed in space, to questions concerning the specific nature of their involvement in spatial representation. The properties of hippocampal place cells have been reviewed by O'Keefe (1979), and more recently summarized by Eichenbaum & Cohen (1988). An illustration of spatially selective firing in the radial maze situation is presented in Fig. 13.9. In the present chapter, we focus primarily on the details and current issues upon which an understanding of the nature of spatial representation appears to us to depend most crucially.

Classes of Hippocampal Single Units

In the early 1970s, it was recognized that neurons recorded in the CA subfields[1] of the hippocampus could be assigned to two mutually exclusive groups based on their discharge characteristics (Ranck, 1973). The dichotomy turned out to be an important one, because neurons of these two classes are distinguished not only physiologically but also on behavioral and anatomical grounds.

One class of hippocampal units, called complex-spike (CS) cells, sometimes discharge bursts of multiple action potentials of declining amplitudes and with interspike intervals of 2 to 7 msec. With the possible exception of a recently discovered class of interneuron, CS activity is generated by pyramidal cells. The other cell class, called theta cells, discharge only simple action potentials of

---

[1]For a review of hippocampal formation anatomy, see Swanson, Köhler, and Björklund (1987).

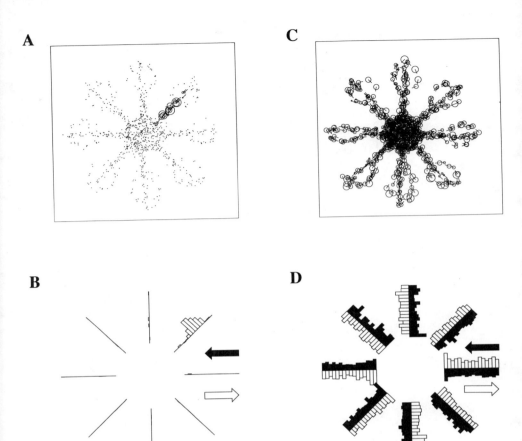

FIG. 13.9. Spatially selective and nonselective discharge, respectively, of a hippocampal complex-spike cell (A, B) and a theta cell (C, D) recorded while a rat freely traversed a radial eight-arm maze. Extracellular single unit recordings were obtained while simultaneously tracking the spatial position of the rat at 20 samples per second. The rat was being rewarded with chocolate milk for repeatedly entering the maze arms in a random order. The plots of A and C were made by integrating the discharge rates of the single unit over sequential five-pixel radii. The area of the plotted circle is directly proportional to the integrated firing rate. Overlapping circles indicate that the cell fired on repeated traverses through the region, and dots indicate that the animal traversed a region but the cell did not fire. The dashed lines originating at the circle centers indicate the direction of motion of the animal. The plots of B and D show the same data averaged over trials. These plots were obtained by first logically dividing the maze surface into equal segments, and then subdividing the segments according to the radial direction the animal was moving if it passed through a given segment. The histograms represent the average number of spikes observed per bin divided by the total time spent in the corresponding location/direction. The firing of the complex-spike cell is highly specific for location and direction, suggesting that something about a particular local view may be represented in its output.

A

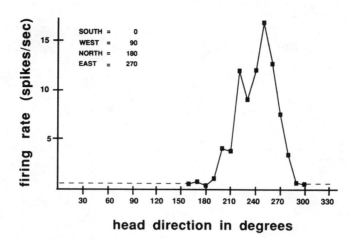

B

relatively constant amplitude, and appear to exhibit increased firing rates only when the theta rhythm, a 7 Hz modulation of the hippocampal EEG, is present. Theta cells exhibit several characteristics consistent with their being inhibitory interneurons (Fox & Ranck, 1975, 1981). CS and theta cells have been found to display very different behavioral correlates across a wide variety of situations, as is discussed presently. As was alluded to in the introduction to this section, hippocampal place cells are CS cells. Theta cells exhibit, at best, marginal spatial selectivity (see Fig. 13.10; Christian & Deadwyler, 1986; Kubie, Kramer & Muller, 1985; McNaughton, Barnes & O'Keefe, 1983).

Fundamental Observations of CS Cell Discharge Correlates

Before an "open-ended" observational approach was used to study the discharge correlates of hippocampal single units (O'Keefe, 1976; O'Keefe & Dostrovsky, 1971; Ranck, 1973), recordings were done exclusively with slightly restrained animals (e.g., Vinogradova, 1975) or with animals that performed highly stereotyped tasks in small darkened chambers (e.g., Segal & Olds, 1972). This latter paradigmatic approach greatly reduced the range of possible behaviors to be correlated with unit activity and perhaps was the reason for not observing the two main classes of hippocampal single units. That restraint can dramatically affect behavioral correlates is clear from recent experiments in which this variable was explicitly manipulated (Foster, Castro, & McNaughton, 1988). In short, body restraint in the rat virtually abolishes the spatial specificity of CS cell discharge.

In O'Keefe and Dostrovsky's preliminary study (1971), they recorded units in CA1, CA4, and fascia dentata while monitoring various spontaneous and elicited behaviors of rats on an elevated platform. Eight of 76 units responded solely or

---

FIG. 13.10. Many single units recorded in the dorsal presubiculum appear to code for absolute head direction independent of absolute spatial location (Ranck, 1984). A. Graph of discharge rates of a "head direction" cell as a function of absolute head direction (courtesy of J. B. Ranck, Jr.). Single units were recorded from a freely moving rat in a cubical apparatus, and action potentials were accepted for analysis when the rat's head direction was constant for at least 1 sec. The resulting discharge rates were sorted into bin widths of 10 degrees and averaged over all spatial locations. B. Spatial and directional plot of firing rates of a "head-direction" cell recorded while a rat freely traversed a radial eight-arm maze. Data collected and analyzed as in Fig. 13.9. (Barnes & McNaughton, unpublished data)

maximally when the rats occupied specific locations, leading the authors to hypothesize that these cells might be involved in the processing of spatial information. These units had no detectable response to simple auditory, visual, olfactory, or tactile test stimuli. However, it was mentioned that the vigor of discharge was related to the animal's directional orientation within the location of increased firing. O'Keefe later called these units "place" cells and their spatial area of maximal firing the place field (O'Keefe, 1976).

These initial observations were subsequently confirmed and extended in a study designed to test more rigorously the hypothesis that spatial location was the primary behavioral correlate of CS cell discharge (O'Keefe, 1976). CS cells were recorded in rats trained to find food at the ends of an elevated T-maze. The maze was open and was situated in a room with numerous extramaze objects. Local olfactory and tactile influences were tested by replacing or rearranging subsets of the maze arms or by covering parts of arms with various materials. The possible contribution of specific reward values and motivation was also assessed by exchanging or removing the type of food or by forcing the rats to traverse the arms in different manners. The distribution of elevated firing on the maze was "mapped" by hand.

Twenty-six of 34 CA1 CS cells had place fields on the maze. Most of the cells had a single field, but two cells had two fields, and one cell had three fields. Place fields were estimated to range in size from 10 cm² to one-half the total area of the maze (2700 cm²) and were found in most areas of the maze.

Local olfactory and tactile stimuli associated with parts of the maze were not responsible for the localized firing, because replacing parts of the maze with identical pieces or rearranging its parts had no effect on the cells' spatial selectivity. The introduction of novel olfactory and tactile stimuli also had no perceptible effect. Specific types of rewards or their absence similarly did not influence the cells' place fields. The only behavior that appeared to modulate the cells' firing in the place field was the animals' walking velocity.

The firing of some CS cells in this study was also strongly influenced by the direction the animal was facing in the place field. Of nine units examined in this way, five showed a clear decrease in firing in one of the two radial directions on the arm that had the place field.

One of the earlier verifications of the spatial firing phenomenon was an experiment designed to assess whether place-specific firing would be evident upon first exposure to a novel environment (Hill, 1978). Rats were trained to run in a shuttle box, and subsequently, CS cells were recorded from the rats as they ran in an enclosed T-maze. The rats had never been exposed to the T-maze prior to recording. For analysis, cumulative average cell discharge rates were calculated manually for six contiguous locations in the maze. CS cells were selected for analysis if the cumulative average for a given location exceeded three times the average of all other locations. For 10 of 12 units that passed the criterion, significant location-specific firing was evident on the first passage through the maze, and there was no trend for firing to increase on subsequent passages through the field. Discharge rates within the place fields averaged 7.0 Hz, whereas outside the field, rates averaged 1.0 Hz. These results suggest that little if any learning is required for the expression of place-specific firing of CS cells. If this is the case, then it is difficult to imagine how place cell firing per se can represent spatial *relationships,* as these presumably are not known until after the environment has been extensively explored.

Hill also observed that for some place cells, the firing rates were different depending on the direction the rat was facing as he sat in or ran through the place field (Hill, 1979). The average rate in the preferred direction was 7.8 Hz compared to 2.4 Hz in the nonpreferred direction.

Similar criteria were also used by Olton, Branch, & Best (1978) for assessing spatial firing of CS cells from rats freely traversing an elevated eight-arm maze for food reward. The mean rate for each unit was calculated separately for each of the eight arms. A grand mean rate was also calculated over the entire maze for comparison purposes. Several conjoint criteria were used to classify units as exhibiting spatially selective firing. These criteria included a sign test for reliability, thus reducing the possibility that one or two visits showing very deviant rates could classify a cell's firing as being spatially selective. This quantification also provided a means for estimating the maximum areal extent of spatially selective firing, because significant rates on multiple arms were possible. Arms on which significant positive rate changes were observed were called "on" arms; those with negative changes were called "off" arms.

Twenty-eight of 31 CS cells were classified as having a spatial correlate of discharge. These 28 were grouped into four types based on the number of criterial "on" arms they exhibited: (a) Nine had a single "on" arm; (b) three had more than one "on" arm; (c) nine had a single "on" arm and at least one other arm on which the mean rate often exceeded the grand mean rate by two standard errors; (d) seven units had no "on" arms but at least one criterial "off" arm. For Type 1 units, the average discharge rate for the relevant "on" arm was 6.9 Hz, while the average grand mean rate was 2.8 Hz. Like previous studies, in this investigation the firing of some place cells was modulated by the animals' direction of travel through the field, although this aspect was not quantified.

The earlier studies just described left little doubt that the discharge of hippocampal CS cells is objectively and statistically related to spatial location, further supporting the general hypothesis that these neurons are involved in some aspect of spatial information processing. Although the point was perhaps underemphasized, *all* of these reports also noted that the discharge rates of place cells are not homogeneous across all orientations of the animal within the place field. The magnitude and generality of this direction-related firing has only recently become apparent through the use of methods that permit explicit quantification of this variable.

Using a video-based automated tracking device first described by O'Keefe

(1983), McNaughton et al., (1983) analyzed the degree to which location, direction, and velocity contributed to CS cell discharge. They recorded from rats traversing an eight-arm maze. Instead of the usual free choice, a "forced choice" procedure was used, in which the rats were required to visit each arm in a random order and an equal number of times. In order to obtain estimates of the reliability of place-specific firing, eight full traverses of the maze were sampled. Spatial coordinates of the rat and cell firings were automatically collected by computer. Movement velocity and spatial location were measured with resolutions of about 5 cm/sec and 0.5 cm, respectively. For statistical descriptions, summed rates over an entire arm was the unit of analysis.

For each cell several indices of spatially selective firing were calculated. *Specificity* was defined as the ratio of summed firing (eight observations) on the arm showing the highest directional rate divided by the grand mean rate calculated over the remaining seven arms. A second measure assessed the degree to which the location-specific firing was related to the direction of movement through the location: *Directionality* was defined as the ratio of the rates in the preferred to nonpreferred directions on the arm showing the highest overall rate. Finally, *reliability* was simply the proportion of the eight trials on which the arm with the overall highest mean rate actually displayed the highest rate. As noted by the authors, reliability was not independent of specificity, because cells with multiple-arm place fields would tend to appear less reliable.

Of the 71 CS cells isolated, 47 discharged sufficiently often to be analyzed for their spatial and velocity characteristics. (The excluded cells fired less than 10 action potentials on the first trial.) Confirming previous research on the eight-arm maze (Olton, et al., 1978), most CS cells showed marked increases in firing rates on only one or two arms. Place fields were generally restricted to $\frac{1}{2}$ to $\frac{1}{3}$ of an arm (i.e., 22 to 34 cm), resulting in an average specificity ratio of 5.7. Place cells in this study also showed a high degree of consistency of place-specific firing. The average reliability index for CA1 CS cells was 0.78. It was also noted that activity was modulated by the velocity at which the animal moved, although the tendency of the relation to asymptote at low velocity led the authors to suggest that the system might not be concerned with coding speed per se.

Of particular interest was the great degree to which place-specific firing in this study was modified by the animals' direction of passage through the place field. This property was reflected in the average directionality ratio of 8.9 for the 25 CA1 CS cells (a directionality ratio of 1 indicates equal rates in the two radial directions). As first noted by Hill (1979), the firing rates in the nonpreferred direction were found to be no different than the "background" rates observed outside of the place field.

With one notable exception, the generality of directionally related discharge of CS cells has now been extended to environments in which the rats' trajectories are not constrained as they are on the eight-arm maze and other linear, elevated mazes (Jones Leonard, McNaughton, & Barnes, 1988; Paul, Weiner, & Eichen-baum, 1987; Breese, Hampson, & Deadwyler, 1987). Kubie, Muller, Ranck, and their colleagues consistently report an inability to find much evidence for direc-tional firing in their current recording apparatus, a 76 cm diameter, 51 cm tall cylinder, the walls of which are grey except for a single white card covering 100°. They find place fields of various shapes and sizes within the arena, that, though determined primarily by the orientation of the card, display little apparent orientation tuning. Although some of this tuning may have been masked by the directionally independent manner in which the earlier data were analyzed, it still appears to be absent when the animal's head direction is explicitly measured using a two-point tracking system (Bostock, Taube, & Muller, 1988; Muller, in personal communication). One suspects that there is a quantitative variation in directional selectivity in different situations, and it remains for the source of this variation to be identified. At present, we can suggest several possibilities. One is that the rat may be more sensitive to the geometrical configuration of its environ-ment than to the absolute luminosity values across contrast borders. This is, in fact, suggested by the behavioral data of the experiments of Cheng, described previously (Cheng, 1986), in which animals confused geometrically equivalent corners of a rectangular box in spite of the presence of strong contrast cues. If this interpretation is correct, then a 100° directional error would be introduced in the cylindrical environment by the equivalent geometrical configurations of the left and right sides of the cue card. Moreover, when facing away from the card there are very few strong directional cues, a factor that also might reduce the apparent directional selectivity of place cells. The performance decrement in a water maze designed explicitly to resemble the cylindrical environment in ques-tion here (Pellymounter, et al., 1987) compared to an environment rich in spatial cues (Rapp, et al., 1987) also lends credence to this interpretation.

We believe that the question of directional selectivity is of fundamental impor-tance because of what it implies about the nature of spatial representation in the hippocampus. If the cells select *location* irrespective of *direction,* then this implies that their discharge represents a map-like relation, in the sense that firing at one point in some way specifies a metric concerned with the relational structure of the environment as a whole, not merely with the immediately perceptible part of it. If, however, the cell firing is dependent on the direction the animal is facing, then one can still accept the simpler interpretation that the firing properties are determined by whatever particular sensory features impinge on the animal at a certain location, facing a certain direction, (i.e., by some "local view" of the world). In other words, there are no spatial relationships, other than the current retinotopic or somatotopic ones, implied by the discharge of these cells. As we shall see, it is clear that the system of which the hippocampus is an essential part must encode something about spatial relations among locations not included in a single "local view." The hypothesis that we propose to account for this property, however, suggests that the relational aspect is coded not by the hippocampal place cell activity per se, but by conditional associations between the local views they represent and the movements that link these views (McNaughton, 1987, 1988a, 1988b). The relation, we argue, lies in the pattern of interconnections that develop between the hippocampus and movement representing systems located elsewhere, and is not implicit in the firing of pyramidal cells themselves.

Before leaving the directionality issue, there is one other aspect of hippocampal cellular activity that sheds considerable light on this issue and on the questions raised earlier in the behavioral section, concerning how trajectories might be computed on the basis of a single landmark and some internal "inertial" direction sense. Very strong evidence for such a sense has come from studies of cells in the dorsal presubiculum (postsubiculum), a region of the hippocampal formation that receives input from association cortex (parietal and cingulate) and projects unidirectionally into the entorhinal cortex. Ranck (1984) found a substantial population of neurons in this region that could best be described as "head direction cells"; cells that fire when an animal faces a particular direction apparently irrespective of where the animal is located in the environment. Ranck (1984) reported that the elevated firing of these cells occurs over an angular range of about 90 degrees in the horizontal plane and appears to be independent of the pitch or roll of the rat's head. An example of the angular specificity and locational independence of the firing of these cells is shown in Fig. 13.10.

Cells with many preferred directions have been found during the same electrode penetration, although some hint of a columnar organization has also been noted (Barnes & McNaughton, unpublished observations). Of particular interest is Ranck's (1984) finding that when the rat is carried to a new environment the absolute directionality of firing persists. On the other hand, observations in both this and Ranck's laboratory indicate that, although the direction heading persists in darkness, it is generally easily shifted if the principal visuospatial cue (in our case, a lamp on one wall of the recording room) is rotated with respect to the geomagnetic compass. One interpretation of this sort of data is that there may be a system of cells that keep track of inertially defined direction on the basis of occasional updates from vestibular input. As the vestibular information is based fundamentally on angular acceleration, however, in the absence of movement the direction signal must be maintained either by the current local view of the world or by the animal's memory for it. It is interesting to note that the parietal cortices of both rats and primates contain a (more or less) well-defined vestibular area (Fredrickson & Rubin, 1986).

The Nature of "Spatial" Coding in the Hippocampus

The notion that either the hippocampal circuitry or its activity is involved in encoding spatial relationships is still somewhat vague. While early experiments clearly identified location and direction as the primary discharge correlate of hippocampal CS cells in most large-scale environments and quantified some of the basic properties of place fields, they did not provide many clues about what specifically these cells are responding to in their place fields.

In order to identify the qualities of the environment or behavioral situation that influence CS cell discharge, a number of experiments have altered these factors. Specifically, this research has examined which aspects of an animal's spatial/sensory world are prepotent in influencing place-cell firing, whether place cells have fields in multiple environments, whether coding was in terms of some metric from a fixed reference, and whether immediate sensory stimulation is a necessary condition for place fields to be expressed.

O'Keefe and Conway (1978) examined two hypotheses concerning stimulus control over place fields: (a) Can individual place cells have fields in multiple environments? and (b) What are the stimuli that determine place-field firing?

Thirty-four CA1 CS cells were recorded from rats in two different environments. One was an elevated platform, open to the room, and where the rat received no behavioral training or reward. The other was an enclosed cue-controlled environment in which the rats were trained to perform a place discrimination on a T-maze. Spatial orientation within this enclosure was defined by a set of four cues that held a constant spatial relationship to each other and to the rewarded arm of the maze. By rotating the T-maze with respect to the four visual cues and by removing subsets of one to four cues from the enclosure, factors could be examined that influenced the expression of place fields.

With regard to the first hypothesis, the data clearly indicated that a given place cell could participate in multiple spatial representations. Fifteen of the 34 units had place fields on both the T-maze and the platform; 10 had fields only on the T-maze, and 7 had fields only on the platform. This finding explains why, in many studies that use a single testing apparatus, a significant proportion of CS cells do not exhibit place fields. Interestingly, no obvious topographic or size relationship between fields in the two environments could be determined.

For 12 units that were tested, all had place fields with a fixed relationship to the controlled distal cues. That is, physically interchanging the maze arms had no effect on the location of the place field, and the place fields rotated an appropriate amount with rotation of the set of cues. For five of eight units tested, the place field remained intact despite the removal of any two cues of the set. These data are consistent with the idea that associative memory, either within the hippocampal circuitry or elsewhere is able to generate a complete representation of any particular local view, given a sufficiently large fragment thereof.

The findings have been extended by observing CS unit activity in three distinct behavioral contexts that all shared some environmental features (Kubie & Ranck, 1983). In the first situation, female rats traversed an elevated eight-arm maze in a working memory task. In the second situation, the rats were operantly trained to bar press for differential food reward in a small chamber. The chamber rested on the center of the maze and was open to the room on two sides. The learned response in the bar-press task could be dissociated from the place in which it occurred by having the rats perform at different locations within the chamber. In the third situation, the lactating rats repeatedly retrieved their pups and pellets of food from different locations in their home cage. The home cage was also open to the room and was placed on the center of the eight-arm maze. In each behavioral situation, the apparatus' orientation within the room was varied to assess whether place-field firing was determined by proximal (i.e., apparatus-contained) or distal cues.

All 28 CS cells that were tested had place fields in at least one environment, and 76% had fields in two or three environments. As O'Keefe and Conway (1978) observed, there was no obvious organizing principle to predict place-field topography across the three environments. Apparently, the cells' place-specific firing was determined by different sets of features in each situation, even though the apparati occupied similar physical locations in the room. Place fields in the operant chamber and home cage maintained their orientation with respect to the *apparatus* after rotation, whereas fields on the eight-arm maze remained constant with respect to the *room* features after maze rotation. Thus, at least on the individual cell level, the existence of fields in multiple environments leads to the conclusion that activity cannot represent absolute space. Although it is still possible to think of individual cells as forming components of distributed representations of many different and separate maps, the stronger implication of these data is that firing is determined by the current input configuration, and not by some relational metric.

As discussed earlier, in their more recent work, Muller, Kubie, Ranck, and their colleagues have used very simply structured apparati over which they have nearly complete control of the visual features. Walled arenas of different shapes (circular or rectangular) and sizes were used in which a single card of contrasting brightness was the single spatially polarizing visual feature. The arenas were placed in a curtained cylinder, further restricting any discriminable visual information. The rats' task was to traverse all parts of the floor of the arena in an unrestricted, semi-random manner. This was encouraged by periodically tossing food pellets into the arena. Several spatial properties of CS cell discharge were quantified with this method (Muller, Kubie, & Ranck, 1987). For estimating the areal extent and "shapes" of elevated firing, they defined a firing field (i.e., place field) as a continuous group of nine or more pixels, in each of which an arbitrary mean rate (usually 1.0 Hz) was exceeded, and each of which shared an edge with at least one other criterial pixel.

For a sample of 34 CA1 and CA3/4 CS cells, the average firing field size was about 1000 cm^2, or 22% of the apparatus floor area. The average in-field firing rate was about 5 Hz, with the peak rates achieving 20 Hz or more. Outside the field, the rates averaged about 0.1 Hz. Like previous and subsequent investigators, Muller et al. (1987) found that some CS cells displayed multiple firing fields within a single environment. For a sample of 40 CS cells, 25 had a single field and 9 had two fields (6 cells were virtually silent in the apparatus). Unfortunately, all such conclusions about the presence of multiple fields must be accepted with some caution, because perfect isolation of units in the hippocampus is difficult with currently available recording techniques. This is unfortunate, because such data are necessary to answer the question about whether there is a lower probability of having two fields in the same room than of having one in each of two rooms. If the former were true, then this would argue for the map-like representation, as it would imply that the firing in one local view is determined by what the animal knows about adjacent ones. On the basis of the frequency of reports of multiple fields, the latter appears not to be the case. However, more quantitative experiments are required.

In the circular arena, firing field shapes could be qualitatively grouped into three categories: radially symmetric, crescentric, and elliptical. Most of the units fell into the first two categories. All of these types of fields tended to have Gaussian contours of elevated firing. This diversity of shape was interpreted as an indication that a place cell's firing does not code for the *distance* from some arbitrary point in the rat's environment. Particularly in the case of the crescentric fields, this shape diversity also indicates a strong influence of the details of the local sensory experience on determining "place" specificity.

In spite of the apparent lack of strong directional tuning in this sort of environment, one major result of these studies provides, in our opinion, rather compelling support for the local view interpretation. Experiments were conducted on the effects of scaling up the environment on spatially selective firing. For example, the cylinder was expanded from the usual 76 cm diameter and 51 cm height to 152 cm and 102 cm, respectively, and the cue card was proportionally expanded. Most place fields maintained their same radial and angular locations, but scaled up with the increase in the size of the environment. Note that, particularly near the center of the cylinder, from the proportional radial and the equivalent angular coordinates, the outline of the expanded cue card would form a visual image occupying nearly *the identical retinal location and area*. The local views would be almost identical.

The spatial distribution and temporal stability of firing fields were also assessed in these studies (Muller, et al., 1987). Field centers of different CS cells showed no statistical tendency to be clustered in any particular concentric ring or in any particular wedge of the circular apparatus. A related question asked whether or not place fields showed a tendency to be located in areas that the rats preferred or avoided. A simple pixel-by-pixel correlation between the firing rate maps and occupancy time maps for a given recording session yielded an average $r = 0.026$, which was not different from zero. O'Keefe and Speakman (1987) found an average correlation between occupancy time and firing rates of 0.006 on an elevated plus maze. Thus, occupancy time in a particular location appears to hold no information about the probability of the presence or absence of a place field, at least not in well-explored environments.

For estimates of temporal stability, a pixel-by-pixel correlation across time for one exemplar cell showed that its field was relatively stable across quarters of a 16-minute recording session. Coefficients ranged from 0.46 to 0.61. The limits of stability for two different place fields was tested by similarly correlating rate maps from sessions separated by 6 days. The resulting rs were 0.70 and 0.45 for the two cells. Others have similarly noted persistence of place fields over days and even weeks (Best & Thompson, 1984; Jones Leonard, McNaughton, & Barnes, 1985). In conjunction with Hill's (1978) data, it thus appears that, whatever sort of spatial representation is implicit in place-cell firing, this representation is largely independent of the degree of experience with the environment.

Recently, O'Keefe and Speakman (1987) have systematically studied the issue of stimulus control and have expanded O'Keefe's earlier results with a larger sample of units. In a very similar behavioral situation (a place discrimination on an elevated plus maze), 33 of 55 CS cells showed a significant relationship to the controlled cues within the enclosure. Sixteen units showed significant relations to the static background cues outside of the enclosure (i.e., the place fields of some units showed a tendency not to rotate completely in register with the controlled cues). However, the magnitude of the firing rate variance accounted for by the controlled cues was four times greater than the variance related to the background cues, suggesting, that for most cells, the immediate visual cues were prepotent in influencing place cell discharge.

Most interesting with regard to stimulus control in this study was the finding that 16 of 43 CS cells showed significant interactions between the controlled and static background cues. That is, the firing of these cells was determined to some degree by the unique conjunction of the location of the controlled cues relative to the cues outside of the apparatus. A similar observation has been reported for CS cells recorded in an odor discrimination task (Eichenbaum, in personal communication). In this situation, some cells have firing relationships with the identity or positions of the odors or to particular configurations of odors and their location of presentation.

Although the foregoing results indicate that place cells are influenced by the details of the current local view, this description is clearly not a complete one. When O'Keefe and Speakman removed the controlled cues *before* introducing the rats into the enclosure, the locations of place fields were unrelated to the experimenter-defined goal arm. Instead, they were located correctly with respect to the geometry of the maze itself, but on an arm that was consistent with the *rats' choice* of the goal arm. In other words, the firing of these cells was not related to the background cues, but to the animal's decision about where it was in relation to the now absent controlled cues. At face value, the latter observation appears to conflict with the local view hypothesis, as one would have to postulate that the cells were firing on the basis of a local view that wasn't there (i.e., a remembered one). This is precisely what we argue.

A complimentary set of observations was made by Muller and Kubie (1987). They found that, with rotations of the cue card in their cylindrical recording arena (i.e., movement to a different angular position), most place fields rotated an almost equal amount, suggesting that the cue card exerted some stimulus control. Curiously, however, the place fields in this apparatus did not hold an *obligatory* relationship to the cue card, because its removal resulted mainly in the fields rotating to a new angular coordinate but a similar radial position.

That, in a highly familiar environment, the immediate presence of the determining spatial cues is not necessary for either accurate behavioral place discrimination or for the maintenance of the location of place fields is shown most thoroughly in O'Keefe's and Speakman's (1987) study. In addition to studying the expression of place fields when the controlled cues were present, they also studied the dynamics of place-field organization when the cues were present for only the first part of a trial, as in the spatial memory studies of O'Keefe and Conway discussed previously. This experiment consisted of three phases:

1. During the "perceptual" period, the animal was introduced into the randomly oriented arena and was allowed to view the controlled cues from the start

---

FIG. 13.11. (See pages 408–409) Place fields of three simultaneously recorded CS cells on the radial eight-arm maze before and during the dark–light–dark experiment (see text). Data collected and analyzed as in Fig. 13.9. A. The stable location of the fields of the three units. B. If the rat was brought into the already-darkened room, presumably disoriented, the units' fields were affected in different ways. Whereas unit 1 stopped firing, units 2 and 3 continued to fire at their "correct" radial distances but on "incorrect" arms. For example, on previous days, unit 3 fixed maximally near the center of the maze when the rat turned from the north to the northeast arm (and not the converse), whereas in PHASE 1 of the experiment it fired when the rat turned from the southeast to the south arm (and not the converse). C. With the room lights on, the fields returned to their stable locations, except for unit 2, which showed some persistent disruption. D. Turning off the room lights *after* the rat had run several trials with the lights on (i.e., PHASE 2) had little effect on the units' fields, showing that immediate visual stimulation is not necessary for the expression of location- and direction-specific firing of CS cells, *if* the rat has experienced the environment beforehand under the normal training conditions.

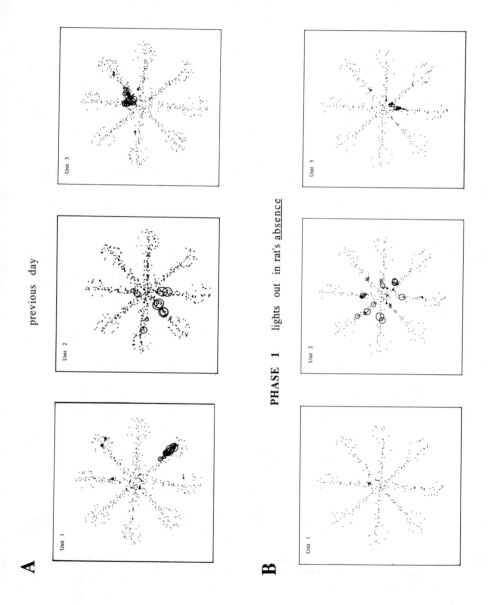

previous day

A

Unit 1

Unit 2

Unit 3

B

Unit 1

Unit 2

Unit 3

PHASE 1   lights   out   in rat's <u>absence</u>

408

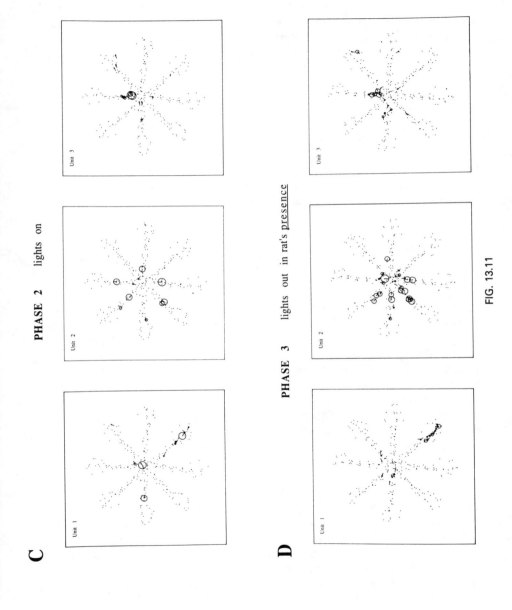

C   **PHASE 2**   lights   on

Unit 3

Unit 2

Unit 1

D   **PHASE 3**   lights   out   in rat's <u>presence</u>

Unit 3

Unit 2

Unit 1

FIG. 13.11

409

arm of the plus maze (i.e., one of the three non-goal arms chosen at random) but was denied access to the maze.

2. During the "memory" period (30–120 secs), the controlled cues were removed from the enclosure in the animal's presence.

3. During the "choice" period, the animal was allowed to traverse the maze and to express its memory for the location of the goal arm. The rats easily attained a high degree of accuracy in choosing the goal arm.

Thirty CS cells with place fields related to controlled cues were recorded during successful performance of the spatial memory trials. The place fields of 90% of these units were maintained during the memory and choice periods, suggesting that place cells truly participate in the internal spatial representation of the rat's environment rather than simply coding for a constellation of immediately impinging spatial information. As described before, if the rat made errors, the place field shifted to where the animal "thought" it was, as inferred from its behavior.

These conclusions were confirmed independently (Jones Leonard, et al., 1985) in a study in which several CS cells were recorded simultaneously and monitored daily for about 3 weeks. The place- and direction-specific firing was plotted daily while the rat performed a forced-choice task on the eight-arm radial maze. The location of the place fields was consistent from day to day, except under a particular experimental condition. This condition consisted of three phases. In the first phase, the animal was brought into the already darkened room in an enclosed box, which was rotated gently several times to disorient the animal. The rat was released onto the maze and allowed to perform the task in the dark. It had little difficulty in doing so, presumably because, although it did not possess information about its angular coordinate, its other senses provided adequate information about its radial coordinate on the maze. This was reflected in the way in which the selectivity of unit firing was disrupted in this phase: Two of the cells continued to fire at the same radial position as on previous days and while the animal was facing the same radial direction. However, they were disrupted with respect to which particular arm they were active on (see Fig. 13.11).

In the second phase of the experiment, the room lights were simply turned on, and the spatial selectivity of firing was assessed again. This situation completely restored the normal firing pattern. In the last phase, the room lights were again extinguished, but this time in the rat's presence. The difference between the two dark phases was that only in the second one did the rat presumably know its starting location. With this information, the normal firing patterns were maintained in the dark, even though the rat was not physically present in the firing field at the time the lights were extinguished.

Interpretations of the Cue Removal and Dark Experiments

The cue removal experiments of O'Keefe and Speakman and of Muller & Kubie, and our own dark–light–dark experiment demonstrate that the spatial selectivity of the discharge of place cells can be determined by the animals memory of the spatial relationships of the visual features of the experimental environment. The neural mechanisms underlying this phenomenon must be more complex than, for example, the persistence of a specific pattern set up when the cues are seen (i.e., reverberation), because the animal may see the cues from a location outside the firing field of a particular cell, and yet that cell fires in its "correct" location when the field is entered.

There are at least two possible interpretations concerning the nature of the underlying neural operations. One explanation, suggested by O'Keefe and Speakman, is that, in their situation, the animal maintains two "maps" of the world, one of the controlled (rotating reference) cues, and one of the uncontrolled (laboratory reference) cues. According to this hypothesis, at the time of exposure to a given orientation of the controlled cues the two maps are mentally rotated into register with each other. Subsequently, the uncontrolled cues available at any given location are used to recall a representation of the corresponding controlled cues. This is reflected in the appropriate "place cell" activity. Such an explanation is very much in keeping with the general notion of spatial representations as global "cognitive maps." It could also be applied to the dark–light–dark experiment, but only if one assumed that the "background" map was formed during the first dark phase (i.e., the map would have to be constructed in a single session, rather than over the course of many sessions as in the O'Keefe–Speakman experiment). According to this explanation, the animal would begin to attend to the previously unnoticed, relatively low salience cues available during the first dark phase, and then link them in associative memory with the normally used, more salient cues available when the room lights are on. The linkage could, in our case, be carried out locally, in the sense that the animal would actually experience all of the required cue set pairings while he traversed the maze in the light phase. The plausibility of this argument is reinforced by the observation that, in our experiments, it turns out to be possible only once or twice to disorient the animal by introduction in darkness. Thereafter, the animal does, indeed, appear to make use of uncontrolled cues in the darkened room, and this is reflected in the fact that the firing fields are not disrupted even in the first dark phase. However, forming a single linkage, or mapping (in the algebraic sense) between two feature sets on a local basis, as would be required in our case, is a relatively simple associative memory problem. It is quite another problem to break and to remake these associations repeatedly and on a global basis, as would be required by the application of the "map-rotation" hypothesis to the O'Keefe

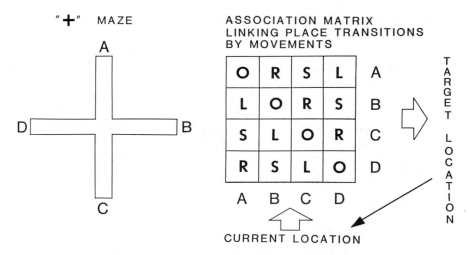

FIG. 13.12.   Illustration of the transition matrix concept of place learning. Imagine that a rat runs on a "+" maze with locations specified by
four distinguishable landmarks, A, B, C, and D. Ignoring, for the moment, that the animal must make 180° turns at the arm ends, learning
about this environment involves "filling in" a square matrix, whose
axes correspond to locations, with the specific movements (*L*eft, *R*ight,
*S*traight) linking these locations. The location information need not be
more complicated than a representation of the "local view" of the
environment (McNaughton, 1988a, 1988b).

and Speakman experiments, in which the animal views the room from a single
location prior to cue removal. In this case, a remapping of internal (remembered)
representations is required. That such a remapping is plausible is strongly suggested by the mental rotation experiments of Shepard and Metzler mentioned at
the beginning of this chapter. However, in those studies there was a considerable
computational load involved even for human subjects, as reflected by the steep
linear relation between reaction time and the number of degrees of rotation
between the reference and target objects (about 20 msec per degree). One would
suppose that even more computation would be required to rotate two global
"cognitive maps." The poor performance of rats on tasks requiring the identification of rotated geometrical forms suggests that the required computational
power is lacking. However, further critical experiments are clearly required. In
particular, one would expect to be able to observe some neurophysiological
correlate of the map rotation operation.

A second possible explanation for these results, one that may be computationally less demanding and that derives some support from available neurophysiological data, was proposed by McNaughton (1987, 1988a, 1988b). Suppose that, during exploration, the animal learns that particular local views of the world that have been experienced sequentially are linked together by particular movements. In more formal terms, the animal learns what can be thought of as a transition matrix (see Fig. 13.12) or "linked list." The elements of such a list would correspond to stored traces of the local views, whereas the linkages are derived from the kinds of motion information available from the vestibular, kinesthetic and visual senses, as well as efference copy from the motor system. Following learning, a previously experienced configuration of an initial local view and a specific movement would elicit recall of the resulting local view. Learning spatial relations is thus seen to be a specific case of the general concept of configural association that has been developed in the animal learning literature (e.g., Hirsh, 1974; Sutherland & Rudy, 1989). If the animal turned left (L) from location A into location B, then the compound representation AL comes to elicit the representation of B, even if the cues normally present in B are removed. The internal representation of B can then be combined with information about movements previously executed in B to recall corresponding locations. Thus, if hippocampal "place cells" reflect recalled local representations, it is easy to see how the appropriate activity in one place can be generated, given only information about a different starting place and a specific sequence of movements. How could this be accomplished in neural circuitry?

A simple model for the neural generation of linked configural associations between local views and movements is illustrated in Fig. 13.13. There are two key elements: a neural network capable of performing simple associative memory (heteroassociation), and a second neural network that forms a unique output pattern for each configuration of local view and movement. The model is flexible with respect to the details of how the associative network is implemented. In recent years, a considerable number of neurally plausible schemes have been proposed, most using some variant of Hebb's learning rule. There is considerable evidence that the hippocampus indeed has the requisite circuitry and properties (see McNaughton & Morris, 1987, and McNaughton, 1988a, for a discussion). One stringent requirement, however, is that the patterns representing configurations of different actions in the same location must be as different from one another as possible. The simplest way to accomplish this would be to have a separate set of "place" units for each fundamental movement. Provided that the latter were restricted to some minimal number, for example, left turn, right turn, and straight, then this solution would not be too expensive in terms of the number of units required and could be "hardwired" into the system during development. There may also be more economical solutions involving learning.

At the present time, the necessary neurophysiological data to distinguish these (and other) hypotheses do not exist. We can cite several recent findings, how-

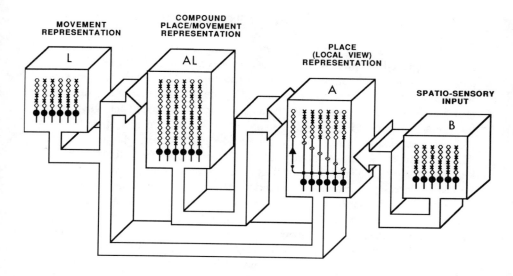

FIG. 13.13. A simple model of implementing the transition matrix idea for conditional association of local view representations with movements. Elements within the boxes represent schematic neurons (see McNaughton, 1988a, for a discussion of the operations that occur inside the boxes). In essence, a compound representation for specific combinations of locations and movements is generated. These event representations can be produced by projecting the output of a hetero-associative matrix representing the local view (A) with the output of the movement representation system (L) onto a third set of neurons (AL) via random excitatory connections. This could produce a system whose output vector was unique for each combination of local view and movement. Projecting this information back into the hetero-associative network via modifiable synapses would permit the *current* local view to be associated with whatever combinations of view and movement that preceded it. Subsequently, that representation could be recalled whenever an appropriate compound place/movement representation was presented. The system would then be capable of internally generating representations of sequences of locations on the basis of movement input alone. Note that only the starting location needs to be specified. A system such as this could account for the finding that hippocampal place cells fire in their correct location in darkness *provided* that the animal is informed about its starting location (see text).

ever, that are at least consistent with the second hypothesis. The first concerns the existence, in the rat brain, of a robust, global representation of motion in space. It turns out that a substantial proportion of single units recorded from the rat parietal cortex distinguish among simple movements such as left turns, right turns, and running straight on the radial arm maze (see Fig. 13.14; McNaughton, Green, & Mizumori, 1986, and unpublished observations). Second, it is possible

414

to find cells in this region that appear to code for specific configurations of movement and visual input (e.g., one cell fired only if the animal's head moved from left to right while the animal faced a particular direction in a particular location). Activity of this sort would be required of the system encoding specific place–movement configurations. Third, some cells appear to respond during spatially equivalent movements (e.g., in one case, a cell was found to fire only during left turns of about 90° or right turns of about 270°). Finally, the notion that spatial representations are developed by learning the conditional consequences of the animals self-generated movements in space suggests that there must be some fundamental interaction between the motor command system and the spatial representational system. It is rather interesting to note, therefore, that virtually all spatially selective firing of hippocampal units is abolished under conditions of restraint in which the animal has learned that movement is impossible. Selectivity returns immediately upon release from restraint (Foster, et al., 1988).

At first glance, the content of the representation proposed in the local view hypothesis appears to be too rigid to guide the kinds of flexible, adaptive spatial behaviors that rats are known to exhibit. However, as with a cognitive map, computations operating on the local-view/movement representation could allow the rat to plan new trajectories between two locations previously reached only on separate occasions from some common point. This can be seen by referring to Fig. 13.12. If any two trajectories through a spatial transition matrix overlap, then a new trajectory can be computed at the point of overlap (e.g., in Fig. 13.12, the trajectory ABCDA could be computed if the animals had experienced on different occasions ABCBA and ADCDA). The cognitive map and local view hypotheses would differ, however, in terms of their predictions about the *duration* that the computation would take. Using a coordinate system (i.e., cognitive map), the computation of trajectory would be independent of the detailed history of exploration. Without one, the duration would be related to the minimum length of local-view movement chain that connects them.

FIG. 13.14. (See pages 416–417) Behavioral correlates of two simultaneously recorded single units in the parietal cortex of the freely-behaving rat. In this task, the rat made repeated traverses between pairs of adjacent arms of the eight-arm maze. Data collected and analyzed as in Fig. 13.9. A. Unit 1 fired during right turns and was relatively quiet during left turns, immobility, and forward motion. B. Perievent-time histograms (PETHs) for right (upper) and left (lower) turns at the ends of the arms for unit 1. Zero indicates the beginning of turns. C. Unit 2, recorded at the same electrode location, fired during forward motion and was relatively quiet during immobility and turns of either direction. D. PETHs for initiation of forward motion (upper) and right turns at the ends of the arms for unit 2.

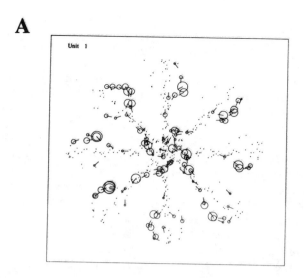

A

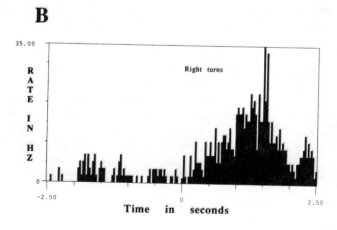

B

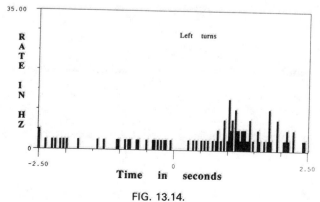

FIG. 13.14.

C

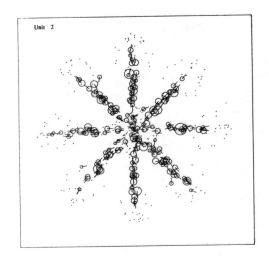

D

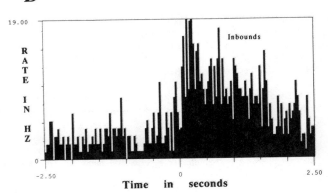

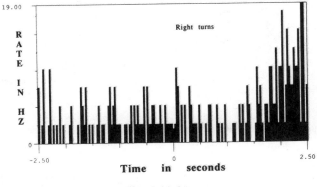

FIG. 13.14. (*Cont.*)

ACKNOWLEDGMENTS

We thank Carol Barnes, Lynn Nadel, and David Olton for helpful comments on a preliminary version of this manuscript. Preparation of this chapter was supported, in part, by a grant from the A. P. Sloan Foundation and by P.H.S. grant NS20331 from the N.I.N.C.D.S.

REFERENCES

Barnes, C. A. (1979). Memory deficits associated with senescence: A neurophysiological and behavioral study in the rat. *Journal of Comparative and Physiological Psychology, 93(1),* 74–104.

Barnes, C. A. (1988). Spatial learning and memory processes: The search for their neurobiological mechanisms in the rat. *Trends in Neurosciences, 11(4),* 163–169.

Barnes, C. A., Nadel, L., & Honig, W. K. (1980). Spatial memory deficit in senescent rats. *Canadian Journal of Psychology, 34,* 29–39.

Beatty, W. W. & Shavalia, D. A. (1980). Spatial memory in rats: Time course of working memory and effect of anesthetics. *Behavioral and Neural Biology, 28,* 454–462.

Best, P. J. & Thompson, L. T. (1984). Hippocampal cells which have place field activity also show changes during classical conditioning. *Society for Neuroscience Abstracts, 10,* #36.18, p. 125.

Birch, D. & Jacobs, G. H. (1979). Spatial contrast sensitivity in albino and pigmented rats. *Vision Research, 19,* 933–937.

Bostock, E., Taube, J., & Muller, R. U. (1988). The effects of head orientation on the firing of hippocampal place cells. *Society for Neuroscience Abstracts, 14,* #51.7, p. 127.

Breese, C. R., Hampson, R. E., & Deadwyler, S. A. (1987). Contingent firing of hippocampal place cells. *Society for Neuroscience Abstracts, 13,* #173.6, p. 608.

Cheng, K. (1986). A purely geometric module in the rat's spatial representation. *Cognition, 23,* 149–178.

Christian, E. P. & Deadwyler, S. A. (1986). Behavioral functions and hippocampal cell types: Evidence for two nonoverlapping populations in the rat. *Journal of Neurophysiology, 55,* 331–348.

Churchland, P. S. (1988). The significance of neuroscience for philosophy. *Trends in Neurosciences, 11(7),* 304–307.

Collett, T. S., Cartwright, B. A., & Smith, B. A. (1986). Landmark learning and visuo-spatial memories in gerbils. *Journal of Comparative Physiology A, 158,* 835–851.

Cooper, L. A. & Shepard, R. N. (1973). Chronometric studies of the rotation of mental images. In W. G. Chase (Ed.), *Visual information processing* (pp. 129–153). New York: Academic Press.

Eichenbaum, H. & Cohen, N. J. (1988). Representation in the hippocampus: What do hippocampal neurons code? *Trends in Neurosciences, 11(6),* 244–248.

Ellard, C. G., Goodale, M. A., & Timney, B. (1984). Distance estimation in the mongolian gerbil: The role of dynamic depth cues. *Behavioural Brain Research, 14,* 29–39.

Field, D. J. (1987). Relations between the statistics of natural images and the response properties of cortical cells. *Journal of the Optical Society of America A, 4(12),* 2379–2394.

Foster, T. C., Castro, C. A., & McNaughton, B. L. (1988). Influence of motor set on place-related hippocampal complex-spike cell activity. *Society for Neuroscience Abstracts, 14,* #160.13, p. 396.

Fox, S. E. & Ranck, J. B., Jr. (1975). Localization and anatomical identification of theta and complex spike cells in dorsal hippocampal formation of rats. *Experimental Neurology, 49,* 299–313.

Fox, S. E. & Ranck, J. B., Jr. (1981). Electrophysiological characteristics of hippocampal complex-spike cells and theta cells. *Experimental Brain Research, 41,* 399–410.

Fredrickson, J. M. & Rubin, A. M. (1986). Vestibular cortex. In E. G. Jones & A. Peters (Eds.), *Cerebral cortex. Sensory motor areas and aspects of cortical connectivity. Vol. 5* (pp. 99–111). New York: Plenum.

Hebb, D. O. (1938). Studies of the organization of behavior. I. Behavior of the rat in a field orientation. *Journal of Comparative Psychology, 25,* 333–353.

Hebb, D. O. (1949). *The organization of behavior.* New York: John Wiley & Sons.

Hill, A. J. (1978). First occurrence of hippocampal spatial firing in a new environment. *Experimental Neurology, 62,* 282–297.

Hill, A. J. (1979). *Investigations of "spatial firing" in dorsal hippocampus of the rat.* Unpublished doctoral dissertation, California Institute of Technology.

Hirsh, R. (1974). The hippocampus and contextual retrieval of information from memory: A theory. *Behavioral Biology, 12,* 421–444.

Honzik, C. H. (1936). The sensory basis of maze learning in rats. *Comparative Psychology Monographs, 13,* 1–113.

Jarrard, L. E. & Bunnell, B. N. (1968). Open field behavior of hippocampal lesioned rats and hamsters. *Journal of Comparative and Physiological Psychology, 66,* 500–502.

Jones Leonard, B., McNaughton, B. L., & Barnes, C. A. (1985). Long-term studies of place field interrelationships in dentate gyrus neurons. *Society for Neuroscience Abstracts, 11,* #320.3, p. 1108.

Jones Leonard, B., McNaughton, B. L. & Barnes, C. A. (1987). A multiple regression analysis of behavioral correlates of rat hippocampal discharge. *Society for Neuroscience Abstracts, 13,* #305.10, p. 1102.

Jones Leonard, B., McNaughton, B. L., & Barnes, C. A. (1988). Location- and direction-specific discharge of rat hippocampal complex-spike cells in an open field and on the radial 8-arm maze. *Society for Neuroscience Abstracts, 14,* #160.14, p. 396.

Keith, J. R. & McVety, K. M. (1988). Latent place learning in a novel environment and the influences of prior training in rats. *Psychobiology, 16(2),* 146–151.

Kelly, J. B. & Glazier, G. J. (1978). Auditory cortex lesions and discrimination of spatial location by the rat. *Brain Research, 145,* 315–321.

Kelly, J. B. & Masterton, B. (1977). Auditory sensitivity of the albino rat. *Journal of Comparative and Physiological Psychology, 91(4),* 930–936.

Kretchevsky, I. (1932). "Hypotheses" versus "chance" in the pre-solution period in sensory discrimination-learning. *University of California Publications (Psychology), 6,* 27–44.

Kubie, J. L., Kramer, L., & Muller, R. U. (1985). Location specific firing of hippocampal theta cells. *Society for Neuroscience Abstracts, 11,* #358.10, p. 1231.

Kubie, J. L. & Ranck, J. B., Jr. (1983). Sensory-behavioral correlates in individual hippocampus neurons in three situations: Space and context. In W. Seifert (Ed.), *Neurobiology of the hippocampus.* (pp. 433–447). London: Academic Press.

Mackintosh, N. J. (1965). Overtraining transfer to proprioceptive control and position reversal. *Quarterly Journal of Experimental Psychology, 17,* 26–36.

Mathews, B. L., Campbell, K. A., & Deadwyler, S. A. (1988). Rotational stimulation disrupts spatial learning in fornix-lesioned rats. *Behavioral Neuroscience, 102(1),* 35–42.

McNaughton, B. L. (1987). Neural association of movement and space: Preliminary steps toward a cartographic theory of spatial representation and learning. *Neuroscience Letters, (Suppl. 29),* S143–S144.

McNaughton, B. L. (1988a). Neuronal mechanisms for spatial computation and information storage. In L. Nadel, L. Cooper, P. Culicover, & R. M. Harnich (Eds.), *Neural connections and mental computations* (pp. 285–350). Cambridge: MIT Press/Bradford Books.

McNaughton, B. L. (1988b). *The Neurobiology of spatial computation and learning.* Five lectures prepared for the Complex Systems Summer School, Santa Fe Institute, June 1988.

McNaughton, B. L., Barnes, C. A., & O'Keefe, J. (1983). The contributions of position, direction, and velocity to single unit activity in the hippocampus of freely-moving rats. *Experimental Brain Research, 52,* 41–49.

McNaughton, B. L., Green, E. J., & Mizumori, S. J. Y. (1986). Representation of body motion trajectory by rat sensory-motor cortex neurons. *Society for Neuroscience Abstracts, 12,* #72.15, p. 260.

McNaughton, B. L. & Morris, R. G. M. (1987). Hippocampal synaptic enhancement and information storage within a distributed memory system. *Trends in Neurosciences, 10(10),* 408–415.

Mittelstaedt, H. (1983). The role of multimodal convergence in homing by path integration. *Fortschritte der Zoologie, 28,* 197–212.

Mittelstaedt, H., & Mittelstaedt, M.-L. (1982). Homing by path integration. In H. Papi & G. Wallraff (Eds.), *Avian navigation* (pp. 290–297). Heidelberg-Berlin: Springer-Verlag.

Mittelstaedt, M.-L. & Mittelstaedt, H. (1980). Homing by path integration in a mammal. *Naturweissenschaften, 67,* 566.

Misner, C. W., Thorne, K. S., & Wheeler, J. A. (1973). *Gravitation.* San Francisco: W. H. Freeman.

Mizumori, S. J. Y., Rosensweig, M. R. & Bennet, E. L. (1985). Long-term working memory in the rat: Effects of hippocampally applied anisomycin. *Behavioral Neuroscience, 99(2),* 220–232.

Morris, R. G. M. (1981). Spatial localization does not require the presence of local cues. *Learning and Motivation, 12,* 239–261.

Morris, R. G. M., Garrud, P., Rawlins, J. N. P., & O'Keefe, J. (1982). Place navigation in rats with hippocampal lesions. *Nature, 297,* 681–683.

Muenzinger, K. F. (1938). Vicarious trial and error at a point of choice. I. Its relation to learning efficiency. *Journal of Genetic Psychology, 53,* 75–86.

Muller, R. U., & Kubie, J. L. (1987). The effects of changes in the environment on the spatial firing of hippocampal complex-spike cells. *The Journal of Neuroscience, 7(7),* 1951–1968.

Muller, R. U., Kubie, J. L., & Ranck, J. B., Jr. (1987). Spatial firing patterns of hippocampal complex-spike cells in a fixed environment. *The Journal of Neuroscience, 7(7),* 1935–1950.

Nadel, L., Wilner, J., & Kurz, E. M. (1985). Cognitive maps and environmental context. In P. D. Balsam & A. Tomie (Eds.), *Context and learning.* Hillsdale, NJ: Lawrence Erlbaum Associates.

O'Keefe, J. (1976). Place units in the hippocampus of the freely moving rat. *Experimental Neurology, 51,* 78–109.

O'Keefe, J. (1979). A review of hippocampal place cells. *Progress in Neurobiology, 13,* 419–439.

O'Keefe, J. (1983). Spatial memory within and without the hippocampal system. In W. Seifert (Ed.) *Neurobiology of the hippocampus* (pp. 375–403). New York: Academic Press.

O'Keefe, J. (1988). Computations the hippocampus might perform. In L. Nadel, L. Cooper, P. Culicover, & R. M. Harnich (Eds.), *Neural connections and mental computations* (pp. 225–284). Cambridge, MA: MIT Press/Bradford Books.

O'Keefe, J. & Conway, D. H. (1978). Hippocampal place units in the freely moving rat: Why they fire where they fire. *Experimental Brain Research, 31,* 573–590.

O'Keefe, J. & Dostrovsky, J. (1971). The hippocampus as a spatial map. Preliminary evidence from unit activity in the freely-moving rat. *Brain Research, 34,* 171–175.

O'Keefe, J. & Nadel, L. (1978). *The hippocampus as a cognitive map.* Oxford: Clarendon Press.

O'Keefe, J. & Speakman, A. (1987). Single unit activity in the rat hippocampus during a spatial memory task. *Experimental Brain Research, 68,* 1–27.

Olton, D. S. (1977). Spatial memory. *Scientific American, 236(6),* 82–98.

Olton, D. S., Branch, M., & Best, P. J. (1978). Spatial correlates of hippocampal unit activity. *Experimental Neurology, 58,* 387–409.

Olton, D. S. & Samuelson, R. J. (1976). Remembrance of places passed: Spatial memory in rats. *Journal of Experimental Psychology: Animal Behavior Processes, 2*, 97–116.

Palmer, S. E. (1978). Fundamental aspects of cognitive representation. In E. Rosch & B. B. Lloyd (Eds.), *Cognition and categorization*. Hillsdale, NJ: Lawrence Erlbaum Associates.

Paul, C. A., Weiner, S. I., & Eichenbaum, H. (1987). Behavioral correlates of hippocampal place cells. *Society for Neuroscience Abstracts, 13*, #364.14, p. 1318.

Pellymounter, M. A., Smith, M. Y., & Gallagher, M. (1987). Spatial learning impairments in aged rats trained with a salient configuration of stimuli. *Psychobiology, 15(3)*, 248–254.

Pico, R. M., Gerbrandt, L. K., Pondel, M., & Ivy, G. (1985). During stepwise cue deletion, rat place behaviors correlate with place unit responses. *Brain Research, 330*, 369–372.

Potegal, M. (1982). Vestibular and neostriatal contributions to spatial orientation. In M. Potegal (Ed.), *Spatial abilities: Developmental and physiological foundations* (pp. 361–387). New York: Academic Press.

Ranck, J. B., Jr. (1973). Studies on single neurons in dorsal hippocampal formation and septum in unrestrained rats. I. Behavioral correlates and firing repertoires. *Experimental Neurology, 41*, 461–531.

Ranck, J. B., Jr. (1984). Head direction cells in the deep cell layer of dorsal presubiculum in freely moving rats. *Society for Neuroscience Abstracts, 10*, #176.12, p. 599.

Rapp, P. R., Rosenberg, R. A., & Gallagher, M. (1987). An evaluation of spatial information processing in aged rats. *Behavioral Neuroscience, 101(1)*, 3–12.

Riley, D. A. & Rosensweig, M. R. (1957). Echolocation in rats. *Journal of Comparative and Physiological Psychology, 50*, 323–328.

Schiffman, H. R., Lore, R., Passafiume, J., Neeb, R. (1970). Role of vibrissae for depth perception in the rat (*Rattus Norvegicus*). *Animal Behavior, 18*, 290–292.

Schöne, H. (1984). *Spatial orientation: The spatial control of behavior in animals and man*. Princeton: Princeton University Press.

Segal, M. & Olds, J. (1972). Behavior of units in hippocampal circuit of the rat during learning. *Journal of Neurophysiology, 35(5)*, 680–690.

Sharp, P. E., Barnes, C. A., & McNaughton, B. L. (1987). Effects of aging on environmental modulation of hippocampal evoked responses. *Behavioral Neuroscience, 101(2)*, 170–178.

Shepard, R. N., & Metzler, J. (1971). Mental rotation of three-dimensional objects. *Science, 171*, 701–703.

Sutherland, R. J., Chew, G. L., Baker, J. C., & Linggard, R. C. (1987). Some limitations on the use of distal cues in place navigation by rats. *Psychobiology, 15(1)*, 48–57.

Sutherland, R. J. & Dyck, R. H. (1984). Place navigation by rats in a swimming pool. *The Canadian Journal of Psychology, 38(2)*, 322–347.

Sutherland, R. J. & Rudy, J. W. (1989). Configural association theory: The role of the hippocampal formation in learning, memory and amnesia. *Psychobiology, 17(2)*, 129–144.

Sutherland, R. J., Whishaw, I. Q., & Kolb, B. (1982). A behavioural analysis of spatial localization following electrolytic, kainate- or colchicine-induced damage to the hippocampal formation in the rat. *Behavioural Brain Research, 7*, 133–153.

Suzuki, S., Augerinos, G., & Black, A. H. (1980). Stimulus control of spatial behavior on the eight-arm maze in rats. *Learning and Motivation, 11*, 1–18.

Swanson, L. W., Köhler, C., & Björklund, A. (1987). The limbic region. I: The septohippocampal system. In A. Björklund, T. Hokfelt, & L. W. Swanson (Eds.) *Handbook of chemical neuroanatomy Vol. 5: Integrated systems of the CNS, Part 1* (pp. 125–277). Amsterdam: Elsevier.

Tolman, E. C. (1948). Cognitive maps in rats and men. *Psychological Review, 55*, 189–208.

Tolman, E. C. & Honzik, C. H. (1930). "Insight" in rats. *University of California Publications in Psychology, 4(14)*, 215–232.

Vincent, S. B. (1912). The function of the vibrissae in the behavior of the white rat. *Behavior monographs, 1(5)*, 1–85.

Vinogradova, O. S. (1975). Functional organization of the limbic system in the process of registration of information: Facts and hypotheses. In R. L. Isaacson & K. H. Pribram (Eds.), *The hippocampus. Vol. 2: Neurophysiology and behavior* (pp. 3–69). Plenum Press: New York.

Whishaw, I. Q. & Mittleman, G. (1986). Visits to starts, routes, and places by rats (Rattus norvegicus) in swimming pool navigation tasks. *Journal of Comparative Psychology, 100(4),* 422–431.

Zipser, D. (1983). *The representation of location.* Technical report of the Institute for Cognitive Science, University of California, San Diego.

Zoladek, L. & Roberts, W. A. (1978). The sensory basis of spatial memory in the rat. *Animal Learning and Behavior, 6(1),* 77–81.

14 Spatial Navigation in Birds

Verner P. Bingman
Bowling Green State University

The emerging synthesis in animal cognition has provided a common theoretical framework for both laboratory-oriented psychologists and field-oriented ethologists to characterize behaviors that are not amenable to interpretations based on classical behaviorism or mechanisms of inheritance (Griffin, 1984; Roitblat, 1987; Roitblat, Bever, & Terrace, 1984). As a consequence, it is now common to hear ethologists discuss memory capabilities as an important evolutionary adaptation that permit organisms to better exploit their environment, thus leading to improved reproductive success. Further, concepts such as information processing and representations are viewed by ethologists as useful heuristic approaches in understanding how memories may be employed in coordinating behavior.

In few other subdisciplines of animal behavior has the synthetic nature of the field of animal cognition met with as much success as in the study of spatial behavior, that is, how organisms recognize locations and coordinate their movements through space. For example, researchers with an ethological perspective, focusing particularly on birds, have benefited from mnemonic models derived from laboratory studies on rodents to understand the impressive ability of some avian species to recover food items previously cached or stored (Sherry, 1985; Shettleworth, 1985), as well as their ability to avoid returning to locations where food levels were recently depleted (Cole, Hainsworth, Kamil, Mercier, & Wolf, 1982). Studies on spatial aspects of avian foraging behavior are justifiably an integral component of discussions on comparative cognition (Roitblat, 1987; Roitblat et al., 1984), yet such behavior involves only a limited aspect of avian spatial behavior: spatial recognition and the behavioral relevance of such recognition. Navigation or goal-directed behavior is another, more sophisticated aspect of avian spatial behavior with a rich ethological tradition, which is only now

423

entering discussions of comparative cognition. Surprisingly, theoretical treatments of avian navigation have nonetheless always had a distinctive cognitive flavor. Forty years of often ingenious experiments on the mechanisms of avian navigation have provided important contributions that permit a good description of how birds move through space. In addition, these studies have done so within the natural complexity of the real world.

I have organized the current chapter into three sections. First, the results from early observational studies on the navigational performance of birds are briefly described. Next, the behavioral mechanisms through which birds regulate their movements in space are discussed, with an emphasis on cognitive properties associated with these mechanisms. Finally, the neural bases of avian navigation are examined.

AVIAN NAVIGATION, FIELD OBSERVATIONAL STUDIES

At the heart of studies on avian navigation is the central empirical finding that, year after year, migratory birds are observed to return to the same breeding and wintering sites. This impressive homing ability intrigued none other than John Watson and Karl Lashley (Watson, 1915), who considered the homing ability of terns who bred on small islands well out in the Gulf of Mexico, as well as homing pigeons. What is truly impressive, however, is that birds will return to goal areas following experimental displacement to places they have never been before (reviewed in Able, 1980), and often do so in a manner that suggests that they can locate the goal direction already from the unfamiliar site of release (manx shearwaters, *Puffinus puffinus,* Matthews, 1968; Layson albatrosses, *Diomedea immutabilis,* Kenyon & Rice, 1958; Leach's storm petrels, *Oceanodroma leucorhoa,* Griffin, 1940; swallows, Hirundinidae, Rüppell, 1937; Sargent, 1962; Southern, 1968; and wood thrushes, *Hylochichla mustelina,* Able, Gergits, Cherry, & Terrill, 1984). These studies have all been important in emphasizing the ability of birds to return to goal areas from unfamiliar locations. As such, they set the foundation for further research focusing on the behavioral mechanisms that form the basis of this navigational performance.

With respect to behavioral mechanisms of navigation, the homing pigeon (*Columba livia*) has been by far the most extensively studied species, and virtually all that is known about the behavioral mechanisms of avian navigation have been derived from studies on this species (excluded here is the more limited question of orientation mechanisms, which has been extensively studied in a number of migratory species as well; Able, 1980; Wiltschko, 1983). As such, I focus this review almost exclusively on experiments performed with homing pigeons and I examine the behavioral and neural mechanisms that permit homing pigeons to consistently return home following displacement to locations never visited before. I work under the tacit assumption that the mechanisms employed by homing pigeons to regulate their movements through space are analogous to those employed by other avian species.

TERMINOLOGY

Before beginning, it is important to clarify some of the terms associated with the study of avian navigation. A homing pigeon displaced to a location 50 km from home where it has never been before will usually fly off in an approximate homeward direction when released. In doing so, the animal is considered to rely on a mechanism of *true navigation* (Baker, 1984; Griffin, 1955). True navigation is based initially on implementation of a *navigational map,* which permits *goal-directed orientation* from unfamiliar areas. For homing pigeons, the navigational map enables a bird to determine its approximate location in space with respect to home from an unfamiliar area where it has never been before and from a direction other than a previous training direction. The northwest orientation of a racing pigeon following release from an unfamiliar area 100 km southeast from home after having been extensively trained up to 50 km from the southeast could be explained by the bird flying a learned compass direction without any reference to a navigational map. True navigation also consists of compass mechanisms, specifically a sun compass and a geomagnetic compass (Wiltschko, 1983), which permit a bird to take up a goal-directed bearing and maintain that course once its location with respect to the goal is determined by use of its navigational map.

Returning from an unfamiliar location, a homing pigeon approaches home and begins to fly over increasingly familiar terrain. Once within this familiar area, the pigeon is thought to rely on landmarks, not necessarily visual, to help in locating its loft (see Landmark Navigation (14-13)). Use of familiar landmarks for navigational purposes is generally called *pilotage* in the field of avian navigation research and is viewed as distinct from true navigation, although it nonetheless permits goal-directed orientation. Pilotage simply implies use of familiar landmarks. The way landmarks could be used for navigation could vary considerably (see Landmark Navigation (14-13)), the most sophisticated version being in the form of a cognitive landmark map that is essentially identical to the cognitive maps described in the psychological literature (Tolman, 1948; O'Keefe & Nadel, 1978). I refer to pilotage as *landmark navigation,* and use *landmark map* when discussing landmarks as part of a system, independent of how it works, which permits goal-directed orientation.

TRUE NAVIGATION, THEORETICAL CONSIDERATIONS

Kramer (1953) was the first to suggest that homing pigeons orient homeward from unfamiliar locations by employing a system involving a map and a compass. Since that time, two major theoretical approaches for understanding the navigational map have been proposed. The most discussed and currently most appealing model is the "gradient" hypothesis of Wallraff (1974). Briefly, the model presupposes changes in stimulus, or stimulus complex strength or quality, which varies in some predictable way with distance and direction from the loft. Ideally, the system is bicoordinate (i.e., based on two intersecting gradient axes that need not necessarily be orthogonal), nor would it be necessary that the stimulus parameter that varies along each of the two axes be perceived by the same or different sensory mechanisms. When displaced to an unfamiliar location, a pigeon would compare the quality of the sensory input at the release site with that at the loft with respect to the two gradient axes, and knowing as a result of experience how stimulus quality varies with distance and direction from the loft, the bird could determine its position with respect to the loft in a bicoordinate fashion. There are variations of this model (see Wallraff, 1974), but in any form, the model emphasizes cognitive elements such as internal representations of stimulus quality at home as well as how it varies from the loft, and the processing of sensory information with respect to these representations at the release site.

The alternative model, the "mosaic" hypothesis of Wallraff (1974), was originally applied to the use of visual landmarks (see Landmark Navigation (14-13)), but has entered discussions of navigational maps primarily as a possible explanation for how homing pigeons may rely on olfactory cues to determine their location in space from places never before visited (Papi, 1982). Using a mosaic map, homing pigeons would compare odors perceived at the release site (or in route to the release site, see Route-Based Navigation (14-2) Wallraff & Sinsch, 1988) with odors perceived at the loft that are carried by winds from different directions. For example, if a bird perceives odor X as strong at a release site, and odor X had previously been associated with northerly winds at the loft, the bird would establish its position as north of the loft and use a compass mechanism to fly south. Two important points regarding an olfactory mosaic map: First, it is not true navigation as previously defined, but more like a landmark map based on odors. Although a homing pigeon could use such a map from locations it has never been to before, the pigeon does rely on cues that it had previously experienced (windborne odors), which permit familiarity with areas without ever having been there. Second, essential cognitive elements are still present in the form of representations of odors and memory of wind directions associated with them, as well as processing of sensory input at a release site with respect to representations acquired at the loft.

TRUE NAVIGATION, SENSORY MECHANISMS

With these models serving as a theoretical background, considerable effort at the empirical level has been directed at revealing the sensory bases of homing pigeon navigational behavior. Discussion has centered on two environmental stimuli:

atmospheric odors and geomagnetism (Baker, 1984; Gould, 1982; Papi, 1986; Schmidt-Koenig, 1987).

Olfaction

The hypothesis that homing pigeons rely on atmospheric odors for their navigational map has been controversial since its formulation some 15 years ago. Intuitive resistance to this hypothesis has been rooted in the belief that olfactory capabilities of birds, as evidenced by the size of their olfactory bulbs (Bang, 1971), are too meager for such a complex behavior. However, olfactory regulation of goal-directed behaviors has been reported in a number of avian species, including turkey vultures (*Cathartes aura*; Stager, 1964) and Leach's petrels (Grubb, 1974). Another conceptual difficulty regards the question of how reliable odors carried in the atmosphere can be (Becker & van Raden, 1986). Despite these considerations, an impressive body of evidence has accumulated indicating that atmospheric odors do indeed play a critical role for the pigeon navigational map.

The possibility that atmospheric elements might play a role in the formation of the navigational map was first suggested by the finding that shielding pigeons in a loft without exposure to ambient winds rendered them impaired in orienting homeward when released from distant, unfamiliar release sites (Kramer, 1959; Wallraff, 1966). Since then, a number of experimental procedures such as olfactory nerve section, temporary anesthesia of the nasal mucosae, the application of nasal tubes to block the perception of odors, and manipulations of the direction of windborne odors at the loft by large fans have all been shown to regularly impair or deflect the orientation of birds when released from unfamiliar sites (Papi, 1982, 1986). Instead of reviewing the massive body of literature associated with this work, including possible problems with it (Schmidt-Koenig, 1987), I focus on a recent experimental approach that provides perhaps the most compelling support for the hypothesis of a navigational map based on olfactory cues.

Using variations of the same basic design, Benvenuti and Wallraff (1985) and Kiepenheuer (1985) have attempted to fool pigeons about the actual location of a release site by manipulating their exposure to atmospheric odors. Homing pigeons were first transported to and exposed to odors, as well as other stimuli, at one location. Subsequently, they were rendered temporarily anosmic and released under anesthesia either at the location where they were exposed to odors or at a location 180° away from the exposure site in an opposite direction with respect to the home loft. The critical result was the following. If a pigeon is brought to location A north of the loft, exposed to odors for a few hours, and then transported to location B at an equal distance south of the loft and released without further exposure to odors, the pigeon is very likely to fly south from location B even though it is a direction opposite that of the home loft. The interpretation of this result is that the bird flies south from location B because the last navigational, presumably olfactory, information acquired was at location A north of the loft, and it relies on this information, anosmia precluding the acquisition of further navigational information, in determining its location to be north of the loft.

The data from both of these studies emphasize the importance of olfactory stimuli for the proper functioning of the pigeon navigational map. However, there is some reason to believe that olfactory cues may be used in conjunction with other contextual information (Kiepenheuer, 1986; but see Papi, 1986). Pigeons exposed to odors from location A while not being at location A, and then released at location B under anosmic conditions, fail to give any indication of homeward orientation with respect to either location A or B. Nonetheless, the earlier experiments, together with the plethora of other studies examining the olfactory hypothesis, emphasize the critical importance of atmospheric odors for the proper functioning of the pigeon navigational map. In addition, the olfactory experiments suggest that homing pigeons have a highly developed olfactory memory system that can be used in an apparent cognitive fashion for determining their location with respect to the loft.

Geomagnetism

Given the well-documented finding that birds can rely on the earth's magnetic field for compass orientation (Wiltschko, 1983), it is not surprising that hypotheses citing a role for geomagnetism in the functioning of the navigational map of pigeons have also appeared. Interestingly, the possible importance of geomagnetism in permitting a bird to determine its location in space was already suggested long before it was firmly established as compass cue (Yeagley, 1947). The supporting evidence indicating a role for geomagnetism for the navigational map includes:

1. Correlations between variations in the initial orientation of pigeons following release with naturally occurring fluctuations in geomagnetic field parameters (Keeton, Larkin, & Windsor, 1974).

2. Impaired initial orientation of homing pigeons when released within naturally occurring magnetic anomalies (i.e., perturbations in geomagnetic parameters along the earth's surface; Walcott, 1978; Kiepenheuer, 1982).

3. Disrupted initial orientation following experimentally induced magnetic disturbances (Benvenuti, Baldaccini, & Ioalé, 1982).

The results of these studies link magnetic stimuli with pigeon homing performance. The effects are plausibly attributed to affect a map mechanism rather than compass orientation, as the experiments are performed under sunny conditions when the birds are known to rely on the sun for compass orientation. However, the possibility of an interaction between magnetic stimuli and sun compass orientation, which manifests itself under conditions of magnetic disturbance, cannot be entirely excluded as an explanation for the reported results. Indeed, until an experiment is performed whereby manipulating the ambient magnetic field exposed to a bird results in predictable shifts in orientation that are interpretable in the context of a map, uncertainties will remain regarding its importance, and the question of a geomagnetic role in the pigeon navigational map will remain open.

I have discussed olfactory and geomagnetic cues as independent sources of potential map information. It remains conceivable, however, that they may work in some collective fashion to permit a pigeon to locate its position in space. For example, if the map does take the form of a bicoordinate gradient system, olfactory stimuli may characterize one axis, and magnetic cues could characterize the other. Although this is as yet a highly speculative notion, Wallraff, Papi, Ioalé, and Benvenuti (1986) have reported that olfactory and magnetic stimuli may interact at some level of the homing process. Homing pigeons exposed to oscillating magnetic fields coupled with anosmia prior to release fail to show the usual deviation in orientation away from the homeward direction characteristic of the magnetic field treatment alone (Benvenuti et al., 1982).

Regional and Individual Differences

Given the possibility of multiple sensory mechanisms associated with the pigeon navigational map, it seems important to consider to what extent regional differences may account for these findings. The currently available evidence indicates that wherever it has been extensively studied, olfaction plays a critical role in the proper functioning of the pigeon navigational map (in Italy, Papi, 1986; in Germany, Wallraff, 1981; Kiepenheuer, 1985). Nonetheless, olfactory treatments have been reported to be less effective in altering navigational performance in other locations in Germany (Wiltschko, Wiltschko, & Mathias, 1987; Wiltschko, Wiltschko, & Walcott, 1987) and the United States (Papi, Keeton, Brown, & Benvenuti, 1978, but see Papi, 1986; Wiltschko, Wiltschko, & Walcott, 1987). At this time, therefore, it is important to consider how and why the salience of olfactory cues for navigation may vary regionally. Indeed, potential regional differences could be based on differences in atmospheric dynamics that may render carried odors more or less reliable as sources of navigational information (Becker & van Raden, 1986; Waldvogel, 1987). Finally, the manner in which individuals from the same loft location are raised (i.e., exposure of the loft and flight training) will also influence whether they rely on olfactory cues or some other unspecified source of navigational information (Wiltschko, Wiltschko, Gruter, & Kowalski, 1987c).

The situation with geomagnetism is somewhat more difficult, insofar as it remains unclear to what extent it may be involved in the navigational map.

Relevant in this context, however, is a finding that indicates that pigeons from different lofts are differentially affected at the same magnetic anomaly (Walcott, in press).

In looking at baseline individual behavior performance, pigeons in different regions are not equally good at returning home following release from unfamiliar locations. For example, birds generally perform better in Italy than in Germany. Raising Italian birds in Germany and German birds in Italy (Foa, Wallraff, Ioalé, & Benvenuti, 1982; Kiepenheuer, Baldaccini, & Alleva, 1979) has indicated that baseline differences are, at least in part, environmentally based, possibly reflecting differences in the way environmental cues are employed in the formation of a navigational map. The available evidence indicates that such may be the case, supporting Keeton's (1974) belief that environmental factors may determine the extent to which specific cues are used for true navigation. However, I wish to close this section by emphasizing that current available evidence implicates olfaction as the primary source of navigational map information, with the demonstration of alternative sources awaiting further empirical support.

LANDMARK NAVIGATION

In the previous discussion, we focused on true navigation, or that mechanism that permits a pigeon to approximate its position in space relative to home *from places it has never been before.* However, when a homing pigeon is in an area where it has been before, either when returning to the loft from an unknown site or when released in a familiar area, it then has available an additional source of potential navigational information in the form of familiar landmarks, which may or may not be visual. As already mentioned, use of familiar landmarks for locating ones position with respect to a goal is referred to as landmark navigation to distinguish it from the true navigation already described.

Despite its intuitive appeal, the extent to which landmarks are used by homing pigeons in generating goal-oriented responses has been one of the most empirically elusive issues in avian navigational research. Nonetheless, there are strong indications that homing pigeons do attend to landmarks and use them for locating their position with respect to home when they are in a familiar area but outside the range of direct sensory contact with their loft. Homing pigeons approaching the familiar area around the loft have been recorded to make appropriate course corrections (Michener & Walcott, 1967). Pigeons wearing frosted lenses that preclude form vision are successful in orienting homeward from a distant, unfamiliar release site, but appear impaired in returning to their loft once in its vicinity (within 5–10 km; Schmidt-Koenig & Walcott, 1978). Finally, homing pigeons, who are not permitted free-flight experience around their loft prior to their first experimental release, orient homeward from a distant location, indicating an ability to perform true navigation, but are impaired in locating their loft once within its vicinity (Wallraff, 1970). This last result suggests that flight experience is important for adequate local navigation near the loft, presumably by permitting familiarization with local landmarks.

Another source of evidence indicating that homing pigeons attend to landmarks for navigation comes from experiments where, as a result of some procedure, birds are initially impaired at orienting homeward from a distant, unfamiliar release site. However, upon repeated exposure to the same, now familiar release site, the birds become better at orienting homeward following the same experimental procedure that originally rendered them impaired. Familiarity with an area enables pigeons to compensate for disruptions in their navigational map, and it seems reasonable to suppose that this familiarity effect is based on the use of landmarks that they had been exposed to. This familiarity effect has been observed under diverse conditions:

1. Olfactory deprived pigeons, who generally fail to orient homeward from unfamiliar locations, do orient homeward when released from locations they had been to previously (Benvenuti, Fiaschi, Fiore, & Papi, 1973; Bingman, Ioalé, Casini, & Bagnoli, 1987, 1988a; Hartwick, Foá, & Papi, 1977).

2. When released within a magnetic anomaly, homing pigeons are often disoriented. However, there is considerable improvement in homeward orientation on subsequent releases from the same anomaly (Kiepenheuer, 1982; Lednor & Walcott, 1988).

3. Homing pigeons who are clock-shifted, a procedure that results in a predictable change in an animal's temporal monitoring of sun movement for sun compass orientation (Schmidt-Koenig, 1960, 1961), typically display a deviation in orientation with respect to home when released from either familiar or unfamiliar locations (Füller, Kowalski, & Wiltschko, 1983). However, they compensate at least partially for that deviation when released under *clock-shift* conditions a second time from the same location (Foá & Albonetti, 1980).

These results suggest that homing pigeons do indeed attend to and use landmarks for navigation. However, it should be emphasized that they are likely used under normal conditions primarily to locate the loft once in its vicinity, vicinity depending on the previous experience of a pigeon (perhaps up to 20 km from the loft). The possible use of landmarks from distant, familiar locations should be viewed as an auxiliary mechanism (Fúller et al., 1983) to be employed when use of their navigational map is disrupted or has previously been associated with incorrect orientation.

Landmark Navigation, Theoretical Considerations

Given that homing pigeons use landmarks for navigation, it becomes important to consider how they may be used. In the following discussion, I consider landmarks within the context of local navigation near the loft, but the ideas can be generalized to landmark use at distant familiar locations as well. Two important questions emerge: (a) What is the nature of the spatial or location information derived from landmarks; and (b) are they used exclusively for location purposes (e.g., "my location is north of the loft") or are they also employed in guiding orientation responses (e.g., "therefore I should fly to this side of the water tower")?

With respect to the first question, two possibilities occur. First, pigeons may rely on landmarks in the form of a mosaic map (Wallraff, 1974; W. Wiltschko & R. Wiltschko, 1982), whereby a pigeon learns the fixed directional relationships of landmarks or landmark complexes with respect to the loft and/or other landmarks. For example, a pigeon relying on such a system, acquired through experience and coded in terms of compass directions, could learn that the water tower lies north of the loft, or perhaps that the water tower also lies northeast of the garbage dump/truck garage complex, which lies west of the loft. Essentially, it is a behavioristic model (Bingman, Bagnoli, Ioalé, & Casini, in press) with pigeons associating a single compass direction, or a limited set of compass directions, with respect to any given landmark. In this model, each landmark or landmark complex is used as an independent source of spatial information. Use of a mosaic landmark map has been hypothesized to occur at familiar release sites where pigeons are able to orient homeward by having presumably associated a site-specific homeward orientation response with a single set of local landmark cues during previous visits (Bingman et al., 1987, 1988a).

A second possibility is that landmarks are not used independently as guide posts, but collectively in the form of an integrative or cognitive map (O'Keefe & Nadel 1978). Such a system is characterized by the use of at least a subset of the same group of landmarks or landmark complexes from effectively any location where sensory contact with them would be possible. Empirically, such a mapping system is advantageous, because the same pool of landmarks could be used over an infinite number of locations within an area of familiarity and could enable a pigeon to direct goal- (loft)-oriented responses even from locations where it has never been before within an area of familiarity. The superiority of such a cognitive mapping system (O'Keefe & Nadel, 1978) compared to the mosaic map described earlier is that the mosaic system is effective only from specific locations, for example, the water tower, where a pigeon would have had the opportunity to associate a limited set of directional responses with respect to goal areas. The cognitive mapping system confers considerably more flexibility in permitting goal-directed responses from anywhere within an area of familiarity (Bingman et al., in press).

Admittedly, the challenge with respect to an integrative landmark map is empirical demonstration that anything like it exists, particularly in a natural setting. One testable prediction that emerges is that such a system should enable a pigeon to use the same group of landmarks from virtually anywhere where sensory contact would be possible. Such use has been suggested in laboratory studies with rodents where goal areas in a maze (O'Keefe & Conway, 1978; Olton & Samuleson, 1976; Suzuki, Augerinos, & Black, 1980), or an escape platform within an opaque milk-bath (Sutherland & Dyck, 1984), need to be located. Interestingly, similar laboratory studies performed with birds (Savannah sparrows, *Passerculus sandwichensis*; Moore & Osadchuk, 1982; and pigeons; Spetch & Edwards, 1986) suggest that they use external landmarks in a manner similar to rodents.

At a functional level, a more important prediction is that such a system should permit goal-directed orientation from *novel* locations within a familiar area. There has been one promising report indicating that homing pigeons can indeed rely on landmarks to orient home from a novel location within a familiar area (Bingman et al., in press).

Both of the models describe behavioral mechanisms that would permit goal-oriented responses and thus fall within the definition of landmark navigation. The possible existence of multiple landmark map systems should not be surprising, given the diversity of conditions under which an animal must travel between locations. Indeed, a recent laboratory study with pigeons emphasizes multiplicity in the way locations may be specified by landmarks (Spetch & Edwards, 1988). Finally, the current models are provided primarily as departure points for future empirical studies, and they certainly do not exhaust the possible mechanisms through which landmarks may be used in the control of spatial behavior.

In whatever manner landmarks may provide location information with respect to a goal, the next question focuses on the extent to which landmarks may be used to regulate the actual movement or orientation of a pigeon once its location is identified. One extreme possibility is that landmarks are only used to determine location (e.g., north of the loft), with a bird then relying on an independent compass mechanism to fly south, as is the case for true navigation (see Terminology (14-4)). One indication that pigeons may, in fact, do this comes from an experiment where birds were clock-shifted and then released within a few kilometers of their loft (Graue, 1963). Assuming landmarks are used both for determining location as well as regulating in-flight orientation, the clock-shift should not affect the birds' behavior, as such a procedure would result in shifted orientation only when pigeons rely on their sun compass (Schmidt-Koenig, 1979). In contrast, if the birds use landmarks solely to determine their position with respect to the loft, and then use their sun compass to take up the appropriate direction home, the clock-shifted birds should show orientation predictably shifted from the homeward direction. In fact, the majority of the clock-shifted birds showed the expected deviation based on sun compass orientation, indicating that, if landmarks are being used, they are used solely in determining one's location with respect to the loft. Interestingly, nutcrackers (Corvidae) tested under clock-shift conditions to locate seeds they had stored prior to being clock-shifted also tended to show the expected deviation in goal orientation, indicating use of their sun compass in regulating their motor response (W. Wiltschko, in personal communication).

In contrast, results from experiments using a different real-world spatial task suggest that landmarks may also be used to regulate a bird's movement in addition to providing information with respect to location. Anosmic pigeons, relying on familiar landmarks to orient homeward from a familiar release site, do not show the characteristic deviation in homeward orientation following clockshift as do clock-shifted controls who had never been to the release site before (Bingman & Ioalé, In press). Therefore, for orientation at familiar release sites, landmarks seem to be used to regulate the flight path of a pigeon (e.g., "fly over the barn"). The remaining clock-shifted birds in Graue's study, those who did not show the change in orientation indicating sun compass use, may have also relied on landmarks for this purpose as well.

Landmark navigation, although still poorly described, is an important aspect of avian spatial behavior. Despite empirical difficulties (how do you move a water tower?), there is considerable evidence demonstrating the integral role that landmarks play for avian navigational performance. The full extent to which landmarks are employed by birds to regulate their movements, however, awaits further innovative field and laboratory studies. The possible uses of landmarks presented here (summarized in Fig. 14.1), which purposely resemble models inspired by the laboratory performance of rodents (O'Keefe & Nadel, 1978; Tolman, 1948), hopefully provide a framework for thinking about the way landmarks may be used in a field setting. The available evidence indicates that all of the various combinations of mechanisms may be used by homing pigeons, further emphasizing the complexity and diversity of mechanisms available to pigeons to regulate their movements through space.

ROUTE-BASED NAVIGATION

Already discussed is how homing pigeons could perform goal-(loft)-directed orientation by a mechanism of true navigation, relying on a navigational map, and by mechanisms of landmark navigation, relying on familiar landmarks. One last navigational mechanism is based on information acquired by a pigeon during its journey to a release site (so-called outward journey information). Outward journey information could be acquired either passively, in the case of experimental displacements, or actively, in the case of its own spontaneous flights from the loft. Homing based on such information has been variously called path integration, displacement navigation, and route reversal (Wallraff & Sinsch, 1988).

Despite a long history of theoretical interest (Barlow, 1964), it is now clear that information acquired en route is not *necessary* for loft-directed orientation in experienced pigeons (Wallraff, 1980). However, experimental treatments such as transporting birds along different routes to the same release site (Papi et al.,

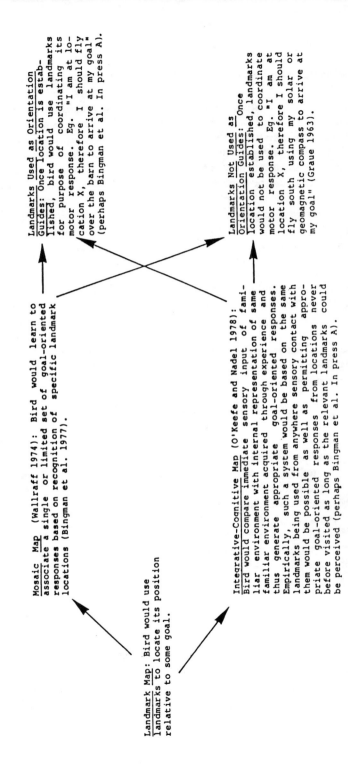

Landmarks Used as Orientation Guides: Once location is established, bird would use landmarks for purpose of coordinating its motor response. Eg. "I am at location X, therefore I should fly over the barn to arrive at my goal" (perhaps Bingman et al. In press A).

Landmarks Not Used as Orientation Guides: Once location established, landmarks would not be used to coordinate motor response. Eg. "I am at location X, therefore I should fly south using my solar or geomagnetic compass to arrive at my goal" (Graue 1963).

Mosaic Map (Wallraff 1974): Bird would learn to associate a single or limited set of goal-oriented responses based on recognition of specific landmark locations (Bingman et al. 1977).

Landmark Map: Bird would use landmarks to locate its position relative to some goal.

Integrative-Cognitive Map (O'Keefe and Nadel 1978): Bird would compare immediate sensory input of familiar environment with internal representation of same familiar environment acquired through experience and thus generate appropriate goal-oriented responses. Empirically, such a system would be based on the same landmarks being used from anywhere sensory contact with them would be possible as well as permitting appropriate goal-oriented responses from locations never before visited as long as the relevant landmarks could be perceived (perhaps Bingman et al. In press A).

FIG. 14.1. Summary of possible uses of familiar landmarks in regulating avian navigation.

435

1972), as well as transport under anosmia (Baldaccini, Benvenuti, Fiaschi, Ioalé, & Papi, 1982) or magnetic field manipulations (Kiepenheuer, 1978; R. Wiltschko, W. Wiltschko, & Keeton, 1978) have all been reported to influence the orientation of pigeons recorded at the release site. These results indicate that homing pigeons attend to information gathered en route to the release site and use it in determining the homeward direction. Unclear, however, is whether such information is used as an independent navigational mechanism or an additional source of input that could be processed in the context of the navigational map (Wallraff & Sinsch, 1988). In any event, with one possible exception, route-based cues are viewed primarily as an auxiliary source of information, perhaps used to supplement information gathered at the release site (so-called location-based information; Baker, 1984).

The one exception is interesting insofar as the effect is so dramatic. Young, inexperienced homing pigeons transported to a release site under conditions of an altered magnetic field are impaired at orienting homeward following release (R. Wiltschko et al., 1978). Similar treatment has only a marginal effect on experienced birds. The results suggest the intriguing possibility that route-based, geomagnetic information is necessary for inexperienced homing pigeons to navigate a homeward course (but see Wallraff & Sinsch, 1988), but such information is no longer necessary with subsequent maturation of alternative navigational strategies (e.g., true navigation).

NEURAL BASES

The numerous studies describing the phenomenon of avian navigational performance and associated behavioral mechanisms have resulted in a good account of this real-world, spatial behavior system, and have thus rendered it amenable to analysis at the neural level. Indeed, considerable effort has been expended in attempting to reveal the neural bases of the various components of avian navigational behavior. Studies have taken somewhat divergent approaches: one concerned with the hippocampus and its integrative role in the regulation of landmark navigation, the other with the central processing of sensory information for true navigation.

Landmark Navigation: The Hippocampus

For more than 30 years, the hippocampus has been a focal brain structure for research examining the neural control of memory. More recently, laboratory studies on rodents have emphasized the importance of the hippocampus in the control of spatial behavior (O'Keefe & Nadel, 1978; Olton, 1983). Studies on the homing behavior of pigeons have gone one step further in examining the importance of the hippocampus in the control of navigational behavior within a real-world setting.

Although the avian hippocampal region, also known as dorsomedial forebrain, is cytoarchitecturally distinct from the mammalian hippocampus, there is considerable similarity both at the level of afferent and efferent pathway connections (Casini, Bingman, & Bagnoli, 1986) and the presence of neurotransmitters and transmitter-related substances as revealed by immunohistochemical techniques (Krebs, Erichsen, & Bingman, 1987). In fact, the avian and mammalian hippocampal regions are thought to be homologous structures, strongly suggesting the possibility of functional similarity in the regulation of spatial behavior (Bingman et al., in press).

The behavior of homing pigeons following hippocampal ablation indicates two relatively distinct functional aspects of the hippocampus, one best understood in the context of spatial recognition, the other in the context of navigation. With respect to the first aspect, the main empirical finding is that following hippocampal ablation, homing pigeons suffer a robust, specific retrograde memory loss, which manifests itself as a failure to recognize salient environmental stimuli, such as their home loft (Bingman, Bagnoli, Ioalé, & Casini, 1984) or locations where they were previously released (Bingman et al., 1987). Important is that the retrograde recognition losses are entirely recoverable with appropriate postoperative training. Hippocampal-ablated homing pigeons quickly relearn to identify their home loft (Bingman, Ioalé, Casini, & Bagnoli, 1985) as well as learn to orient homeward from a familiar release site when tested under anosmic conditions (Bingman et al., 1988a) in a manner that does not differ from controls.

From a comparative perspective, it is interesting to note that similar retrograde recognition deficits occur for both spatial and nonspatial tasks in rodents (Olton & Papas, 1979; Walker & Olton, 1984) and monkeys (Salmon, Zola-Morgan, & Squire, 1987) following hippocampal ablation.

The second, more significant finding is that despite unimpaired recognition of salient environmental stimuli (following postoperative training), hippocampal-ablated homing pigeons show a persistent impairment in homing performance, from which they do not recover. One year after surgery, hippocampal-ablated homing pigeons are found to consistently take more time to return home compared to control-ablated pigeons whether released from familiar or unfamiliar locations (Bingman et al., 1987, 1988b). The available evidence indicates that this deficit is rooted in impaired navigational ability (Bingman et al., in press). Given this chronic impairment in homing performance, it is now important to consider what type of navigation system may be disrupted and thus identify the nature of the cognitive process(es) that involve the hippocampus.

Hippocampal-ablated homing pigeons released from a location where they have never been before succeed in orienting homeward in a manner that does not differ from controls (Bingman et al., 1984, 1988b). For experienced pigeons, therefore, the hippocampus is not necessary for true navigation as described previously, which would be employed from such unfamiliar locations. (Recent results, however, indicate that the hippocampus is critical for navigational map acquisition in young, inexperienced pigeons.)

An alternative possibility is that for experienced pigeons, the hippocampus is necessary for landmark navigation. As such, the hippocampus would be primarily involved in regulating a pigeon's movements once within its familiar range around the home loft, and indeed there is considerable evidence in support of this hypothesis (Bingman et al., in press). One prediction that emerges from this hypothesis is that, when released in the vicinity of the home loft, within the familiar range, hippocampal-ablated homing pigeons should be impaired in their ability to direct a course home. Presented in Fig. 14.2 are results from a radio-tracking study designed to examine the flight path of homing pigeons near the loft (Bingman & Mensch, in preparation). Although limited, the data clearly reveal an impairment on the part of the hippocampal-ablated homing pigeons compared to ablated controls in their ability to direct a course home. These results provide the most compelling evidence indicating impaired landmark use following hippocampal ablation. Indeed, the flight paths taken by the hippocampal-ablated pigeons is remarkably reminiscent of the paths taken by hippocampal-ablated rats in the Morris milk bath (Morris, Garrud, Rawlins, & O'Keefe, 1982).

A more difficult question is whether the suggested impairment may be associated with landmark use in the form of something like a mosaic map or an integrative-cognitive map (see the scheme of Fig. 14.1). The existent data are consistent with an interpretation based on impaired use of an integrative map. Hippocampal-ablated homing pigeons can learn a site-specific homeward orientation response from a familiar location, which is expressed when they are tested under anosmia (Bingman et al., 1988a). Successful acquisition of a single, appropriate directional response with respect to a landmark or landmark complex, as indicated by this result, reveals that hippocampal-ablated homing pigeons can use landmarks when used in a manner that is consistent with implementation of a mosaic map.

Although it is difficult to unequivocally identify the existence of an integrative-cognitive map, certain predictions (see Landmark Navigation, Theoretical Considerations 14-16) can be generated, assuming that such a map exists. Indeed, homing pigeons are ideally suited for testing predictions generated from a cognitive map model (O'Keefe & Nadel, 1978). One prediction is that an integrative map should permit an organism to successfully use familiar landmarks for navigation even when the landmarks are perceived from novel locations. In one study, control homing pigeons that were dependent on the use of familiar landmarks successfully oriented homeward from a *novel* location within a familiar environment, suggesting that the use of a cognitive map (Bingman et al., in press). Importantly, hippocampal-ablated pigeons failed to orient

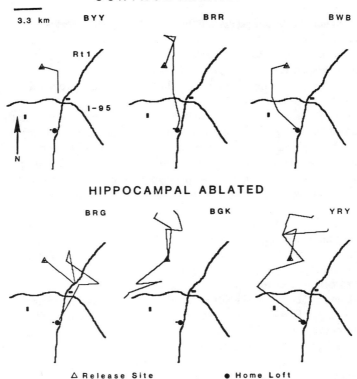

CONTROL ABLATED

3.3 km   BYY   BRR   BWB

Rt 1

I-95

N

HIPPOCAMPAL ABLATED

BRG   BGK   YRY

△ Release Site   ● Home Loft

FIG. 14.2. Flight paths taken by control anterior forebrain ablated and hippocampal ablated homing pigeons, recorded by radio telemetry, following release from a site approximately 7 km north of the home loft. Triangle identifies the location of the release site, circle the home loft, and the various rectangles large conspicuous buildings. The two thick lines identify the two major roads in the area; the primarily vertical thick line is Route 1 and the primarily horizontal thick line is Interstate 95. The fine line that originates from the triangle is the flight path taken by the bird, whose identity can be found in the upper right corner of each diagram (eg. BYY). Breaks in the flight path identify locations where the transmitter signal was lost. BYY returned within 10 min. of release and it is likely that the path taken by BYY following loss of the signal was more or less directed toward the loft. All the birds eventually returned home.

homeward on the same task, indicating that if the behavior of the control animals was based on the use of an integrative or cognitive landmark map, hippocampal ablation severely disrupts the use of such a map (Bingman et al., in press).

Further evidence linking the hippocampus to spatial performance comes from work with food-storing birds and operant studies with pigeons (Good, 1987; Reilly & Good, 1987). The essential finding with respect to food storing birds is that, having cached seeds in a manner that does not differ from controls, hippocampal ablated birds are impaired in their subsequent recovery of the seeds (Eurasian nutcracker, *Nucifraga caryocatactes,* Krushinskaya, 1966; black-capped chickadee, *Parus atricapillus,* Sherry & Vaccarino, In press). Interestingly, within taxonomically related species, species that store seeds are found to have a larger hippocampus than those that do not (Krebs, Sherry, Healy, Perry and Vaccarino, In Press).

Although these studies clearly identify a spatial memory deficit following hippocampal ablation, it is not clear to what extent failed recovery of stored seeds can be explained in the context of navigation. It would be interesting to establish whether the reported deficits simply reflect failed recognition of cache sites, an impairment with respect to specifying the location of cache sites when displaced from them at various points within a test aviary (navigation), or a combination of the two.

The diverse set of results just described provide considerable evidence linking the hippocampus to avian spatial behavior. For homing pigeons, the hippocampus is not necessary for the recognition of salient environmental stimuli, use of an already functional navigational map and associated compass mechanisms, and homeward orientation from familiar areas presumably based on a mosaic-like landmark map. The most plausible hypothesis is that for experienced pigeons, the hippocampus is specifically involved in the use of landmarks for navigation, and particularly the use of landmarks in the form of a integrative-cognitive map (O'Keefe & Nadel, 1978; Bingman et al., in press). Although they are somewhat less clear, the results from food storing birds can at least be interpreted in a similar fashion.

The performance of hippocampal-ablated homing pigeons, together with the spatial behavior of hippocampal lesioned mammals, offer an exciting opportunity to examine hippocampal function in a comparative or evolutionary context. First, a mechanism of true navigation as described for homing pigeons has not been described for mammals. If true navigation is a uniquely avian phenomenon, a hypothesis of functional similarity between the avian and mammalian hippocampus in the neural control of specific spatial behavior processes would be supported if the avian hippocampus was not necessary for the neural processes associated with true navigation. As described earlier, homing pigeons who undergo hippocampal ablation after having already acquired their navigational map are unimpaired in relying on a mechanism of true navigation.

Additionally, the avian hippocampus is not necessary for the *acquisition* and maintenance of a mechanism of landmark navigation consistent with the use of a mosaic map. A mosaic map has several properties that are similar to a system of spatial reference memory that can be used by rodents in an eight-arm radial maze (Olton, 1983). Primarily, both spatial reference memory and a mosaic landmark map are characterized by fixed, temporally invariant responses with respect to external cues or landmarks. Interestingly, the mammalian hippocampus is also not necessary for the *acquisition* and maintenance of spatial reference memory

(Olton, 1983). Therefore, with respect to neural processes common to a mosaic landmark map and spatial reference memory, both the avian and mammalian hippocampus are similarly unimportant.

Finally, the performance of hippocampal-ablated homing pigeons can be best described as reflecting impaired use of landmarks in some spatially novel context. Hippocampal-lesioned rodents are also impaired in tasks that require the use of familiar landmarks to navigate to (Morris et al., 1982) and recognize goal areas (Jarrard, Okaichi, Stoward, & Goldschmidt, 1984; O'Keefe, Nadel, Keightley, & Kill, 1975) in some novel spatial context. As such, the hippocampus of both birds and mammals seems to be involved in spatial behaviors that are consistent with the use of something like an integrative or cognitive map.

These considerations indicate striking similarity in birds and mammals with respect to the relative importance of the hippocampus in the neural control of different spatial behavior processes. If we assume, as suggested by anatomical considerations, that this similarity cannot be accounted for as a result of evolutionary convergence or parallelism, then it seems that a functionally similar "hippocampus" existed in reptiles at the time when bird and mammalian lineages diverged from their common reptilian ancestor some 250 million years ago.

True Navigation: Central Processing of Sensory Input

Studies on the mechanisms of true navigation have focused on the sensory nature of environmental information used by birds to locate their position in space. Current and likely future work on neural mechanisms will focus on the central processing of olfactory and geomagnetic stimuli.

The importance of olfactory cues for the navigational map has been well described (see True Navigation Sensory Mechanisms (14-7)). Equally well described is the projection pattern of olfactory bulb efferents (Reiner & Karten, 1985). As such, there is now an excellent opportunity to begin examining the relative importance of these central olfactory projections for avian navigation. The telencephalic targets of olfactory bulb efferents can be divided into a limbic component, consisting of projections to the medial septum and to a subdivision of the avian amygdala known as the nucleus taenae (Zeier & Karten, 1971), and a cortical component, consisting of a projection to the pyriform cortex. One important future experiment, therefore, will be to examine the relative role of these olfactory subsystems in the functioning of the pigeon navigational map and associated olfactory memories.

Indeed, some progress has been made in determining central brain structures involved in the processing of olfactory input. In addition to primary recipient areas of olfactory bulb efferents, processing of olfactory information may occur in other brain locations (Macadar, Rausch, Wenzel, & Hutchinson, 1980; Rieke & Wenzel, 1978), with interhemispheric transfer mediated, at least in part, via the anterior commissure (but see Reiner & Karten, 1985). In one fascinating experiment, anterior commissure transection, which presumably resulted in the creation of an olfactory split brain, led to homing pigeons that acquired two functional navigational maps following experimental manipulation of odors exposed to each nostril and thus each hemisphere (Foá, Bagnoli, & Giongo, 1986). The results implicate the anterior commissure in the neural regulation of the pigeon navigational map.

Clearly, the most compelling challenge to workers in the field of avian orientation and navigation is to reveal the mechanism(s) that control the transduction of geomagnetic stimulation into a neural signal and its subsequent processing within the central nervous system. With respect to the transduction mechanism, neither the physicochemical model of Leask (1977) nor a mechanism based on ferromagnetic particles (Presti & Pettigrew, 1980; Walcott, Gould, & Kirschvink, 1979) has accounted for the sensitivity of birds to geomagnetism.

Another approach has been the use of electrophysiological unit recordings to identify brain areas that may be involved in the central processing of geomagnetic stimulation in birds. Cells that are responsive to changes in the ambient magnetic field have been found in the pineal body (Semm, Schneider, Vollrath, & Wiltschko, 1982), mesencephalic recipient areas of retinal ganglion fibers (the optic tectum and nucleus of the basal optic root; Semm & Demaine, 1986), vestibular nuclei (Semm, Nohr, Demaine, & Wiltschko, 1984), and the trigeminal nerve (Beason & Semm, 1987). It is not clear what this set of results may mean with respect to the use of geomagnetic cues for compass orientation or the possibility of their use for the navigational map. One major obstacle for further clarification is that all of the reported responsive areas function in some other known sensory capacity (vision, acceleration, or somatosensory), thus confounding interpretation of any eventual behavioral effects that one might observe following possible lesion experiments. In one relevant study, pinealectomized homing pigeons were essentially found to be unaffected under conditions where geomagnetic stimuli are thought to be employed, indicating that the pineal body is not necessary for geomagnetically based orientation or navigation (Papi, Maffei, & Giongo, 1985).

CONCLUSIONS

The spatial behavior of birds, as manifest in seed-storing, migration, and homing, ranks as among the best-described, real-world experimental paradigms in ethology and behavioral ecology. Neuroanatomically, the avian brain (particularly the forebrain) has been similarly well described. As such, the requisite behavioral and anatomical data exist to permit insightful investigations into the neural mechanisms of avian spatial behavior. Indeed, birds are exceptional in that one can readily examine relatively independent spatial processes embedded in a larger, more complex spatial task; for example, the various processes associated with pigeon homing behavior such as the navigational map, compass mechanisms, and landmark use. Additionally, avian behavior is easily observed either in the field or under simulated naturalistic conditions in the lab, with many aspects being quantifiable (e.g., initial orientation, homing time) thus facilitating experimental design and between-group comparisons. In short, birds offer a unique opportunity to examine the neural bases of spatial behavior while maintaining natural complexity found under real-world conditions.

Despite the various advantages of working with birds, our understanding of the underlying neural mechanisms of avian spatial behavior remains limited. With respect to the most studied form of avian spatial behavior, the homing behavior of pigeons, the number of unanswered questions is essentially infinite and includes the relative importance of cortical and limbic olfactory recipient areas for the regulation of the navigational map, identification of relevant visual pathways for sun compass orientation, central processing of geomagnetic stimuli, and further clarification of hippocampal and nonhippocampal regulation of landmark navigation. As a first approach, all of these questions are amenable to conventional lesioning techniques for the generation of an initial data base. Looking further into the future, such component analyses will hopefully yield to studies that attempt to examine how the various spatial behavior elements are integrated (e.g., for true navigation, identifying the brain regions where the processing of navigational map information may interface with the neural regulation of compass orientation), eventually leading to a fuller understanding of the neural control of overt spatial responses.

REFERENCES

Able, K. (1980). Mechanisms of orientation, navigation and homing. In: S. Gauthreaux (Ed.), *Animal Migration, Orientation, and Navigation.* New York: Academic.

Able, K., Gergits, W., Cherry, J. & Terrill, S. (1984). Homing behavior of wood thrushes (*Hylocichla mustelina*). *Behav. Ecol. Sociobiol., 15,* 39–43.

Baker, R. (1984). *Bird navigation.* London: Hodder and Stoughton.

Baldaccini, N., Benvenuti, S., Fiaschi, V., Ioalé, P. & Papi, F. (1982). Pigeon orientation: experiments on the role of olfactory stimuli perceived during the outward journey. In: F. Papi & H. Wallraff (Eds.), *Avian Navigation.* Berlin: Springer.

Bang, B. (1971). Functional anatomy of the olfactory system in 23 orders of birds. *Acta Anat. Suppl. 58, 79,* 1–76.

Barlow, J. (1964). Inertial navigation as a basis for animal navigation. *J. Theoret. Biol., 6,* 76–117.

Beason, R. & Semm, P. (1987). Magnetic responses of the trigeminal nerve system of the bobolink (*Dolichonyx oryzivorus*). *Neurosci. Letters, 80,* 229–234.

Becker, J. & van Raden, H. (1986). Metereologische Gesichtspunkte zur olfaktorischen Navigationshypothese. *J. Ornith., 127,* 1–8.

Benvenuti, S., Baldacinni, N. & Ioalé, P. (1982). Pigeon homing: effect of altered magnetic field during displacement on initial orientation. In: F. Papi & H. Wallraff (Eds.), *Avian Navigation.* Berlin: Springer.

Benvenuti, S., Fiaschi, V., Fiore, L. & Papi, F. (1973). Homing performance of inexperienced and directionally trained pigeons subjected to olfactory nerve section. *J. Comp. Physiol., 83,* 81–91.

Benvenuti, S. & Wallraff, H. (1985). Pigeon navigation: Site simulation by means of atmospheric odours. *J. Comp. Physiol. A, 156,* 737–746.

Bingman, V., Bagnoli, P., Ioalé, P. & Casini, G. (1984). Homing behavior of pigeons after telencephalic ablations. *Brain Behav. Evol., 24,* 94–108.

Bingman, V., Bagnoli, P., Ioalé, P. & Casini, G. (in press). Behavioral and anatomical studies of the avian hippocampus. In: V. Chan-Palay & C. Kohler (Eds.), *The Hippocampus, New Vistas. Neurology and Neurobiology Vol. 32.* New York: Liss.

Bingman, V. & Ioalé, P. (in press). Anosmic homing pigeons released from familiar sites maintain homeward orientation following clock-shift. Behaviour.

Bingman, V., Ioalé, P., Casini, J. & Bagnoli, P. (1985). Dorsomedial forebrain ablations and home loft association behavior in homing pigeons. *Brain Behav. Evol., 25,* 1–9.

Bingman, V., Ioalé, P., Casini, G. & Bagnoli, P. (1987). Impaired retention of preoperatively acquired spatial reference memory in homing pigeons following hippocampal ablation. *Behav. Brain Res., 24,* 147–156.

Bingman, V., Ioalé, P., Casini, G. & Bagnoli, P. (1988a). Unimpaired acquisition of spatial reference memory, but impaired homing performance in hippocampal ablated pigeons. *Behav. Brain Res., 27,* 179–188.

Bingman, V., Ioalé, P., Casini, G. & Bagnoli, P. (1988b). Hippocampal ablated homing pigeons show a persistent impairment in the time taken to return home. *J. Comp. Physiol. A., 163,* 559–563.

Casini, G., Bingman, V. & Bagnoli, P. (1986). Connections of the pigeon dorsomedial forebrain studied with WGA-HRP and 3-H proline. *J. Comp. Neurol., 245,* 454–470.

Cole, S., Hainsworth, F., Kamil, A., Mercier, T. & Wolf, L. (1982). Spatial learning as an adaptation in hummingbirds. *Science, 217,* 655–657.

Foá, A. & Albonetti, E. (1980). Does familiarity with the release site influence the intitial orientation of homing pigeons? Experiments with clock-shifted birds. *Z. Tierpsychol, 54,* 327–328.

Foá, A., Bagnoli, P. & Giongo, F. (1986). Homing pigeons subjected to section of the anterior commissure can build up two olfactory maps in the deflector lofts. *J. Comp. Physiol. A, 159,* 465–472.

Foá, A., Wallraff, H., Ioalé, P. & Benvenuti, S. (1982). Comparative investigations of pigeon homing in Germany and Italy. In: F. Papi & H. Wallraff (Eds.), *Avian Navigation.* Berlin: Springer.

Füller, E., Kowalski, V. & Wiltschko, R. (1983). Orientation of homing pigeons: compass orientation vs. piloting by landmarks. *J. Comp. Physiol., 153,* 55–58.

Good, M. (1987). The effects of hippocampal-area parahippocampalis lesions on discrimination learning in the pigeon. *Behav. Brain Res., 26,* 171–184.

Gould, J. (1982). The map sense of pigeons. *Nature, 296,* 205–211.

Graue, L. (1963). The effects of phase shifts in the day-night cycle on pigeon homing at distances of less than one mile. *Ohio J. Sci., 63,* 214–217.

Griffin, D. (1940). Homing experiments with Leach's petrels. *Auk, 57,* 61–74.

Griffin, D. (1955). *Bird navigation.* In A. Wolfson (Ed.), Recent studies in Avian Biology. Urbana: Univ. Illinois Press.

Griffin, D. (1984). *Animal Thinking.* Cambridge, Massachusetts: Harvard University Press.

Grubb, T. (1974). Olfactory navigation to the nesting burrow in Leach's petrel (*Oceanodroma leucorrhoa*). *Anim. Behav., 22,* 192–202.

Hartwick, R., Foá, A. & Papi, F. (1977). The effect of olfactory deprivation by nasal tubes upon homing behaviour in pigeons. *Behav. Ecol. and Sociobiol., 2,* 81–89.

Jarrard, L., Okaichi, H., Steward, O. & Goldschmidt, R. (1984). On the role of hippocampal connections in the performance of place and cue tasks: Comparisons with damage to hippocampus. *Behav. Neurosci., 98,* 946–954.

Keeton, W. (1974). The orientational and navigational basis of homing in birds. *Advances on the Study of Behavior, 5,* 47–132.

Keeton, W., Larkin, T. & Windsor, D. (1974). Normal fluctuations in the earth's magnetic field influence pigeon orientation. *J. Comp. Physiol.*, *95*, 95–103.

Kenyon, K. & Rice, D. (1958). Homing of Layson albatrosses. *Condor*, *60*, 3–6.

Kiepenheuer, J. (1978). Pigeon navigation and the magnetic field: information collected during the outward journey is used in the homing process. *Naturwissenschaften*, *65*, 113.

Kiepenheuer, J. (1982). The effect of magnetic anomalies on the homing behavior of pigeons: an attempt to analyse the possible factors involved. In: F. Papi & H. Wallraff (Eds.), *Avian Navigation*. Berlin: Springer.

Kiepenheuer, J. (1985). Can pigeons be fooled about the actual release site position by presenting them information from another site? *Behav. Ecol. Sociobiol.*, *18*, 75–82.

Kiepenheuer, J. (1986). Are site-specific airborne stimuli relevant for pigeon navigation only when matched by other release-site information? *Naturwissenschaften*, *73*, 42–43.

Kiepenheuer, J., Baldaccini, N. & Alleva, E. (1979). A comparison of orientational and homing performances of homing pigeons of German and Italian stock raised together in Germany and Italy. *Monit. zool. ital.*, *13*, 159–171.

Kramer, G. (1953). Die Sonnenorientierung der Vögel. *Verh. Dtsch. Zool. Ges.*, *1952*, 77–84.

Kramer, G. (1959). Recent experiments on bird orientation. *Ibis*, *101*, 399–416.

Krebs, J., Erichsen, J. & Bingman, V. (1987). The immunohistochemistry and cytoarchiotecture of the avian hippocampus. *Soc. Neurosci. Abstracts*, *13*, 1125.

Krebs, J., Sherry, D., Healy, S., Perry, V. & Vaccarino, A. (In press). Hippocampal specialization of food-storing birds. *P.N.A.S.*

Krushinskaya, N. (1966). Some complex forms of feeding behaviour of nutcracker *Nucifraga caryocatactes*, after removal of old cortex. *Zhurnal Evoluzionni Biochimii y Fisiologgia II:* 563–568.

Leask, M. (1977). A physicochemical mechanism for magnetic field detection by migratory birds and homing pigeons. *Nature*, *267*, 261–264.

Lednor, A. & Walcott, C. (1988). Orientation of homing pigeons at magnetic anomalies. The effects of experience. *Behav. Ecol. Sociobiol.*, *22*, 3–8.

Macadar, A., Rausch, L., Wenzel, B. & Hutchinson, L. (1980). Electrophysiology of the olfactory pathways in the pigeon. *J. Comp. Physiol.*, *137*, 39–46.

Matthews, G. V. T. (1968). *Bird Navigation*. Cambridge: Cambridge University Press.

Michener, M. & Walcott, C. (1967). Homing of single pigeons-an analysis of tracks. *J. Exp. Biol.*, *47*, 99–131.

Moore, F. & Osadchuk, T. (1982). Spatial Memory in a passine migrant. In: F. Papi & H. Wallraff (Eds.), *Avian Navigation*. Berlin: Springer.

Morris, R., Garrud, P., Rawlins, J. & O'Keefe, J. (1982). Place navigation impaired in rats with hippocampal lesions. *Nature*, *297*, 681–683.

O'Keefe, J. & Conway, D. (1978). Hippocampal place units in the freely moving rat: why they fire where they fire. *Exp. Brain Res.*, *31*, 573–590.

O'Keefe, J. & Nadel, L. (1978). The Hippocampus as a Cognitive Map. Oxford: Clarendon.

O'Keefe, J., Nadel, L., Keightley, S. & Kill, D. (1975). Fornix lesions selectively abolish place learning in the rat. *Exp. Neurol*, *48*, 152–166.

Olton, D. & Samuelson, R. (1976). Remembrances of placed passed: spatial memory in rats. *J. Exp. Psychol.: Anim. Behav. Proc.*, *2*, 97–116.

Olton, D. (1983). Memory functions and the hippocampus. In: W. Seifert (Ed.), *Neurobiology of the Hippocampus*. New York: Academic.

Olton, D. & Papas, B. (1979). Spatial memory and hippocampal function. *Neuropsychologia*, *17*, 669–682.

Papi, F. (1982). Olfaction and homing in pigeons: ten years of experiments. In: F. Papi & H. Wallraff (Eds.), *Avian Navigation*. Berlin: Springer.

Papi, F. (1986). Pigeon navigation: solved problems and open questions. *Monit. zool. ital.*, *20*, 471–517.

Papi, F., Fiore, L., Fiaschi, V. & Benvenuti, S. (1972). Pigeon homing: outward journey detours influence the initial orientation. *Monitore zool. ital., 7,* 129–133.

Papi, F., Keeton, W., Brown, A. & Benevenuti, S. (1978). Do American and Italian pigeons rely on different homing mechanisms? *J. Comp. Physiol, 128,* 303–317.

Papi, F., Maffei, L. & Giongo, F. (1985). Pineal body and bird navigation: new experiments on pinealectomized pigeons. *Z. Tierpsychol., 67,* 257–268.

Presti, D. & Pettigrew, J. (1980). Ferromagnetic coupling to muscle receptors as a basis for geomagnetic field sensitivity in animals. *Nature, 285,* 99–100.

Reilly, S. & Good, M. (1987). Enhanced DRL and impaired forced-choice alternation performance following hippocampal lesions in the pigeon. *Behav. Brain Res., 26,* 185–197.

Reiner, A. & Karten, H. (1985). Comparison of olfactory bulb projections in pigeons and turtles. *Brain Behav. Evol., 27,* 11–27.

Rieke, G. & Wenzel, B. (1978). Forebrain projections of the pigeon olfactory bulb. *J. Morphol., 158,* 41–56.

Roitblat, H. (1987). *Introduction to Comparative Cognition.* New York: Freeman.

Roitblat, H., Bever, T. & Terrace, H. (1984). *Animal Cognition.* Hillsdale, New Jersey: Erlbaum.

Rüppell, W. (1937). Heimfindeversuche mit Rauchschwalben, Wendehalsen, Rotrückenwürgern und Habichten. *J. Ornith., 84,* 180–198.

Salmon, D., Zola-Morgan, A. & Squire, L. (1987). Retrograde amnesia following combined hippocampus-amygdala lesions in monkeys. *Psychobiology, 15,* 37–47.

Sargent, T. (1962). A study of homing in the bank swallow (*Riparia riparia*). *Auk, 79,* 234–246.

Schmidt-Koenig, K. (1960). Internal clocks and homing. *Cold Spring. Harb. Symp. Quant. Biol., 25,* 389–393.

Schmidt-Koenig, K. (1961). Die Sonne als Kompass im Heimorienttierungssystem der Brieftauben. *Z. Tierpsychol., 68,* 221–244.

Schmidt-Koenig, K. (1979). *Avian Orientation and Navigation.* New York: Academic.

Schmidt-Koenig, K. (1987). Bird navigation: has olfactory orientation solved the problem. *Q. Rev. Biol., 62,* 31–47.

Schmidt-Koenig, K. & Walcott, C. (1978). Tracks of pigeons homing with frosted lenses. *Anim. Behav., 26,* 480–486.

Semm, P. & Demaine, C. (1986). Neurophysiological properties of magnetic cells in the pigeons visual system. *J. Comp. Physiol. A, 159,* 619–625.

Semm, P., Nohr, D., Demaine, C. & Wiltschko, W. (1984). Neural basis of the magnetic compass: interactions of visual, magnetic and vestibular inputs in the pigeon's brain. *J. Comp. Physiol. A, 155,* 283–288.

Semm, P., Schneider, T., Vollrath, L. & Wiltschko, W. (1982). Magnetic sensitive pineal cells in pigeons. In: F. Papi & H. Wallraff (Eds.), *Avian Navigation.* Berlin: Springer.

Sherry, D. (1985). Food storage by birds and mammals. *Advances in the Study of Behavior, 15,* 153–188.

Sherry, D. & Vaccarino, A. (In press). The hippocampus and memory for food caches in black-capped chickadees. *Behav. Neurosci.*

Shettleworth, S. (1985). Food storing by birds: implications for comparative studies of memory. In: M. Weinberger, J. McGaugh & G. Lynch (Eds.), *Memory Systems of the Brain.* New York: Guilford.

Southern, W. (1968). Experiments on the homing ability of Purple Martins. *Living Bird, 7,* 71–84.

Spetch, M. & Edwards, C. (1986). Spatial memory in pigeons *Columba livia* in an open-field feeding environment. *J. Comp. Psychol., 100,* 266–278.

Spetch, M. & Edwards, C. (1988). Pigeons', *Columba livia,* use of global and local cues for spatial memory. *Anim. Behav., 36,* 293–296.

Stager, K. (1964). The role of olfaction in food location by the turkey vulture (*Cathartes aura*). *LA County Mus. Contrib. Sci., 81,* 3–63.

Sutherland, R. & Dyck, R. (1984). Place navigation by rats in a swimming pool. *Canadian J. Psych.*, *38*, 322–347.

Suzuki, S., Augerinos, G. & Black, A. (1980). Stimulus control of spatial behavior on the eight arm maze in rats. *Learning and Motivation*, *11*, 1–18.

Tolman, E. (1948). Cognitive maps in rats and men. *Psychol. Rev.*, *55*, 189–208.

Walcott, C. (1978). Anomalies in the earth's magnetic field increase the scatter of pigeon's vanishing bearings. In: K. Schmidt-Koenig & W. Keeton (Eds.), *Animal Migration, Navigation and Homing*. Berlin: Springer.

Walcott, C. (In press). Homing in pigeons: effects of olfactory deprivation and magnetic anomalies on Cornell pigeons. *Proc. XIX Int. Ornithol. Cong.* (Ottawa, 1986.)

Walcott, C., Gould, J. & Kirschvink, J. (1979). Pigeons have magnets. *Science*, *205*, 1027–1029.

Waldvogel, J. (1987). Olfactory navigation in homing pigeons: are current models atmospherically realistic? *Auk*, *104*, 369–379.

Walker, J. & Olton, D. (1984). Fimbria-fornix lesions impair spatial working memory but not cognitive mapping. *Behav. Neurosci.*, *98*, 226–242.

Wallraff, H. (1966). Über die Heimfindeleistungen von Brieftauben nach Haltung in verschiedenartig abgeschirmten Volieren. *Z. vergl. Physiol.*, *52*, 215–259.

Wallraff, H. (1970). Über die Flugrichtungen verfrachteter Brieftauben in Abhängigkeit von Heimatort und vom Ort der Freilassung. *Z. Tierpsychol.*, *27*, 303–351.

Wallraff, H. (1974). *Das Navigationssystem der Vögel*. Munchen: R. Oldenbourg Verlag.

Wallraff, H. (1980). Does pigeon homing depend on stimuli perceived during displacement? I. Experiments in Germany. *J. Comp. Physiol. A*, *139*, 193–201.

Wallraff, H. (1981). The olfactory component of pigeon navigation: steps of analysis. *J. Comp. Physiol. A.*, *143*, 411–422.

Wallraff, H., Papi, F., Ioalé, P. & Benevenuti, S. (1986). Magnetic fields affect pigeon navigation only while the birds can smell atmospheric odors. *Naturwissenschaften*, *73*, 215–217.

Wallraff, H. & Sinsch, U. (1988). The role of "outward journey information" in homing experiments with pigeons: new data on ontogeny of navigation and general survey. *Ethology*, *77*, 10–27.

Watson, J. (1915). Recent experiments with homing birds. *Harper's*, *131*, 457–464.

Wiltschko, R., Wiltschko, W. & Keeton, W. (1978). Effect of outward journey in an altered magnetic field on the orientation of young homing pigeons. In: K. Schmidt-Koenig & W. Keeton (Eds.), *Animal Migration Navigation and Homing*. Berlin: Springer.

Wiltschko, W. (1983). Compasses used by birds. *Comp. Biochem. Physiol.*, *76*, 709–717.

Wiltschko, W. & Wiltschko, R. (1982). The role of outword-journey information in the orientation of homing pigeons. In: F. Papi & H. Wallraff (Eds.), *Avian Navigation*. Berlin: Springer.

Wiltschko, W., Wiltschko, R., Grüter, M. & Kowalski, U. (1987). Pigeon homing: early experience determines what factors are used for navigation. *Naturwissenschaften*, *74*, 196–198.

Wiltschko, W., Wiltschko, R. & Mathias, J. (1987). The orientation of anosmic pigeons in Frankfurt A. M., Germany. *Anim. Behav.*, *35*, 1324–1333.

Wiltschko, W., Wiltschko, R. & Walcott, C. (1987). Pigeon homing: different effects of olfactory deprivation in different countries. *Behav. Ecol. Sociobiol*, *21*, 333–342.

Yeagley, H. (1947). A preliminary study of a physical basis of bird navigation. *J. Appl. Phys.*, *18*, 1033–1063.

Zeier, H. & Karten, H. (1971). The archistriatum of the pigeon: organization of afferent and efferent connections. *Brain Res.*, *31*, 313–326.

Author Index

449

Subject Index